CRUCIBLE OF LIGHT

Also by Elizabeth Drayson

Lost Paradise: The Story of Granada

The Moor's Last Stand: How Seven Centuries of Muslim Rule in Spain Came to an End

ELIZABETH DRAYSON

CRUCIBLE OF LIGHT

Islam and the forging of Europe from the 8th to the 21st Century

PICADOR

First published 2025 by Picador
an imprint of Pan Macmillan
The Smithson, 6 Briset Street, London EC1M 5NR
EU representative: Macmillan Publishers Ireland Ltd, 1st Floor,
The Liffey Trust Centre, 117–126 Sheriff Street Upper,
Dublin 1 D01 YC43
Associated companies throughout the world

ISBN 978-1-0350-0859-9 HB
ISBN 978-1-0350-0860-5 TPB

1 3 5 7 9 8 6 4 2

A CIP catalogue record for this book is available from the British Library.

Typeset in Dante MT Std by
Palimpsest Book Production Ltd, Falkirk, Stirlingshire
Printed and bound in the UK using 100% Renewable Electricity by CPI Group (UK) Ltd

In memory of my parents
John and Kate Drayson

'I am human, I think nothing human alien to me'
('Homo sum, humani nihil a me alienum puto')

Terence the African

'I am a Palestinian Christian. We also say "Allahu Akber", which you normally hear from a Muslim, as well as "In shaa Allah", "Ma Shaa Allah, Alhumdulillah". This is simply because Arabic is our language, and the Arabic word for God is Allah, whether you are a Christian or a Muslim!'

Archbishop Theodosius of Sebastia

'This clash of the culture. East and West. Us and Them. Muslim and Christian. Does not exist.'

Marjane Satrapi

Contents

List of Illustrations

INTEGRATED IMAGES

Photographic credits are shown in italics.

PLATE SECTIONS

26. Abd el-Ouahed ben Messaoud ben Mohammed Anoun (1558 – ?), ambassador to the court of Queen Elizabeth I of England in 1600, to promote the establishment of an Anglo-Moroccan alliance. *Photo: CPA Media Pte Ltd / Alamy*
27. 'Battle of Vienna', 1683. Anon. Military History Museum, Vienna. *Photo: Wikimedia Commons*
28. Coat of arms of Isabella I of Castile and Ferdinand II of Aragon, after 1492. *Photo: Wikimedia Commons*
29. 'Landing of Columbus', 1847. Jon Vanderlyn. *Photo: Wikimedia Commons*
30. 'Bonaparte before the Sphinx', 1886. Jean-Léon Gérôme. Hearst Castle, San Simeon, California, USA. *Photo: Wikimedia Commons*
31. The first President of the Republic of Turkey, Mustafa Kemal Atatürk, in a top hat and white tie. *Photo: Wikimedia Commons*
32. A British UN soldier in the UN buffer zone, Nicosia, Cyprus. *Photo: Agencja Fotograficzna Caro / Alamy*
33. 'The Temple of All Religions', Tatarstan, by Ildar Xanov. *Photo: Wikimedia Commons*
34. The Alhambra, Granada, Spain. *Photo: Wikimedia Commons*
35. Berat, Albania. *Photo: Prisma by Dukas Presseagentur GmbH / Alamy*

Maps

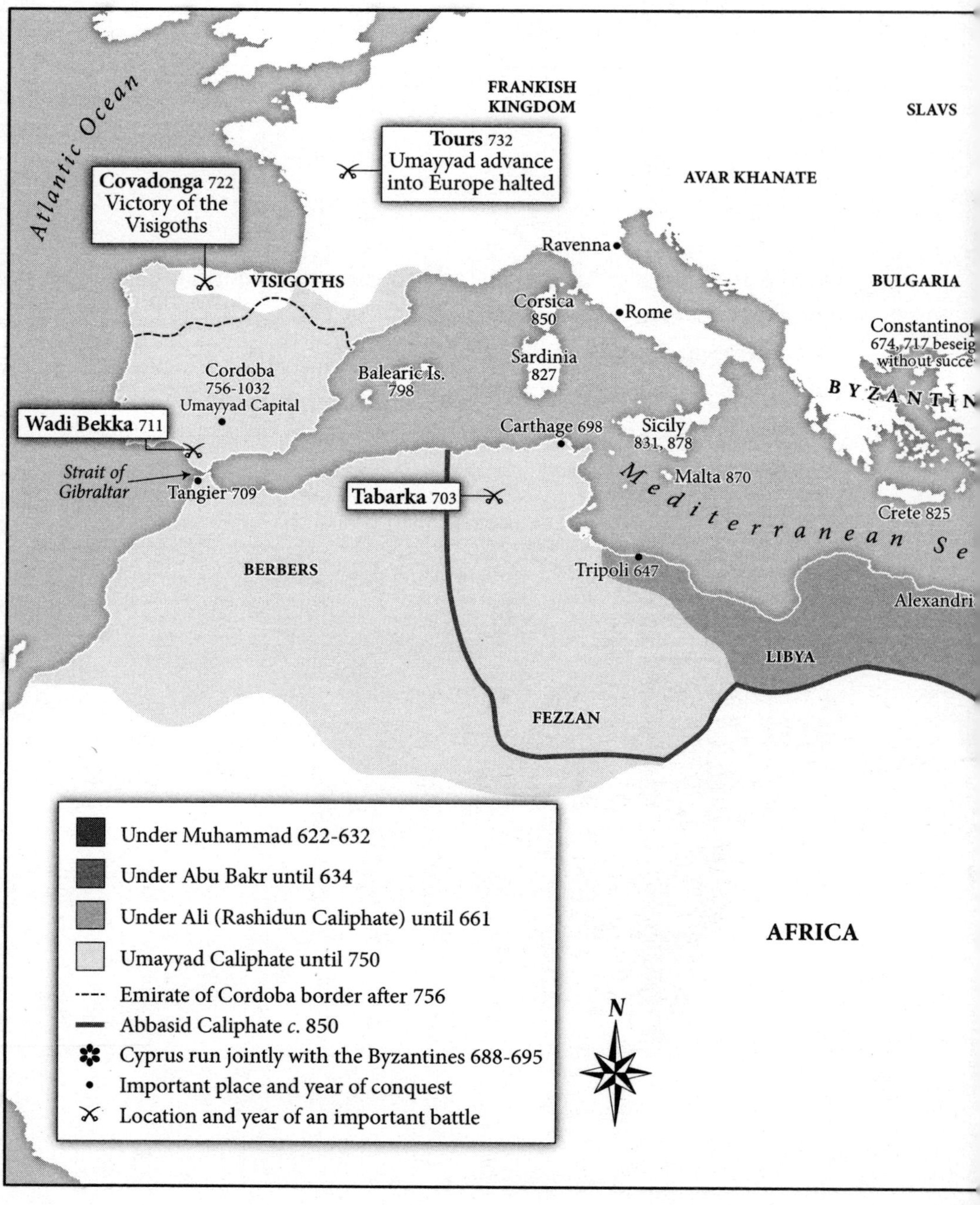

Atlantic Ocean
FRANKISH KINGDOM
SLAVS
Tours 732
Umayyad advance into Europe halted
AVAR KHANATE
Covadonga 722
Victory of the Visigoths
Ravenna
VISIGOTHS
BULGARIA
Corsica 850
Rome
Sardinia 827
Cordoba 756-1032 Umayyad Capital
Balearic Is. 798
BYZANTIN
Wadi Bekka 711
Carthage 698
Sicily 831, 878
Strait of Gibraltar
Tangier 709
Tabarka 703
Malta 870
Mediterranean Se
Crete 825
BERBERS
Tripoli 647
Alexandri
LIBYA
FEZZAN
Under Muhammad 622-632
Under Abu Bakr until 634
Under Ali (Rashidun Caliphate) until 661
Umayyad Caliphate until 750
Emirate of Cordoba border after 756
Abbasid Caliphate c. 850
Cyprus run jointly with the Byzantines 688-695
Important place and year of conquest
Location and year of an important battle
AFRICA
N

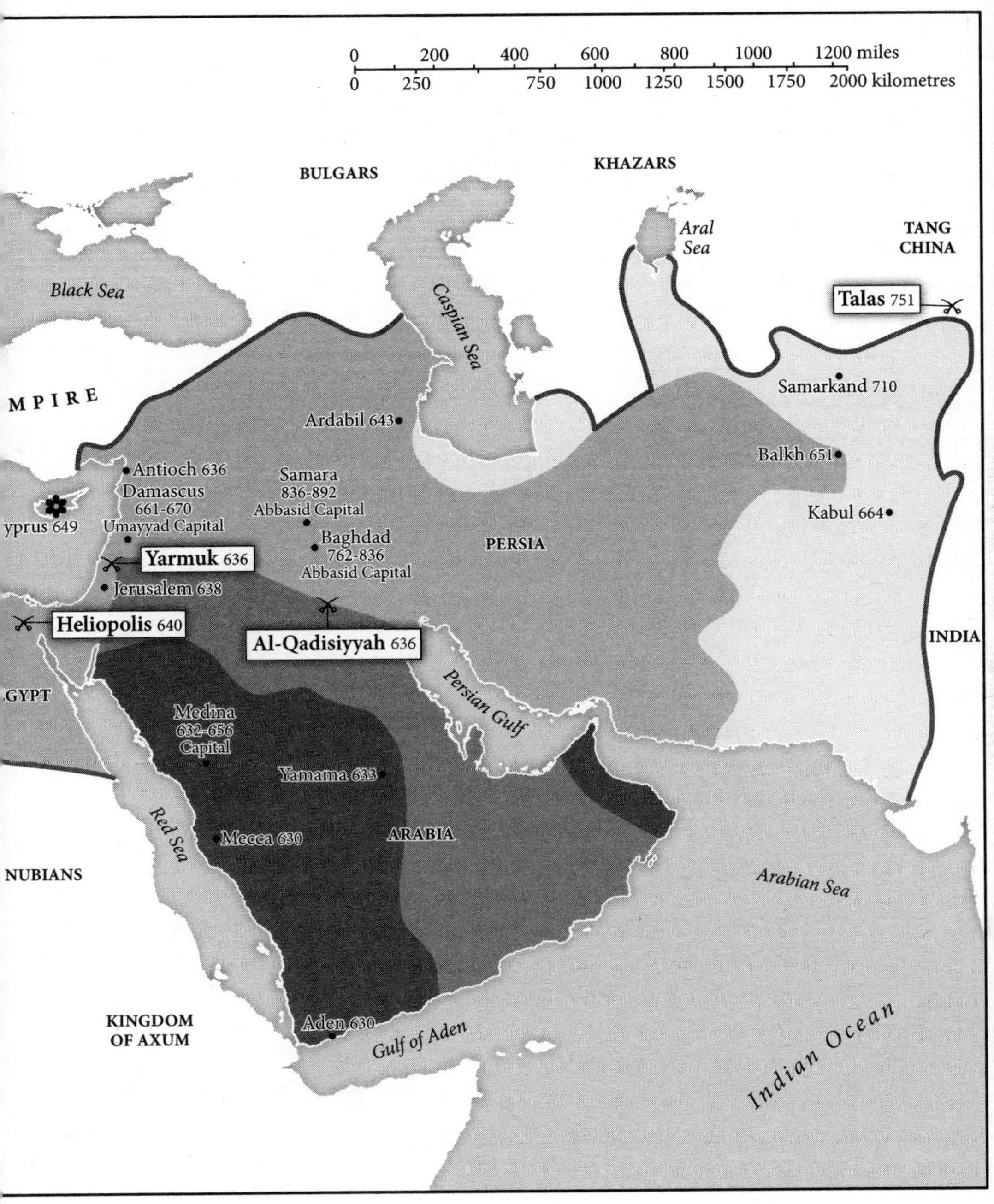

1. Islamic conquests from the seventh to the ninth century.

2. The Holy Roman Empire in 800.

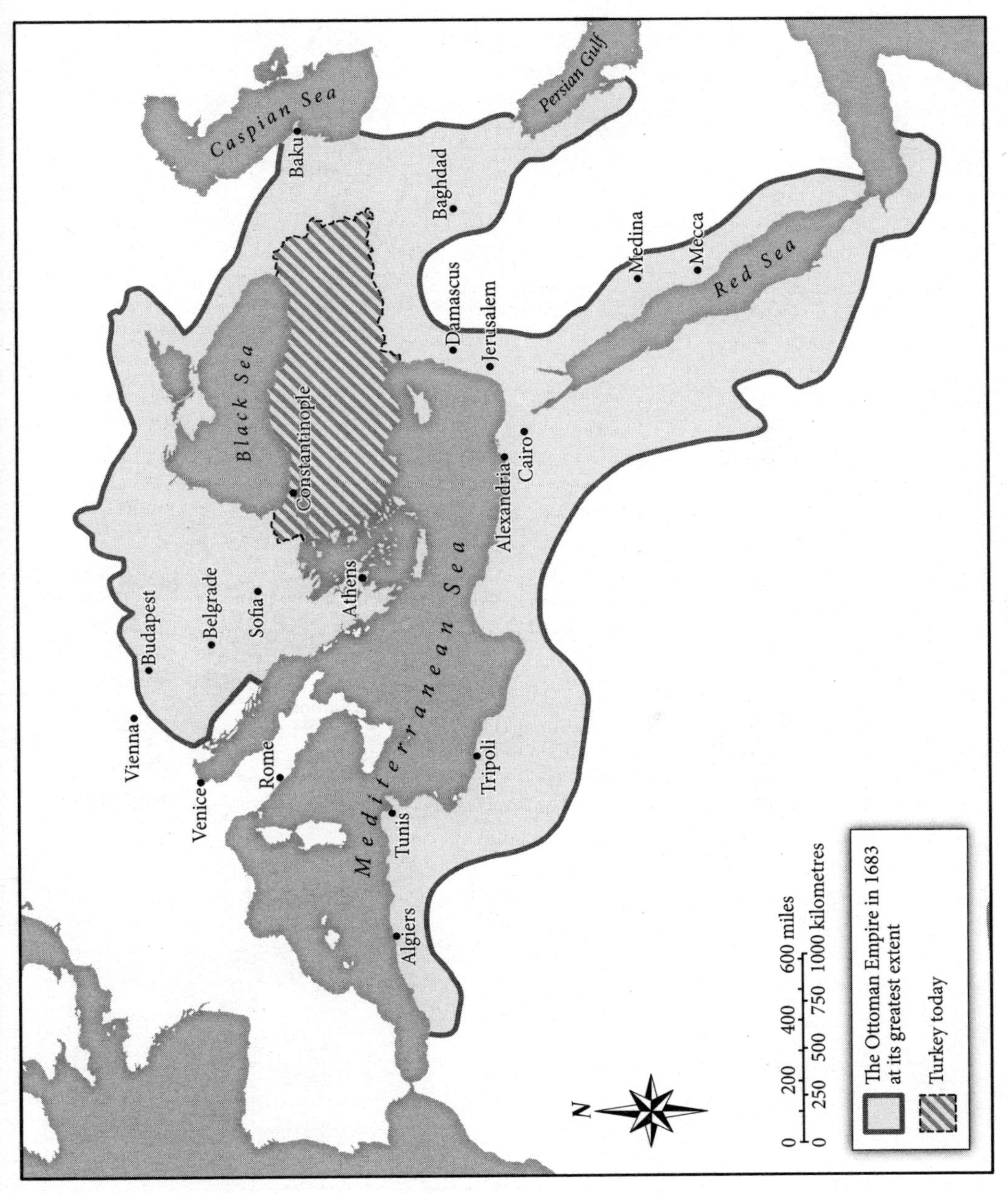

3. The Ottoman Empire at its greatest extent.

4. *The Austro-Hungarian Empire in 1910.*

Introduction

PERSPECTIVES PAST AND PRESENT

'Christian and Muslim playing chess', from The Book of Games of Alfonso X, *folio 64r, between 1251 and 1285*

'The one duty we owe to history is to rewrite it.'

Oscar Wilde

The King's Gambit

THIS HISTORY BEGINS with a picture, a medieval miniature painted in glowing indigo, vermilion and ochre, that appears in an illuminated manuscript known as the *Book of Games* (*Libro de los juegos*). Commissioned in Spain long ago by King Alfonso X the Wise of Castile and completed in his scriptorium in Toledo in 1283, the book contains the oldest known descriptions of a variety of board games, including dice and chess. At first glance, we might think the miniature illustrates two warriors planning their battle strategy over a game of chess. They sit inside an Arab military tent, its war pennant fluttering at the apex, with two long spears at the ready just outside, and one man has a sword slung round his body. In the late thirteenth century, when the image was painted, Christians and Muslims in the Iberian peninsula were battling for territory and dominion in a conflict known as the Reconquest (*Reconquista*), when Spanish Catholic armies fought to recover, as they saw it, the lands they had lost to Islam 500 years before. The visual references to warfare are echoed by the chess game, one of the oldest methods used to teach war strategy. It has been played in Spain longer than anywhere else in Europe, by Spanish Muslims since their arrival in the eighth century, and by Spanish Christians and Jews since the early tenth century. The game came from ancient India, and the original pieces represented the units of the Indian army – foot soldiers, cavalry, armed chariots and elephants. The infantry, or pawns, were led on the chessboard, as in life, by the king and his senior minister, his vizier. Some think it was a game modelled on Alexander the Great's campaigns in Persia, in which his squadrons were aligned in ranks of sixty-four squares, the number of squares on a chessboard. The Indian game spread to the rest of Europe from Islamic Spain, where opening moves had romantic names such as the Sword Opening, the Pharaoh's Fortress or the King's Gambit. Over time, the pieces changed to reflect the feudal social environment of the rest of medieval Europe – the elephant was replaced in Christian chess by the bishop, a powerful figure in the medieval Church, while, in Spanish Muslim chess, the equivalent is just an *alfil*, meaning a chess piece and nothing more. King Alfonso's book was the first in Europe on the subject, translated and compiled using Arabic manuscripts.

The painting's implicit reference to the ongoing conflict between Christians and Muslims in the 1280s seems to bear out our first impression, but closer inspection reveals something quite different. The chess player on the right is a turbaned Muslim, but the one on the left is a Christian. They have set aside any hostility and difference in favour of an alliance, as friends, or perhaps as soldiers, who have come together in peace to play a board game. The unknown artist has created a scene of respect and understanding, and of amiable coexistence. His painting suggests a quite different aspect of the so-called clash between the civilizations of Islam and Europe so controversially expounded by the American scholar Samuel P. Huntington, an aspect which has been overlooked, unappreciated or has simply been unknown.[1] The image portrays friendship and collaboration between two individuals perceived as enemies and becomes a painted paradigm of the tolerance and exchange that catalysed Europe's cultural illumination and gave rise to its associated and immeasurable debt to Islamic civilization. It is this paradoxical yet profound intertwining of the lives of Europe's Christians and Muslims at all levels, from the most intimate to the most universal, that this book explores.

It recounts the development of European civilization as it evolves through the many encounters between Islamic and Christian peoples that have taken place in Europe from the eighth century to the present day. It reveals how their vexed cultural and religious exchanges, which often occurred in scenarios of severe trial, war and persecution, created and continues to create a hybrid European society, a civilization in progress. This central idea is expressed through the image of the crucible as a vessel of transformation, a metaphor for the European continent as a place of transmutation, progression and enlightenment, its civilization emerging through struggle and strife, but also through the cooperation and dialogue between Muslims and Christians. The idea of a shared continental culture shatters conventional distinctions between Christian Europe and the Islamic empires and discloses the profound influence of Muslim life on a continent that has been moulded as much by Islamic civilization as by Latin Christendom.

The perspective of this book reflects changing attitudes to the writing of history in the twenty-first century, which abandon established views of the past and set out to recover hidden heritages that have been erased from memory. Conventional histories tend to chart the legacy of a centuries-long mutual antagonism and violent conflict between the Muslims and Christians of Europe, born of the age-old fear of invasion and conquest, of ancient attitudes of militancy expressed in Crusade and jihad, and of an unwaveringly negative perception of racial and religious difference. But the mood is shifting: together with Black history, denunciations of the abuse of women and the controversy over colonialism, a new, alternative kind of history is bringing to light the suppressed cultural and religious elements that have contributed to the creation of modern Europe. Forgotten voices tell a different story, not just of divergence, violence and repression, but also of alliance and cultural collaboration between Muslims and Christians. That complex interplay between conflict and coexistence, disparity and resemblance is a key element of this book. It is not just a story of war but also a story of dialogue and interaction, of extraordinary learning and creativity, of modes of thought and ways of being that have substantially determined the modern European world.

Finding the Past in the Present: Current Conflicts with Ancient Roots

The dominant perception of relations between Christians and Muslims today is one of strife. European civilization has defined itself as Christian, and Christianity remains the most widespread religion in the European Union. Three of Europe's greatest challenges in this century – immigration, religious and racial difference and terrorism – are strongly associated with Islam, aggravating a sharp rise in Islamophobia, a term that only came into regular usage in the 1970s. Yet ancient clashes between Muslims and Christians have contemporary echoes in a number of terrorist activities that have traumatized several European countries. In 2015, a terrorist atrocity laid bare the deep rift between Islam and Europe. Stéphane Charbonnier, who worked as a cartoonist and editor of the satirical left-wing French magazine *Charlie Hebdo*, left his Paris home for work on 7 January and never returned. He was at an editorial meeting that morning with three other cartoonists when two masked gunmen dressed in black forced their way in and opened fire with Kalashnikov rifles. They massacred eleven people at the offices of the magazine and later shot dead two gendarmes before the police finally caught up with them and killed them on an industrial estate on the outskirts of Paris. The gunmen were Saïd and Chérif Kouachi, the latter a known terrorist with links to al-Qaeda, who had spent time in jail. Both were French citizens, born in Paris, of Algerian parents.

What led these French Muslim citizens to commit such an extreme act of barbarism was a series of satirical cartoons of the Prophet Muhammad, published by *Charlie Hebdo* in 2012, one of which showed the Prophet naked, on all fours, with a star covering his anus. Visual images of Muhammad are conventionally forbidden in Islam, and the cartoons were denounced as blasphemous by Muslims the world over. But such a shocking act of militant terrorism, which struck at the heart of European freedom of speech and expression, intensified the fear and hostility felt by non-Muslims towards Islam and its followers; it also intensified the feeling of prejudice and persecution experienced by Muslims in today's European society.

France was not alone in suffering violent upheavals in the name of Islam, the repercussions of which have transformed the face of politics, social policy and popular feeling. Eleven years earlier, on 11 March 2004, ten bombs tore through four commuter trains coming into Madrid's Atocha station during the rush hour, killing 193 people and injuring almost 2,000 in the deadliest attack in Europe since the Lockerbie plane bombing in 1988, and an extreme Islamic terrorist group was held responsible. More recently, the threat of terrorism has fuelled the anti-Muslim propaganda of the right-wing Spanish political party Vox, not long ago a serious contender for power in Spain's government. In November 2018, Vox tweeted a short film clip showing Santiago Abascal, the party leader, dressed up as their early medieval hero, Don Pelayo of Asturias, riding alongside his comrades to music from the *Lord of the Rings* films, to lead a new Spanish reconquest. His crusading rhetoric imitated the language of the Spanish dictator Franco's fascist ideals and harked back to the medieval victory of Catholicism over Islam in Spain.

Santiago Abascal's discourse of national Catholicism aligns itself with the ultra-right-wing ideology current in politics across Europe, the associated Islamophobic, anti-immigration stance of which targets the Muslim immigrants who currently live in the European Union and the United Kingdom, where they came to find work. In these countries, there is antagonism towards Muslims, both immigrant and native, who are feared as a threat not just to national security and to the nature of society, but to European identity itself. Muslims themselves feel like outsiders, often rejected and mocked. Some countries, such as France and Switzerland, have sought to erase visible signs of religious difference by banning Muslim women's use of the burka or niqab. In 2021, the populist right-wing Swiss People's Party paid for campaign adverts showing a woman wearing a niqab and sunglasses alongside the slogan 'Stop extremism! Yes to the veil ban', a stance supported by the Swiss government, who stated that the burka was a symbol of the repression of women. Swiss Muslims themselves felt strongly that the ban aimed to stigmatize and marginalize Muslim women even more. Meanwhile, over the border in Austria, which had over a million new Muslim immigrants in 2015, the government went so far as to shut down certain mosques because they were considered a security threat.

The word 'immigrant' has become synonymous with 'Muslim' in some countries, and racial prejudice is inextricably tied up with religious difference. Nowhere was this more apparent than in the terrible conflict in Bosnia-Herzegovina from 1992 to 1995, in which a hundred thousand people died and two million were displaced in one of the largest ethnic cleansings since the Second World War. After the peace treaty was signed in 1995, a divided country was created in which two borderless nations, with their own laws, parliaments and capitals, exist within a larger nation. Bosnia-Herzegovina now encompasses both Bosnia and Herzegovina, whose majority population is Bosniak and Muslim, and the Republic of Srpska, with a majority population of ethnic Serbs and Orthodox Christians.

*

There is no doubt that contemporary Europe is at political, religious and cultural loggerheads with Islam. The constant tide of immigrants, together with the fear of religious extremism in the wake of 9/11, the attacks in France, London and Madrid, and the late Osama bin Laden's declaration of a global jihad, has reinforced stereotypes and fostered persisting conflict. Immigration, terrorism and racial and religious difference are issues that confront us worldwide, and the way in which the history and legacy of Islam in Europe are perceived will have a major impact on how those challenges are eventually resolved. With some justification, we might see current encounters with Islam precisely in terms of migration, extreme violence and religious hostility, all issues with deep roots going back to the birth of Islam itself and its arrival on the European continent. Nowadays, migrants come to find work, but the history of Islam is distinguished by the constant movement of peoples, of transition from city to city, country to country. Their earliest migrations were religious conquests, or jihad, a word that means 'struggle', which has nowadays come to signify a war against Christian infidels. In turn, Christian armies adopted an inverted image of jihad with Crusades against peoples considered to be Muslim heretics. It turns out that the problems we confront today mirror many of the tensions that have existed in historical relations between Muslims and Christians in Europe since the eighth century.

If we look closer, ancient resonances appear. France's first violent encounter with Islam goes back to the time of the Frankish kingdoms of the eighth century, out of which France itself would eventually emerge. In the early sixth century, Clovis, chieftain of the Franks, brought the Catholic faith to his vast kingdom, which stretched from the Rhine to the Pyrenees, with its capital in Paris. Their laws proclaimed the Franks as God's chosen people, free of heresy – ideas which became the foundation of the evolving European mindset. But, in 719, Muslim armies swept up to southern France and took Narbonne as the capital of Muslim Septimania. Almost one fifth of what was then Gaul came under Muslim occupation, as far north as Autun, 180 miles south-east of Paris. In the year 732, al-Ghafiqi, then emir of what is now southern Spain, advanced along the ancient paved Roman road from Zaragoza into south-west Gaul, with conquest in mind. His army entered Poitiers and ravaged the basilica, desecrating the tomb of St Hilary and setting the building on fire. Al-Ghafiqi's defeat by Charles Martel, Charlemagne's grandfather, at the Battle of Poitiers lies deep in collective memory as the crucial, mythical moment when Europe defined itself in opposition to Islam.

Nor was the satirical depiction of the Prophet Muhammad that aroused such violence in Paris in 2015 anything new. Antipathy sprang from the quills of early medieval historians such as the eighth-century Syrian priest John of Damascus, who refuted Islam, and the Venerable Bede, who believed that Muslims were descended from Hagar, Abraham's concubine, whereas Christians came from his lawful son

Isaac. Bede referred to the prophecy about Ishmael in the book of Genesis 16.12, which condemned his descendants, the Saracens, to wander in the wilderness. In Bede's version of the story of origins, all Muslims were illegitimate, while only Christians belonged to the legitimate bloodline. This antagonistic attitude was adopted by later Arab and Christian writers, who set the moral tone for centuries to come. Muhammad was also denigrated in medieval visual images. In Canto 28 of the thirteenth-century Italian poet Dante's *Divine Comedy*, the Prophet appears in Hell, where he is depicted in early manuscripts with his entrails hanging out.

Spain traces its violent encounters with Islam back even further, to the year 711, a turning point in world history, when Berber and Arab tribes from North Africa, led by their Muslim general Tariq ibn Ziyad, entered Spain and defeated the last Visigothic king, Roderick, taking over his lands and conquering all of what is now Spain and Portugal, save for the kingdom of Asturias in the far north. From that time on, there would be Muslim rulers in the Iberian peninsula for nearly 800 years, until their final defeat by the Catholic Monarchs Ferdinand and Isabella in 1492. Throughout those centuries, Muslims and Christians often fought each other with brutal enmity, but they also made alliances and signed peace treaties. Yet the memory of what is known as the invasion of 711 cast a long shadow and is still vividly alive in popular festivals throughout Spain, where the battle between Moors and Christians is re-enacted each year. Today, anti-Muslim, anti-immigration graffiti in Spain's public places convey an ever-present anxiety about invasion and a fear of modern terrorism in the wake of the calamitous Madrid attacks.

In central Europe, Switzerland's current preoccupation with the outward signs of Muslim identity also has a long history, revived in the late twentieth century with the arrival of large numbers of Muslim immigrants, mostly from Kosovo and Turkey. As far back as the tenth century, Switzerland had already encountered Islam in the form of Arab raiders, who left their fortress of Fraxinetum in southern France to take control of the Alpine passes. In the old chronicles, Fraxinetum was a symbol of the terror and panic caused by the Arab expeditions of that time, and it is repeatedly mentioned in Swiss chronicles as the source of all evil. In 939, Arabs attacked the Vallais region of southern Switzerland and destroyed an abbey. Twenty years later, a group of Muslim invaders assailed the great Carolingian monastery of St Gall, the historian Ekkehard tells us, but were slaughtered by the deacon Waldo. Local stories confirm that some names of villages and mountains, and even some present-day ruins, are the legacy left by the Saracen marauders. Further east, the horror of twentieth-century religious and racial war in the Balkans brings to mind the medieval wars of the Ottomans with Bulgaria, Serbia and Anatolia, before Sultan Mehmed the Conqueror won the longed-for prize of Orthodox Christian Constantinople in the watershed of 1453. The conquest of the Balkan states, which became part of the Islamic Ottoman Empire in the sixteenth century, prefigures more recent warfare.

Beneath and sometimes alongside this legacy of war and conflict is a different kind of heritage. It is not solely political and economic, but belongs to communal memory, often tangible and visible, sometimes hidden, even secret. It can take the form of architecture, music, art, writing, intellectual history, or it can inhere in the landscape, in territory, spaces and structures, in everyday life. Islamic civilization was informed by Greek culture and Roman architecture; in turn, Muslim scholars became first the guardians of that learning, and, later, the creators and transmitters of Europe's intellectual and artistic inheritance, generating a cultural evolution in which Spain played the most vital role. It is the intricate entanglements of many parallel histories, past and present, in war and peace, that shape this narrative.

The Panoramic View

Crucible of Light is a book about the nature of European identity. The continent of Europe has been carved out over millennia by the creative forces of its geography, history, politics and culture, which have given it its unique character. Its past is an epic tale that sweeps across cities, countries and continents, through the powerful empires of the Carolingian Franks, the Byzantine Greeks and of Islam, in a drama enacted across the Mediterranean and beyond, that challenges the foundations of Europe's perceived identity. As one of the great cultural conflicts of the world, and also one of its great alliances, is played out between its Christian and Muslim citizens, disturbing questions erupt from its turbulence to challenge the status quo and demand that we rethink exactly what European civilization is, that we probe deeper to find it and comprehend why it matters. Scrutiny of the divergences and commonalities between Islamic and Christian cultures demands that we view Europe's history in a quite different way.

This book is structured around a sequence of historical turning points, interwoven with the stories of outstanding individuals and of the great landmarks of Islamic culture in Europe, in architecture, science, technology, philosophy, art and music. Thirteen hundred years of religious, political and social conflict, yet also of collaboration and coexistence, are brought to life through the lives of people of all social levels – monarchs and scholars, slaves, pilgrims and diplomats – men and women who speak in letters, historical records, ancient manuscripts, poetry and song.

My aim is to create a compelling account that brings to light a long history of cultural role reversals, of surprising mirror images, of political power won and lost, in which we can glimpse the seeds of the vexed conflicts of our own times: love/hate relationships that triggered epic battles and sieges yet also created cultural diversity; the inverted images of Crusade and jihad that led to centuries of warfare yet resulted in unexpected alliances and cooperation; the transfers of knowledge, at first from Muslim to Christian Europe, and then, in more recent times, from Europe to the Muslim world. This is a tale of hybrid nations in which Islamic and Christian cultures have remoulded each other at different times, and it requires us to rethink the history of the last thirteen centuries. It is a book for general readers, whatever their beliefs, but it is not a theological history of either Islam or Christianity, although those religions are of prime importance to the past and present history of Europe.

The book has seven parts, constructed around seven major historical turning points. Its narrative begins in the sixth century AD with the last epic conflict between the fading Persian and Roman Empires, which sets the scene for the birth of Islam in the deserts of eighth-century Arabia, home to the nomadic clans who came to subdue the Iberian lands south of the Pyrenees and stayed to create the resplendent civilization of al-Andalus. It tells the story of the rise and fall of the Muslims and Christians of western Europe from the time of the first Muslim conquest on European soil in 711, and the creation of the caliphate of Cordoba, which ruled the western Islamic empire in the ninth and tenth centuries, until the demise of the last western Islamic state in Europe. It charts the progress of the crusading armies that sacked Constantinople before that great city finally succumbed to the powerful Ottoman sultan Mehmed II in 1453, shortly before the last Islamic emirate of Granada fell to Christian powers in 1492. The focus then turns to eastern Europe, which bowed to Ottoman rulers whose vast empire was not finally dissolved until 1923. The narrative explains how Christian Europe gained ascendancy through the conquest and colonialism that grew out of the triumph of Christian Spain in 1492, as Portuguese and Spanish explorers set sail for the New World, and it explores the imprint of Islamic civilization on Europe today.

The first two parts span a thousand years, starting from the fall of the Persian and Roman Empires, the rise of Islam in the seventh century and the earliest great battle between Muslims and Christians in western Europe in 711, up to the Christian conquest of Granada in 1492. The narrative pinpoints the origins of the hostility and sense of otherness that has bedevilled relations between Muslims and Christians. It then lingers a while in medieval Cordoba in southern Spain, seat of the first Islamic caliphate in Europe, before moving to Sicily under Muslim and Norman dominion. The story follows the waxing and waning of Islamic rule, as new Muslim dynasties arrive on the scene and make their capital in Seville. At the same time, the idea of the Christian reconquest of Spain takes hold, while Catholic crusaders travel to wage a holy war against the infidel in the Near East. In northern France, the growing strength of European Catholicism symbolized by the founding of Chartres Cathedral is thrown into question by its hybrid religious identity, disguised by a Gothic style with deep roots in Islamic architecture. Part II then moves on to Toledo in central Spain to explore the crucial transfer of knowledge through translation, and culminates in the rise and fall of the Nasrid dynasty of Muslim rulers of Granada, the last Islamic state in Europe at that time. The epoch-making history of the Nasrids' earthly paradise reached a climax in 1492, when the city fell to Christian conquerors, ending Islamic rule in western Europe after nearly eight centuries.

Part III looks to the east, where a new Islamic power rises when Constantinople is captured in 1453 by the Ottoman Turks, who created one of the most majestic empires in world history in the fifteenth and sixteenth centuries. Themes of trade, cultural exchange and the power of architecture emerge along the great commercial highway of the Silk Road, across the sea and on to Venice, capital of commerce, before we return to Constantinople to encounter the great Ottoman architect Sinan, Islam's Michelangelo. From there, the narrative pursues the adventures of travellers on land and sea, and the rediscovery of lost knowledge in Part IV, which returns us to Europe in the aftermath of 1492, as the consequences of that momentous year threaten the lives of the Spanish Moriscos, before and after their exile in 1609. We meet wandering Sufis, as well as Muslim and Christian pirates further east, and discover the revival of Arabic knowledge in the Renaissance amid the European obsession with Ottoman art.

In Part V, there are reversals of roles and shifts in the balance of power as the theme of invasion resurfaces. At the fifth historical watershed, the great titans of early modern Europe lock horns; the Ottomans have conquest in mind and the Habsburgs fear an attack prefigured in the fifteenth-century siege of Belgrade. They meet at last at the gates of Vienna in 1683, where Sultan Mehmed IV's armies are roundly defeated, finally thwarting all Ottoman plans to expand further westwards. A century or so later, the European colonization of Muslim lands in the early 1900s echoes the fifteenth- and sixteenth-century colonization of the Americas, Africa and India by the Spanish and Portuguese, and takes place in parallel with the rise of travel, tourism and Romanticism on the continent. Napoleon Bonaparte's campaign in Egypt at the end of eighteenth century appropriates the stones and splintered fragments of the Middle East in a cultural crusade that foreshadowed the cultural invasion of that region by western European travellers during the next hundred years, and sparks the controversial trend of orientalism. Meanwhile, in the east, Russia annexes the Crimea, homeland of the Ottoman Tatars. Part VI steps outside the linear narrative to turn a spotlight on three very different abodes of Islam: the state of Tatarstan in eastern Europe, a living example of an interfaith utopia, and the divergent islands of Cyprus and Malta, one divided and the other shaped by the meeting of Islam and Christianity in those places.

The story of Europe's Islamic past concludes in Part VII by turning to its living legacy, set against the backdrop of the demise of the Ottoman Empire from 1800 up to the creation of the secular republic of Turkey in 1923. Here, the narrative picks up the threads of the first chapter and returns to the theme of ethnic and religious cleansing in Armenia and in Serbia after Tito's regime ended. It delves into and expands on the ways that the presence of Islam lives on across Europe in contemporary politics, in the landscape, in our everyday life, building on cutting-edge research by international groups of scholars that reveals how Islamic culture has always been and still is an integral part of Europe, west and east. This includes the Ottoman revival in Turkey after the demise of Kemal Atatürk, the impact of the Ottoman legacy on identity, culture and politics in twenty-first-century Slovakia, and the restoration of mosques and Muslim cemeteries in the predominantly Catholic Poland of today. The narrative culminates inside the Alhambra palace of Granada, perhaps the most resonant and poignant expression of the tangible presence of Islamic civilization in Europe.

Close-ups and Snapshots

Europe does not have a single, linear history. The span of time from 711 to the present demands a narrative structure that reflects its complexity. This book responds to that by stepping outside the historical chronology at key points to focus on recurrent motifs, ideas and themes that stitch the narrative together, weaving a pattern not only of difference and rupture, but also of continuity and coherence, highlighting mirror images, oppositions between frontiers and territories, between Crusade and jihad, migration and settlement, cross-fertilization and cultural repression, tolerance and intolerance. They uncover echoes, harbingers and continuities across the continent. The first significant motif in this history is the ambivalent role of books and words, with their ability to persuade, instruct, record, debate and delight. The very foundations of Islam, Judaism and Christianity rest on their sacred books, which demonstrate that a written culture based on scholarship and learning is fundamental to these faiths – and their cultures. Nonetheless, language itself is ambiguous and its effects can be pernicious. We have seen how the antipathy towards Muslims expressed in the writings of early medieval historians left a lasting negative legacy that fostered intolerance and religious prejudice, and accentuated ideas of religious difference.

At the same time, words and books record and preserve human knowledge. Essential to this story is the crucial contribution of the Islamic world to written learning. That contribution begins with their early copying of Greek and Persian scholarship into Arabic in Baghdad, and the subsequent introduction of paper to Europe via Muslim Spain, a piece of technology that revolutionized book production and paved the way for the printing press. The books and learning of Islamic culture formed the basis of European scholarship; Muslim intellectuals reread the writings of classical scientists, such as the mathematician Archimedes and the physician Galen, and created their own innovative theories, which spread to the rest of Europe through Muslim Spain. The new learning that galvanized the continent was the result of Muslim, Christian and Jewish scholars working together in the great centres of scholarship in Toledo in Spain and Palermo in Sicily, in the Middle Ages, where they produced translations of Arabic texts into Latin and vernacular Spanish. Their collaboration laid aside prejudice and hostility to create an environment of tolerant coexistence and collaboration. Yet a climate of fear and secrecy once more pervaded Spain in the sixteenth and early seventeenth centuries. Translation, ambiguity and the power of books, words and the Arabic language were central to the life of Miguel de Luna, who fabricated his mysterious Lead Books in Granada in a last-ditch attempt to save his fellow Moriscos, or Muslim converts to Christianity, from expulsion from their native land.

The second important motif relates to journeys, to the nomad, the wanderer, harking back to the movement of nomadic tribes and clans in Arabia, where the Prophet Muhammad was born in the late sixth century. As Islam took hold, this natural movement of clans was inspired by religious faith, so that migration became linked to land and dominion, to the militancy and violence that inspired the Muslim conquest of Spain in 711. Later, Christian soldiers fought Crusades against the Muslims of Europe, and the Catholic reconquest of Iberia got under way, reaching its nadir with the expulsion of its Morisco and Jewish populations, condemned to roam strange lands in search of a new life. Those nomads of Islam may have been conquered by the Christian sword, but their wanderings contributed to the creation of Europe's multicultural heritage.

Commerce was fundamental to the foundation of the Islamic empire, and the exchange of goods and knowledge relied on alliance, collaboration and understanding. Scholars, merchants and diplomats were constantly on the move, and at times left surprising legacies. The young diplomat Leo the African, born in Muslim Granada and enslaved by Christian pirates, nomads of the sea, was forced to convert to Christianity, and eventually became a great scholar and travel writer. His mirror image appears in the story of Samson Rowlie, born in Great Yarmouth in Norfolk and captured by pirates in 1577. Samson was castrated by the Ottomans, converted to Islam and took the name Hassan Agha, in which guise he became chief eunuch and treasurer of Algiers until he died, or was possibly murdered, in 1588. The ceaseless movement of Muslims in Europe continues today with its twenty-first-century wanderers, the immigrants who come not to conquer, but to find work and a better life.

The geography of the continent of Europe and the Middle East, the history of its borders and frontiers, the transmigration of both the desert peoples of Arabia and the agricultural workers of northern Europe to a settled life in towns and cities, and the movement from a wandering to a sedentary lifestyle have all had significant repercussions on the history of European Muslims and Christians. The importance of place takes many forms, which often relate to war and conquest, to Crusade and jihad, where borders and frontiers have created a sense of difference, separation and opposition. There are places of authority, of worship, war, triumph, transition, as well as places of memory, which form part of a tangible, multilayered heritage visible in what are often contested sites. The narrative travels through countries and cities, enters buildings, scales mountains and crosses rivers, lingering at places of prominence to discern the meaning of an Islamic heritage writ large on landscapes and cityscapes. It takes us to Cordoba, place of illumination, to Palermo, city of wisdom, to Seville and the Almohad triumph, and north towards Chartres and its mysteries. The journey turns eastwards to Istanbul and its hybrid identities, returns to besieged Belgrade and pauses at the gates of Vienna, before heading towards France, England and Holland, architects of Muslim repression, then alights again in Turkey. The final leg takes us to the utopian state of Tatarstan, then south-west to the island of Cyprus, with its violent schisms, and on to Malta, whose greatest Islamic inheritance is its language, before returning finally to Granada. The route leads the reader inside majestic buildings: the Mosque of Cordoba, the Cappella Palatina in Palermo, Istanbul's Hagia Sophia, the Alhambra of Granada. It guides us along the great trade route of the Silk Road and into the oriental coffee houses of England in the seventeenth and eighteenth centuries.

Books, journeys and places reveal new motifs and ideas. The lost and the hidden rise to the surface, the legacy of forgotten Islamic knowledge and the Renaissance in Europe, which turned back to ancient Greece and Rome, but also reclaimed Arab science to begin its scientific revolution. A heritage of concealment, of false identities and secret languages emerges as we learn of the lives of crypto-Muslims in sixteenth-century Spain, and the crypto-Christians of Cyprus persecuted under Ottoman rule. Europe's discovery of Ottoman art from the sixteenth to the eighteenth centuries ignited an obsession with all things Turkish – turbans, carpets, the rise of the coffee house. Queen Elizabeth I of England wore clothes in Turkish style and turbans were sported by the modishly dressed. Later, nineteenth-century tourism fostered the fashion for orientalism that found expression in books, images and architecture. Islamic heritage created hybrid identities as Europe's Christians adopted the outer appearances of Islamic civilization, torn between the desire for resemblance and the fear of difference. The deep-rooted connection between Christians and Muslims, whose shared European history lives on in the twenty-first century, west, east, north and south, in politics, national culture, architecture and everyday life, began in ancient Persia and Rome, where this book also begins. It roams across nations and travels through many centuries to trace the emergence of a common European identity forged in the burning crucible of religious and political strife, the deep significance of which this present-day saga brings into the light.

Part One

THE RISE OF THE CRESCENT MOON IN EUROPE

'Saint Helena and Heraclius taking the Holy Cross to Jerusalem', Martín Bernat and Miguel Ximénez, c. 1483

Chapter 1

Fire, Wood and Stone: A Phoenix Ascends

'Gather up the fragments that remain, that nothing be lost'

John 6.12

The story of the time before Islam came to Europe is one of fragments. Our vision of the seventh century after Christ is often shadowy and spectral, a distant view of a vibrant, evolving world, rich in ideas yet beset by violence, division, war and migration, glimpsed partially through incomplete documents, ancient records and faded images. It is not solely our perspective that is fragmented, but the times themselves, rocked by the multiple changes writ large across fractured states and polities reshaped by invasions and conquests whose pole star was religion. The importance of the seventh century is neglected yet vital, because its history marks the end of the ancient regime and the transition into an emerging European continent. The events that led to this were determined by battles fought in the name of both mighty empires and migrating tribes, each represented by storied individuals and the sites of power they created. These were struggles for supremacy over land, peoples, trade routes, over money and power, but above all they were struggles not just for hearts and minds, but for souls too, as three major religions met on European soil, their creeds objectified in wood, fire and stone.

The origins of Europe's encounters between Muslims and Christians lie in the last great battle of classical antiquity. It began in the early seventh century and was the finale of a long-standing drama enacted between the Roman and Persian Empires for 700 years, a colossal tussle between two martial superpowers from different civilizations, each struggling for supremacy. By the summer of 603, when the Persians, led by the ruler of the Sassanid dynasty Khusro II, attacked the Roman province of Mesopotamia, religion had become the focus of the conflict. Long before the time of Christ, the Iranian prophet Zoroaster (Zarathustra) wrought his new faith of moral truth from the legends of Persian sky and war gods, creating the world's first known monotheistic religion, whose supreme deity Ahura Mazda was the Lord of Wisdom. Its teachings of individual judgment, Heaven and Hell, the resurrection of the body and everlasting life became crucial tenets of Judaism, Christianity and Islam. Fire and water formed the life-sustaining elements of ritual purity, ever present in the fire temples where worshippers prayed. In Sassanid Persia, Zoroastrian ethics fused theology and law in the role of its priests, who oversaw both faith and justice.[1] Yet the Persian Empire, whose trade connected Arabia with central and south-east Asia, China and India, embraced many other creeds, including Christianity, and its peoples were of many nationalities, diverse races, and spoke numerous languages. Over the 400 years of Sassanid rule, Persian civilization was multicultural and tolerant of its religious variety. It was also confident of the ethical and intellectual superiority of Zoroastrianism over the newly arrived Christianity.

While the Roman and Persian Empires of classical antiquity were mirror images in terms of military expansion, legal systems, cultural and architectural attainment, the Romans of the late Byzantine Empire judged Persian Zoroastrians as impious worshippers of a false god, whose rulers delighted in violence and sacrilege. Their last mighty battle with the Persians became a direct clash of warring faiths. Christianity had triumphed in the Roman Empire in the fourth century, when its one God superseded rival pagan deities. The catalyst in the adoption of the new religion was the controversial emperor Constantine the Great, whose legendary victory over his challenger, the emperor Maxentius, at the Milvian Bridge over the river Tiber in Rome, in AD 312, was inspired by a famous vision of the Holy Cross in the sky. On the eve of battle, as he dozed fitfully, its meaning was revealed to him in a dream, in which he was told to mark the sign of the Cross on his soldiers' shields. During the battle Maxentius was drowned in the river Tiber; Constantine converted to Christianity and became ruler of half the Western Roman Empire. In 330, he made the ancient city of Byzantium its new capital, the new Rome, renaming it Constantinople, after himself. In 391, Christianity was finally formalized as the only legitimate faith of the Roman Empire by the emperor Theodosius. Constantine's conversion was a watershed moment which moulded the future religious tenor of Roman and European history as essentially Christian.

Although the Roman Empire stretched from Mesopotamia to the Atlantic, from Scotland to the Sahara, the power of Rome waned and Constantinople grew stronger, so that a schism developed between East and West, each with its own senate and emperor. The authority of the patriarch of Constantinople, leader of the Eastern Church, was only second to that of the principal religious figurehead, the Bishop of Rome. By the sixth century, the supremacy and splendour of the Eastern Empire found its greatest expression in Christian architecture. The enigmatic and brilliant emperor Justinian (482–565), nephew of an illiterate Balkan soldier, ordained the construction of the Church of Holy Wisdom, St Sophia, consecrated for the first time in 537. Breathtaking in its beauty and fabulous in construction, it became the religious heart of the Byzantine Empire, an image of its ostensibly supreme power. The new cathedral embodied Justinian's desire to eliminate all dissidence and unite the Roman Empire under a single faith. But it would be the destiny of another Roman emperor, Heraclius (575–641), to snatch victory from the jaws of defeat and turn the tables on the might of Sassanid Persia.

The sacking of Byzantine Jerusalem by the Sassanids in 614, during which they seized fragments of the True Cross of Christ's Crucifixion, was a bold provocation to retaliate. Heraclius had been emperor since he deposed the tyrant Phocas, parading his dismembered body through the streets before having it burned, and organizing his own coronation in Constantinople on 5 October 610. But his empire was soon scourged by the coordinated attacks of the Persian armies of Khusro II, whose driving ambition to eliminate

Roman rule from the Middle East was achieved by the early 620s, when all such territories, including Egypt, came under Persian rule. Khusro next set his sights on the invasion of Asia Minor, the last substantial territory under Roman control. The great Iranian king seemed to have won decisively, but there was an unexpected twist to the plot.

Against all odds, in the winter of 627, Heraclius carried out a daredevil raid into Mesopotamia, the Persian heartland that had been wrested from the Romans at the start of the conflict in 603. He crushed the Persians at Nineveh and sacked Khusro's magnificent palace at Dastagird. Khusro fled to Ctesiphon, where he was suddenly overthrown in a palace coup in the night of 25 February 628 and was murdered the next day by his son, Kavadh II, who also had all his brothers and half-brothers executed to avoid any challenge to his kingship. Kavadh immediately surrendered to Heraclius, agreeing to Persian withdrawal from all the lands they occupied. The Roman Empire had triumphed, and the emperor's victory dispatch was read out in St Sophia on 15 May, a personal eulogy in which Heraclius cast himself as the biblical King David and announced the defeat of the 'arrogant Khusro, opponent of God.' A war that had lasted a generation had ended, and the people of Constantinople rejoiced, taking to the streets with lights and olive branches to acclaim their great emperor and praise the power of God. Their civilization had been defended, and Heraclius' conquest, prefigured in the epic conflicts between the Hellenes and the Persians in the fifth century BC at Salamis and Thermopylae, reinforced the cultural identity of the West.

In 1464, the famous Florentine painter Piero della Francesca (*c.* 1415–92) finished his masterpiece, a cycle of frescos called *History of the True Cross*, which adorns the basilica of San Francesco in Arezzo and in which Roman piety plays a key role. Two frescos are devoted to the emperor Constantine, one showing his dream in which an angel from the star-studded heavens brings the sleeping emperor a tiny gold cross that presages his victory over Maxentius, the other portraying his victory on the Milvian Bridge. The last fresco of the cycle shows a triumphant Heraclius, distant heir of Constantine, arriving in Jerusalem to return the True Cross to its rightful place of rest. Most precious and holy of Christian relics, the wooden fragments of the original Cross now merged with Heraclius' sensational victory to heighten the religious status of the Roman Empire. Nicephorus, ninth-century patriarch of Constantinople, gives an account of Heraclius' entry into Jerusalem, on 21 March 630, bearing those fragments. Amid the shrines inside the Church of the Holy Sepulchre, Heraclius handed the reliquary of the Cross to Modestus, Jerusalem's senior cleric, who inspected the seal and declared it intact. A hymn was sung as Modestus removed the holy relic and restored it to its rightful place at the centre of the church, the site of the Rock of Calvary, where Christ was crucified.[2] The ceremony was a powerful statement of Christian supremacy; with the Persians subdued and the True Cross restored to Jerusalem, it seemed that the Eastern Roman Empire was now all powerful, even if depleted by the ravages of war. Despite the open fissure between Rome and Constantinople, the entire Middle East was set to become Christian.

The Birth of Islam

That certainty was shattered by a series of startling events. Out of the ashes of two fallen civilizations, a new religion, Islam, emerged in the Arabian desert, and its followers, against all expectation, defeated the powers of Rome and Persia in only twenty years, and went on to rule an empire that stretched from western Europe as far as southern central Asia, a feat they achieved in less than a century. Nothing in the Arab peoples' prior history or way of life suggested that they might do so. Nomads by nature and known as Sarakenoi (Saracens) or the 'people of the tents' to the Greeks, the desert peoples led a tribal life enforced by the harsh, rocky geography of their homeland. Stateless raiders who had ruled themselves since biblical times, their militant, predatory clans fought for booty and to avenge wrongs inflicted on their kinsfolk. Every Arab belonged to a tribe or clan group, which gave them security in the absence of a formal government, and tribesmen were fiercely proud of their ability to defend themselves and their dependants. The shift in trade routes that involved new caravan trails connecting Yemen and Syria brought great riches, which threatened the traditional equilibrium of the clans and substituted economic values for their tribal ones. Not all were nomadic, as many settled in towns and cities as traders, though their population was relatively sparse and lacked any extensive political organization. Both the Persians and the Romans had dealings with Arabia – the Romans had first encountered the trading and raiding of Arab tribesmen in 63 BC, when the general Pompey annexed Syria and Palestine. Neither of the two superpowers could have imagined them as world conquerors, but rather saw them as a marginal border people who posed no significant threat.

Nor could they have known that an oasis on the old caravan route that linked the Mediterranean world with South Arabia, East Africa and South Asia would become a global spiritual centre. The city of Mecca, in present-day Saudi Arabia, is surrounded by arid mountains and is located midway between Marib in the south and Petra in the north. In Roman and Byzantine times it had become a thriving commercial centre, controlled by the powerful Quraysh tribe and benefiting from Arabia's trade with the African continent through the Nile. Sea routes to India connected with the Persian Gulf, which enabled the Arabs to sell their wares to the eastern markets of the Roman Empire. But it was Mecca's reputation as a centre of pilgrimage that boosted the local economy, as pilgrims streamed in to visit its holy temples, said to house over a hundred pagan deities. The city's most sacred sanctuary was the Ka'aba, shrine of the Quraysh tribe and home to the idols that represented the manifold gods of the Arabian clans.

*

Around AD 570, a man called Muhammad ibn 'Abd Allah ibn 'Abd al-Muttalib was born into the Quraysh tribe. Muslim tradition recounts that he spent the first five years of his life with a Bedouin tribe, according to Arab custom, so that he could learn the pure speech and manners of the desert. Orphaned at the age of six, he was then raised in Mecca and worked as a merchant. When he was twenty-five, he became the commercial agent of a wealthy widow and distinguished businesswoman, Khadija, whom he married. Although Khadija was about forty when she became his wife, she bore him several children. As he grew older, Muhammad became more inclined to reflection and solitude, often retreating to a cave on Mount Hira, just north of Mecca. There, at the age of forty, he had a vision of an angel, who told him 'I am Gabriel and you are the messenger of God.' Gradually, through Gabriel, and for the rest of his life, Muhammad was instructed to recite and remember the holy words that eventually became the Koran. It was the moment that Islam was born.

As Muhammad started preaching, initially to his family and friends and later in public, his visionary message of the need for submission to the will of a single, all-knowing God (which is what the word 'Islam' means) at first shocked and then antagonized the citizens of Mecca, whose many deities were enshrined in the Ka'aba. The ancient Black Stone set inside it was worshipped long before Islam. A dark, fragmented piece of rock, resembling a meteorite, it was thought to date back to the time of Adam and Eve, before whom it fell from Heaven in the place where they built an altar. After the Ka'aba was destroyed by a flash flood in 608, the Quraysh squabbled over who should lay the sacred stone in position in the rebuilt shrine, and it fell to Muhammad, who showed great wisdom in his first public act, laying the stone in position and kissing it. Today the focal point of Islam's greatest shrine, all Muslims yearn to kiss it during the hajj or annual pilgrimage. Like the Cross of Christ, the Black Stone became the symbol of unity that brought disparate clans together instead of dividing them.[3] As Zoroastrianism had been embodied in fire, and Christianity in the wood of the Cross, so Islam was manifested in stone.

The Muslim calendar starts in the year AD 622, when Muhammad fled from Mecca with his followers to the city of Yathrib, to escape the hostility and violence of the Meccan pagans and restore order to the feuding Jewish and Arab populations. Yathrib later became known as Medina, the City of the Prophet, and Muhammad's flight there was seen as the first emigration, the Hijra, marking the beginning of a communal organization of Muslims, known as the umma, established by Muhammad in the Constitution of Medina. In December of 630, the year that Heraclius returned the True Cross to Jerusalem, Muhammad agreed to a truce with the hostile tribes of his home town and returned triumphant to Mecca as the prophet and leader of an egalitarian religious movement set to rock the political and religious foundations of the known world. His victory was won with bloodshed and violence. Muhammad's choice of the direction of prayer (qibla), facing towards Mecca instead of Jerusalem, destroyed his good relations with Medina's Jews. His followers subdued rebel tribes, mainly Jewish, who were massacred and their women and children enslaved, in the first jihad, or struggle against the enemy. Islam, with its one God, had triumphed over paganism in Arabia, as Christianity had 300 years earlier in the pagan Roman Empire. Upon his unexpected death, two years later, in 632, Muhammad bequeathed a religious and cultural legacy of astonishing originality and permanence. It ignited a revolution with its radical commitment to a new ethic of the family and a return to the ancient values of monotheism, in which Muhammed aligned himself with the tradition of the great Jewish prophets.

*

Less than a century later, a thriving new Islamic empire stretched beyond Samarkand in central Asia to Tangiers in North Africa. Quite how this was achieved perplexed early Christian scholars and clergy, who sought an explanation in God's divine retribution, and it is not clearly understood even today. Without doubt, the first four successors of the Prophet, known as the Rightly Guided Ones, established the idea of the caliphate and set the religious, political and economic framework on which the emerging empire was founded. The Prophet died without appointing a successor, and it was clear that the umma could not exist without a leader. Muhammad's friend, Abu Bakr, was elected, and inaugurated the role of caliph or 'deputy', but died of a fever just two years later, aged sixty-two. Omar, the second caliph, led the faithful for ten years, shaping Islam as a political ideology and beginning to build an empire. A born military strategist, Omar added the designation 'Commander of the Faithful' to the title of caliph, thereby fusing his spiritual and military roles. His armies took on the conquest of the known world, inspired by the new faith, which promised them booty and riches in their fight against the evil and misguided.

By the early 640s, Omar's soldiers had conquered Egypt, Lebanon, Syria and Palestine, and Persia would soon follow. As David Levering Lewis explains, 'The religion and language of the Arab conquerors spread over the Iranian plateau like a prayer blanket, smothering an 1,100-year-old civilization that would rebound, *mutatis mutandis* its Islamicisation, slowly and almost stealthily in less than a century.'[4] The full-scale military operation, resulting in the invasion of both the Byzantine and the Sassanid Empires in a matter of only twenty years, was viewed by the Romans as an incomprehensible military disaster, as well as a religious debacle. It was achieved not by massive armies, but by disconcertingly small Arab forces, just a few thousand to overcome Roman Syria and subdue Iran. The crown jewel for the Muslims was Jerusalem, which had appeared in one of the Prophet's visions. In 638, Omar entered the city in person to accept its surrender, some say riding on an ass and wearing ragged robes to meet the emperor Sophronius. Omar ordered a small wooden mosque to be erected, in the place where his successors were to build the Dome of the Rock, near the Al-Aqsa Mosque, two of Islam's most venerated sites. Both men signed a pact to confirm that there would be no compulsion in religion, which later became sura 2.256 of the Koran.

In 644, this great leader of men was stabbed by a Persian slave and died the same day. He was succeeded by a distant cousin of Muhammad, Othman, of the Umayyad clan, who became the third caliph at the age of sixty-eight. In his twelve-year rule, Othman oversaw the compilation of a definitive version of the Koran, the one still used by Muslims today, as well as building over 5,000 mosques across the new empire, but, like Omar, he was brutally murdered, dying at the hands of a group of rioting Egyptians. The fourth caliph and beloved cousin of the Prophet, the mystical Ali, led the umma for four short years, until he too was assassinated, in 661, by one of his own radical followers. The first era of Islamic history ended in the shadow of violence, and all eyes turned to Othman's cousin, Muawiya (r. 661–80), the man who became the first Umayyad caliph of Damascus.

*

Muawiya and a splinter group of the Umayyad clan had fled to Damascus when Othman was murdered, and Muawiya was appointed governor of the city. The caliphate he created there would preside over what was in effect a free-trade zone from one end of the known world to the other, and his dynasty set Muslims on the path to greatness. With the main tenets of the new religion now enshrined in the authority of a written text, Islam began to evolve as a civilization and a political entity, in part forged out of the ruins of the empires it had replaced. Like the old pre-Christian Roman Empire, the caliphate depended on tax collecting and was tolerant of religious and cultural variety, as was the multicultural Sassanid Empire. Islam had emerged from the preaching of a visionary seer, as had Zoroastrianism, with which both Islam and Christianity shared the promise of personal judgment and eternal afterlife. The early Islamic world was defined by its system of values, by a political and cultural model whose driving forces were religious belief, power, factionalism and the family. The Islamic state, in the form of the ruling dynasty, guaranteed salvation, but also justice and social harmony, unifying religion and politics. Arab pride in the honour, independence, virility and language of the tribe was rooted in the purity of family descent, tribal hierarchy and the solidarity of patriarchal links. This was mapped onto the Umayyad state and the Muslim army, the former a means of bringing aristocratic families to power, in which the legitimizing role of lineage was crucial.

But the social model conflicted with this structure, as it was predicated on an egalitarian society of believers and a system of government in which caliphs ruled in the name of Allah. The monotheism of Islam rose above tribal divisions to unite Arabs in a single community of believers, following a single law and fighting the holy war, jihad.[5]

As a result, from the start, the Umayyad government existed in an atmosphere of continual conflict, a kind of civil war, at once political, ideological and familial, that originated in the great schism caused by the question of succession after Muhammad's death. The split centred on the Sunni conviction that the caliphate should be elective, at odds with the Shi'ite belief that it should be hereditary. Yet the Umayyads achieved a certain balance between an egalitarian, universalist message and their hierarchical power structure, since they were sensitive to their duty to the community of believers, and to the need to set standards of morality, justice and liberality. But future generations of Muslim rulers were nevertheless beset by this fundamental conflict over how to define legitimacy of power, an issue that harked back to the biblical perception of Abraham's son Ishmael as illegitimate.

The adoption of hereditary succession of the caliph and the appointment of governors from the Umayyad family to rule the huge provinces of the Muslim empire helped to sustain political unity for a century. But it destroyed the traditional life of the nomadic tribesmen, who now lived in a society of great wealth, as well as belonging to a social and political hierarchy in whose running they had no say. Even so, Muawiya's newly minted caliphate saw the birth of an Islamic civilization forged from the scattered fragments of Persian, Roman and Arabian culture, expanding its borders and heralding an era of learning and scholarship that would indelibly mark European life.

*

The seismic shift in eastern civilizations had so far barely touched the west of the European continent. The Muslims had first turned to the east, paying scant attention to a Europe that seemed to have very little to offer in terms of commerce and knowledge. The west had its own trials to deal with as the Western Roman Empire gradually segmented and was refashioned from the fifth to the seventh centuries, with the Persian and the Eastern Roman Empires crumbling and succumbing to the Arab Muslims. Invasion was a keynote in both east and west. Around 375, the Huns, a nomadic tribe from the central steppes of Asia, crossed the river Don into the Eastern Roman Empire, where they were given short shrift and hastily departed westwards, reaching Italy in 408. The fall of the Eternal City of Rome to Alaric and his tribe of Germanic Visigoths in 410 shocked the West; in response, and by way of appeasement, the Roman commander Constantius set up the first barbarian kingdom of Visigoths in 418, in the region of Aquitaine, giving them the status of federates or allies of the empire. But when, on 4 September 476, the young Roman emperor Romulus Augustulus was stripped of his insignia and exiled by his own army, rebels led by a Germanic chieftain, it marked the end of the Roman Empire in the West.

Eventually, the German Frankish tribes who had arrived in the fifth century created the most powerful Christian kingdom in medieval Europe in the land we now call France. Akin to the desert Arab tribes who were raiders and fighters, the Franks came from a tribal society geared to war. Their chief was a warrior, and their Germanic civilization was founded on violence as the supreme virtue. Like the Arabian nomads, they were bound by ties of fidelity and service. Separated from the Romans by their ignorance of Latin, they were Christians disdained for adopting the perceived heresy of Arianism, which did not accept Christ's divine nature. Yet, after the Spanish Visigoths converted to Catholicism in 589, Christianity, still a comparatively new faith, enveloped the west. It held firm amid migrations and swings in the balance of power, an intermediary between Rome and the Visigoths.

*

The rise of western Christianity contributed to an economic decline in Europe in the early Middle Ages, the roots of which lay in its teachings. The Church took exception to individual wealth, preaching an ideal life of poverty and asceticism, and it also banned usury at the Council of Nicaea in 325. Money itself was almost obsolete and was replaced by a barter economy, which deprived western Europe of 'its financiers, bankers, great merchants and contractors; in other words, specialists in production and exchange.'[6] Alongside this lack of economic prosperity, churchmen became more deeply embroiled in statesmanship, with bishops taking on a political role and leaving monks to bridge the gap between God and Christians, under the influence of St Benedict. The rise of monasticism meant that the Christian religion and the monasteries would be the guardians of Western learning.

As Violet Moller explains, the Church attempted to absorb or destroy the philosophy, science and literature of the ancient pagan world.[7] The emperor Justinian closed the Athens Academy, centre of pagan intellectual resistance and of Neoplatonist philosophy, upon which its scholars fled to Persia, taking their learning with them, in an act that impoverished European cultural life. Secular book production around the sixth century took place in secret, while monastic scriptoria filled the gap with new types of religious writing, including the lives of saints. By 500, the most important centre of learning in the world, Alexandria, was declining, as the power and importance of Constantinople grew. The papyruses in the legendary Library of Alexandria, founded around 3000 BC by the Egyptian king Ptolemy I, crumbled into dust. The rich, opulent Byzantine Empire also aggravated the existing antagonism between Rome, capital of the West, and the Greek capital of the Eastern Roman Empire, whose people were contemptuous of western European intellectual and technological backwardness.

By the early eighth century, the situation in the Islamic empire was virtually the opposite of that in Europe. While cultural and religious changes in the Western Roman Empire had a negative impact on its economic and intellectual life, in the Damascus caliphate equivalent changes were supported and financed by a more stable economy and political structure. At the same time, invasion and migration were central to the history of both Europe and the Islamic world from the fifth to the seventh century, and their effects had been amplified by momentous religious change.

Islam's earliest history was marked by events that were to shape the nature of its eventual presence in the West. Its founding act, the Hijra, or emigration to Medina, associated the new religion with exile, while Muhammad's first war against the Meccans established a military dimension that found expression in the idea of jihad, or holy war.* When the Prophet arrived in Medina, he built the very first masjid, or mosque, there – an iconic place of worship specific to Islam. At once religious and secular, the mosque was a defensive stronghold, a political and military assembly place, and a place of worship, an inward-facing sanctuary. It enshrined the military, political and religious dimensions of the religion in tangible form. The new unity and commitment of Arab and Berber Muslims in the late seventh century that arose when the civil wars of the Umayyad caliphate were quelled was expressed in greater military expansion and movement of its peoples. The migration of troops to fight holy wars was fundamental to the evolution of the Islamic empire.

The origins of Europe's relationship with Islamic civilization turns on an axis of invasion and conquest, violence and power, of warring empires and cultures, around which swirl migrating tribes, nomads of the deserts and steppes, whose exchanges in trade and war brought forth a fractured, divided world. In this great evolution of peoples and faiths, a Christianity divided by Schism held sway on the European continent, unconcerned by the new religion that it scarcely understood and deemed a heresy. Meanwhile, on the edge of Europe, the Islamic empire wrought unity out of fragmentation, fusing faith and politics in its revolutionary egalitarian state. By the

---

* The word *jihad*, in Arabic, means 'struggle', often against the unbeliever, but through usage it has come to mean 'holy war' in common parlance.

early eighth century, the caliphate of Damascus had the European mainland in sight. But no one foresaw that eighth-century Spain would soon be shattered by conquerors from overseas – conquerors who fought in the name of a new prophet, Muhammad.

Chapter 2

The King and the Slave: Roderick, Tariq and the Great Battle of 711

> 'Men, where can you fly when the sea is behind you and the enemy before you?'
>
> Tariq ibn Ziyad, 711

The story of the first defining moment in Europe's encounter with Islam has a veneer of clarity and coherence. The essential historical facts camouflage the intricate relationships between four enigmatic individuals: Roderick, last king of the Spanish Visigoths; Count Julian of Ceuta; the Berber leader Tariq ibn Ziyad; and Musa ibn Nusayr, governor of North Africa, who all took centre stage in the Muslim conquest of Visigothic Hispania. On 19 July 711, the armies of King Roderick were defeated by Muslim troops under the command of Tariq ibn Ziyad on the banks of the river Guadalete in Andalusia. Over the next three years, between 711 and 714, almost the entire Iberian peninsula came under the rule of Islamic leaders from North Africa, echoing the pattern of whirlwind conquests that preceded the supremacy of the Umayyad dynasty of caliphs in Damascus. It was part of a sequence of invasion, conquest and expansion that had created the ancient Roman and Persian Empires, as well as the new Islamic superpower.

In that context, the events of 711 were familiar, yet unique. No one could have anticipated the indelible impact the decisions and actions of these four men would have on the history of both Spain and Europe. Their intense personal antagonisms, rivalries, betrayals and desires reflected the widespread upheavals born of the collapse of the empires of antiquity and the construction of a new world order created by the empire of Islam. Yet the history of the dawn of Islam in Europe was forged in a climate of both conflict and cooperation, inspiring a narrative thread that would be woven into foundation myths of extraordinary importance and longevity, and whose dominant strands were ambiguity and hybridity.

The Tragedy of Roderick

In the remote desert of Jordan, traversed only by Bedouin tribes, lies the ruined palace of Qusayr 'Amra, its reddish stone blending into the tones of the barren landscape. Built as a retreat for the Umayyad sultans, this eighth-century relic is famous for its magnificent wall paintings, especially the *Six Kings* fresco. A fragmented image of a vital moment in ancient times, it shows six kings gesturing towards an enthroned figure encircled by a nimbus on the wall opposite. This royal personage appears to be a caliph, whose pre-eminence the kings are acknowledging in a visual statement of Islamic imperial power.[1] The emperors of Byzantium and Persia are there, along with the Negus of Abyssinia, their rich robes and crowns faded yet still symbolic of greatness, while the images of two other sovereigns, maybe from India and China, have deteriorated beyond recognition.

The sixth monarch is the most unexpected, as his depiction personifies the earliest known record of Roderick, aside from coins minted during his brief reign. The fresco was painted sometime between 711 and 715, at the end of the Umayyad caliph al-Walid I's reign in Damascus, and precedes all written accounts of Roderick's monarchy. He is aligned, not with the authority and power of Byzantium or Christianity, as on the Visigothic coins, but with that of the Muslim empire. Roderick is without question a king conquered by Islam, and if not subjugated by it, then certainly deferential to its military power. He was a Christian ruler, and the image also hints at Islam's superiority over his religion. Roderick himself is an ambiguous, Janus-like figure, looking back towards Christian imperialism and forward to the new empire of Islam. Most crucially, Roderick's fractured portrait and its context represent the first ever allusion to the dramatic loss of his kingdom in the Muslim conquest of 711.

The last Visigothic king of Spain is a man shrouded in legends, whose actions were governed by circumstances and by a destiny that prevailed over a conflicted, ambivalent personality. We know only the barest details about Roderick, who was probably a duke and military commander. Even his accession to the throne in 710 was bedevilled by murky conflict. The warlike Visigoths had entered Hispania, the Roman name for Spain, in the early fifth century AD and made Toledo their capital city. Their legacy of learned literature, fine arts and crafts, a pioneering legal system and a strong tradition of Catholic Christianity was diminished by endless coups and feuding, and, by the early eighth century, their kingdom was corrupt and decadent. After the death of the dissolute King Witiza in 710, certain Visigothic noblemen ignored the claims of his sons and encouraged Roderick to take the throne in a bold coup d'état, despite accusations that he was a usurper and not a direct heir to the crown.[2] The early Latin *Mozarabic Chronicle of 754* (*Crónica mozárabe de 754*) states that 'Roderick seized the throne with force and at the instance of the Senate'.[3] This account carries great weight due to its early date, and is the best-informed source on this era, reflecting a Christian viewpoint, though its brevity renders it ambiguous, if not cryptic. The narrative is framed by the principle that divine providence was the agent of history, and the conquest of 711 looms large as a catastrophic event on a par with the fall of Troy, a punishment for the sexual corruption and decadence of the Visigothic realm. The narrator blames Roderick's ambition, as well as the treachery and cowardice of those around him.

The events of 711 were infused with an apocalyptic quality for both Christian and Arab historians, who merged history with legend, above all in the earliest Arabic chronicles, some of which construct that Muslim victory as the fulfilment of a prophetic, supernatural warning sent to Roderick. The king's ambition, combined with a boldness that verged on the foolhardy, are vital aspects of his character in one legend, which tells of an enchanted tower near Toledo, allegedly built by Hercules. No Visigothic king had ever entered it, since a curse was laid upon it that forbade its violation. Each newly crowned king came to the tower and added another lock to the door, for fear of breaking the spell. Against the advice of his counsellors, Roderick ignored the evil hex and broke in, only to find auguries of his own downfall prefigured in the depiction of Arab horsemen on the walls inside. The curse was set out in an Arabic inscription forewarning the reader that whoever broke the locks would lose his kingdom to the men depicted in the frescos.

The Betrayal of Count Julian

Roderick's fate was inextricably entwined with a man named only once in the *Mozarabic Chronicle* – Urbanus, though he is more usually referred to as Count Julian. Even less is known about him than of Roderick, yet all Arab sources are unequivocal in underlining the crucial importance of Julian's actions. We do know that he was a Christian based on the north African coast. Several historians describe him as Roderick's governor in Ceuta, which was then under Visigothic control, though the Muslim chronicler Ibn al-Qutiyya (d. 977) wrote of him as a merchant who brought Roderick fine horses and falcons from Tangiers. Julian is said to have had a beautiful daughter, whom he sent to the Visigothic court at Toledo to be educated. That decision unleashed a chain of events with disastrous consequences for Roderick, who became passionately involved with her. She subsequently became known as La Cava, the Whore, and when the king's illicit relationship with her came to Julian's attention, he was furious at her dishonour and Roderick's betrayal of his trust. He conceived a terrible revenge, colluding traitorously with the Muslims to expedite the occupation of Spain.[4]

This saga of transgressive passion, vengeance and treason has been retold throughout the centuries as a way of explaining what was viewed as a disastrous defeat for Christian Spain. The ensuing conquest of the peninsula by mixed Arab and Berber tribes gave rise to a defining myth for the Spanish people, in which Roderick's love affair with La Cava was seen as the original cause of war, leading to the cataclysm of invasion and a powerful Arab presence in Spain for over 700 years. While the existence of Roderick and Julian is certain, no historical evidence remains to prove the existence of La Cava, later known as Florinda, nor is it clear whether she had a love affair with the king or whether she was a victim of rape. Roderick would not have been the first monarch to abuse his power through sexual violation, and the Muslim conquest of Spain was an event of such magnitude that a narrative of mythical scope was needed to justify, reconcile, or simply answer the question of why it happened. Christian legend makes it clear that, from the perspective of the conquered, the loss of the Visigothic kingdom to Islam was God's punishment for sexual corruption, dishonour and betrayal.

The Triumph of Tariq

On 29 April 711, a Berber chieftain and governor of Tangiers, who was once a slave, sailed at the orders of the governor of North Africa, Musa ibn Nusayr, on a surprise raid of the south coast of Spain, with several thousand troops. Legend has it that he burned all his boats on landing and climbed to the top of a towering rocky outcrop to scrutinize the fertile plains and wide sandy bay below. He was Tariq ibn Ziyad, whose name lives on today in the place where he landed, Jabal al-Tariq, the Arabic name for Gibraltar. Like that of Roderick, the life of Tariq ibn Ziyad is a patchwork of fiction and truth, of fragments pieced together as part of the much broader story of Islam's first arrival in Europe. He too was a man of destiny, beginning life as a slave and rising to enduring prominence, his ambitions entangled with those of his mentor and rival Musa ibn Nusayr. Long before the events of 711, in the 630s, an Arab Christian was captured in Iraq by the Quraysh tribe, became a slave and then a freed *mawla* or affiliate of the Umayyad clan. Musa was his son. In the first decade of the eighth century, Musa led the Muslim forces across North Africa into Tangiers, becoming Umayyad governor of North Africa, then known as Ifriqiya. His troops were partly Arabs, but mainly Berbers, formidable fighters whom he had originally been sent to attack. As soon as he had a foothold in North Africa, Musa maintained a strategy of respecting Berber traditions without enforcing Islam; this was highly successful, leading to the religious conversion of many Berbers, who then joined his army, making him at once their conqueror and their general. One of them was probably Tariq. Musa's victories had taken the Muslim armies as far as the north-westernmost tip of Africa, and all before them was sea – where should they go next? The historian David Levering Lewis regarded Musa as a 'visionary jihadist', the finest Islamic military strategist west of Damascus.[5] In 710, at the age of seventy, this exceptional soldier knew what he must do. He embarked on a bold mission to bring the message of Islam to Visigothic Hispania and beyond, into the declining Roman Empire.

Musa knew his Berber *mawla* Tariq ibn Ẓiyad was a magnificent horseman and natural leader, and had already appointed him as governor of Tangiers, capital of the Maghreb, after its capture early in 710. Now, he planned to send Tariq north, across the narrow strait of water that separated North Africa and Hispania, whose peoples had traded with each other for centuries, but not under the banner of Islam. On Musa's orders, a small Berber raiding party of about 500 men, led by Tarif ibn Malik, had already crossed over to the peninsula in August 710, landing where the present-day city of Tarifa stands, which took his name. Tarif and his men were the first Muslims to set foot on European soil. The local Christians fled and Tarif returned laden with booty, bringing tidings of the rich pickings to be had. But, next time, things took a more serious turn. Arabic sources relate that, before Tariq ibn Ziyad crossed the Strait of Gibraltar with between 7,000 and 12,000 Berber troops in boats supplied by Count Julian, he had a dream in which the Prophet assured him that Christian Hispania was destined for Islam. It would take a terrible battle, a holy war, before that dream was fulfilled.

When Tariq landed on the southern shore, Roderick was as far away as he could be, fighting his first recorded campaign against the Basques, in the north of the peninsula. In panic, he hurried south, meeting Tariq's invading army as they were en route to Cordoba, in the valley of the river Guadalete, near Medina-Sidonia. In *The Breath of Perfume*, the historian al-Maqqari evokes the scene as Tariq harangues his men before battle, in the words that begin this chapter, promising them the rewards of untold riches and beautiful women.[6] That battle ended Roderick's reign and the Visigothic kingdom with it, his demise no doubt hastened by his predecessor's usurped sons, who colluded with the Arabs, deserting their king in his final hour of need. The Arab and Berber victory in that year of Ramadan 92, less than a hundred years since the birth of Islam, was astonishing in its speed and finality. The Muslim army, far outnumbered by Roderick's troops and unfamiliar with the lie of the land, were lightning fast on their small Arab horses, and their improvised tactics were not familiar to the Visigoths, who moved in Roman-style squadrons from set positions. The mayhem of the Visigothic retreat before the Berber cavalry was later vividly imagined in a painting by the nineteenth-century artist Salvador Martínez Cubells.

The result was the slaughter of almost all the Visigothic nobility, a scene of devastation lamented in a famous series of ballads on Roderick's demise, though his final fate remains a mystery. His white horse was found, still saddled, but Roderick's body was never discovered. One legend has it that he escaped to Portugal, where he has a tombstone in Viseu, while another claims that one of his gold sandals was found in the river Guadalete. The unresolved question of his death opened the door for future generations to challenge the truth of the old story, revisiting the cultural and emotional site of conquest and rewriting the history of 711 in an attempt to confront and resolve tensions between Christianity and Islam, Europe and Arabia.[7]

What had been a cataclysm for Christian historians barely caused a ripple in Damascus. The events of 711 were reported by Arab chroniclers as the fulfilment of the general expansionist policy of the government of Damascus, part of the much wider Islamic conquest taking place outside the Peninsula and late Roman Empire. Strictly historical elements were infused with fiction and fantasy, sometimes designed to reinforce the validity of Islam's message, evident in its military triumph. In 'The City of Brass', a tale in *One Thousand and One Nights*, Musa ibn Nusayr is ordered to explore a strange Andalusian city with towers of brass; inside the city's palace, he finds the embalmed corpse of a beautiful woman, surrounded by jewels and gold treasure. His soldier Talib, a thinly disguised Tariq ibn Ziyad, wants to seize the treasure, but Musa advises him to refrain. Ignoring the warning, Talib is slaughtered by two statues as he attempts to steal the booty. This may seem far-fetched, but it contains a seed of historical truth in its allusions to the violent greed of Tariq's Muslim army, and to the repercussions of Tariq's incursions, which sparked a burning rivalry between Tariq and Musa that would eventually bring about the great general's downfall.

After his victory on 19 July 711, Tariq decided to press on towards the Visigothic capital of Toledo despite the loss of a quarter of his army. He split his remaining men into divisions, one heading to Cordoba, led by Mughith al-Rumi, where the Muslims entered through a breach in the colossal Roman walls to find a welcome from the city's Jewish population. The Visigothic governor and the Christian army fled and were slaughtered on the road to Toledo. Their execution sent a fatal message to those who resisted, but those who surrendered were shown tolerance. When Mughith moved on, he left a garrison of Jews, Christians and a few Muslims in charge of defending the city – the first instance of an alliance between peoples of the three faiths, something that would become such an important feature of life in medieval Spain.

After finding fresh horses at Écija, Tariq pressed on in the burning heat to Toledo, along the old Roman road from Jaén, and arrived to find a city almost deserted, save for its Jewish population. Tariq was after a priceless treasure, the Table of Solomon, son of David, believed to have entered Spain with Alaric the Visigoth in the fifth century, and of great mystical resonance as well as monetary value. The ninth-century historian al-Hakam recounts what happened at the fortress of Firas, near Toledo, which was under the command of Roderick's nephew:

> Tarik said: 'Hand over the Table to me', which he did; it had gold decoration and precious stones such as he had never seen. Tarik removed one of its legs together with its ornamentation

> of gold and jewels and made a replacement leg for it. The Table was valued at 200,000 dinars because of its precious stones. Tarik took all the jewels, armour, gold, silver and plate he found there . . . He collected it all up and went to Cordova, where he made his base. He then wrote to Musa b. Nusayr informing him of the successful conquest of Spain and of the booty he had acquired . . .[8]

Tariq's astuteness in replacing a leg of the priceless table turned out to be crucial upon his return to Damascus. But, for the time being, his mission was fulfilled. By the autumn of 714, the Muslim victory was complete and Hispania had become al-Andalus, the Arabic name for the region now under Muslim rule.

The Undoing of Musa

The bond between Tariq and Musa was akin to that between Roderick and Julian: a relationship between master and subordinate, in which the subordinate brought about the downfall of his master. After the conquest of Toledo, Musa's *mawla* and general, Tariq, became the effective governor of al-Andalus. After being apprised of Tariq's victory, Musa arrived a year later, it is said, with an army of 18,000 Berbers and Arabs, who besieged Seville for three months before it surrendered, and then moved on to capture Mérida, the capital of Lusitania, now western Spain and modern Portugal. Musa then marched north to meet Tariq at Toledo, leaving his son Abd al-Aziz in the south. Arab historians record Abd al-Aziz's forging of a prototype treaty with the Duke of Murcia, the generous terms of which revealed Musa's policy of cooperation with the indigenous peoples.

It was in Toledo that things began to go wrong. Tariq and Musa argued over Tariq's booty; at the same time, Mughith al-Rumi, who had been sent to Caliph al-Walid I in Damascus to inform him of events in al-Andalus, returned with orders for Musa to withdraw and report to al-Walid in person. The caliph feared the campaign was a distraction from Umayyad plans to attack Constantinople – an alluring yet dangerous prospect that would require significant manpower. Musa made the fateful decision to ignore the caliph's demands and capitalize on the advances already made by his troops. Instead of returning to Damascus, he headed north and joined forces with Tariq, their conquests reaching as far north as Oviedo and the Bay of Biscay. Only the small kingdom of Asturias remained unconquered.

Once Muslim governors were in place throughout the peninsula, Musa headed back to Damascus with the booty. Tariq preceded him, having already sent severed heads wrapped in camphor-soaked cloth along with gold rings and bejewelled swords to the capital as proof of his impressive victory. As fate would have it, Musa's arrival coincided with the caliph being taken ill, so his brother Sulayman took charge and asked Musa to delay his grand cavalcade from entering the city. Musa ignored the request and triumphantly processed into the city, laying his booty before the languishing al-Walid, who died a few days later.

This was his undoing, and Musa's triumph soon turned to tribulation. Not only did he incur the new caliph Sulayman's displeasure, but his own *mawla*, Tariq, the man he had raised to greatness, turned against him. The Persian historian Ibn al-Faqīh described Musa's attempts to claim the glory for the discovery of the Table of Solomon and the conquest of Spain. In his account, he records a showdown between Musa and Tariq in the presence of Caliph al-Walid. Tariq claimed he, not Musa, had discovered the table, but Musa accused him of lying: 'So Tarik said to al-Walid "Send for the Table". The caliph looked at its foot; it was not the same as the others. Tarik said "Ask him about it". So al-Walid asked Musa and he replied "I got it like this". Tarik then brought the real foot, that he himself had removed and al-Walid realized that he had been telling the truth.'[9] Musa was stripped of his rank, and his booty, including the Table of Solomon, was confiscated. Even worse fortune befell him when his son Abd al-Aziz was murdered by a group of Arabs. His head was sent to the caliph in the presence of his father, who was cruelly asked if he recognized it. Musa never recovered his reputation, dying at the age of about seventy-five, in 715. In contrast, Tariq's fate remains mysterious, as no historian mentions him again.

The Muslim conquest of Spain in 711 sprang from a set of political, religious and cultural circumstances refracted through the lives of these four powerful men, whose decisions had colossal repercussions. Our understanding of their interaction is woven from a patchwork of fragments, a partial knowledge of events, laced with legend and pieced together from the words of the earliest Christian historians, who saw history as moral philosophy, and from the records of their later Arab counterparts, who tended to write history as victory propaganda. Dominant notes of violence and invasion, conquest and empire, religious difference and cooperation modulate the actions of the men whose lives hover in the margins of historical narratives.

The first crucial encounters between Muslims and western Christians began at the Rock of Gibraltar and were played out on the banks of the river Guadalete and in the streets of Visigothic Toledo. The long, glorious history of al-Andalus arose out of one complex defining event that engendered strife and violence between individuals and peoples, while later being marked by pragmatic collaboration and tolerance. Yet, as European Christendom first began to absorb the reality of the Islamic presence on the continent, cooperation and alliance were far from the minds of Catholic clerics and intellectuals. The perceived threat to the Christian faith found expression in a verbal animosity that was to spread through theological writing, history and fictional literature, as authors and poets harnessed their linguistic virtuosity to demonize the Prophet and his supposedly heretical religion.

Chapter 3

Words of Hostility: The Fabrication of Otherness

'Words, so innocent and powerless as they are, standing in a dictionary, how potent for good and evil they become in the hands of one who knows how to combine them.'

Nathanial Hawthorne, 1848

In scrolls, codices and illuminated manuscripts painstakingly crafted on metal, parchment, vellum or paper, the written foundations of Judaism, Christianity and Islam came into being, and the followers of these religions became known in Islamic belief as peoples of the Book, united by revelation and scripture. The three religions are grounded in their texts of holy power – the Jewish Torah, which includes the first five books of the Christian Old Testament, the Christian Bible and the Muslim Koran – and a written culture based on scholarship and learning is fundamental to the religious life and customs of these faiths. The compilers of these holy texts harnessed the potency of language to create living testimonies that persuaded, instructed and guided their readers in the search for divine truths. Nonetheless, language is inherently ambiguous, its written objectives often as pernicious as they are pious. While eastern Christianity, which included the Syriac, Coptic, Greek and Armenian branches of the Church, has had a long history of close, often constructive engagement with Islam, the antipathy towards Muslims expressed by certain early medieval Christian historians left a tenacious and negative legacy that fostered intolerance and religious prejudice often linked to race, accentuated ideas of difference and sharpened religious identities.

In the early centuries of Islamic conquest, eastern Christians were ambivalent towards the new religion. They began to assert their faith in theological works composed in Syriac and Arabic that sought to stem the tide of conversions to Islam, which were encouraged by the eighth Umayyad caliph Umar (r. 717–20). During his brief reign, he had adopted an enlightened policy of tolerance towards the *dhimmis*, the subject populations of Islamic conquest. But the earliest productive encounters between the two religions came in the form of exchanges of letters and debates between Muslim and Christian theologians. In one instance of a face-to-face encounter, the Iraqi patriarch Timothy I (d. 823) had a discussion in 781 with the third Abbasid caliph al-Mahdi (744–85), in which the latter raised objections to the nature of God and the image of Christ, claiming that Christians had corrupted their scriptures.[1] Timothy was known for his diplomacy, and while defending his own faith against these accusations, he also showed an open mind in acknowledging the goodness of the Prophet: 'Muhammad deserves the praise of all reasonable men because he walked the path of the prophets and of the lovers of God.' Thirty years later, at the court of Caliph al-Ma'mun (r. 813–33), formal debates were held in which members of each religion discussed the principles and practices of their creeds openly and freely. It was an intellectual environment where Christians played a crucial role as wordsmiths in the caliph's project to translate scientific and cultural works from Syriac and Greek into Arabic, a task of immense importance that eventually led to the creation of the famous translation school known as the House of Wisdom in Baghdad.

These dialogues, while always polemical, were often profitable and sought what the two religious communities had in common, but such exchanges stopped in the mid-ninth century due to a change in attitude towards Christians on the part of Caliph al-Mutawakkil (822–61). Despite these early interchanges, a number of Syrian Christians had expressed their antagonism to Islam openly. Other eastern Christian writers wrote in apocalyptic terms of Islam as the religion of the Antichrist, while some saw it as a deviant heresy derived from Christianity. Sometime in the late seventh century, a

Syriac priest recorded his thoughts on the Islamic conquest of the Near East, giving it authority by pretending it was written by a fourth-century Church father, Methodius, hence its arcane title, the *Apocalypse of Pseudo-Methodius*. He believed that the sons of Ishmael had risen from the desert as God's punishment for the depraved sexual behaviour of Christians, whose alleged sins included homosexuality, cross-dressing and swinging. The *Apocalypse* was translated into Greek and Latin in the early eighth century and had a strong influence on western Christian views of Islam for centuries to come. The ninth-century chronicler Dionysius of Tel-Mahre, patriarch of Antioch (d. 845) and head of the Syrian Orthodox Church, described Muslims as 'the most despised and disregarded of the peoples of the earth', despite conceding that the 'sons of Ishmael' had liberated his peoples from the oppression of imperial Rome.[2]

These perceptions underlined the initial view of Christian writers that Islam had been sent by God as a punishment for their sins, but it had also now become a serious rival, comparable with Christianity itself. Around the time of the *Apocalypse of Pseudo-Methodius*, Yuhanna ibn Mansur ibn Sarjun, otherwise known as John of Damascus (d. 749), wrote his own version of anti-Muslim propaganda. John came from a prominent Damascene family and was in his late thirties by the time the Muslim conquest of al-Andalus was complete in 714. His father was probably an Arab Christian who spoke no Greek, but John had a foot in both Christian and Islamic worlds as an ascetic and Church elder, and also as one of the chief financial administrators of two Umayyad caliphs, Abd al-Malik (r. 685–705) and al-Walid I (r. 705–15). In about 725, John abandoned city life and his role in the caliphate for one of religious seclusion. In the ancient monastery of Mar Saba, hewn out of the yellowish rocks of the Kidron Valley in Palestine, where he would end his days, he cloistered himself away to write over 1,500 pages of religious reflections and treatises.

Few of those pages addressed Islam directly, but those that did made a lasting impression. In *On the Heresies*, Islam appears merely as the last of a hundred different heresies that had beset the Church, showing that John considered it a deviant form of Christianity rather than a religion in its own right. Long before the tradition of debates had been established at the Islamic court, John wrote his seminal *Dialogue between a Saracen and a Christian*, a defence of Christianity that offered practical arguments to use when confronted with Islamic scepticism. In the written argument, the monk asks a hypothetical Muslim counterpart to prove, among other things, the legitimacy of the Prophet's revelations, given that Muhammad experienced them alone in the desert, unlike the revelations made to Moses, who received God's law on Mount Sinai before a large crowd of people. Through this hypothetical debate, John developed one of the first Christian refutations of Islam.

Far to the west, on the remote Scottish island of Iona, sometime in the 680s, Adamnan, a local abbot, had a chance meeting with Arculf, a Frankish bishop who had been on a pilgrimage to the Holy Land, but was shipwrecked on the shores of Iona on his return journey. As he recovered in Adamnan's care, he told him of his travels to Jerusalem, Bethlehem, Alexandria and Constantinople. The abbot then wove Arculf's story into a book, *On the Holy Sites*, which found its way to the monastery of Jarrow, near Newcastle – a renowned centre of medieval learning, with the largest library north of the Alps. There, it chanced to fall into the hands of the Venerable Bede, the Anglo-Saxon scholar regarded as the father of English history, who spent most of his life at the monastery. Bede's early views of the Arabs and Islam were formed in part by Arculf's account and in part by the work of the Spanish saint Isidore. At first, Bede wrote of the distant Muslim conquerors, whom he calls Saracens, with some admiration and little sense that they had become a new world power. He described Arabia as a land of sweet-smelling myrrh and mentions the Saracen caliph Muawiya's alliance with the Christians against the Jews of Jerusalem.

At that time, Bede had little knowledge of or interest in the details of the new religion. Historians and intellectuals far into the Middle Ages followed the same path, turning to the Bible for an explanation of exactly who the Saracens were. In the famous Latin translation of the Bible by St Jerome (347–420), the Book of Genesis describes the Saracens as descendants of the biblical figure Ishmael, the firstborn son of Abraham with an Egyptian slave, Hagar, his wife Sarah's handmaid. When Sarah herself later conceived a child, Isaac, she sent Hagar and Ishmael away. In Genesis 17.20, God speaks of Ishmael to Abraham: 'Behold, I have blessed him, and will make him fruitful and will multiply him, exceedingly; twelve princes shall he beget, and I will make him a great nation.' Ishmael, forebear of the Ishmaelites or Hagarenes and an ancestor of Muhammad, is described in the Koran sura 19.54 as 'a man of his word, an apostle and a prophet', and was buried with his mother next to the Ka'aba. He is also seen in Muslim tradition as the common father of the Abrahamic religions. Yet Jerome, and Bede after him, had a more negative interpretation. Jerome pointed out that the angel of the Lord told Hagar in the desert that her son 'will be a wild man; his hand will be against every man, and every man's hand against him' (Genesis 16.12). He deduced that therefore the Saracens were wanderers of no fixed abode, who invaded all nations and were attacked by all; as desert marauders, their wildness and aggression formed the inherited character traits of the line of Ishmael. Bede added to the negativity by claiming that 'Agareni', or Hagarenes, derives not from the name Hagar but from the Hebrew word *ger*, meaning 'enemy'. Both Jerome and Bede fomented the belief that Ishmael, the illegitimate son, the exiled outcast and father of the wandering warrior tribes, prefigured the advancing Saracen armies of Islam.

By the time Bede embarked on his great work, the *Ecclesiastical History of the English People*, around AD 731, the threat of Saracen invaders, who had by then reached Frankish Gaul, was on the horizon. He recorded the emergence of two comets around the sun in AD 729, visible for a fortnight, at which time '. . . a swarm of Saracens ravaged Gaul with horrible slaughter; but after a brief interval in that country they paid the penalty of their wickedness'.[3] Bede makes no reference to their religion – to him, they were more non-Christian invaders, without legitimacy. It was the changing of the imperial guard that was more important; it had brought new protagonists to the western Christian territories in the form of the Germanic kings, Catholics who deferred to the Church as the heir of imperial Rome. While verbal hostility towards Islam and the Saracens set the mood in the west of the old Roman Empire, the Muslims took their holy war further north into what is now central and southern France. Three battles distinguish the history of this time as focal points in the wider struggle for territory and religious supremacy between the advancing soldiers of Islam and the warriors of the Christian west. They took place in Covadonga in northern Spain, Poitiers in central France and at the Roncevaux Pass in the Pyrenees. Each conflict came to be seen as decisive in very different ways, not so much on the basis of known facts, but as a result of the historical and poetic constructions later placed on them.

The Battle of Covadonga

After Musa and Tariq had been ordered to return to Damascus in 714, a homecoming that had ended in disgrace for Musa, Caliph Sulayman ibn Abd al-Malik picked up the gauntlet thrown down by the Prophet Muhammad in the letter he had sent the emperor Heraclius asking him to surrender and convert to Islam. Sulayman deployed his great army and navy to besiege Constantinople in 717–18. It was a disaster, a shock defeat of the Muslim war machine by the wily emperor Leo III, and it prompted the caliphate to reassess the scope for expanding the Islamic conquest north of Iberia instead. In the wake of this unexpected setback, in around 719, the armies of Muslim Iberia moved north into Gaul, still under Visigothic rule, and seized the city of Narbonne, which became the capital of Muslim Septimania, now south-east France. The western territories conquered by Islam were expanding, but the new rulers had sidestepped an area along the coastal regions of central northern Spain, the harsh, mountainous geography of which made it virtually impenetrable and unassailable. The newly established emirate of Cordoba in the south took little notice of a growing band of

Christian rebels who inhabited these remote crags and valleys of the north.

The leader of the Christian resistance was the fabled Pelagius (Pelayo, in Spanish), who first appears in a ninth-century Spanish annal, the *Chronicle of Albelda*. A born rebel, he is said to have been a grand-nephew of King Roderick, making his home in the mountain fastnesses of the north after being expelled from Toledo. Time has obscured much of his story and there are gaps in the manuscripts, hints and partial explanations that were and still are open to interpretation. It seems that Pelagius made a stand by refusing to pay the *jizya*, the tax on non-Muslims, and by attacking the small Umayyad garrisons guarding the northern reaches of the peninsula. Some records say a Muslim expedition was sent expressly to punish Pelagius for his insurgency. Others claim that Muslim troops returning from their first defeat in the west, when they had been overcome by Frankish forces at Toulouse on 9 July 721, determined to put Pelagius in his place on their way home. They arrived in the Asturian mountains, headed by the commanders Alqama and Munuza, in May 722, ready to take on the rebellious Christian nobleman. Refusing to surrender, the guerrilla leader and his band of followers, possibly as few as 300 men, fled to the cave of Covadonga, in a narrow valley amid high mountains.

A battle began, during which the Christian rebels shot arrows and threw stones from higher ground until, at a vital moment, Pelagius led his soldiers out from the cave into the valley, surprising the Muslims, whom they routed, and killing their leader Alqama. In Cordoba, the reaction was minimal – the eleventh-century Muslim historian Ibn Hayyan later wrote: 'What are thirty barbarians perched on a rock? They must inevitably die.'[4] For the Christians, though, it was a splendid victory that would be magnified out of all proportion by local chroniclers and would eventually become the foundational story of the kingdom of Asturias, with Pelagius as its first king. The Battle of Covadonga became a symbol of Christian resistance to Muslim rule, and Asturias the cradle of what would later be known as the Christian Reconquest of Spain.

The Highway of the Martyrs – the Battle of Poitiers

The Battle of the Highway of the Martyrs, as the Muslims call it – or, for Christians, the battle of Poitiers* – was the first significant defeat of Muslim military forces by Frankish armies. But it is scarcely remembered in the twenty-first century, though it has mythical status for certain historians. On 10 October 732,[5] the emperor Charlemagne's grandfather, Charles Martel, and his Frankish and Aquitainian troops met the army of the Umayyad emir of al-Andalus, al-Ghafiqi, on a plain familiar to Martel, outside the village of Moussais-la-Bataille, between Tours and Poitiers in today's western France. Al-Ghafiqi had marched his troops, possibly as many as 30,000, from Zaragoza, through the northern mountain passes of the Pyrenees, into Basque Aquitaine, on a mission to conquer south-western Gaul. His army had reached Poitiers, on the old imperial highway, and his soldiers set about plundering the tomb of St Hilary, stripping it of gold and precious stones before torching the building.

The destruction of Christian Gaul's most sacred basilica was a catastrophe for the Christian Franks, and a desecration of their religious treasures. In retaliation, Charles Martel attacked al-Ghafiqi, and brutal fighting lasted for seven days, during which the badly outnumbered Frankish squadrons managed to hold off al-Ghafiqi's army. The greed for booty was the downfall of the Muslim army; many troops broke away to rescue their stashes of rich plunder from Poitiers, leaving their commander al-Ghafiqi unprotected. When he was killed by an arrow fired by the Frankish infantry, it proved disastrous. The next day, the ethnic and tribal groups of the Muslim army failed to agree on who they should appoint as their new commander and the army was forced to beat a hasty retreat. Charles Martel's hard-won victory marked the first important Islamic defeat in their campaign of conquest in the west.

---

* It is also known as the Battle of Tours, as it took place at a location between Tours and Poitiers.

On this basis alone, the battle was highly significant, but just how significant has given rise to ambivalence, even to quite opposing views. Historians from Edward Gibbon onwards have claimed the Battle of Poitiers was one of the great decisive battles of world history, saving Christian Europe and western civilization itself, while others have viewed it as a conflict glorified by the propaganda of the papacy and the Franks, important but not crucial. Arab historians have paid scant attention to it. After all, the Battle of Poitiers did not stop Arab incursions into Frankish territory, which continued for some years afterwards. Muslim expansion north of Iberia was halted far more convincingly by the civil wars that plagued the caliphate in the form of Berber uprisings in North Africa, which led to Berber unrest in al-Andalus.[6]

But what makes the Battle of Poitiers a genuinely key event in the history of encounters between Christians and Muslims west of the Islamic empire is the importance of its modern legacy. The popular historian Philip Guedalla's short alternative history of western Europe under Muslim rule was written in 1931. His vision of Granada as the great centre of enlightened culture whose informed policies were respected across the continent in contemporary times was definitively quashed.[7] The dominant historical theme became the crucial role of the battle in defining western Europe as Christian rather than Muslim, the latter scenario seemingly averted by the Frankish Christian defeat of the Islamic jihadists. From this perspective, the early-twentieth-century German historian Hans Delbrück claimed there was no more important battle in the history of the world. Yet the American historian David Levering Lewis, writing in the first decade of the twenty-first century, argued outspokenly that, instead of saving western Europe from Islamic dominion, the Christian victory largely fostered 'the creation of an economically retarded, balkanized, fratricidal Europe, that, in defining itself in opposition to Islam, made virtues out of religious persecution, cultural particularism and hereditary aristocracy.'[8]

The Battle of Roncesvalles

Out of the shadows of the late eleventh century, an unknown poet composed France's oldest surviving poetic work, the *Song of Roland*. The stirring deeds and tragic demise of Roland, count of the march of Brittany, who died fighting for the emperor Charlemagne in the Spanish Pyrenees in the late eighth century, have been immortalized not only in France's national epic, but in the glorious stained-glass windows of the abbey of Saint-Denis and Chartres cathedral. This tale of chivalric heroes, or *chanson de geste*, paints Roland as a model of knightly virtue, fighting for Christianity and for the Frankish kingdoms against the Muslim enemy. But this is the creation, albeit magisterial, of the poet's imagination. The historical reality was entirely different.

It began with tribal conflict among the Muslim leaders of al-Andalus. The new Umayyad emirate of Cordoba was independent of the Abbasid caliphs of Damascus, and its first emir, Abd al-Rahman I, had grown powerful. The Muslim governors further north remained loyal to the Abbasid regime and saw their independence threatened by Cordoba. Meanwhile, much further north, at the Diet of Paderborn in 777, Charlemagne, king of the Franks, presided over his clergy and noblemen inside the huge wooden hall built for the occasion. They were concluding their discussions on the religious and secular regulations of the new Carolingian regime when some unexpected guests interrupted their deliberations. Three leaders from the northern lands of al-Andalus – Sulayman ibn al Arabi, governor of Barcelona and Girona, al-Husayn, the custodian of Zaragoza, and the unnamed governor of Huesca – had made the long journey north to propose a military alliance with Charlemagne against the emirate of Cordoba. The plan was to their mutual advantage and would enable the Frankish armies to invade and occupy northern Spain, giving Charlemagne access to Zaragoza, while giving the rebel towns security against incursions from the south.

Charlemagne had just conquered the fearsome Saxons and was widely seen as the defender of Christianity. It seemed a divinely ordained opportunity to bolster his frontiers and create a buffer zone between him and Abd al-Rahman I, with booty thrown in. He agreed to the Muslims' plan and, in the summer of 778, mustered two huge armies of up to 25,000 men, among them Roland, commander of the elite Breton cavalry. They were to cross the Pyrenees and converge on Zaragoza, endorsed by Pope Hadrian I, who saw this campaign as the struggle of Christianity against the threat of Islam, a holy war against the Hagarenes, enemies of God. But the great scheme was ill fated. Charlemagne reached the gates of Zaragoza in May 778 to find that al-Husayn had changed his allegiance and now supported the Cordoba emirate; entry was barred to the Franks. Suspecting treachery, Charlemagne besieged the city for a month before cutting his losses and abandoning the whole enterprise, destroying the Basque city of Pamplona in an act of revenge on his way back.

Worse was to follow. As his army crossed the Pyrenees at Roncesvalles – Orreaga, in Basque – Count Roland, bravest of the brave as the *Song of Roland* states, held back to see the baggage wagons, laden with Spanish jewels, coins and silks, wend their way through the narrow, perilous mountain pass. On the morning of 15 August 778, they were assailed by a calamitous rockfall and a deluge of arrows, with Roland and his men trapped between the baggage train below and their attackers above. Too late, Roland sounded the oliphant, his famous ivory battle horn, and, to a man, the entire Frankish rearguard was killed by a handful of Basque guerrillas determined to avenge the destruction of Pamplona.[9]

No contemporary written chronicle ever mentioned the battle. Perhaps no one dared do so while Charlemagne still lived. After his death, the emperor's chronicler Einhard acknowledged the role of the Basques in what had been a significant military event, as did chroniclers sixty years later. The Battle of Roncesvalles put an end to any aspirations Charlemagne might have had to conquer Islamic Spain. But it is the influence the battle exerted that is remarkable, with the direst of defeats transformed into a national epic pitting Christians against Muslims. Whether or not the *Song of Roland* poet believed his work might inspire crusading Frenchmen to fight against the Saracen enemy, it lionizes Charlemagne as the champion of Christianity against Islam, creating what Levering Lewis calls 'one of the great constitutive myths of Christendom'.[10] This powerful poetic trickery framed historical events as an epic struggle between the two faiths, and the narrative persuasively reinforced religious and cultural divisions, provoking antagonism towards Islam in the minds and hearts of twelfth-century European Catholics.

*

In the mid-eighth century, no one used the term 'European'. The geographical concept of Europe was barely formed, its boundaries vague. The Greek historian Herodotus (*c.* 484 BC–*c.* 425 BC) described the territorial division of the known world in three parts: Europe, Asia and what he called Libya, by which he meant Africa. The first-century-AD geographer Strabo (*c.* 64 BC–*c.* AD 24) originally defined the boundary of eastern Europe as the river Don, and St Isidore of Seville (*c.* AD 560–636), who gathered together the traditions of late antiquity in his famous *Etymologies*, declared that the three divisions of the world derived from their allocation to the biblical sons of Noah. Isidore claimed that Shem was the originator of Asia, land of the Semitic peoples, while Japheth had Europe, land of Gentiles, Greeks and Christians, and Africa was the lot of Ham, who was to be subject to both Shem and Japheth. The early biblical supremacy of Europe evident in Isidore's account had played no part in the world view of the Roman Empire, which straddled the Hellenistic east, North Africa and western Europe. That world view had been uprooted by the seismic shock of the Islamic conquests, and the former imperial territories were beginning to redefine themselves in religious rather than geographical terms.

In the *Mozarabic Chronicle of 754* (*Crónica mozárabe de 754*), the word 'Europeans' is used for the first time to describe the Frankish armies who defeated the Arabs, as the chronicler calls them, at the Battle of Poitiers in 732.[11] He does not refer to either the Muslims or the Christian Franks in terms of their religion. He defines the former by their ethnicity, while the latter are seen as part of a new, wider social group that replaces the now defunct idea of citizenship of the Roman Empire. This was a sea change in how the western world was viewed, and it pitted the inhabitants of the former Roman Empire against the peoples of Arabia. Over the next fifty years, this new mindset was reinforced as kings and Christian religious leaders came together to forge the foundations of western Christendom.

The Carolingian dynasty had come into being in 751, when Pippin the Short became king, and with it a Frankish empire that stretched across west and central Europe as we know it. An alliance was built between king and pope when Pippin met Stephen II at Ponthion, near Metz, after the pontiff had endured a freezing winter journey across the mountains. The king showed his deference by walking the last mile to his palace beside the pope, holding the horse's bridle. Neither had any inkling of how profound the consequences of their deliberations would be for the future of Europe. Stephen had brought with him a document outlining the vital importance of the king's protection of the papacy. Known as the Donation of Constantine, it is one of history's most notorious and consequential forgeries.* It appeared to establish the supremacy of the bishop of Rome over the Eastern Orthodox Church, thereby making the papacy all powerful, while Pippin's coronation at the Abbey of Saint-Denis in 754, legitimized by Pope Stephen, intertwined Church and Crown and elevated the papacy to secular sovereignty.

In the year of Pippin's coronation, St Boniface, reformer of the Frankish Church, died ignominiously at the age of seventy-nine, slain by a group of armed robbers. Hailed as the man who fashioned early Christian Europe and the Latin Church, he had encouraged

* The Donation of Constantine was a fake imperial decree which stated that Constantine the Great had transferred power over Rome and the Western Roman Empire to the pope. It bestowed supreme power on the pope over the clergy and over secular leaders and was one of the most important and influential documents of the Middle Ages. It was not until the middle of the fifteenth century that it was declared to be a forgery.

the close relationship between the Carolingians and the papacy and became known as the 'apostle of Germania'. Pippin's association with Pope Stephen followed Boniface's lead. The largest Roman Catholic community in the west was the land of the Franks, where a militant religious ethos arose, governed by a hierarchy of priests who insisted on their authority as intermediaries between man and God. Charlemagne inherited the emerging Frankish kingdom from his father and was unexpectedly crowned Holy Roman Emperor by Pope Leo III in 800, a move which irrevocably alienated the Eastern Empire. In strong contrast with the first emir of Cordoba, Abd al-Rahman I, the new emperor could not write and probably could not read, but spoke Latin easily and understood Greek. Yet he had a thirst for learning, and his court became the centre of a renaissance within the western Church, graced by scholars such as Alcuin of York and the Lombard Paul the Deacon. Monks dominated the cultural agenda, and the books found in monastery libraries were mainly religious works, lives of saints, elementary Latin primers and theology written in the vernacular, along with some classical Latin literature. There was a sprinkling of scientific and medical works, but few had read or understood them. Although Charlemagne himself did not shine as a scholar, on the battlefield he was a military genius, a figurehead who embodied all the martial aggression of the Germanic tribes, along with deep Christian piety. As Europe evolved, he became the mythical saviour of Catholic Christianity, the scourge of Muslim interlopers.

*

If the seventh century had been a time of unprecedented global change in religion, society and civilization, the next hundred years witnessed the crystallization of a new world order which was dominated by religion. History and literature together created a narrative that began to shape a new identity for the peoples who lived west of Constantinople. Not only were those people embryonic Europeans, who defined themselves according to a geopolitical framework that separated them from Asia and Africa, but the term

'European' was strongly associated with Christianity. The growing perception of European selfhood evolved out of opposition to the new religion that was challenging – even threatening – Roman Catholic dominance. Europe's response was hostile language, forged documents, newly coined words and fabricated versions of historical realities, all of which planted the idea of the alienness of Islam in the European psyche.

Chapter 4

City of Illumination: Cordoba

'Oh, Cordoba! How beautiful and pleasant you are!
How delicious your nights! How delightful your days!'

Musa ibn Nusayr, governor of Ifriqiya, 698

'Everything, the whole happy and perfumed world
Of my childhood in Damascus, I have found it here . . .'

Nizar Qabbani, 1955

Cordoba is a city of light, bathed in a radiance at times mellowed by its golden stone, at times glittering in the blazing summer sun. Cordoba's natural luminosity has a symbolic parallel in the social, cultural and religious enlightenment of its three centuries of Muslim glory, a golden age between the eighth and tenth centuries which brought it fame as both a meeting place of creeds and also as a model of cultural collaboration which forged an intellectual epicentre. Cordoba became a site of power that embodied a new idea of what might constitute the identity of emerging Europe. The early perception of European selfhood as fundamentally Christian was challenged by the society that evolved under Islamic rule in al-Andalus. Whatever the impression that pervaded Europe north of the Pyrenees, the continent was not solely Christian, but partly Muslim too.

The First Emir in Europe

The transformation of Cordoba (Qurtuba, in Arabic) into the first emirate in Europe was achieved by one exceptional man, Abd al-Rahman ibn Mu'awiya, who became the first emir of the city in

756. His astonishing life story began in Damascus when Syria was under the rule of the powerful Umayyad dynasty. In 731, the year before the Battle of Poitiers, a Berber slave named Raha gave birth near Damascus to a son, Abd al-Rahman, whose father Mu'awiya, son of Caliph Hisham ibn abd al-Malik (r. 724–45), died young. The boy's grandfather took charge of his education at the caliphal court, where he spent time at the magnificent palace the caliph had built on the outskirts of Rusafa in Syria, amid shady courtyards, calming fountains and flourishing palm trees. This life of luxury and liberty ended abruptly when Abd al-Rahman was twenty. The palace was burned to the ground and most of his family brutally murdered in a dramatic coup by the rival Abbasid tribe, who seized the caliphate between 748 and 750.

Abd al-Rahman, however, managed to get away, in an escape both perilous and tragic. He fled from Damascus with his brother Yahya and his Greek freedman Badr, and headed for the river Euphrates, hiding in forests and taking refuge in small villages until they reached the water. With their pursuers still hot on their heels, they decided to swim for it. The historian al-Maqqari recounts how tragedy struck when Yahya, fearing he was drowning, started to turn back towards the riverbank. Abd al-Rahman implored him to keep swimming, shouting: 'Come to me, come to me!'[1] But Yahya turned back anyway and, before his brother's eyes, he was promptly beheaded by Abbasid horsemen, who left his body to rot in the mud. When Abd al-Rahman reached the far side of the river, he flew in horror from the scene, with only Badr to help him. Somehow, they kept going for four years, travelling through Palestine, the Sinai peninsula, across Egypt and the deserts of North Africa. They narrowly escaped capture on several occasions, once by hiding beneath a pile of clothes belonging to a Berber chieftain's wife, until they reached Ceuta in Morocco and made contact with the Nafza Berbers, the tribe of Abd al-Rahman's mother. Here, Abd al-Rahman, the exiled grandson of a caliph, with a natural aptitude for command and a strong sense of personal destiny as sole survivor of an illustrious dynasty, looked across the water to newly conquered al-Andalus. He first set foot on Spanish territory at Almuñécar, east of Malaga, in 755, at the age of just twenty-four.

The First Emirate of Western Islam

Allegiances came easily as the story of Abd al-Rahman's miraculous survival spread, and supporters rushed to greet him, among them Syrians with Umayyad connections who had themselves emigrated to al-Andalus in the 740s. With their support, he captured Seville peacefully and headed towards Cordoba, where, beside the roiling waters of the river Guadalquivir in spate, he defeated its governor al-Fihri and entered the city as its emir in 756. It was a decisive moment. The sole survivor of a devastated dynasty was now the leader of the first Muslim emirate in Europe, and in al-Andalus he would create 'a political and cultural experiment of unique brilliance that would have no counterpart on the other side of the Pyrenees.'[2]

Abd al-Rahman immediately launched an extensive construction plan for his new capital city, bestowing its buildings with both functional and symbolic meaning. He renovated the ruins of the old Roman city's temples, baths, statues and mosaics, and the remains of an extensive irrigation system. The ancient alcazar or fortress lay on Roman foundations, allegedly discovered by King Roderick while hunting and later inhabited by Cordoba's first Arab conqueror, Mughith. It was a huge administrative complex, yet, when Abd al-Rahman arrived, it had been neglected for forty-five years. The new emir lived there, but not for long. Still yearning for his childhood idyll at al-Rusafa, he brought it to life in a new palace outside Cordoba, better suited to his status and power.

In fallow land on the edge of a mountain stream just north-west of the city, Abd al-Rahman I began what the historian al-Maqqari called a 'green revolution', creating a garden palace the like of which had never been seen in Europe.[3] It was named Munyat al-Rusafa, after his grandfather's retreat in Syria, and had nature at its heart. Irrigated by water from wells or aqueducts that channelled the mountain streams, its spectacular gardens were stocked with rare and wonderful plants. The emir sent scouts out across the Middle East and North Africa in search of the seeds and flora reminiscent of his childhood. There is a legend that he was sent a basket of pomegranates from Syria; although the fruit rotted on the hot journey, the seeds were planted at al-Rusafa, from where the pomegranate spread across southern Spain. In a poignant poem, Abd al-Rahman honoured the palm trees he imported and naturalized – trees displaced, like him, in a foreign land:

> A palm tree stands in the middle of Rusafa, born in the
> West, far from the land of palms.
> I said to it: 'How like me you are, far away and in exile, in
> long separation from family and friends.
> You have sprung from soil in which you are a stranger; and I,
> like you, am far from home.'[4]

'Al-Rusafa was a pioneer of the many celebrated Andalusian botanical gardens, visited by scholars who studied the plants and their medicinal uses. The remedies derived from those herbs and other flowers were fundamental to the evolution of Andalusian Arab medicine. In northern Europe, monastic communities used plants as remedies too, but not until years later. The famous monastery of St Gall did not commission its own botanical garden until half a century after al-Rusafa, between 816 and 836, and although the tradition of monastic physic gardens continued, there were no other European gardens specializing in the scientific study and domestication of foreign varieties until the sixteenth century.

Nature also propelled much of Cordoba's new agricultural economy, which flourished in a landscape transformed by terraced slopes, diverted mountain streams and crops irrigated with waterwheels or norias, all husbanded by tenant farmers who, under the Islamic system, tithed a percentage of their harvest, a marked improvement on the feudal Visigothic tax system. Abd al-Rahman's ambitious vision enabled the cultivation of monsoon crops like sugar cane, bananas, rice and watermelons, and daily fare included dates, apricots, peas, peaches, figs and saffron, as well as citrus fruits. This abundance both fed the growing population and brought in 100,000 dinars a year.

Governance of the emirate was equally enlightened, fostering a sense of community which held races and religions together under a regime Levering Lewis describes as increasingly congenial to justice and liberality.[5] Dhimmis, the protected peoples under Muslim rule, were guaranteed their own religious rights and privileges, subject to tax – the Christians under the old Visigothic law and the Jews under rabbinic law. Christians converted to Islam more often than Jews, though there was a great deal of freedom of interaction, and also intermarriage between the peoples of different faiths. Sarah, the granddaughter of the Visigothic king Witiza, is said to have known Abd al-Rahman I personally; she married a Muslim, and their two sons became high-ranking Andalusian aristocrats. In contrast with the Frankish rulers who enforced religious conversion and conformity as absolute law, Abd al-Rahman I allowed people to convert without coercion, as advised in the Koran. A tolerance of religious and cultural difference bore the seeds of future collaborations between Andalusian scholars of different faiths. Slaves, too, were treated with humanity, many of them Slavs with blond hair and blue eyes, captured by the Franks and sold to al-Andalus. The emir's personal bodyguard were Black Africans, many of whom converted to Islam, which gained them their freedom; some rose to become eminent at the Muslim court and they eventually formed an influential class of their own.

Even though the people of Cordoba lived in stability and affluence, the threat of war was never far away. From 763 onwards, Abd al-Rahman had to quash local rebellions almost constantly, as well as incursions from the north by the Franks and attacks in the south from his Abbasid rivals. The caliph al-Mansur sent an army from Damascus to depose the man who dared to assume the title of emir of al-Andalus, but, in a daring sortie at the gates of besieged Carmona, Abd al-Rahman and his troops slaughtered most of the Abbasid army. Their leaders' heads were cut off, packed in salt and sent in a ghastly bundle to al-Mansur, who was on pilgrimage in Mecca.

By the time he died, aged fifty-seven, in 788, Abd al-Rahman, had risen from his position as an impoverished immigrant to become the all-powerful, enlightened and wealthy ruler of Islam's first European emirate. He had overseen the metamorphosis of crumbling Visigothic Cordoba into a site of urban splendour, reflected in the exquisite silver dirhams he had minted in the city at a time when the Franks had no coinage and lived from barter. Two years before his death, he laid the foundations for what would become the greatest medieval mosque in the western world. Poet, eloquent orator, a man of great culture as well as a born leader and ruthless warrior, Abd al-Rahman was a visionary ruler who, seen in retrospect, raised the prospect of a Europe where Christians, Muslims and Jews could share a civilized coexistence.

The greatest tribute came from his greatest enemy, the Abbasid caliph al-Mansur (714–75), who gave Abd al-Rahman I the exalted title of Falcon of the Quraysh, symbol of the Prophet's clan, declaring:

> The Falcon of the Quraysh is Abd al-Rahman, who escaped by his cunning the spearheads of the lances and the blades of the swords, who after wandering solitary through the deserts of Asia and Africa, had the boldness to seek his fortune without an army, in lands unknown to him beyond the sea. Having naught to rely on save his own wits and perseverance, he nonetheless humiliated his proud foes, exterminated rebels, organized cities, mobilized armies, secured his frontiers against the Christians, founded a great empire and united under his sceptre a realm that seemed already parcelled out among others. No other man before him ever did such deeds . . . but Abd al-Rahman did it alone, with the support of none other than his own judgment, depending on nothing but his own resolve.[6]

Cordoba and Baghdad

In 762, Caliph al-Mansur had left Damascus and founded a new capital city, Baghdad, on the banks of the river Tigris. There, learning and culture prospered in a multicultural and multi-ethnic environment, in an era known as the Islamic Golden Age. Its renowned library and intellectual centre, the House of Wisdom, became synonymous with the city itself. By the ninth century, rivalry between Umayyad Cordoba and Abbasid Baghdad was as strong as ever, but the two cities also began to develop close trade and cultural connections. Cordoba was the furthest Muslim outpost in the known world and aspired to become another Baghdad.

Abd al-Rahman I was succeeded by his son Hisham I, famous for his piety, charity and great learning, who ruled peacefully, but he died young, after just eight years on the throne. In contrast, Hisham's son al-Hakam I (796–822) had a longer, if conflicted, reign, in which constant rebellions provoked his tyrannical nature, but Abd al-Rahman II (822–52), who succeeded him, took up the mantle of his great-grandfather, as well as his name, and soon became celebrated as a patron of the many scholars, poets and musicians who made his court the cultural centre of western Islam.

In September 844, the emir had some unwanted visitors, who brought the first contact between European Muslims and Scandinavia. In a dramatic assault, Viking longships sailed south from Galicia, ransacking Lisbon en route, and set their sights on Seville, then known by its Muslim name of Išbīliya. They captured the city in early October after heavy fighting, and, according to Muslim accounts, the inhabitants were terrorized and threatened with imprisonment or death. Abd al-Rahman II acted swiftly. He sent troops, who, it was said, destroyed thirty longships, burning them with the incendiary weapon 'Greek fire'; they may have killed as many as a thousand Vikings. Those captured were hanged from palm trees, though some accepted Islam to save their lives. Seville was left in ruins and its people traumatized, so Abd al-Rahman II ordered a shipyard to be built, with a new fleet to guard the river Guadalquivir approaches, which successfully deterred future attacks. Yet it seems the Scandinavians wanted to make peace; a year later, in 845, they sent an embassy to Abd al-Rahman, who responded by appointing his famous court poet al-Ghazal as ambassador to the Vikings.

The light that was Cordoba had its inevitable shadows. The flourishing Arabic culture had beguiled many Mozarabs, the Christians living under Islamic rule. The Cordoban Christian scholar Paul Alvarus lamented their fascination with Arabic language and poetry – to such an extent, he claimed, that they had forgotten their own language. Yet a group of local Mozarabs felt that, despite the freedom of worship and protection under Islamic law from which they benefited, they were often treated with contempt, as inferior. Paul Alvarus and his friend Eulogius, a priest, both documented their resistance, claiming that Christians were harassed by Muslims, their churches destroyed and their priests subjected to public abuse and even stoning. Things escalated when, in 850, the priest Perfectus publicly denounced the Prophet Muhammad as an agent of the devil, as an adulterer and a liar, and was executed for blasphemy.

His death led to a harrowing episode of self-imposed martyrdom. Over the next nine years, more than fifty Christians denounced Muhammad before Muslim authorities and were executed, including Eulogius himself in March 859, despite his admission that the majority of Christian clergy were against such fervour. But whether the martyrs were genuinely provoked by Muslim persecution or by overzealous preaching is ambiguous. Often, the Muslim authorities showed mercy and gave offenders a chance to retract, as in the case of Isaac from Tábanos, a village in the foothills of Cordoba, who left his monastery and went down to the city square, where he approached a judge and accused him in good Arabic of promoting devilish delusions. The amazed judge replied: 'Maybe you are drunk, or prey to some frenzy, and cannot really control what you have said.' He reminded the Christian that he would incur the death penalty, but Isaac would not budge and insisted that he welcomed a violent death, which he met when he was hanged head down on the gallows.[7] In the end, Abd al-Rahman II called a Church council, presided over by Recafredo, bishop of Seville, to try to resolve the problem. Fearing they might provoke the Muslims to withdraw the conditions of relative liberty and tolerance under which they lived, the council strongly discouraged the quest for martyrdom, but that did not end it. In fact, Abd al-Rahman II's death under suspicious circumstances in 852 was seen by the Cordoba Christians as a divine judgment for his persecution of them.

The Blackbird

Cordoba continued to flourish, and the growing lustre of the Umayyad court under Abd al-Rahman II was reflected in the life of the musician Abu l-Hasan 'Ali ibn Nafi (*c.* 789–857), known in Baghdad as 'Ziryab the Jay-bird' and in al-Andalus as 'the Blackbird' because of his extraordinary singing voice and his talent as a lute and oud player. His origins remain elusive, but it seems he was born a slave in Iraq but became the pupil of the eminent Persian teacher and composer al-Mawsili in Baghdad, where he was famed as a performer at the Abbasid court. Ziryab left the city for North Africa, from where he was invited to Abbasid Cordoba in 822. It is said that Abd al-Rahman II rode out to meet him and entertained him in his palace for some months, after which he became a close friend and confidant of the emir. Ziryab established one of the first music schools in Cordoba, with students of both sexes, and five of his many children also became celebrated musicians and kept his school alive. The extent of his influence on Andalusian music has been much debated, though it is likely that he introduced new instruments and added a fifth string to the oud, coloured red to represent the soul.

Ziryab exerted a remarkable influence on the Umayyad court in Cordoba, to which he brought all the panache and elegance of Abbasid Baghdad. Deodorant, toothpaste, hair shampoo with salt and fragrant oils in it, changing clothes according to the seasons, and new hair fashions were all part of Ziryab's repertoire of innovations. The use of tablecloths and cutlery, and three-course meals of soup, a main course and dessert are all ascribed to him too, as well as drinking out of crystal glasses rather than metal cups. His many civilizing innovations imperceptibly formed fundamental aspects of European daily life that are still familiar today. During his lifetime and in the years immediately after his death, he embodied not only the cultural interaction between Cordoba and Baghdad, but also their growing cultural equality. His arrival had eclipsed the gifted Christian-Basque woman musician, Qalam, a former slave who graced the royal palace; it was a symbolic changing of the guard that aligned the Cordoban court with that of Baghdad. Ziryab modernized court music along Baghdadi lines, making it a match for music in the eastern Islamic empire; such prestige even hinted that the western Islamic empire might potentially be superior to its Abbasid rivals.[8] The success of the emirate of Abd al-Rahman I and his heirs sent a clear message to both Muslim and Christian worlds, and paved the way for Umayyad Cordoba's most brilliant incarnation.

Abd al-Rahman III – The Defender of God's Faith

One hundred years after the death of the great Abd al-Rahman I, around 890, a child was born in Cordoba and given his forebear's name. This child's destiny was to become the self-proclaimed supreme leader of the Islamic empire in the west. His father, Muhammad, was the son of Abdullah ibn Muhammad al-Umawi, emir of al-Andalus, and his mother was Muzna, a Christian concubine. His father's mother was the infanta Onnéca Fortuna, who came from Christian royalty as a Basque princess, and whose marriage linked Christian and Muslim ruling families in the peninsula. Pale skinned, blue eyed and auburn haired, Abd al-Rahman dyed his beard black to look more Arab. When he succeeded his grandfather on 16 October 912 and donned the regal ring that symbolized power, he began a reign that would last for fifty years.

*

Abd al-Rahman III believed in strong central government, which he enforced through consolidating his realms and challenging the pattern of local rebellions within al-Andalus and external threats to its northern and southern borders that had been a feature of Muslim rule since 711. He quelled regional uprisings, tamed his long-time adversary Ibn Hafsun and entered into alliances with the Byzantines against the Franks and the Abbasids, which opened up trade in the Mediterranean. He also gained Christian territory in the north of Spain, in particular obliging his Navarrese aunt Queen Toda to submit to him. At times, he used a mercenary army that included Christian soldiers, so Muslims were pitted against Muslims and Christians against Christians in a struggle that was more often for supremacy than for religion.

With new treaties and diplomatic ties with Byzantium and Christian Spain, and the North African ports of Ceuta and Melilla secured to naval advantage, Abd al-Rahman III made a dramatic decision. In January 929, he declared himself Caliph of Cordoba, the political and religious leader of all Muslims in al-Andalus, and protector of his Christian and Jewish subjects, his power symbolized by the throne and sceptre. As he saw it, the original Umayyad caliphate had been usurped by the Abbasids, and its legitimate reinstatement in al-Andalus cut ties with both the Abbasids and the Tunisian Fatimid dynasty. His new status effectively proclaimed that al-Andalus and its capital Cordoba had now reached an apogee, and the declaration of the caliphate became the catalyst for a comprehensive evolution in administration, religion and intellectual life that found expression in the material structures in and around the city. Córdoba was no longer the rival of Baghdad but had surpassed it in a magnificent act of Umayyad revenge.

Madinat al-Zahra

Like Abd al-Rahman I, the new caliph of Cordoba was touched by genius. Abd al-Rahman III commissioned a magnificent palace to be built west of the capital in the Sierra Morena mountains, on a site halfway up Jabal al-Arus, the Hill of the Bride, offering commanding views over the plain of the Guadalquivir river. Madinat al-Zahra*

---

* It has been suggested that Zahra was the name of Abd al-Rahman III's favourite concubine, but to me it seems more likely that it meant 'City of Flowers',

was an entirely self-sufficient palatine city conceived on a monumental scale, with its own mosques, baths, markets, bakeries, barracks and urban administration. There was even a prison, and a zoo with lions, ostriches and camels. Even at the time, it was recognized as being extraordinary – both palace and city, rural and urban. We know of it from the histories of Ibn Hayyan, Ibn Idhari and Ibn Khalliqan, who described it as among the wonders of the world. Begun in 936, Madinat al-Zahra was modelled on the Abbasid caliphal city of Samarra; Abd al-Rahman III oversaw the entire project throughout the forty years it took to build.

The kilometre-square complex echoed the palace of al-Rusafa, but on a larger scale. Mountain streams were diverted along renovated Roman aqueducts and the water stored in huge cisterns to supply the site, which was divided into three terraces, with palaces at the top. Behind a modest exterior, the Hall of the Caliphs glittered and shone. The roof was made of gold and silver, and the walls of thick marble, rose-coloured and green from Carthage and white from Tarragona. Marble columns, plundered from the ancient ruins of Rome and Narbonne, supported arches of ebony and gold, inlaid with gems and mosaics. A huge pearl, sent as a gift from Constantinople, hung from the centre of the ceiling above a basin of quicksilver that astonished visitors. According to al-Maqqari, 'it sparkled with light, confounding all vision. When al-Nasir (the caliph) wished to impress visitors, he would signal to slaves to cause the mercury to vibrate, whereupon in the chamber there would appear a flash like that of lightning bolts that would fill our hearts with fear.'[9]

Outside, the caliph surveyed a terrain planted with fig and almond trees, which replaced dark native ilexes, creating a leafy Umayyad landscape of gardens and orchards. This site of natural and architectural drama was the stage on which the caliph performed his new role as a world ruler. Few were allowed entry to Madinat al-Zahra.

---

which is the meaning of the word *zahra* in Arabic, given its superb gardens and the close connection between the urban and the rural there.

It was a place for international show as well as the caliph's personal residence, and access was reserved for the aristocracy, selected scholars and poets, and visiting ambassadors from the Franks, the Lombards, the Byzantine Empire and the Christian kingdoms of northern Spain. Madinat al-Zahra symbolized the centralized structure of the state and the all-powerful authority of the caliph. Yet it seems that Abd al-Rahman III could never rest easy. Not long before he died at the age of seventy in October 961, he wrote: 'I have now reigned above fifty years in victory or peace; beloved by my subjects, dreaded by my enemies and respected by my allies. Riches and honours, power and pleasure, have waited on my call, nor does any earthly blessing appear to have been wanting to my felicity. . . . I have diligently numbered the days of pure and genuine happiness which have fallen to my lot: they amount to fourteen. Place not thy confidence in this present world!'[10]

Abd al-Rahman III's reign was the time when Cordoba truly became what the German nun Hrotsvitha of Gandersheim described, despite her natural reservations as a Christian, as the ornament of the world. At night, its clean streets were illuminated by lamplight, at a time when London streets were made of mud and the city was lit by candles. Running water fed innumerable fountains in shady patios, and artisans and merchants grew wealthy from their trade in luxury goods – leather, jewellery and their celebrated copper green and blue pottery. If Madinat al-Zahra represented the power of the caliph, Cordoba's places of learning reflected its intellectual enlightenment; there were over seventy libraries in the city, containing at least 400,000 books. Abd al-Rahman III, as supreme religious leader, was renowned for his tolerance of non-Muslims, Jews and Christians, and Cordoba boasted a multicultural, multi-religious environment second to none in Europe. Yet, while there were churches and synagogues, it was Cordoba's 3,000 mosques that dominated the skyline. Islam's religious authority was vested in the Great Mosque, the foundations of which were laid in the reign of the first emir of Cordoba and which, by the time of Abd al-Rahman III, seemed to be overshadowed by Madinat al-Zahra's radiance. Nevertheless, Abd al-Rahman did not forget his obligations, building a new minaret and remodelling the outer wall of the Great Mosque, Europe's oldest Muslim place of worship, an emblem in light and stone of the evolving religious identity of the European continent.

Chapter 5

A Space of Ambiguity: The Great Mosque

'It embodied what came before. Illuminated what came after.'

Abd al-Rahman I, first emir of al-Andalus

In the Great Mosque of Cordoba, space, form and light converge in the service of art, religion and politics. The mosque's spectacular architectural innovation, the form and decoration of which vividly convey the religious laws, political grandeur and authority of Islam, creates a place of worship that is both hybrid and ambiguous. For 800 years, it was the second-largest mosque in the world after the Sacred Mosque in Mecca, great in dimension but greater in status, meaning and value. The Great Mosque's irregular plan, both inside and out, unsettles and surprises visitors, as if its very stones reflect its controversial status as a building resolutely Muslim in conception and material reality, yet also shaped later by Gothic, Renaissance and baroque architecture.

The Palm Trees of Syria

Abd al-Rahman I, the Falcon of the Quraysh, was a man of the people. He often left his country retreat of al-Rusafa to walk freely through the streets of Cordoba in his white djellaba and turban, joining and often addressing the growing congregation at Friday prayers. In 785, three years before his death at the age of fifty-four, he ordered the construction of a new Friday mosque more commensurate with the power and status of his emirate. The site he chose was a striking setting for the most important building in the city, lying beside the Guadalquivir river and fringed by the well-populated

Jewish quarter, just across the street from the administrative palace or alcazar. Later Arab historians suggested that he had bought the land on which a church stood, possibly the monastery of St Vincent, which was demolished before the construction of the mosque began, in order to consecrate the site as an Islamic sanctuary.[1] Abd al-Rahman I was deeply involved in the project, overseeing much of the work and consulting with stonemasons. Although many of its craftsmen were probably local Iberians and people of Syrian ancestry, the stones on view inside the mosque today bear masons' marks and names that are mostly Arab. The emir called the new structure the Ka'aba of the West, at once aligning it with the holiest place of Islam. The qibla, or direction of prayer, is not orientated exactly towards Mecca, like most mosques, but appears to reflect the emir's wish to face towards Muhammad's first Great Mosque in Quba, Medina, towards the south-east. It is said that the pillars and arches of the main prayer hall were designed to evoke the palm trees of Abd al-Rahman I's native Syria. Its orderly rows of treelike columns appear to stretch orchard-like into infinity, their regular, repeated intervals giving the space an order of rhythm, not hierarchy, that suggests the egalitarian pillars of Islam. It was a place for communal prayer, without privileged spaces or priestly intermediary.

From the outset, the Great Mosque was a startling achievement, a fusion of Christian and Muslim creativity that brought together the heritage of Spain's Roman architecture and Visigothic church-building techniques with local innovations and early Islamic traditions. The past is inherent in a building constructed from recycled and repurposed materials, which were reconfigured with striking originality, enabling the mosque to be finished in just two years, so Abd al-Rahman I saw its completion before he died. Its craftsmen reused the remains of old Visigothic and Roman structures in the area, especially for columns and capitals. The mosque's first incarnation was roughly a square of seventy-five metres, divided equally into an open courtyard and the iconic prayer hall, whose double tiers of alternating red and white horseshoe arches, known as voussoirs, were revolutionary. Balanced on delicate supporting columns, this highly evolved and impressive superstructure, which had no Islamic precedent, raised the height of the wooden roof and increased the drama of the entire building. Abd al-Rahman I and his architects, who remain anonymous, may well have known of or been inspired by the old Roman aqueduct in the city of Mérida, in the west of the peninsula, founded by the Romans in the first century BC, the double-tiered arches of which were made of alternating red and white stones, coinciding with the dynastic colours of the Umayyads. There is great nostalgia, too, for the homeland Abd al-Rahman I left behind, not only in the architectural echoes of its palm trees, but also in the reminders of the Great Mosque of Damascus, with its arcade of arches on slender columns. The Cordoba mosque marked the zenith of Abd al-Rahman I's reign and was a powerful symbol of the rival power of Umayyad al-Andalus. It was a clear religious and political statement of the supremacy of his dynasty and was the place in which Umayyad tradition and new western Islamic customs met. Abd al-Rahman I's words, quoted in the epigraph to this chapter and carved into the masonry of the mosque, perfectly expressed his open-minded ethos – respect for the past and enlightenment for the future.

Sculpting the History of the Caliphate in Stone and Light

Over the next two centuries, the Great Mosque evolved and expanded in harmony with Cordoba and the Umayyad dynasty. The late-thirteenth-century historian Ibn Idari recounts how the first emir's son Hisham I (r. 788–96) built a modest minaret, paid for with some of the booty won in successful military campaigns against Narbonne and Gerona. Hisham I's grandson Abd al-Rahman II (r. 822–52) extended the prayer hall by adding eight bays, in keeping with the form and decoration of Abd al-Rahman I, maintaining the subtle harmony of proportions and the tranquil geometry of the arches. The progressive transformation of the mosque through a process of innovation that honoured the past reflected the spirit of the Umayyad court at this time, whose rulers promoted sciences and arts by surrounding themselves with scholars and teachers in the style of prestigious rulers since ancient Greek times. The Umayyad sultans of al-Andalus saw themselves as heirs to ancient classical culture as well as the legacy of the Romans and Visigoths that enabled them to develop their own political, cultural and architectural knowledge, a mindset encapsulated in the reusing of building materials to fashion new Islamic structures in the Great Mosque.

Umayyad glory shone during the tenth-century caliphate of Abd al-Rahman III, who did not neglect Cordoba's most important religious building, despite his enthusiasm for the construction of the brilliant palatine city of Madinat al-Zahra. In 951–2, Abd al-Rahman III enlarged the courtyard and pulled the old minaret down to replace it with a much taller, more imposing version. It was the first true minaret in al-Andalus and influenced all later versions in the Islamic west. It is the minaret we see today. The early modern Arab historian al-Maqqari tells us that, in those times, the minaret had one silver and two gold apples at the top on a metal rod, crowned by a small golden pomegranate.[2] It was forty-seven metres high, a visual symbol of the caliph's power as well as a means of encouraging the faithful and urging them to prayer. By the time Abd al-Rahman III died in 961, the Great Mosque was grander and more monumental, in both its horizontal and vertical dimensions. Its finest incarnation awaited the reign of al-Hakam II (961–76), son of the first caliph.

A Luminous Spectacle of the Sacred and the Secular

Patron of knowledge and pursuer of peace with the Christian kingdoms of the north, al-Hakam II used his wisdom and energy to raise Cordoba to even greater heights. In the tenth century, the Great Mosque acquired a religious and secular standing that established it definitively as one of the supreme buildings of Islamic and European architecture. In the four years from 962–6, al-Hakam II expanded the space by twelve bays, using a design that built on the existing architectural concept of the mosque, yet lifted it to new levels through the creation of a *maqsura*, an area designated for the caliph's private worship and intended to shield him from potential assassins. The four domes of the roof were borne by a complex pattern of interlocking arches, no longer horseshoe-shaped, but made up of circular arcs or leaf shapes, interlaced in alternating colours and set on delicate columns, linking it to but also setting it apart from the rest of the prayer hall. At the far end of the space, glowing in the half-light, was a magnificently decorated qibla of gold, green and blue mosaics. Its shadowy opening to the mihrab had a mystical aura to it, a sense of the divine presence in a holy sanctum, and it could be lit on occasion as a beacon for the faithful. Its brilliant display of arches and domes resting on elegant columns was unique to Spanish Islamic architecture.

In the new space, those local Mozarabic building traditions rubbed shoulders with Byzantine and Islamic practices. The Arab historian Ibn Idhari recorded that al-Hakam II asked to borrow a mosaics expert from the Byzantine ruler Nikephoros II, 'in imitation of that which al-Walid (r. 705–15) had done at the time of the construction of the mosque of Damascus'.[3] The shimmering effects of the gold, green and blue mosaics he created reflected the atmosphere of a Byzantine church, while also renewing the Cordoba mosque's cultural and ideological links with the Umayyad caliphate of Damascus.

What further set al-Hakam II's design apart and asserted the legitimacy of his dynasty and its political ambitions was the importance he assigned to the written word and to the symbolism of colour and light, in which flowers, leaves and geometric patterns were interwoven with written inscriptions. The mosque was part of his religious and political propaganda, and the gilded letters and mosaics that imitated precious stones in his new personal prayer space were royal and imperial, yet also suggested a sacred unveiling of holy light in the darkness. Light was the symbol of justice and the intellect, creating beauty through its radiance. The vault of the mihrab was decorated with a carving of a scallop shell, metaphor of that divine light.[4]

The Great Mosque housed a copy of the Koran so large that two men were needed to lift it. In the book were four pages from the original Koran attributed to Caliph Uthman, who was said to have been assassinated while he was reading it, as its bloodstained pages suggested. The holy book with its precious text was carried out of the treasury in a candlelit procession, its very presence aligning the Umayyad caliphate of Cordoba with Uthman's religious authority. The written iconography of the mosque was one of the earliest of its kind to be created. It endowed the building with a ceremonial and religious meaning that was rare in the Muslim world and hinted at the latent influence of the Christian rites and rituals of many of Cordoba's inhabitants. Unusual Koranic verses and countless historical writings were inscribed on the inside walls, reminders of spiritual obligations, expressions of the caliph's gratitude to be chosen as the builder of this temple. All of them present the mosque as a universal Islamic shrine, akin to the Prophet Muhammad's mosque in Medina, linked by virtue of their creation as the culmination of a story of exile and migration, arising from conquest and renewal. The Cordoba mosque narrated the history of the western Umayyad dynasty through its physical forms, building materials, decoration and in the symbolism of its light and colours. It marked Abd al-Rahman III's restoration of the Umayyad caliphate as part of a divinely ordained heritage, which reached its greatest glory in the lifetime of al-Hakam II. Yet, when he died in October 976, Cordoba's splendour slowly began to wane, along with the power of the caliphate, while the fourth incarnation of the Great Mosque took on form and substance.

The Cathedral Bells of Santiago de Compostela

During the last twenty-five years of the tenth century, the tenor of life in al-Andalus changed, as it fell under a dictator known as Almanzor (al-Mansur). Hisham II (976–1009) was the heir chosen by al-Hakam II, but, at the time of the caliph's death, Hisham was just ten years old. He took the throne after a conspiracy against him was quelled by Ibn Abi Amir, the future Almanzor, who became his counsellor of state. A descendant of the original Arab conquerors of Spain, Abi Amir was cunning, intelligent, ruthless and ambitious, and he was famed as a military commander. He assumed the role of prime minister, exerting a stranglehold over the young caliph, but, in his favour, he continued the policy of tolerance and assimilation of Christians in al-Andalus. His armies contained many Christians, who were well treated and were allowed to celebrate their own religious festivals. Beyond the borders of al-Andalus was another matter, however, and Abi Amir waged almost constant warfare against the Christian kingdoms, fifty-two campaigns in all, an incessant holy war that cast the Christian states in the role of aggressors against Islam, thereby successfully diverting public attention from his total usurpation of the power of the caliph.

The new dictator styled himself Almanzor, the Victorious through Allah, the scourge of Christian Spain, and he ruled from his newly built palace Madinat al-Zahira, east of Cordoba, built specifically to upstage Madinat al-Zahra on the other side of the city. Almanzor was deeply pious, which had positive and negative consequences. To curry favour with the rigorous theologians of Cordoba who disapproved of secular learning, he ransacked al-Hakam II's magnificent library and burned as many as 10,000 books on science and philosophy. The silver lining was that his craving for power and glory was not only destructive but constructive, as it was the incentive for the last important expansion of the Great Mosque in 987–8.

Because the building was close to the river, it could not be extended southwards, so Almanzor decreed that there should be an expansion of forty-eight metres to the east, adding another eight naves, which increased the size of both the courtyard and prayer hall, making it the largest mosque in existence in the Muslim world outside Iraq. More than a hundred new columns were needed to support the new double arches, all simpler and less detailed due to the haste in which they were constructed.

A decade later, in 997, Almanzor fought his most daring campaign to capture the great Christian pilgrimage centre and shrine of Santiago de Compostela in the north of the peninsula, one of the holiest cities in Catholic Christendom. Arriving in the city on 11 August, he sacked it and razed the church built over the Apostle St James's tomb. Only the human remains of St James survived the devastation, which was imprinted on Christian memory for generations. Almanzor's soldiers carried off the church doors to use for shipbuilding, and its bells were looted and taken back to Cordoba, borne on the shoulders of Christian captives. On his return, a triumphant Almanzor was recorded as ordering them to be converted into lamps to hang in the Great Mosque. His success prompted him to sum up his life in verse: 'Thus I surpassed in power all men of power, excelled them all in glory until I found none to excel.'[5]

From Mosque to Cathedral: Destruction, Restoration and Transformation

'After many horrible massacres of Christians, Almanzor was seized in the great city of Medinaceli by the demon which had possessed him while he was alive, and he was buried in hell', wrote an unknown Christian author of the twelfth century.[6] The dictator's sudden death in 1002 unleashed events leading to the equally sudden collapse of the caliphate in 1031, which broke into over twenty minor kingdoms, known as *taifas* – small states ruled by Berbers from North Africa, northern European slaves and local Arab or Berber chieftains – and Cordoba itself became a republican emirate ruled by a local sheikh. Al-Andalus began to disintegrate, and the star of the Christian kingdoms in the north of the peninsula rose as their rulers focused more intently on the idea of reconquest of the lands they perceived as lost to Islam. The eleventh century saw a shift in the balance of power as Christian Spain built stronger ties with north-western Christendom, and the new Spanish kingdoms of Castile and Aragon took advantage of the fragmentation of the caliphate to push ever further southwards. The glory of nearly 300 years of Umayyad rule had been eclipsed in just three decades.

The Great Mosque, the single most powerful symbol of Islam in the peninsula, suffered a degradation that reflected the surrounding political chaos. It was looted and damaged during the civil conflict, when the golden door of the *maqsura* was stolen, and, between 1145 and 1146, the Christian army of King Alfonso VII of León and Castile briefly occupied Cordoba and entered the mosque after its ruler surrendered. It was a significant moment for the man who claimed to be 'king of the men of the two religions' and protector of Muslims. The Granadan historian Ibn Ghalib recounts how Alfonso's soldiers 'carried off the golden and silver apples that were on the minaret, and about half of the *minbar*'.[7] Lamps, ornaments made of precious stones and metals, everything valuable disappeared. For the first but not the last time, a Christian Mass was held inside the mosque, led by King Alfonso VII and Raymond, Archbishop of Toledo. But Christian victory was short-lived and almost a century passed before the Great Mosque faced a new transformation.

On 7 February 1236, King Ferdinand III of Castile rode through floods and rainstorms to help his vassals mount a siege of the city. The former 'ornament of the world', heart of the Umayyad caliphate, Cordoba finally capitulated on 29 June to the 'accursed Christians', as al-Maqqari put it. It was a crucial date in Spain's history, a moment of conquest that opened up the south to the Christian armies, who, by 1248, had captured the great city of Seville, with only the emirate of Granada still under Muslim rule. In his history of Ferdinand's reign, the king's chronicler Archbishop Jiménez de Rada tells us that, to right an ancient wrong, Ferdinand ordered the bells of Santiago de Compostela, which had been removed by Almanzor, to be carried back and restored to their rightful place.[8]

Almost at once, the Great Mosque was consecrated as a cathedral, named Santa María after the Virgin. From the start, the Christians realized the magnificence of the treasure they had captured, and few changes were made to the actual fabric of the building. Ferdinand understood the inordinate power of the mosque-turned-cathedral to symbolize their conquest and appreciated its status as an embodiment of the Muslim faith as well as being the model for all other mosques in al-Andalus. So, instead of succumbing to demolition, the Great Mosque was used as a church, to which were added side chapels and burial spaces, and a pantheon for Catholic royalty, built in the Mudejar style by Muslims living under Christian rule. Ferdinand and his son Alfonso X of Castile embarked on a restoration programme in which the dangerous roof and ceiling were repaired, along with masonry and the hydraulic water system, undertaken mostly by skilled Mudejar craftsmen. Muslims continued to work on the building under Christian rule, as had Christians under Islamic rule, and clearly the latter felt comfortable worshipping in what was still essentially a Muslim religious space. As the art historian Heather Ecker points out, what differed was the intention of those who created and recreated it, whether the mosque represented legitimate rule, embodied the past and the new future, or was seen as the spoils of war, transformed yet restored as Spain's most sacred Muslim building.[9] The enlightened view of King Ferdinand III and those who came later allowed the Islamic form and decoration of the mosque to be preserved for the next 300 years.

'Something that was unique in the world' – the Cathedral-Mosque of Cordoba Today

In the twenty-first century, the cathedral-mosque of Cordoba is a UNESCO World Heritage Site of Outstanding Universal Value, defined as a masterpiece of human creative genius that reveals an important interchange of human values, a site with a cultural significance so exceptional that it transcends national boundaries and is of importance to present and future generations. So far, the potential of the Great Mosque to inspire the interfaith and cross-cultural dialogue intimated by this definition has not yet been fulfilled, for political and religious reasons embedded deep in the history of Catholic Spain and its relationship with Europe's first Islamic caliphate. At the start of the sixteenth century, the Catholic Church had embarked on a programme of religious conversion, after the conquest of the emirate of Granada in 1492 by Isabella I of Castile and her husband Ferdinand II of Aragon. It was not just an attempted conversion of Muslim minds and souls, but also a widespread conversion of Islamic buildings, mainly mosques, into churches. The physical environment, as well as the spiritual one, was to be made Christian, and the canons of Cordoba wasted no time in lobbying to convert the Great Mosque into a cathedral. Their plan to remove the centre of the mosque and replace it with a Gothic cathedral choir was forcefully opposed by the city council, which was overruled after King Charles V, the first Habsburg king of Spain and Holy Roman Emperor, gave his permission for a project that lasted until the eighteenth century.

In 1523, the chief architect Hernán Ruiz started work on the great nave and transept, which soars above the flat prayer hall of the mosque, its towering, radiant space bedecked with Renaissance sculptures and Gothic tracery, some in abstract designs that mark the fusion of Andalusian Spanish church style with an Islamic patterning that today discloses the influence of 700 years of coexistence.[10] The minaret was appropriated as a bell tower, which, along with the dome and nave of the cathedral, announce a Christian identity to the world outside. Its dominating presence at the heart of the old mosque usurped its Islamic meaning and appropriated the space to assert Christian power, authority and ascendancy. When Charles V finally saw the new cathedral, he was appalled and is reported to have said, 'You have taken something that was unique in the world and turned it into something mundane.'

The dramatic transformation of the Great Mosque into a Christian cathedral created a distinctive yet controversial space which is a visual testament to one of Islam's vital European encounters with Christianity. It is hard, on entering the prayer hall and suddenly glimpsing the cathedral for the first time, not to share Charles V's shock and outrage at what feels like an act of sacrilege. In recent years, the monument has become the focus of a new battle, between the city council and the people of Cordoba on the one side and the ecclesiastical authorities on the other, revolving around the legitimacy of ownership of the land, which the Church council asserts is a Christian one on the basis that the original mosque was built on the site of a Christian church. It is an irony that Muslims are forbidden to pray inside a mosque that was once the glory of the Islamic world. Old tensions between Muslims and Christians are now mapped onto a contemporary politics in which ancient fears of invasion and conquest have resurfaced as numbers of immigrant Muslims rise and the political extreme right promotes a new Christian reconquest. In this confrontational climate, the contested identity of the mosque-cathedral is a crucial part of Spain's ongoing battle to come to terms with its Muslim past.

The Great Mosque of Cordoba tells a story of artistic, political and religious ambiguity and hybridity, written in stone, light and shadow. An enduring monument to the Islamic life, culture and architectural traditions of the Umayyad dynasty, it is part of the wider history of architecture in Islamic lands, creating a distinct tradition in its own right. That tradition also belongs to the story of European architecture, which it influenced – a fact rarely acknowledged because it is not perceived as part of mainstream European, and therefore by definition Christian, architecture. The Great Mosque embodies the imprint of Umayyad power and splendour, and the presence of Islamic civilization in Europe. Yet it is also a vehicle of expression of the earliest relations between Muslims and Christians on that continent and imparts the complex intertwining of each through its hybrid construction and its ambiguous and vexed later history. It remains important to us now in its affirmation of the ties that bind Europeans of both faiths, whether in conflict or in harmony.

Chapter 6

The Paths to Enlightenment: Books, Scholars and the Search for Knowledge

'He who travels in search of knowledge travels along Allah's path to paradise.'

Hadith

The Spirit of a New Age

Along the highway to Baghdad International Airport, the towering statue of a man with outspread wings, his eyes fixed on the horizon, arrests the gaze. The sculpture connects modern air travel with its distant origins in its representation of Abbas ibn Firnas, a multi-talented genius born of Berber parents in the town of Ronda, in the emirate of Cordoba, around the year 810. Cordoba has its own material tribute in the form of the Ibn Firnas bridge spanning the river Guadalquivir, a magnificent structure, 365 metres long, whose sweeping arches represent a pair of wings with an abstract sculpture of the polymath at its central point. The memorial next to the bridge honours Ibn Firnas as an aviation pioneer and the father of aeronautics, in a poignant homage to one of Cordoba's greatest sons, who is said to have travelled to Baghdad to study before returning to live in Cordoba itself. In that city, almost 1,200 years ago, in 852, at the age of forty-two, he attempted what was the first human flight.

Abbas had trialled his flying machine successfully a number of times in the local desert before testing his designs in the urban setting of Cordoba. One morning, he wrapped himself in a loose cloak stiffened with wooden struts and jumped from the minaret of the Great Mosque, the cloak acting as wings so that he could glide as if he were using a kind of parachute or hang-glider. The flight was a failure, but the cloak slowed his fall enough to prevent any serious injury. Undeterred, he upgraded his design, building a flying machine with wings made out of eagle feathers and silk. Near al-Rusafa, where Abd al-Rahman I had built his royal palace, Abbas ibn Firnas, aged almost seventy, climbed up a hill near the Mountain of the Bride and explained to a large crowd of onlookers how he planned to fly by guiding the wings fitted on his arms up and down: 'I should ascend like the birds. If all goes well, after soaring for a time I should be able to return to your side.' He flew to a good height, hovered for ten minutes, then plummeted to the ground, breaking the artificial wings and one of his vertebrae. Only afterwards did he realize that birds land using their tails, a detail which he had omitted from his design. He had belatedly discovered the very principle used by modern aircraft when they land on their rear wheels first.

Ibn Firnas's intellectual originality and powers of innovation were not limited to early aviation. He grasped the scientific properties of glass, from which he made what he called 'reading stones', early corrective lenses which were prototypes of reading glasses. Beautiful glassware inspired by the work of glassmakers in Samarra and Old Cairo was crafted in al-Andalus, and Ibn Firnas developed a technique of cutting quartz crystal from mined rocks, impelling a thriving crystal industry. By converting a room in his house, he constructed a kind of glass planetarium that showed the night sky, similar to those used today, complete with artificial thunder and lightning. His exceptional erudition and inventiveness were fuelled by eastern writings, many of which he brought back from Baghdad to Cordoba, including the celebrated *Sindhind*, an Arabic translation of the first highly influential work on astronomy by the Indian mathematician Brahmagupta. Scientist, engineer, musician and poet, Ibn Firnas died aged seventy-seven, in 887, his life the perfect expression of the burning desire for knowledge that instigated a great tradition of scholarship and learning and created a golden age of Islamic cultural and intellectual achievement in medieval Spain for the next 600 years.

The Search for Knowledge

The quest for knowledge that led to one of the world's greatest cultural and scientific revolutions was fired by multilingual, multicultural collaborations and fusions born of a shared vision, lighting up medieval Europe and setting it on the path to modernity. The cult of the book and a deep reverence for scholarship emerged from the convergence of Islam with Greek and Persian learning that began in the eighth century and inspired the intellectuals of al-Andalus – and of Cordoba, in particular – to tread new paths of exploration. Their discoveries fuelled the development of a profound and extensive body of learning that formed a unique European written culture composed of Islamic, Christian and Jewish elements. From the start, Christians and Muslims worked side by side, often in the company of Jews and scholars of other faiths, assimilating, transferring and extending human knowledge, sharing ancient learnings that combined the diverse intellectual traditions crucial to the evolution of European civilization.

From the birth of Islam, study was considered a religious duty comparable to prayer, and the search for knowledge a holy obligation. The first book written in Arabic was the Koran, in the reign of the caliph Uthman, and it needed a degree of sophistication in its expression, grammar and calligraphy that demanded a link between scholarship and devotion. The *rihla*, a journey seeking religious enlightenment, became a search for earthly understanding too, and scholars were sent far and wide to find and exchange learning, weaving complex networks that connected the sages of both Islamic and Christian lands and fostered the circulation of books. From the time of Caliph Harun al-Rashid (786–809) and his great library inside the House of Wisdom in Baghdad, the Abbasid caliphs set a tone of multicultural, multifaith tolerance that cultivated an age of intellectual enlightenment and progress. Muslim and Christian scholars and polymaths of all stripes gathered to undertake a translation programme of startling range and importance, the aim of which was to convert all known classical knowledge into Aramaic and

Arabic. Caliph al-Ma'mun (r. 813–33) and his Abbasid successors were bewitched by the lure of Persian culture, which was also translated into Arabic, and they well understood the importance of cultivating arts and sciences to acquire prestige. Their cultural policy was based on assimilating the literary heritage of the ancient past, supported by the circle of philosophers and sages assembled at the royal court. The conservation of treasured knowledge and the compulsion to learn were vital ways of legitimizing and strengthening their political power. The caliph ruled as a kind of philosopher king, inspired by Plato's belief that the ideal state could only be created by a ruler who possessed supreme philosophical knowledge.

East and west met in Cordoba in the reign of the Umayyad caliph al-Hakam II (r. 961–76), who embraced the cultural policy of Abbasid Baghdad and surrounded himself with wise men and intellectuals at court. They built a body of Andalusian knowledge that unfolded from the synthesis of ancient Greek and Persian learning with Hispanic and Roman heritage, creating an independent national cultural identity that validated his status as Umayyad ruler.

Cordoba's economy was thriving, and al-Hakam spent vast sums of money on acquiring books, sending his scholars to the East to bring back all the written texts they could find. Their task was made easier because trade routes had opened as roads were built and repaired and the Muslim empire stretched ever further, allowing merchants' caravans to travel great distances. Andalusian sages from the royal court travelled through the desert along with pilgrims; many merchants were scholars themselves, now with access to specialist booksellers, who traded and passed books between the famous souks in Cairo, Baghdad, Timbuktu and Fez, before bringing them back to Cordoba. The constant movement and migrations of intellectuals across countries and continents allowed the spread of knowledge to the furthest reaches of the Islamic empire.

Cordoba became the largest book market in the western world. As the city flourished, a mania for book collecting and building a personal library took hold, expedited by the technology of papermaking, new to the world beyond China. By the year 651, the first paper mill inspired by Chinese expertise had been built in Samarkand, on the Silk Road between China and the West. By 794, papermaking had travelled west to Baghdad, then to Damascus, and paper markets became common, heralding a boom in the production of new dyes, ink, glue and leather. Paper was produced in Cordoba and Seville, and turned out to be cheaper than papyrus or parchment, a boon even for poor people, who could then own books, as well as for the large teams of scribes employed to copy all the written learning brought back to the heart of al-Andalus.[1] Hundreds of people were involved in the production of some 70,000 to 80,000 books in Cordoba each year. Al-Hakam II had a personal library that held almost half a million volumes, the largest library in western Europe. The biggest in Christian European territory owned just a few hundred manuscripts. The library catalogue is mentioned with awe by the eleventh-century Cordoban polymath Ibn Hazm because it alone filled forty-four volumes of fifty pages each. In his writings, Qadi Iyad (d. 1149) gives a high profile to what he calls al-Hakam's 'House of Wisdom', linking it directly with the Houses of Wisdom that existed in Baghdad and Raqqada in the ninth century.[2] It set al-Hakam's Cordoba at the pinnacle of intellectual discovery in the western Islamic empire.

Star-takers, Algebra and Algorithms

The most common kind of symbolic representation of numbers used in the world today is called the Hindu–Arabic numeral system, based on decimals. We use it in daily life for weighing and measuring, in working out our finances, in telling the time. It is the basis of modern computing, helps create virtual worlds in film and measures new records in the arena of sport. Yet, when Ibn Firnas returned to Cordoba from Iraq with copies of the mathematical work of the brilliant Muslim scholar Muhammad ibn Musa al-Khwarizmi, he had no idea that he was bringing knowledge that would underpin the entire mathematical system of the western world. Around the year 820, Muhammad al-Khwarizmi was appointed astronomer and head of the House of Wisdom in Baghdad, where he studied sciences and mathematics using translations of early Greek and Sanskrit works. At that time, astronomy, mathematics and astrology were closely interwoven, and the latter was considered a branch of knowledge in its own right. The Umayyad rulers employed astrologers to forecast their future, including al-Dabbi, who had moved from Algeciras to Cordoba as court astrologer to Emir Hisham I (r. 788–96), where he successfully predicted that Hisham's reign would be lucky but would last just eight years.[3]

The Abbasids were fascinated by Persian culture, and its Zoroastrian myths were infused with astrology. Despite the Prophet's disapproval of fortune-telling and divination, the caliphs revived astrology as a respectable branch of knowledge after 850, ordering the translation of the key texts from Middle Persian into Arabic. The skill of plotting star positions for horoscopes was considered a scientific discipline, which depended on star charts and mathematical tables. It is very likely that Ibn Firnas brought al-Khwarizmi's astronomical tables based on Indian astronomy, the *Zij*, back with him from Baghdad. These tables, which enabled the movements of the sun, moon and the five known planets to be calculated, marked a turning point in the evolution of scientific investigation. The *Zij*, and the Greek scholar Ptolemy's work on astronomy known as the *Almagest*, one of the most influential scientific texts in history, formed the basis for Arabic astronomy. In the time of Abd al-Rahman III, the mathematician al-Majriti adapted the *Zij* to the longitudinal coordinates of Cordoba, which allowed him to calculate the direction of Mecca and the correct times of day for prayer using the phases of the moon.

Astronomy began to diverge from astrology and acquire a practical dimension, which inspired a synthesis of science and art in the creation of the astrolabe. What seems a mysterious and arcane object to us was in fact the most important device for calculating the position of the stars, telling the time, casting horoscopes and plotting locations before the invention of digital computers, and the most important instrument before the telescope.[4] Made sometimes of wood, but often of brass, the astrolabe was based on the conception of the Earth as the centre of a spherical universe. It had fixed and rotating parts, consisting of a hollow round plate called a 'mater' that held a pierced star map, with a viewing device on the back, along with various mathematical tables. In essence, it was a graphical computer, and it bore the latitudes of different cities, which were used to find the qibla, the Muslim direction of prayer.

The late-tenth-century Cordoban sage Ibn al-Saffar made a newer version of the *Zij* better adapted to the geographical position of Cordoba and, with the help of his father, a brass maker, created an early Andalusian astrolabe, uniting the craft of the smith with the inventiveness of the scientist. In 1387, the English poet Geoffrey Chaucer so admired the astrolabe that he wrote a treatise on it for his ten-year-old son, Lewis. At the end of the fifteenth century, it became a vital tool in ocean navigation, opening up the world to sea trade and travel, used by Christopher Columbus on his great sea voyages of discovery to the Americas. Louise Devoy, curator at the Royal Greenwich Observatory in London, which houses a collection of astrolabes, believes the concept of the instrument has been revived in the stylishness, adaptability and multifunctionality of today's smartphones.[5]

Al-Khwarizmi wrote the earliest treatise on the astrolabe, but it was the influence of his mathematics on the Muslim empire, as it grew in wealth and geographical size, that was most exceptional. Arithmetic was crucial to keeping accounts and in the early forms of banking that arose from burgeoning trade routes, and geometry, of which the Arab Muslims were already masters, became ever more vital to projects such as building bridges with stone arches, waterwheels and canals. Al-Khwarizmi is known as the father of algebra, used to represent numbers and quantities in formulae and equations, unifying mathematics and giving it a whole new broader dimension. It is indispensable today in computer programming, graphics, facial recognition and the development of software.

When we use a recipe for baking, solve a long-division problem, wash our laundry or use an internet search engine, we are using algorithms, exact lists of mathematical instructions that conduct specified actions step by step, in either hardware- or software-based routines. We owe the discovery and use of algorithmic instructions once again to al-Khwarizmi, whose Latinized name gave us the term 'algorithm' itself. The bedrock of these revolutionary advances was al-Khwarizmi's textbook, *On the Calculation with Hindu Numerals*, written about 820, which introduced what we now call Arabic numerals in English, the numbers 1 to 9, based on the use of angles (1 has one angle, 2 has two angles and so on), along with the decimal point and the concept of zero. By the end of the ninth century, this knowledge had passed from the Middle East to Andalusian scholars like Ibn Firnas and his successors, who had obtained many of the translated Greek texts as well as the works of some of the great geniuses of Baghdad's House of Wisdom. Using these translations, and building on the advances made by the scholars of Iraq, Andalusian astronomers and mathematicians studied, challenged and amended the work of Ptolemy, harvested ideas from Indian mathematics and developed their own scientific innovations. This body of learning was to be translated into Latin and circulated through the rest of Europe, establishing the foundations of modern mathematics and astronomy on the continent.

The Power of the Book: Herbal Healing and al-Zahrawi's 'The Method of Medicine'

The origins of European medicine dwell in the pages of two books – one Greek, one Arabic – that opened new horizons. The first, entitled *On Medical Materials* (*De materia medica*), was a precious gift given in 949 to the Umayyad caliph Abd al-Rahman III by the Byzantine emperor Constantine VII. Written in the first century AD by the Greek physician and pharmacologist Dioscorides, it was an exquisitely illustrated five-volume herbal pharmacopoeia, listing hundreds of plants and minerals and the medicines they can be used to make. For Constantine's gift to be useful to the scholars of the Cordoban caliphate, a big obstacle needed to be overcome: it was written in Greek, and there was no one in al-Andalus with a knowledge of the language. Hasdai ibn Shaprut, the Jewish physician to

Caliph Abd al-Rahman III, wrote to Constantine VII for help; two years later, the emperor sent a monk called Nicholas to join a team of translators in Cordoba. It was a painstaking process, as Nicholas had to teach Greek to the Latin-speaking local Christian scholars, so they could interpret between him and their Arab counterparts, but gradually *De materia medica* was translated into Arabic.

In this way, the passion for learning rose above all differences of creed and race in a multilingual collaboration between Christians, Jews and Muslims that brought ancient Greek knowledge into the purview of western Islamic lands, and from there to the rest of Europe. The gift of Dioscorides' book led to a defining moment in Andalusian medicine, allowing it to build on the botanical work on medicinal plants instigated by the first emir of al-Andalus, Abd al-Rahman I. It came to eclipse the achievements of the eastern Islamic empire in that field and fostered an independent medical tradition in al-Andalus. *De materia medica* was the authority on herbal medicine for 1,500 years, passing from Arabic into Latin, French, German, English and Spanish, and laying the foundations of many Renaissance herbals. Its wonderful illustrations continued the tradition of botanical drawing started in eighth-century al-Andalus – a tradition that still flourishes. Muslim Spain was the wellspring of herbal medicine; 3,000 plant-based medicines had already been created there by the thirteenth century and the first royal botanical gardens in Europe bore fruit in Toledo and Seville.

Towards the end of the golden age of Islamic Cordoba, sometime after 936, Abu al-Qasim Khalaf ibn Abbas al-Zahrawi, one of the titans of Muslim Spain, was born. Known in the Christian West as Abulcasis, he was named after the place where he lived most of his life, Madinat al-Zahra, where he rose to be court physician to Caliph al-Hakam II. In the middle of the tenth century, he travelled with many Andalusian scholars to Baghdad to study the work of Persian physicians and the Arabic texts of the great Greek doctor Galen. After his return, al-Zahrawi found fame as the most celebrated surgeon of the medieval world. Later in life, he wrote a huge thirty-volume compendium of medical knowledge known as *The Method of Medicine* (*Kitab al-Tasrif*), a practical guide containing treatises on disease, symptoms and treatment, diet and the preparation of drugs and ointments. One fifth of the work is devoted to the surgery for which he was most famous.

Al-Zahrawi's medical techniques and inventions were revolutionary and enduring. He pioneered over one hundred surgical instruments, many still used today, such as forceps, the speculum, bone saw, surgical needle and syringe. He was the first to use catgut for internal stitching, made advances in dentistry and devised the use of anaesthetics that are inhaled, using sponges soaked with narcotics including cannabis and opium. He illustrated his books himself, and his drawings of surgical instruments were the first of their kind; his description of the syringe is the first accurate account of it in the history of medicine. Al-Zahrawi died in 1013, just two years after Madinat al-Zahra was sacked and ruined, not knowing that his great work would soon be translated into Latin by the Christian scholar Gerard of Cremona (1114–87) and would become a principal source of medical knowledge in Europe for centuries.

The Shifting Sands of Confrontation and Alliance

When Rome fell in the fifth century, the rest of western Europe beyond al-Andalus gradually lost contact with Greek philosophy and erudition. Scientific study declined as education became confined to cathedral schools and monasteries, where syllabuses were focused on Bible study. The great reformation of education and revival of learning known as the Carolingian Renaissance, ushered in at the start of the ninth century by Charlemagne and the scholar Alcuin of York, relied on ancient Roman texts, works by learned Romans such as Martianus Capella (*fl. c.* 410–20), who introduced the study of the seven liberal arts that shaped medieval education, and Boethius (*c.* 480–524), who translated many Greek classics into Latin. Learning was preserved rather than developed, and clerical scholars devoted themselves mainly to the rudimentary study of astronomy and mathematics, which enabled monks to calculate prayer times and the correct date of Easter. But the scholarly agenda in northern Europe was to be revolutionized by the scientific legacy of al-Andalus, a great tree of knowledge that slowly took root in the Iberian peninsula and branched upwards and outwards to the northernmost reaches of the continent. It did so through movement and migration, as Christians travelled to al-Andalus to seek illumination, some remaining, but others returning, as Andalusian scholars had returned from Iraq, with copies of the latest Arab scientific and philosophical texts, which were then transformed by the vital and powerful act of translation.

The dawn of a great era of translation and transfer of learning rose with the birth of a humble monk in France around 946, in the time of Abd al-Rahman III. Gerbert of Aurillac (*c.* 946–1003) was sent to the monastery of St Gerald of Aurillac, sixty kilometres north of Barcelona, to study mathematics and Arab science, and he probably also studied at the nearby monastery of Santa María de Ripoll, on the border between the Islamic empire to the south and the Christian Franks to the north, an important seat of learning with an extensive library. The monastery of St Gerald was led by Bishop Atto, who had travelled to Cordoba and met Caliph al-Hakam II. Atto told Gerbert about the wonders of Arab culture and science, including mathematics, astronomy and the new Hindu–Arabic numerals.

Smitten by Arabic culture and learning, Gerbert was the first Christian scholar to take Arabic science out of Spain into the Christian West. His adaptation of the abacus, based on Roman numerals, to the Arabic counting system and his introduction of the armillary sphere, an instrument akin to the astrolabe, brought back lost knowledge, with cutting-edge Arabic modifications, to Christian Europe. Gerbert was one of the most illustrious scientists of his time, a real humanist long before the Renaissance and a lifelong advocate of Muslim Arab learning, whose destiny was to rise to supremacy in the Christian Church as Pope Sylvester II. There can be no better example of the harmonious conjunction of Muslim and Christian cultures than the learned pope who first introduced the groundbreaking science of the Islamic empire to Christian Europe.

*

The caliphate of Cordoba at the end of the tenth century was a place of paradox and divergence. It was at a pinnacle of cultural splendour, its path-breaking mathematics, astronomy and medicine paving the way for the great advances in European wisdom of the next 500 years. Yet it was in a state of imminent political collapse. The first thirty years of the eleventh century were beset by a factionalism that led to civil war, as rivals for the caliphate fought among themselves. Seven caliphs came and went, some of them with multiple brief reigns, as the former majesty of the Cordoban state disintegrated into a series of massacres, pillaging and destruction, amid which al-Mansur's palace of Madinat al-Zahira and the Falcon's al-Rusafa were obliterated almost without trace, and the wondrous library of al-Hakam II was ruined. When the Umayyad caliph Hisham III was forced to abdicate in 1031, the reign of the great Umayyad dynasty ended and the caliphate was abolished. Centrality had given way to marginality as al-Andalus fragmented into small local kingdoms, many ruled by Berber chieftains whose star was rising.

The search for knowledge that had glorified the western Islamic caliphate for almost 300 years had originally been in the service of religion, power and politics, a holy duty that bestowed prestige and authority on its emirs and caliphs. The ephemerality of that power and the instability of politics had engendered a descent into confrontation, corruption and collapse – yet, alongside that division and fragmentation, a unity was born of a common aim and passion for learning. It cultivated a sense of democratic sharing of knowledge, a feeling of community among Muslims, Christians and Jews that evolved beyond racial and religious hostilities or differences. On the eve of some of the most harrowing conflicts between Christians and Muslims, scholars across the religious divide were beginning to collaborate on the great transmission of learning from Muslim to Christian Europe, engaged in the pursuit of knowledge for the universal good.

Chapter 7

Sicily: Crossroads of Civilizations

'Sicily is an island, extensive and important. The Muslims have no island more splendid, more prosperous, or with more cities.'

Al-Muqaddisi, tenth-century Palestinian geographer

'Do you not harmonize the inharmonious and mix together the unmixable . . . with wise foresight blending and uniting into a single race disparate and incongruent peoples?'

Eugenius, minister of King William II of Sicily, *c.* 1175

The geography of Sicily is the lodestar which has guided and shaped its historical and cultural contours. The triangular shape of the island inspired its earliest name, Trinacria, which means 'three-pointed' in Greek, its three capes pointing west to Europe, south to Africa and north-east to the Balkans and Asia. With links to all three continents, Sicily was at times the seeming heart of the civilized world, at times a place where empires collided. The largest Mediterranean island, its mountain streams flowed into rivers that watered the arable land and created an abundant agricultural economy; the rivers met the sea at great ports – Messina, Catania and Palermo among them – making Sicily a crucial strategic location for Mediterranean trade. Yet its geographical situation also made it vulnerable to external forces, to invasion, conquest and control by Greek, Roman, Byzantine, Muslim and Norman powers, successive colonizations which sometimes evolved into significant phases of independence. Throughout, the powerful ever-active volcano Mount Etna, cast on the island in Greek myth by the goddess Athena, slumbered and occasionally erupted, the geographical reflection of Sicily's vexed and varied past.

An aura of myth and mystery surrounds the island, legendary abode of the fabled Cyclops sighted by Jason's Argonauts on their travels and seat of a Greek civilization that was home to the most talented scientist of the ancient world, Archimedes, who lived in Syracuse. In Roman times, the great plays of Terence and Aristophanes were staged in Sicily's theatres, shining with mosaics and beaten gold, and there was close social and commercial contact with the cities of the wider Greek empire. By the Middle Ages, Sicily had become a place of contradictions; it was both the centre of Mediterranean trade and cultural interchange, and a crossing point where slaves and captives, exiles and refugees, pirates, smugglers, fortune seekers, wandering merchants and scholars met and departed. It had a changing, fluid society that lived simultaneously on the edge of other empires and within an interlinked cross-cultural system. As the geographical centre of the Mediterranean, it lay between western Christendom, the Islamic empire and Greek Christendom. Sicily was a frontier land that seemed both to unite Christianity and Islam through a network of culture and trade, and to divide them.

Much earlier, in AD 535, Belisarius, the Greek commander-in-chief of the Byzantine army, was sent by the emperor Justinian I, with a force of just 8,000 soldiers, to undertake the reconquest of Italy from the Ostrogoths. Landing on Sicily in the summer, he had the entire island under his control by the end of the year, bequeathing a legacy for the next 300 years that established Greek as the official language of government, while the Church adopted Greek rites and allegiance to the patriarch of Constantinople. So it remained until the early ninth century. No one knew that in just a few years, this Byzantine Christian island, main outpost of its western empire, would be overcome by new conquerors from the south, familiar yet fearsome, bearing the banner not of Christ, but of Muhammad.

Echoes of an Emirate: Muslim Sicily 827–1072

The story of Muslim Sicily is obscure and fractured, and deciphering it is akin to poring over the tattered fragments of an old manuscript, full of gaps and silences. There is little written information to draw on; the few early chronicles that refer to this period of Sicily's history briefly record Muslim raids on the island as early as 652, becoming more regular between 700 and 800 as North African troops attacked its shores to capture booty and slaves. Syracuse was stormed by marauders from Egypt in 669, and the treasures of its Roman churches were plundered and taken to Alexandria. Ambassadors of the Byzantine governors of Sicily negotiated peace treaties with the African princes and exchanged gifts, to no avail. Political changes in the Muslim world of the early ninth century were conspiring to turn these Muslim raids into an invasion.

Almost a hundred years earlier, in 711, Musa ibn Nusayr and Tariq ibn Ziyad had taken control of the Iberian peninsula as part of a holy war, a concerted westward expansion of the new and united Islamic empire. Now, in contrast, on the eve of the Islamic conquest of Sicily, the Muslim world had become fractious and divided. It was the third Islamic century, and the nation of believers, the umma, had begun to fragment into conflicting factions and Baghdad had lost its sole authority over all Muslims. Abd al-Rahmann III had proclaimed his own caliphate in al-Andalus, while Sunnis, Shi'ites and Kharjites had developed their own clashing visions of legitimate authority and rule across North Africa and Arabia. In 800, a new dynasty of Sunni Arab princes, the Aghlabids, built their royal palace just outside Kairouan in Tunisia, and ruled Ifriqiya, an area stretching from Algeria to Libya. Their first ruler, Ibrahim ibn al-Aghlab (r. 800–12), was appointed hereditary emir by the Abbasid caliph. But it was the contact between his son, the emir Ziyadat Allah (r. 817–38), and a Byzantine general, Euphemius, that changed Sicily's fortune for the next 250 years.

The legendary story of the Muslim occupation of Sicily, like that of Spain, rests on the violation of a woman. At the start of 827, Ziyadat Allah caught wind of news that the Byzantine armed forces in Sicily were holding Muslim soldiers captive. The intelligence came from a rebel commander of the fleet in the Byzantine army, Euphemius. Latin chronicles report that he had invaded the sanctity of the cloister, abducting a nun called Homoniza from her convent and marrying her. The Byzantine emperor Michael II found out and inflicted the appropriate Greek penalty of cutting off the offender's nose. In an act of revenge, Euphemius colluded with the Aghlabid emir, asking for help to overthrow the emir's enemies in Sicily, in exchange for vital military secrets. This was of great interest to Ziyadat Allah, who saw the island's potential for new commercial and military ventures.

One morning in June 827, a fleet under the emir's orders set sail for Sicily, carrying Arab, Berber and Persian warriors in what was presented as a jihad to liberate Muslims from the infidel, allowing the Aghlabids to conquer the island. Sicily came late into the Muslim world, and at great cost – a surprising aspect of the Islamic conquest was how long it took the Muslims to gain control of the island, in comparison with the speed of the conquest of Spain. The first landing at Mazara in 827 and the siege of the capital Syracuse failed, but, in 830, Palermo was captured after a year-long siege, and, in twenty years, half the island was under Muslim control. Nearly fifty years later, the monk Theodosius described the fall of Syracuse in 878, after 1,500 years as Sicily's main town. He wrote of huge siege engines and subterranean mines breaching the walls, and lamented the bloodshed where no living thing remained in a city that once rivalled Athens and Alexandria. The archbishop was spared after he showed the conquerors where the cathedral treasure was hidden, although the division of land and enormous booty led to squabbles among the troops. By the end of the ninth century, the Byzantines had almost entirely withdrawn from Sicily; in 902, the Aghlabid emir captured the last fortified outpost of Taormina, massacring the inhabitants and setting fire to the town. Muslim control of Sicily was complete.

The new rulers discovered a society made up of many ethnic and religious groups: Greek-Byzantine Sicilians, Jews, Lombards, who were the Germanic rulers of Italy, and Latin peoples. The cities that surrendered were allowed to practise their religions, but any resistance was supressed with brutality. As in al-Andalus, many churches became mosques, but Christians mostly lived by their own laws, despite the obligation they shared with Jews to use distinguishing marks on their clothes and houses, pay greater taxes and not to ring church bells or read the Bible in earshot of Muslims. From the start of Muslim rule, immigrants moved north from Africa in large numbers, fleeing dangers and looking for a new life. The Arab Muslim colonists were the new elite, and Berbers, Jews and local Sicilians were the lower classes and farmers.

Sicily had a completely different status as a colony of North Africa. The island was the central point of a large commercial network stretching from Spain to Syria, Alexandria to Ceuta. It basked in the light of Kairouan's civilization, with its rich architectural heritage and renowned scholarship, and its exquisite pottery, textiles and carpets. Palermo became the Arab capital of Sicily, with a population which now included Slavs, Tatars and Black Africans. It was also a centre for Arab travellers from Spain, Syria and Egypt and the haunt of Persian traders in cereals, cattle and slaves. In the ninth century, the monk Theodosius, who had known the glories of Byzantine Syracuse, acknowledged it as a magnificent town. In the countryside, the same Muslim skill in irrigation that made al-Andalus a fertile paradise watered market gardens and arable land to give abundant crops of sugar cane, date palms, sumac for tanning and dyeing, pistachios, melons, lemons and bitter oranges. Spain and Sicily were the first places in Europe to grow rice, and cotton plants and mulberries were introduced along with silkworms to make the finest silk. The economy expanded and Palermo developed in line with other great cities of the medieval Muslim world, focusing on social and cultural rather than military institutions.

Political upheaval in North Africa, which had fomented the conquest of Sicily by the Aghlabids, brought about the demise of their dynasty. In the early tenth century, civil war and the rise of the Shia Fatimids of Egypt overturned the Tunisian rulers, and the Fatimid Mahdi became caliph, founding Cairo as his capital. The last Aghlabid ruler of Sicily, the drunken and abusive Ziyadat Allah III, who had conspired to assassinate his father, fled to Egypt in 909, leaving the island in the control of a Fatimid governor. It was as if the bold and pioneering Aghlabids vanished into nothing. If few written sources on Aghlabid Sicily exist, almost nothing of their material culture remains; what was built was destroyed, reused or built over in later eras. But the chance survival of a fragment of marble from the altar of a church in Agrigento in the south-west of the island, one of the earliest cities to be converted to Islam, tells us that Christians were still able to practise their faith. The marble relief shows a Tree of Life, Byzantine symbol of the Cross of Christ, in the form of a date palm, a tree introduced by the Arab settlers. The use of its image in Christian church art suggests that the Byzantine Christians of Sicily had quickly absorbed Muslim features of daily life.

Fatimids and Kalbids: Sicily 909–1044

The Fatimid dynasty made a powerful assertion of its legitimacy by claiming descent from Fatima, the daughter of the Prophet. The first Fatimid caliph, 'Ubayd Allah al-Mahdi, was very interested in Sicily. He had already embarked on a campaign of jihad in southern Italy that promised him political power and wealth, and Sicily was in a strategically important location for consolidating his ambitions. He acted quickly to install a trusted proxy who could lead the island's Muslim population, but there were rebellions, particularly in Taormina in the east, which, though conquered, was never fully converted. Its inhabitants still felt they were part of Christian Byzantium instead of the Muslim world, and the Fatimids had repeatedly to intervene in their uprisings. Across the sea, yet again, political chaos in Ifriqiya blighted Muslim Sicily. Its appointed local rulers came and went like the flickering images on an old film reel, until finally, in 944, a new Muslim clan, the Kalbids, were sent by the Fatimids to govern the island by direct proxy, as a reward for their unfailing loyalty to the caliphate. In 948, al-Hasan al-Kalbi became the first emir of Sicily, his line eventually forming their own dynasty, which brought enough stability to the island to create an environment in which scholarly and social institutions with a specifically Sicilian Muslim identity saw the light.

A century after the first assault on Sicily, interactions between Muslims and Christians had become more complex and nuanced, as fruitful collaborations emerged through commerce and scholarship. Under the Kalbids, while minor local unrest and Muslim confrontation with the Byzantines continued, there was also a growing peace and prosperity, bolstered by burgeoning trade and cultural growth. The contact between Sicily, North Africa and Egypt stimulated lucrative commerce between Muslim, Christian and Jewish merchants, craftsmen, importers and exporters, which thrived amid the shipping trade round the Mediterranean. In 973, the island was visited by the Shi'ite Fatimid traveller and geographer from Baghdad, Ibn Hawqal (d. after 978), who left a forthright contemporary account of Sicily in his great work of geography *The Face of the Earth* (*Surat al-Ard*). His description of the markets in Palermo at that time reflects the more general expansion in trade in its rich array of merchants and craftsmen: 'Most markets are there . . . the olive market, all the flour merchants, the money-changers, pharmacists, blacksmiths, burnishers, the grain markets, embroiderers, fish-sellers, . . . butchers, greengrocers, fruiterers, herb-sellers, potters, bakers, rope-makers, a section for perfume-sellers, slaughter-men, shoe-makers, tanners, carpenters, joiners and wood-workers.'[1]

At the same time, Arabic writing on Muslim history began to paint a picture of Sicily's growing international reputation as an intellectual centre, especially in Islamic sciences, to which the abundant references to the prodigious scholarship of Sicilian Muslim jurists, Koranic scholars, grammarians, scientists and poets bear witness. Sicilian works on Islamic law in the Maliki tradition, which relied on the Koran and the sayings of the Prophet known as Hadiths as sources, underlined a scholarly connection with North Africa, where Maliki Sunnism was strong even under the influence of the Fatimids' strict Shi'ite beliefs. The Fatimid emphasis on an individual's intellectual and ethical merit rather than their class or ancestry embraced an idea of fairness which enabled an education to be offered to some 40 per cent of children, both boys and girls. The insistence on the Koranic injunction that encouraged reading to enable study of the Koran, and the use of the Arabic number system, which was relatively easier to use than the Roman or Byzantine systems, created an unprecedented level of literacy in the Arabic language and sciences. The study of Arabic itself flourished in the scholarship of the Sicilian Arabs, perhaps because of the importance of teaching it to the many Sicilians to whom it was not their native language. Erudite works on grammar, syntax, how to compose poetry and prose, even on the study of vocabulary, were plentiful, and represented the high point of Islamic culture in tenth-century Sicily. The monastic schools run by members of the island's Jewish and Byzantine Christian populations also had a high level of literacy, creating a remarkable level of education across Sicilian society that gave individuals opportunities for much greater social mobility.

In the second half of the tenth century, the Kalbid court was the place for those who aspired to self-advancement, especially if they had a gift for poetry. As in the caliphate of al-Andalus, the writing of poetry, fostered by scholarship on the Arabic language, gave the royal court a veneer of high culture and helped consolidate the political legitimacy of the Kalbids. Sicilian poets emerged from all walks of life, some of them scholars, some princes, some court panegyrists, all keen to display their learning and skill in praising, commiserating with and congratulating the emir on his military campaigns. Yet no amount of poetry could stave off the impending demise of the dynasty. In 970, the Fatimids conquered Egypt and built a new capital city that would become modern Cairo; they barely glanced back towards their western kingdoms. Powerless without the patronage and support of their overlords, the Kalbids fell into decline and Sicily suffered fatal political disintegration. The last Kalbid emir, al-Hasan al-Samsam, was deposed in 1044 and the island fragmented into small kingdoms ruled by local warlords, one of whom, Ibn al-Thumna, was to play a minor but crucial role in the history of Sicily.

Ibn al-Thumna of the Kalbid dynasty had control of Syracuse and Catania to the east, while his great rival, the provincial commander Ibn al-Hawwas, ruled Agrigento in the south-west of the island. By chance or by destiny, Ibn al-Thumna, who was prone to rages, was married to Ibn al-Hawwas's sister, whom he left to die after having her veins bled following a drunken argument. Her son discovered her and managed to find a doctor, who saved her life. Ibn al-Thumna begged for forgiveness, but his wife fled to Ibn al-Hawwas, who refused to let her return to her husband. Incensed, Ibn al-Thumna fought his brother-in-law and lost, leaving his army in tatters and his power undermined. Turning to the Norman army, which had southern Italy under its control, for assistance, he was fortunate that they saw an opportunity to expand their Italian territory and seize Sicily. The Normans agreed to collaborate, with consequences that were devastating for Muslim supremacy in Sicily, yet providential for the future of the island. The emirate of Sicily ended as it had begun, with an act of violent aggression towards a woman that, this time, provoked a regime-changing betrayal.

Disintegration and Demise: The Fall of Islamic Sicily

The Muslims had brought their religion, laws, technology, art and science to create a thriving agricultural society and a hub of intellectual achievement, a truly cross-cultural society of peoples of three different cultures, religions and languages. Sicily had become part of the dynamic civilization of North Africa, a place where Arabic, Byzantine and Latin cultures met. Its towns and cities reflected this mixed status in their mosques and churches, as did the longevity of the use of Arabic on the island, where today, after nine centuries, over 300 words of Arabic influence are still in common use. Now, it is only words, just a few scattered inscriptions, that testify to the lustre of the Sicilian emirs, whose imposing baths, palaces and mosques have disappeared with barely a vestige remaining, destroyed or refashioned, as if, in later centuries, a concerted effort were made to obliterate all signs of a Muslim past.

The disintegration of the Muslim dynasties of North Africa left Sicily isolated and vulnerable to attack from Christian Europe, for whom the Islamic conquest that began in 827 had seemed a fearful threat, leaving Rome vulnerable to Muslim assaults and weakening the Christian presence in the Mediterranean Sea. In 1038, George Maniakes, a Byzantine general, had attacked the Sicilian Muslims with the help of Harald Hardrada, future king of Norway, plus a contingent of Norman mercenaries, one of whom, 'Iron Arm' William de Hauteville, defeated the emir of Syracuse in single combat. The Muslims quickly regained control, but the Normans had a whiff of success which convinced them that Sicily could be conquered.

Religious conflict served as the backdrop to events in the central Mediterranean in the first half of the eleventh century. It was conflict not solely between different religions, but also between different branches within the same religion. As the Islamic empire succumbed to strife between Sunnis, Shi'ites and warring Berbers, Sicily too fell prey to dissenting tribal factions. In comparison with the emirates and caliphate of al-Andalus, with their strong, focused government at the highest level, the emirate of Sicily had always been contended and ill-governed, its power diluted and confused by its dependence on a foreign caliphate. But, if there were serious divisions between Muslims, there were equally destructive clashes between Christians. The Great Schism of 1054 split the Latin Roman Church from the Greek Byzantine Church, each with major religious, cultural and ethnic differences, and each accusing the other of falling into heresy, a rift which has not yet been reconciled. In search of dominion, the Roman papacy made a plausible but inaccurate claim to the feudal lordship of Sicily, based on the dubious premise that the Carolingian kings had owned the island and later donated it to the pope. The Normans were Christian descendants of the Vikings and cast themselves as protectors of the pope, so it was with a degree of Christian fervour, and an even greater lust for land and power, that they set their sights on Sicily.

Two of the twelve sons of the Norman landowner Tancred de Hauteville led the Norman conquest of the island. Robert Guiscard, 'the Fox', his sixth son – tall, fair-haired, cunning and brilliant in battle – had gone to Italy from Normandy as a professional soldier, a mercenary recruited by the Lombards, who controlled southern Italy. He reached Calabria in south-west Italy in 1046, living as a bandit in the hills, pillaging towns in the region and amassing a fortune. Just three kilometres across the Strait of Messina, one of the frontiers of Christian civilization, lay Sicily, and the Roman Church wanted to reclaim it from Islam. They saw in the Normans an opportunity either to oust or convert the Muslim population and Latinize the Greek Church on the island. In 1059, Robert swore allegiance to Pope Nicholas II, with a promised reward of power over Sicily. With the help of his younger brother Roger, Robert wielded the papal banner and waged a holy war against the Sicilian Muslims. It is said that St George appeared on a white horse during one battle, a divine affirmation of the legitimacy of their purpose, which resulted in three years of bloody fighting and violent plunder in the name of Christ. By 1064, they had reached the outskirts of the Muslim capital of Palermo, making the mistake of camping on a rocky outcrop that was crawling with tarantulas. The Christian chronicler Geoffrey of Malaterra gives us a vivid account: 'Anyone who was stung by them found himself filled with gas and suffered so much that he was unable to keep the same gas from coming out of his anus with a disgusting rattle. Unless a poultice or some form of hot pad was applied quickly, the victim was said to be in danger of dying. When some of our men were afflicted in this disgusting way, the brothers were forced to change sites.'[2]

Roger (1031–1101) met the Muslim armies outside the city in 1068 and defeated them in a ghastly battle. Geoffrey of Malaterra describes Roger as 'of the greatest beauty, of lofty stature, of graceful shape, most eloquent in speech and cool in counsel. He was far-seeing in arranging all his actions, pleasant and merry . . . strong and brave'.[3] He was also a ferocious and merciless fighter who used the Muslims' own homing pigeons to send messages written in blood back to Palermo announcing his victory. Six years after the Norman conquest of England, Roger finally entered Palermo as its ruler in 1072, and was declared count of Sicily by his brother Robert, his overlord.

A Model Society: Norman Sicily between Islam and Christianity

What happened next was truly remarkable. Roger, a medieval Norman warlord who had lived as a bandit, paved the way for the creation of a state that was exceptional. From the start, Roger was magnanimous in victory, although the last major stronghold of Muslim Sicily, Noto, did not fall until 1090. He treated all civilians with tolerance, allowing Jews and Muslims to practise their faith, and some of the latter even joined his army. Under Roger's jurisdiction, the nature of the island changed from Muslim to Roman Catholic, to a western European culture whose basic language was Latin, with a few remaining pockets of Greek Orthodoxy. Roger had unusual political skill and adaptability; he quickly saw the superiority of Islamic culture and eastern administration and adopted it. Coins were minted with Kufic inscriptions dated using the Muslim Hijra. He used the Saracen title of emir for the new count of Sicily, while laws and taxation were based on existing Byzantine traditions.

From the moment Roger took charge, immigration was encouraged, in a steady flow of peoples from northern Europe, France and northern Italy, many of them Lombards. In this great gallimaufry of races, urban life tended to encourage friendly cooperation, even if there was an element of ghettoizing of those of different faiths. In the country, fault lines appeared as Muslims and Christians lived in specific areas and suffered raids from newly arrived settlers, as well as being prone to violence and antagonism among themselves.

In many ways, the new state was the antithesis of al-Andalus. The tone was conciliatory, though Muslims and Jews had to pay a special tax. Norman charters continued the Islamic precedent of ensuring that Latins, Greeks, Jews and Saracens should be judged by their own laws. Muslim culture was encouraged, and while Norman French and Latin were the official languages of the court, Arabic and Greek were used alongside them. Roger I put politics before religion and aimed to be even-handed with all his peoples, carefully cultivating his Muslim subjects, endowing more Greek than Roman Catholic monasteries and installing a Latin archbishop at

Palermo by 1083. He fused in his person western feudalism and the eastern idea that the ruler was sovereign and divine, which endowed him with a kind of imperial authority as the pope's representative. Roger even wore an ecclesiastical ring and carried a crozier like a bishop, announcing a blend of temporal and spiritual power that made him one of the most successful rulers in the world. When he died, in 1101, he was interred in an ancient Roman marble sarcophagus, like a Byzantine emperor. His legacy brought Sicily a unity, prosperity and prestige not seen since its ancient Greek era.

Roger II of Sicily: A King for All Times

One of the supreme treasures held in the Imperial Treasury of the Hofburg Palace in Vienna is the Royal Mantle of Roger II of Sicily (1095–1154). Fashioned for a Christian king by Muslim and Byzantine craftsmen in the royal Palermo workshop, using vermilion silk imported from the Byzantine Empire, it is embellished with gold embroidery, thousands of pearls from the Persian Gulf, enamel, garnets and rubies. The Arabic inscription in imposing Kufic script on the hem dates it from year 528 of the Hijra, or 1133–4, and its panels depict two lions, each attacking a camel, on either side of a palm tree. The lions stood for Roger himself, the palm the tree of life and the camels suggested the North Africans whom he subdued and ruled. Worn on state occasions and to welcome guests, it was used as a coronation robe by Roger's Germanic descendants, the Holy Roman Emperors, who marked the sacredness of their Catholic investiture with Muslim Arab finery and eventually took it to Austria. It is a woven history of Roger's reign, a eulogy to a king, but also the product of the collaborative society of Christians and Muslims he oversaw.

Unlike his ancestors, Roger II was an Italian, born in Mileto in Calabria in 1095. From his father Roger I, he inherited what was then the County of Sicily at the age of nine, with his mother acting as regent until he reached his sixteenth birthday. Roger's support of Pope Anacletus II earned him the reward of the kingdom of Sicily, and he was crowned in Palermo on Christmas Day 1130, in the tradition of priest kings, against whom rebellion would be sacrilege. In the church of Santa Maria dell'Ammiraglio in Palermo, founded by Roger's vizier George of Antioch, a magnificent gold mosaic depicts the king being crowned by Christ himself.

Tall, with a loud voice, high intelligence and insatiable ambition, Roger II advanced his father's principles by departing from the familiar style of north European courts and embracing the great diversity of his people. His new kingdom, which now included southern Italy, needed to be seen as legitimate. To achieve this aim, Roger strove to appeal to the different cultures of the island. Growing up in Byzantine Calabria, he spoke in Greek, but he also knew Arabic and had a genuine fascination with Islamic culture; it is said that an Arab cook oversaw the royal kitchens and that Roger sat in state beneath a bejewelled parasol given him by the Fatimid caliph. Muslims were still the majority population and he needed their allegiance, which was perhaps consolidated by his dealings with the emirs of Zirid Ifriqiya and Fatimid Egypt, whose institutions, splendid courts and scholarly prestige he greatly admired. Roger proved his authority by synthesizing elements from Rome, Constantinople and Fatimid Egypt, all part of a deliberate policy to orchestrate his reign as a model of absolute monarchy. In this he was aided by a few trusted officials, such as George of Antioch, chief minister around 1125, an Orthodox Christian who was fluent in Greek and Arabic. Under Roger II's aegis, Sicily would come to rival the grandeur and military skill of the Byzantine Empire, the splendour of the Muslim court in North Africa and the diplomatic skills of northern courts such as those in France and England.

Multicultural and multi-religious cooperation was expressed in Norman Sicily through its art, customs and languages, but perhaps its most splendid incarnation was the peerless royal chapel or Cappella Palatina, built in the 1130s and consecrated in 1143, standing as a focal point at the centre of the royal palace in Palermo. Seen from the city, its Byzantine dome and rounded bell tower might be mistaken for a mosque and minaret. Inside, there is no mistaking the hybrid nature of the building. In its creation, craftsmen of three different religious traditions worked side by side. Western Christian artisans from across Italy constructed its marble pavements; the magnificent mosaic of the Christ Pantocrator inside the dome was fashioned by Greek artists using Byzantine and Latin iconography; and the wooden stalactite ceiling carved with winged genii, veiled houris and turbaned chess-players was the creation of Muslim craftsmen, its star and cross pattern a purely Islamic version of the Byzantine patterns in the floor beneath. On the ceiling are lively scenes from daily life at court: men playing chess, sitting by a fountain, hunting; there are dancers, musicians, folk eating and drinking. Roger himself appears seven times, portrayed as an Islamic ruler, sitting cross-legged and wearing a kaftan and three-pointed crown. The Greek Sicilian monk Philagathos of Cerami described the chapel as 'brilliant with lights, shining with gold, glittering with mosaics, and bright with paintings. He who has seen it many times, marvels when he sees it again, and is as astonished as if he were seeing it for the first time'.[4]

If there had been a mass exodus of Muslim scholars and intellectuals at the start of Norman rule in Sicily, they now flocked to Roger II's court – Greeks, Muslims and western Europeans alike – to breathe in its rarefied air of learning and erudition. Scholars from all over the world met in Palermo, still a hub of learning and invention specializing in science and astronomy, as it had in Muslim times. In Roger's reign, and that of his son William, the Greek and Arabic texts lost to the west were translated into Latin, including the works of Plato, Euclid and Ptolemy's *Almagest*, the latter by the Italian Henry Aristippus with the help of the Byzantine scholar Eugenius, who knew Arabic and Latin. It may have predated the more influential version by the great translator Gerard of Cremona, and it was the first time Ptolemy's seminal work could be read in Latin.

Geography inspired the zenith of Roger II's cultural patrimony, not in its practical topographical dimension, but in the form of a book. In 1139, the king commissioned a Muslim scholar, Muhammad al-Idrisi (1100–1165), to come from Cordoba to make him a map of the world. Muslim expertise in geography in part derived from their early environment as nomads searching for pasture, so the subject developed as a practical necessity. The orienting of mosques towards Mecca was another impetus for the study of geography, combined with astronomy, to calculate the exact direction of the city, and combined with the increased need for geographical knowledge due to the expansion of the Muslim empire and trade within it. Al-Idrisi spent fifteen years in Sicily interviewing thousands of travellers, and from the knowledge gleaned he wrote the greatest single work of geography of the Middle Ages. It became known as the *Book of Roger* and was based on previous work done by the great al-Khwarizmi and Ptolemy's work on geography, which had survived in Arabic translation, as well as the information gathered in the melting pot of global trends and ideas that was Sicily at that time. Al-Idrisi depicted the world as a globe 22,900 miles in circumference, close to the actual distance of 24,902 miles measured at the equator. His book and seventy maps showed the entire continents of Europe, Asia and Africa north of the equator, and was the first work to integrate Greek, Latin and Arab scholarship in a single compendium of the known world. Before then, Orosius's fifth-century description of the Earth was the only thing of this kind known in the West. Al-Idrisi's book was global in its scope, an ethno-geographic account of peoples and cultures that included information on the caste system in India, rice cultivation in China and an account of England, shaped like an ostrich head. It would remain the most accurate map of the world for the next 300 years. The *Book of Roger* matched and epitomized the king's enormous cultural ambition. He had all seventy maps engraved on huge silver disks, and al-Idrisi created a flattened hemisphere weighing 400 pounds, the acme of contemporary geographical knowledge.

For about half a century, Sicily was a cultural utopia, a model society where Christians of both denominations lived side by side with Muslims and Jews, brought together by learning, art and custom. There was still conflict over religion, land and power, and Roger II's desire to embrace a society of many cultures and religions went hand in hand with an equal desire to overtake the Islamic empire as the military, commercial and cultural power of the Mediterranean. Yet it seems clear that he and his successors aspired to unify the island populations into one Sicilian people. This aspiration takes solid form in the marble inlaid tombstone made for Anna, the mother of Grisandus, one of Roger II's priests. Dated in Palermo in 1149, Anna's eulogies are written in four different languages and scripts: Judaeo-Arabic, Latin, Greek and Arabic. They are not literal translations of each other but take account of the different cultures and religions of each group, so that the dating systems respect different calendars and the pope is referred to as the imam of Rome. They reflect both Roger's official policy, and what may well have been the funeral rites of a truly multicultural family.

The Turning Tide: Sicily and Latinization after Roger II

By the time Roger II died in Palermo, in 1154, little had been done to resist the gradual transformation of Sicily from a mainly Muslim and Greek Christian culture into a Latin one. Latin-speaking immigrants from France, England and Italy came to settle there in droves, and late in his life, Roger had attempted to convert leading members of the Islamic communities to Christianity and had one of his most trusted Muslim confidants executed. The contemporary Arab historian Ibn al-Athir saw this as a sign of impending doom for Sicilian Muslims. Roger was succeeded by his son William I (1121–66), and then his grandson William II (1153–89), who between them ruled Sicily for more than half a century. Over this time, the island's relatively peaceful pluralistic society responded to the changing tide of history by flaring up, its growing turmoil mirrored by the spectacular volcanic eruption of Mount Etna in 1160, when lava flowed as far as the sea just north of Catania. A paradox arose in so far as both Williams espoused the Muslim lifestyle as well as the growing Latinization of the island. William I kept even more of a Muslim entourage than his father and was tolerant of Islam; yet, overseas, Sicily lost its foothold in North Africa as the advance of the rising Berber Almohads held sway. At home, Muslims came under threat as his barons rebelled in an attempt to overthrow the king, not only sacking the royal palace but pillaging Muslim communities and seizing their land. His son William II took the throne in 1172, a just, lenient king, who lived like an oriental sovereign, patronized Arab learned men and had a harem and a bodyguard of negro slaves. The Andalusian traveller Ibn Jubayr was shipwrecked off Messina in 1184 and recorded William's kind-heartedness in arriving in person to help the stranded passengers. Ibn Jubayr's description of his visit to Palermo suggested that, on the surface, it had barely changed in 200 years: 'The Muslims of this city preserve the remaining evidence of their faith. They keep in good repair the greater number of their mosques and come to prayer at the call of the muezzin. In their own suburbs they live apart from the Christians.'[5] He also recounted how, during a powerful earthquake, William told everyone to pray to whichever god they wished, and that, in Catania, Christian abbots let their serfs swear on the Koran.

While Christians and Muslims met at court and in everyday dealings, they nevertheless lived separately in the city, as the monk and later court poet Peter of Eboli made clear in a miniature painted at the time of William II's death in 1189, which shows Latins, Greeks, Arabs and Jews living in different quarters, coexistent but not equal. Muslims became more and more oppressed by their increasing obligation to conform to the ideas and customs of the Roman Church, as both William I and William II turned irrevocably towards western Christianity, despite their love of Islamic culture. William II turned the royal palace, marriage of three creative traditions, into a church by adding a pulpit, font and candelabrum and removing the inlaid Arabic inscriptions. In rural areas, Muslim and Greek serfs became tied to the land and could be bought and sold like any possession, part of the wave of anti-Muslim feeling that emerged from the unceasing flow of Latin-speaking settlers from western Europe. By the late twelfth century, the prosperous, diverse society of equals that Roger II had genuinely envisaged during his reign finally succumbed to the changing tide of religious and political pressures of the world outside.

In his magisterial world geography, al-Idrisi waxed lyrical about

Sicily, the 'pearl of this century, for its qualities and its beauty, for the uniqueness of its towns and inhabitants.' He praised 'its strengths and the various gifts it enjoys, because it brings together the best aspects from every other country.' Alongside its Jewish population, Christians and Muslims at times crossed swords but also coexisted in comparative tolerance. While it shared many parallels with al-Andalus, under Norman rule it diverged from the civilization of the western Islamic caliphate. For two brief centuries, Norman Sicily was the antithesis of al-Andalus, as its Christian kings assimilated Islamic culture and showed that cultural crossings can move in opposite directions. Along with medieval Spain, the Muslim, Christian and Jewish scholars of Sicily enabled scholarship to reach the rest of Europe via translation, influencing secular life for the first time in its Christian history. Muslim learning in Latin translation was to shape the intellectual life of the rest of Europe irrevocably. For a brief span of 200 years, the Normans built a model society forged from the island's Islamic past. But the European encounter between Islam and Christianity had reached its second great turning point, as Islamic sovereignty waned and the power of the Catholic Church grew strong.

Part Two

THE WANING OF THE CRESCENT MOON: RECONQUESTS, REVERSALS AND RAPPROCHEMENTS

Cronica del muy
esforçado caualle
ro el Cid ruy diaz
campeador.

A page from the Chronicle of the Most Valiant Knight El Cid

Chapter 8

Nomads of War: Christian Heroes, Muslim Puritans

'Come hither; I will shew unto thee the judgment of the great whore that sitteth upon many waters: with whom the kings of the earth have committed fornication, and the inhabitants of the earth have been made drunk with the wine of her immorality.'

Revelation 17.1–3

'I would rather be a camel-driver in Africa than a swineherd in Castile.'

Al-Mu'tamid, eleventh-century emir of Seville

The Rise of the Cross and the Birth of Crusading

Against a vibrant background of red and gold, the Whore of Babylon accepts the wine goblet that represents her lust, seated on a cushioned divan in the style of an Islamic princess and flaunting a crenellated diadem with a crescent moon at its centre. Her biblical portrayal in St John's Book of Revelations as a symbol of iniquity and corruption is here transposed into an image of the seductive yet sinful power of Muslim civilization in al-Andalus. The tenth-century illuminated manuscript in which this miniature appears is known as the Morgan Beatus, created by the artist Magius to illustrate one of the most important of all Spanish manuscripts, the *Commentary on the Apocalypse*, written in 776 by the monk Beatus (730–85). His *Commentary* associated the Whore of Babylon with wickedness in general, but, by about 960, when Magius created his masterpiece, Beatus's book, conceived in the heartlands of the Asturian leader

Pelayo's emerging kingdom, had taken on a new meaning. The Antichrist no longer signified the Roman Empire, but the caliphate of Cordoba, and, as Spanish Christians saw it, the Whore was now the alluring yet dissolute culture of the Muslims. The *Commentary* was thought of as the definitive book of the Reconquest, the long campaign of the Christian kingdoms of the Iberian peninsula to eliminate Muslim rule, first conceived in Pelayo's mountain fastnesses.

The tone of the evolving relationship between Christians and Muslims in western Europe was reflected in the ambiguous reactions of Catholics to Islamic civilization in Spain, manifested in the co-existing aversion and attraction to it signalled in Magius's portrait of the Whore of Babylon. The history and heritage of that relationship in the eleventh and twelfth centuries shows an important shift in the balance of power, foreshadowing the second major turning point in Europe's Islamic history. As the Islamic caliphate of Cordoba collapsed in 1031 and was restructured as a series of smaller *taifa* kingdoms, Christian Spain began to look both north and south. The desire to conquer the lands of al-Andalus grew ever stronger, while, at the same time, the Catholic states sought a closer bond with the rest of Europe, especially with France, and with the authority of the Roman Catholic Church. The new attitudes were reflected in the arrival in Spain and Portugal of a new kind of population, migrants from beyond the Pyrenees who came for adventure, but also as settlers, among them knights, monks, pilgrims, merchants and scholars, creating an increased and more diverse Christian population. As Muslim authority ebbed in the first decades of the eleventh century, the fortunes of King Ferdinand I of Castile (r. 1037–65) rose. Acknowledged by his chroniclers as *rex magnus*, 'the Great', he united Castile with the kingdom of León in 1039 in a move which paved the way for the frontier kingdom of Castile to become the premier power in the peninsula. Ferdinand exacted hefty tributes from the *taifa* rulers and threatened them with invasion; when he convened a council of bishops in León in 1055 'for the restoration of Christendom', it seemed as if the equilibrium of power had tipped firmly in favour of the Christians.

Ferdinand's intentions were strengthened by two important influences from France. Monks from the reformed Benedictine order of Cluny had arrived in Christian Spain at the end of the tenth century and were well established by the 1040s. Zealous, celibate and scholarly, the Cluniacs embraced the ideals of militant Catholicism and aimed to impose their faith and strict adherence to its rules universally. North of the Pyrenees, the concept of a crusade was starting to emerge, and in 1064, a year before Ferdinand's death, an international force of 3,000 nomads of war entered the peninsula through Roncesvalles and headed for the north-eastern Spanish city of Barbastro. With French, Normans and Italians among them, they were mercenaries, often second-born sons with no prospects of inheritance, who had come in answer to the appeal of Pope Alexander II (1061–73) to take God's message to the infidels, and had been granted freedom from penance and the remission of sins by the pope himself. If not a formal crusade, it certainly had the crusading spirit and papal blessing. After a forty-day siege, Barbastro surrendered when its water supply ran out. Although its Muslim defenders had been granted safe conduct as they left the city, as many as 6,000 were slaughtered, Muslim women violated and children seized as slaves; it was a victory for which the Christian troops were rewarded with immense booty. These terrible deeds reveal an important aspect of the relations between European Catholics and Muslims at this time. The anti-Islamic zeal and fanaticism of those Christians not in continual contact with Muslims marked a stark contrast with the comparative tolerance of those who were.[1]

A Moment of Truth: The Fall of Muslim Toledo

On Christmas Day 1065, Ferdinand I of Castile laid his crown on the altar of St Isidore's Church in León and donned the robes of a penitent. He died two days later of an illness contracted during the siege of Valencia in November; his realm was divided contentiously among his three sons, a legacy that entirely unravelled their father's ambitious unification of the kingdoms. Sancho II, the eldest, inherited Castile; García, the youngest, took on Galicia and part of

Portugal; and Alfonso VI, his father's favourite, was given León and the tribute money from Toledo. Sancho was murdered by his sister Urraca's hired assassin, possibly in cahoots with Alfonso, with whom she allegedly had an incestuous relationship. Then, with García safely imprisoned under lock and key until his death, the ambitious Alfonso, who had been exiled in Toledo by his brother Sancho, returned to the fray when he was twenty-five to take control of Castile and León, reunifying the kingdom once again.

Alfonso had his sights set on the important and centrally located city of Toledo. The ancient seat of the Visigothic monarchy, Toledo had flourished under Muslim dominion for over 300 years and was greatly coveted by the Christians. Pope Gregory VII (1020–85) applauded Alfonso's ambitions to reconquer Muslim territory, but insisted that the kingdoms of the Iberian peninsula had belonged to St Peter since olden times and now belonged to Rome. Refusing to acknowledge the pope's jurisdiction over the Hispanic kingdoms, Alfonso declared himself emperor of all Spain and pursued his own agenda of reconquest. In his memoirs, Abd Allah (r. 1074/5–90), the last Zirid emir of Granada, revealed that agenda, declaring that Alfonso's plan was to turn Muslim rulers against each other, draining them of money through tribute payments and exhausting both their resources and power to resist.

Alfonso VI was well acquainted with the sophisticated and highly educated ruler of Toledo, al-Ma'mun (r. 1043–75), who had sheltered him during his exile from León. Like many *taifa* emirs, al-Ma'mun was a patron of poets and scholars, raising his city to great prosperity and enlarging its territory by annexing Valencia and Cordoba. He lived in a luxurious residence – the Mansion of the Hours, beside the river Tagus – which sparkled with mosaics, gilded stuccos and marble fountains. Alfonso would have been familiar with the splendours of the palace, which boasted a water clock, or clepsydra, said to have been made by the famous Toledan astronomer al-Zarqali; the clock told the time using a system of water basins filled and regulated according to the phases of the moon. In the palace gardens, a pavilion had been constructed in the centre of a gigantic fountain made of coloured glass and decorated with gold and silver arabesques. When the emir's court sought refuge from the sun, they would enter the pavilion through the spray of the cool fountain water that cascaded upon them in a rainbow of light.[2]

Yet, despite his name, al-Ma'mun's grandson al-Qadir, 'the Powerful' (r. 1075–85), who inherited his throne and his fascination with clocks, did not have his grandfather's wits or resolve. His obsession with timepieces led him to neglect politics, and he failed to defend Toledo from attack from other *taifa* states. When he fled the city in 1080, Alfonso grasped the opportunity, promising to restore him to power if he eventually surrendered the city. And so, on 6 May 1085, King Alfonso VI entered Toledo mounted on a white stallion to claim his prize. He guaranteed the safety of all residents and their property subject to the payment of a poll tax, despite the fact that this tolerant attitude to the Muslim population appalled the French clergy and royalty. Alfonso sent al-Qadir to Valencia with some troops to install him as ruler and protect him. Toledo was the heart of what became New Castile, and it became the political centre of Catholic Spain. In just three years, Pope Urban II (d. 1099) declared the supreme authority of the archbishop of Toledo over all other Hispanic sees. The Christian capture of Toledo was seen as the glorious reconquest of the old Visigothic capital, marking a crucial moment in the ebb and flow of power between the kings and emirs of western Europe that appeared to set Catholic Spain on the road to dominion over Islam. But Alfonso's great triumph had ironic and very unexpected consequences.

The Advance of the North African Berbers

Two years before Alfonso VI seized Toledo, he had rampaged through southern al-Andalus as far as the coastal town of Tarifa, where Muslim scouts had landed nearly four centuries earlier. Legends describe how he rode his stallion into the sea and proclaimed: 'This is where the land of Spain ends, and I have walked upon it.' The king's ambitions struck fear into the heart of the powerful emir of Seville, al-Mu'tamid (1040–95), whose city he had already threatened. Bizarrely, it was a game of chess that turned out to be the broker of peace between them. The Moroccan historian al-Marrakushi (1185–1250) recounts how al-Mu'tamid's beloved yet ill-fated vizier Ibn Ammar was unbeatable at chess. He took the emir's personal sandalwood chessboard to the Christian camp poised at the gates of Seville; when Alfonso caught sight of the board's glittering jewels and exquisite gold and silver embellishments, he challenged the vizier to a game. Ibn Ammar agreed to play on the basis that, if Alfonso won, he could keep the chessboard, and, if not, then he must grant the vizier's first request. The Christian king fell for the ruse, and was easily beaten by Ibn Ammar, who at once demanded Alfonso's immediate withdrawal from al-Andalus. Seville did not fall into Christian hands for another century and a half.

The apparent strangeness of two battling enemies meeting to play a board game underlines the complicated relationships between the Christians and Muslims of western Europe at this time. The business of war between them had an ostensible religious agenda which was often secondary to matters of territorial sovereignty, such that at times Christians fought for Muslims against other Christians and vice versa. Outside the theatre of war, there were liaisons, friendships, marriages and kindred mindsets across the religious divide that were natural among peoples who had lived in close proximity for centuries. Alfonso VI and al Mu'tamid, two rulers of the same age, shared both a liberality that allowed their subjects to follow their own religious customs, and an admiration for scholarship that rose above theological differences. But, on one occasion, Alfonso VI seems to have overstepped the mark, asking the emir to allow his pregnant wife to visit the former Christian church in the mosque of Cordoba and take up residence in Madinat al-Zahra, so that she could benefit from the clean air and visit the mosque regularly. Al-Mu'tamid was so affronted that he threw a desk at Alfonso's emissary, splitting his head, then had him crucified. It did not seem to harm their good relations permanently though, as Alfonso's only son and heir was born of his marriage to a former daughter-in-law of al-Mu'tamid.

Al-Mu'tamid belonged to the Abbadid dynasty founded by his grandfather Muhammad ibn Abbad (984–1042), the first emir of Seville, and he was the third and last of his line. His reputation as a cosmopolitan and benevolent ruler was surpassed by his gifts as a bard – he was one of the most outstanding Andalusian poets of a brilliant poetical age in which satire, diplomacy and love all found expression in verse. Passionate and romantic, he met his favourite wife, Rumaykiyya, while walking beside the river Guadalquivir reciting a poem he was composing. At the time, she was washing clothes; she overheard him and offered to finish his verse for him, and al-Mu'tamid fell in love with her witty improvisation. But, while the emir was an idealist in love, he was a realist in politics.

Fifty years before, the *taifa* rulers had looked northwards and enlisted the help of Christian kings to fight for them. Now those kings were fighting against them. Al-Mu'tamid and the rulers of Granada and Badajoz all realized they were ill-equipped to fend off Alfonso VI, so they turned to the south for deliverance. It was a risky move, but the emirs of al-Andalus were between a rock and a hard place. Conquest from the Christian north was imminent, yet an equivalent danger threatened if they invoked the assistance of North Africa. On the horns of a dilemma, al-Mu'tamid's laconic remark – 'I would rather be a camel-driver in Africa than a swineherd in Castile' – made it clear that he preferred to be in thrall to Muslims rather than Christians. He decided to send his emissaries to Marrakesh to beg for the help of a charismatic Berber ruler, Yusuf ibn Tashufin (r. 1061–1106).

Ibn Tashufin was the leader of a fundamentalist group of Muslims from Mauritania known as the Almoravids, whose warlike name means 'Defenders of the Frontier Forts', alternatively known as 'The Veiled Ones'. Their founder, Abd Allah ibn Yasin, had his own fort, a monastery or 'ribat', on an island in the river Niger, from where he strove to inspire the Berber tribes of the Sahara with devotion to Islam. His followers were desert nomads, half monks, half soldiers, extreme ascetics and militant Muslims who covered their faces with a veil and insisted on strict observance of the Koran, forbidding the drinking of wine and also the custom of having more than the permitted four wives. Their belligerent zeal was akin to the French Cluniac monks' equally extreme enthusiasm for Christianizing Europe along Benedictine lines of reform. Yusuf ibn Tashufin was a military genius, respectful of the Abbasids in Baghdad, yet known as the emir of the Muslims. His tribe of Sanhaja Berbers had overcome the rival Zanatas who controlled the famed hub of the Sahara gold trade, Sijilmasa. Ibn Tashufin captured Fez, Oran and Tlemcen in 1082, and soon had control of all Morocco and western Algeria. He then founded Marrakesh as the new capital of the Almoravid dynasty.

There was the utmost contrast between the poet king al-Mu'tamid and the warrior monk Ibn Tashufin. The scholarly emir of Seville enjoyed a heritage of enormous wealth and tolerant religious belief, counting Christians among some of his closest acquaintances. The Berber soldier dressed in wool, ate barley and camel meat, and drank milk, believed literally in the Koran and demanded absolute obedience. He saw the *taifa* rulers of al-Andalus as over-refined lovers of luxury, who were lax in their religious observances. To many Muslims of al-Andalus, the Almoravids, who spoke little or no Arabic, appeared to be terrible, mysterious barbarians, with their dark veils, scimitars and poniards, and their strange alien tongue, although the Zirid rulers of the kingdom of Granada were themselves Sanhaja Berbers and celebrated the advance of the Almoravids with displays of drumming and public festivities. Ibn Tashufin might have been an ascetic, but his decision to enter Spain at the request of the *taifa* rulers afforded the chance of both military distinction and political advancement, and had the merit of protecting the Islamic faith. He seized the opportunity to invade Spain knowing the Andalusian Muslims were on the back foot, landing his troops at Algeciras in June 1086 and advancing north towards Seville in pursuit of jihad.

The overconfident Alfonso VI hurried south with a relatively small army and met the combined forces of the Almoravid army and the troops of the *taifa* kings on 23 October 1086, 200 kilometres north of Seville, at a place the Arabs named Zallaqa – or Sagrajas, in Spanish – its meaning referring to the ground made slippery by the bloodshed of battle. The Christians drove the Muslims back to

Badajoz amid great slaughter, but, undaunted, Yusuf ordered his warriors to advance to the beat of war drums, launching a ferocious counterattack that left the Catholic army defeated by nightfall. The Moroccan historian Ibn Abi Zar (d. 1315) relates in his influential history *The Gardens of Pages* (*Rawd al-Qirtas*) how piles of the severed heads of Christians were loaded onto carts and sent to the cities of al-Andalus as grisly proof of the decisive Muslim victory.[3] Ibn Tashufin had sent a fearful message to both Christians and Muslims, but failed to capitalize on it when he suddenly departed for North Africa, allegedly due to the death of one of his sons. Alfonso had suffered a dire defeat, but had lost no territory, and he still controlled Toledo. It was at this time that the king was also reconciled with his most powerful and dangerous vassal, whom he had sent to Valencia as protector of the exiled emir of Toledo, al-Ma'mun.

The Greatest Knight of All: The Enigma of El Cid

Marcilla Castle in Navarre was plundered by the republicans in the Spanish Civil War of 1936, but later fell into nationalist hands. Inside a crate, they found a magnificent broadsword bearing a note: 'Comrade, respect this sword, it is the sword of El Cid'. Now on display in Burgos Museum, its broad gleaming blade, over three feet long, is etched with the name *Tizona*, meaning 'Firebrand'; it dates from the eleventh century and may well have belonged to Spain's national hero Rodrigo Díaz, El Cid (*c.* 1043–1099). Tizona symbolizes the military prowess, courage and virility of the knight who became the figurehead of Spain's Christian Reconquest, his story sung in epic and ballad. Lionized as the saviour of national Catholicism, his image appeared on Francoist flags during the Spanish Civil War, hence the reverence of nationalist soldiers when they found his sword. This is the Cid of romance, the model of Christian virtue and chivalry, but the Cid of history remains an enigmatic character, whose controversial relationship with both King Alfonso VI and with the Muslim leaders and populace is a measure of the growing complexities of the multi-religious societies of eleventh-century al-Andalus and the Christian north.

In 1889, the Cuban artist Armando Menocal painted his imposing historical work *The Oath of Saint Gadea (Jura de Santa Gadea)*, in which the Cid, the king's vassal, obliges Alfonso VI to swear upon the altar of St Gadea church in Burgos that he had no part in his brother Sancho's assassination. The oath may be a legend, but Menocal's artistry draws out two important facets of the Cid: his Christian piety and his moral power over the Castilian ruler. A minor nobleman from the village of Vivar, near Burgos, Rodrigo Díaz became the greatest Christian warrior. When al-Andalus was caught between the resurgent Christian kingdoms of the north and the North African offensive from the south, his life was intertwined with that of Alfonso VI in a power dynamic that ebbed and flowed as he alternately lost and won the king's favour. Alfonso had given his niece Jimena to Rodrigo in marriage, a sign of preference and distinction which at once elevated the social and political status of his vassal. He entrusted Rodrigo to be his legal representative in court cases, and, in March 1075, they travelled together to Oviedo Cathedral to open a chest alleged to contain Christ's sudarium, the cloth wrapped round his head when he died. Some decades earlier, the bishop of Oviedo had attempted to open the chest, which emitted a dazzling light when the lid was lifted, preventing the monks from seeing what was inside. A royal document bearing the Cid's signature records the precious relics found inside, including fragments of the True Cross, and flasks containing Christ's blood and the milk of the Virgin. In awe, Alfonso ordered a new solid-silver chest to be made to house them.

In 1079, Alfonso dispatched the Cid to Seville to collect tribute money from al-Mu'tamid, but, shortly after, their close association fell apart. It seems that certain men at the royal court became jealous of the king's favourite and made false accusations against him. Rodrigo had been raiding areas of Castile with his own private army and amassing huge riches in booty. Perhaps his expanding power, prestige and dissident attitude was seen as a threat by Alfonso, because, in 1081, the king sent Rodrigo into exile, marking the start of his career as a frontier knight. His services as a mercenary were eagerly engaged by the new *taifa* king of Zaragoza, al-Mu'tamin, for whom he fought and defeated Sancho I of Aragon (1042–1094) and the Count of Barcelona, Berenguer Ramón II (1053/54–1097/99), the ally of al-Mu'tamin's brother who aspired to usurp him. It was not unusual for *taifa* rulers to seek the paid help of Christian armies in their conflicts against fellow Muslims. A great military leader and strategist, the Cid aimed to serve his own interests; he was happy to obey Muslim masters during his exile, only to turn their trust to his advantage to regain favour with the Christian kings. Five or six years after his banishment, in 1086–7, Alfonso became reconciled with Rodrigo and readmitted him to his service as protector of the emir al-Qadir in Valencia. Just three years later, he would cross paths with the advancing Berber armies of Yusuf ibn Tashufin. The Cid's hour had come.

The *taifa* rulers had summoned Ibn Tashufin once more, and this time the outcome was serious. The Berber leader arrived in 1090, armed with a fatwa from the revered Imam al-Ghazali delivering the verdict that the *taifa* kings were corrupt, unfit to rule and must be removed from power. His first victory was the deposition of the Zirid emir of Granada, Abd Allah, who recounts in his memoirs that he went to surrender his city to Ibn Tashufin like someone led to his execution. He describes his humiliation at the hands of the Berber emir's general, who commanded him and his mother to '"Take your clothes off in front of me, because the sultan knows you are hiding the choicest pearls in your clothing." Despite protesting our innocence, I had to undress before him. He also pulled all the wool out of the cushions, turned the chests upside down . . . and even dug up the ground our tent stood on, in case we'd buried something.'[4] The Zirid sultan was forced to depart into exile in North Africa, after which the Almoravids deposed his brother Tamim, king of Malaga, in September 1090.

The Battle for Valencia

The Cid had the upper hand over al-Qadir, the emir of Valencia, whom he protected under Alfonso VI's orders, but the Muslim

Valencians, discontented with high taxes and the fact that their weak ruler was in thrall to a Christian knight, sought help from the Almoravids. The Valencians finally rebelled in 1092, killing the emir. Eventually, an Almoravid garrison arrived on the scene, but the Cid forestalled any Berber conquest of Valencia by besieging the rioting city to pre-empt an Almoravid takeover; Valencia surrendered to him in June 1094. Ibn Tashufin finally advanced on Valencia in October with a large army, but the Cid clashed with his troops near the city walls and forced them to retreat in what was the first Almoravid defeat on the Iberian peninsula.

The Cid became undisputed ruler of Valencia until his death in 1099. He was liberal and tolerant to its Muslim inhabitants, allowing them to practise Islam freely, liberating all Muslim slaves on entry to the city and sentencing their owners to death. Known to both Muslims and Christians by his Arabic title 'Cid' – either from *al-sayyid* ('the nobleman') or *al-sīd* ('the lion') – Rodrigo Díaz seems to have reconciled his religious beliefs and military obligations with a respect and admiration for Muslim culture. He could write in Latin, as a document signed in his own hand confirms, and the contemporary Arab historian Ibn Bassam observed that, during his years in Valencia, the Cid studied books and read heroic deeds in Arabic, openly expressing his admiration for them. The absence of any reference to an interpreter during his negotiations with Muslims suggests a knowledge of spoken Arabic that smoothed relations between them. It is said that when his tomb was opened in 1541, his body was found wrapped in a Moorish mantle embroidered with arabesques and Arabic inscriptions, a story perhaps corroborated by a Spanish woodcut of the late fifteenth century depicting the Cid dressed in Arab costume, on a horse wearing Arabic equestrian trappings.

Yet Arab historians were unanimous in their condemnation of the material destruction and human suffering caused by the Cid's capture of Valencia, which they tried to understand in the context of the more general destruction of al-Andalus in the eleventh century. The violence and devastation experienced by the people of al-Andalus at this time arose in part from the militarization of the Christian society of the peninsula, of which the Cid is the epitome. It also stemmed from the extreme militant Islam of the Almoravids, which was at odds with a deep-rooted aspect of Andalusian Muslim society that affirmed social, religious and cultural progress over and above its martial nature.

By any standards, Rodrigo Díaz was an exceptional and original figure with the political and military profile of a king, a man of his time yet also beyond it. He shared elements of his life with his near contemporary, the Norman, Robert Guiscard. Both men fell out with their overlords and went into exile, creating their own military forces and living on the spoils of war, and both created small territorial states which they ruled. It was a way of life born of the nature of European aristocracy, which harnessed violence in the service of survival. Over many centuries, the Cid's persona evolved into a central pillar of the history of the medieval Castilian mentality, part of the history of Spain that lived on in myth and legend, epitomized in the great epic *Poem of the Cid* (*Poema de mio Çid*), and which bolsters right-wing national Catholicism there today. Yet it is the ambivalence of Rodrigo Díaz which is truly interesting. His political and military autonomy undermined the status quo and challenged royal authority in a clash with the traditional political order of the Christian kingdoms of Spain. He was also a hero of hybrid identity: Christian, yet aligned with the Muslim society and culture of al-Andalus; not just revered by Catholic historians, but by Arab historians too. Ibn Bassam's perception of the Cid speaks for itself: 'All in all, this man, the scourge of his time, in his manly strength of character and heroic bravura, was a miracle among the great miracles of God.'

Building a Hybrid Heritage: The Glories of Almoravid al-Andalus

When the Almoravids finally seized the burning ruins of Valencia in May 1102, they had complete control of Muslim Spain within their grasp. Only the *taifa* of Zaragoza remained. The poet king of Seville, al-Mu'tamid, had been banished to Tangiers, his family sailing into exile on black barges before a grief-stricken crowd that lined the banks of the Guadalquivir river. He ended up, not as a camel-driver, but as a destitute poet in the desert village of Aghmat, stricken by the sight of his wife and daughters spinning wool for a pittance. In contrast, Yusuf ibn Tashufin's empire stretched for 3,000 kilometres, from the Atlantic to the Mediterranean and across the straits of Gibraltar as far as the borders of Sudan. In that world of mercurial changes of fortune, Almoravid dominion over al-Andalus was to last less than half a century, yet it left a decisive mark on the evolving society and culture of the Islamic west – even more remarkable from a tribal dynasty with scant knowledge of statesmanship.

The legacy of Almoravid culture in al-Andalus gives material form and substance to their ethos in fabric, books and stone. Fragments of silk inscribed with the name Yusuf ibn Tashufin, which ironically survived as a Christian church vestment, bear witness to the genius of the nomadic Berbers. Famed for their carpets woven for bedding, blankets or floor coverings adapted to the harsh climate of the desert and mountains, their skills found expression in the woven silk textiles made by the Almoravids in al-Andalus. Manuscripts in the famous collection known as the Cairo Genizah point to the heart of the Islamic west as the leading textile-producing country of its time. Almería, with its extensive connections with the rest of the Muslim world and its role as a port for European ships, was the hub, and its heyday was the first twenty-five years of the twelfth century. It boasted 800 looms for silk weaving, 1,000 for splendid brocades and 1,000 for other textiles. There, and in other textile centres in Murcia, Malaga, Granada and Seville, weavers created brightly coloured fabrics in orange, red, blue and green on an ivory background, decorated with roundels and gold brocade, using designs that were copied from Baghdad. Ibn Tashufin's garment was richly embroidered with lions, palm trees and sphinxes, a new fashion that bespoke the wealth, opulence and power of the ruler. Those textiles that have survived have done so because they were often looted as booty – when Alfonso VI captured Almería from the Almoravids, two brocades were taken to Sigüenza Cathedral to shroud the relics of a saint. At times they have survived, like Ibn Tashufin's robe, as clerical vestments, or in royal burials, where they still had associations of wealth and authority, though in a Christian context. The basic designs of Almoravid textiles must have already been known in France by the late twelfth century, as they were the model for the painted ceiling of the crypt in Clermont-Ferrand Cathedral. In this way, the fluid dynamics of relations between Christians and Muslims in the Islamic west were mirrored in the incorporation of the Islamic material culture of al-Andalus into the Christian religious and regal contexts of the rest of Europe.

The Almoravids' strict adherence to the word and letter of the Koran was embodied in the beautiful manuscripts they produced. The Almoravid Koran, dated 1090, written in Maghrebi script in black ink on vellum and created in al-Andalus, is the earliest known illuminated manuscript to have survived from the Islamic world. Yusuf ibn Tashufin's piety was also proclaimed in his mosque-building programme. The minbar from the Kutubiyya (Booksellers') Mosque in Marrakesh was said to have been ordered by Ibn Tashufin when he was in Cordoba and modelled on the minbar of the Great Mosque, which was made of inlaid sandalwood, ebony and ivory. The elaborate carving and marquetry of the Almoravid preaching platform fused the North African tradition of the minbar as the sign of Islamic sovereignty with the exquisite carpentry of the Cordoban tradition, creating a heritage with a uniquely Andalusian flavour.

Consistent with the military focus of the Berber dynasty, Ibn Tashufin also fortified the city walls and castles in his territory, in particular in Granada, where new districts were created, with their own walls joined to the main ramparts. By the twelfth century, Seville too had a new urban landscape that reflected its role as a military base and significant port, with its political centre in the royal alcazar or palace, close to the main mosque. Huge four-sided towers were built in the city walls to bolster defences against attack from both Muslims and Christians, and many buildings were decorated in highly complex geometric patterns in red on a white background, an aesthetic that heralded an independent Almoravid art closely tied to Sunni doctrine in the Islamic west. House-building was inspired by the palace of Madinat al-Zahra in Cordoba and was based on a new type of inner patio, with a water feature and plants, often decorated with motifs of palm trees, pineapples and acanthus. As artists and craftsmen moved freely between al-Andalus and North Africa, their styles intermingled; the Almoravids also brought the *riyad*, the orchard garden that was to spread across Andalusia, as well as the stunning honeycomb decoration later used in the ceilings of the Alhambra palace. Caught at the interstices of northern Europe and North Africa, al-Andalus evolved a culture that would provide a heritage for the entire continent.

The Berber zealots reached their zenith under the leadership of Yusuf ibn Tashufin. His heirs were no match for their illustrious general, and his empire was stricken by disunity in both North Africa and al-Andalus, ripe to be overtaken by a new Islamic power, more zealous and mystical even than the Almoravids. It is a great irony that those warlike ascetics who followed Ibn Tashufin were soon condemned as unfaithful and materialistic, as dangerous enemies of the Islamic faith. At the start of the reign of Alfonso VI, it had seemed that the Christian reconquest of al-Andalus was certain, yet the crusade against the Whore of Babylon that had propelled his great triumph in Toledo had been thwarted by al-Mu'tamid's desperate petition to ask Ibn Tashufin for help. Rather than winning back the lands perceived as lost to Islam, Muslim rule in the westernmost outpost of the Islamic empire was set to remain for another 350 years.

Chapter 9

Seville: City of Triumph and Transition

'Seville is a bride, whose groom is Abbad,
The Aljarafe is her crown, her necklace the River'.

Al-Mu'tamid ibn Abbad, emir of Seville

The Meeting of Opposites

From the perspective of outer space, a grey-green ribbon of water stands out, curving sinuously through the brown, ochre and viridian tones of the great fertile valley stretching out beyond the urban confines of Seville. This satellite view of the river Guadalquivir, which means both 'great valley' and 'great river' in Arabic, shows how it flows through a vast, marshy plain as far as the Atlantic Ocean, opening the river port of Seville to world trade, but leaving it vulnerable to attack. Moving in closer, the panoramic view from the air that picks out the modern bullring and the football stadium draws the eye to a well-known landmark, the great tower known as La Giralda, named after the weathervane or *giraldilla* at its summit. To ancient travellers still several days away from the city, who saw it from afar, it seemed to reach the stars, the four golden balls at its pinnacle gleaming high in the sky. Those who climb the fifty metres to the top are rewarded with a prospect that expands endlessly, over rooftops, fields and orchards, with the gleaming river waters snaking westwards. La Giralda is an iconic monument, a metonym for Seville, or Išbīliya in Arabic, that tells the story of domination and defeat in the eleventh and twelfth centuries. At ground level, the shifting perspectives of the narrow maze-like streets in the old city, its brightly coloured houses gay with geraniums, all converge at the largest

Gothic cathedral in the world, raised on the ground plan of the former mosque, whose minaret, La Giralda, is now its belltower.

These religious structures are mighty and imposing, sites of power and dominance that dwarf their surroundings and embody the struggle between Muslims and Christians that took place there long ago. They manifest an appropriation of one culture by another, but also a synthesis of both, and mark the crucial importance of Seville at the juncture of Christian ascendancy and Berber triumph and decline. Seville has endured many assaults and invasions, among them Phoenician, Roman, Visigothic and Viking. Following the Muslim conquest of 711, Seville was the first Arab capital in the peninsula, from 713 to 716. The Cordoban Arab historian Ibn al-Qutiyya describes how his own ancestor, Sara, daughter of the Visigothic king Witiza, sailed from Seville to Damascus in the 730s to ask the Umayyad caliph Hisham to settle a property dispute. Hisham upheld her rightful claim and married her to a freedman, 'Isa; one of their sons, Ibrahim, was the great-grandfather of Ibn al-Qutiyya. When 'Isa died, Sara married Umayr, an Umayyad with royal blood, and the descendants of this union between a Gothic princess and an Arab aristocrat became the long-standing and prominent Banu Hajjaj of Seville. This early mingling of Christian Visigothic and Muslim Arab blood introduced a hybrid element in the character of Seville, a new aspect that contrasted with the more dominant note of strife between opposing faiths and took on other dimensions as the twelfth century came into view. By that time, Seville had been under Muslim rule for 400 years, and, with the demise of the imperial Almoravid dynasty, the fulcrum of Berber power was about to shift westwards from Cordoba, driven by a powerful threat to Christian Spain and insurgent al-Andalus lying in wait on the coast of North Africa.

The Evolution of Islam: A Quest for Mastery

The thriving Berber trading town of Aghmat, at the foot of the High Atlas mountains of Morocco, thirty kilometres from the Almoravid capital of Marrakesh, had become a favourite place to exile the rulers of al-Andalus. The last Zirid emir Abd Allah wrote his memoirs in Aghmat, and, before him, al-Mu'tamid of Seville was banished there with his family. Destitute and broken at the end of his days, al-Mu'tamid acquired a certain posthumous glory in Morocco. In 1970, a mausoleum was built to house his tomb, with an Almoravid-style dome adorned with lines of his celebrated verses, which has become a place of pilgrimage.

Aghmat was the capital of the Masmuda Berbers, who worked the land and preferred town and village life to nomadic wanderings. A charismatic man arose from their tribe named Ibn Tumart (*c.* 1080–*c.* 1128–30); he had been a child so pious that he loved to light the candles in the mosque, and he became the spiritual leader of a new sect practising extreme asceticism. In search of religious guidance, he had travelled to Cordoba in 1106, then made a pilgrimage to Mecca, before studying in Baghdad, where he came across the Sufi teachings of al-Ghazzali (d. 1111), which had been outlawed in Cordoba. Taking on the trappings of a saint, Ibn Tumart declared he was the Mahdi, the rightly guided one, descended from the family of the Prophet, and called his followers the Almohads, meaning those who believe in the absolute unity of God. This revolutionary preacher of virtue who addressed the masses in the Berber language also had the Koran translated from Arabic into Berber.

Both holy and militant like their predecessors the Almoravids and the Christian Crusaders, Ibn Tumart and his disciples launched a jihad that destroyed the entire Almoravid empire in the twelfth century, accusing its rulers of impiety and corruption. The rebellious native Muslims of al-Andalus got wind of the African revolt and rose up against the Almoravids. In just one year, between 1144 and 1145, al-Andalus collapsed once again into a discord soon compounded by the advancing Almohad armies, who crossed the Strait of Gibraltar in May 1147. They expelled the Almoravids from Seville in the same year, making it their capital city in western Europe, twinned with Marrakesh. Soon, Malaga, Granada and Almería fell under the Almohad banner and, by the middle of the twelfth century, the Berber religious revolutionaries controlled al-Andalus. This new stage in the evolution of Islam created a western European province of the Almohad Empire through jihad and colonization. A new social order held sway, in which the minorities in that empire came under attack – in particular, the Jews, who were the only minority left in al-Andalus. The Almohads obliged them to emigrate or convert to Islam, and many made the decision to leave for the Christian north, while some, like the great Jewish scholar Maimonides, forswore their faith and remained. The Almohad caliphs began to look northwards as well, their aim to wreak havoc on the Christian states.

The Shaping of Catholic Spain and the Battle for al-Andalus

While Muslim fought Muslim in al-Andalus and in North Africa, the Christian territories to the north were also undergoing a sea change as they began to acquire the political structure that would remain for centuries. The kingdoms of Castile, León, Aragon, Navarre and Portugal all vied for authority and power, with the frontier territory of Castile starting to show its dominance. In the last quarter of the twelfth century, their constant discord and in-fighting distracted them from outside threats and allowed the Almohads to inflict calamitous attacks on their kingdoms, which were defended by the new Christian military orders of Calatrava, Alcántara and Santiago. Their troops were warrior monks who sought to combine monastic ideals with chivalry, as did the Berbers, and swore to defend Christendom against the infidels. Their crusading spirit coincided with the zeitgeist of the time, when thousands of Catholic soldiers elsewhere in Europe prepared to launch the Third Crusade to liberate Jerusalem, a city controlled by the sultan of Egypt and Syria, Saladin (*c.* 1137–93), since 1187. Nonetheless, in the Hispanic peninsula, the Christian rulers' overriding obsession with power outweighed all other concerns as they prepared to fight King Alfonso VIII of Castile, whom they believed was hell-bent on dominating and subjecting them all. This civil warfare caused great scandal in the rest of Europe, where the general opinion was that, instead of harming each other, the Catholic kingdoms should have been collaborating against the Almohads. Pope Celestine III (1106–98) was so outraged that he sent a legate to restore order, and, in 1194, the kings of Castile and León made peace, albeit still harbouring deep-rooted rancour. Meanwhile, the Almohads had ongoing conflicts in North Africa which for a while curtailed their operations in Spain and allowed the Christians to take advantage of what had become a second era of *taifa* states to launch raids on Muslim territory.

Two battles proved decisive in this fierce struggle between the Berber Almohads and the kings of Christian Spain. The first was a triumph for Islam. Al-Mansur Ya'qub (1160–99), the third Almohad caliph, was tall, dark-skinned and a man of action; he had mixed blood, since he was the son of a Christian concubine called Sahir. The historian al-Himyari tells us that, in June 1195, al-Mansur Ya'qub got wind of enemy aggression that threatened his territory around Seville and left his capital in Marrakesh in anger, heading for al-Andalus with a large army and landing at Tarifa.[1] They marched northwards through Cordoba and on towards Toledo, pitching camp in the desolate, hilly plains near the ancient settlement of Alarcos. Alfonso and his troops hastened to meet al-Mansur without waiting for the promised reinforcements from the king of León, and battle began on 19 July 1195, 484 years to the day from King Roderick's fateful battle with the armies of Tariq ibn Ziyad by the river Guadalete.

Al-Himyari described the combat, which lasted from early morning until noon, the two forces meeting at the bridge of Alarcos, where Alfonso's side fled or were put to the sword, and the Christian camp was plundered. The historian claimed that 30,000 Christians were killed, and fewer than 500 Muslims, figures that may not be accurate, but which convey the huge scale of a Muslim victory that left Alfonso VIII running for his life to Toledo with just a handful of knights. Instead of capitalizing on his success, al-Mansur retired to his capital of Seville with enormous booty, unaware that the Battle of Alarcos was to be the last important Muslim victory over Christians in Spain.

'Las Navas de Tolosa' is a resonant phrase in Spanish history. It evokes the treeless, often marshy plains lying near the southern slopes of the Sierra Morena mountains of al-Andalus, sixty kilometres north of Jaén, where the second major battle between Almohads and Christians was fought. After Alfonso VIII's debacle at Alarcos, several years of peace reigned and Toledo remained in Christian hands. The peace might have lasted longer had not Pope Innocent III (1161–1216) fomented war by writing to Rodrigo Jiménez de Rada, archbishop of Toledo, pressing him to persuade Alfonso VIII to take up arms again in another crusade against the infidel. Alfonso's son Prince Ferdinand dedicated his sword to the new crusade, and the renewal of Christian raids on al-Andalus prompted al-Nasir (1181–1213), the fourth Almohad caliph, known in Spain as Miramamolín, to cross the Strait of Gibraltar in May 1211 and make for Cordoba.

Innocent III still orchestrated the Hispanic crusade from Rome, the Muslim recapture of Jerusalem in 1187 remaining a sharp thorn in his side. His assertion of papal power involved coercing the French bishops to send the believers to help the king of Castile, as well as granting crusading indulgences that released Alfonso VIII and his followers from the penalties of religious penance. The combined army of Crusaders reached Las Navas de Tolosa on 13 July 1212, where they were met by al-Nasir and the Almohad army, who intended to block their advance southwards. The archbishop of Toledo carried the Virgin's banner into battle and later wrote a full account of the engagement, while Alfonso's queen Berenguela sent a letter to her sister Blanche, wife of Louis VIII of Francc, that revealed some interesting details. The difficult terrain and extreme heat were hard to bear, and nearly all the foreign, mainly French, troops defected, ostensibly because they could not stand the conditions, but in fact because they were undisciplined, violent and governed by the obsessive desire to kill infidels and harvest booty, which did not chime with Alfonso VIII's lenience in dealing with the garrison soldiers of captured towns, whose lives he spared, allowing them to depart.

The fighting was brutal and lasted several days. Twice the Almohads blocked narrow passes, until the Christians were forced to retrace their steps, abetted by a local shepherd who showed them a way through to the Muslim camp. The Arab historian al Marrakushi's account, written in 1224, claimed that the Muslims were not battle ready, and there was dissent and rebellion among the ranks because their pay was in arrears. Alfonso's men drove through the circle of negro slaves chained together to guard the caliph's tent, upon which al-Nasir fled as far as Jaén. The Muslim defences crumbled and thousands died on the battlefield, resulting in the resounding triumph of the Christian armies and a complete reversal of the outcome of the Battle of Alarcos. Al-Nasir was of mixed blood, the son of a Christian concubine, like his father, yet light-skinned, with blue eyes and a red beard, and his regnal title meant 'Champion of God's Religion', a name not without irony, for his commitment to the jihad against the Christians ended in ignominy. The booty was immense – the rich tapestry shielding the entrance to al-Nasir's tent was sent to the monastery of Las Huelgas, near Burgos, as a war trophy, and it still hangs there today. The Christian victory has been seen as the greatest of the Reconquest, a pivotal moment ending the Almohad grip on al-Andalus and tipping the balance of power in favour of the Catholic north.

Transition and Transformation: The Forging of a New Society

As northern European currents began to shape Catholic Spain, and North African unrest took its toll on the Islamic caliphate in Europe, a different kind of society started to evolve. The European economy was growing, and many north European immigrants arrived in the peninsula to try their fortune, in parallel with the presence in al-Andalus of new Berber incomers, creating an overall increase in the population and in the variety of racial groups. The Iberian peninsula had always been diverse in its ethnicities, harking back to ancient Iberian peoples, Romans and Germanic Visigoths, along with varied regional identities, among them Basque, Galician, Catalan, Portuguese and Castilian. To this were now added Franks from Germany, France and England, and new tribes from the Maghreb, many of whom were pilgrims, crusaders, traders and monks, creating rich seams of cultural and social associations and fusions.

New words were coined to describe new categories of identity.

Many Arabized Christians who had lived under Muslim rule and knew Latin, Arabic and the local vernacular language had emigrated to Catholic territory. They became known as Mozarabs (*mozárabes*) and were crucial in fostering connections between north and south. At the same time, Jews and Muslims who stayed put under the new Christian regime could, under the authority of royal Christian law, still practise their religion and be governed by their own legislation, subject to paying a poll tax. Such Muslims were called Mudejars (*mudéjares*), a term which meant those who submitted to Christian rule, and they often lived in separate quarters of towns and cities, were obliged to wear identifying clothes and could not marry Christians. The Christians and Jews living in al-Andalus, who had basked in the light of a relative tolerance under the *taifa* kings, found themselves treated with contempt and hostility by their Berber overlords. Both Almoravids and Almohads attacked churches and synagogues, and deported to Morocco all those Christians and Jews who did not flee to Christian lands.

In the south, by the eleventh century, the inhabitants of al-Andalus saw themselves as indigenous to the Hispanic peninsula, no longer foreigners from the east but Andalusians with a very specific identity that fused Arab, Berber and Syrian ancestry with the bloodlines of the old pre-conquest peoples of Spain and Portugal. When the emir of Seville al-Mu'tamid wrote to Ibn Tashufin in 1086, he had lamented what he saw as the dissolution of the Arab tribes and the loss of their genealogies. Those lineages were modified again by the Berber dynasties, who overlaid the native royalty with a new aristocracy. By the time of the great Battle of Las Navas de Tolosa in 1212, the Iberian peninsula had evolved into a highly complex multicultural society, forged out of religious conflict and coexistence, with an intellectual and artistic life to match.

The Pearl of Andalusia: Seville and a New Golden Age of Islamic Culture in the West

Seville and its iconic Giralda was the glory of Almohad Spain and the high point of its culture. Like the Almoravids, the twin poles of

Almohad art and architecture were religion and militancy, which gave birth to one of the most significant eras of artistic creation in western Islam. Religious function and ideology combined in an aesthetic of mosque-building founded on absolute simplicity. The formal and forbidding Giralda minaret announced far and wide the presence of an impressive mosque and its central importance in the life of Almohad Seville. The construction, which began in Ramadan 1172 and was finally finished in 1198, used a bold combination of recycled materials and innovative new ones, its foundations huge ashlar blocks upon which the main walls rested, their stone resurrected from the remains of buildings created under the Abbadid dynasty of Seville. The minaret was decorated with the coloured glazed bricks called *azulejos*, new to both Morocco and Spain, that also adorned the mosque in Marrakesh, their vivid colours contrasting with the minaret's austerity of design. The Almohads embraced the ancient heritage of western Islamic architecture and exploited it in their prestige buildings; the Giralda nodded to Abd al-Rahman III's minaret in Cordoba, but its original towering height of seventy metres made it even taller than its source of inspiration.

Both the minaret and the mosque it signalled were designed by the famous Ahmad ibn Baso, director of Almohad architecture in Gibraltar. The huge Friday mosque showed a remarkable harmony between its ground plan, geometry and ornamentation. Its enormous spaces, housing seventeen aisles and twelve bays, were arranged on a T-plan that recalled the Great Mosque in Cordoba. Little now remains of the mosque itself, obliterated by the majesty of the largest Gothic cathedral in the world. One surviving portal, the Door of Forgiveness (*Puerta del Perdón*), displays the pointed horseshoe arch of the Almohad era, and its bronze door knockers in the shape of palmette leaves are masterpieces of Spanish Islamic metalwork.

The Tower of Gold (*Torre del Oro*) watches over the river Guadalquivir on the Santa Cruz side, opposite the district of Triana. Said to take its name from the shimmering gilt lustre tiles that once clad it and cast a golden light on the river, the twelve-sided watch-tower guarded the entrance to the harbour by means of a great chain that linked it to a now vanished tower on the opposite riverbank. Its formidable yet stylish form, with crenellated battlements, demonstrated the power of the Almohad defences, which were reinforced by barbicans with towers erected in front of the high city walls of Seville. In their short reign, the Almohads built or restored fortresses and defences throughout al-Andalus, and constructed new castles. The ruins of ancient walls that outline many Andalusian hillsides remain as a testament to their desire to consolidate Muslim rule in the face of both the challenge of the Reconquest and the hostility of the residents of al-Andalus to Berber sovereignty. They are the fragmentary traces of the penultimate military conflict between the Cross and the Crescent on Spanish territory.

The rigour, simplicity and asceticism embraced by Ibn Tumart and embodied in the religious buildings of Almohad Seville gave way to a riot of colour, decoration and sensory delight in the construction of domestic buildings and gardens. The Andalusian historian Ibn Sahib recorded that, in 1171, Caliph Abu Ya'qub Yusuf rebuilt the city walls, alcazar and aqueduct in the wake of an earthquake and disastrous floods in 1168–9. Water was supplied from a subterranean canal dating from Roman times, renovated by the engineer al-Yalish to replace the old system of hoisting water from the river, providing a supply to the inhabitants of Seville. He built magnificent palaces and botanical gardens in the Buhayra public park using government funds and requested special species of pear, apple and plum to be brought from Granada and Guadix, which were transported to Seville on mule convoys. The caliph had a keen interest in gardens and liked to watch the planting of olive trees. He employed the qadi and the imam of the mosque, who were expert in surveying, soil preparation and cultivation, charging them with the design and creation of palace parks on the barren land. Their gardens stand alongside the rural landscaping of the Umayyad caliphs of Cordoba in the history of western Spanish Islamic horticulture. The hilltop palace, al-Zahir, built by al-Mu'tamid's father and restored by his son, stood high above the river, surrounded by olive groves. It fell into ruin after his exile and was damaged by Christian troops in 1182, yet a century later was rebuilt by al-Mansur, its great halls looking down over Seville. The riverbanks were planted with gardens, orchards and vineyards that produced olives, figs, cotton and sugar cane.

Almohad buildings both religious and secular, and their gardens, were displays of power, given authority by architectural references to the splendour of the caliphate of Cordoba and, through that, to the Umayyad heritage in Syria. The hostilities between Christians and Almohads did nothing to quell the admiration of Christian rulers for the artistic talents of their enemies. The beautiful former synagogue of Santa María la Blanca in Toledo and the Chapel of the Assumption in the Cistercian convent of Las Huelgas in Burgos have pure Almohad designs in their stucco capitals and wall decoration. The stucco *muqarnas* and vegetal motifs in the chapel ceiling reveal the heights reached by Almohad decorative arts, probably created in these cases by Almohad Mudejar craftsmen, where Islamic and Romanesque architectural forms came together as part of the coherent Christian symbolism of salvation.[2] These influences on the Christian north bear witness to a hybrid legacy that would have a lasting impact on Christian art.

The Meeting of Great Minds: A Zenith of Islamic Learning in the West

The intellectual life of Christian Spain lay in the shadow of Islamic scholarship, though a distinctive Christian culture began to grow as the Catholic Church was reformed and Roman and canon law started to confer coherence on it. Thrown into disarray by the Berber conquests and the early Crusades, the role and legislation of the Church became more clearly defined by the pope. The monasteries advanced the formal study of the scriptures, the writings of the Church Fathers and religious law, while annals and other historical works became popular and a literature written in regional vernaculars came to life. Peoples of the two religions interacted more closely as important Muslim cities such as Toledo, Zaragoza and Lisbon were captured by the Christians, with both positive and negative repercussions. In 1197, King Peter II of Aragon decreed that all heretics must leave his kingdom or be burned by fire, the first time such a death penalty was inflicted in western Europe. A less violent approach had been used by the abbot of Cluny, Peter the Venerable, who visited Spain in 1142 and commissioned what was the first European translation of the Koran, which the English scholar Robert of Ketton converted into Latin in 1143. His aim was to acquire an accurate version of the original, so that Islamic doctrine could be disclaimed more convincingly.

The scholars of Muslim al-Andalus had other things on their minds. Intellectuals and writers flocked to the court of Seville. The fascination with science and astronomy that had gripped Umayyad polymaths grew ever stronger in the eleventh and twelfth centuries. In 1091, one of Islam's great medical clinicians, Ibn Zuhr, was born in Seville into a family that had produced six consecutive generations of physicians. He began as court physician to Ibn Tashufin, but fell out with him and fled to Morocco, where he was imprisoned in Marrakesh. He felt safe enough to return to his home city when it came under Almohad rule, where he wrote *The Book of Moderation*, a seminal treatise on general therapy, which shaped future medical practice. Intended for Ibn Tashufin, it ranged over diseases, therapeutics and hygiene, as well as giving advice on the use of cosmetics. He was the pioneer of plastic surgery, which he recommended for the improvement of thick lips, crooked teeth and the reshaping of noses. Ibn Zuhr was praised by the famous Ibn Rushd as the greatest physician since Galen.

In Berber al-Andalus, astronomy reached new heights. The Toledan astronomer al-Zarqali (*c.* 1029–*c.* 1100) developed a new version of the astrolabe, later known as the Saphaea, that could be modified to use anywhere in the world, unlike earlier models tied to a specific latitude. He was just one of two Islamic astronomers mentioned by Copernicus, who also benefited from the Toledan Tables, the best, most accurate set of astronomical measurements produced by Arab and Jewish scholars at the court of Toledo. The prodigious Ibn Bajja, known as Avempace, born in the *taifa* of

Zaragoza in 1089, deduced that the Milky Way was made up of myriad individual stars, whose glow came from refraction through the Earth's atmosphere. Like Ibn Zuhr, his life was intertwined with the Berber caliphs – he was vizier to the Almoravid ruler of Zaragoza and then to Ibn Tashufin, but twice suffered imprisonment, and finally died in Fez in 1138, probably from poisoning. An intellectual giant, he was also an important Islamic philosopher, botanist, physician, poet and musician, whose vast knowledge had an impact on European science and philosophy.

*

The Arab passion for the rational nature of mathematics and other sciences found its natural extension in the abstract thought of philosophy. The Italian artist Raphael's stunning masterpiece *The School of Athens* (1510) hangs in the Vatican and portrays the world's greatest philosophers. Only one Muslim appears, wearing a turban, alongside the likes of Plato, Aristotle, Leonardo da Vinci and Pythagoras – the genius from Cordoba, Ibn Rushd (1126–98), known in Latin languages as Averroes. His life spanned both Almoravid and Almohad times and was one of perpetual motion as he moved between his home city, the regular meetings of poets and luminaries in Seville, and trips to Marrakesh. A distinguished jurist and qadi of Seville and, later, Cordoba, like his grandfather, he attended the caliph as court physician. He is esteemed as the founder of secular thought in Europe, famed for his work on the ideas of Aristotle, who represented the apogee of human intellect to him.

Averroes' major idea was to reconcile religion and philosophy without compromising either, which meant harmonizing faith with rational thought. Using the work of Aristotle, he tried to overcome the conflict between science and religion, and his critique and commentaries on Aristotle started the revival of classical philosophical thought, 200 years before the Renaissance. His approach proved contentious in Muslim religious circles, though the Almohads under caliph Abu Yaqub authorized his views, since their own creed, the *Aqida*, summed up their essential beliefs in 'a triumph of rationalism mobilized in support of Koranic authority', the first sentence of which – 'It is by the necessity of reason that the existence of God, praise be to Him, is known' – is attributed to Averroes.[3] He was finally exiled to Morocco by the Malikites, who banned his works, and he died there two years later, in 1196. It is a strange irony that later Muslim scholars had little time for Averroes' rationalism, and as a result hardly any of his writings in Arabic survive, with many burned or lost. A great debt is owed to Michael Scot and Herman the German, who translated his work into Latin in Toledo, from where it reached northern Europe and ignited controversy. There was heated debate for years at the University of Paris as the Christian Church banned the philosophy of both Aristotle and Averroes. The Italian philosopher Thomas Aquinas disagreed with Averroes, despite his admiration for the Cordoban, whom he called The Commentator, although his own synthesis of Aristotelian thought and Christian doctrine, which influenced Catholic doctrine for centuries, echoed Averroes' efforts to bring together Aristotle and Islam.

*

In the classic BBC radio programme *Desert Island Discs*, which has run for over eighty years, a guest pretends to be a castaway on a desert island and, during the course of an interview with the presenter, has the chance to review and reflect upon their life. This idea of an island castaway evokes Daniel Defoe's novel *Robinson Crusoe*, but less well known is Defoe's source of inspiration. His novel was published in 1720, not long after the rescue of the Scottish sailor Alexander Selkirk from four years of solitude on a remote island. Yet he may also have drawn on the first ever philosophical novel, written in twelfth-century al-Andalus by the Granadan philosopher Ibn Tufayl (1105–85), mentor and vizier to the Almohad caliph Abu Yaqub Yusuf, and published in English translation just eleven years before *Robinson Crusoe*.

The manuscript of Ibn Tufayl's novel *The Story of Alive, Son of Awake* is kept in the Bodleian Library in Oxford. It is the allegorical tale of a child, cast away on a desert island and raised by a gazelle, who, with no human contact, discovers ultimate truth through reasoned enquiry. There are sufficient similarities with *Robinson Crusoe* to make it plausible that Defoe knew the work, not solely through the comparable storylines, but also because of Defoe's published reflections on his own novel, which range across various moral, religious and philosophical questions. A bestseller in the rest of Europe in the seventeenth and eighteenth centuries during the European Enlightenment, *The Story of Awake, Son of Alive* is known to have influenced the thought of the great northern European philosophers Thomas Hobbes, John Locke, Isaac Newton and Immanuel Kant. In this way, the great brilliance of Islamic intellectual and cultural life in al-Andalus under Berber dominion endured, undimmed by the turbulent shadows of an almost perpetual strife that was both holy war and a contest for land and power. The enlightened legacy of Berber culture made a permanent imprint on European life in the centuries to come.

The Road to Seville: The Great Siege of 1248

As the glorious golden age of learning and invention shone brightly, Seville's pole position as second capital in the Almohad caliphate of the west, in parallel with Marrakesh, began to lose its lustre. Al-Andalus, once the axis of Berber power, became overshadowed by new North African cities such as Fez, Ceuta and Marrakesh itself, which began to eclipse the two foremost cities of Cordoba and Seville. The Almohad caliphate fell to the Marinid dynasty of Morocco in 1269, and, to make matters worse, its government in al-Andalus collapsed and the rebel ruler of Zaragoza, Ibn Hud, started a campaign to massacre the Almohads as oppressive heretics. During a great uprising in 1228, he took control of much of al-Andalus after the Almohad caliph al-Mamun fled to Morocco. The Christian rulers of the north had been on the rampage since their great victory over the Almohads in 1212. Seville still lay out of reach, the glittering object of the Christian desire to dominate and colonize. In 1230, Ferdinand III (*c.* 1201–1252) became king of Castile and León, uniting the two kingdoms in a bid to overcome what remained of

Muslim territory in Spain. He wanted not only the opulence and prestige of Seville, but also its seaport, which led to the Mediterranean and the Atlantic Ocean, and now the way was clear.

By lucky chance, that path led Ferdinand III to Cordoba, where a small group of Castilians had entered one of its suburbs with the help of its Muslim inhabitants. Breaching his peace treaty with Ibn Hud, the Christian king galloped through rainstorms and floods to answer their plea for help, and for four months laid siege to the city, which surrendered on 29 June 1236. Ferdinand was magnanimous with the Cordoban Muslims, who were free to leave if they wished, or to remain and practise Islam. But, on that day, the Great Mosque was consecrated as a Christian cathedral dedicated to the Virgin Mary, and Jiménez de Rada wrote that Ferdinand returned the bells to Santiago de Compostela that had been looted long ago by Almanzor.

Over a decade passed before Ferdinand and his army stood outside the gates of Seville. In July 1247, exactly one hundred years after the Almohad conquest of the city, a siege was imposed, and Christian troops blockaded access to the sea. With no hope of any help from the Almohad caliph in North Africa, and haunted by the spectre of certain starvation, the Sevillians gave in on 23 November 1248. Ferdinand made his triumphant entry to the city on 22 December, but three years later he was dead, leaving a powerful kingdom and rich lands to his son, Alfonso X, who had been present at the siege of 1247 and who buried his father in Seville Cathedral.

Alfonso became one of the greatest European monarchs, and he was captivated by the charms of Seville, which became the implicit capital of his realm. The man who was to be known as the Learned King admired Islamic culture, and in his eulogy of the city enthused over the Tower of Gold and was deeply impressed by La Giralda: 'with such mastery was it made and so fine is the staircase leading to the tower, that kings and queens and important men who wish to ride on horseback can go up to the top whenever they wish.'[4] He refused to countenance plans for its destruction, and it was forbidden to lay a finger on it upon pain of death.

Alfonso founded the General Studium (*Estudio General*) in Seville in 1254, which provided instruction in Latin and Arabic, and encouraged the study of science and philosophy, taking his lead from the principle of wise rule that had guided the Umayyad rulers of al-Andalus and the Almohads after them. Although the Studium did not ultimately survive, it heralded Alfonso's celebrated court in Toledo, the seat of Christian learning and translation in the peninsula. When he buried his father, Alfonso ordered a gold and silver tomb for him bearing an epitaph in all four languages of al-Andalus: Latin, Castilian, Hebrew and Arabic.

Transition and Transformation: Shaping a New Identity

The capture of Seville in 1248 left most of the Iberian peninsula under Catholic dominion. This major transition of power from Muslim to Christian hands signalled a historical circumstance at once new and ancient. Christianity had been held in check on the peninsula by Islamic dominance since 711, before which it had existed in a very different form as the state religion of the Visigoths. By the middle of the thirteenth century, something original had emerged out of half a millennium of coexistence under Muslim jurisdiction. Both religions had evolved in distinctive ways. Christianity had become more precisely formalized as an institution with its own canon law, under the aegis of the Church of Rome. Islam, under the Umayyad caliphate in al-Andalus, had developed through the Malikite legal rite, with deep Arabian roots, and its culture embraced an Arab passion for learning, poetry and genealogy. It was not until the coming of the Berbers that a more rigorously Islamic element came to the fore, sparking an asceticism that shaped its material culture and expression. At the same time, culture and society had been transformed as al-Andalus began to metamorphose into Catholic Spain, causing a unique situation to arise in which Hispanic, Arab and North African features merged into a cultural identity that was a blend of all three. At the western outpost of the Islamic world, al-Andalus had created unique architectural and artistic traditions that looked to the Umayyad heritage in Syria and also to local

Hispanic ones forged from Roman and Visigothic precedents. In turn, Christian Spain began to evolve not just in its religious dimension, but through the integration of Islamic elements compelled by interaction with the Muslim world, as if the very struggle for existence against their alleged enemy began to define the culture and society of Catholic Spain. As Montgomery Watt and Pierre Cachia observed, it found in its interaction with Muslim al-Andalus those non-religious elements which gave it its fundamental nature – elements not foreign to it, but fused as a symbiosis of Arab, Islamic and Iberian societies.[5]

One striking and consistent aspect of that great symbiosis is the alternative, parallel history of Muslim and Christian encounters in everyday life – a history that cuts across and also underpins the main narrative of conflict. The ancient patina of reconquest hides the reality of human relations that were so often tolerant and cooperative, and led to some of the greatest intellectual collaborations in European history. These parallel lives jarred with the spirit of militancy and the fight for power which had led the Christian north to a place of near supremacy that was lamented by the great thirteenth-century Andalusian poet al-Rundi:

> Where is Cordoba, the seat of great learning,
> and how many scholars of high repute remain here?
> Where is Seville, the home of mirthful gatherings
> on its great river, cooling and brim-full with water?
> These centres were the pillars of the country.
> Can a building remain when the pillars are missing?
> The white wells of ablution are weeping with sorrow,
> as a lover does when torn from his beloved;
> they weep over the remains of dwellings devoid of
> Muslims,
> despoiled of Islam, now peopled by Infidels!
> Those mosques have now been changed into churches,
> where the bells are ringing and crosses are standing.[6]

It may have seemed like the end of his world to al-Rundi, but out of the blue a new Muslim dynasty sprang up that saved Islamic rule from defeat in the peninsula for another 250 years. Meanwhile, further afield, the eyes of the world turned to the east, where the ongoing conflict between Europe's Christians and Muslims took a critical turn.

Chapter 10

The Pageant of Death: Crusades, Conquests and Colonization

'Regard the Franj. Behold with what obstinacy they fight for their religion, while we, the Muslims, show no enthusiasm for waging holy war.'

Saladin

'Pagans are wrong, Christians are right'
(*'Paien unt tort e crestiens unt dreit'*)

Chanson de Roland, v. 1015

The First Procession: A Pilgrimage to the Holy City

Across the horizons of cold, grey northern skies, river valleys and mountain peaks, a danse macabre was silhouetted, a terrible pageant of death enacted by emperors, noblemen, peasants, hermits and children, wending its way towards the shining goal of the holiest city in Christendom. The participants had no idea they were on a Crusade, yet they had donned a costume bearing a large red cross, sewn into their clothing. Shivering in chilly churches or monkish cloisters, they had learnt of the power of pilgrimage, a spiritual journey of respect and devotion akin to the Muslim hajj, and no site was more sacred than Jerusalem. Few could afford to travel as far, so instead they could make an armchair pilgrimage and envisage the Holy City at home, inspired by its glorious image in stained-glass windows or colourful frescos. In the province of Soria, near the Iberian frontier between Islamic and Christian lands, around 1125, the Master of Tahull painted such a fresco in tempera inside the

Hermitage of St Baudilus of Berlanga, a church built a century earlier by Mozarab craftsmen. It showed the entry of Christ into Jerusalem, riding a donkey, on Palm Sunday. The motley band of travellers who formed the pageant aspired to make their own procession into the city on the pilgrimage of a lifetime. But theirs was not an interior pilgrimage – it was physical, armed, and driven by the powerful urge to free Christianity's most sacred site from Muslim dominion.

Jerusalem had an aura as a place of divinity, both terrestrial and imaginary, at once the city of the Jewish king David, the place of Christ's crucifixion and his tomb, and the location of the Prophet Muhammad's first night flight from Mecca, from where he ascended to Heaven. Though the three religions of the Book met in the city, that proximity did not unite them, but rather divided them as each strove for the treasured prize they craved to possess in the name of their faith. So it was that, in the year 1095, Christ's Vicar on Earth, the French Pope Urban II, gave the performance of his life. In Clermont, standing in a field muddy with November rains, he used the most masterly yet dangerous rhetoric to inveigle the vast crowd gathered before him to take up arms and travel east to wrest Jerusalem from its Muslim rulers: 'Not I, but God exhorts you as heralds of Christ to repeatedly urge men of all ranks whatsoever, knights as well as foot soldiers, rich and poor, to hasten to exterminate this vile race from our lands and to aid the Christian inhabitants in time . . . May you deem it a beautiful thing to die for Christ in the city where he died for us.'[1]

Antagonism to Islam had grown bolder since Charlemagne's first efforts to rebuff the Muslims in northern Spain, where Catholicism had resurged in the campaign to reconquer the lands judged as lost to Islam. Urban's predecessor, the ambitious Pope Gregory VII, aimed to expand the power of the head of the Roman Church in worldly matters and had already dreamed up the plan of a great military expedition to claim the Church of the Holy Sepulchre, site of Christ's crucifixion and burial in Jerusalem. With Urban's call for a military expedition to the Holy Land, the western European response had hardened into a trenchant yet ignorant hostility towards Islam. He had given the invasion of the East a credible religious purpose.

The plan to bring the Holy Land under the control of the Roman Catholic Church had a snag. A Christian kingdom, Byzantium, already existed in the East, technically part of the Eastern Roman Empire, but ruled by emperors guided by the Greek Orthodox Church, which had a far more plausible claim to Syria and Palestine. Both Gregory and Urban had paid lip service to the idea of healing the Schism between the two Churches, but Latin and Greek Christianity had drifted too far apart for reconciliation. The Latins failed to understand the Byzantine Empire and saw its inhabitants as alien, though they envied its opulence. But it turned out that Urban's mobilization of western Europe had in part been sparked by a plea for help that caused a commotion in Catholic circles. Anna Komnene, the first major woman historian in the western world, wrote in her *Alexiad*, the life of her father the emperor Alexios I, of his fateful decision to ask Urban II for military assistance against the Turkic tribesmen known as the Seljuks. Expert horsemen and fierce warriors, the Seljuks had recently converted to Islam, and they ruled a huge empire across Asia Minor known as the Sultanate of Rum. Alexios had warned Urban that they were close to the gates of Constantinople and might eventually threaten Rome. But the emperor's plea for a united Christian front against the Muslim threat was doomed to backfire, exposing the East to crusader armies.

A year after Urban's inflammatory speech, in the summer of 1096, the Seljuk prince Kilij Arslan had intelligence of a crowd of odd-looking warriors who had entered his eastern Anatolian territory. They were, he was told, wearing poor garments on which a red cross was crudely sewn, and bore basic or home-made weapons. He was told they called themselves Franks who had come from distant lands to kill Muslims and win the Holy Sepulchre. Arslan slaughtered most of them, some 60,000 according to accounts, including women and children. Here, at the Battle of Civetot in October 1096, the Grim Reaper ended the danse macabre that was the People's Crusade, led by a French priest, Peter the Hermit. Peter wore woollen tunics and walked barefoot, a man of eccentric and intense piety who had visited Jerusalem in person. He told the tale of a dream in which Christ roused him to call upon his fellow Christians to rise up against the Muslims of the Holy Land. The first and least likely leader of a Crusade, he led tens of thousands of mostly poor folk – butchers, cobblers, peasants, women and children, mixed in with a few low-ranking soldiers – along the Danube towards Constantinople on their armed pilgrimage. It was a long, dangerous journey that left them prey to robbers gunning for the gold and silver with which they were obliged to pay their way. En route through Germany, the French and German mobsters among them committed atrocious acts of mass murder against the Jews of the Rhineland, before they were themselves annihilated by Arslan I. The first Catholic foray into crusading turned out to be a brutal and pointless calamity from start to finish.

Undeterred, a second deathly cavalcade marched on towards the rising sun of Levant, this time led by the high aristocracy of western Europe – mostly French troops led by such nobles as Raymond IV of Toulouse, Godfrey of Bouillon and the mighty Norman Bohemond, prince of Taranto, son of Robert Guiscard, who headed the procession as it took the scenic route across central Europe, via Hungary, towards Belgrade on the outskirts of the Byzantine Empire. Anna Komnene described her distrust of Bohemond, a man magnetically charming and beautiful, with fair hair and blue eyes, but, in her view, malevolent, deceitful and treacherous. After pledging a nominal allegiance to the emperor Alexios, these heroes of the First Crusade marched on the Muslim city of Antioch in October 1097, laying a siege masterminded by Bohemond, who took control of the city and ruled as its prince, despite his promise to return it to Byzantine command. Soon after this triumph, in 1098, Edessa too fell to the Christians. An almost unimaginable scenario now presented itself – the journey of military pilgrimage, some 2,000 miles long, had reached its destination. The road to Jerusalem lay open before them and, by 7 June 1099, the great and mighty of Catholic Europe stood awestruck before the gates of the

Holy City, the place Pope Urban II saw as the 'navel of the world', its riches ripe for reaping.

The assault on Jerusalem began in the light of dawn on 14 July. The attack was a brutal combination of great battering rams and siege engines, catapulted stones, firebombs made of pitch, wax and sulphur, and hails of arrows. By the next day, Godfrey of Bouillon and his men had breached the outer wall, but the casualties were devastating – as a Latin chronicler wrote, 'death was present and sudden for many on both sides.' Soon, the French had scaled the walls and broken through, at which the horrified Muslim defenders collapsed completely, deserting their posts. The contrast with the peaceful occupation of the city by Arab forces 360 years before was startling. The dreadful sack of Jerusalem began at midday on 15 July 1099 and lasted for two days. There was no immediate thought of reverence or Christian piety, only a horrifying lust for blood, ghastly in its savagery and excess in a massacre that left corpses piled high, then burned, the stench lingering in the city for six months.

In the *Deeds of Tancred* (*Gesta Tancredi*), the Norman chaplain Raoul de Caen tells the story of the Norman knight Tancred de Hauteville's destruction of a statue of the Prophet Muhammad standing in the Dome of the Rock in Jerusalem. The statue was adorned with precious gems, a crown of gold and royal purple robes. Raoul points out the stark contrast with the equivalent attributes of Christ hanging from the cross – nails in his hands and feet and wearing a crown of thorns. Tancred's act of vindictive vandalism is probably a fiction, yet it speaks of a scorn and loathing of the Muslim faith, incarnated in the act of inhumanity that was the sack of Jerusalem. That act was sealed with hymns and prayers inside the Holy Sepulchre, a ghoulish paradox that exposed the shocking simultaneous contradiction and reconciliation of extreme violence and religious faith. From the crusaders' perspective, it seemed a miracle had happened. Jerusalem was now in Christian hands, and Baldwin I, count of Edessa, was crowned king of Jerusalem on Christmas Day 1100. Their success was exalted in verse, song and saga across the Latin west. The Cross was now in the ascendant in a victory won by violence, marking a profound political shift parallel to the Catholic Reconquest of the Iberian peninsula, while it seemed the Crescent moon had begun to wane across Europe.

Crusade versus Jihad

The concept of a Christian crusade acquired clarity through its focus on the Holy Land. At the time of the First Crusade, the word *croisade*, meaning 'the way of the cross' in French, was unknown, and 'journey' and 'pilgrimage' were used for the military campaign. The term *crucesignatus*, one signed by the cross, was adopted to designate a crusader at the start of the twelfth century, when Jerusalem came under Christian rule as one of the territories of Outremer, the new Latin Christian colonies beyond the seas. A crusade then meant a military expedition with a symbolic and religious purpose, which was the liberation of perceived Christian lands or cities from the infidel Muslims. Its prime motivation purported to be the religious reward of the remission of sins, a spiritual salvation like no other, which drew in thousands of pious Christians willing to die a glorious death for the cause and be absolved of divine punishment for their misdeeds.

The popes extolled the religious angle of crusading, yet harboured far more pragmatic reasons for their military campaigns. Fighting holy wars was a way of controlling and directing violence, nominally for the common good, yet often in a way advantageous to the ruling classes. The Crusades are thought of as religious wars, yet their consequences were more worldly. The First Crusade was not propelled by any overwhelming and urgent threat, nor by any disastrous defeat; it was an act of Christian aggression, perhaps even a long-delayed reaction to, or inverted image of, the early unprovoked invasions of Islam 400 years earlier. It was the first large-scale struggle between Christian and Muslim powers for land, wealth and status, in which the Cross of Christ's sacrifice became the emblem of war. As a result, the Crusades embodied a dismaying contradiction: vast war machines were created in the name of Christ the peacemaker; mass murder was justified, even glorified, by the ironic aim of peacekeeping, and its perpetrators were absolved by confession.

The meaning of holy war is the most potent element of difference between western Christianity and Islam. Jihad, the continuous striving on the path of faith, has a lesser form, which is striving by the sword, a meaning warranted by the permission given to the first Muslims in Medina to fight against those who broke their solemn pledges. The Islamic idea of religious war is historically and fundamentally inseparable from the state and its political order, where it is a unifying, not divisive, force. Here, it diverges entirely from the western Christian separation of State and Church, in which the former is a part of secular society, without hierarchy. For Muslim culture, that western concept of a non-religious state is offensive to Allah's will to create order in the human community.

At the time of the Christian conquest of Jerusalem in 1099, jihad had lost some of its impetus in Muslim societies, who barely acknowledged the First Crusade and certainly not as an epic clash between Islam and Christianity. It was scarcely reported in contemporary Arabic chronicles, and not described in detail until the 1150s, when Arab historians referred to what would be two centuries of violence as the 'Franj wars' – the 'wars of the Franks'. The Muslim world at that time knew little about western Europe except for al-Andalus. They saw it as primeval, primitive, a world where the word 'Christians' meant the Greek Byzantine Church. The glories of ancient Greece and Rome were mere memories. They still harboured prejudices against Christianity's polytheism, as they saw it, and against its use of figurative religious images. But the Muslims of the Near and Middle East saw no serious threat from the Frankish armies, whom they believed to be mercenaries fighting for the Byzantines in their campaign to win back territory. They had no idea the crusaders aimed to conquer and settle Syria and Palestine – if they had, they might have joined forces to combat an enemy hostile to Islam. Instead, the fractured relations between the Syrian Sunnis and the Shi'ite Fatimids in Egypt, strife between Turkish rulers and discord in Baghdad drained their energies. The coast was clear for the Latins to strengthen their hold on their newly won states in the Holy Land.

The Procession Travels to Outremer

On a limestone peak strategically set between the former Syrian cities of Homs and Tripoli, the great fortress of Krak des Chevaliers rises to dominate the landscape. Built to be impregnable, with two layers of concentric walls, the castle was given in 1142 to the Knights Hospitaller by Raymond II, count of Tripoli, and it signals an overriding preoccupation with defence. By the early twelfth century, a frontier land had arisen in the East, a distant outpost of Latin Christianity in the land beyond the Mediterranean Sea, known as Outremer. The Crusader states created a new arena for the ongoing drama between Muslims and Christians, in some ways a mirror image of the Islamic conquest of al-Andalus, this time with the Christians venturing out of Europe into Muslim territories. The four main outposts were the kingdom of Jerusalem, the principality of Antioch and the counties of Edessa and Tripoli, all ruled by Frankish noblemen whose astonishing achievement was the control of the entire coastline of the eastern Mediterranean, the result of the first acts of Christian colonization of Muslim lands. Krak des Chevaliers was one of many permanent garrisons of religious soldiers set up across those states to protect pilgrims and defend the new Christian Holy Land. They were commanded by international military orders, the Knights Templar and Knights Hospitaller, founded by the western Church and backed by the patron of the Templars, the French abbot Bernard of Clairvaux. These monkish warriors, akin to the pious jihadis of the Almohads, represented the twin poles of Christian holy war as part of an official crusading institution that formed permanent links between the Latins of the west and east. Their purpose was to defend the new Latin states from the impending threat to their existence posed by their Muslim neighbours.

The danger was not long in materializing. The Turkish general Zangi (1085–1146) was the son of a warlord, a courageous, powerful soldier with a gift for leadership and a legendary reputation for merciless and brutal violence, 'like a leopard in character, and a lion in fury', as a Muslim chronicler described him. In 1144, he recaptured

1. 'The Panel of the Six Kings', Qusayr 'Amra, Jordan.

2. The Cathedral-Mosque in Cordoba, Spain.

3. 'Abbasid Public Academy, The House of Wisdom' *c.* 1237. Yahya ibn Mahmud al-Wasiti, Baghdad. Manuscript depicting scholars in the library.

4. Statue of Abbas ibn Firnas outside Baghdad International Airport.

5. World map, 1154, by Muhammad al-Idrisi. Reproduction of the planisphere engraved on a silver plate for King Roger II of Sicily. On display at the Sharjah Museum of Islamic Civilization, UAE.

6. 'The Whore of Babylon', *c.* 950. *Commentary on the Apocalypse*, fol. 194v. Morgan Beatus.

7. Fragment with wrestling lions and harpies, 12th century shroud of San Pedro de Osma.

8. La Giralda, the tower of the Cathedral of Seville, as viewed from the Plaza Virgen de los Reyes in Seville, Spain.

9. Notre-Dame de Chartres.

10. Stained-glass window depicting Charlemagne in the Cathedral of Notre-Dame de Chartres.

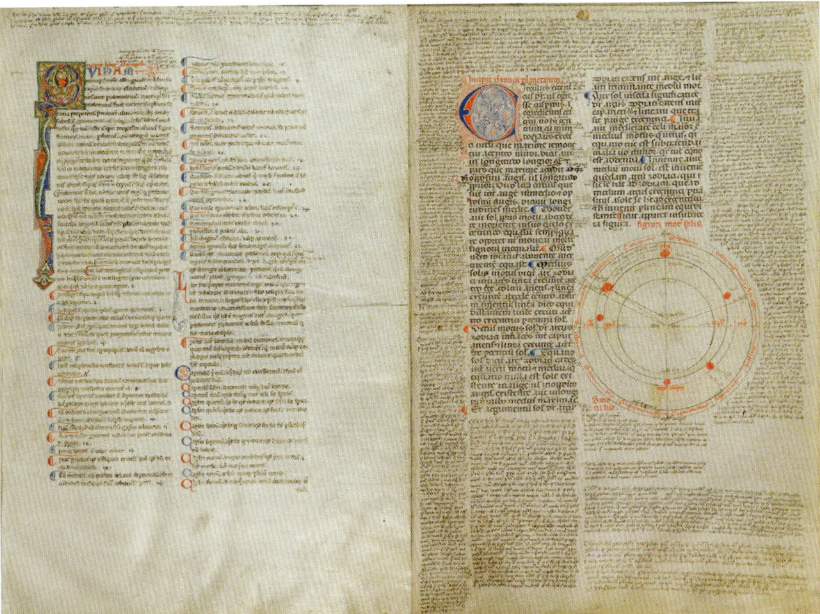

11. Pages from Ptolemy's *Almagest*, *c.* 1200. Translated by Gerard of Cremona.

12. 'View of Toledo', between *c.* 1596 and *c.* 1600. El Greco.

13. Astrolabe, *c.* 1320. Ibn al-Raqqam, Granada.

14. 'The Taking of Granada', 1890. Carlos Luis de Ribera y Fieve.

15. 'Entry of Sultan Mehmed II in Constantinople', 1876. Jean-Joseph Benjamin-Constant.

Left 16. Full-size portrait of Vlad Țepeș, 17th century. Anon.

Right 17. 'A slave-market in the town of Zabid in Yemen', 1237. Al-Wasiti, Yahya ibn Mahmud. Book illustration produced in Baghdad, manuscrit arabe 5847, fol. 105.

18. 'The Three Philosophers', between *c.* 1508 and *c.* 1509. Giorgione.

19. Statue of Mimar Sinan, the legendary imperial Ottoman architect. Located in front of his masterpiece, the Selimiye Mosque, in Edirne, Turkey.

20. Engraving of Suleiman I's crown, *c.* 1535. Agostino Veneziano.

the Crusader kingdom of Edessa, to which Bernard of Clairvaux's ill-advised response was to call for the launch of the disastrous Second Crusade, the first to be led by European kings – Louis VII of France, accompanied by his wife Eleanor of Aquitaine, and Conrad III of Germany. The armies of both kings were defeated, on separate occasions, by the Seljuk Turks, and, although Louis and Conrad both reached Jerusalem, their attempt to seize Damascus in 1148 ended in their retreat.

Zangi himself had an ignominious end in September 1146; he was murdered by a Frankish slave in Damascus who had joined forces with the Christians against the general. This was one step too far for the Muslims of the Levant. The concept of jihad, which had fallen into disuse, was about to be revived in a dramatic way by Zangi's second son, Nur al-Din. Devout, diplomatic and warlike, he galvanized his people to unite under Sunni Islam and make jihad their main objective. In doing so, Nur al-Din revived the image of the charismatic, pious leader who put the Muslim community above wealth or power, and he aroused its fervour. When the crusaders fled before a relief army led by Nur al-Din in the dismal five-day siege of Damascus in 1148, relations between the newly arrived crusaders and the established colonists soured, while Muslim hopes of victory rose. As the curtain fell on Catholic humiliation and the renewal of jihad, a new and powerful character was waiting in the wings.

Jerusalem Reclaimed

The holy wars took a new turn in the middle of the twelfth century as circumstances aligned against Latin Christendom and in favour of the Islamic kingdoms. Out of the ashes of Fatimid Egypt arose a legendary leader who became the thorn in the side of the Christian states in Levant. Under the Fatimid dynasty, Cairo's beauty and wealth reached its zenith; the city was known as 'the wings of the world' and the glory of Islam. Yet the assassination of the twelfth Fatimid caliph al-Zafir in 1154 was the prelude to the downfall of the caliphate in sixteen short years. In 1163, Nur al-Din's general Shirkuh entered Egypt accompanied by his Kurdish nephew, Salah al-Din Yusuf ibn Ayyub, known as Saladin, a name meaning 'righteousness of the faith'. In 1169, the Fatimid caliph al-Adid appointed Saladin as his vizier, and it was in this role that he took an army and defeated a colossal force of Byzantine and Crusader troops at the siege of Damietta later that year.

In May 1174, Nur al-Din died quite suddenly, leaving Saladin with political independence in Syria. Just two months later, the king of Jerusalem, Amalric, also died, leaving his kingdom to his thirteen-year-old son Baldwin IV, who suffered from incurable leprosy and was doomed to die young. With a weakened Jerusalem and political autonomy in Syria, the way was open for the great Saladin to unite Egypt and Syria under his own unchallenged leadership, before focusing his efforts on the Crusader lands. Although Saladin's legend, like that of El Cid, diverged from reality, this ruler of a vast kingdom that now included Syria and Egypt was seen as a saviour by the Muslims, and as a hero even by the Black Prince, son of England's King Edward III, who had Saladin's great deeds embroidered on his bed curtains. Much of the Kurdish ruler's power lay in the fact that he was beloved of his people as a man who was humble and charismatic, ascetic but not dogmatic. As a military man, he was astute and a good strategist, though his campaigns against the Franks in the 1180s swung between victory and defeat. Saladin set his sights on the recapture of Jerusalem, winning a famous victory against Guy of Lusignan, king of the Holy City, in July 1187, luring the vast Christian army into the harsh, hostile terrain of the Horns of Hattin, near an extinct volcano, without water supplies.

Saladin had captured almost all the Crusader cities, but Jerusalem was his key objective because of its great significance to Islam. He wanted to take the city without bloodshed and on generous terms, in complete contrast with the crusaders' shameful orgy of killing and destruction. But its inhabitants refused to leave, and a siege was raised, without massacres or looting, until the citizens capitulated on 2 October 1187. Saladin offered fair terms to the Franks, setting free all prisoners upon payment of a ransom, then he summoned the Jews and permitted them to resettle in the city. Jerusalem was returned to Muslim rule, and it is said that Pope Urban II died when he heard of the Christian defeat.

The Pageant's Dying Cadence: The Loss of Outremer and the Failure of Crusading

For Latin Christendom, there was no silver lining to the loss of Jerusalem to the Muslims. The jewel in the crown now belonged to Islam again and the Crusader states were threatened with annihilation. This incited a new, Third Crusade, which set off down the Danube in the autumn of 1187, led by Henry II of England's son, Richard the Lionheart, in a desperate attempt to reverse crusader fortunes. The tense engagements between the English prince and Saladin, which lasted off and on for a year, were later idealized in the awkward yet respectful friendship between the two antagonists so movingly evoked in Sir Walter Scott's novel *The Talisman*. Saladin's city of Acre fell to Richard's armies in July 1191 and became the new Crusader capital. Then, the crusaders laid siege to Jerusalem in June 1192, but Richard had become ill and weak; it is reported that Saladin sent him fresh fruit and cool snow to reduce his fever, and waited patiently for his adversary to realize he lacked the men to take Jerusalem. Later that year, the English prince was obliged to return home with the news that he had reinstated Frankish rule in the coastal cities from Jaffa to Acre, and that Saladin had granted Christian pilgrims access to Jerusalem for worship.

As the thirteenth century dawned, the immediate danger to Outremer seemed to have been averted, but the dance of death went on. Five more Crusades marched to the Holy Land before their vigour diminished and died away. The Fourth, Fifth and Sixth Crusades each brought new perspectives on the encounter between Muslims and Christians in the Near East, both in terms of the betrayal of crusading aims and the surprising importance of meetings between key individuals on both sides. Pope Innocent III announced a new Crusade in 1198, its goal the submission of Egypt, with Jerusalem as the prize. The Republic of Venice played a crucial role in supplying a huge armada to transport up to 30,000 crusaders, at enormous cost, although many ended up travelling from other ports. Then, things began to go wrong. The Christian troops had seen little action, no booty and certainly no glory in the East, and they arrived outside the walls of Constantinople in 1203 unavoidably complicit in a plot to overthrow the emperor Alexios III in favour of his exiled nephew Alexios IV. Their incentive was the proposed unification of the Roman and Greek Churches.

The crusaders spent a cold, hungry winter outside the city, until they were leaned on by their leaders to rise up against the enemy, who were presented to the Christian army not as their co-religionists, but as their old adversaries, the Greeks. They attacked Constantinople for four days and sacked it for five, and the devastation was horrifying – a ghoulish spectacle of rape, burning, impaling and ransacking of holy shrines, in which a spine from Christ's crown of thorns was stolen. Great fires took hold that consumed vital equipment such as silk looms, a disaster from which the silk trade never recovered. A prostitute sat on the throne in the great Hagia Sophia basilica, and donkeys loaded with treasure slipped and skidded on the blood and gore on the floor. Priceless knowledge stored in codices of parchment and vellum was pillaged or set alight, obliterating centuries of fine scholarship and peerless beauty in a few hours, leaving a defiled and scarred city with no trace of its former glories.[2] Violence and sacking were part and parcel of the military ethos of the time, but this was extreme. The contemporary Arab historian al-Athir saw it as an atrocity that destroyed centuries of classical and Christian civilization. In this ignominious way, Constantinople came under the rule of a Latin emperor, Baldwin I, and the Crusade against infidel Muslims had mutated into the assassination and oppression of fellow Christians.

Undeterred by that terrible betrayal of the crusading raison d'être, the next, Fifth Crusade, sent with the same aim of conquering Egypt and Jerusalem, rolled on across the continent and had the Nile city of Damietta surrounded by 1219. An unexpected guest at the crusader camp on the sandbanks of the river was the thirty-seven-year-old

Francis of Assisi, founder of the Friars Minor. Inspired by the Crusade, he had travelled to Egypt in the hope of making a spectacular conversion. Morale in the Christian camp was low after their attack in late August on the Ayyubid sultan al-Kamil's camp was heavily defeated. Under truce conditions, the sultan offered the crusaders their longed-for Jerusalem on condition that they left Egypt, a proposition that caused disagreement and turmoil in the Latin camp. In September, Francis left the crusaders to meet al-Kamil in a tent in his armed encampment, and returned unharmed a few days later. Although no Arab author mentions their meeting, Christian chronicles record that the sultan received Francis politely and respectfully, but rejected the monk's offer of peace in exchange for his conversion to Christianity. Amused but unswayed, he sent Francis back to the crusader camp empty-handed. The story of Francis's mission to the sultan of Egypt has echoed down the centuries, not because it achieved its aim, but more as an example of a surprisingly peaceful encounter between a Muslim ruler and a Catholic priest at the height of a violent confrontation between the faiths.

Al-Kamil's generous efforts at diplomacy and reconciliation found a more sympathetic ear during the Sixth Crusade, led by Frederick II, king of Sicily and Holy Roman Emperor, who was crowned king of the Germans in Aachen in July 1215. Unorthodox and rebellious, he had a passion for learning which was unconstrained by religious or cultural divides. Surrounded by Jewish, Latin, Greek and Muslim advisers, poets and scholars, he spoke Arabic fluently, had a personal Arab tutor in logic and showed a natural understanding of Islam. Frederick and al-Kamil understood each other at once and had a close relationship, which left the Sicilian open to scorn and criticism from Christian Europe. Gerold, the patriarch of Jerusalem, reproved him for living and dressing like a Saracen, and for feasting and drinking with dancing girls sent by al-Kamil.

It had surprised many when Frederick took the Cross and joined the Sixth Crusade, yet it was in large part his liberal views on religion and culture that paved the way for a treaty agreed between the two men in 1229, unique in crusading history because it was achieved through diplomacy and without a major military conflict. The sultan agreed that Jerusalem was to be returned to Christian rule, with a ten-year armistice and exchange of prisoners, and Frederick accorded Muslims access to the Temple Mount to worship freely at the Al-Aqsa Mosque. Frederick ignored ritual anointing and crowned himself king of Jerusalem in the Church of the Holy Sepulchre in March 1229. He had achieved through tolerant understanding and negotiation what the crusaders had failed to achieve in almost a century of killing, plundering and hostility. Yet he died in 1250, in the wake of a Crusade preached against him by the bishops and friars of the Catholic Church. For, while Jerusalem had been returned to Latin Christendom once more, it was not enough to prevent the downfall of the Crusader states, ravaged by the Mamluk sultan Baybars, who burned Caesarea to the ground. By 1291, all of Outremer was under Muslim rule.

The Shattered Mirror: The Legacy of the Crusades in the Holy Land

The phantasmagorical pageant of Christians and Muslims who had waged war for the Holy Land for 200 years grew insubstantial, a shadow show of fleeting figures who fought, slayed, triumphed and faded away. The Crusades had been the tragic performance of a piety that was real to the crusaders, yet was in part a papal subterfuge, a great theatrical charade of religious enmity that masked a lust for land, power and wealth. What remained in the immediate aftermath was a deeper split than ever between Islam and Christian Europe, as Catholic crusading aggression had revived an Islamic zeal for jihad. Both sides were linked by holy war, jihad and Crusade, similar in purpose, but different in conception. King Frederick II's legendary tolerance of Muslims was deeply distrusted by Latin Christendom, a suspicion that saw Dante relegate him to Hell with the wizards in *The Divine Comedy*. Things had changed and views were reversed – a century before, the intermingling of the Christian and Muslim cultures of Norman Sicily had been taken for granted.

The psychological effects of the loss of the Crusader states on Christian Europe combined with adverse practical changes. France and Germany had incurred huge expenses in funding the mammoth crusading expeditions, which brought social and economic consequences, and whole families and sections of the nobility had died in the conflicts. The power of the military orders in the short term threatened to undermine Church and State, although the popularity of crusading reinforced the popes' aim of wielding authority over the state as figureheads with independent military and political capabilities, who could subject monarchy to their control. On the Muslim side, it might have seemed as if little had changed in the end. When the Mamluk Turks reconquered Jerusalem in 1244, the city remained under Muslim rule until 1917. The Crusades aroused little curiosity about western Europe in the rest of the Muslim world. Though they were appalled at crusader atrocities, the Muslims never saw them as an intellectual challenge to their beliefs, and they had never threatened Mecca, Medina or Baghdad. Not for a moment was it considered a never-ending contest between the peoples of the two faiths – only the Christians came to see it like that.

Alongside the narrative of warring faiths was another story, this time of peaceable interchange. A ceaseless procession of merchants and pilgrims passed through the frontier lands of Outremer, going between western Europe and the Muslim realms of the Levant and further east. Exotic eastern goods including spices like nutmeg, black pepper and cloves, silk, satin and cotton all found their way into kitchens and wardrobes as far north as France, England and Germany. The Crusader routes and their states in Outremer altered the nature of trade. The Muslims of the North African seaboard had traded with Europe long before 1095, but the volume and importance of their commercial interactions was transformed in the twelfth and thirteenth centuries. The Crusader states consolidated the power of the great Italian trading cities of Genoa, Pisa and, above all, Venice. The growth of Europe's booming markets was based on a deep irony – at a time of direst conflict, commerce flourished because of the stability and good relations between the Christians on the continent and in the Holy Land and the Muslims. Successive waves of crusaders and their entourages were amazed that trade with the infidel enemy took place every day. The twelfth-century Muslim historian from al-Andalus, Ibn Jubayr, observed the mostly friendly relationships between Christians and Muslims in everyday life, which even involved reciprocal almsgiving at times. Not only western European societies and economies grew rich. One Muslim, Abu 'l-Qasim Ramisht, from Siraf in the Persian Gulf, made a fortune as a middleman in the early 1100s.[3] He bought goods from India and China and sold them to the West, his agent recording shipping goods worth over half a million dinars in a single year. Ramisht was a man of legendary wealth and generosity, and his largesse in paying for a new golden waterspout to replace the silver one in the Ka'aba earned him the distinction of burial at Mecca.

Some cultural exchange was born of violence and trade. The twelfth-century Muslim historian al-Qalanisi wrote in his *Damascus Chronicle* that, when the Franks attacked Tripoli in Syria, the amount of merchandise in its storehouses and the quantities of books in its libraries and in private ownership were beyond calculation. Some precious volumes fell into the hands of the Genoese who led the attack, and may well have been sold or copied before they found their way to Christian Europe. Some military innovations were imported from the East, such as crossbows and carrier pigeons, and the first properly organized European hospitals may have been modelled on those in the Levantine region. Words transliterated from Arabic became commonplace in European languages. Even English has well over 2,000 words of Arabic origin, such as 'cheque' from *sakk* (a written agreement), or 'carafe' from *ghiraf* (a grain scoop). When we mention alcohol, sofas, satin, muslin or mattresses, we are using words that come from Arabic.

Some Franks stayed on in Outremer and their descendants founded families whose names reveal their origins – Bardawil from Baldwin, Salibi from the word for a cross – but the crusaders lived on an urban frontier inhabited originally by people living at a higher level of civilization than the invaders had known in Latin Christendom. The Islamic tribes of the Levant lived in richer, more advanced cities, unrivalled in Europe. Some, such as Antioch and Jerusalem, had histories older than Rome itself. The crusaders never put down deep roots. They were always outsiders who showed little interest in Muslim culture and science, and most of them returned to the cool lakes and forests of north-western Europe with little to show for their fleeting assumption of a new identity.

The saga of the Crusades against Islam is a chronicle of reversals, inversions, heroism, bathos and legend. As the power of the Cross waxed and waned, the Crescent moon of Islam fell and rose again. If either side looked at each other and saw reflected a simultaneous otherness and sameness, that mirror image was shattered. If the Crusades had been an act of revenge for the conquests of the early Muslim empire, the Christian states of Outremer foreshadowed future European colonialism and imperialism. The holy wars had intensified the idea of Christianity as defining the common identity of Europe, a perception that could only magnify the conviction that Muslims were heretical and alien outsiders. Nowhere was Europe's Christian identity more apparent than in the Gothic cathedral of Chartres in north-west France.

Chapter II

A Space of Enigmas: Chartres Cathedral

'The face of Europe was changed. Well, the face of architecture was changed too! Like civilization, it turned the page, and the new spirit of the times found it ready to write at its dictation. It returned from the Crusades with the pointed arch, like the nations with liberty.'

Victor Hugo

'This we now call the Gothic manner of architecture . . . I think should with more reason be called the Saracen style.'

Sir Christopher Wren

The cathedral of Our Lady of Chartres, seat of the bishop of Chartres, is one of the greatest monuments of western Christianity, an awesome stone book which has survived fire and war in its five incarnations. It is a UNESCO World Heritage Site and the zenith of French Gothic architecture, built in the form of a cross and adorned with exuberant Gothic sculpture which tells the story of the Christian faith in limestone and stained glass. Chartres is an ancient place of pilgrimage, focused on its veneration as a site of devotion to the Virgin Mary, whose sacred tunic is the cathedral's most precious relic. It also became a seat of learning in the eleventh century, when Bishop Fulbert created a cathedral school there which grew into a famous centre of scholarship attended by theologians and scholars who kindled a twelfth-century renaissance of learning. While no place better embodied the medieval European Catholic spirit, the cathedral also hides a deeper truth. It is a space of enigmas, of outer appearances, masterly imitations and spectacular innovations, including some that conceal their Islamic origins beneath the overlay of Catholicism.

The Architectural Illusion: The Saracen Style

Fire has refined the metamorphosis of Chartres Cathedral. At the top of a hill on the left bank of the river Eure, rising from the fertile plain of Beauce, eighty kilometres south-east of Paris, a holy building has existed since the fourth century AD. That first church was burned to the ground in 743 by the Duke of Aquitaine, and by 962 it had been damaged by fire and rebuilt four times. Another serious fire broke out in 1020, which prompted its bishop, Fulbert, to build a new, much larger cathedral, funded by donations from the monarchs of Europe. Yet another fire in the town in 1134 damaged its façade and its octagonal belltower, built after the Second Crusade. Then, on the night of 10 June 1194, a sixth major fire ravaged the building, destroying all but the crypt, towers and the new façade, leaving just a shell. Chartres's fame as a place of pilgrimage, a journey undertaken to revere the relic of the Holy Virgin's tunic, persuaded the great and good of Europe to rally once more in response to the latest conflagration and fund its immediate reconstruction, with contributions coming from King Philip II of France, Pope Celestine III, local gentry, merchants and craftsmen, and King Richard the Lionheart of England. The reconstruction was mostly completed in an astonishing twenty-five years, and the building was finally consecrated in 1260. It was as if, through a trial of many fires, the cathedral had finally found its ideal form, the epitome of High Gothic style, which remains almost unchanged today.

'Gothic' was a term coined in the sixteenth century by the architect Vasari to distinguish between classical Roman architecture and what he considered the inferior architecture of buildings erected by the Goths after they sacked Rome. But Gothic architecture has little to do with the Goths. The definitive version of Chartres Cathedral was built in a style known as Frankish work, which originated in the region around Paris called the Île-de-France. The defining feature of Frankish work, or High Gothic, was the pointed arch, as well as rib vaulting for ceilings, flying buttresses for support, stained-glass rose windows, towering spires and elegant windows whose stonework was divided into decorative patterns. Some of these architectural elements had already been used in religious buildings outside France – Durham Cathedral, built in the north of England between 1093 and 1104, was the first to use rib vaults – but the first fully Gothic building was the abbey of Saint-Denis, on the outskirts of Paris. In the early twelfth century, Abbot Suger (*c.* 1081–1151) had begun the reconstruction of the abbey, and his masons incorporated the latest features introduced into Romanesque architecture, including the pointed arches, rib vaulting and flying buttresses used at Chartres, plus the first-known circular rose window above the west portal. The reconstruction was an international undertaking – as the abbot himself remarked, the anonymous craftsmen who brought about this architectural revolution were 'many masters from different nations'.[1]

Chartres Cathedral became a landmark of the new style, which increased the vertical dimension of religious buildings so that, in reaching skywards, they seemed to link Heaven and Earth. They were transformed into spaces suffused with a jewelled light that shone through their stained glass, in a grand imitation of divine luminance. Like medieval narrative paintings, stained-glass windows tell visual stories both holy and worldly: the lives of saints, Bible stories and tales of historical heroes. One of Chartres Cathedral's 172 bays of stained glass is called the Charlemagne window, which portrays Charlemagne's deeds in two major Crusades, in Jerusalem and Muslim Spain, in which he is shown violently vanquishing the Saracen enemy. The window makes a statement at once religious and political, depicting the king of the Franks as the great defender of Christianity. More emphatic still is the presence of Roland in scenes taken from the epic *Chanson de Roland*, where the hero is shown sounding his oliphant horn and slaying Muslim assailants. Above him, the hand of God descends from the heavens to bless the battle. In the crusading era in which the stained glass was created, the decision to represent scenes from the French epic that lionized the defeated Charlemagne and his army, and told a false history, set a tone of militant Catholicism primed to assert itself over the Muslim enemy. It revealed the political power of the Church and the message it sent to the faithful. The Gothic cathedrals and churches of western Europe, among which Chartres is peerless, are one of the great glories of its civilization, built as testaments to the overarching power of Christianity on the European continent. Even so, a different, parallel narrative emerges, shaped by the everyday lives and interactions of the Christians and Muslims who traded, travelled and crafted those monuments. It is little known that almost all the elements of Gothic architecture had their origins in earlier Islamic buildings.

One of the world's most eminent architects, Sir Christopher Wren (1632–1723), knew that Islamic architecture was deeply intertwined with the Gothic style, and his views proved controversial. In *Parentalia*, a family history written by his son, the latter describes how his father's study of European Gothic cathedrals led him to believe that Gothic architecture was a style originally invented by the Arabs and imported to the rest of Europe by returning crusaders, and via Muslim Spain: 'Such buildings have been vulgarly called Modern Gothick, but their true appellation is Arabic, Saracenic or Moresque.'[2] Christopher Wren cited comparisons between the mosques and palaces of Fez in Morocco and Burgos Cathedral in northern Spain. Two decades earlier, the French writer Florent le Comte had expressed a similar opinion in his *Study of Architectural Peculiarities* (*Cabinet des singularitez de l'architecture*) of 1699. For those who saw Gothic architecture as an original and fundamentally Christian form of artistic and intellectual expression, invented in northern France, these may have been unpalatable opinions, yet they have been validated by modern evidence.

The Arch Never Sleeps

The pointed Gothic arch was taken from Syrian Byzantine architecture by the Muslims, who were master arch builders. Their proverb

'The arch never sleeps' expresses the dynamic, living presence of the Islamic arch, which could imitate the branches of the palm tree or reflect the spherical nature of the globe. Their superb knowledge of geometry and the laws of physics enabled them to draw on past knowledge and improve on it, and their arches proved far more robust that the semicircular versions built by the Romans and Byzantines. The pointed arch, the defining feature of High Gothic, was thought to be an invention of Christian European architects. In fact, it came to Europe from Cairo, via Sicily.

The pointed arch was adopted in Islamic architecture to establish a cultural identity for the new religion, and was first used by Muslim architects in the Dome of the Rock. Around the millennium, Christian merchants from Amalfi trading with Egypt probably saw the pointed arches of the Mosque of Ibn Tulun in Cairo. The Benedictine abbey of Monte Cassino, near the Amalfi coast, was in its heyday in the eleventh and twelfth centuries and employed Byzantine and Islamic craftsmen to work on the building. It was also home to the Tunisian scholar Constantine the African, a man knowledgeable about the building techniques of Fatimid North Africa. It was at Monte Cassino that the first pointed arch in Europe was constructed, and, when Abbot Hugh of Cluny visited the abbey in 1083, he returned to France with new architectural knowledge that was used in the church of Cluny, which boasted 150 pointed arches. Abbot Suger visited Cluny sometime between 1135 and 1144, after which his own masons went on to build Saint-Denis abbey. The pointed arches of Chartres had precedents in the two most influential churches in Europe in their time, and the style spread to Germany and later to Great Britain in the mid-twelfth century.

In Spain, the Umayyads had been inspired by the horseshoe arches of the Great Mosque of Damascus, which they had imported and developed to perfection in the Great Mosque of Cordoba. The horseshoe arch travelled north with the Christian Spanish Mozarabs, and the monastery of San Miguel de Escalada, close to the pilgrimage route of Santiago de Compostela, was built using horseshoe arches by monks from Cordoba in AD 913. In France, the twelfth-century

Puy Cathedral cloister is also adorned with red and white patterned arches, some with Arabic inscriptions.

The magnificent Gothic rib vaulting of Chartres Cathedral also had its roots in earlier Islamic buildings, as Muslim architects sought ways of creating edifices that were stronger, finer and higher. The style of the vast ribbed vaults and intersecting arches of the Great Mosque of Cordoba travelled north, appearing in the intersecting roof arches of Durham Cathedral and Bolton Abbey in England, as well as the High Gothic cathedrals of northern France. The Muslim minaret – a word that derives from *manarah*, meaning 'radiator of the light' of Islam – was an innovative feature of Muslim architecture first seen in the minaret of the eighth-century Great Mosque of Damascus, and probably reached northern Europe via Muslim Spain. Minarets grew more refined, their rectangular towers bearing slender, spire-like forms that influenced the creation of spires on Christian buildings.

Perhaps the greatest glory of Chartres Cathedral is the west rose window, created about 1215, where the dead are shown rising from their tombs, summoned by the trumpets of angels to the Last Judgment. The prototype of the Gothic rose window with ornamental stonework may have its origins in an octagonal window with rosettes in the Umayyad palace of Khirbat al-Majfar in Jordan, built between 740 and 750. Fifty years later, the Great Mosque of Damascus had stained-glass windows in the form of carved marble window grilles to let in light, the oldest known Islamic geometric interlace work. In 1184, the Muslim traveller Ibn Jubayr described the magical effects of the coloured light from the seventy-four windows, so bright they dazzled his eyes. In northern Spain, the church of St Michael of Lillo, in Asturias, is a World Heritage Site. Its round tracery window high on the south wall, sculpted from a single piece of stone and decorated using geometric patterns and plant motifs, suggests a very early Islamic influence in the heartlands of the Asturian reconquest, and presupposes a very early route of transmission to northern Europe through Spain. Whatever the case, the 167 stained-glass windows of Chartres Cathedral, along with its other crucial architectural innovations, owe a debt to Islamic prototypes. There, they were transformed into a didactic programme in glass and stone that unveiled a vision of the global importance of the Christian Church advanced by Pope Innocent II at the height of the worldly power of the papacy.

The Riddle of the Virgin's Tunic

A faded fresco of the Virgin Mary on her throne in the crypt of Chartres Cathedral was given new life in the most famous of its stained-glass glories, the window of the Blue Virgin, created in 1180. There, she is seated on a throne and wears a deep blue robe, Mary's colour, with the Christ child on her lap, in a composition known as the Throne of Wisdom. Pilgrims who flocked to Chartres to worship the Virgin would have been in awe of the majesty, wisdom and maternal love portrayed in her luminous image, the defining qualities of the cult of the Virgin Mary that thrived in the twelfth and thirteenth centuries in Christian Europe. The Catholic Church had perceived a need for a more human approach in its teachings, for a motherly figure who could intercede between God and sinners, and, fuelled by the preaching of Bernard of Clairvaux, the mother of Christ became the focus of pious devotion.

Catholics were drawn to Chartres not just because of its dedication to the Virgin, but because of the precious relic it housed: the undergarment or tunic of Mary, the *sancte chemise*, which she was said to have worn at the conception and birth of Christ. Devotees had seen images of the tunic, because they could buy a souvenir in the form of a pilgrim badge made of lead to wear on their hats. Puzzlingly, the image on the badge looked like a plain western linen shirt, yet, in medieval accounts, Charles the Bald, ruler of the Carolingian Empire and son of Charlemagne, brought the original tunic to Chartres from Constantinople, a place famous for its costly silk fabrics.[3] It was even more baffling when the reliquary holding the tunic at Chartres was opened in 1712 and found not to contain such a garment, despite its highly embellished gold cask being decorated with images of chemises. What was inside were two lengths of cloth, one of embroidered silk and the other a gold fabric adorned with birds and geometric and plant motifs.

The embroidered cloth has been associated with tenth- or eleventh-century Byzantium, although it seems more likely that it came from Muslim Spain. Charles the Bald was known to have received gifts of textiles from Spain as early as 865, specifically from Cordoba, which produced luxury silk. He was also the founder of the medieval fairs of Champagne, sites of trade between Muslim Spain and northern France. Silks from al-Andalus were traded throughout the Mediterranean, and those from Almería, the hub of silk production, were used by the French aristocracy and in ecclesiastical vestments. Some were brought back as war booty and used to wrap Christian relics, and Islamic textile patterns were used in border decorations for columns of statues in twelfth-century French cathedrals, including the west façade of Chartres. So it transpires that the Virgin's tunic, a sacred relic that underlines her Christian divinity and maternity, was not a plain chemise but took the form of luxurious Muslim silk; it is a hybrid artefact, whose very fabric is testament to cross-cultural trade and exchange between people of both faiths.

The Scholastic Illusion

Aldebaran stands out in Taurus
Menke and Rigel in Gemini,
and Frons and bright Calbalazet in
Leo. Scorpio, you have
Galbalagrab; and you, Capricorn,
Deneb. You, Batanalhaut, are
alone enough for Pisces.[4]

Bishop Fulbert of Chartres (d. 1028) wrote this short poem as an aide-memoire in his study of the stars, which all had Arabic names. For the first time in history, he used Arabic loan words in his Latin verses to identify the heavenly bodies, and also consulted his Arabic–Latin glossary of terms relating to the astrolabe, which he compiled from the oldest known western treatise on that instrument, the

Sententie astrolabii, which came from north-eastern Spain in the tenth century, probably written originally in Arabic by the Muslim scholar al-Khwarizmi. Such knowledge was highly unusual in northern Europe in Fulbert's time and his interest in Arab science sheds an intriguing light on the man who, from humble beginnings, rose to become Bishop of Chartres in 1006 and established a place of learning there that, for 200 years, was one of the leading cathedral schools on the continent, attracting great scholars of the time, both French and foreign.

In 789, Charlemagne had ordered the founding of schools in cathedrals and monasteries to teach reading, singing, numbers and grammar, and to train future priests and clerical administrators. More advanced learning was based on the seven liberal arts, the trivium, which taught logic, grammar and rhetoric, and the quadrivium, devoted to mathematics, music and astronomy. Bishop Fulbert was the powerhouse of Chartres Cathedral, and was instrumental in its construction and in creating its educational prestige. Once, when Fulbert was gravely ill, the Virgin healed him with a drop of her milk, and this miracle led him to foster the cult of the Virgin and make Chartres a vital centre of Marian worship. The bishop also wrote poems and hymns, and the entire focus of his life was the Catholic faith. Yet he embraced what would have been seen as profane wisdom through his fascination with Muslim science, and the Chartres school prioritized mathematical arts and natural philosophy, subjects in which the latest advances had been made by Muslim scholars.

Fulbert's intellectual interests may be accounted for by the likelihood that he was the pupil of Gerbert of Aurillac (946–1003) when a student at the cathedral school of Reims. Gerbert was one of the outstanding personages of the Christian Middle Ages, born in France but a student in Catalonia, probably at the monastery of Ripoll. There, in northern Spain, he was introduced to Muslim mathematics and Arabic numerals, and also to astronomy, for which he developed a passion. He is credited with bringing the abacus and the armillary sphere back to Europe, and in his lifetime became a magisterial scientist and scholar, before he was elected as the first French pope, Sylvester II, in 999. Gerbert found no contradiction in his roles as both head of the Roman Catholic Church and advocate for Greek and Arabic mathematics, astronomy and philosophy, and for Muslim culture.

Other great scholars who belonged to Chartres Cathedral school in the twelfth century were the Neoplatonist philosopher Bernard of Chartres (d. after 1124), the English philosopher John of Salisbury (d. 1180), who later became bishop of Chartres, and the French scholastic philosopher William of Conches (*c.* 1090/1–*c.* 1155–70). As they strolled in the cloisters, they read and discussed books, many of which were in the cathedral library. Among the familiar Latin works by Cicero, Donatus and Priscian listed in the scholar Thierry of Chartres' compendium, the *Heptateucon*, there were books translated from Arabic. For teaching geometry, Euclid's *Elements* was recommended, translated by Adelard of Bath from the Arabic text. There, too, were Ptolemy's *Canons* and the *Zij*, al-Khwarizmi's ninth-century astronomical tables, also translated from the Arabic by Adelard. The scholars of Chartres were intellectually curious, seeking new knowledge to broaden their horizons, as Thierry's inclusion of Latin translations of Arabic scientific treatises shows.

William of Conches read the works of Greek and Arab physicians translated into Latin by Constantine the African, and it may be that he read those translations at Chartres. He was at the forefront of a period of intense intellectual reconfiguration that led to the twelfth-century renaissance, when scholastic philosophy rose to prominence across Europe, fuelled by the great Muslim sage Averroes' commentaries on Aristotle. William was one of the first Christian scholars to study Islamic physical science and philosophy in translation from Arabic, treading in the footsteps of Fulbert before him and adopting a rational approach to knowledge, through which he sought verifiable truth. William of Conches appeared radical to his contemporaries, but he was humble, and quick to acknowledge his debt to his sources: 'We [moderns] are not more learned than the ancients, but we yet have a wider perspective. For we possess their books and moreover a natural ingenuity by which we discover something new. We are dwarves on the shoulders of giants: we perceive much on account of their merit, but little on account of our own.'[5]

The Enigma of Identity

Gothic architecture, the cult of the Virgin Mary, the cathedral school – all define Chartres as unerringly Christian in conception, purpose and heritage, and indisputably French in its material nature and geographical location. Out of the great fire of 1194 came a renewal born of both imitations and innovations: imitations because the new cathedral turned back to both the Romanesque architecture of the past and to an Islamic style dating as far back as the eighth century, and innovations because the incorporation of Islamic elements into a Christian building forged something new that denoted a distinctive mixed identity. The features that determine its western, Gothic and Christian nature – pointed arches, rib vaulting and flying buttresses, spires and rose windows – all derive from an eastern Muslim paradigm. Chartres Cathedral is a space where architectural, devotional and intellectual illusions are dissolved as each lays bare the hybrid identity of a place of unerring Christian Catholicism, but one which is founded on and fortified at its deeper levels by the influence of Muslim architecture, artisans and scholars.

Chapter 12

The Light from the East: Translation, Transmission, Transition

'Western Europe owes its civilization to its translators'

L. G. Kelly

Claudius Ptolemy lived in Alexandria, in Egypt, in the second century after Christ, when the city was under Roman rule. He was probably part Greek, part Egyptian, a scholar famed as a supreme master of mathematics and astronomy. In his fifties, he wrote a work in Greek later named *The Great Treatise* or *Almagest* by its Arabic translators, which became one of the most influential scientific works in history. It traced the movements of the planets and stars based on the ancient understanding that the Earth was at the centre of the cosmos, and it supplanted previous Greek knowledge of astronomy. Nearly 700 years later, in ninth-century Baghdad, the Abbasid caliph al-Ma'mun received a copy of the *Almagest*, one of several choice Greek manuscripts he was given each year from the Great Library of Alexandria as a condition of maintaining peace with the Byzantine emperor Theophilus. The manuscript was then translated into Arabic in Baghdad by the Syrian Christian astronomer Sali ibn Bishr (d. *c.* 845), but remained unknown in Christian Europe until the Italian scholar Gerard of Cremona translated it into Latin around 1150. It remained the most important work on astronomy for 1,500 years. The journey of the *Almagest* from the Great Library of Alexandria to the cloisters of the monasteries and cathedral schools of Catholic Europe was accomplished through the power of the translated word.

In the early days of Islam, Christian theologians had first manipulated the inherent ambiguity of the written word to spawn a pernicious hostility between Muslims and Christians. Now, at the start of the twelfth century, the written word fostered collaboration and communication between them, as the translation process became the vehicle for a cultural transfer on a prodigious scale. Christian scholars were eager to unravel the secret code of language that would allow them to decipher important books that were mainly secular rather than religious. They needed to bridge the gap between Latin and Arabic to assuage their thirst for the learning of Muslim Europe, a thirst that stemmed in part from the historical isolation of western Christians from the Byzantine Church and its Greek heritage after the fall of the Western Roman Empire. Only one of Plato's Dialogues, and no work by Ptolemy, Galen, Hippocrates, Euclid or Aristotle, had so far been translated into Latin. The Roman senator and philosopher Boethius, who wrote the *Consolation of Philosophy*, and the great Iberian polymath Isidore of Seville had both written potted versions of important Latin texts, but they barely touched on Greek thought. Knowledge of cutting-edge science was no better, although trade in medicines between the East and Charlemagne's Rhineland is reflected in a Latin treatise from the 790s, composed near Mainz, on the banks of the Rhine.

Yet this sparse harvest of new ideas left medieval Christian scholars afraid of being left behind and disadvantaged by their comparative intellectual poverty. By the twelfth century, the outlook had changed, and Christian Europe was infused with the new energy of transition. People, books, materials, produce – all were in transit as trade flourished and towns sprang up across the continent. Europeans were introduced to innovative ideas and technologies, which were expressed in new vernaculars and found form in Gothic cathedrals like Chartres. Central to this renewal was the translation of works from other cultures, many of which had begun to come fully into the Christian purview since the Christian Reconquest of al-Andalus, which brought northern Spanish Christians more closely into contact with the intellectual treasures of Muslim Spain. Many scholars from Latin Europe embarked on a quest for Greek and Arab science and philosophy, the Greek works of which were lost, while Arab learning remained unknown to Christians on the continent, and they travelled thousands of miles to find it.

Travel and Translation: Three Wandering Scholars

As early as the eleventh century, Christian scholars migrated southwards in search of knowledge. Their travels were the equivalent of the *rihla*, the Muslim concept of a journey made for the sake of learning. One exception to this direction of travel was the physician Constantine the African (d. before 1098), whose journey began in Muslim North Africa and ended in Christian Italy. The twelfth-century monk Peter the Deacon wrote that Constantine may have travelled to Babylon, Ethiopia and even India, where he acquired scientific knowledge. Constantine emigrated to Sicily, then moved on to Salerno, home of the famous medical school, where he was known as Constantine Siculus. He spoke no Italian, but made friends with a doctor, Abbas, who became his interpreter. His life's work was revealed to him when he fell ill and noticed his friend's poor medical knowledge when Abbas failed to ask him for the customary urine sample. Constantine realized there were no good books on medicine in Italy, so, once recovered, he returned to Carthage to practise medicine for three years, before returning to Salerno laden with treasured medical volumes. Constantine converted to Christianity and became a Benedictine monk, spending the rest of his life at the abbey of Monte Cassino. There, he devoted himself to translating into Latin the Arabic works of the great geniuses of Arab medicine, such as al-Razi's comprehensive medical compendium, as well as writing his own treatise on sexual intercourse, *De coitu*. His translations reached libraries in Italy, Germany, France, Belgium and England, and were used as textbooks until the seventeenth century, the fruit of a life's work that brought Muslim enlightenment to the teachings and practices of healing in northern Europe.

Adelard of Bath was born around 1080, shortly after the Norman conquest, in the English city after which he is named. In his twenties, he embarked on a mission to study science, making a long journey south that brought him into contact with Arab scholars. Adelard recorded his travels to the 'lands of the Crusades', probably Rome, Greece, Sicily, Salerno and Asia Minor, including Antioch, during which time he must have learnt to speak Arabic. Ten years later, around 1116, he returned to England, where he became a civil servant in King Henry I's government. He eventually retired to his home town of Bath, laden with books, including the Arabic translation of Euclid's *Elements*, with the ambition of communicating what he had learnt about Arab philosophy, astronomy and geometry to a lay audience. He cut an uncharacteristically dashing figure as a scholar who liked finery, and appears in a Paris manuscript of about 1400 wearing a bright green cloak and emerald ring. His important original work *Questions on Natural Science*, written before 1133, in which he often refers to his experiences in Antioch, is in the form of a Platonic dialogue intended to be used as a framework to discuss Arabic theories on the natural world.

Adelard's greatest gifts to medieval Christian Europe were his translations of key mathematical works. First, al-Khwarizmi's astronomical tables, the *Zij*, making the great mathematician's invention of algebra widely available in Latin, and then, the first full translation of Euclid's *Elements*. Not only did Adelard's work exert a strong influence on natural philosophy and the ideas of Roger Bacon, William of Conches and Peter Abelard, but he introduced algebra to Christian Europe.

The third member of this trio of medieval pioneers who kindled the evolution of European culture was born around 1170, in the Italian town of Pisa, three years before the foundations of the famous Leaning Tower were laid. His name was Leonardo Bonacci, known later as Fibonacci. Like Constantine before him, an early trading life opened a portal into the world of Muslim science that shaped his future. Leonardo's father, Guglielmo, was a customs official for the Pisan Chamber of Commerce in Bugia, on the coast of modern-day Algeria, where Leonardo grew up. There, he was taught by the finest Arab mathematicians, and learnt the Hindu–Arabic number system. Leonardo watched the way merchants conducted their business and saw that the old number system of Roman numerals did not serve the practical demands of contemporary commerce, an observation that became a significant focus in his later writing.

The splendid court of the emperor Frederick II (r. 1198–1250) drew Europe's finest scholars as it migrated from Palermo to Naples, Bologna to Pisa, Vienna to Verona, Brindisi to Jerusalem. This intellectual powerhouse brought great opportunities for the transmission of knowledge due to its itinerancy. Leonardo Fibonacci found his way to Frederick's court, where he became the emperor's guest, engaging him and the scholar and Sicilian Arab, John of Palermo, in discussions of mathematical problems, including those debated by the Persian polymath Omar Khayyam. In this dynamic scholarly environment, Fibonacci wrote books that would form the basis of mathematical study in Christian Europe, and his *Book of Calculation* (*Liber Abaci*) became a seminal text. It explained the number system of ten digits, including zero, that today we call Arabic numbers, and showed its importance in business transactions such as bookkeeping, converting weights and measures, currency exchange, the calculation of interest and all those mathematical operations essential to commerce today. Fibonacci's calculations were made using an updated version of the abacus, which Gerbert of Aurillac had reintroduced to northern Europe in the tenth century, and they were essential to the growth of accounting and banking on the continent. Fibonacci is also famous for his implementation of the ancient Indian number sequence where each number is the sum of the preceding two numbers. The Fibonacci sequence continues to fascinate the creative worlds of literature, music and the visual arts, and is still used in today's financial trading.

Constantine, Adelard and Leonardo Fibonacci were scholars of inestimable value in terms of their European legacy in the fields of medicine, mathematics and astronomy. Equally significant is the dialogue they shared with an elite group of Christian and Muslim intellectuals who moved easily between West and East and showed that knowledge has no barriers. This cultural exchange of ideas, while it moved only in one direction, from east to west, brought men together in a common pursuit, the sharing and transmission of learning, and, remarkably, it took place at the height of one of the most violent and antagonistic series of wars between Christians and Muslims in history.

Toledo: The Fulcrum of Europe's Cultural Future

One of the most famous landscapes in European art is El Greco's *View of Toledo* (*Vista de Toledo*), painted at the turn of the sixteenth century. It is a work of breathtaking drama, casting a light that is lurid yet mystical on the Castilian city of Toledo, caught between storm and sunshine. El Greco's use of chiaroscuro, the way the black sky outlines the silver-grey buildings and the elongation of the composition give a sense that this is both an important, almost supernatural place and one of strife and conflict. His revolutionary landscape caught the essence of the city, perched high on a mountain in the Castilian plain, with the river Tagus encircling it on three sides, almost at the geographical centre of the Iberian peninsula. Its superb natural defences were desirable to the Romans, who named it Toletum, and the Visigothic kings made it their capital city, until the Berber Tariq ibn Ziyad overthrew its rulers in 711–12. It then remained under Muslim rule until 1085, when King Alfonso VI of León claimed it for the Catholic kingdoms. Known as both the Imperial City, since it became the court of the Holy Roman Emperor Charles V in the sixteenth century, and as City of the Three Cultures, because of its multicultural history, it reached its zenith in the period of 150 years between 1150 and 1300, when it became a site of convergence, the beating heart of a cultural interchange unprecedented in Europe.

This came about through a unique set of circumstances. At the start of the twelfth century, local laws show that Toledo was a city of cultural hybridity, with a mixed population of Jews, Muslims and Christians, as well as a growing number of Mozarabs – Christians who had lived under Muslim rule and were Arabic-speaking or bilingual. This means that up to 10,000 of the estimated 30,000 inhabitants of Toledo at this time were Arabic-speaking. It was a combination of cultural, racial and religious factors, together with the intellectual ambition and dynamism of Raymond (Raimundo de Salvetat), the archbishop of Toledo from 1125 until 1152, that created a centre of Islamic learning that drew scholars to the city from across Europe, from as far afield as England and Hungary.[1] There, in the hundred years from about 1150 until 1250, the diverse elements of Christian Platonic thought and Aristotelian Arab science were fused together. It was possible to find works by Arab scholars in the libraries of Toledo that might be translated into Latin, and later into Castilian Spanish. Daniel of Morley (*c.* 1140–1210), a philosopher from a village in Norfolk, travelled to Paris, which he found 'dominated by law and pretentious ignorance, and . . . hastened to Toledo, as the most famous centre of Arabic science, in order to hear the wiser philosophers of the world.'[2]

Archbishop Raymond was the sponsor and driving force behind the initial translation enterprise, an era that ran from 1130 until 1187. A Benedictine monk from Gascony in France, he was a man with many foreign contacts, and was fighting for the supremacy of the see of Toledo, hoping to rival other cathedral cities in Europe. Raymond was something of a visionary, who believed that, without Islamic knowledge, the Christian west would remain culturally paralysed. Under his aegis and that of his successor, Archbishop John of Castellmorum, a Jewish *converso* scholar, John of Spain (*c.* 1130–50), translated works of astrology, philosophy, mathematics and medicine from Arabic into vernacular Spanish, including Avicenna's important *Book of Healing*. These were then translated into Latin by his colleague Domingo Gundisalvo, a Castilian scholar specializing in philosophy, who went on to translate Avicenna's *On the Soul* and other works of Arabic philosophy into Latin. Between them, they translated many works of ancient Greek, Persian, Indian, Arab and Hebrew thought, across all branches of knowledge, which found their way northwards to Christian lands.

The brightest star in the constellation of learned men who flocked to Toledo in the early twelfth century came from Cremona in northern Italy. Gerard of Cremona (*c.* 1114–87) left his home town with a passion for astronomy and a burning desire to find a copy of the greatest known work on the study of celestial phenomena, Ptolemy's *Almagest*. Some time before 1144, and a thousand miles later, he stood travelworn at the gates of Toledo, where a seemingly superhuman energy drove him to translate into Latin upwards of seventy of the most brilliant and wide-ranging works of Arabic science over the course of his life. This feat was even more surprising because Gerard did not know a word of Arabic when he arrived. His brief biography, penned by his students, informs us that 'seeing the abundance of books in Arabic on every subject and regretting the poverty of the Latins in such things, he learnt the Arabic language in order to be able to translate.'[3] Toledo was also a place of teaching, where Gerard held lectures, often on astrology, for groups of listeners with whom he debated in the Arabic style of the ancient schools of learning of Baghdad, testing philosophical and scientific questions daily.

His pupil, Daniel of Morley, recalls that Gerard was helped by his Mozarab friend Ghalib, who translated some of the Arabic texts into vernacular Spanish, which Gerard then translated into Latin. His version of the *Almagest*, dated 1175, became the most widely known in western Europe up to the Renaissance. A century before Gerard reached Toledo, the scientific-instrument maker and genius al-Zarqali, born in Toledo, designed a new universal astrolabe, the Saphaea, which was replicated from Europe to India. To complement his invention, al-Zarqali wrote an explanation of how to use the Toledan Tables, and Gerard's Latin translation of this work became fundamental to European astronomy for centuries. In addition to astronomy, Gerard also translated ten medical works of Galen and one by Hippocrates, thereby providing the Latin world with the complete theoretical foundation of ancient Greek medicine. Somehow, his great body of work, including several original scientific treatises by Gerard himself, found its way to the centres of learning of Christian Latin Europe, miraculously preserved in its perilous journey along bumpy, dangerous roads and across rough, wild seas. More than any other scholar of his time, Gerard of Cremona equipped major cathedral schools, monasteries and universities with the Greek and Arab scholarship that completely recast Christian European learning and thinking.

A 'detestable and damnable' Pagan Heresy: Latin Korans and a Christian History of the Arabs

These new developments fostered an equal interest in, and animosity towards, the religion of Islam, aspects that combined in the innovative scholarship of two Catholic churchmen whose lives spanned the eleventh to thirteenth centuries. Around the time Gerard of Cremona arrived in Toledo, the abbot of the Benedictine abbey of Cluny, Peter the Venerable (*c.* 1092–1156), began a tour of Spanish monasteries. A professor at twenty and an abbot at thirty, he was gifted with an almost encyclopaedic knowledge of theology that propelled a keen desire to study Islam using its primary sources. His trip to Spain was in part to commission the first ever translation of the Koran into Latin, along with other works in Arabic. It represented a landmark in the intellectual history of Europe, one which sought to reassess Islam from the Christian perspective. The manuscripts commissioned probably came from Toledo, although Peter met his translators – principally the Englishman Robert of Ketton, who was archdeacon of Pamplona, Herman of Carinthia and a Muslim called Muhammad, among others – at a northern Spanish monastery in La Rioja. Their collaborative and pioneering version of the Koran was finished by the summer of 1143, and this and other translated Islamic works allowed Christian scholars to study Islam seriously for the first time.

For all Peter the Venerable's open-mindedness, he was a man of his age and a devout Catholic, whose reading of the new translations confirmed that, for the Catholics of Europe, Islam was a heresy that verged on paganism – 'detestable and damnable', as he called it. But, this time, amid the cultural revival of Christian Europe, the intellectual approach was based on rational study, a far cry from the uninformed propaganda of the early Christian commentators. Despite his predictably negative theological stance, Peter wrote respectfully of Muslim scholars as 'clever, learned men whose libraries are full of books dealing with the liberal arts, and the study of nature, and that Christians have gone in quest of these.'[4] Peter was the first western European scholar to make an effort to understand Islam, and he had divergent opinions on Muslim culture, on the one hand being quick to condemn the Islamic faith, while on the other expressing admiration for Muslim scholarship.

This ground-breaking version of the Koran in Latin was the first specifically religious Muslim text to be translated for a Catholic readership, in contrast with the Latin versions of so many secular scientific and philosophical works in Arabic; but it also embodied that fundamental paradox of religious hostility alongside intellectual esteem and collaboration that underlay relations between Christians and Muslims in Europe at this time.

*

Sixty years after Peter died at Cluny, King Alfonso VIII led the knights of Spain to a defining victory over the Almohad army of Caliph Muhammad al-Nasir, at Las Navas de Tolosa, in 1212. Among the Christian ranks was Rodrigo Jiménez de Rada (1170–1247), the militant and scholarly archbishop of Toledo, who had stirred up the popular outrage felt at earlier Almohad victories and exhorted Pope Innocent III to proclaim a Crusade against the Berbers. Both warrior and historian, Jiménez de Rada wrote an eyewitness account of the Christian conquest in his *On Spanish History* (*De rebus Hispaniae*), a nine-volume chronicle of Spanish and Portuguese history up to 1243. He was also the first western Christian scholar to write a Latin history of the Arabs, which describes the birth and spread of Islam. As archbishop of Toledo, Rodrigo carried on the tradition of his two predecessors by sponsoring Latin translations of important works in Arabic, hoping to strengthen his own theological arguments through a grasp of the religious ideas of his Muslim political adversaries. Under his patronage, scholars who came to translate in Toledo were made canons of the Church, which entitled them to a maintenance stipend. Among these were Michael Scot, whom Dante consigned to Hell in the *Divine Comedy* as a necromancer and fortune teller, and

Herman the German, the bishop of Astorga, who arrived in the city in 1240, twenty years later. Scot's translation of a book on concentric spheres by Aristotle was later used by the thirteenth-century English philosopher Roger Bacon. Herman, too, translated some of Averroes' writings, including his commentary on Aristotle's *Ethics* and works by Avicenna. The third member of the translation team was a local, Marcus of Toledo, whom Jiménez de Rada allotted the task of creating a new Latin version of the Koran and a translation of the *Aqida*, a theological treatise ascribed to the Berber reformer Ibn Tumart.

We know that the translators worked in pairs at this time – one skilled in Arabic, who was often a Jew, and one skilled in Latin. The Jewish or Mozarabic scholar translated the Muslim works orally into the vernacular, and the Christian converted it into a written Latin text. This process highlights the vital role of Jews and Mozarabs in the translation project, their common language being the local vernacular Spanish, yet many of them remain anonymous. Although the two great patrons of the translation enterprise, Peter the Venerable and Archbishop Jiménez de Rada, never used the translated texts explicitly as anti-Muslim propaganda, their political and religious leanings left no doubt as to their moral position. Yet the collaboration between Muslims, Jews and Christians in the transformation of Arabic learning into Latin scholarship bore no trace of hostility or antagonism, a characteristic that was to become a defining feature of the third great proliferation of translation later in the thirteenth century.

From Arabic to Castilian: Translation at the Court of Alfonso X the Wise

When King Alfonso X of Castile, León and Galicia came to the throne in 1254, he was monarch of a domain that extended from the northern coast as far south as his beloved Seville. He was a man of great political and cultural ambition, who admired Islamic learning and lifestyle, and he founded 'general schools of Latin and Arabic' ('escuelas generales de latin e de arabigo'[5]) in Seville in the year of his accession to the throne. He ruled in the style of the Platonic poet king, espoused the idea of wisdom as the vital ingredient of harmonious government, and surrounded himself with a cosmopolitan court of scholars who cooperated in the production of monumental works of history as well as translations from Arabic. Alfonso aspired to unite and educate his kingdom so that it was on a par with Muslim culture, and he aimed to give it international standing through the use of vernacular Castilian as the new national language. Now, patronage of translation passed from the Church to the royal court, where the king's scriptorium became a government office and its translators court officials. It became a Castilian institution that represented the cultural supremacy so crucial to Alfonso's political programme.

Alfonso himself took an active part in the translating, editing and polishing draft versions of texts that focused on Greek and Arabic astronomy and astrology, which could be used as tools of political control. Unlike the programme of Archbishop Raymond, philosophical treatises were avoided, as were religious works. Alfonso's scholars produced great compilations and miscellanies, such as *Picatrix*, on talismanic magic, originally written by the tenth-century Andalusian scholar al-Qurtubi, and *The Lapidary* (*Lapidario*), on the magical properties of precious stones. These two works were translated by the Jewish scholar Yehuda ben Moshe, the king's personal physician. The team of translators was fifteen strong, five of them Arabic-speaking Jews, plus ten Christians, three of them local Spaniards, seven foreigners, and only one Muslim converted to Catholicism, Bernard the Arab. They acted not just as translators, but as compilers, organizers, editors and authors, and used a similar process to that employed in Jiménez de Rada's time. An Arabic speaker gave a direct spoken translation into Castilian, which was then written down, while a Christian cleric converted it into written Latin simultaneously.

The miniatures in the illuminated manuscript of Alfonso X's own poetical composition, the *Songs to the Virgin Mary* (*Cantigas de santa María*), show Christians, Jews and Arab Muslims working together in the great scriptorium, and sometimes depict Alfonso instructing his scribes. Yet the circumstances of their collaboration were complex and hindered by certain limitations. These thirteenth-century paintings portray a degree of close cultural contact between people of the three faiths which is contradicted by a polemical propaganda, similar to that used by the Cluniacs, which emerges in the historical and legal works created during Alfonso's reign. Those works show no sense of tolerant mediation between Islam and Christianity, often a gross ignorance of Islam itself and sometimes downright hostility. Relations between Muslims and Christians were based on notions of opposition and contrast, on an awareness of otherness born of a society that lived on a frontier defined not solely by geography, but also by religion. The discrepancy between the everyday living together in relative tolerance in Alfonso's reign and his anti-Muslim political agenda reveals how religious understanding failed to exist, while intellectual admiration and respect among those of different faiths still prevailed in scholarly circles.

To a degree, Alfonso's transition to an egalitarian policy that made learning more accessible to his Castilian subjects had the effect of limiting the resonance of Islamic learning beyond the Pyrenees. The essentially international nature of Archbishop Raymond's team of translators was lost in Alfonso's time, as over half of his linguists came from the Hispanic peninsula. But his fostering of Castilian as the main language of higher learning, law and science enabled Christian Spain to take a prominent place on the European stage.

The Light from the East: Transmission, Transference and Transposition

Despite, or maybe because of, the Christian Crusades against the Muslims, western Europe experienced one of the greatest transfers of cultural knowledge in world history. Over a period of 200 years, Spain and Italy were vehicles for the transmission of lost or unknown Greek and Arab learning, mainly via the city of Toledo, to north-western Europe. Spain's primordial role in this crossover is rarely acknowledged, but it was vitally important to the history of western civilization; without it, Europe would have become culturally ostracized and the scientific and cultural development of the early modern

Renaissance in western Europe would have been greatly hindered. The great intellectual endeavour in Toledo that produced this transference of learning has parallels with an equivalent venture in the House of Wisdom of ninth-century Baghdad. The House of Wisdom was founded to safeguard and translate the knowledge of earlier civilizations, which in turn served to impel the creation of a strong Arab Muslim civilization. The aims of the translation programme in Toledo were very similar: to rediscover Greek and Latin scholarship translated into Arabic, spread the knowledge of Arabic science and philosophy, and bring enlightenment to Christian Europe. Both centres were intellectual magnets that attracted the brightest minds of their times. Yet there is one significant difference between them. The scholars of Baghdad donned the mantle of ancient learning to acquire the status of a great civilization by absorbing its cultural and intellectual past. The Greek, Latin and even Persian scholarship they revived came from civilizations that were essentially defunct in terms of political and religious dominion. The Arabs then added their own contributions to science, philosophy and theology. The scenario was quite different in the case of the savants of Toledo, who bathed themselves in the light of an Islamic Arab civilization that is still alive today.

The transfer of learning was a familiar idea in the Middle Ages, when it was known as *translatio studii*. History was conceived of as a succession of transfers of knowledge from one place and time to another, and it was closely connected to the dominance of empire. In the case of the Muslim empire centred on Baghdad, its imperial power was strengthened by the re-establishment of the intellectual heritage of the defeated cultures within its own political framework. When Charlemagne established his Carolingian Empire, it could be seen as the transference of Roman imperial rule to another people, an idea that later gained momentum as leaders of the medieval Church appropriated the pagan culture of Greece and Rome into the Latin culture of Catholic Europe. The transfer of learning related to the written word – to translating, commentary and interpreting – and was believed to move always in a westward direction, from Greece, to Rome, then to France.

The idea of the westwards transfer of Arab learning is less familiar, but its consequences are important and concern the close link between empire and learning. References to imperialist ideas began to surface in the passing metaphors of translators, strikingly in a letter from St Jerome to the Roman senator Pammachius, where Jerome describes a fellow translator 'like some conqueror, he (the translator) marched the original text, a captive, into his native language.'[6] The image of ransacking and taking the spoils of conquest appears much later, in a letter Daniel of Morley wrote on the subject of translation to his friend John of Oxford, around 1175: 'Although not numbered among the faithful, some of the gentiles' words are full of faith and should be incorporated into our teaching . . . Let us then borrow from them and, with God's help and command, rob the pagan philosophers of their wisdom and eloquence. Let us take from the unfaithful so as to enrich ourselves fully with the spoils'.[7] Daniel's letter casts light on the surprising attitude of some Christian scholars to the translation of Arabic wisdom into Latin. It suggests the ancient idea of *translatio imperii* still held sway as Latin Christian churchmen and intellectuals sought to increase the power of Catholic Europe by means of the absorption of Muslim knowledge into its own political and religious constitution.

The transfer of Muslim learning to Christian Europe involved a mighty migration of Arabic books, people and knowledge, whose secrets were deciphered and transformed into Latin and the vernacular languages of Europe. That collaborative achievement gave translation the power to shape culture. In medieval Spain, it influenced the evolution of western civilization by acting as the shaping power of one culture upon another. The translators themselves could never have envisaged how far-reaching and pervasive the work they produced would be. To translate a great work, or even a minor one, for posterity is one thing. To influence western European thought is another. This influence is arguably the most profound product of the fusion of East and West in the medieval Spanish peninsula. Yet it came at the price of an unexpected and ironic reversal of fate, an ill-starred inversion of the status quo. Christian Europe, which had lagged so far behind the brilliant European civilization of Muslim al-Andalus, harnessed its learning to grow strong and build an empire of its own that would in turn assert its dominion over the Islamic civilization of the continent.

Chapter 13

Granada: A Place of Destiny

'Granada strikes me as a pleasant, extensive country, one of the largest in al-Andalus. It is the capital of the Muslim king of al Andalus and his royal residence, and has a marvellous position, splendid buildings, it is lovely, agreeable and in an admirable location. I saw many kinds of craftsmanship there, and it resembles Damascus in Syria.'

Abd al-Basit, 1465

'Granada is a bride whose tiara, jewels and garments are the flowers, her tunic is the Generalife, her mirror the peace of strangers, her pendant earrings pearls of dew.'

Ibn Zamrak

The Islamic civilization that had existed in Europe for half a millennium was on the brink of extinction by the thirteenth century, as the clash of faiths on the frontiers of al-Andalus and Christian Spain threatened to destroy the land of cultural diversity created by the Muslims. As King Ferdinand III of Castile rode into Cordoba in June 1236 to consecrate the Great Mosque as a cathedral dedicated to the Virgin Mary, the relentless progress southwards of the Christian Reconquest seemed inexorable. The irony was that Muhammad ibn al-Ahmar, the very man who helped him defeat Cordoba's emir Ibn Hud, became the first sultan of a new Muslim dynasty and established the city of Granada as the capital of his state just one year later. The Granadan emirate of Sultan Muhammad I secured the presence of Islam in Spain for another quarter of a millennium, just at the point when its future seemed doomed.

'Conqueror by the grace of God': Ibn al-Ahmar and the Islamic State of the Nasrids

On 18 April 1232, after Friday prayers at the mosque in the small town of Arjona in the rolling hills near Jaén, a local chief named Muhammad ibn Yusuf ibn Nasr ibn al-Ahmar rose up against the emir of al-Andalus, Ibn Hud, and boldly proclaimed himself ruler of a small area that included Baeza to the east, Guadix to the south and the city of Jaén itself. Just five years later, in 1237, the city of Granada became his capital, and the Nasrid dynasty was born, its identity taken from the new chief's resonant name of Nasr, meaning 'Victory'. Born into the clan known as the Banu Nasr, this daring fighter proclaimed himself emir of the Muslims of al-Andalus, taking the title of Muhammad I and creating a dynastic line that would rule the city and province of Granada for more than 250 years. Chivalrous, mystical and charismatic, a warrior who could wield a mace weighing ten kilos in battle as if it weighed nothing, his military prowess was a vital asset at a time when the Christians were pushing ever further south. The fourteenth-century Andalusian historian Ibn al-Jatib describes him as 'a valiant warrior, a hero, a tough man, of great strength, who disdained a life of calm and leisure and preferred simplicity and poverty.'[1] Ibn al-Ahmar, a farm labourer, had no prestigious family lineage, though he soon acquired one from Muslim genealogists, who linked him to the first caliph of Islam after the Prophet.

Granada was already ancient in 1237, with its old citadel or *alcazaba* at the heart of the fortified city built on the hill on the right bank of the river Darro. The Berber Zirids had reinforced the old ramparts, taking them to the edge of steep natural slopes that made potential attacks very difficult. By the early thirteenth century, Granada had developed into a large urban centre, with its medina – the traditional Arab walled city, centred on a castle or citadel – divided in two by the river. At the start of the twelfth century, if not before, the main mosque of Granada stood in what is now the Calle de los Oficios, in the city centre, and was said to be very beautiful, with marble columns, and pillar heads and doors brought specially from Cordoba.

Such was the setting for the first Nasrid emir's entrance into the city. One Friday during Ramadan 1238, he came to the outskirts of Granada at dusk, humbly dressed, with the intention of arriving the following morning, but changed his mind and carried on through the city gates at sunset. The early fourteenth-century Moroccan historian Ibn Idhari describes the moment, with eyewitness details from Abu Muhammed al-Basti: 'I saw the day of his entry into Granada with my own eyes. He wore a tunic of striped cloth, torn at the shoulders. When he stopped at the gate of the Aljama mosque in the Alcazaba, the muezzin was calling the faithful to evening prayer . . . Then he reached Badis's [the Zirid sultan's] palace, his way lit by candles.' Ibn Idhari adds that al-Ahmar had girded his sword, and, with torches burning at the gate of the Zirid palace, he entered with his chief ministers like a bridegroom hastening to meet his bride.[2]

In the first year of his reign, Muhammad I embarked on an undertaking which became the symbolic and representative hallmark of the Nasrid era, and an iconic and defining feature of the history of Granada: the city's new fortress, the Alhambra, meaning 'the red one'. For a while, the emir stayed in the old fortress known as the Alcazaba, with the idea that he could live alongside some of his subjects, but he decided that this did not befit a sultan, who should instead live apart from his people. He thoroughly inspected the site of the Alhambra, marking the foundations of the building and organizing the excavations. In less than a year, tall defensive structures had been raised, supplied with water from the Darro, carried there by a specially created irrigation channel. There were stores for food and arms, and a public treasury in this place that had served as a refuge for rebels and leaders since the earliest times of al-Andalus. The walled city of the Alhambra, with its flowing water and lofty fastness, had come into being.

Throughout his reign, Muhammad I cultivated close ties with North Africa. He adopted the honorary title 'al-Galib bi-Llah' ('Conqueror by the grace of God'), the future motto of the Nasrid dynasty, reflecting the pious yet combative character of the first Nasrid emir, aligning him with the ethos of the Almohads and matching both the role his dynasty assumed and the time in which they lived, fraught with violence, oppression and domination.

By the time Muhammad I made the city the capital of his new Islamic state in 1238, Granada both looked like and functioned as a city in Muslim North Africa, rather than in Christian Spain. The status of the city created two different categories of Muslims in the Iberian peninsula at this time: first, the numerous Muslims who lived as subjects of the Christian kingdoms of Castile, Aragon and Navarre, known as Mudejars; and, second, those who lived in the small, crowded, independent Muslim kingdom of Granada, who spoke Arabic and were part of the Islamic world. Although most of the Iberian peninsula was under Christian rule by 1248, from Muhammad I's time onwards, there is no record of native Christians anywhere in Muslim Andalusia. Those who do get mentioned are slaves, merchants, refugees or resident foreigners. As a result, the culture of Nasrid Granada was purely Arabic in its expression. The living side by side of three different religious communities – known as *convivencia* – which had been such an important feature of Islamic Spain in earlier centuries, was entirely absent from Granada from this time until 1492.

Christians and Muslims were simultaneously attracted to and repulsed by each other, and this magnetism left an indelible mark on relations between the Catholic kings of Spain and the Nasrid sultans. Those long-established contradictions between love and hate, collaboration and confrontation were uppermost in the dealings between Granada and Castile until 1492. Muhammad I's sights were always set on seeking the best way to prolong the Muslim presence in Spain and Portugal and increase the power of his realm, and that often involved shrewd strategic diplomacy.

In the next decade, Muhammad I became the most powerful

Muslim ruler in the peninsula. His brilliant statesmanship ushered in an era of understanding and alliance with his Christian counterpart Ferdinand of Castile, at a time when Granada was newly established and vulnerable. There had been hostility between them, incursions into each other's lands, culminating in Ferdinand's capture of Muhammad I's home town of Arjona in 1244. Two years later, the Muslim emir took the decision to relinquish the city of Jaén to Castile, upon which a treaty was signed, bilateral and symbiotic, a pact that brought a twenty-year peace. It enabled Ibn al-Ahmar to define the boundaries of his kingdom and stabilize and strengthen his position. The reality involved a promise to serve Ferdinand in peace and war, attend the parliament of Castile and pay a large tribute over two decades, which became the king's main source of income. The Castilians saw the surrender in feudal terms, which demanded that the emir kiss Ferdinand's hand as a symbol of vassalage, yet no such word existed or was acknowledged in the Islamic Arabic vocabulary of that time. For them, the peace treaty meant an act of conciliation between two equal powers, but it set a pattern of subservience which would be repeated throughout the existence of the Islamic state of Granada.

Ibn al-Ahmar's promise of service to Castile obliged him to take part in Ferdinand's conquest of Seville in 1248–9, when the emir's troops supported the Christians against their fellow Muslims. There appeared to be a genuine mutual respect on both sides. Ferdinand was greatly admired by the Muslims, who both feared him and loved him for his loyalty towards them. When the king died in 1252, Muhammad I ordered his emirate to go into mourning, sending a large number of candles to Seville to burn beside his tomb. This was not an act of disloyalty to the Muslim people. In this fluid landscape of alliances and reversals, the underlying motive for these struggles was power and territory, and religion was a pretext – there were no Muslim leaders who had not done deals with the Christians.

The Nasrid dynasty was destined to fall prey to a series of repeating political and dynastic patterns arising from a history beset by intense disorder, conflict, betrayal and murder. When Muhammad

I took the title of emir and leader of believers in 1232, that title implied an absolute dominion over his subjects, though it was also modulated by the power of the leaders of clan-based social groups or lineages. One aspect which became a critical complication was the absolute power of the emir to designate his successor. There was no written law on the subject, yet it was logical in Sunni Muslim political tradition for the eldest son to succeed his father, a right dramatically disputed on occasions. The visual reinforcement of Muhammad I's power was a heraldic shield with a band across it bearing the Nasrid motto, said to have been granted to the emir by Ferdinand III. The colour of the standard, and the sealing wax, seals and paper of documents from his chancellery were red, in recognition of his name, al-Ahmar, meaning 'the Red'. It was a fearful omen of the bloody future of his line.

The turbulent conflicts on both sides of the frontier between Castile and Granada in the thirteenth century were reflected in the character and reign of its first emir. The military nature of his personality and the pronounced military purpose of the earliest institutions in the province of Granada, including the role of the Alhambra as a fortress, were the corollaries of a hundred years of warfare. Muhammad I's childhood as a farmworker and his dedication to frontier fighting had left him with little interest in intellectual life until he took on the role of sultan, at which point he realized that, politically, his status demanded his patronage of chroniclers and poets to record his sovereignty and write his eulogies. Poetry became important propaganda that gave authority and legitimacy to his policies and government. What began as a political pose was the precursor of Granada's evolution into the main intellectual point of reference of the realm, focused on the exquisitely elegant main mosque, with its white marble columns and running water. Under the sultan's aegis, religion and Islamic law were studied, along with Arabic language and the arts of poetry and prose writing.

Ibn al-Ahmar, Muhammad I, died in January 1273, in the Alhambra, at the age of seventy-eight, after falling from his horse, and was buried in the cemetery on the hillside. He had reigned wisely for almost forty-four years, over an emirate created from nothing, which was to play the decisive role in the history of Islam in the west. All that came after stemmed from Ibn al-Ahmar, frontier chieftain, trailblazing sultan and precursor of a new Islamic cultural centre in western Europe. He was the epitome of his time and of the history of Granada itself, and his life story reflects the texture and quality of the relations between Granada and Castile, Christians and Muslims. Ibn al-Ahmar came out of nowhere to forge a relatively safe refuge for Islam in the peninsula, built on perhaps unheroic but crucial compromises with the enemy, and hindered by discords caused by the alienation of his supporters. In the Alhambra, he left a building that would become the iconic symbol of Muslim Spain, yet his legacy would still reflect a need for perpetual vigilance in dealing with the Christians, and a willingness to compromise and switch alliances as political power shifted, all and anything required to maintain Granada's survival.

The Red Fort: The Alhambra as Microcosm of Islam in Western Europe

The Alhambra crowns the Sabika hill, an oasis of perfumed gardens and flowing waters, evoking the image of paradise penned by the great court poet Ibn Zamrak. The famous red fort is a site of power – architectural, political, religious, historical and cultural – and a permanent reminder of Granada's incarnation and heritage as a Muslim city, encapsulated in this supreme image of an Islamic fortress. To a remarkable degree, its evolution as a building matches the rise and fall of the final Islamic dynasty of medieval western Europe and hints at the ambivalent interchange between the Muslims of the state of Granada and the Christians of Castile. Like their relationship, that great walled citadel is not what it seems. It harbours secrets, illusions, mysteries; it is a place of the hidden and unexpected, of strange contrasts, contradictions and ambiguities.

A satellite view of the Alhambra would show us the palatine city on a craggy outcrop of the Sierra Nevada mountains, almost unassailable from the north and west, while, to the south-east, we would see a narrow, deep ravine separating the spur from its mountain. The aerial perspective reveals the Alhambra's superb natural defensive position, as well as its reliance on cisterns or aqueducts to store its water, making it vulnerable to attack. Viewed from the ground, and from a distance, the Alhambra inspires awe in its monolithic majesty, and its imposing military configuration speaks to us of conquest and victory. The great red fortress is a symbol of the power of the Nasrid dynasty who created it, and it watches over the city and interacts with it as a dominating Islamic presence.

Few Christians ever saw the Alhambra at close hand until the end of Muslim rule. To them, it was awe-inspiring, a prize viewed from afar whose possession they desired. The fifteenth-century Spanish ballad *Abenámar* recounts how King John II of Castile brought his army within sight of Granada in 1431 and marvelled at the buildings rising on the distant hill before him. When his Moorish captain Abenámar tells him they are the Alhambra and its mosque, John exclaims, 'Granada, if you wished, I would marry you, / and give you Cordoba and Seville as a dowry' ('*Granada, si tu quisiesses, contigo me casaría: / darte yo en arras y dote a Córdoba y a Sevilla*').[3] This ancient poem reveals how the Christians associated Granada and its buildings with femininity, and how, despite being on enemy territory, a Christian king could admire a city and culture alien and inaccessible to most Spanish Catholics. Much later, at the end of the fifteenth century, King Ferdinand II of Aragon and Queen Isabella I of Castile would also admire the Alhambra from afar, just days before they conquered the city.

Yet that imposing exterior hides the secrets of an astonishing interior, of a citadel transfigured into a palace, a place of mystery, camouflage and ambiguity. Perfect proportion and symmetry suggest order and harmony, which is constantly unsettled by a perplexing spatial complexity. There is the disturbing sensation of being in a maze. Courts and rooms are set at odd angles to each other, with access through inconspicuous doors or gloomy passages, and winding, offset approaches lead to inner chambers. No portals or vistas lead from one part to another. For the visitor, this dislocation of one's spatial awareness is disorientating; there is no sense of the overall ground plan. Perhaps, in Nasrid times, it created in outsiders a feeling of vulnerability, of potential surprise at any moment. The sultan was inaccessible, and therefore powerful. Only those in the know could navigate the entrances and exits to inner courtyards, creating a suspicion of intrigue heightened by interior passageways and shifting levels. This intentional confusion is mirrored below ground in the sixteen kilometres of underground galleries, some leading to dungeons, others to secret passageways down which the sultan could flee in dire circumstances.

The Alhambra's architectural design speaks clearly of the obsession with defence of a dynasty of rulers who lived in perpetual fear of attack. As if in defiance of this ever-present threat, the Nasrids created a palace of mythical style and opulence, a dreamlike setting for the pleasure and refuge of those who lived there, but conceived on an intimate, human scale, lit by night at ground level by vast standing candelabras to welcome the returning sultan. In a similar way to medieval European cathedrals, no plans exist of its design, nor records of its architects and builders, the anonymous masters who worked their magic with running and still water, reflections of light and shadow, scented and colourful plants, marble, stucco and wood.

Sultan Muhammad I's inspired vision had brought the Alhambra into being, and, when he died, his third son, Muhammad II, reigned for almost thirty years, until 1302. Unlike his father, who had been a soldier, not a scholar, Muhammad II was highly educated, interested in medicine, astrology and philosophy, and wrote poetry and music. He broadened the group of learned men who had served the first sultan's political ambitions, and created a literary court at the Alhambra whose sages aspired to emulate the immense learning of the Muslim, Jewish and Christian scholars at the court of the Castilian king Alfonso X. Even so, Muhammad's relations with Christian Castile at this time were soured by Alfonso X's deception of him in Seville, where both monarchs pledged their friendship, while Alfonso connived with the sultan's adversaries, the Banu Ashqilula. Then, suddenly, in April 1302, the second sultan of Granada died in gruesome circumstances, amid rumours that he had been poisoned by a cake made for him by his son and heir, Muhammad III. The reign of this third Nasrid sultan, recorded as a superstitious, unpredictable man, with a liking for brutish cruelty, was bedevilled by an instability and violence which would last for over a hundred years, creating a paradigm of bloodshed and savagery that saw four sultans come and go in short order, culminating in the murder of the sixth Nasrid ruler, Muhammad IV, as he was returning to Granada from Gibraltar in 1333.

*

The evil spell was broken in the reign of Sultan Yusuf I (1333–54), when a glorious age of Nasrid cultural achievement began. The arts flourished and many of the foremost writers of the time graced the royal court. It was in Yusuf's reign that the Alhambra came into its full glory, when the monumental Gate of Justice was built on his order, as well as the Comares Palace, which contained rooms for royal receptions and had an enormous rectangular patio, fountain and wooden roof representing the Islamic conception of Heaven, one of the supreme examples of Nasrid carpentry. At the height of a plague epidemic, in the spring of 1349, Yusuf inaugurated the Madrasa Yusufiyya, whose teachers specialized in Islamic law, Sufism, logic, mathematics, medicine, astronomy and the literary arts. The Muslim passion for knowledge was not dimmed by the dire circumstances of conflict and pestilence, and there was no sense that Hispanic Islam was moribund, for it was at this time that the kingdom of Granada became an important seat of learning which generated the last significant scientific, historiographical and literary works of al-Andalus. These included a number of practical treatises on the plague that advised on hygiene and how to avoid contact with people, and agricultural works that were effectively landscaping manuals giving instructions on levelling land, gathering water and designing gardens in relation to their houses. The Nasrids continued to expand Muslim expertise in astronomy, preparing tables and producing advanced instruments. Before Yusuf's reign, Muhammad al-Qallusi (d. 1308) wrote a book on the movement of the sun, which still survives, while Ibn al-Raqqam (d. 1315) introduced the navigational compass to al-Andalus and calculated Granada's modern latitude for the first time.

Yusuf I's patronage of a new flowering of Muslim scholarship overlaid a backdrop of constant political and military strife. Like his predecessors, the sultan made a truce with Castile, and then entered into an agreement with both the Castilians and the North African Marinids, situating Granada as a pawn wedged between these two strong powers. The most disturbing reversal of the Muslim cause in Spain before 1492 took place during his reign, in the Battle of Salado of 1340, where his troops were roundly beaten by Christian armies. Their victory came down to superior weaponry, as the Castilians pounded the enemy with heavy cavalry charges that devastated the lightly armed and manoeuvrable Muslim cavalry. Two years later, the Castilian king Alfonso XI's crusading zeal inspired him to have another go at capturing Algeciras in 1342–4, which ended in a ten-year truce. Once again, the machinery of war was crucial, this time in favour of the Muslims. The siege of Algeciras was the first major engagement in the Iberian peninsula, and one of the earliest anywhere, in which cannon were used. The mighty guns were introduced by the Muslims, not the Christians, as the latter made out in their own chronicles.

Ten years later, Yusuf I's enlightened reign had a terrible end. As he was praying in the Great Mosque in Granada in 1354, an assassin, described as a lunatic in Arabic accounts, stabbed him to death. It seemed the Nasrids had a curse of violent, bloody death upon them, yet Yusuf's genius as a ruler enabled his kingdom to last another 150 years and established its reputation as one of the great sites of Islamic cultural achievement in the world.

*

The interweaving pattern of political upheaval and cultural evolution continued in the reign of Yusuf's son, Muhammad V. The Alhambra became a hotbed of sedition and treachery as the new emir was overthrown by two successive rivals for the Nasrid throne, prompting him to invoke his close allegiances with both Castile and the Marinids in Fez to quash members of his own clan. His relative Ismail II ousted the sultan in a palace coup in 1359, upon which Muhammad V fled to exile at the Marinid court in Fez for two years. When Muhammad VI the Red, a nephew of Yusuf I, took the throne in 1360, the usurped Muhammad V, a staunch vassal of Castile in true Nasrid fashion, received the help of King Peter I of Castile against his usurper. True to his nickname, 'the Cruel', Peter imprisoned Muhammad VI, then led him out to a great field in Seville mounted on an ass and clad in a scarlet robe, where he ran him through with his lance. Muhammad V finally won back the kingdom of Granada in April 1362 and negotiated a series of truces which led to the longest period of peace Granada had experienced in its history, during which he reigned for nearly thirty years, until his death at the age of fifty-three. Soon after his return, in 1365, the far-sighted sultan had the Maristan of Granada built, the first European hospital to make provision for the mentally ill.

Under his direction, the Alhambra took on the appearance it has today; the Court of the Lions and many of the beautiful royal buildings whose style has never been equalled were the work of his architects and craftsmen. Muhammad V's relations with the Christians and the Marinids were not merely political but involved a degree of cultural exchange, and the Palace of the Lions, built after his return from Fez, bore some of the qualities of Marinid architecture. The exchange worked both ways. Muhammad's ally Peter the Cruel extended the Alcázar palace in Seville in a blatantly Nasrid style, and the sultan sent him some of his artisans to help with the construction.

As the Alhambra was transformed into its full glory, the written word came to the fore. The second emir Muhammad II's love of poetry lived on at the Nasrid court, along with other kinds of writing, including the Arabic *maqama*, a form of narrative story written in rhymed prose, which had later echoes in the complex metaphors and language of Spanish baroque poetry and in picaresque narratives across Europe. The court was graced by scholars of both sexes, including Umm al-Hasan, the talented daughter of a doctor from nearby Loja, who was not only an esteemed poet but an expert in readings of the Koran and a student of medicine. But poetry reigned supreme, and the phenomenon of mural poetry, which evolved in the lifetime of Muhammad II, was unique in the Muslim world of the west. Visual art merges with the word in almost all the rooms and walls of the Alhambra, often in a form that endows the building itself with a first-person voice that speaks to us directly in verse.

The Tragic Tale of the Scholar and the Poet

The saga of minister poets, often viziers to the sultan or other high officials, began with Ibn al-Jayyab (1274–1349), secretary to the royal chancellery, who introduced the custom of inscribing his poetry on the walls of the Alhambra. He praised the Nasrid sultans for nearly half a century, until he died peacefully in bed, aged seventy-five. His death saw the rise of his disciple, Sultan Muhammad V's first vizier, Lisan al-Din ibn al-Khatib. Born into a Yemini aristocratic family, he succeeded al-Jayyab as court poet and became head of the chancellery. This office, founded by Muhammad II, was where state documents were written on red paper, denoting the Nasrid line. As court poet, Ibn al-Khatib wrote *qasidas* – poems of praise for official celebrations, the circumcision of emirs, military campaigns and funerals – and *muwashshahs* – poems about love's cruelty and hopelessness, set to music.

Ibn al-Khatib's literary talents were not solely those of a poet; his remarkable scholarship, range of knowledge and prolific output of sixty or so works encompassed travel writing, treatises on political theory and medicine, biographical dictionaries and histories. His complex, highly ornate official letters contrast with the scientific stringency of his treatise on the plague, written about 1362 and perhaps inspired by Avicenna, in which he explored the idea of transmission of the disease through contagion, 500 years before the first vaccinations against infectious diseases became widespread. His crowning glory was the great historical work *The Complete History of Granada* (*al-Ihata fi akhbar Gharnata*) of 1369, which tells his own life story, describes the city and kingdom of Granada, and recounts its history.

The Andalusian genius Ibn Zamrak composed the majority of the Alhambra's mural poetry. Brilliant, devoted to study and the pupil of a glittering generation of North African and Granadan scholars, he harboured political aspirations alongside his literary ambitions. He became secretary of the North African Marinid prince Abu Salim Ibrahim, until Ibn al-Khatib found him a niche in the Granadan royal administration. Both men were on excellent terms with each other, to the extent that Ibn al-Khatib dedicated his great history of Granada to his pupil, who in turn wrote eulogies about his mentor. Ibn Zamrak is considered the greatest poet of the Alhambra. His verses appear in the Patio of the Myrtles, the Hall of the Two Sisters, and on the bowl of the fountain in the Court of the Lions. Expert in the secrets of cadence and symmetry, his grammatical perfection and impeccable musicality make him a master of his art, unique as a poet in witnessing the completion of the palace buildings. His lyrical descriptions of the place, though conventional, are often sublime, evoking the natural world, gardens, flowers and life's pleasures, which were standard topics of Arabic poetry. He often expressed his preference for artifice over nature, which combined in perfect measure in his eulogy of the city:

> [Granada] is a bride whose garland is the Sabika,
> And whose jewels and garments are the flowers . . .
> Her throne is the Generalife;
> Her mirror, the surface of the pools,
> Her earrings, the pearls of dew.[4]

Ibn Zamrak showed his deep gratitude to and affection for the man who educated and employed him, but, amid suspicions that Ibn al-Khatib was plotting to overthrow him, Muhammad V replaced him immediately with Ibn Zamrak as chief vizier, who achieved the defining goal of his political career. Arrested on trumped-up charges of heresy and betrayed by his own beloved pupil, Ibn al-Khatib was murdered in a Moroccan prison. But, when Muhammed V died in 1391, Ibn Zamrak lost his job as chief vizier and, one night, probably in 1393, the sultan's thugs attacked him while he was at home reading the Koran with his two sons. All three of them were murdered in front of his wives, daughters and servants. One terrible assassination was avenged by another, as intrigue, treachery and ambition destroyed the lives of two exceptional scholars, and politics ultimately extinguished Arab Andalusian poetry, one of the brightest lights in western Muslim culture.

The Waning of the Crescent Moon in Western Europe

At the rise of the fifteenth century, the Islamic state of Granada was unique in Europe. Isolated from the rest of the peninsula by its mountain frontiers and governed by a Muslim dynasty whose rule had never extended beyond those confines, this Arabic-speaking emirate on the edge of Europe mirrored the customs and even institutions of the Marinid dynasty of North Africa, with which it had strong ties. Before, Granadans had rubbed shoulders with the Christians to the extent that their ways of dressing and the arms they used looked similar, and Muslims had rarely worn turbans in al-Andalus. But now Granadan troops wore Moorish armour and golden helmets, used Arab saddles, leather shields and light Moorish lances. Isolation also determined the layout of the emirate's capital city, the narrow streets, labyrinthine passageways, mighty walls and entry gates of which all spelled out a primordial need for defence against attack. They signified a society closed off from the outside world, living with the ever-present threat of assault and persecution born of the long history of Christian reconquest, a threat which had pushed the boundaries of the Islamic kingdoms further and further south, until only Granada remained. The comparatively tolerant coexistence of the peoples of three faiths that had been a feature of al-Andalus was no longer the case inside the emirate. While the frontier between Granada and the Christian kingdoms was still a place of barter, trade and diplomatic negotiation, as well as skirmishes for territory, the last Muslim emirate in Europe had hardened its relations with Catholic Spain. There was no indigenous Christian population at all, although there were still Christian residents, well established and tolerated, but they were and remained outsiders – merchants, political and ideological refugees, outcasts and, above all, captives. Many religious renegades, or *elches*, who had converted to Islam and escaped from Castile, found asylum and important positions in the Nasrid army and at court. There were no Christians native to Granada because the Mozarabs had disappeared from the area before the emirate was formed. Nasrid Granada was a city of two, not three, faiths: Islam and Judaism. North of the frontier, people of the three monotheist religions still cohabited, but never on equal terms, for there had never been equal terms on offer anywhere in the peninsula at any time.

After the great Muhammad V died in 1391, sultans came and went at a bewildering rate, and their history reads rather like something from tales of the *Arabian Nights*. The Nasrids continued to indulge their fatal predilection for palace intrigue and bloody violence, while the strength of the Christian kingdom of Castile was growing. Castile had recovered from the Black Death, which had ravaged the peninsula from mid-century, and was developing the formidable power which would eventually lead it to dominate both Europe and the New World. The skilful diplomacy that had previously enabled the kingdom of Granada to stand up to Castile grew less effective as the Christians began to wield their military muscle, refusing to accept the kind of easy truces made in the past. The Christian campaigns involved horrific violence. In 1457, a Swabian knight, Jorge de Ehingen, travelled to Spain in the service of Duke Albert of Austria. He recorded one of their ruinous raids: 'We had to assault most of the fortresses and towns and put all the Moors to death, and their assistants and servants were ordered to knife to death the women and children, which they did.' In his words, they crossed the kingdom of Granada, 'bringing blood and fire to everything we found.'[5]

Sultan Sa'd was fifty-five when he acceded to the Nasrid throne in 1453, supported by the new Castilian king Henry IV after he came to the throne just a year later in 1454. But when Sa'd finally took possession of the Alhambra in 1455, he promptly rejected all Castilian demands for truce, vassalage and tribute, in spite of benefiting from their support. In a bizarre turn of fate, Sa'd was overthrown by his own son, Abu l-Hasan, in a midnight coup in late August 1464. Banished to Salobreña castle under house arrest, he died there on 20 April 1465. Abu l-Hasan had his father's cruel, warlike nature, and a weakness for sensual indulgence. He favoured fighting over diplomacy and refused to pay the tribute which denoted subservience to Castile – because, he claimed, the places in Granada where coins were minted were forging lance-heads to make war.

This was the state of affairs between the Islamic emirate and the Catholic kingdoms as the balance of power began to shift permanently in favour of the Christians. The Nasrid era had seen a glorious, late flowering of cultural creativity and learning that had brought the Alhambra into being in its symbolic synthesis of classical and eastern motifs, akin to that ancient synthesis of Greek and eastern knowledge that took place in Baghdad, Cordoba and Cairo long ago. The old, traditional forms of Arabic poetry had come to life, as well as new scientific and philosophical knowledge, but the collaboration and camaraderie between scholars across the religious divide that had prevailed earlier in Toledo was non-existent. The Alhambra was not solely a monument to Muslim architecture and civilization, a palace of pleasure and delight, but also a military fortress against the enemy – one that manifested the history of relations between the Muslims and Christians of western Europe in stone.

Chapter 14

1492: A Year that Changed the World

'Sir, these are the keys of this paradise. I and those inside it are yours.'

Sultan Muhammad XI of Granada, Boabdil

'That January by strength of arms I saw the flags of your royal majesties placed atop the towers of the Alhambra. And I saw the Moorish king leave through the city's gates.'

Christopher Columbus

The third watershed in the history of Muslims and Christians in Europe fell on 2 January 1492, when Abu Abdallah Muhammad b. Ali, Muhammad XI, known as Boabdil, the last Muslim sultan of Granada and head of the Nasrid dynasty, handed over the keys of his city to the Christian rulers of Castile and Aragon. The first great cycle of European Islam came to an end and a new era of domination by the Christian faith began in the west of the continent. It was a time of transition from a society of diverse religions, races and languages to one with a single faith and a single official language, a society bent on purging all traces of racial and religious otherness. A veneer of apparent national unity was won at the cost of the terrible pain of exile, upheaval and betrayal experienced by the Muslims and Jews of the Iberian peninsula, and the sense of tragic and irreparable loss that overcame them. Christopher Columbus himself witnessed the first of many widespread departures and arrivals, symbolized on that fateful day by the flags of Catholic Castile and Aragon flying on top of the embodiment of Muslim power in western Europe, the Alhambra.

The fall of Granada was the culmination of the ancient battle between two major and opposing civilizations, which not only settled the cultural fate of a large part of Europe but also established the basis for the discovery of the Americas. The year 1492 is generally seen as a beginning, whether of modern Spain or the discovery of the New World. But what had ended was equally significant. The conquest of Granada was one of the most memorable events in Spanish and European history, and the pivotal role was played by Sultan Muhammad XI.

A Man of Destiny: The Rise of Sultan Muhammad XI, known as Boabdil

An anonymous monochrome engraving is the only contemporary portrait we have of one of the most important men in European history, Sultan Muhammad XI of Granada, known to the Christians as Boabdil. It shows an affable, good-natured man, his modest Muslim dress revealing a lack of pretentiousness and natural humility. Abu Abdallah Muhammad b. Ali was born in the Alhambra in either 1459 or 1460, in the reign of his warlike father Abu l-Hasan. From the start, a dark shadow of destiny lay over him, as court astrologers predicted that he would suffer great misfortune, and he became known to the Christians by the nickname *El Zogoibi*, 'the unlucky one'. He was educated at the madrasa of the Alhambra, where his schooling was designed to turn him into an educated and widely read man, an image hinted at in Christian chronicles. He also became a skilled horseman, adept at hunting, a pursuit that was a measure of his nobility as well as excellent training for fighting, which made him deft in battle. His mother, Abu l-Hasan's legitimate wife Aixa, was an important and powerful Nasrid princess, allegedly descended in a direct line from the Prophet Muhammad. Their marriage was harmonious for twenty years, during which time they had three children: Abdullah, Yusuf and Aixa. But when Isabel de Solís, the daughter of a knight commander of a local town, was captured during a raiding party and sold into the emir's household, things changed. Isabel was converted to Islam and given the name Zoraya, after a star in the Pleiades cluster. Legend has created an image of her dazzling beauty, which bewitched the sultan, and he gave her land, houses and a privileged position at court, bribing certain judges into legalizing a new marriage, which created furious resentment in Aixa and her sons. From then on, the sultan made his life with Isabel, recognized her as queen, and never spoke to or saw his wife Aixa again.

The emir's impetuous, cruel and angry nature made Aixa fear for her children, so, despite her bitter jealousy, she let things pass for a time, while he indulged his passions. But when Zoraya's sons Sa'd and Nasr were considered as royal princes, Aixa played her trump card, exercising her right to the throne as mother of the next true Nasrid sultan. With the support of Boabdil's in-laws, she incited him to revolt against his father, and he was proclaimed Sultan Muhammad XI in July 1482. Abu l-Hasan, a man who had ousted his own father Sa'd, was overthrown in turn by his son, and fled to Malaga. This extreme discord in the Granadan royal family damaged the Islamic emirate irreparably, but, in its final ten years, the coup de grâce would come from across the frontier between Granada and the Christian north. Events had reached a tipping point, and a new drama was set to be played out on the political stage of Granada.

A Symbol of Doom: The Sultan in Chains

A contrasting and surely Christian image of Sultan Boabdil shows him in sombre mood, with an iron ring and chain around his neck, yet wearing a crown that denotes his royalty. The circumstances that led to this abject picture of ostensible slavery had their roots in the history of the Christian kingdoms of Castile and Aragon when a twist of fate brought the princess Isabella to the throne of Castile in 1474. Isabella was married to Prince Ferdinand of Aragon, who in 1479 became king, thereby uniting the two kingdoms. In the same year, civil war in Castile ended and peace was made between Castile and Portugal. This advantageous marriage of monarchs and kingdoms created a Christian union so powerful that it proved fatal to both the Nasrid kingdom and to western Islam, as Ferdinand and

Isabella together could now give their concerted attention to war against Granada. Isabella had always harboured the ambition to drive the Muslims from Spain, and that intention had been written down plainly in the terms of her first marriage contract with Ferdinand, signed in 1469. She saw that intention not solely as a reconquest, but as a veritable crusade that would unite the unruly and disordered kingdom of Castile around a single cause – to extinguish the Muslim state for ever.

Arab historians recorded ominous warnings given to the Granadan Muslims of what was seen as their imminent divine punishment and ruin. Al-Maqqari recalled an ancient weathercock in the old kasbah of the city which bore a notorious rhyme foretelling some dreadful calamity that would ruin both the Alhambra and its owner. Hernando de Baeza described the appearance of a comet, broad and long like a sword, which appeared from two hours before dawn until daylight for a period of thirty days, which the emir's astrologers declared to be a portent of war and destruction. The year 1478 had brought another omen when Abu l-Hasan organized a grand parade and inspection of all his troops, a marvellous public spectacle to demonstrate his military might. But this culminated in disaster, as al-Maqqari vividly describes:

> One day when the sultan was as usual seated under the pavilion and the troops were passing before him, the summit and the sides of the neighbouring hill of As-sabíkah being crowded with spectators who had left their dwellings for the purpose of witnessing the pageant, God permitted that all of a sudden the rain should fall down in torrents, and that the river Darro should overflow its banks. Such was the fury of the devastating element, which came pouring down from the neighbouring mountains, carrying along large stones and whole trees, that it destroyed everything in its way, and that houses, shops, mills, inns, markets, bridges and garden walls were the prey of the devastating flood . . . So frightful an inundation had never before been experienced in the country, and the people naturally looked

> upon it as the harbinger of the dreadful calamities which awaited Muslims in just chastisement for their perversity and their sins.[1]

Despite this calamity, which had a terrible psychological effect on him, Abu l-Hasan still remained active on the frontier between Granada and Castile, raiding and skirmishing in Christian territory. His decisive capture of the Christian town of Zahara in December 1481, in a stealthy night attack, prompted Ferdinand and Isabella to retaliate, capturing Alhama near Granada in February 1482. Alhama had been Muslim for over 700 years, yet Isabella ordered the town's three mosques to be converted into churches fully equipped with the silver crosses and religious paraphernalia needed for Catholic worship. It was a Christian victory sung for centuries in Spanish ballads that laid bare the shock and outrage of the Muslim foe, and it began a decisive ten-year struggle between the two sides.

Disaster struck in April 1483, less than a year into Boabdil's reign as sultan, when he reluctantly followed the advice of his ministers and took 1,500 cavalry and 7,000 infantry out of the kingdom of Granada into enemy territory to raid the Christian town of Lucena and destroy its wheatfields and vineyards in a countermove to Ferdinand's devastation of the crops in the Vega of Granada. As the sultan and his troops left the city, they passed through the Gate of Elvira, where the point of Boabdil's lance hit the arch of the gate and was broken. This sinister omen was followed by another, more alarming one, when a fox crossed the path of the army, ran through the ranks and, despite the showers of missiles thrown at it, escaped unhurt. At Lucena, the portents were fulfilled; Boabdil's army fell prey to a surprise Christian rearguard attack, during which the sultan attempted to fight back, but his soldiers panicked, fleeing across the stream. Boabdil's white horse entered the water and sank down into the mud, stuck fast and unable to move. Hernando de Baeza gives us another vivid picture of those moments:

> While the king was in this state of anguish and distress, a Christian foot-soldier came to the edge of the riverbank and

> raised his lance to strike the king. A cavalryman named Santa Cruz who was a Muslim living under Christian rule in Toledo, whose own horse was stuck in the stream alongside the king, shouted to the foot-soldier 'Stop, stop, you fool, don't kill him, he's the king.' The soldier stopped in his tracks and at that moment another infantryman came up, this one from the town of Baena, along with another man riding a pack mule laden with baskets. The other soldier said to him 'That's the Moorish king!' and together they lifted him from his saddle and put him on the mule.[2]

On that catastrophic day, when up to a thousand Muslim troops and nobles were killed, the captured sultan was imprisoned in the castle of Porcuna, one hundred miles from Granada. In a matter of hours, the Muslim sultan had become a Christian pawn. He was obliged to pay the price of his freedom by pledging homage and fealty to the Catholic Kings, who had taken his baby son Ahmed as hostage. A two-year peace treaty was signed, in which the sultan swapped his freedom for vassalage and undertook to make war against his own father, who had reclaimed the throne of Granada in his son's absence. Ferdinand used that deadly antagonism between father and son to win a diplomatic victory, but Isabella wanted to go further, insisting that the time was right to conquer the kingdom entirely. The Castilians began a policy of relentless aggression against Granada in 1484. Boabdil, who had returned to the city, was forced to flee again to Cordoba, which was in Christian hands, when his uncle, Abu Abdullah Muhammad, el Zagal, seized control and deposed his brother, Boabdil's father. El Zagal ruled from 1485 to 1487 as Muhammad XII but Boabdil and this second rival for the throne, his uncle, decided to present a united front against the intensifying Christian campaign. Boabdil was unlucky enough to be captured a second time, at Loja, in the far west of the province, and was obliged to renew his vassalage to Ferdinand and Isabella. In 1487, Granada fell once more into his hands, and El Zagal was forced to withdraw to Almería, allowing the Catholic rulers to put pressure on Boabdil to agree to surrender the city in exchange for a lordship. Unable to countenance such drastic measures, Boabdil reneged on the agreement and continued to resist, but he had small chance of success. He was up against a queen obsessed with Joan of Arc and the idea of crusade, and a king of Machiavellian cunning.

From the first encounter between Sultan Boabdil and his nemesis King Ferdinand II of Aragon and Castile, the tone was set for their future relationship. The sultan was never hostile in his manner, but shrewdly compliant. Unlike his father, he was statesmanlike and often effusively courteous in the face of his enemy. Ferdinand, ten years older than Boabdil, had the upper hand not only because of his age, but because the sultan was his prisoner. His apparent generosity and benevolence to his captive disguised an underlying coldness and suspicion, a calculating quality. His reluctance to meet Boabdil in person and the insistence on the sultan's subservience to Castile and Aragon all belie his façade of friendliness and bonhomie. While the capture of Boabdil seemed to play into Ferdinand's hands, he clearly saw the sultan as a serious threat to his ambitions, and one that needed to be held in check.

Those ambitions had grown and taken full hold of Ferdinand since the start of 1482. If the stars had predicted Boabdil's unfortunate destiny, great things had been prophesied for Ferdinand. Ancient documents were said to reveal that he was destined to conquer both Jerusalem and Granada. Beneath his apparent amiability with Boabdil, Ferdinand harboured the intention of using him to worsen the internal divisions in the Nasrid camp. In a letter written to his sister Juana, the queen of Naples, on 26 August 1483, just a few days after seeing the captured sultan, he told her that it had been decided to release the Nasrid sultan because Ferdinand's objective was 'to create such division in the kingdom in Granada that it would bring about its complete and utter ruin.' This strategy of sowing discord between the leaders of the Nasrid dynasty bore fruit. Ferdinand sent Christian troops to help Boabdil win the fight against his uncle on the streets of Granada, a collaboration which caused dissent among the Muslim population. Later, in 1487, during the Christian siege of

Malaga, Boabdil was constrained to attack a Muslim force sent by his uncle as reinforcements – an act which cast him as a traitor in the eyes of many of his people. Nevertheless, the Granadans still agreed to support the emir, accepting his obedience to Ferdinand and Isabella because they lived in great fear of the Christian army and the devastation it could bring to their crops and livelihoods. The sultan had to perform the tricky balancing act of being appropriately subservient to Castile while maintaining his own supremacy as ruler of his beleaguered people. His plan was to play along with the Catholic Monarchs while still harbouring the hope of saving his kingdom. But the most terrible days still lay ahead for the Nasrid capital.

The Surrender of Granada and the End of Islam in Western Europe

Ferdinand was not only cunning and immensely powerful, but also an expert military strategist, versed in the newest trends of warfare in the fifteenth century. Alongside new weapon capabilities and tactical and administrative advances, almost every European army had adopted the gunpowder weapons used so successfully in siege operations during the Granadan war. Siege artillery had been used in Spain before the fifteenth century, but by Islamic forces – Sultan Isma'il I was reported to have captured the town of Huéscar in 1324 and Baza in 1325 using gunpowder artillery, and we know that the Spanish Muslims used cannon against the Castilian army of Alfonso XI at the siege of Algeciras in 1342. Ferdinand used great artillery guns, employing gangs of road-builders to flatten out hillsides and rough terrain in order to drag the heavy weapons close to castles and city walls, which disintegrated before their explosive power. The Christian king was remorseless and unstoppable, and by 1490 he had taken the fight for Granada to a new level.

Ferdinand and Isabella had built a military headquarters in the form of an entirely new town called Santa Fe that they had constructed just west of Granada. This proximity allowed them to sever the city's communications with the outside and threaten it with the spectre of starvation. Boabdil could not inflict that fate upon his people, so he opened secret negotiations with the Castilians and reluctantly decided to surrender, finally agreeing to the terms of the Capitulation on 25 November 1491. His royal chancellery prepared a long document on behalf of the sultan, setting out his proposals for the surrender of Granada. First and foremost, on the day that they received the Alhambra, the Christians had to release Boabdil's son, still held prisoner in Moclín, and hand him over to his father, along with all the other Muslim hostages and their servants.

There followed a long series of practical conditions and religious stipulations. In essence, all Granadan Muslims should be allowed to keep their religion, mosques and leaders, and the muezzin's call to prayer should continue, for all time. Boabdil also stipulated that Jews living in Granada should have the same rights as Muslims under the terms of the surrender. He was sensitive to his people's feelings and took pains to try to avoid any sense of the inferiority of Muslims under Christian domination, stipulating that no Christian would have the right to speak cruelly of the past. The practice of Islam and its material manifestations of the mosque, minarets and muezzins were paramount, as was the *aljama*, or Moorish quarter of the city, from where Muslim lawyers, judges and community leaders operated. Boabdil's inclusion of the minority group of the Granadan Jews in the terms of surrender, where he states that they 'should benefit like us from these terms', is particularly poignant in the knowledge that, just months later, in the spring and summer of 1492, all Jews, not just those from Granada, would be expelled from their native Spain by Ferdinand and Isabella.

On 2 January 1492, Boabdil surrendered the city of Granada to Ferdinand and Isabella. It was a moment that has captured the imagination of writers and artists up to the present day, initially as a day of supreme conquest and later because of the extreme pathos of that moment of transition and loss, so sympathetically evoked in Francisco Pradilla's famous painting. A contrasting, more triumphalist scene was painted by another nineteenth-century artist, Carlos Ribera y Fieve, showing Queen Isabella and her retinue, including Christopher Columbus, watching in wonder and jubilation from just outside the city, on the banks of the river Genil, as the Christian flag of St James the Moor-slayer and the Holy Cross are hoisted in the Alhambra. As Boabdil handed the keys of his city to Ferdinand, he addressed the king in Arabic: 'God loves you greatly. Sir, these are the keys of this paradise. I and those inside it are yours.' His words marked a crucial moment in the centuries-old encounter between two great religions and cultures, and a defining hour in European history. It symbolized the epoch-changing transition of the kingdom of Granada from Islamic state to Christian territory, a moment which set Spain on a course to become the greatest power in early modern Europe.

The Path to Exile and Betrayal

There is a well-known Morisco legend that, when Boabdil and his entourage left their city for the Alpujarras, where he had been granted a country estate by the Catholic Monarchs, upon reaching the town of Padul, the furthest place from which Granada can be seen, Boabdil sighed heavily, invoking the Muslim god of war, and began to weep. His unkind mother is said to have unjustly scolded him with the words: 'You do well, my son, to cry like a woman for what you couldn't defend like a man.' The French artist Dehodencq's dynamic painting catches the sultan's last glimpse of the city he loved, and which symbolized the zenith of Islamic life in western Europe.

In October 1493, the last sultan made the decision to abandon his country estate and set sail for exile in North Africa, a move prompted by the death of his wife Moraima. Mystery surrounds the date and place of Boabdil's own death – some say he died soon after his arrival in Fez, others that he lived in Tlemcen in modern-day Algeria. Overtaken by political and cultural events beyond his control, the man destined to relinquish the last Islamic state in western Europe played the foil to King Ferdinand as hero, and, where his life was retold in fictional stories of conquest, he was cast as the betrayer. Deprecated in the past as a cowardly traitor or tragic victim, he has become a potent symbol of resistance to repression, a man who always preferred negotiation and diplomacy to violence and war. Boabdil was the scapegoat of history, at once the Muslim invader and the native Hispanic self, and he encapsulates the enduring presence of Spain's cultural distinctiveness and its crucial role in the history of Islam in Europe.

As Boabdil departed from Granada to lead his family into internal exile, Isabella and her retinue entered the city. Ironically, it looked as if the Christian royalty and knighthood had in fact turned Muslim, since all were wearing Moorish dress, decked out in brocade and silk tunics, with the Moorish waist sash or *marlota*. This purported to be a mark of respect, a visual statement to placate, reassure and suggest commonality. To the people of Granada watching in fear from a city vanquished after a long period of siege, it did not seem that way, but felt more like an act of insolent appropriation, of absorption of what was Moorish by the Catholic enemy. It was an entirely ambiguous symbolic act, hinting on the one hand at the centuries-old covert Christian admiration for Moorish culture, for what was forbidden, which militated against the entire ethos of the Reconquest, and on the other betraying a longing to usurp and eliminate that culture and religion.

The triumphant King Ferdinand expressed his elation in the letter he wrote on the very day, 2 January, to the councillors and people of Murcia:

> I write to inform you that it has pleased our Lord, after enormous effort, expense and fatigue in our kingdoms, and the spilling of blood of our native subjects, to bring the war that I have engaged in with the Moors of the kingdom and city of Granada to a happy conclusion. That city, held and occupied for over seven hundred and eighty years, today, 2 of January of this year 1492, has come under our power and dominion, and the Alhambra and city and all its forces, together with all the other castles, fortresses and townships that remained in this kingdom for me to win, were handed over to me.

Much of Europe joined Ferdinand in celebrating what they saw as a great victory. Te Deums were chanted in St Paul's Cathedral in London, and, in Rome, the pope and his cardinals attended a special High Mass. Venice and Naples joined in the festivities, and Europe congratulated itself on the victory of this Christian crusade. In stark contrast, a resident of Cairo, Ibn Iyās, the last oriental witness, both emotional and historical, of the death throes of the Nasrid kingdom in Andalusia, records in his diary for the year 1492 the news of the fall of Granada as 'one of the most terrible catastrophes to befall Islam.'

In North Africa, there was great lamentation for the conquest of Granada, which was seen as a lost paradise to the Muslims. Yet, the Marinid dynasty of Berber rulers of Morocco, who had tried without success to help the emirate of Granada stand firm against the Christian threat, had been taken over in 1465 by another Berber dynasty, the Wattasids, who were too busy fending off their enemies to lend any support to the Nasrids. Boabdil's people may rightly have felt abandoned by their fellow Muslims abroad, who were benevolent to them in spirit but provided no sustained practical support. If Granada had resisted Christian domination, it is possible that it may have formed strong alliances with North African and even Turkish leaders and become part of a larger Islamic political entity, perhaps acting as an intermediary between the Islamic empire and Europe. We might also envisage a scenario where the emirate of Granada had become an Ottoman state, to form part of a mighty Islamic empire that could have changed the face of western Europe.

But that is speculation. The reality was that racial and religious cleansing was on the minds of the Catholic Monarchs. Barely four months after Sultan Boabdil had stipulated in the terms of surrender of the city that all the Jews of his kingdom should benefit like the Muslims from the deal agreed, his conquerors sat in state in his former throne room in the Alhambra to give their final approval to the Edict of Granada. Sometimes known as the Alhambra Decree, this new law stated that all Jews must either become Christians or leave the kingdoms of Spain by 31 July 1492. It would not be long before other terms of surrender of the city agreed with Boabdil would also be cast aside. For the next eight years, Islam remained the religion of most of the inhabitants, the muezzin still called the faithful to prayer from the 200 or more mosques that rose in the urban landscape, and the Great Mosque, with its imposing minaret, dominated the skyline until it was demolished in 1588. But the city was ruled by a small group of upper-class Christians, soldiers, lawyers and clergymen, and, just five years later, the peerless Granada where Islam still flourished, described so clearly by the German doctor Hieronymus Münzer, had become a place of further trauma for its Muslim inhabitants.

Ferdinand and Isabella soon reneged on the terms of the surrender agreement, and the failure of the Christian authorities to fulfil the terms of the Capitulations meant that not only did the Muslim community lose its privileges and freedoms, but its very religious and cultural identity was under threat. The crucifix, Catholic statues and images were worshipped, and bells replaced the call of the muezzin as mosques were transformed into churches. In the fragments of his poetry that survive, Ibn al-Qaysi al-Basti denigrated the betrayal of the Christians, who forced his people to convert to Catholicism and, in doing so, raised the dilemma of apostasy, punishable by death in Islamic law. He stressed the intention of the Granadans to remain Muslims in secret, invoking the doctrine of *taqiyya*, a legal dispensation for an individual Muslim to dissimulate or commit acts which would otherwise be blasphemous, if there was a risk of persecution. Al-Basti described the violation of the terms of the surrender treaty, Cardinal Cisneros' terrible public book-burning in the Plaza de Bib-Rambla, punishments for not attending Mass, and the forced consumption of pork and wine. The poet exposes the duplicity of Ferdinand and Isabella, who had informed the Egyptian and Turkish envoys at court that any conversions of Moriscos had been entirely voluntary, when in fact, he says, it was fear of death and burning that made them comply. The significance of this last poetic vestige of Islamic Spain is considerable, as it reveals a major religious crisis in a community shrouded in dissimulation, plainly contrasting the previous tolerant attitude of Islam to other religions in the past with subsequent Christian intolerance and persecution.

But Granada only nominally became a Christian city in January 1492 – it was rather a Muslim city under Christian political control. The western Christian visitors who travelled there still felt the full shock of the revelation of a different civilization, and so did the Catholic authorities in charge of the conquered city, who believed they had a mission to reconstitute the urban landscape. Granada seemed intolerable to them in its Muslim incarnation and, in their eyes, needed to be made safer, more beautiful, nobler. Mosques gradually became churches, and Muslim cemeteries, of which there were many outside the city walls, became the sites of new parish churches or convents. Yet, strive as they might, the new Catholic authorities in Granada could not change the essentially Islamic character of the city, especially in the centre.

What did change after 1492 was the nature of Spanish society throughout the peninsula. It went from being a place where members of three different religions lived side by side to a closed, suspicious society desiring to repress and eliminate difference. In the same year that Granada was conquered and the Jews were exiled, Ferdinand and Isabella funded Christopher Columbus's first voyage of discovery to the Americas, in August 1492. The light of the glorious 800-year-old civilization of Islam in western Europe was extinguished, as Spain gained new territories and headed what was to become a vast empire, with colonies worldwide, that would be a harbinger of the European colonialism of the nineteenth century. It seemed that Christianity had reaped the profits of Muslim knowledge and turned it against their cultural benefactors.[3]

Part Three

THE ETERNAL STATE: THE ISLAMIC EMPIRE OF THE OTTOMANS IN EUROPE

Sultan Selim I. 16th century miniature by Nakkaş Osman

Chapter 15

Guardians of the Past, Architects of the Future: The Rise of the Ottomans

'That city, placed at the junction of the two seas and two continents, seemed like a diamond set between two sapphires and two emeralds, to form the most precious stone in a ring of universal empire.'

The dream of Osman[1]

'Halt not, conquerors! God be praised! You are the conquerors of Constantinople.'

Sultan Mehmed II, 1453

The Dream of a Nomad

A MIGHTY TREE grew from Osman's navel, its leaves the shape of scimitars, its shady branches covering the entire world. There were valleys, mountains, streams and gardens alive with sweet birdsong, all a vision of earthly paradise, where domes and cupolas, minarets and towers graced the skylines of great cities. The vision settled over Constantinople, the meeting place of two worlds, where the crescent moon presided over the muezzin's call to prayer – a city formed, in the logic of his dream, of a jewelled ring Osman was poised to place on his finger. The dream displayed symbols of warfare, utopia and Islam, and though he could not have imagined its full meaning at the time, it prophesied his rise to power and the transformation of his nomadic tribe into the Muslim rulers of a majestic empire that would survive for 600 years and stretch from south-east and central Europe as far as western Asia.

The legend of Osman's dream has endured, but many details of his life are a mystery. His nomadic ancestors came from the Turkic and Mongolian tribes who roamed the steppes of Europe and Asia, tent dwellers not of the desert, but of the wild, windy grasslands, where they rode sturdy Turkish ponies instead of camels. Osman was born around 1281 into a family of Turkic horsemen who migrated annually with their herds of horses, oxen, goats and sheep, moving between winter and summer pastures. His fabled dream was a call to action that spurred him on to migrate west to the lands of Anatolia, with a makeshift army of Christian renegades, Sufis and allied princes, fighting both Turks and Byzantine Christians. There, he created a small principality, known as a *beylik*, with its capital at Söğüt in north-west Anatolia, and his followers were known as Osmanli, from which the word 'Ottoman' is derived. These wandering warriors were bound by ties of personal loyalty, and they gradually adopted Islam, their fighting acquiring a religious dimension. The earliest Ottoman rulers were described in the oldest existing account of the dynasty, *History of the Kings of the Ottoman Lineage and their Gaza Against the Infidels*, as champions of the faith, or *gazis* – jihadists who battled the unbelievers.[2] Osman would become known as Lord of the Horizons, though we are told that, when he died in 1326, he left few possessions behind him – just one kaftan, one suit of armour and a mess kit with a salt cellar and spoon rack. He owned a single pair of high boots, and no books, silver or gold, nor even a prayer mat. What he did leave was a Muslim dominion that would rise to global power in centuries to come.

If Osman was an ascetic, his son and successor Orhan (r. 1324–62) was the opposite. His ambitions to expand Osman's territories drove him like wildfire through north-west Anatolia, where he captured the imposing Byzantine citadel of Bursa in 1326, commemorated as the first capital of the Ottoman dynasty. There, Orhan developed a love for the good life, and his court imbibed fine Greek wines. He married Theodora, the daughter of the Byzantine emperor John VI Kantakouzeno, and later his son married his maternal cousin, Irene Palaiologina, two unions that permanently entwined Ottomans and

Byzantines through their bloodlines. As the second Ottoman ruler, Orhan was in control of almost a hundred fortresses, and grew rich in lands, material wealth and military resources. In 1331, he captured the Byzantine stronghold of Iznik, in the Turkish province of Bursa, and for a short period the town became the capital of the now expanding Ottoman territories.

Late in 1331, soon after Iznik came under Orhan's control, the Moroccan traveller Ibn Battuta stayed there, describing it as a beautiful city, with 'fine bazaars and wide streets, surrounded on all sides by gardens and running springs'.[3] Inside the outer walls were gardens and cultivated plots, each house encircled by an orchard, and the town produced abundant fruit and nuts, including walnuts, chestnuts and sweet grapes. Orhan set about restoring its buildings, shaping the town's new Islamic character, converting the large church of Hagia Sophia in the centre into the Orhan Mosque and building the first Ottoman Islamic theological college and bathhouse nearby.

Orhan proved to be the longest living ruler in Ottoman history, but tragedy struck in 1357 when his eldest son and likely heir, Suleyman Pasha, died after falling from a horse. Such was the importance and value of horses to the early Ottomans that Suleyman's steed was buried beside him. Orhan was greatly affected by the death of his son and died soon after, in 1362, in Bursa, aged eighty, after reigning for thirty-six years. Ibn Battuta thought him a great man: 'The greatest of the kings of the Turcomans and the richest in wealth, lands and military forces. Of fortresses he possesses nearly a hundred, and for most of his time he is continually engaged in making a round of them, staying in each fortress for some days to put it in good order and examine its condition. It is said that he has never stayed for a whole month in any one town. He also fights with the infidels continually and keeps them under siege.'[4] Orhan's main legacy was to take the Ottomans from Asia to the edge of Europe, allying them with the Byzantines through marriage, and fighting both Christians and Muslims along the way, a feat he achieved in less than four decades.

Orhan's second son, Murad I (r. 1362–89), took the throne in place of his deceased brother and raised the emerging Ottoman dynasty to another level of power and influence. Lauded as both *gazi* warrior and miracle-working saint by Ottoman chroniclers, it was nevertheless his political and strategic genius that wrought an astonishing transformation upon the prospects of his people. While Osman and Orhan had styled themselves as beys, or chieftains, Murad put the Ottomans on a whole new footing by designating himself as sultan, the secular and military leader of the resulting sultanate, and his new title appeared on coins minted in his reign. He backed this new status up with an elite military force, an infantry loyal to his person, units of highly trained soldiers made up of non-Muslim boys, mainly Anatolian and Balkan Christians, taken from their homes, who became known as the *yeni çeri*, or 'new army', the Janissaries.* While these troops were effectively slaves, the sultan treated them like his own sons, and inspired such devotion that they became willing to sacrifice themselves for him. Their diverse regional origins also made special intelligence about any newly conquered territories easily accessible.

To maintain the peace and unity of a sultanate liable to be destabilized and fragmented by succession wars, Murad instigated the policy of murdering all male relatives of a new sultan – in his case, his brothers and uncles. This law of fratricide was legalized in the reign of a later sultan, Mehmed II. Meanwhile, Murad I's reign was rooted in absolute control by the sultan and in the subordination of his subject peoples, creating a system in which hierarchy and difference were paramount. It was this vice-like grip on his people and his army that allowed Murad I to push his boundaries further, deeper into Europe itself.

Orhan had already crossed into Europe in 1354 and found a stronghold in the town of Gallipoli in Thrace, which he had

* It is likely that Orhan's vizier Alaeddin and his associate Çandarlı had established the collection of Christian boys to form an elite paid army, but it seems it became institutionalized in the reign of Murad I.

conquered in the aftermath of a devastating earthquake. Murad I also took his armies into Thrace and seized the beautiful Greek city of Adrianople in 1362, changing its name to Edirne and making it the new Ottoman capital, which it remained until 1453. As the Byzantine Empire waned on the continent, the Ottomans soon ran up against the local warlords of south-east Europe, who were also eyeing opportunities to expand their varied territories. Bulgaria sought to revive the cultural and spiritual supremacy of its first empire in southern Europe, but in the end became Murad's vassal in 1372, while Hungary would continue to challenge the Muslims well into the sixteenth century. Serbia had been ruled by Steven Dusan, a self-proclaimed Christ-loving tsar who had set out to conquer Constantinople in 1356 but died on the way, leaving his empire open to Murad I's advances. The sultan's armies fought the Serbians on the Field of Blackbirds at Kosovo in 1389, where his troops won the day and Serbia became a vassal of the Ottoman Empire. It was a victory that led to almost 500 years of Ottoman rule over the Serbs. Their success was gravely undermined when a Serbian nobleman, Milosh Obravitch, entered Murad's tent and stabbed him to death with a dagger, an act glorified in old Serbian ballads and epic poetry. The sultan's sons Bayezid and Yakub Bey rushed to his tent from the battlefield, where Bayezid at once invoked the law of fratricide and had his younger brother strangled. He was then made sultan on the spot.

Bayezid I was half Turkish, half Greek, and nearly forty when he became head of the Ottoman dynasty in 1389. The dramatic murder of his brother and his sudden, impetuous nature earned him the nickname Thunderbolt. He was so fiercely ambitious that he named himself Sultan of Rûm, the old Islamic word for the Eastern Roman Empire. He was not a model ruler by Muslim standards, but rather a hardened alcoholic who lived a life of decadence and failed to attend mosque. Yet, by 1390, he had already strengthened Ottoman sea trade with Venice and Genoa, annexed the entire west coast of Anatolia and made the Byzantine emperor in Constantinople his vassal.

Four years later, in 1396, Bayezid launched the first Ottoman siege of Constantinople, attempting to isolate the city and starve its inhabitants. He was met by King Sigismund of Hungary, at Nicopolis in today's Bulgaria, on the banks of the Danube. Sigismund headed an army of 10,000 crusaders, in a new holy war to relieve the city, but the Ottomans won decisively, and Bayezid, who had now shored up his western boundary, celebrated by building the Ulu Cami Mosque in Bursa. With Constantinople still under siege, his western empire now stretched from Thrace, through Macedonia, Bulgaria and parts of Serbia in Europe, and as far as the Taurus Mountains in Asia. His army was considered one of the best in the Islamic world.

It was in 1402 that he met his nemesis, Tamerlane the Great, a Turkish general and emir from central Asia, descended from the Mongols. On 20 July 1402, they fought at the Battle of Ankara and the Ottomans were roundly defeated; Bayezid tried to escape, but was captured and, according to legend, Tamerlane imprisoned him in an iron cage, where the sultan killed himself in despair with a dose of poison he had kept hidden in his jewelled ring. There followed an eleven-year hiatus, an interregnum in which the Ottomans endured the destructive rebellion of the dervishes, Muslim Sufis known for their ecstatic rituals and led by the subversive Sheikh Bedreddin, until one of Bayezid's four sons, Mehmed Çelebi, claimed the Ottoman throne in 1413 and seated himself on its gold, bejewelled divan. After an appalling bloodbath in which the dervishes were subdued, he executed the rebel sheikh, hanging him naked from a tree in Siroz in 1416, and went on to rule for eight years as Mehmed I. His reign saw the construction of the stunning Green Mosque in Bursa and the revitalization of the floundering Ottoman Empire, but his life came to a sudden end when he was crushed to death by his own horse, in Edirne, in 1421. Mehmed was succeeded by his nineteen-year-old brother Murad II (r. 1421–44, 1446–51), who promptly had their remaining two brothers murdered.

The ever-growing power of the Ottoman Empire provoked Pope Eugenius IV to call on the leaders of Christian Europe to take the Cross against Murad's armies in a desperate attempt to prevent the

Ottomans reaching central Europe. The papal command incited one of the most significant events of Murad II's reign, the Crusade of Varna, led by the Byzantine emperor John VIII and Vladislav I, king of Hungary, who narrowly missed defeating the sultan's armies at Zlatitsa Pass in Bulgaria in the summer of 1444. Murad saw what he was up against and wisely negotiated a ten-year peace treaty with the Hungarians, then promptly abdicated in favour of his twelve-year-old son, Mehmed II (r. 1444–6, 1451–81). No one knows why he retired to Anatolia, but his absence was brief. Murad had modelled himself on the *gazis* of old, the warriors of Islam who fought for religion and justice. He had ordered the translation into Turkish of old Persian, Arab and Anatolian epics, seeking the ancient legends of his people and likening himself to a fictional Arab hero who fought the Byzantines. It was no surprise that his viziers soon implored him to return to the throne as *gazi* in the face of a new threat of imminent invasion by the Hungarian crusaders, who had reneged on the peace treaty.

In November 1444, the steel-clad Hungarians matched the ferocity of Murad's Janissaries in an encounter at Varna, on the west coast of the Black Sea, that saw 'heads and legs, fingers and fingernails, axes and hammers, arrows and lances, shields and weapons' litter the theatre of war.[5] Thousands of Christian crusaders died, including the king of Hungary, defeated by the sultan's cavalry in a resounding victory that gave the Ottomans total control of south-eastern Europe. Murad retired once more, returned Mehmed to his throne, then promptly reclaimed it when called to control a rebellion of the Janissaries in 1446. He remained as sultan until, one day in 1451, as he was riding near Edirne, he met a dervish who forewarned him of his impending death. The sultan went to bed with a headache and died three days later. His viziers hid his corpse for almost a fortnight, until Mehmed could reach Edirne and finally take his place on the Ottoman throne.

*

In the 200 or so years since the creation of the Nasrid dynasty of al-Andalus in 1237 and the birth of the Ottoman regime around 1288,

European Islam's axis of power had shifted from one side of the continent to the other. The Catholic regime of Spain and Portugal had gained the upper hand and eclipsed the brilliant civilization of al-Andalus in 1492. While western European Islam waned as Christian power increased and Muslim rule was weakened by internal fighting, its eastern counterpart waxed strong.

Mehmed II inherited an empire of great wealth and economic stability, created by his father's military success and the expansion of trade. Since Osman's first successful battle against the Christians, the Ottoman line had witnessed an extraordinary transformation from minor statelet to majestic sultanate. While the Ottoman rulers shared the uncanny political acumen of the earlier Abbasids and Umayyads, their decisive polices were very different – in particular, those of Murad I, whose cruel statesmanship had established the Janissaries and a rule of succession based on fratricide, and whose pole stars were tolerance of diversity and the absolute imposition of hierarchy. The dynasty also came into being at an auspicious moment, when the Byzantine Empire was crumbling, impoverished, and ravished by the bubonic plague that had devastated Europe in the 1340s. Osman's nomadic statelet escaped disease and fostered trade routes on the imperial frontiers, while Ottoman rulers married Byzantine Christians and intermingled with local sheikhs, creating scope for changing alliances and loyalties. Six sultans had come and gone before Mehmed II stepped into the limelight and rose to stardom on the world stage.

The Seventh Sultan and the Red Apple

Mehmed was brilliant, cruel and obsessively ambitious. He wanted to achieve what no man had done – to win the Red Apple or supreme goal of conquest, the city of Constantinople. Learned in philosophy, geography, and Islamic, Latin and Greek history and literature, Mehmed was a gifted speaker of Turkish, Greek and Slavic, as well as Arabic. He was also an exceptional military strategist and had formulated a plan to wage war against the Byzantines and besiege their capital. That once great city was in a state of decline, poignantly symbolized by the four empty plinths in the hippodrome, whose bronze equestrian statues had been carried off to Venice after the great sack of the city by the crusaders in 1204, a ghastly deed for which Pope John Paul II apologized on behalf of the Catholic Church in 2004, on the 800th anniversary of the destruction.

Since the sacking of Constantinople, the legacy of bitterness between Western Catholics and Eastern Orthodox Christians had remained. Venice, Genoa and Ragusa were too deeply embroiled in Ottoman trade to get involved, and only a few western Catholics came to the emperor Constantine XI's aid, leaving the final Christian outpost in the Near East weak and vulnerable. The last Byzantine emperor was a practical man, well aware of the weight of history and the heritage he felt obliged to defend. The great strength of his city lay in the depth of its as yet impenetrable fortifications. To the Ottomans' advantage, Mehmed II could muster huge numbers of soldiers, and his strategists could master military techniques speedily, including the use of cannon.

In 1453, the sultan reached the age of twenty-one; he was insolent, violent, ceaselessly energetic and warlike. Perhaps he saw Constantinople as an irritant in the midst of his empire, as well as a vital commercial centre, serving traders from the Black Sea to the Mediterranean. But the city state also had deep personal and religious meaning for him. As a Muslim, he knew the prophecies dating back to the failed Arab sieges of the seventh and eighth centuries, which foretold a cycle of defeat, death and final victory. Also, as the site of the demise of the Prophet's standard-bearer, Abu Ayyub al-Ansari, it was a holy place for Islam. He also knew of his great-grandfather's unsuccessful siege in 1396, and of his ancestor Osman's famous dream. Mehmed realized the momentousness of his desire, sensed the city's power and suspected it might rouse 'the whole west against us, from the ocean and Marseilles, and the western Gauls, the inhabitants of the Pyrenees and Spain, from the Rhine river, the Celts and the Cantiberians and the Germans.' But he did not waver.

The Ottoman Conquest of Constantinople

On 5 March 1453, Mehmed II sent an ultimatum to the emperor Constantine XI demanding his immediate surrender of the city. Both sides knew that a failure to surrender led automatically to the imposition of a siege, and, as the emperor refused to cede the city, both sides prepared for war. Inside the city, Constantine had about 4,700 Greeks, including monks and 3,000 foreigners, who were capable of bearing arms – a shocking deficit the emperor saw fit to keep secret. Outside the city gates stood possibly 60,000 Ottoman troops, assisted by many mining engineers, and Mehmed had positioned between fifty and eighty war galleys in the Bosphorus, poised for action. Despite the great military superiority of the Ottomans, Constantine believed he could hold out. He had the help of heroic Genoese nobleman and captain Giovanni Giustiniani, an expert in siege defence, who had brought 700 soldiers with him at his own expense.

Mehmed arrived outside Constantinople in April 1453 and harangued his men, telling them it was now only a city in name, just an area overrun with plants, vineyards and ruined walls. Sixty churches remained in the city, including the magnificent Hagia Sophia cathedral, along with many roofless chapels. Fighting began on 6 April, the massive Ottoman cannons bombarding the walls, but they took so long to load, the Byzantines were able to patch up most of the damage after each shot. The noise was colossal, the sound of the cannons terrifying, and, to frighten the enemy, trumpets and drums were taken to the battlefield by both sides. Bells were rung in the city to warn of the impending attacks, and the entire population joined in the defence effort, with women and children in lines carting stones to be thrown from the walls. Ottoman casualties were high and, to make matters worse, the sultan found his fleet unable to enter the Golden Horn – the curved inlet of the Bosphorus Strait that forms the harbour – due to the massive iron chain Constantine had ordered to span the entrance to keep out invading armies.

Furious, Mehmed conceived a solution of breathtaking originality and boldness, commanding his soldiers to lay down huge wooden beams greased with olive oil, leading overland from the Bosphorus to the Golden Horn. Sixty warships were fastened to robust cables and thousands of men were deployed to drag them along the oiled beams, up the steep hill, then down into the Golden Horn. It must have been a sight both awe-inspiring and horrifying to the Byzantines, to see great ships moving across land as if on water, complete with sails and crew. Their already shattered morale was dealt a further blow when Mehmed played his trump card.

He had employed a cannon-maker from Hungary called Orban, a man who, having already offered his services to the emperor, who lacked the money to pay him, switched sides. Mehmed ordered Orban to build a monstrous cannon, offering him four times the price he had asked of the Greeks. The enormous war-machine was unveiled in Edirne in January 1453, measuring eight and a half metres long, with a bronze barrel 76cm in diameter with 20cm thick reinforcements that fired balls weighing 544 kilos. Orban told Mehmed it could blast through the very walls of Babylon. Dragged from Edirne by 400 men and sixty oxen, it was hauled to the St Romanos Gate, close to where Mehmed had pitched his red and gold tent.

The final assault came on 29 May and the mood was apocalyptic. Sudden storms whipped up, fogs enveloped the city and there was a partial eclipse of the moon. A procession was carrying an icon of the Virgin Mary, to whom the population prayed for protection, which slipped and fell into the mud. There had been three days of fasting and ritual prayer in the Ottoman camp, where huge bonfires burned at night, and at 1.30 a.m. Mehmed II moved his men forward in waves. A huge cannonball, fired from the bombard an hour before dawn, breached part of the outer wall, and Mehmed himself led the Janissaries forward, but still the Muslims had not broken through the inner wall. Then the decisive moment came – the great Giustiniani was gravely wounded by a crossbow and left his post to be carried to a Genoese ship in the harbour. His presence had been crucial to the defenders, who lost heart, and at daybreak the Ottomans burst through the breach made by Orban's cannon in the Theodosian Walls and invaded the city. After the battle, it is said that a corpse was found wearing purple shoes, which identified it as the remains of the emperor Constantine.

*

The conquest of Constantinople by the Ottomans is the fourth turning point in the history of Europe's Muslims and Christians. Osman's prophetic dream was fulfilled and Mehmed II made sure the Hadith 'Constantinople will be conquered. Blessed is the commander who will conquer it, and blessed are his troops' was inscribed in Arabic above the entrance to his imperial mosque. At the ceremonial hour, when the sultan entered the city, it is reported that he carried the Prophet's sword before him, took the city in the name of Allah and had Muhammad's prayer mats brought into the Hagia Sophia cathedral. Mehmed had halted the statutory three-day sacking of the city by his soldiers after just one day, in which they had already stripped out everything of value. Much of the looting was in the form of people taken for the slave trade. The sultan had been taken aback by the scale of the devastation they had wrought and by the desolation and abandonment of the great metropolis. He is said to have recited the words of the Persian poet Saadi as he walked through the deserted Byzantine palace: 'The spider is the curtain holder in the palace of the Caesars. The owl hoots its night call on the Towers of Afrasiyab.'*

Mehmed at once set about rebuilding and reviving his new capital. First and foremost, he remade Constantinople as an Islamic city. He converted the Hagia Sophia cathedral into a mosque by adding a single minaret and left the Byzantine frescos and mosaics as they were. The former imperial church and monastery of St Saviour Pantocrator was transformed into the city's first Islamic college, and many other churches became mosques. The sultan ordered the Holy

---

* Afrasiyab is the mythical hero and main antagonist of the Persian poet Ferdowsi's epic work *Shah-Nama*, but the lines Mehmed recites were probably written by Saadi or Rumi. It is also the oldest part and ruined site of the ancient Persian city of Samarkand.

Apostolic church to be razed in order to build the Mosque of the Conqueror, a symbolic architectural statement of the imposition of Islam upon Christianity in a building which survives today. The city also acquired an aura of sanctity in the shape of a new Muslim pilgrimage site along the Golden Horn, where the burial place was apparently discovered of the Prophet's companion al-Ansari, who was reportedly killed in AD 669 in the first siege of Constantinople.

The transformation was not just architectural. Its populace underwent a metamorphosis born of Mehmed's wish to reinforce the cultural traditions of a historically cosmopolitan, multi-religious, multiracial city where many languages had always been spoken. He did not want Constantinople to be a city for Muslims alone, so Christians and Jews lived in their own quarters, subject to the *jizya* tax, and many were forcibly deported to the city from all over the empire to build up the population. The sultan wished all resident craftsmen to remain, as well as bringing others in from elsewhere, forcing them to live in the city. It was a policy that demanded tolerance, institutionalized under Mehmed's determined direction, and Constantinople began to flourish once again. New mosques, churches and even synagogues were built, although the latter were forbidden by Islamic law, and the new Imperial Palace, later known as the Topkapı Palace, came to define the Muslim capital, along with its supreme mosque Hagia Sophia. Mehmed's new palace was the centre of political and social authority, and a space of ritual power, whose eery silence and absence of mirrors lent it, and the sultan, an aura of holiness. Mehmed II adopted the title 'Caesar' after 1453, assuming the inheritance of the Roman Empire and reconstituting its eastern capital as the heart of the Ottoman dynasty with a new imperial administration.

The conquest of Constantinople brought scant reaction from the rest of the Islamic empire, but western Christendom was traumatized by the loss. People recalled exactly where they were when they heard the news, and it is said that Romans wept and beat their chests in despair, while Christian chroniclers recorded it as a terrible global catastrophe. The newly developed printing presses spread news of the terrible Turk throughout Europe, and the perceived disaster sparked a renewed crusading zeal fomented by Pope Pius II. In this history – written, unusually, by the losers – it was crystal clear that the new ruler of Europe's ancient Roman Empire was now a Muslim.

The Strange Story of the Sultan and the Impaler: Mehmed II and Vlad Ţepeş

The ancient Romanian city of Târgovişte lies at the crossroads of long-standing trade routes, eighty kilometres north-west of Bucharest. Today, it is a leafy urban centre of stately buildings and well-built houses, associated with the trial and execution of the Communist leader Nicolae Ceauşescu on Christmas Day 1989. In the botanical garden of Chindia Park, near the old city centre, a huge statue of Vlad Ţepeş the Impaler (*c.* 1428–*c.* 1477), dressed for battle and wielding a broadsword, hints at an even darker history dating back to the time when Târgovişte was capital of the medieval region of Wallachia. In the fifteenth century, it was ruled by the Dracul (Dragon) family of aristocrats, so called because they belonged to the Order of the Dragon, a militant brotherhood founded by the king of Hungary with the aim of halting the Ottoman advance into Europe. Vlad Ţepeş is one of Romania's national heroes and belonged to the Dracul family, reigning as voivode, or semi-independent ruler, of Wallachia three times. His stormy fate was closely entwined with the Ottoman Empire, and in particular with Sultan Mehmed II, and their fraught relationship remains one of the most compelling episodes in the long history of the dynasty.

Vlad the Impaler in some degree inspired Bram Stoker's legendary Count Dracula, but the historical reality was something else. Vlad was the only Christian leader to accept Pope Pius II's challenge and take the Cross after the latter's declaration of a three-year crusade in 1460. Vlad may have harboured a true desire to defeat the enemies of the Cross of Christ and to uphold the religious statutes of the Order of the Dragon, but there were other motives, more complex and personal, that induced him to wage war against the Ottomans.

Wallachia had been a vassal state of the Ottomans during the reign of his father, Vlad II Dracul. Vlad and his brother Radu, both Wallachian princes, were raised as hostages at the Ottoman court when they were teenagers, alongside young Mehmed. No other Christian ruler knew Mehmed personally, and it was the intimate knowledge of his obsessive ambition and how to provoke him that gave Vlad the upper hand. Upon the death of Vlad's father in 1456, Mehmed sent him from the Ottoman court as his vassal to rule Wallachia, leaving his brother Radu a hostage in Constantinople. Vlad formed a dubious alliance with the king of Hungary in 1460, and the trouble began. Vlad had sent the sultan a letter claiming he could no longer pay the tribute money Mehmed demanded, nor leave Wallachia, for fear of losing his kingdom to Hungary. In return, Mehmed sent an embassy to insist on the tribute payment, but Vlad had them all murdered by impaling them on large stakes, a horrific method he had learnt from Mehmed. Provoked to a fury, Mehmed decided to invade Wallachia, and the first battle of wits began.

Vlad had nothing like the military clout of Mehmed, but he knew the terrain better and had a brilliant strategic mind, like the sultan. Mehmed set a trap by luring him to the Ottoman fortress of Giurgiu on the river Danube, ostensibly to prove his good faith by promising him gifts of children, horses and more personal offerings of his own.[6] But Vlad was forewarned about the impending ambush and, knowing Mehmed would attack, he planned to strike first. He took his cavalry into the fortress cleverly disguised as Turks, mingling with the crowd, then took control and burned the Ottoman stronghold, boasting to the Hungarian king that they had killed 20,000 people. In the rest of Europe, Vlad's exploits were greeted with admiration and amazement. The would-be crusaders could not believe his daring, nor his success. William Wey, an English pilgrim on his way home, wrote that, on the island of Rhodes, the army had Te Deums sung in honour of the Wallachian victory.[7]

Through the long, hot summer of 1462, Vlad's scouts lay in the reeds of the Danube, watching and waiting. They were local men who knew every inch of the land, every water source and village, and they scanned the river and its surrounds night and day. And so, they were prepared when Mehmed crossed the river in late September, accompanied by his grand vizier and Vlad's brother Radu, the sultan's favourite, wearing eastern armour. Their aim was to dethrone the Impaler and install Radu in his place. With them came the Janissaries, flying their white and gilt banner of the faith, alongside other flags bedecked with stars, crescent moons, spearheads and animals. The sultan's army numbered around 80,000 men, a mighty cohort that dwarfed Vlad's military forces, causing him to withdraw to the north, burning the villages and crops of his own people as he went. Rotting animal corpses were left in wells and rivers, and it was reported that he even adopted a kind of germ warfare, paying plague-infected Wallachians disguised as Ottomans to mingle in Mehmed's camp and spread disease.

The Night Attack and the Forest of the Impaled

Years later, Vlad told the papal legate Niccolò Modrussa that, while Mehmed's army pursued him, he and his 24,000 troops were holed up in rough country, as the Ottomans looted towns and carried off children. On 17 June 1462, Vlad's men were close enough to hear the highly organized Ottoman camp at prayer an hour before sunset, its tents pitched in perfect order in what was a microcosm of Ottoman society and the epitome of the sultan's authority. It seems Vlad himself may have wandered through the camp in Turkish disguise, to reconnoitre before launching a celebrated and daring attack. Using arrows torn from the bodies of the dead, Vlad took his cavalry of almost 8,000 men and rode at full tilt through the Ottoman camp, massacring horses, camels and several thousand Turks. In the end, the Janissaries repelled the attackers, but Vlad's audacious night attack, another strategy learnt from Mehmed and turned against him, came nail-bitingly close to succeeding. If he had managed to reach the sultan's tent and capture or kill him, history would be quite different. But, in the end, many of his cavalry fled with their wounded leader into the darkness.

Mehmed and his men found no living creature, nor food, nor

water, as they marched on Vlad's capital of Târgovişte. All had been laid waste by Vlad's retreating army. A hundred kilometres from the city, they came across a unique and terrible sight. No Ottoman annal records it, but the Greek historian of the Ottomans, Laonic Chalkondyles, described the scene, which consisted of 'a field of stakes, about three miles long and one mile wide. And there were large stakes on which they could see the impaled bodies of men, women and children, about twenty thousand of them . . .'[8] The forest of the impaled left a lasting, ghastly impression on all who witnessed the outcome of an act far more terrible than any vampire legend. Mehmed pressed on and, nearly a month later, defeated Vlad's troops, removing the Impaler from the throne and replacing him with Radu, from whom his brother escaped, traversing wild and dangerous country to reach Hungary, where King Matthias Corvinus kept him under house arrest until around 1475. Legends relate how he met his death at the hands of an assassin near the Danube, who had his head sent to Mehmed in Constantinople, where it was displayed in the city on a tall stake.

On the surface, the conflict between Mehmed II and Vlad *Tępeş* was a war between two European leaders – one Christian, the other Muslim. But it was no ordinary religious war. It was also a battle for territorial advantage, in which Vlad fought to consolidate and increase his power, and maintain authority over his homeland. Mehmed's aim was to replace the first in line to the Wallachian throne with his younger brother, but it seemed that he had no desire to conquer; rather, Mehmed wished to use Wallachia and neighbouring Moldavia as buffer states against the Hungarian threat that persisted, and to secure the Danube as a line of defence. Yet, their battle was more than religious and political; it was a deeply personal fight for power between two men who were bound by the ties of youthful companionship, but riven apart by individual ambition and a drive for supremacy complicated by shattered loyalties.

On the European stage, Mehmed II was invincible: he was Caesar of Rome, the Sultan of Two Lands and Khan of Two Seas. He had achieved what seemed impossible, conquering Constantinople, creating a new Muslim capital on European soil and elevating a dynasty that would rule for almost another 500 years. He was the guardian of the Greek and Roman heritage of Europe, enshrined in his capital city, and architect of a cultural, political and religious future that bolstered the Ottomans as well as the European continent. In April 1481, he marched with the Ottoman army on a new campaign, some say to overthrow the Mamluk sultanate of Egypt, but death met him on the road. He died on 3 May 1481, at the age of forty-nine, after falling ill, possibly poisoned by his eldest son and heir Bayezid II, and was buried in the Fatih or Conqueror Mosque in Constantinople.

Chapter 16

Istanbul: City of Manifold Meanings

'If the earth were a single state, Istanbul would be its capital'

Napoleon Bonaparte

'Bishop-mated was the King of India by my queenly troops, when I played the chess of empire on the board of sovereignty.'

Sultan Selim I

The Hybrid City

A CHANNEL OF water less than four kilometres wide, known as the Bosphorus, separates the landmasses of Europe and Asia, flowing south into the Sea of Marmara and the Aegean, and northwards into the Black Sea. The venerable city that lies on its opposite shores is part of both continents, a place of manifold names that embody its diverse identities. The bygone people of Thrace in south-east Europe first named the settlement there Lygos in their language, according to the Roman natural historian Pliny the Elder (AD 23–79). In the seventh century BC, Greek settlers colonized the eastern shores of the Bosphorus and renamed the place Byzantion, said in legend to honour the sea god Poseidon's son Byzas, but perhaps in reality after a king of Thrace of the same name, who gave his wife the land that was to become Istanbul. Then the Romans came, carving out a magnificent highway, the Via Egnatia, from the Adriatic coast to Byzantion, creating a path from Rome straight to the Bosphorus. They Latinized the name of Byzas' city to Byzantium, and it was absorbed into the Roman Empire in AD 73.

The emperor Constantine the Great made the already legendary city his capital in the year 330, after his miraculous conversion to Christianity at the Milvian Bridge, when pagan Byzantium became Christian Constantinople, the New Rome named after the emperor and founded on seven hills, like the Eternal City itself. Over a thousand years later, after Mehmed II's victory over Constantine XI in 1453, Constantinople's name changed yet again, to the Ottoman Turkish Kostantiniyye, and also to its new Muslim name of Istanbul, a fusion of the Greek phrase 'in the city' and the Turkish word *Islambol*, meaning 'abounding with Islam'. The name 'Istanbul' is a metonym for a city that is the meeting place of two worlds, one Byzantine Christian, the other Turkish Muslim. Both names were used by the Ottomans, although the city was not officially named Istanbul until 1930, and Christians, both resident there and those living in the rest of Europe, continued to use 'Constantinople'. The city's many denominations emphasize a past of cultural, ethnic and religious hybridity epitomized in its Ottoman names, which honour both its Christian heritage and its dominant Muslim status. The Ottoman conquest of Constantinople was a vital moment in the evolution of Islamic Europe, whose history so far had encompassed the fall of its western European stronghold in the Iberian peninsula and the virtually concurrent rise of its eastern European territories, where Islam had arrived much later. Though migrating Seljuk Turks from central Asia had first brought Islam to Anatolia in the eleventh century, it had not taken hold until Öz Beg (1282–1341), Khan of the Mongol Turkic dynasty known as the Golden Horde, was converted to Islam by a Sunni Sufi in the fourteenth century and adopted Islam as his state religion. It began to spread across eastern Europe among the Turkic tribes, including the tribe of Osman, who may initially have been a client of the Mongols. As a result, the history of eastern and central Europe followed a diametrically opposite course to that of western Europe.

*

To obey *Fight hard for Allah* is my aim and my desire,
'Tis but zeal for faith, for Islam, that my ardour doth
inspire.
Through the grace of Allah and assistance of the Band
Unseen,
It is my earnest hope to crush the infidels with ruin dire.
On the saints and on the Prophets surely doth my trust
repose,
Through the love of God to triumph and to conquest I
aspire.[1]

In this ghazal, a lyric poem written in Arabic by Sultan Mehmed II, it is clear that Islam is his lodestar. Holy war against the infidel was his deepest duty as the man who had been destined to win Constantinople for Islam. Yet Mehmed highly valued the diverse history of the city and its varied cultures and aspired to maintain them. Religious tolerance was key to his revival of a city he had found in ruins and fractured, and it was a policy that obliged him to restore amicable relations with other religious leaders. He lost no time in inviting the Armenian patriarch Hovakim I to return from the town of Bursa and institute the Armenian Church in the new Ottoman capital, creating a community permitted to rule itself by its own laws. Mehmed also summoned the chief rabbi Moses Capsali from Jerusalem to lead the Jews of Turkey, a man he greatly admired and whom he elevated to a position in the Islamic government ministry under the jurisdiction of the grand mufti, religious head of the Muslims. Gennadius the Scholar was also reinstated as patriarch of the Eastern Orthodox Church, in a ceremony during which Mehmed invested him with the crozier and mantle of his office. Gennadius appointed thirty-six bishops to serve the same number of churches preserved in the city, but a panoramic view of the horizon left no doubt that Kostantiniyye was now an Islamic place, with a skyline dominated by minarets.

While Mehmed II was breathing new life into Kostantiniyye, the western continent was at the height of the era later known as the Renaissance. The movement to revive and surpass the learning of classical antiquity that set Florence on fire caught hold in other areas of Europe, bringing momentous changes in art, literature, politics, architecture and science. The new Islamic empire in the east of Europe was deeply involved with the Renaissance in two very different ways, which have tended to go unacknowledged. The first relates to the consequences of the emigration of Greek scholars from Constantinople to western Europe after 1453. Like the Umayyads, Abbasids and Muslims of al-Andalus before them, the Muslims of eastern Europe generally had little to learn in scholarly and cultural terms from western Christendom. Ancient Greek and Arabic learning had travelled from east to west and had impelled the expansion of north-western European culture. The transfer of knowledge continued in that direction when Greek intellectuals fled from Kostantiniyye after the Muslim conquest. Many found their way to Italy, Crete and Dalmatia, where they set themselves up in universities as teachers of the Greek language.

The perception of Renaissance humanism as a thing apart from Islamic intellectual knowledge is flawed. The evolution of Renaissance science, literature and philosophy had already been influenced by the Greek and Arabic scientific and philosophical learning that had reached western Europe from al-Andalus. But Renaissance scholars were interested first and foremost in Latin works of history, philosophy and literature, such as those by Seneca, Lucretius and Livy, and also in the recovery of ancient Greek historical, literary and religious writings by Homer and dramatists such as Demosthenes, which had not been studied in Latin Christendom due to its scant knowledge of the Greek language. The Greek refugees from Kostantiniyye brought some of these ancient works to western Europe, where they were rediscovered. In contrast, the Islamic world, and the Ottomans themselves, had never been cut off from Greek knowledge as Latin Christendom had, and they never needed to rediscover it.

What the Greek emigres also brought to western Europe was a renewed hostility towards Muslims, which rekindled the old medieval animosity that sprang from the quills and parchments of early

Christian writers. A rhetoric of barbarism and civilization framed the cultural prejudices of the Greek refugees, who penned a discourse that fostered the opposition between the 'civilized West' and the 'barbarian East'. One of its most vocal advocates was Bessarion, a Greek humanist who hailed from Anatolia, rose to become a cardinal and was appointed Latin patriarch of Constantinople by Pope Pius II. He lived in Italy from the 1440s onwards, where he made every effort to commission new translations of Greek scholarship into Latin and was known as the original patron of the Greek exiles after 1453. The news that Constantinople had fallen to the Ottomans prompted him to write eloquently to the doge of Venice, lamenting what he saw as a terrible loss to western culture: 'A city which was recently flourishing, with such a great emperor, so many illustrious men, such very famous and ancient families, so prosperous, the head of all Greece, the splendour and glory of the East, the school of the best arts, the refuge of all good things has been captured, despoiled, ravaged and completely sacked by the most inhuman barbarians and the most savage enemies of the Christian faith, by the fiercest of wild beasts'.[2] Clearly Bessarion had forgotten about the Fourth Crusade and the horrific sack of Constantinople by Christian crusaders in 1204. This kind of language was common in western accounts of the conquest of 1453, which deplored the loss of an ancient, magnificent empire, the sacrilege wrought upon holy buildings and the enslavement of the inhabitants. Yet, while Mehmed II was aware of this antagonism and declared that he had avenged many of the injustices inflicted on the East by the West, most of his chroniclers presented him as a sultan who wanted the integration and unity of Asia and Europe.

Those values were reflected in Mehmed's life as the ruler of Kostantiniyye and head of the Ottoman Empire, and were embodied in his persona. He was deeply interested in the intellectual pursuits and scholarship of the Renaissance, gathering Greek and Italian scholars at court and building a library of Greek and Latin works, as well as Islamic and Jewish writings. Perhaps he saw it as part of his Roman inheritance, a duty to understand those realms he was perceived to have conquered. Along with the Arabic tales of chivalry he enjoyed, and works on Sufism, Islamic law, medicine and philosophy, the library contained Homer's *Iliad*, Maimonides' *Guide to the Perplexed* in Hebrew, and books in Armenian, Persian and other languages, many of which came from the Byzantine Imperial Library. Particular favourites were the sources for the life story of Alexander the Great. The Greek scholar George Amiroutzes, who came to his court, made a map of the world for the sultan based on Ptolemy's *Geographia*, but with Arabic text.

Mehmed had a passion for the art and literature of the Renaissance, and wrote to the king of Naples and the Medicis of Florence asking them to send him their artists. Lorenzo de Medici's personal sculptor Bertoldi di Giovanni minted a medallion of the sultan showing him as a heroic gladiator on a chariot. Mehmed commissioned the Venetian painter Gentile Bellini to paint him a view of Venice and a depiction of the Virgin and Child. Bellini also painted a portrait of Mehmed II in full Renaissance style in 1480, a work now held by the Victoria and Albert Museum in London. Mehmed seemed fascinated by Christianity, commissioning the Greek patriarch to write him a treatise explaining the religion, and he accumulated a bizarre collection of Christian relics, such as the corpse of the prophet Isaiah, complete with hair and ears. Isaiah is often mentioned in Islamic sources because he was said to have predicted the coming of Jesus and also of Muhammad. In some sense, Mehmed was the forerunner of the western Renaissance princes Charles V, the Holy Roman Emperor, and King Francis I of France. He was a man whose cosmopolitanism brought together two religions and cultures and built on the remarkable exchange of knowledge between Christians and Muslims that had started in al-Andalus and spread to north-western Europe.

Set in Stone: The Rebirth of a Metropolis

Constantinople had its own renaissance under Ottoman rule, its rebirth as a Turkish, Muslim city enshrined in its new names, Kostantiniyye and Istanbul. That new identity also found expression in the buildings and gardens of the urban centre. Mehmed II's rehabilitation programme began with the repair of buildings and infrastructures neglected for centuries, in particular the vital flow of water through the hydraulic systems of the city – cisterns, aqueducts and drains – and with the creation of new architecture, as well as the incorporation of what already existed into the Islamic framework. Two of Kostantiniyye's most famous landmarks, the Imperial Palace and the Hagia Sophia basilica, became icons of that fusion of cultures and religions that made the city unique. Its role as the capital of the great Muslim empire was the accomplishment of Mehmed's will, represented in the new sultan's main imperial residence, known as the Topkapı. In 1458, Mehmed had led the conquest of Athens, and had been deeply impressed with the beauty of its ancient monuments, issuing an edict forbidding their looting or destruction. Overawed by the magnificence of the hilltop fortress of the Athenian Acropolis, he studied the principles of its siting and architecture, which he applied to the construction of his own acropolis in Kostantiniyye. The location he chose was the Seraglio Point, on a hill overlooking the Golden Horn, where the Bosphorus meets the Sea of Marmara. The new palace was to be built on the site of the old acropolis of Constantinople, and the sultan had the land levelled and terraced into the steep slopes. He established the layout of the buildings himself, situating his personal quarters at the highest point, a suitably commanding location for the ruler of a vast empire.

From afar, it is a serene symphony of rounded domes, towers and spires, a formal garden of bushes and trees carved in stone. Close up, the perimeter has a martial air, whose high, defensive walls speak of authority, strength and seclusion. Through the Gate of Salutation, there is a disconcerting sense of asymmetry, of being off-centre. The inner buildings are places of grilled windows for secret spying and secret passages for flight. Their layout and appearance are unique among Islamic palaces and are based on the principle of imperial seclusion from the world, a tradition formalized by Mehmed, who imposed a rule of complete silence in the inner courtyards. The Ottomans called it the Palace of Felicity.

Mehmed would enter the palace from the Mese avenue, through the massive Imperial Gate built in 1478 on the south side of the precinct, its high arch glittering with verses from the Koran and the sultan's signature in gilded Ottoman calligraphy. It announced the diverse nature of the Ottoman dynasty, referring to him as 'khan' and 'sultan', with reference to his Turco-Mongol heritage, and as 'the shadow of God', in Islamic style, and 'sovereign of the two continents and two seas' – sovereign of Europe and Asia. It announced the fusion of divine and secular power in words and stone, in a citadel that reinforced the imperial authority of the sultan as supreme leader of the Ottoman state. The sultan's palace replaced what went before, superimposing a Muslim stronghold over the footprint of the old Christian acropolis.

From the Imperial Gate, the road led directly to the Hagia Sophia mosque, visually and tangibly linking the sultan and all he stood for with that new and powerful representation of Islam. When Mehmed entered the Christian cathedral in May 1453, there had been a church on the site for over 900 years. Originally named Church of the Holy Wisdom and designed by Greek mathematicians Isidore of Miletus and Anthemius of Tralles, it became the epitome of Byzantine architecture and the world's largest cathedral, only superseded by the Catholic cathedral of Seville. The two Greeks had been appointed by the emperor Justinian to construct a new basilica on the site of the previous one, built in the reign of Theodosius and burned to the ground during city riots. It was originally finished with a marble veneer, which, in combination with areas of gilding, made it shimmer from afar, a sight that would have struck awe into sea travellers approaching the harbour. Over 10,000 people worked on its construction and no cost was spared. Polychrome marble in green and white, purple porphyry and gold mosaics were imported from all around the Mediterranean, and when Justinian first saw it completed, he is recorded as saying: 'Solomon, I have surpassed you!' The building was briefly converted to a Catholic cathedral in 1204, during the disastrous Fourth Crusade, under the aegis of the Latin Roman Empire, but it was restored to Eastern Orthodoxy when the Byzantine Empire was reclaimed in 1261.

Mehmed II treated the great church with veneration during its conversion. The bells, altar, baptistery and pulpit were removed, and eventually four minarets, a minbar and a mihrab were added. The golden crescent of Islam was mounted on top of the dome, and the mausoleum became the burial place of forty-three Ottoman rulers. Nowadays, the Hagia Sophia, or *Ayasofya* in Turkish, is a UNESCO World Heritage Site and a cultural icon of modern Istanbul. It was a church for almost a millennium, a mosque for nearly 500 years, then a museum, and recently it has become a mosque once more. In the time of Mehmed II, the newly converted mosque was the symbolic heart of the Islamic empire of the Ottomans, sending a clear message to all who saw it from afar or close up: the primary religious and cultural identity of Constantinople was Islamic.

The City of Books and Refugees

The ancient Forum of Theodosius was probably the largest square in Constantinople and lay along the Mese, the main road leading from the Imperial Palace to the Hagia Sophia. Under Ottoman rule, its name was changed to Bayezid Square when Sultan Bayezid II ordered the construction of a mosque. Nowadays, it is the oldest original imperial mosque complex remaining in Istanbul. Bayezid was Mehmed II's eldest son, who had travelled to Constantinople on hearing that his father had died, rushing from Amasya in Anatolia, where he was governor, to arrive before one of his younger brothers, Çem, who also claimed the throne. Bayezid came to the throne in 1481, and his reign began a struggle for accession which embroiled Christian Europe directly with the Ottomans and divided secular and religious leaders on the continent who sought to use Çem as a pawn against the Muslim state.

The king of Hungary wanted Çem to lead his armies against the Ottomans, who already had the backing of the Egyptian Mamluks, but rivalry between Hungary, France and the pope split European forces rather than united them. While Bayezid was not as cruel to his siblings as his father, his troops defeated Çem, who fled to Rhodes for shelter, where it was thought Bayezid had brokered a deal with the Knights Hospitaller to keep his rival imprisoned for a yearly payment. Instead, they sent him to France in 1483 as a prisoner, from where he was taken to Rome. Pope Alexander VI had plans for him to head a new papal crusade, but it came to nothing, and Çem eventually died in Naples in 1499. The complex negotiations between Bayezid, Çem and European leaders drew the Ottomans into the sphere of Renaissance diplomacy. Çem had his portrait painted by the Renaissance artist Pinturicchio, and Bellini drew him in a standing pose, like a Renaissance prince. The Italian Baldassare Castiglione mentioned him in his early-sixteenth-century *Book of the Courtier*, a philosophical discussion of what makes the ideal royal adviser. The Ottomans were now a part of European culture.

Although Bayezid II was a patron of both western and eastern culture like his father, he was severe in his disapproval of figurative art. He had the frescos and paintings commissioned by Mehmed, including his portrait by Bellini, packed up and sold in the city bazaars, using the profits to finance the building of the Bayezid II mosque complex. He also sold Mehmed's collection of Christian relics. He did not have his father's thirst for military conquest – even though he thwarted a rebellion of the Iranian Safavids and consolidated the Ottoman Empire in his thirty-two-year reign, perhaps his most enduring legacy was in the realm of knowledge. Bayezid commissioned the collection and compilation of the many tales and oral narratives that circulated in the fifteenth century about the House of Osman, in effect a family history, that was to be written in Ottoman Turkish and Persian. The creation of written texts that set down the oral history, myths and legends surrounding the origins of his 200-year-old dynasty resulted in the first major body of written Ottoman history. It included different versions of popular accounts of the past in the *Deeds of the House of Osman*, many of which were fictions, and formed a body of heroic-style narratives that remains a vital source of information and speculation on early Ottoman history. That history served two purposes: it shored up Bayezid's authority as sultan, and also fostered loyalty to the dynasty, whose Turco-Mongol heritage and ancestry from the Oğuz Turks of central Asia was given strong emphasis. To reinforce his spiritual authority, Bayezid had himself proclaimed a saint.

In 1502, Bayezid ordered the librarian of the Imperial Palace, al-ʿAtufi, to prepare a catalogue of library holdings. The Register of the Library revealed an archive that matched or surpassed the great Islamic libraries of the past in Cordoba, Damascus and Baghdad, and consisted of 5,000 volumes and 7,000 titles on every conceivable field of human knowledge at that time. The books came mostly from the combined libraries of Mehmed II and Bayezid II, many brought as gifts, or acquired through the vast and thriving Mediterranean and global book trade, or taken as part of the booty of conquest. As such, it was an unmatched encyclopaedic collection of scholarship that constituted one of the most precious treasures of the Ottoman dynasty.[3]

While Bayezid established himself on the European cultural and political stage, he was also keeping a close eye on developments in the western Islamic state of Granada. On the eve of its conquest by Christian Spain, Sultan Muhammad XI, Boabdil, of Granada had made desperate pleas for help to defend his kingdom against the impending threat of the Christian armies of Ferdinand and Isabella, contacting both the Berber Wattasid dynasty in Fez and the Mamluks in Egypt, and sending envoys to the Ottoman Empire to beg for assistance. Moral support, but no practical help, was forthcoming from the Berbers or the Mamluks, but, in 1487, Bayezid sent the naval commander Kemal Reis on a mission to defend the Islamic emirate of Granada.*

Kemal landed his troops at Malaga, captured the city and local villages, and took many prisoners, before sailing up the Mediterranean coast to the Balearic Islands and Corsica. On various occasions in the last two years of the Granadan emirate, in 1490–2, he returned to al-Andalus and took on board ship Muslim and Jewish refugees

* Kemal Reis was the uncle of the celebrated Ottoman cartographer Piri Reis.

fleeing from the besieged province of Granada, sailing them into the lands of the Ottoman Empire. Although Bayezid could afford little extra practical help as his resources were focused on fighting the Mamluks in the east, Kemal Reis continued to assault al-Andalus and hinder the Spanish advance by bombarding the ports of Elche, Almería and Malaga. His attacks alarmed Ferdinand and Isabella, prompting the king to bolster the defences of Sicily, which was then under his jurisdiction. He also curried favour with the Mamluks and forged a brief alliance with them against the Ottomans between 1488 and 1491, shipping grain to the Mamluks and providing a fleet of fifty caravels against the common enemy. It was an ironic and calculating move, given that Ferdinand was determined to destroy Islam in the Iberian peninsula.

The Ottoman navy's efforts to avert the catastrophic conquest of the emirate of Granada were to no avail and the city fell into Christian hands on 2 January 1492. When, just three months later, in April, King Ferdinand and Queen Isabella proclaimed the Alhambra Decree that ordered the expulsion or conversion of all Jews throughout their Spanish and Portuguese territories, Bayezid II evacuated many Sephardic Jews from Spain, settling them in Ottoman lands, especially in Salonica. He sent out proclamations across his empire requesting that the refugees should be welcomed, granting them permission to become Ottoman citizens, and he threatened with death anyone who treated Jews harshly or refused them the right to settle in the empire. He cast ridicule on Ferdinand and Isabella's expulsion of two groups of people so useful to their realms, rebuking his courtiers: 'You venture to call Ferdinand a wise ruler, he who has impoverished his country and enriched mine!'[4]

The proof of Bayezid's wisdom lay in the great contribution made by the exiled Muslims and Jews of al-Andalus to the rising power of the Ottoman Empire, where they brought new ideas, methods and craftsmanship. The first printing press in Kostantiniyye was founded by Sephardic Jews in 1493, and, during Bayezid's reign, Jewish culture flourished, led by the famous Talmudic scholar and scientist Mordecai Comtino and the astronomer poet Solomon ben

Elijah, among others. A family of Jewish doctors from Granada travelled to the Ottoman capital, where they became famous. José Hamon became Bayezid's physician, and also that of his son, Selim, who took him on his victorious Middle Eastern campaigns.

It was Selim who brought a sudden end to his father's illustrious sovereignty, marching on Edirne in 1511, where Bayezid and his court had fled to escape the aftermath of a great earthquake in 1509 that had shaken the capital. The sultan defeated his son on the battlefield, but, three years later, Selim assailed the Imperial Palace in Kostantiniyye with his Janissaries and confronted his father as he sat on his dark marble and gold throne. It is said that Bayezid wept as he abdicated that throne and empire to his son. Selim sent him off to retirement in his native town of Dimetoka, accompanying him to the city gates and bidding him an affectionate farewell. But Bayezid never made it, and died en route on 26 May 1512, either poisoned at the order of his son, or of despair.

The City of the Caliph

The sword of Sultan Selim I is one of the Sacred Trusts, the name for the collection of Islamic sacred relics on show at the Topkapı Palace. In close proximity to Selim's sword is hair from the beard of the Prophet Muhammad, his Seal, an autographed letter written by the Prophet, and his own swords and bow. These venerated objects, brought back to the Ottoman capital by Selim I after his campaign in Egypt, associated the sultan with the supreme leader of Islam, elevating him to the position of revered spiritual ruler. Selim ruled for just eight years, and his reign has lain in the shadow of his celebrated grandfather Mehmed II and his own son and successor Suleiman the Magnificent. But some historians believe his short reign was momentous in its impact on world history, since his series of wars in the Middle East left a lasting mark on the globe.[5]

Selim had a fiery temper and a taste for executing his viziers, which earned him the epithet 'the Grim'. He also had both his half-brothers strangled within a month of each other, to prevent any accession challenges. In 1513, the Italian diplomat Machiavelli wrote

The Prince, a guide for princes in diplomacy and statecraft, in which Selim is held up as the archetypal ruthless, dominant and strategic politician that Machiavelli so greatly admired. He also had a cultivated side to his personality – he could speak both Turkish and Persian fluently, and was a distinguished poet, whose Persian verses are in print today. Like his grandfather, his cultivation existed side by side with a love of war, and with a ferocious ambition. He saw the Shi'ite Safavid dynasty of Iran (1501–1736) as the greatest military and ideological danger to the Sunni Muslim Ottoman Empire. At the outset of his reign, he had instigated the largest domestic purge of the population in Ottoman history when he ordered the massacre of all Shi'ites aged between seven and seventy in Anatolia. He defeated the Safavids in 1514 at the Battle of Chaldiran, when they surrendered their capital Tabriz, from where Selim sent its finest artisans, poets and intellectuals back to Istanbul. It was a resounding victory, which fuelled the sultan's ambition to fulfil his birth prophecy that he would rule all seven climes. His vision was one of Sunni Ottoman global domination, and he aspired to become the first Ottoman caliph, chosen by God to cast his shadow over all creation. What stood in his way was the Mamluk sultanate of Egypt, with its capital at Cairo.

The Mamluks were a warrior class that emerged from the ranks of slave soldiers, akin to the Janissaries, who ultimately became the knightly military class of Egypt. Selim moved in and won a superb victory against the Mamluks in Aleppo, then took Damascus, and conquered Jerusalem itself in December 1516, pledging to protect the city's Christians and Jews. With Cairo now in his sights, he led his armies, camels, horses and twelve large cannons on a remarkable 200-mile trip amid the winter rains, crossing the Sinai desert in just five days. By mid-January 1517, they were at the gates of Cairo. The final battle for the city took place on 22 January and was over in barely an hour, giving Selim victory and with it the Egyptian empire, a historic conquest that paved the way for global domination. He now ruled large areas of three continents, controlled more territory than any living person and boasted the world's two largest cities,

Kostantiniyye and Cairo. His next step was decisive in establishing him as not just the Ottoman sultan of a majority Muslim population, but as their spiritual leader too.

Soon, Selim took control of the desert cities of Mecca and Medina, the holiest places of Islam, and demanded the keys of the Ka'aba. It was at this point that he sent the sacred relics of the Prophet back to Kostantiniyye, a city which then played a crucial role in Muslim pilgrimage for the next four centuries. Selim adopted the title 'Servant of the Two Holy Cities', a designation of crucial personal and political importance that denoted his guardianship of the two holiest mosques in Islam and indicated that he was – nominally, at least – the caliph of Islam. From 23 January 1517, Ottoman historians boasted that Kostantiniyye was the new European centre of the Islamic caliphate, ruled by Islam's caliph himself.

This was the start of new traditions in the city, as it controlled the route of the hajj to Mecca and dominated the Middle East commercially and spiritually. The long-established annual tradition of sending gifts from the sultan to Mecca and Medina continued, but their journey now began in Kostantiniyye and not Cairo, leaving on white camels, decorated, perfumed and loaded with handmade gifts, which were taken on barges across the Bosphorus amid songs and devotional chanting. Charity money was sent in leather pouches, amounting in Selim's reign to 200,000 gold pieces, as well as pearls, chandeliers and silk rugs that adorned the caravan. After 1517, Selim really lived up to his title 'God's Shadow on Earth', as he ruled the entire middle world, including trade routes between the Mediterranean, India and China, and the ports in all the great oceans of the Old World, and he had unmatched religious authority among Muslims. He also introduced coffee from Yemen, and brought back great cultural wealth to Kostantiniyye, which absorbed the traditions of the Egyptian empire, alongside its economic riches.

So far, Selim had shifted the cultural and geographical centre of the Ottoman Empire away from central Europe and the Balkans towards the Middle East, but his relationship with Catholic Spain and Portugal was about to take on great importance. In 1499, King

Ferdinand and Queen Isabella had captured the North African town of Melilla, their first territory on the African mainland. It was part of what they called a new crusade against Africa, designed to quash any ideas of a potential Muslim reconquest involving the exiled Muslims of al-Andalus and their North African allies. It was part of Queen Isabella's will, after she died in 1504, that she wanted her legacy to be the conquest of Muslim Africa and a crusade against Islam as a defence against what she perceived as further invasion.

Bolstered by the newfound wealth from the Americas, Spain recalled many of its soldiers from the New World to renew its North African campaign, after Ferdinand recaptured Bougie on the Algerian coast in 1510. As his father had done before him, Selim sent the Barbarossa brothers to the kingdom of Granada to rescue and resettle Muslims from the province by taking them across the water to North Africa. But Selim had also captured Algiers, and, when Ferdinand died in 1516, the sultan was freer to formulate his plan to invade Morocco and drive Spain off the continent. Once again, Muslims stood at Spain's borders, and Morocco took on the nature of a frontier land between Islam and Christianity, between Eurasia and the western Atlantic continent. It might have seemed to Selim that control of Morocco would lead to a truly global Ottoman state, but then, on 22 September 1520, he succumbed to a mystery illness and died, aged forty-nine. It was a 'What if' moment that might have seen Islam prevail over Christianity, but hopes of an Ottoman takeover of Morocco vanished with the caliph. After eight short years, he left behind an empire that had expanded to vast dimensions, spanning nearly 3.5 million square kilometres geographically, and had conquered and brought together the most holy lands of Islam. His body was brought back to Kostantiniyye and was buried in a tomb in the Selim I Mosque, on the fifth hill of the city overlooking the Golden Horn.

*

In the seventy years since the conquest of Constantinople and the death of Selim I, the Ottoman Empire and its capital had been transformed. The city had experienced a religious conversion from

Greek Eastern Orthodox Christian heartland to an Islamic site of power, and that conversion was writ large on its urban horizon as church towers and spires became outnumbered by minarets. At the same time, hybridity and diversity were the hallmarks of both capital city and empire, as Kostantiniyye retained and developed a multicultural, multi-ethnic society whose rich and varied heritage gave it a unique character. In parallel, the Ottoman Empire had expanded exponentially to embrace the peoples of three continents and had established itself as part of Renaissance Europe politically and culturally. Its history had evolved through the written word, through its architecture and in the storied deeds of three generations of sultans whose ambition, religious fervour and brilliance raised their dynasty and imperial dominions to global prominence. Old reflections and parallels surfaced between these Muslims and Christians of early modern Europe, familiar alliances and conflicts, Muslim tolerance and Christian hostility, a persisting sharing of knowledge and of commerce, and the brokering of diplomatic deals as well as calls to war. But the world had changed since 1492. Religions tensions had intensified within Christianity as Protestantism threatened Catholic Europe, and within Islam as Selim's Middle Eastern conquests had stirred up the antagonism between Sunnis and Shi'ites. Maritime exploration and Europe's expansion into the Americas had set a new agenda and new struggles for supremacy. Yet Selim I had prepared the way for his successor to inherit a mighty empire that extended far into Europe and was poised on the threshold of Catholic Spain.

Chapter 17

Trading Titans: Venice and Constantinople in Commerce and Conflict

'Going down upon the margin of the green sea, rolling on before the door, and filling all the streets, I came upon a place of such surpassing beauty, and such grandeur, that all the rest was poor and faded, in comparison with its absorbing loveliness.'

Charles Dickens

'All the actions of Venice, in war and in peace, were determined by the interests of commerce.'

Peter Ackroyd

The Marriage of the Sea

Venice is built on water and gold. It shimmers with golden mosaics, gilded ceilings, palaces and towers that are the incarnation of once prodigious riches born of trade and the sea. That fusion of water and wealth is honoured each year on the day of Christ's Ascension, when the mayor of Venice assumes a doge's mantle of sumptuous gold and silver brocade, lined with ermine, and bears a ceremonial rod in his hand. In an ancient ritual of propitiation, he boards his barge and sails out of the lagoon that cradles the city, into the Adriatic Sea, where he throws into the depths the gold ring that symbolizes the marriage of Venice to the sea, and her maritime dominion. The Venetian ceremony began in the year 1000, but illuminates the time when the Ottoman Empire stood on the threshold of its greatest era, after the death of Sultan Selim I, a time when

Venice ruled the waves of the Mediterranean as the most powerful and prosperous city in western Europe, standing at the gateway to the East. Fundamental to that prosperity was the intense relationship between Muslim Constantinople and Christian Venice, an encounter at times antagonistic but also mutually beneficial. To understand that deep connection between the two powerhouses of eastern and western Europe, we first need to go back in time and chart the progress of commerce in Europe and the Mediterranean as it evolved from the ebb and flow of the civilizations of Latin Christendom and the Islamic world in Europe and beyond.

Bazaars, Slaves, Spices and Silk: The Rise of Mercantile Capitalism

The sharpest contrast in the growth of trade between the Christian and Muslim lands of Europe lay in the rural and the urban. At the birth of Islam in the early seventh century, the largest city in Christian Europe was Constantinople, the heart of the Eastern Roman Empire and the impetus behind commerce with the main western cities of Rome, Ravenna and Carthage, plus Alexandria and Antioch in the east. Latin Christendom was then a rural society, its feudal structures invented by monks, whose monasteries were the sole centres for education and writing until the twelfth century. The coming of Islam wrought great changes in European trade. The Arabs were masters of a desert landscape marked out by trading posts like Medina, where Islam began, and Islam's founder was himself a trader, along with his wife, and his immediate successor Abu Bakr, a cloth merchant. The value of commerce is explained in the Koran and the Hadith, which express the profound connection between trade and Islam remarked on by the American financial theorist William Bernstein, who believed that their interrelation transformed history: 'This extraordinary fact suffuses the soul of this faith and guides the historical events that ricocheted over the land routes of Asia and the sea lanes of the Indian Ocean through the next nine centuries.'[1]

As Islamic armies seized the largest and wealthiest cities of the old Byzantine and Persian Empires from the seventh century onwards, peoples and traditions intermingled, while urban culture and monuments became central to Islam and to the authority of the caliph in cities like Jerusalem and Damascus under Umayyad rule. In Latin Europe, castles were its sites of power and were associated with defence, while in Islamic lands power lay in cities, political, economic and cultural hubs which became supreme expressions of their civilization. Urban design focused on the main mosque and imposing minarets, on the royal palace, baths and souks defended by ramparts that spoke of power and military might. The souk or bazaar was a fundamental element in the development of Muslim cities. Its most striking feature was its separation from residential areas, to allow customers and traders easy access. Bazaars were created along closely interwoven labyrinths of streets and lanes, and sold spice, food, cotton, silk, leather, metal and jewellery, and exchanged money, much as they do today. In each city was a *funduq* or courtyard with a warehouse and lodging for caravans. By the ninth century, the largest European cities apart from Constantinople were in the west, in Muslim al-Andalus, where Cordoba shone as capital of the Umayyad caliphate and Almería produced silk and built the ships vital for Mediterranean commerce. Islamic trade looked eastwards, connecting al-Andalus with North Africa, Egypt and Syria; it rarely looked north beyond the Pyrenees.

In the early eleventh century, Fatimid Egypt became the epicentre of international commerce, standing at the crossroads of major world trade routes between the Mediterranean and the Red Sea. Pepper, cinnamon and ginger sailed from India to a Red Sea port, where the spices and other goods were taken by caravans across the desert to Cairo, including the annual pilgrimage caravan to Mecca, which brought back Eastern goods to the Egyptian capital. Muslim attention to the needs and comfort of travelling merchants was outstanding. The construction of rest stations known as caravanserais, at intervals of thirty kilometres along the caravan routes, were fundamental to Muslim trade, and were charitable foundations that provided travellers with three days of free shelter, food and sometimes entertainment. Like the *funduq*, they had a courtyard bordered with halls and rooms for lodging, depots, guard rooms and stables.

Merchants crisscrossed not just the deserts but also the seas between Europe and North Africa and the Pacific, selling a vast variety of goods. One such merchant was Nahray ibn Nissim, leader of the Iraqi Jews in Cairo, who traded across the Mediterranean for fifty years between 1045 and 1096. Nahray was a respected religious scholar, but became a wealthy businessman by specializing in the export of spices, pearls and indigo to his native Tunisia and to Sicily. He also bought Egyptian linen, Spanish silk, Byzantine cotton and dried fruit from Syria, as well as perfumes and cosmetics. It was during his lifetime, in the eleventh century, that the Italians, including the Venetians, began to make their mark on world trade, also venturing to Egypt in increasing numbers, especially to Alexandria. There, they sold wood, cheese and wine, as well as silver, a desirable product for trade with the Muslim East, which enabled them to mint silver coins as well as their customary gold pieces.

*

The growing complexity of buying and selling across many different countries and cultures using varied currencies demanded new trading practices and procedures. The whole enterprise of fitting out a ship, loading it with goods and sailing it across the Mediterranean was a highly risky undertaking that called for new types of contract and associations to protect profits and share risks. It was an Arab style of contract that the Italians adopted in the 1200s, called a *commenda* in Italian – a simple arrangement which involved a financial sponsor who provided capital, and a merchant who transported and sold the goods. Another type of Arab contract, the *shirka*, involved a partnership in which everyone invested a share and acquired a percentage of the gains or losses. To avoid transporting large amounts of currency, and to avoid the prohibition on usury in both Muslim and Christian law, Italian merchants frequently used bills of exchange; Islamic countries used a *sakk*, later adopted in Europe as the cheque, which authorized payment on an account.

By the twelfth century, the ships of Latin Europe began to dominate the trade routes, partly because the Islamic countries along the Mediterranean lacked forests to provide wood for shipbuilding, and partly as a result of the prohibition on the sale of ships to Muslims by many Christian councils. But west European traders were still reliant on the nautical charts and astrolabes used by Arab pilots to measure latitude, forerunners of the nautical compass that was introduced in the thirteenth century. Trading ships could become warships in an encounter with the enemy, and the fear of pirates, thieves and swindlers loomed large in the letters of passengers, who often included crusaders, mercenaries, emigrants and pilgrims to Jerusalem or Mecca. Yet, despite the risk of shipwreck, robbery and the imposition of taxes, commerce was often very lucrative – a merchant selling pepper in the mid-eleventh century could buy it in Egypt and hope to sell it at an 80 per cent profit in Tunisia.[2]

*

Trade between European Christians and Muslims was not only in luxury goods and vital manufacturing supplies. For around 500 years, the main export from Europe to the Islamic countries was slaves. Early in the eighth century, the Venetians had purchased slaves on the Roman market to resell to Muslims, an enterprise shut down by Pope Zachary, who redeemed and freed them. Before AD 1000, merchants from Christian Europe sold slaves at the markets of al-Andalus and North Africa, but the scenario started to change at the historical pivot point of the eleventh century, when Muslim Spain came under threat from north and south, and the Crusades got underway. Muslim captives of European Christians went on sale in the Rialto market in Venice, in the south of Spain and in the lands of the East. From the thirteenth century onwards, Venice was deeply involved in slave-trafficking, from the Black Sea region in particular, so much so that, a hundred years later, as many as 10,000 slaves may have been sold in Venice itself.

The Black Sea slave trade had existed since ancient times, and women were frequently active dealers. Under Ottoman rule, the strongest slaves worked in the fields, harvesting sugar and other crops, but the most attractive of both sexes went to the sultan's harem or into service in the royal household. Many local families in Ottoman lands saw being traded as a vital opportunity to progress, and their sons and daughters were sent to halfway houses to learn the ways of nobility before they were sold as marriageable commodities.

Aside from slaves, spices and gold, wool was a crucial element of trade between the Latin Christian and Islamic worlds, and this thriving business brought changes to Muslim dress habits and wealth to the sheep farmers of Italy, Flanders and Castile. At the same time, trade sparked the evolution of both Christian and Islamic monetary systems, giving Latin Europe access to African gold from the Maghreb to mint their coinage, while, conversely, Egypt turned central European silver into coins to promote international retail trade. As western Europeans discovered the delights of bananas, silk and spices, and Muslims bought iron, wood and wool, it was the city of Venice that came to the fore in this climate of reciprocity and cultural and economic exchange.

The New Alexandria: Gateway to the East

As ghostly figures flee from a thunderbolt across a dark, stormy Venetian sky, a man's corpse is reverently unloaded from the back of a camel. This is the scene set in an imposing painting by the dyer's son and visionary artist Jacopo Tintoretto, born in Venice and known as 'Il Furioso' for his powerful creative energy. His picture captured a legendary moment in the early history of his city: the secret arrival of the corpse of St Mark the Evangelist. Mark was a North African who founded the Church of Alexandria around AD 49 and, according to Egyptian Coptic tradition, was its first bishop. He was martyred in the city in AD 68 when Alexandria was ruled by the Muslim Abbasids of Cairo, and legend has it that two opportunist Venetian merchants snatched his body with the help of Greek monks and hid it in a barrel of pork until they docked in Venice. At that time, the see of the city was St Peter's Cathedral, where the alleged stone seat of Peter himself resides, either a gift from the Byzantine emperor or booty from the sack of Constantinople, ironically fashioned from an Islamic gravestone inscribed with verses from the Koran.

To honour and house the priceless relic of St Mark's cadaver, the majestic basilica that bears his name was built, which came to represent the city's wealth and power. Known as the Church of Gold on account of its glittering mosaics, this great Christian building is a breathtaking fusion of Byzantine and Islamic architecture, an exotic hybrid mixing the oriental and the occidental. Many of the profuse mosaics inside St Mark's Basilica depict Egyptian backgrounds – the pyramids, palm trees, camels and the lighthouse of Alexandria – markers of the place of origin of the saintly relic. Out of this grand appropriation of St Mark, the myth of Venice as the New Alexandria took hold, forging the deep connection between the city and the Islamic East epitomized in the very structures and stones of St Mark's Basilica, and enshrined in the legend of the city's patron saint.

Venice, the Serenissima, created its own mystique, coming out of the water, rootless, undefined, free of boundaries, so all its myths, including the very miracle of its construction on the lagoon, honour the sea. Its unique geographical location later allowed a special relationship with great Islamic dynasties to take hold over hundreds of years, although its maritime expansion began at the end of the tenth century with trade agreements with Constantinople. In 1082, the Venetians traded their assistance to the Byzantine emperor in curbing Norman incursions for permission to ply their wares across the eastern Mediterranean, and the true extent of their trading ambition began to appear after the pope's summons to the First Crusade in 1095. The religious mission filled them with a zeal more focused on profit than on piety. Rival trading cities Genoa and Pisa had already joined up, and Venice would not countenance any competition for the lucrative markets that lay in Syria and Egypt. The city also capitalized on its location as a staging post for pilgrims as they stopped off and embarked on Crusades and pilgrimages, wayfarers who needed food and lodging before boarding Venetian galleys to carry them overseas. As their tourist industry gained momentum, merchants explored new trade routes in the south and east Mediterranean to the degree that their maritime power came to equal that of Constantinople.

Then came the Fourth Crusade, spearheaded by the controversial doge Enrico Dandolo in 1204. It was to be one of the most reprehensible events in the history of Venice, which at that time was a rich, pious, aristocratic republic, ruled by an elected head of state and respected by the great powers of the Holy Roman Empire. In the twelfth century, Venetian crusaders had helped seize Tyre and establish independent trading colonies in every city in the Frankish East. When Pope Innocent III called for the Fourth Crusade, three Frankish lords, rulers of Champagne, Blois and Flanders, turned up at the Venetian court and asked the doge for ships. Dandolo agreed to the largest military contract in their history, to build and supply a huge armada fit to transport 33,500 crusaders and 4,500 horses to the East, in return for 85,000 marks, equal to twice the annual revenue of the kingdom of France. The deal promised either great riches, or complete bankruptcy.

Twelve months later, 200 galleys lay waiting, stocked with vast quantities of meat, wine, cheese and horse fodder – but barely a fraction of the planned number of crusaders arrived. Their leaders could only pay 50,000 marks, and so the Venetians were faced with financial ruin. The ninety-year-old doge decided to cut his losses. He sailed in October with the fleet, attacked the Dalmatian port of Zara, whose inhabitants were themselves crusaders, then headed not for Jerusalem, but for Constantinople, his aim to gain the 200,000 silver marks guaranteed by the exiled Byzantine prince Alexios for help in regaining the imperial throne of Alexios's father John II Komnenos. The horrific sacking and slaughter of the great Byzantine city has been related previously; there, Venice won fame or notoriety for its looting of the much celebrated four bronze horses adorning the Hippodrome, which took pride of place on the façade of St Mark's Basilica, where they remain. St Mark's treasury became legendary in Europe as the repository of unimaginably precious luxury objects, many of which had been gifted to the Byzantine emperor by Muslim courts, such as the Fatimids, or taken as booty by the Venetians. These dubious trophies of victory initiated the history of collecting Islamic artworks in Venice.

Between Two Worlds: Conflict, Trade and Diplomacy

Marco Polo (1254–1324) was the most famous of thousands of Venetian merchants who plied their trade by buying luxury goods and spices in the East and selling them at a profit on the Venetian market. Marco Polo's journey to China lasted a quarter of a century, and his meeting with Kubla Khan of the Mongol Empire is legendary. His story set the tone for the future merchants of Venice who explored the great trading cities of Constantinople, Damascus, Cairo, Aleppo, Tripoli and Alexandria with the help of Muslim astrolabes and the recondite navigation charts known as portolans, and wrote of their experiences in travel diaries. In such places, Venice set up trading colonies where its merchants could find lodging, food, public baths and a church, and communications were assisted by the hire of multilingual interpreters known as dragomans, although many Venetian merchants learnt Arabic so that they could negotiate with Muslim traders and customs officials directly. In this way, Venetian dialect absorbed many Arabic words. By the end of the thirteenth century, the republic was not only trading with Muslims but supplying them with materials to make the siege engines that battered Christian towns and forts.

Venice's pivotal trading role between Christian Europe and the East was modulated by an attitude of ambivalence, expressed through both a fear of and fascination with their Muslim counterparts. The republic needed to reinforce good diplomatic relations, first with the Mamluks, then with the powerful Ottomans, in order to build thriving commercial links. In 1454, an ambassador had reached sultan Mehmed II's court to convey their desire to live in peace and friendship with the new Ottoman Empire. The result was freedom of trade throughout Ottoman lands and a new merchant colony in Constantinople.

At the same time, the Venetians were obliged to reconcile that diplomacy with their role as defenders of Christendom in Europe. Conflicts emerged between Venetians and Muslims, although these were not religious, but arose out of disputes over territory. The

Ottomans threatened Venetian merchant colonies in Cyprus, Crete and Corfu, and the two empires first met on the sea at Gallipoli in 1464, where the Venetians emerged the victors of a lengthy battle. The fight for land continued in the Balkan borders, leading to a series of intermittent wars between Venice and the Ottomans over a period of a century, starting in 1463. Yet the Ottoman Empire was so crucial to Venice that the ambassador to the Sublime Porte, as the central Ottoman government was called, held the most senior, most highly paid post in the diplomatic service. In 1553, the ambassador emphasized Venetian economic dependency on Muslim trade: 'Being merchants', he said, 'we cannot live without them.' Finally, Venice had to sue for peace with the Ottomans, resulting in the treaty of Constantinople in 1479, whereby the Venetians managed to retained Crete and Corfu. The republic's aims went against the grain of those of Christian Europe, and their mindset was different – they saw the Muslims not as infidels but as customers.

It was in fact the continuous presence of Venetian diplomats and merchants in the cities of the Islamic Near East that differentiated Venice from all other European powers.[3] The Italians were entirely pragmatic in their approach, focusing on diplomatic and political rather than religious issues and adopting a role of absolute neutrality. Above all, it was vital to maintain peace, which enabled trade to flourish. As a result, their sustained contact with the Islamic world gave them a first-hand, frequently intimate knowledge of all aspects of Muslim life and culture, which often aroused the suspicions of the rest of Christian Europe.

From the thirteenth century, Venice had also been in close economic and diplomatic contact with the Muslim Mamluks, rulers who had defeated the last crusaders and halted the advance into Europe of the Mongols. Their capital in Cairo was magnificent, opulent and vast, the biggest city of its era, and their spice traders acted as the lynchpin between South Asia and Europe. Venice fostered ties with the Mamluk court – the longest-reigning doge, Francesco Foscari (1423–57), was in fact born in Mamluk Egypt – and trade between them produced a vibrant mercantile exchange of textiles, spices, medicines, metals, pigments, precious stones, glass and paper. Through this contact, Venice began to absorb aspects of Islamic culture, developing a fashion for Islamic-style bookbindings, for blue and white ceramics and inlaid metalwork. But this reciprocity ended abruptly when Sultan Selim I conquered Syria and Egypt in 1516–17, and all eyes turned to the Ottoman Empire.

*

Not only were the Venetians supreme traders, but they were experts in diplomacy, 'unrivalled in graceful self-presentation', as Peter Ackroyd points out.[4] Key to their polished statecraft was the ritual exchange of gifts, exemplified in records showing that the Venetian envoy Benedetto Sanudo presented the sultan of Mamluk Alexandria with gifts of fine cloth and Parmesan cheese, and in turn received chicken, sweetmeats and watermelons. The exchange of presents between Venice and the Ottomans had an enduring cultural impact on both sides, and sometimes the boundaries between gifts, bribes and actual purchases were blurred. Ottoman envoys made frequent prolonged visits to the city, often to discuss Near East policies. The Venetian doge adopted the Muslim practice of bestowing robes upon visiting diplomats, and textiles were also the most frequent gift taken to the Sublime Porte. Sometimes the Venetians showed consummate sensitivity towards Islamic culture – in 1586, in the interests of creating good relations, Lorenzo Bernardo, who was the *bailo* or consul to Constantinople, gave the grand vizier Siyavush Pasha two water clocks for the mosque he was having built. The vizier was so taken aback to receive a gift for a mosque from a Christian, he insisted the accompanying message should be translated twice to make sure. Sometimes the Ottomans bought precious items from Venice at enormous cost. The Rialto jewellers Caorlini and Levriero sold an encrusted gold tiara to Sultan Suleiman the Magnificent for the staggering sum of 115,000 ducats, not far off two million dollars today.[5] Often the Venetians were overtly asked for certain items by the Ottoman rulers and their wives, usually textiles, jewellery and mechanical gadgets such as automata and clocks, but cheese, lapdogs and maps of the world were also popular. For the Muslims, these so-called gifts underlined their diplomatic and political power and the extent of their personal contacts, while, for the Venetians, they were a vital element in achieving their central diplomatic purpose, which was to ensure a sustained period of peace that would enable trade to blossom.

Between the Serenissima and the Sublime Porte: The Creation of a Hybrid City

In the great bazaar of the Rialto and on the quays of Venice, carpets, silk, perfumes, pepper, cloves and cinnamon were stacked high as trading vessels docked on their return from Cyprus, Egypt and the Crimea. From there, Venetian merchants sent the exotic goods to the rest of Europe, including fragrant wax, spices and sandalwood from the Indies, Timor and Malabar, giving their business deals romance, mystery and status. Silver, gold, jewels and porcelain also swelled their markets, and made the fortunes of Venice's earliest private banks, which appear in official records from 1270 onwards; its first public bank was opened in 1625, over a century before the Bank of England. Art, too, was big business, and the art trade was fundamental to Venetian diplomacy and economy. In practical terms, the city's trade in pigments – vermilion, lead-tin yellow, bone black, the vivid purple purpureus beloved of Byzantine artists, mosaic gold and lapis lazuli from the mountains of central Asia – bolstered the golden age of European art. Piero della Francesca, Fra Angelico, even Michelangelo all worked with pigments sold in the Venetian markets.

Islamic art began to suffuse private and public life in Venice, which took on many features of an Eastern city. Portraits of its ruling families started to include depictions of a prized possession – their oriental carpet – and Islamic textiles, inlaid woodwork, glass, ceramics and metalwork were all imported as home furnishings. A wealthy merchant, Stefano Ravagnino, died in 1455 and left among his possessions a writing stand from Damascus with silver scales, a silver writing stylus with a copper nib and Moorish cover, Arab-style knives with bone handles and Damascene embroidered handkerchiefs.[6] The carvings of turbaned Muslims that adorned the wall-niches and paintings of fifteenth-century Venice echoed the appearance of the Islamic traders who rubbed shoulders with the locals at the docks. What was striking, and even unique in Europe, was the degree of realism of their artistic portrayals, probably inspired by the sketches made by Gentile Bellini during his two-year sojourn at the court of Mehmed II, who had commissioned the artist to paint his portrait. His drawings of people he saw on the streets of Constantinople were copied in Venice in great religious paintings, often in the shape of Muslim onlookers in works that eulogized Christian saints and martyrs, such as Carpaccio's depiction of St George, before whom the Muslim king of Trebizond on the Black Sea coast humbles himself and receives baptism. Yet, Carpaccio's paintings of the life of St George, the ultimate crusader and conqueror of the infidel, convey no sense of fear or aversion towards the enemy, but instead portray a coexisting community of Christians and Muslims. Later, in the sixteenth century, portraits of Ottoman sultans became a fashion that evolved from Bellini's landmark painting of Mehmed II. As Suleiman the Magnificent won a great victory in Hungary in 1526, he too took his place in European royal galleries of paintings of powerful men.[7]

The portrayal of one particular Muslim in Venetian art had surprising and long-lasting consequences on a broader European stage. The life and work of the mysterious Venetian painter Giorgione, an apprentice to Bellini, who died in his thirties in 1510, have haunted art historians, perplexed by the significance of one of the six surviving works attributed to the artist, known as *Three Philosophers*, painted around 1505. A plausible interpretation of the work favoured by recent scholars identifies the three men depicted as Aristotle on the right, the Muslim scholar Averroes in the centre, wearing a turban, and a young Christian philosopher on the left.[8] It seems that Giorgione had tapped into an important development in Venetian culture: the astonishing revival of the Cordoban polymath Averroes' philosophy, banned in France but debated heatedly in

Venice and at Padua University between the fourteenth and seventeenth centuries. Michael Scot's Latin translations of Averroes' commentaries had been sent to Bologna University by the emperor Frederick II of Sicily, and from there they went on to Paris. When the use of printing presses began in Venice in 1469, multiple copies of Averroes' works were issued – it is through the Latin editions published in Renaissance Venice that his philosophy is mainly known to us today. Averroes' fame and status in Venetian culture marks the resurgent heritage of Islamic al-Andalus and the pre-eminence of a European Islamic intellectual who played a major part in European civilization far into the seventeenth century. There is a great paradox in the fact that Averroes' writings, as we have seen, were mostly ignored in other Muslim countries, but were translated and hotly debated by European Christians and Jews.

There was a sorry sequel to this brave Venetian reinstatement of a Muslim thinker in a cultural oasis on the northern shores of the Adriatic. The Italian poet Francesco Petrarch (1304–1374) lived for many years in Venice and, as an early humanist who turned to the Platonism of St Augustine to understand Christianity, he reviled all associated with Arab Muslim culture. 'I hate the whole Arab race', he wrote to a physician friend, enraged at the influence of Arab physicians on the Venetian doctors of his day. Petrarch strove blatantly to extinguish all vestiges of Arab Muslim contributions to humanism, expelling their ideas as they themselves had been expelled from western Europe. The poet's denunciation of Averroes, Avicenna and other Arab thinkers left its imprint on European humanists, universities and even scientists, so that, by the middle of the seventeenth century, the study of classical Islamic authors in the Christian West was almost extinct.

The Destiny of the Sea

Venice's fortune was its marriage to the sea. The ever-changing, ever-moving waters lent its people a fluidity in their character, an openness to the new, an obligation to be in perpetual motion. It made them global travellers, traders whose cultural identity was fashioned from its dialogues with the Muslim world and honed by their differences. In part, the story of Venice and Islamic Europe can be told as a by-product of war, of looted objects, relics and manuscripts that found their way to Christian lands. But most of all it was the story of fortunate encounters fostered by a trade and diplomacy that disregarded religious conflict, a tale of mutually beneficial economic and cultural transactions that drew together two great cities, Venice and Constantinople, the latter already cosmopolitan and multicultural, the former moulded by a hybridity acquired through intense and prolonged contact with what was perceived as its cultural Other, which in reality became a vital element in its distinctive civilization.

That hybridity was apparent in all spheres of Venetian life. Its labyrinthine networks of alleys, secluded courtyards and covered balconies all linked its domestic settings to its overseas Venetian colonies in Muslim lands. Venetian women in the fifteenth century wore mostly black and were veiled in public, much to the surprise of one anonymous European visitor, who remarked that 'one cannot see their faces for all the world.' Venice's ruling class desired self-definition through architecture. As the city began to emulate aspects of Alexandria, home of their patron saint, and Egyptian themes appeared in St Marks's mosaics and rounded domes, as Venice aspired to the wisdom and justice of Solomon in echoing biblical accounts of his residence in the main cedarwood hall of the doge's palace, to which were added two giant outer columns like Solomon's Temple, a subtle irony arose. With its location as a point of embarkation for pilgrims to Jerusalem, Venice aimed to take on the identity of a holy city, but in every case, that inevitably involved elements that were essentially Islamic. As that pervasive tension between Christian and Muslim cultures extended to its artworks and its scholarly life, the city evolved into a refuge of intellectual freedom and religious tolerance. In doing so, it stood firm as a bastion of independent religious, political and cultural thought that defied the papacy and the powers of the rest of Christian Europe.

Things were about to change. The Battle of Lepanto at the end of the sixteenth century was to put an end to the many sustained, friendly and lucrative trading deals between Venice and the Ottoman Empire. As Venice aligned itself more with Christian Europe, the Ottomans lost interest and turned towards a global sea trade, opened up by Portuguese merchants. In the end, the demise of the Republic of Venice came not from the Islamic world but from within Christian Europe under Napoleon. It rang the death knell of the Serenissima's great mission of symbiosis with the East, which had lasted over a millennium.

CHAPTER 18

AN ARCHITECTURE OF POWER AND FAITH: ISLAM'S MICHELANGELO IN THE REIGN OF SULEIMAN THE MAGNIFICENT

'Architecture is the most difficult of professions, and he who would practise it must, above all things, be pious.'

Sinan

'If there is anywhere in the world any majesty of empire and of true monarchy, it must radiate from the sultan.'

Jean Bodin, sixteenth-century political theorist and traveller

'The greatest victory since Moses parted the Red Sea.'

Juan Fernández de Espinosa, on the Battle of Lepanto

The Rise of a Genius

A GEOMETRY OF divergent shapes creates the skyline of modern Istanbul. From some perspectives, the brutal glass and metal rectangles of skyscrapers dominate the densely packed clusters of urban dwellings, while from other vantage points, the pure forms of cubes, spheres, slender cylinders and the spires of ancient mosques rise up to tell the history of the city in stone and define its religious identity. The points, lines, planes and curves so fundamental to Euclid's geometry converge in a perfect harmony of shape and form that is both hybrid and distinctly Ottoman. Along a sightline that links the Hagia Sophia and the Mosque of the Conqueror, the two minarets considered the most beautiful in the city soar above the domes of the Şehzade or Prince's Mosque, its exterior embellished with elaborate geometric decorations, its luminous interior graced by red and white horseshoe arches and *muqarnas* that echo those of the Great Mosque of Cordoba and the Alhambra palace. Built between 1543 and 1549 to honour Prince Mehmed, son of Sultan Suleiman I, who died of smallpox in 1543, aged twenty-one, it is an imperial mosque on a monumental scale, designed by the architect Sinan (*c.* 1488–1588), a man of genius, often thought of as Islam's Michelangelo. He saw four sultans take the throne during his long life, which spanned the era that dawned more than 250 years after the Ottomans had first emerged as nomadic chieftains, an era when they had been transformed into the rulers of a global empire that stretched from North Africa to Sumatra.

The fortunes of Mimar* Sinan waxed in parallel with those of the Ottomans, and were closely linked to those of Sultan Suleiman I (1494–1566). Even though Sinan was rarely mentioned by contemporary historians, and was almost totally ignored by European travellers of his time, the Ottoman writer and traveller Evliya Çelebi wrote a fulsome account of his works half a century after Sinan's death. The fullest and most intriguing source for his life was the one the architect wrote himself in collaboration with his lifelong friend, the poet and painter Mustafa Sa'i Çelebi, compiled shortly before Sinan's death. It comprises five separate documents, brought together in the *Record of Construction* (*Tezkiretū-'l-Būnyān*), forming an autobiography that emphasizes the close relationship he had with his much loved yet mercurial patron Suleiman I, and portrays a man with a unique vision, a man with star quality.

Sinan, whose name may have been Yusuf, was born in Anatolia, in the town of Ağırnas (near Kayseri), sometime between 1488 and 1490, to parents who were either Armenian or Greek Christians. His father was a stonemason, from whom he perhaps inherited his feeling for working with stone. Sinan was in his mid-teens when he was recruited to the Janissaries, and was sent to work on a farm outside Istanbul to learn the language, religion and customs of the Ottomans.

---

* 'Mimar' is an honorific title meaning 'architect' in Turkish.

His carpentry skills soon enabled him to become a military engineer, travelling on major campaigns with the Janissaries in the sultan's army to Rhodes and Belgrade in 1521, Mohács in 1526 and Vienna in 1529. In the Iran and Baghdad campaigns of 1534–5, he built three fully equipped and armed galleys, which brought him promotion to the rank of sergeant-at-arms in the Imperial Guard. He became an expert in building roads, bridges and aqueducts, and after his final military campaign in Moldavia in 1538, at the age of fifty, Sinan was appointed chief of the Imperial Architects by Suleiman I, a post he would retain for almost half a century, during which time he is known to have designed, renovated or overseen a prodigious 400 or more building projects.

*

The army had given Sinan great discipline and organizational skills, which enhanced his talents for design and administration. His military travels in Asia and parts of Europe gave him the chance to observe Islamic, Christian and Byzantine architecture, and he may have been familiar with concepts of Italian Renaissance architecture inspired by the Roman architect Vitruvius. A Latin manuscript copy of Vitruvius's *On Architecture* (*De Architectura*) had been in the Imperial Library of the Topkapı Palace since it was acquired during the conquest of Hungary in 1526, and Sinan would have had access to it, as well as to treatises on geometry and astronomy.[1] But the Ottomans tended not to embrace the classical Greek and Roman traditions of the Renaissance, and Sinan was grounded in a practical knowledge that came from his close study of 200 years of Turkish building practices and his admiration for Byzantine buildings, especially the Hagia Sophia, its great dome inspiring Sinan's lifelong desire to emulate or supersede its magnificence.

As court architect, he was responsible for repairs and maintenance of water supplies, cisterns, aqueducts and dams, a position of importance which prepared him for his role as chief architect on construction projects for major religious buildings. The first was Suleiman's commission to build a mosque as a birthday present for his wife, Haseki Hürrem, known as Roxelana. Just after this, Sinan designed and built the stunning Şehzade Mosque for Suleiman's deceased son, a task he accomplished in only two years, between 1543 and 1545. To build such a testament to the Islamic faith in so short a time bore witness to Sinan's creative genius; it also confirmed the increasingly significant relationship between architect and sultan, a synergy that would lead to ever greater achievements, as each man attained his highest eminence.

An Auspicious Conjunction: The Rise of Suleiman I

When Suleiman I became sultan in 1520 upon the unexpected death of his father, Selim I, his first given title was 'Master of the Auspicious Conjunction', arising from the fact that he was the tenth Ottoman sultan, born at the turn of the tenth Islamic era. Astral readings foretold that such a person would become the preordained universal ruler who could unite East and West under one crown and one religion. Yet, he was not the only monarch aspiring to boundless dominion at that time. Europe was gripped by a major dynastic conflict between King Francis I of France and the Habsburgs, who governed Austria, Germany and Spain under Charles V, Holy Roman Emperor and King of Spain. Their clash was intensified by religious tension between European Catholics and certain Protestant states whose allegiances with the Ottomans were considered dubious. Charles's battle with Francis, coupled with the schism between European Christians, thwarted the emperor's ambition as Charlemagne's heir to rule a Europe united by a single religion, as his grandparents Ferdinand and Isabella had united Spain. Charles also desired a crusade against the Turks, which set Francis further against him. It incited the French king to form an alliance with Suleiman I that firmly established the sultan as a major European statesman.

All the same, Suleiman's inexperience, combined with the appointment of his childhood friend and palace favourite Ibrahim Pasha to high-level military and administrative roles with no experience whatsoever, failed to inspire confidence in his government. To prove himself, the new sultan launched into a decade of incessant military campaigns, starting in 1521. At the time when Hernán Cortés was expanding the dominance of Christianity by seizing Tenochtitlán from the Aztecs on the other side of the world, the sultan's armies were taking Belgrade, at that time part of Hungary, for Islam. The besieging and capture of the island of Rhodes soon after, in 1522–3, was followed in 1526 by a grand campaign against Hungary, assisted by King Francis I. It culminated in the decisive Battle of Mohács, in which the Ottomans crushed the Hungarian royal army in less than two hours, killed King Louis II, sacked the capital of Buda, then retreated. One unforeseen repercussion of their victory was the creation of the Habsburgs' monarchy on the Danube, when Charles V's younger brother Ferdinand seized the empty Hungarian throne, forming a sovereign state that would endure until the First World War.

But Suleiman had his sights on greater conquests, that would take him deeper into central Europe. In 1529, the Ottoman army set off on a 1,500-kilometre journey across difficult terrain to Vienna, an expedition that would take three or four months. Among the Janissaries was Sinan, braving torrential rain, floods, snow, hunger and the loss of men and horses before arriving outside the city gates in late September. It proved to be a logistical step too far for the huge army, which failed to break down Vienna's defences, and resulted in a peace treaty between the Habsburgs and the Ottomans that lasted twenty years. Even so, Suleiman believed he was the rightful inheritor of the Holy Roman Empire, not Charles, and his military presence on the threshold of the dynastic capital of that empire was deeply fearful to Christian Europe.

Suleiman the Magnificent and the Transformation of the Ottoman Empire

'Enthroned on cushions of cloth of gold, he wore a gown of white satin with a medium-sized turban over a pleated crimson velvet bonnet. On the turban was a gold rosette set with a sparkling cut ruby the size of a hazelnut and in his right ear was a pear-shaped pearl.'[2] This description of Suleiman's splendour was written by Jérome Maurand, a French priest who saw the sultan when he was present at an audience with him in August 1544, as part of the Franco-Ottoman alliance. The sultan's extravagant appearance more than matched the title Suleiman the Magnificent by which he had become known in the west of Europe, as did all public festivities and state ceremonial where he made an appearance amid pageantry that took place on a colossal scale, enhancing his glory as head of religion and state, and inspiring dread in his enemies. As Ottoman caliph, and therefore ruler of the entire Muslim world, Suleiman projected an image of himself as the Mahdi, a messianic redeemer, an invincible hero who would rule the Earth as last world emperor before the final judgment. His aspiration was to achieve this grandiose ambition by conquering Vienna, Rome, Baghdad and Tabriz, thereby uniting Asia and Europe under Islam, and ruling as both temporal and spiritual leader of Muslims and also as Holy Roman Emperor.

The Ottoman Empire that Suleiman now governed operated with a precision and sophistication echoed in the perfect geometry of Sinan's architecture. To his people, the sultan was known as Suleiman *Kanuni*, the Lawgiver, for his role in codifying Ottoman civil and military law, and the extent of his vast influence is immortalized in a marble relief of the sultan that appears in the House Chamber of the US Capitol building in Washington DC, alongside twenty-two other lawgivers whose work to establish legal systems influenced the Founding Fathers of America and helped shape the principles that underlie American jurisprudence. All administrative law in Ottoman lands was harmonized with religious law, akin to parallel legal innovations in France and Spain at that time. Yet the Ottoman policy of religious tolerance was the antithesis of religious attitudes in the rest of Europe. In direct opposition to other European countries that were expelling their Jewish populations, Suleiman took in 100,000 Jews exiled from Spain, who were allowed to live in Ottoman lands as *dhimmis*, without forced conversion, although without democratic rights or equality within the strict legal hierarchy. Those Sephardic

Jews who made new lives there saw the sultan as the scourge of Catholic Spain and proved to be the most devout believers in the redemptive qualities of the Ottoman emperors. Between the late fifteenth and seventeenth centuries, Sephardic Jews streamed into Ottoman society, bringing new medical and geographical knowledge, holding roles at court and translating key scholarly works.

Wealth flooded into the royal coffers, which swelled from a combination of the spoils of war in the form of exquisite porcelain, royal crystals, amber and jade from Tabriz, Aleppo, Damascus and Cairo, plus tribute money and a flourishing global network of trade. As in Venice, the arts blossomed on the proceeds of commerce, as virtuoso artisans wrought priceless jewellery, and the royal collections boasted an eclectic range of artefacts, among the most extravagant of which were clocks and watches from France and Germany, decorative items rather than accurate timepieces, and elaborate automata, such as the magnificent silver planetarium Ferdinand of Austria sent Suleiman as a peace token. This golden era of art was in part funded by the flow of treasure to Europe from the New World, from which Suleiman benefited, and, by 1560, many of the emeralds used by Ottoman jewellers came from Colombia.[3]

Solomonic Glory: The Construction of the Süleymaniye Mosque

By the time Suleiman reached the age of fifty-six in 1550, he was at the pinnacle of his glory. He saw himself as the Solomon of his era, whose splendour was to be eternally captured in stone in the great architectural triumphs of his reign. Suleiman may well have inspired Sinan to recreate a Solomonic temple that would outdo Justinian's Hagia Sophia when he commissioned the Şehzade Mosque. But now Suleiman was a mighty player on the European stage, a ruler of boundless wealth who had subdued and humiliated Habsburg Austria, and he demanded a building to match. He charged Sinan with creating an imperial mosque in his name on the summit of the third hill of Istanbul, overlooking the Golden Horn. Money was no object, and the complex was to include four colleges, a soup kitchen, a hospital, an asylum, baths and a caravanserai and hospice for travellers, all focused on benevolent services to the community, with the mosque itself at the centre.

The Süleymaniye Mosque was a new expression of Sinan's archetypal vision, a synthesis of Christian Byzantine and Ottoman architecture that closely followed the plan and basic structure of the Hagia Sophia, while surpassing its impact on the city skyline due to its greater mass and its impressive location. Its four minarets housed ten galleries, to mark the fact that Suleiman was the tenth Ottoman sultan. It was no accident that it could be viewed most clearly from the suburb of Galata, where the non-Muslim population lived. The Süleymaniye was a building that spoke to all, whether Muslim, Christian or Jew. During the previous decade, Suleiman had tasked his craftsmen with the restoration of the Al-Aqsa Mosque and Dome of the Rock in Jerusalem, giving the city a renewed focus on pilgrimage for both Muslims and Christians, and increasing the sultan's religious and military authority. The Süleymaniye Mosque echoed the Dome of the Rock, built on the site of Solomon's temple, thereby connecting Suleiman to the cultural heritage of both Jewish king and Byzantine Emperor Justinian, while outshining them.

Inside, the mosque was entirely different from the Hagia Sophia. Its main beauty lay in its unity of space, reflecting the oneness of God and, in particular, the unity of empire and sovereign. No longer did Ottoman architecture reflect the Arab style of mosque-building that produced the forest of piers and pillars in the Great Mosque of Cordoba. Instead, there was just a single overarching dome supported by two half-domes, creating a vast central space. Sinan's lifelong obsession was to fuse the dome structure into a whole, joining it to the rest of the mosque using Euclid's principles of rigorous geometry, thereby permitting nothing to divide or fragment the inner luminous space. This was quite unlike anything in Renaissance architecture, where one structure was laid on top of another, and obeyed a harmonic relation. The dome of the Süleymaniye was not, in the end, larger than that of the Hagia Sophia, but it was the highest dome measured from sea level in the Ottoman Empire. Sinan's interior decoration is simple and restrained, with stained-glass windows on the wall of the qibla, where plaster skeletons are filled with coloured glass that shows no human forms. The walls are adorned with natural materials – wood, marble, ivory and mother of pearl – and limited areas of the celebrated Iznik tiles, that introduce shades of red, blue, turquoise and black. Sinan regarded the Süleymaniye Mosque as a work of his qualification stage as an architect, yet it proved to be one of his greatest, most original and famous achievements, a landmark that rises above the urban sprawl to proclaim the majesty and greatness of its patron.

The Mirrored Crown: Suleiman the Magnificent and Charles V

In 1532, Grand Vizier Ibrahim Pasha obtained an imperial crown for his beloved Suleiman I, a headpiece fashioned in solid gold by elite Venetian jewellers and decorated with fifty diamonds, forty-nine pearls, forty-seven rubies, twenty-seven emeralds and a large turquoise. Crowns were not habitually worn by Islamic monarchs, but formed part of the ceremonial dress, alongside the sceptre and throne of gold, that befitted a Muslim ruler. Suleiman's headdress was in the form of a helmet consisting of four tiers of crowns that represented not just the Ottoman ruler but also European Christian imperial and papal regalia. He first donned it in a tent in Belgrade at a meeting with astonished European ambassadors, before he marched on to Vienna.

The sultan was emulating, or mimicking, the ceremonial attire of the Holy Roman Emperor Charles V, who had recently been crowned by Pope Clement VII and had proclaimed himself the successor of Julius Caesar and the emperor Augustus. Three years before, in Vienna, Charles had worn a similar crown, though with just three tiers; Suleiman was sending a crystal-clear message that it was he, not Charles, who was the rightful heir of the Holy Roman Empire. Magic, prognostication and prophecy swirled around both men. It was said that Suleiman and his soldiers were surrounded by an invisible army of angels, prophets and saints, actually reported as visible at the Battle of Mohács; while Charles V was associated with apocalyptic prophecies of a Roman emperor who would unite Christendom, reform the Church and conquer the Ottomans, thereby reuniting Constantinople with Rome under a global leader.[4] A clash between the two colossi of Europe seemed inevitable, but was their motivation fuelled by inordinate ambition, or was this highly complex situation really the familiar trope of a clash of two world religions?

In many ways, the Habsburg Empire was the mirror image of the Ottoman Empire. In the great game of politics, power and faith, they shared a desire for global supremacy that was grounded in religious ideology, an aspiration that on the surface seemed set to provoke yet another episode in the age-old conflict between Christians and Muslims. But the reality was far more complex and nuanced. The political and strategic situation demanded alliances and sparked discords across the religious divide, as well as among co-religionists. Charles V was at war with France for ascendancy in the west of the continent, while attempting to fend off Ottoman expansion in the Mediterranean and central Europe, specifically in Hungary, where his younger brother Ferdinand ruled. Like Charles, Suleiman was motivated by his perceived inheritance of the Holy Roman Empire, and believed he was its rightful successor. The sultan never recognized Charles's imperial title, referring to him solely as the king of Spain. At the same time, Charles's enemy King Francis I had allied himself with Suleiman I against the Habsburgs in what was essentially a struggle for power and European territory.

Even so, religion unquestionably played an important role in the evolving drama, in part because it was used as the justification for war. The soldiers in both Habsburg and Ottoman armies believed they were fighting for their own God, though their war was not a clear-cut battle between Muslim East and Christian West. The Ottomans were as much a part of the West as the East, and their military allegiances created an ambiguous series of cross-religious, cross-continental connections. Catholic France had allied with Muslim powers against fellow Spanish Catholics, while the Ottomans aligned themselves with rebel Protestants in south-east and central Europe. The world views of the Ottomans and the Habsburgs were shaped by religion, and a fundamental difference lay in their attitudes to religious divergence and to ethnicity. On the Christian side, the end of the Reconquest of Spain and Portugal in 1492 had fostered severe religious intolerance in Catholic Europe, with an accompanying ethnic cleansing and forced religious conversion. Conversely, the Ottomans had encouraged a multicultural, multi-religious society since the time of Mehmed II the Conqueror. They sought international dominion but not obligatory religious conversion. As a result, each side had opposing concepts of universal sovereignty strongly influenced by their religious ideologies.

Suleiman's military pressure on central Europe had some unexpected repercussions on the Protestant Reformation movement which criticized the Catholic Church and the papacy in particular. Initially, the religious reformer Martin Luther had written that the Ottomans, whom he described as the 'scourge of God', were a divine punishment for the iniquities of the Catholic Church, and, although he changed his rhetoric in later years, his words struck home among rebel Protestants, some of whom preferred the idea of being ruled by Muslims rather than by Catholics. Suleiman is reported to have declared that Ottoman Muslims had sympathy for Protestant iconoclasm and opposition to the pope, and his government formed an alliance with the Hungarian Calvinists, supporters of the French Reformation theologian Jean Calvin (1509–1564) and his branch of Protestantism. The sultan's secret agents were also sent into the Habsburg Netherlands and German-speaking territories whose inhabitants had Protestant leanings and rejected both the pope and the Holy Roman Emperor. By the time Sinan began working on the great Süleymaniye Mosque in 1550, the majority of Christians in Ottoman Buda in Hungary and their vassal state of Transylvania had converted from Catholicism to either Protestantism or Islam.[5] Yet religious turmoil was not confined to the continent of Europe. The schism that split the western Church apart in the sixteenth century had a counterpart in the deepening chasm that had developed between the Sunnis and Shi'ites of Anatolia and Iran under Shah Ismail of the Safavid Empire, a rift that had already resulted in the beheading of tens of thousands of Shi'ites in Anatolia in 1514, under the aegis of Selim I.

Love and Death: The Private Tragedies of Suleiman I

Beneath his fearsome mien, the great warrior and spiritual leader of the Muslims was a man of passion and intensity, and the two great loves of Suleiman's life were both Christian slaves. The love of his youth was Ibrahim Pasha, the son of a sailor or fisherman from Adriatic Greece who was captured in a raid at the turn of the sixteenth century and entered the sultan's service as a slave. They slept in the same bed, as Venetian sources state, and the multilingual, intelligent and canny Ibrahim exerted a powerful influence on his master. Suleiman had taken the unorthodox step of appointing him as grand vizier, a job at which he excelled, despite his complete lack of experience, and during which he engineered very close diplomatic relations with Venice, where he was wryly known as 'Ibrahim the Magnificent'.

This all changed when, as he was nearing the age of forty, the sultan fell for the beautiful, red-haired daughter of a Christian Orthodox priest from what was then Poland. She, like Ibrahim Pasha, was captured in a raid, sold as a slave in Kostantiniyye and joined the royal harem. Her name was Hürrem, known to western diplomats as Roxelana, to whom the sultan wrote love poetry under his pen name Muhibbi. Around 1533, Suleiman made the unprecedented, extraordinary decision to marry his concubine, who took the new title Hürrem Sultan, meaning principal and legal wife, and once again broke with tradition by allowing her to live with him in the Topkapı Palace for the rest of her life, bearing him five sons and a daughter during their monogamous relationship. Meanwhile, Ibrahim Pasha had become vastly wealthy, powerful and arrogant, and, like many influential viziers, he made the mistake of acting as if he were in charge of state affairs. Having fallen out with Hürrem Sultan over who would be the rightful heir to Suleiman's throne, he was strangled in his bed by the monarch's assassins. Hürrem then took on the role of chief political adviser on matters of state, an unconventional role for a woman, giving her power and international status.

Suleiman's many sons caused great strife and rivalry for the succession of the dynasty. In 1553, the sultan had his firstborn son Mustafa executed during the campaign in Safavid Persia on suspicion that he was planning to usurp him. Mustafa's mother was Mahidevran, Suleiman 's concubine, not Hürrem, who may have plotted against him to ensure that her own son Selim would be the sultan's successor. When Hürrem died in 1558, Suleiman turned away from luxury and towards a more spiritual life and greater piety, a life change akin to that of King Charles V, who spent his final years in a monastery, also after a thirty-year reign. Suleiman ordered the destruction of all musical instruments and strictly enforced a prohibition on figural art; from that time until his own death from unknown causes in September 1566, aged seventy-one, on a campaign in Hungary, the sultan only wore green woollen vests, like the Prophet Muhammad.

The Reign of Selim the Sot and Sinan's Great Masterpiece

Such was the shock and unexpectedness of the demise of Suleiman in the midst of a campaign that his men were obliged to bury his corpse temporarily inside the imperial tent and keep his death a secret for three weeks until his son Selim II (r. 1566–74) reached Kostantiniyye to take the throne. His father was buried in the city six weeks later amid great pomp, a major state event depicted in a series of miniatures in which the architect Sinan is portrayed wielding a measuring stick. In his new role as both sultan and caliph, Selim was in pious mood, visiting the tomb of al-Ansari, the companion of the Prophet, on the Golden Horn. But his piety was soon dissipated by a devotion to the pleasures of the flesh and a lack of interest in government. In complete contrast with his father, he rarely went to the mosque, preferring instead wine, women, boys, poetry and music. His miniature portrait reveals a portly personage who, it is said, was barely able to saddle a horse.[6]

In 1543, Selim had taken a beautiful, highly intelligent woman named Nurbanu as his concubine, and he made her his legal wife in 1571. Nurbanu may have been Venetian or an Orthodox Christian from Cyprus, and she followed in her deceased mother-in-law

Hürrem Sultan's footsteps in acting as her husband's adviser. She bore Selim a son who would become Sultan Murad III, making her valide sultan (mother of the sultan), and she became a formidable and influential diplomat during the era of the Sultanate of Women, a period mainly in the sixteenth century when the mothers and wives of Ottoman sultans exerted great political power, exchanged gifts and letters with foreign rulers, endowed many important public buildings and engaged in philanthropic projects such as building mosques, schools and women's medical centres.

Nurbanu maintained a regular correspondence with the Italian noblewoman Catherine de Medici, to whom she sent items of exquisite embroidery from Istanbul, prompting Catherine to employ several Turkish seamstresses to create the soft furnishings in her houses in France and Italy. Nurbanu also contributed to Ottoman life on a scale few women had achieved. She inaugurated the first library to be endowed by an Ottoman woman in one of the mosques in Istanbul, as well as building a mosque in the Anatolian town of Üsküdar, along with hostels for travellers and soup kitchens for the poor. In her will, she decreed that, on her death, 150 of her female slaves should be freed and each be given 1,000 gold coins.

*

Meanwhile, Selim attempted to reform himself, vowing to give up drinking and partying, and his efforts to clean up his image included one important commission: he instructed Sinan to build a mosque in his name. In 1569, when he was eighty, Sinan embarked on the Selimiye Mosque in the old Ottoman capital of Edirne. Raised on a floor plan that incorporates a circle inside an octagon inside a square, its dome is the largest in Ottoman architecture, spanning thirty-one metres (102 feet) and achieving his ideal to surpass the dome of the Hagia Sophia. During its construction, Sinan was also at work repairing the structure of Hagia Sophia, work sometimes regarded as the most important architectural achievement of Selim's reign and giving Sinan greater insight to its design.

The genius of the Selimiye Mosque, Sinan's supreme building, resides in the way its dome is supported on eight massive piers, an innovation that rendered the half-domes of earlier mosques redundant. Outside, four slim, fluted minarets soar into the sky at a height of seventy metres (230 feet) around the dome. The beauty and elegance of the mosque are expressed in the geometric clarity of its structure, and in its striking contrasts between geometric forms, all in subtle shades of grey, and the tensions between horizontal and vertical space and the curved domes and external semi-domes that mark the movement from octagon to square. Inside is a glorious harmony of marble, wood, Iznik tiles and horseshoe arches in familiar red and white tones, adorned with swirling arabesques and carved geometric motifs.

Despite the striking influence of the Byzantine architecture of the Hagia Sophia, the vast inner space of the Selimiye Mosque beneath the immensity of its dome reflects a sharp difference in stylistic taste between the Islamic world and the rest of Europe. The prayer hall is a totality of uninterrupted space, where the faithful arrive from and depart in all directions. There is no order or procession. Nothing is arranged according to the rules of perspective, which are foreign to Islamic and Ottoman sensibilities. Perspective imposes a specific view upon the spectator, whereas, in the Ottoman style of mosque, and also in the Umayyad mosque of Cordoba, no viewpoint dominates as all are equal.[7] Sinan's Selimiye Mosque is peerless in its visual coherence, and its geometric perfection reflects the perfection of the divine. It is believed to be the supreme achievement in Islamic architecture.

A Day of Reckoning: The Battle of Lepanto

In September 1571, Spain's greatest writer, Miguel de Cervantes Saavedra (1547–1616), went to Naples to board the *Marquesa*, a battleship in the armada commanded by Don John of Austria, the illegitimate son of the Holy Roman Emperor King Charles V. They were heading for the Gulf of Lepanto, in the Ionian Sea, west of Greece, to take on the might of an Ottoman fleet which lay waiting in the bay off the Ottoman-held port of Lepanto. In the famous battle that followed, Cervantes was wounded in the chest and lost the use of his left arm, but he proudly proclaimed that he had fought in the 'grandest occasion the past or present has seen, or the future can hope to see.' It was a view shared by most of Christian Europe.

Selim was credited with the Ottoman occupation of Cyprus in 1570. The island had belonged to the Venetians and, on its takeover, they sought help from other Christian powers in the Mediterranean. Pope Pius V greeted their request for aid with enthusiasm, as he spied the opportunity for a crusade against Islam, pinning his main hopes on King Philip II of Spain and Portugal, the legitimate son of the Holy Roman Emperor Charles V. Pius arranged a Holy League to combat the Ottoman threat, consisting of the Catholic states of Spain and its Italian territories, certain independent Italian states headed by Venice, and the military order of Malta. Philip II had eventually agreed to join the League because he saw himself as the most powerful of the holy partners, and thought he might use the combined fleets to his advantage to regain Tunis from the Hafsids. The Ottoman danger must have lurked at the back of his mind, as he would have known that western intelligence services had been watching the Hungarian and Mediterranean frontiers of Christian Europe with the Ottoman Empire since 1566, in anticipation of Suleiman making a final bid for control of the continent. After some tough negotiation, Philip agreed to pay the lion's share of the logistical costs of the Holy League, and Venice, the papacy and the other member states agreed to pay the other half between them.

The terrible wars fought over three years in the province of Granada between Morisco rebels and state troops led by twenty-four-year-old Don John of Austria came to an end in 1571 after some brutal interventions on the part of the Spanish commander. That left the arrogant, cruel, illegitimate half-brother of Philip II free to take charge of the combined fleets, which gathered at Messina in August 1571. He headed the largest Christian naval force ever seen in the Mediterranean, comprising 208 galleys and thirty warships, which sailed to meet the entire Muslim fleet already at sea and ready for action. Though Spain provided the most men, it relied upon its allies for support, and so the fleet of warships was predominantly Italian and, above all, Venetian. On 7 October 1571, 170,000 men joined battle, of whom 7,500 were killed and 20,000 wounded, including Cervantes. Yet they won an extraordinary victory, capturing 130 Ottoman warships, 400 pieces of artillery and almost 3,500 prisoners. One hundred and ten Ottoman galleys were sunk, and 1,500 galley slaves were freed. The Turkish navy lost a startling 30,000 men.

Christian Europe was ecstatic over a triumph celebrated as Spain's greatest ever military feat, yet the Venetians and other Italian partners firmly believed the victory had been theirs and that the Spanish had failed at Lepanto. The reality was that Philip was unable to pay Spain's half share in the costs, and, in Venetian eyes, he had failed to capitalize on the conquest by pressing on to recapture Greece. Yet the pope, who was overjoyed at the turn of events in favour of the Christians, offered Philip II the crown of Emperor of the East if he could regain Constantinople. For Europe, the defeat of the Ottomans was both a military and moral victory, which seemed to signal an attenuation of Ottoman authority under Selim's rule. Even so, it could be seen as a hollow triumph, as the Ottomans remained in control of Cyprus and rebuilt their fleet in about six months, which enabled them to reassert their dominance in the Mediterranean. Selim's grand vizier boasted to the Venetian emissary that the Lepanto debacle had caused no lasting harm: 'You come to see how we bear our misfortune. But I would have you know the difference between your loss and ours. In wresting Cyprus from you, we deprived you of an arm; in defeating our fleet, you have only shaved our beard. An arm when cut off cannot grow again; but a shorn beard will grow all the better for the razor.'[8]

Despite the seemingly casual attitude of the Ottomans, the Battle of Lepanto was a major naval encounter that temporarily put a stop to their western advances, and it continued to be memorialized in Christian lands in painting, sculpture, poetry and song for centuries after.

*

Selim II enjoyed fine wine, an indulgence that proved to be his downfall. In 1574, aged fifty, he died after slipping and falling on the marble floor of his bathroom while drunk. His eldest son succeeded him as Murad III (r. 1574–95) and promptly ordered the murder of his five younger brothers. If wine had been Selim II's nemesis, Murad's was women. He is recorded as initially impotent and unable to father an heir, yet his physicians found a cure that left him with an insatiable, indiscriminate sexual appetite that generated over one hundred children during his reign of twenty-one years. On the diplomatic front, he maintained important contact with Queen Elizabeth I of England. In one letter, he advocated an alliance between the Ottoman Empire and England, suggesting to Her Majesty that Islam and Protestantism had much more in common than either did with Catholicism. When war broke out between Spain and England in 1585, a joint military operation was mooted against the Spanish, but, in the event, the great Armada was defeated by the English in 1588 without Ottoman assistance.

The Crescent Moon Wanes

Sinan had lived through an era of unprecedented Ottoman growth and glory, and his life had in many ways reflected the metamorphosis of the empire as it rose to its zenith. It was also a series of major personal transformations: from Christian to Muslim, from carpenter's son to Janissary, from decorated soldier and military engineer to the supreme architect of Ottoman civilization. During that time, he amassed a fortune; the charter of the charitable organization he founded in 1563 lists among his possessions eighteen mansions, thirty-eight shops and nine houses, plus land, mills, mosques and schools. He was a true visionary, changing the skyline of Kostantiniyye into the spectacle of a cosmopolitan city across which rose hundreds of new buildings standing alongside existing Byzantine structures. As chief architect, Sinan headed a team of constructors who built far and wide, spanning the territories of the empire from Bosnia to Baghdad, Crimea to Yemen. His school of architecture continued to expand and produce remarkable buildings in far-flung places from Algeria to India.

In his mid-nineties, in 1583, he made his pilgrimage to Mecca, five years before his death, aged one hundred – the inscription on his tomb gives his date of death as 1588. Sinan was a European Muslim architect, and his momentous contribution to the history of European civilization mirrored the magnificence and prestige of Europe's eastern Muslim empire. The utopia of an Islamic Kostantiniyye had been achieved largely through warfare, as the dream of Osman had foretold centuries earlier. But the Ottomans never regained the glory they had acquired in the lifetimes of Suleiman the Magnificent and his principal architect, though they had not given up their ambition to conquer Vienna.

Part Four

FEAR AND FASCINATION: ISLAMIC LIFE AND CULTURE IN EUROPE AFTER 1492

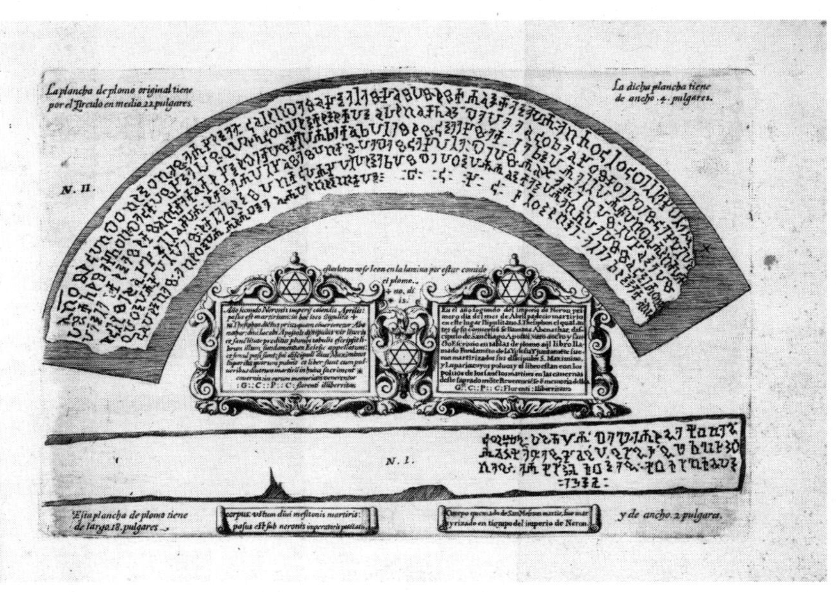

Funerary plaque of Saint Cecilius

Chapter 19

A People Betrayed: The Spanish Moriscos and the Repression of Western European Islam

'On the last evening
we contemplate mountains surrounding the clouds,
invasion and counter-invasion,
the ancient era handing our door keys over
to a new age.
Enter, O invaders, come, enter our houses,
drink the sweet wine of our Andalusian songs!'

Mahmoud Darwish

'. . . perhaps the first major episode of European ethnic cleansing'

Kwame Anthony Appiah

The Betrayal: 'A war of fire and blood'

Abdelghafar el Akel lives in the blue-tinted town of Chefchaouen, near the Moroccan coast. Taking pride of place above his fireplace is his most prized possession – a collage of objects consisting of a large key, a lock and some fragments of wood. These survived centuries of war, emigration and poverty, secretly stashed in an old sack and hidden as revered possessions of his ancestors, the Spanish Moriscos. They are the remains of the door of the house his family once owned in Granada, relinquished when his forebear Ibrahim Ben Ali fled in desperation to North Africa to escape religious persecution, just before the city came under Christian rule in 1492. They are a vital, tangible memento of his individual history and of the broader history of the native Spanish Muslims from whom he descends.

In just forty years, the vital force of Islam in Europe had shifted from west to east. As Kostantiniyye grew strong as the eastern capital of Islam on the continent, the surrender of the Islamic emirate of Granada in January 1492 marked a crossroads in European history, a critical point at which Christian Europe sought to eradicate its western Islamic peoples permanently. Over the next 120 years, Catholic Spain was to break the promises made in the Capitulations of Granada and betray the Muslim citizens of their dominions in a war that resulted in a brutal programme of ethnic and religious cleansing in the name of purity of blood and religion. The tone was set in April 1492, mere months after the fall of the city, when Ferdinand and Isabella announced the shocking Alhambra Decree that ordered all Jewish citizens to convert to Catholicism or leave the country within three months. That stark choice between forced conversion or permanent exile served as a terrible warning to the Muslim population of the Iberian peninsula, who were still practising Islam, but under Christian control.

The Muslim population of Granada whose families had lived for many generations on Spanish soil, and who considered it their native land, became known as *mudéjares*. This term redefined them as Muslims living protected under Christian jurisdiction – yet the word, taken from the Arabic word *mudajjan*, meaning 'tamed', and originally used as a taunt, underlined their subjection to Christian domination. At first, Islam appeared unthreatened, in line with the terms of the surrender agreed by Sultan Boabdil and the Catholic Monarchs, which safeguarded the religious and cultural freedom of resident Muslims.

The German physician Hieronymus Münzer was an eyewitness to this situation when he visited Granada in October 1494, and he wrote a detailed travelogue that recorded important aspects of Muslim life under Christian authority. His doctor's eye perceived the advanced Muslim sewerage system, with running water, urns used as urinals and plentiful wells of clean drinking water. He described the splendid main mosque, with rush mats on the floor, a patio with a central fountain for ablutions, and an enormous candelabrum bearing over a hundred candles, used for festivals. 'We saw many beautiful lamps lit and priests wearing a white tunic and white headcloth chanting their hours in their own way, which was a very sad clamour rather than singing. The temple was made with extraordinary richness.'[1] Münzer witnessed Muslim beliefs and rites, the Friday prayer meetings, the ritual washing before entering the mosque. His travel diary shows that, over two and a half years since Granada fell, Islam was still thriving in the city, which very soon would become an abode of fear and despair for native Muslims.

The prospect of a new Muslim conspiracy or uprising, and a suspicion that the constant interaction of Christians with Muslims would somehow contaminate Catholicism, fomented a religious persecution that was introduced in insidious stages. On 2 March 1498, Catholic authorities decreed that Granadan Christians were forbidden to sell wine to Muslims, rent out houses to them or to use Muslim baths or Muslim midwives; each community was obliged to operate separate storehouses for oil, honey, cheese, raisins and fruit. In short order, the Muslims found themselves ghettoized or moved outside the city. These measures and the growing uncertainty in their besieged community over whether all Muslims were safe from forced conversion to Catholicism led to a tipping point. The blatant betrayal of the 1492 Capitulations provoked a fierce Muslim revolt in the city between December 1499 and January 1500, where street fighting broke out, a Christian law officer was killed and the Inquisitor General Archbishop Cisneros narrowly escaped attack. Order was restored, but a point of no return had been reached. The Christian authorities declared that the rebellion rendered the terms of the Capitulations null and void, and a familiar-sounding ultimatum was issued: convert to Christianity or face exile. The Muslims felt they had been hoodwinked over the guaranteed right to pursue their own religion and had resorted to violence. The end of Islam as a public religion in Spain had come, and, along with it, the birth of crypto-Islam, the secret adherence to that faith while professing another.

The Muslims were redefined yet again – no longer as Mudejars, but as Moriscos, a word whose diminutive ending has a pejorative sense. The later meaning of 'Morisco', which came into being in the sixteenth century precisely because of these events in Granada, is much more specific. It describes those Muslims who remained living in Spain as baptized Christians, but who were forced, unwilling converts. At least 8,000 Muslims were forcibly converted in Granada around the turn of the century. In 1501, in the Plaza de Bib-Rambla in the city centre, the zealot Cardinal Cisneros gave the order to burn all books and manuscripts written in Arabic, which his men had gathered throughout the city, as part of a series of measures to eliminate all tangible signs of Islam. Juan de Vallejo, Cisnero's servant, described the events:

> In order to uproot them from their perverse and evil sect completely, he [Cisneros] ordered the Muslim expounders of the Law to take their Korans and other private books, as many as they owned, and build large fires and burn them all; and among them were an infinite number with silver bindings and other Morisco patterns on them, worth eight or ten ducados, and others worth less than that. . . . So they were all burnt, without leaving a trace . . . except for the books of medicine, of which there were many, which he ordered to be kept; of which his Lordship ordered thirty or forty volumes to be brought, which today are in the library of his distinguished college and university of Alcala[2]

In just five years, the peerless Granada where Islam still flourished had become a place of trauma for its Muslim inhabitants. The New Capitulations, or solemn agreement, dated 26 February 1501, aimed to ensure that Islam was eliminated as soon as possible. The choices it announced were harsh and drastic: remain and accept baptism, refuse baptism and become a slave, or emigrate and become a refugee in an Islamic country. A further royal decree of 12 February 1502 removed choice and obliged all inhabitants of Castilian territories to become Christians, as they were forbidden to remain Muslims. The Moriscos had no recourse to help from the rest of western Europe, which had celebrated the Christian victory of 1492 as an act of revenge for the loss of Constantinople, suffered forty years earlier. The only option was to approach Muslims abroad for assistance, but appeals to the Egyptian Mamluks and the Ottoman Turks proved fruitless, as neither was in a position to make a successful strike against Spanish territory because they were fighting each other. The irony was that Spain, a world imperial power at that time, felt threatened from within its borders by a minority group who, without substantial overseas aid, could never have posed a military threat to them.[3]

Islam in the west went underground. In the early sixteenth century, a young man of unknown name from the town of Arévalo in Castile lived as a crypto-Muslim, practising Islam clandestinely after the forced conversion decrees of 1501 and 1502. He was learned in Arabic, Hebrew, Greek and Latin, and his treatises concerned the fundamentals of the faith and rites of Islam. He wrote in Aljamía, a secret language invented by crypto-Muslims, written in Castilian but using the Arabic alphabet, and his record of several interviews with certain survivors of the fall of Granada gives us a moving insight into the tragedy of the Muslim community in Spain at this time.

One survivor he interviewed was an elderly woman known as the *Mora de Úbeda,* originally from the border between Granada and Castile. When he met her, she was ninety-three years old and lived in the Albaicín district. The Mora, who wore rough twill clothes and esparto grass sandals, had a body and limbs so large they perturbed the young scholar. She lived alone in great simplicity, although she had been very influential in Boabdil's time and maintained a privileged role at the Nasrid court, signing and sealing the books of the sultan of Granada, who gifted certain volumes to her when he went into exile. Latterly, she had withdrawn from public life to weep over the fall of the Islamic state and had witnessed the terrible destruction of Arabic books in the Plaza de Bib-Rambla. The young man reports her very words: 'I saw the Holy Book in the hands of a merchant who was tearing it up to use as paper for children, and I gathered up all the pieces, which broke my heart.'

Another distinguished figure in the local community was a teacher of Islam, Yūse Banegas, whose classes on the Koran were attended by the young man from Arévalo, held in the strictest secrecy and at risk to their lives. Yūse was an expert in Arabic and Hebrew, and his possession of books in those languages shows that their prohibition by the Christians was scorned by the Morisco minority. Yūse clearly perceived the Morisco tragedy and described his personal losses and the pain and indignation he felt in witnessing the shaming and selling of Muslim women at public auction: 'In my opinion nobody ever wept over such a misfortune as that of the sons of Granada. Do not doubt what I say, because I am one myself, and an eyewitness, for with my own eyes I saw all the noble ladies, widowed and married, subjected to mockery, and I saw more than three hundred young women sold at public auction. . . . I lost three sons, all of them died defending our religion, and I lost two daughters and my wife . . .'

In the decades to come, the Moriscos' plight worsened, bedevilled by the apparent desire both to assimilate them wholeheartedly into the Catholic fold and to contain, control and isolate what was perceived as the alien element in the new Christian Granada. Soon, the converted Muslims fell prey, like the Jewish *conversos*, to the unholy practices of the Inquisition, hell-bent on banning the whole inherited culture of the Moriscos.

In 1504, the mufti of Oran pronounced a fatwa, or considered legal opinion, setting out for the benefit of persecuted Muslims in Spain a list of modifications they could legitimately introduce into the religious obligations they must observe under circumstances of oppression. It is an exceptional document, still known today throughout the Muslim world, which essentially permitted Muslims to stay in Spain by allowing them to pretend to be Christians while maintaining their inner determination and intention to be Muslims. It gave detailed instructions on how this double life could be led.

In the secrecy enforced upon them by external pressures, the Moriscos invented a new written language, Aljamía, as used by the young man from Arévalo. It was similar to Jewish Ladino – Spanish written in Hebrew characters – adopted by the Jews prior to their expulsion in 1492, which had continued to flourish in the diaspora. Aljamía was not only an assertion of loyalty to Muslim religion and culture, but also a vital way of maintaining the Moriscos' threatened Islamic identity. Yet its message was ambivalent. The use of Arabic marked cultural difference, but its Spanish vocabulary showed that Moriscos were Europeans too. The new language expressed their embracement of two cultures, their Spanish identity as well as their Arabic and Islamic origins.

The ever more threatening attitude of the Christians and the clandestine lives of the crypto-Muslims built towards a conflict that would end in violence, as secrecy, falsity and ambiguity reigned in everyday life. Just before 1560, a petition was drawn up by Christian lawyers insisting on the revision of all property titles in the kingdom of Granada. This move was disastrous for Moriscos, who were obliged to show ancient title deeds from the time of the Nasrid dynasty, dating from the thirteenth century. If they could not, they were stripped of their land and property, which was put up for sale. In 1567, the Granadan authorities banned not only the use of Arabic, but also the use of Arab names, and of Moorish baths, while wearing Moorish clothing was officially prohibited in January 1568. Granada had become a place of panic and terror for the Moriscos. Prophecies or *jofores* containing obscure predictions circulated freely, and Moriscos met secretly to debate the situation. They decided to resist, and in an upsurge of enthusiasm they staged their first rebellion at Christmas 1568.

The Morisco uprising lasted for virtually two years, until November 1570, and became a savage battle involving appalling atrocities committed by both sides. After the anarchic violence and terrible rage of their uprising in the city on Christmas Eve 1568, when churches were robbed and burned, altars pulled down and priests dragged through the streets naked then shot with poisoned arrows, their rebellions focused on the mountainous region in the province of Granada known as the Alpujarras, longtime refuge of bandits and outlaws. There, the Moriscos fought under local commanders headed by the last indigenous Muslim pretender to the emirate in al-Andalus, known as Aben Humeya, assisted by foreign military experts sent by the Turks from Algiers. Aben Humeya's claim to be a descendant of the Umayyad Muslims who first ruled Spain sent the powerful message that his rule had a legitimacy predating any claimed by the Christian Habsburgs of Austria. The Moriscos were up against the Christian might of royal troops and urban militia, led by the Habsburg Don John of Austria. While the Moriscos sorely lacked manpower and firearms, their knowledge of the rocky mountain passes, mule trails and deep valleys of the Alpujarras meant they could outwit the royal troops, who lacked experience of the terrain or mountain weather conditions.

In the autumn of 1569, King Philip II removed all restrictions on rape and plunder on the part of the Christian army, giving his troops free rein in what he declared to be 'a war of fire and blood.' In January 1570, Don John of Austria led 12,000 Spanish troops and heavy artillery to besiege the ancient village of Galera, 150 kilometres from Granada. The 3,000 locals were armed with rocks, rubble and the few weapons they had, plus an indomitable spirit. As heavy cannons blasted gaps in the walls, the Christian knight Juan Pacheco rushed through the gap into the village, where he was promptly hacked limb from limb. Enraged at the terrible casualties among his troops, inflicted by mere civilians, Don John ordered the slaughter of over 400 women and children, a gruesome atrocity which tells us as much about John of Austria as it does about the extraordinary courage and determination of the Morisco villagers, whose resistance was inevitably overcome.

What the Morisco rebels did not know was that around March 1570, a decision had been taken to deport the entire Muslim population of the kingdom of Granada to destinations in the kingdom of Castile, where they were unlikely to cause a threat. Don John of Austria returned directly from the Alpujarras campaigns to oversee the critical first stages of the deportation. In June, squadrons of royal soldiers rounded up all Morisco men and boys aged between ten and sixty and barricaded them into parish churches, where they spent the night under armed guard. The Granadan soldier and chronicler Luis del Mármol Carvajal was moved at the plight of his neighbours: 'It was a miserable spectacle to see so many men of all ages, heads held low, hands crossed, their faces bathed in tears and their expressions sad and suffering as they left their comfortable homes, their families, their homeland, their native identity, their possessions, without knowing for certain if they would keep their heads on'.[4]

The deportation carried on into the harsh Castilian winter, during which these internal exiles suffered cruelly from snow, cold and typhus, and many died. All Muslim inhabitants of Granada were relocated, except for artisans and a very small, privileged elite judged useful to the Crown.[5] Yet there emerged from this minority band a group of men who brought hope to the crypto-Muslim community of Spain, not using arms, but words.

The Fusion of Identities: The Lead Books of Granada

Nearly twenty years after the first banishment of the Moriscos, Granada was rocked by a number of archaeological discoveries, first at the construction site of the new cathedral, and later on a hill outside the city, where a series of mysterious books written on lead discs were unearthed and enthusiastically hailed as very early Christian texts.[6] It all began on 19 March 1588, Armada year, as workmen demolished the minaret of the former great mosque, known as the Torre Turpiana, to make way for a third nave in the new cathedral. They unearthed a lead casket inside which was a small panel bearing an image of the Virgin Mary, a fragment of linen, a small piece of bone, a folded parchment and some blackish-blue sand. What caused the greatest stir was the parchment, on which a text, written in Latin, Arabic and Castilian, described the contents of the casket as the bone of the first Christian martyr, St Stephen, the cloth the Virgin dried her eyes upon at the Crucifixion, and a prophecy by St John the Divine relating to the end of the world. Yet the writing on the parchment caused such trouble to decode that eventually expert translators were called in to decipher the full script, one of whom was the Morisco Miguel de Luna, translator to King Philip II.

De Luna and his colleague Alonso del Castillo studied it separately, each deciphering the same great revelation. It transpired that the prophecy of St John, which foresaw the advent of Muhammad in the seventh century, the division of Christianity into sects and the coming of the Antichrist, had been translated into Castilian by a St Cecilius, who described himself as the earliest bishop of Granada during the first century AD. Despite the conundrum posed by such an early saint being able to write not only in Arabic but also Castilian Spanish, a language that did not exist in the first century, Granada was exultant to learn that he was its first bishop.

The genuineness of the relics and parchment seemed vindicated when, in April 1595, treasure-seekers digging on the hillside near Granada, later known as the Sacromonte or Holy Mount, unearthed a strip of lead engraved in archaic Latin, which claimed that the cremated remains of an early Christian martyr were buried there. Immediately, the site was excavated, revealing two more lead plaques, one of which stated that St Thesiphon, one of the seven bishops of Rome, who was allegedly an Arab convert to Christianity, had written a book on lead tablets called the *Fundamentum Ecclesiae*, or *Fundamental Doctrines of the Church*. Amid great excitement, ashes presumed to belong to the saint were also discovered.

Then, the first of a mysterious series of texts later known as the Lead Books was unearthed beneath a large stone, still visible today. It was wrapped in a lead cover and consisted of five round plates, ten centimetres across, hinged together by a twist of lead. The plates were inscribed in Arabic on both sides, with the Latin title on the inside, which translated into English as *The Book of the Fundamental Doctrines of the Church Written in the Characters of Solomon*. This was presumably the book written by St Thesiphon, referred to on the lead plaque. The new revelation was celebrated with parties, fireworks, artillery salutes from the Alhambra and general bell-ringing.

Over a period of many months, a total of twenty-two lead books were found on the hillside. Due to the complexities of the texts, written in ancient Arabic, professional translators were called in, including Miguel de Luna, who declared that the books contained doctrinal material of the greatest importance, including the instructions and sayings of the Virgin Mary, St Peter and St James. Experts of all kinds, including scribes, parchment makers, anatomists and charcoal burners were called in to scrutinize the relics. Strong supernatural predictions of their discovery bolstered the belief that they were genuine. As long as fifty years before the excavations took place, mysterious lights had repeatedly been observed over the site, and this was considered conclusive evidence of the divine revelations.

King Philip II was fascinated by this affair that involved his royal translators, but rumours began to circulate that the relics were not authentic, and several scholars and churchmen appeared to corroborate this. Yet, a group of local theologians, including the new archbishop of Granada, Don Pedro de Castro, had already decided that the relics and texts were genuine. It was inevitable but unfortunate that the Vatican got involved, firmly applying pressure to have the finds investigated further. After many years of resistance, the Lead Books were taken to Madrid for examination in 1631, and were eventually forcibly removed to Rome amid great protest. Finally, in 1682, they were condemned as heretical Islamic writings. The Lead Books had caused a religious sensation in Granada, as well as in Catholic Europe, and many involved ignored the Vatican's damning accusation, including Diego de Yepes, the king's confessor, who deemed them to be as precious to Granada as the Ark of the Covenant to the Israelites.

Archbishop Pedro de Castro was profoundly involved in the whole Sacromonte affair, commissioning the translators to work on the Lead Books and the testing of the relics, with the encouragement of royal and religious authorities. The fact that their message involved rewriting Church history to provide Granada with a Christian heritage that predated its Islamic incarnation was a marvellous boost to the project of transforming the city from Islamic state to Christian enclave. In April 1600, at a meeting of forty-nine Church elders in the cathedral to authenticate the relics, it was unanimously agreed that they were genuine. Granada celebrated for several days, an unbridled spectacle of imitation ships, knights, serpents and fireworks. The archbishop began to foster the cult of the Sacromonte, keeping the relics there on the hillside in a small chapel, later to become the Abbey of the Sacromonte, which he founded in 1610 on the site of the discoveries and conceived as a sanctuary to house the bones of the first Christian martyrs and ultimately the Lead Books. The Vatican has never challenged the authenticity of the relics of the Sacromonte martyrs to this day.

From the start, the out-and-out apologists for the artefacts were their first translators, the Moriscos Alonso del Castillo and Miguel de Luna, the latter of whom was the most mysterious and complex of all those involved in the saga of the Lead Books. Born into a noble Morisco family in Granada around 1550, Luna learnt Arabic as a young man and studied medicine at the newly founded university in the city. He worked as a physician in Granada, but it was writing that became fundamental to his life as the vehicle through which he conveyed his radical, subversive views. Luna's up-to-the-minute medical treatise on bathing was written in 1592, a thinly veiled political and religious statement about the importance of restoring the prohibited Morisco practice of taking baths, which purported to discuss their therapeutic value from a solely scientific, pragmatic perspective. The treatise was never published, but his next work, written in the guise of his other profession of translator and entitled *The True History of King Roderick* (*Verdadera Historia del rey don Rodrigo*), was published in 1592 as a crucial reinterpretation of the events surrounding the Muslim invasion of Spain in 711. It was allegedly the translation of an unknown Arabic source he found in the library of El Escorial, and was very popular, with seven reprintings and translations into several European languages. But it transpired that this 'true history' was in fact a colossal fabrication, which fooled many learned people, including the two Inquisitors who assessed whether it should be censored or not. Boldly dedicated to King Philip II, Luna's alternative history aimed to legitimize the political and religious claims of the Moriscos to live in Spanish territory at a time when the Church was acting fast to eliminate any traces of religious otherness.

For Miguel de Luna, words were power at a time when Moriscos in Granada, as well as those in internal exile, were a powerless minority. The most crucial aspect of his life was his ambiguous connection with the Lead Books, initially as their translator in his capacity as a converted Muslim member of the elite Christian royal establishment. He began work on translations of the first two lead texts in May 1595, and issued a persuasive report for the king in October, adamantly supporting their antiquity because, he said, the age of the lead they were made from proved they were too ancient to contain any reference to the Koran. In addition, their script predated Koranic language and was called Solomonic script, of the kind he claimed he had seen in ancient magical books like the *Key of Solomon*. He also declared that no one alive in Spain could have faked them, as no Moor was sufficiently learned or adept at such a script. But, in fact, Miguel de Luna was just that person.

A native of Granada, he loved the city, describing it as an earthly garden of delights; yet, in February 1611, in a letter to the archbishop of Granada, he wrote how his paradise had turned into purgatory. Fearful of the expulsion that had overtaken his fellow Moriscos, he described being on the verge of the same fate: 'the authorities entered my house to remove arms and exert other extortions, which has made me so furious that I can't sleep at night for thinking about these offences.' In the same letter, he lamented 'the injustice of wanting to take away my property, lineage, honour and the value of services I have rendered'.[7] Torn between his desire to belong to the Christian establishment and wanting to remain true to his Morisco roots, he succeeded in acquiring the status of a nobleman, thereby avoiding deportation, and Archbishop Castro wrote that his faithful translator lived as a Catholic and died a good Christian death with all the sacraments in his beloved Granada in the summer of 1618.

But Miguel de Luna never ceased to be a Muslim, living a double life. Outwardly, he was a Christian doctor and translator, but he attended secret meetings with other crypto-Muslims, where he expounded on the Lead Books, using them as evidence that Jesus was not divine but a prophet. He presented their purpose not as upholding the longevity and power of Christianity in Granada, which he had so vehemently defended when in the city, but as polemical Islamic texts presenting an improved version of Christianity and asserting that the perfect religion was Islam. As such, Miguel de Luna lived a life of great risk as a heretic, at once a Muslim yet an apparent Christian, and almost unquestionably the author of the Lead Books and Torre Turpiana parchment, in concert with others, including Alonso del Castillo.

The fabrication of the Lead Books is a story of resistance and creative ingenuity in the face of overwhelmingly powerful religious and political forces, a resistance embodied in a hidden network of courageous, idealistic men who fought to defend their culture and language. Miguel de Luna was never denounced in his lifetime and never suffered exile. Daring, radical, right at the heart of the establishment as the king's translator from Arabic, Miguel de Luna was a prolific wordsmith who delighted in the art of ambivalence, in constructing an outer appearance contrary to the inner reality, in using language as a compelling yet subversive weapon in the desperate fight to reinstate Morisco cultural and religious values in Spanish society. In doing so, he fabricated and fused Muslim and Christian identities so that they appeared indistinguishable.

Abandoning Paradise: The Exile of the Iberian Muslims

Amid the intrigues and drama of the Lead Books affair, the Spanish monarchy and the Catholic Church worked doggedly to find an effective solution to what they perceived as the Morisco problem. The desire to banish the Moriscos, who were objectively native Spaniards who had converted to Catholicism, was fuelled by a racial and religious antipathy which went back a very long way, to the Muslim invasion of 711. Expulsion was to be the final stage of reversing that ancient historical turning point, and such a measure reveals how deeply unsatisfactory the apparent completion of the Reconquest in January 1492 had been. Islam had not disappeared, and both secular and sacred authorities were nonplussed. The Christian perspective was that, despite all efforts at conversion, the Moriscos could not be assimilated into the Catholic scheme of things. Everyone knew they were still Moors – 'as Moorish as the Algerians' became the refrain.

The proposal for a solution, sent to King Philip II in 1587 by the bishop of Segorbe, Martín de Salvatierra, shrank from a prior recommendation to send the Moriscos to sea and drown them, suggesting instead that they could all be deported to America, the males castrated and the women sterilized, so they would die out quickly. The fact that this horrifying scenario was prompted, the bishop stated, by the fear of a Morisco alliance with North Africa, which might see them launch an attack on Spain, underlines how potent the ancient horror of invasion continued to be in the Christian psyche.

The reason given for the expulsion, in the decree issued by King Philip III, was Morisco disloyalty, though the real reason was most likely to compensate for the failure of Spanish policy in northern Europe by a measure that would restore the prestige of the sovereign. Philip even commissioned a series of narrative paintings depicting vital moments in the expulsion, amid a flurry of books and manuscripts on the subject, in which the king was praised as 'the last and ultimate conqueror of the Moors in Spain.'[8] This propaganda was intended to rouse public approval for an expulsion of highly questionable legitimacy. Opinion in the rest of Europe was divided: the Venetian ambassador to Spain in 1611 spoke of Moriscos as 'the worst of people', while Francis, Lord Cottington, English ambassador to Madrid, called the expulsion 'a cruelty never heard of in any age.'[9]

Over the next five years, like the Jews before them, the marginalized, persecuted Moriscos were banished region by region and herded onto galleys at ports around Valencia, to be taken to North

Africa, initially to Oran in present-day Algeria. A few greeted their exile joyfully and looked forward to returning to the land of their ancestors. Most of the Granadan Moriscos had been sent into internal exile in the 1570s, but they had not settled in, and many managed to find their way back to Andalusia, where there was work. Some had even illegally slipped back into Granada itself. The edict of January 1610 declared that these Moriscos were to be expelled without exception, within thirty days, taking no money with them, only permitted goods. By March 1611, there was really no escape – Moriscos from the city who had not left when summoned, including former slaves and even those who possessed a formal statement that they lived as good Christians, were forced to leave. In 1614, this ethnic cleansing was supposedly complete, and Islam, which came to the land in 711, had been driven out after 900 years.

The Aftermath

Best guesses estimate that 300,000 Moriscos were exiled from the realm, plus some 10,000 or 12,000 who died en route. Of those who survived, many were scattered across Egypt, Turkey, the Balkans, Lebanon, Greece and sub-Saharan Africa; some even reached the American continent, but the vast majority ended up in Morocco, Tunisia and Algeria, where their agricultural know-how, artistic and cultural heritage and Hispanic family names live on today. The transition was hard, since they were Spanish, and their language, customs, way of life and even religion did not blend in easily with North African ways. As many as 80,000 Moriscos settled in Tunis, which still has a district known as Andalusia Alley, and the old songs of their people forbidden in Spain formed what became the national Tunisian musical genre *ma'luf*.

In Spain and Portugal, the consequences of the expulsion were severe. Across the peninsula, key members of the workforce were lost, including silk-workers, agricultural labourers and horticulturalists on whose skills both religious and secular institutions depended. Valencia lost 30 per cent of its population, and many landlords faced poverty and ruin. This crisis of manpower was later seen as a major factor in the rapid decline of Spain, though it was not just the economy that was stricken. The country abruptly changed from a multicultural society, where members of three different religions lived side by side, to a society with a sole religion and one official language unified under Catholicism. It became a closed, suspicious society, desiring to repress and eliminate difference, further cut off from Europe by its abhorrence of Protestantism and its own Counter-Reformation. Inquisitorial suspicion of heresy also cut ties with important cultural currents in north-west Europe due to the prohibition on foreign literature, leading to intellectual repression and the resulting creation of a uniquely Hispanic cultural tradition in the sixteenth and seventeenth centuries.

★

By 1614, Granada had been transformed into a Spanish-speaking Castilian kingdom with almost no native Muslims. Or at least that was the theory. The practice was quite different. In the first half of the eighteenth century, the Inquisition in Granada rooted out several hundred crypto-Muslims, all married and living within their own community completely incognito, many of whom were silk dealers, artisans, livestock breeders, sugar traders and leasing agents. Alongside these middle-class Moriscos, a new elite group of families lived on who had become integrated into seventeenth-century Granadan society. Often, they were wealthy, competing with and even surpassing the Old Christian elite, and working in public offices as scribes, law enforcers, doctors, castle governors and even as priests, some of whom attained a high rank in the Church. They had been able to acquire nobility by establishing a legal case, using fake documents and genealogies to concoct a plausible ancestry. They were all protected by a network of powerful local Christian aristocrats who enabled them to hide in plain view. Between 1728 and 1731, the Holy Inquisition persecuted about 250 of these Moriscos, some of whom fled to Istanbul and Tunis, while others lost their possessions, were imprisoned for years or exiled. It is astonishing that the majority of those on trial continued living in Granada and, to all appearances, became completely absorbed into the community by the late eighteenth century. Try as they might, the Spanish Church and monarchy never entirely eradicated the native Muslims from the Iberian peninsula, and certainly not from Granada, nor could they obliterate their cultural traces. In the lavish disguise of a great Renaissance Christian city, Granada unmasked still bore the indelible imprint of its Muslim heritage – in its lineages, in its architecture, in its very cityscape.

CHAPTER 20

BEYOND THE PALE: SUFIS, SLAVES AND PIRATES

'Beware of confining yourself to a particular belief and denying all else, for much good would elude you – indeed, the knowledge of reality would elude you. Be in yourself a matter for all forms of belief, for God is too vast and tremendous to be restricted to one belief rather than another.'

Ibn al-Arabi, Andalusian Sufi

'"Go home, go home!" says Captain Ward, "And tell your king from me: Although he's king of all dry land yet I'm king of the sea!"'

'Captain Ward and the Rainbow', old pirate ballad

'I come from no country, no city, no tribe. I am the son of the highway, my country is a caravan . . . all languages, all prayers belong to me.'

Amin Maalouf, *Leo Africanus*

FAR FROM THE pomp and circumstance of Europe's royal courts, beyond the confines of the officialdom and regal power that resisted all change and dictated religious and political policy, motley waves of European Muslims and Christians rose, fell and intersected on the borders of human society. Wandering mystics, slaves and nomads of the sea dwelled in the transitional spaces between two worlds and two religions. Most were mavericks, rebels and non-conformists who crossed boundaries and broke rules, transgressive anarchists and social pariahs who lived on the fringes of European life. On sea and land, religious zeal and an appetite for trade created alliances and interchanges in the margins, where religious identities were swapped and cultural and religious exchanges sprang into life. Destinies were changed by chance and by religious conversion. Pirates, the renegades of the high seas, governed the flourishing Mediterranean slave trade and made alliances of convenience, often with unexpected repercussions, while, in eastern Europe, mystical Sufis at odds with traditional Sunni Islam roamed the highways of the Balkans under the Ottoman Empire.

Religious Rebels: Learned Sufis and Deviant Dervishes

In 1451, Sultan Murad II met a Sufi on a bridge near Edirne who foretold his imminent death. The encounter was a terrifying omen for Murad that also entailed an unexpected reversal of roles, in which the Sufi was the master and the sultan his disciple; it identified the Sufi as both an outsider, as wandering diviner, and an insider who had the most potent of influences on the monarchy. The ambivalence of the Sufi order is also apparent in its objectives as both the chosen path of a group of elevated mystics and an Islamic way for all levels of society, combined in a tradition of powerful knowledge, practices and charismatic leaders. The name 'Sufi' comes from the Arabic word *Suf*, meaning 'wool', which refers to the coarse, foul-smelling wool garments worn originally by both Christian and Muslim ascetics to emphasize their rejection of the worldly in favour of the spiritual.

Some of the founding myths of Islam in Africa refer to the arrival of wandering holy men, and the earliest version of a Sufi lodge anywhere in the world is in Guardamar, in the Spanish province of Valencia, where there is a *ribat* dating from the tenth century AD, in the time of the caliphate of Cordoba. Originally a fortress, it had a communal mosque, lodgings for pilgrims and thirteen residential cells for holy men, each with a prayer niche. Muslim sources point to a wide network of *ribats* in al-Andalus by the eleventh century, from Almería in the east to Toledo and Badajoz in the west, where Sufis were often involved in jihad and were linked to militant spirituality. Sufism became popular, in part because many Muslims had ceased to learn the Arabic of the Koran, and the Sufi shrines of saints brought believers back to Islam through a cult that fused the arcane with an everyday idiom that spoke to the Muslim community. Its influence spread across all social levels, from princes to peasants, nomads to town dwellers, the educated and the uneducated. It flourished on the frontiers of Islam, in places where kin and tribal organization were predominant, where Sufis assimilated boundless local religious traditions with Islam. They worked as intermediaries between religions and cultures and drew in non-Muslims by sharing their experiences with people from other religious traditions, including Christianity.

Sufi Islam was a religion of saints and miracles, and as its orders sprang up, it became inspired by the mystical ideas of a Spanish Sufi, Muhyi al-Din ibn al-Arabi (1165–1240), who went on pilgrimage to Mecca and had a vision of the divine throne, and received the holy knowledge that he was foremost among saints. Ibn al-Arabi was born into a noble Arab family in court service in Murcia, and he moved between west and east, travelling to North Africa before spending most of his life in Seville. Greatest of all Sufi visionaries, he claimed he could summon the presence of any dead souls and spoke regularly with Jesus, Muhammad and Moses. His masterwork was *The Meccan Revelations*, a grand vision of cosmic existence in which he saw all human history as explorations of divine being. His doctrine of the unity of being was a magisterial synthesis of Sufi, philosophic and Neoplatonic ideas, in which God was transcendent, yet identical with man in essence, since all creation was a manifestation of God. Banned for pantheism for centuries by both Muslim and Christian scholars, Ibn al-Arabi set the agenda for Sufism after 1300. He died in Damascus in 1240 at the age of seventy-five.

Just forty years separated Ibn al-Arabi and the other great Sufi sage of the thirteenth century, Jalal al-Din Rumi (1207–1273), who fled from east to west to escape the Mongol terror and spent his life among the Seljuk Turks of Konya in Anatolia. Rumi is considered the greatest Sufi poet, and his *Masnavi*, a colossal compilation of fables, tales of the everyday, metaphysics and sayings from the Koran, is thought to be the greatest poem ever written in Persian. Rumi was a Muslim scholar who followed the example of Muhammad, yet his message of universal love embraced music, dance and poetry as a path to the divine, and led to the ritual dance or *sama* of the Whirling Dervishes, practised by the Mehlevi order established in his name. The Ottomans funded the expansion of the brotherhood of Whirling Dervishes, which became their favoured religious association, strengthening their conviction that the Sufi brotherhoods were crucial in maintaining social order. Selim I granted to the Sufis a Christian monastery, with its vineyards and olive groves, in the Christian village of Dayr Bi'na, in Galilee, in 1516. In this way, new forms of combined religious practice evolved as Christian and Sufi communities came to tolerate each other. In an age of severe conflict between the faiths, Sufis played an important part in creating new kinds of religious synthesis.

*

In 1493, Sultan Bayezid II was almost assassinated by a Sufi. Ottoman patronage of the mystical orders did not prevent rebellions against imperial authority, led by anarchist dervishes who overtly transgressed social norms. In a way akin to certain Christian mendicant orders such as the Carmelites, the dervish fraternities espoused material poverty, doing without proper food, shelter or clothing, in accordance with the views of Ibn al-Arabi that God was present in all creatures and that dervishes were saints. Hajj Bektas, an Iranian immigrant to Anatolia and contemporary of Rumi, was known as a miracle worker who cured the sick, resurrected the dead and conjured up huge quantities of food to feed the poor. He formed the order of Bektashi dervishes, whose twin poles were asceticism and anarchy, and who became known among scholars as deviant dervishes. The Bektashis, who were the favoured order of the Janissaries, renounced all social norms and indulged in repellent behaviour to prove it. They were men who had severed their social ties, left their families, flouted authority and become dropouts. They dressed in woollen sacks or furs, or went barefoot and stark naked, with just a few leaves to cover their genitals, which were adorned with strange metal piercings. They wielded primitive weapons such as clubs, bones and hatchets, and unabashedly indulged in marijuana, hashish and wine. The Bektashis had a strong following in the Balkans, and their sect spread across Bulgaria, Bosnia, Greece and Albania, where it still exists. By the sixteenth century, towns such as Prizren and Đakovica in Kosovo and Skopje in modern Macedonia had Sufi centres of education for scholars, and books circulated widely in that region. The Ottoman explorer Evliya Çelebi, whose own father was a famous dervish, travelled to the Balkans in 1664 and came across the first recorded Bektashi *tekke*, the Turkish name for a Sufi lodge, in Blagaj in Bosnia.

The behaviour of deviant dervishes was the cause of major tensions among the ulema, Muslim scholars who abhorred their undisguised flouting of Islamic law or sharia. After the death of Bayezid I, the biggest rebellion in Ottoman history was led by the infamous Sheikh (Master) Bedreddin, born around 1359 to a Muslim father and a Christian mother, a man half Greek, half Turkish, and a revered scholar said to have the power to resuscitate the dead. The sheikh flouted Islamic tradition by adhering to the views of Ibn al-Arabi, but succeeded in winning the favour of the Ottoman rulers as a spiritual guide, as well as acquiring a large following of Anatolian townsfolk, peasants, Christians and Jews. It is telling that Bedreddin's two main disciples were originally a Christian and a Jew.[1] When Mehmed I came to the throne, he saw Bedreddin as a potential threat to the dynasty who might stir up unrest, and kept him under house arrest in Iznik. In 1416, and still under arrest, Bedreddin sent his deputy and disciple Börklüce Mustafa to lead thousands of Christian and Muslim followers in a rebellion in west Anatolia. They were eventually quashed by Mehmed I's armies, while Bedreddin somehow escaped to whip up rebellion in Bulgaria, taking refuge with the Christian prince of Wallachia. Mehmed I finally caught up with him later that year, sentencing him to be hanged stark naked from a tree and his corpse left on public display in Siroz. The uprisings were quashed, but what had shaken the Ottomans to the core was the unprecedented prospect of more popular peasant uprisings that united Christians, Jews and Muslims against the empire.

Even while the dervishes were seen as threats to conventional Islam and viewed with suspicion as the instigators of civil unrest, learned Sufis travelled to Anatolia and the Balkans, teaching religion and founding centres of learning throughout the Ottoman Empire. As they created important social, cultural and economic networks in rural areas and towns, they strove to find common ground between Islam and other religions. Their powerful mysticism was closely connected with the Kabbalah of the Sephardic Jews and had a strong influence upon Roman Catholic mysticism. Sufism embraced pagan, Christian and Persian rituals, and echoed the individual pursuit of love, virtuous action and faith of Christian mysticism.

Between Two Worlds: Pirates and Privateers in the Mediterranean

As Sufis roamed the highways of early modern eastern Europe, Muslim and Christian pirates ruled the high seas, making alliances of convenience across the Mediterranean. They came to be known as Barbary pirates, after the Berber states where they operated, dominating the length of the North African coast along the Ottoman borderlands whose territories were ruled from Algiers, Tunis and Tripoli, as far west as the sultanate of Morocco. For almost 300 years, from the sixteenth to the nineteenth centuries, these renegades worked the shadowy zones between Christianity and Islam, moving easily between two worlds. Many pirates began as privateers, state-authorized raiders of merchant shipping who could turn their hands to warring when required. In the sixteenth century, Algiers, Tunis and Tripoli were military states that elected their own rulers, who made a handsome living from war booty pillaged from Spanish and Portuguese shipping. The Barbarossa brothers, who operated out of Algiers, were early privateers who waged war against the Christians on behalf of the Ottomans and fought in a maritime jihad against the knights of St John, who retaliated in kind by attacking Muslim shipping in the eastern Mediterranean, spurred on by their Christian duty to fight the infidel.

Privateering evolved from a state-sanctioned and regulated system of robbery into the sophisticated criminality of piracy, peopled by disenchanted and impoverished sailors. After the defeat of the Spanish Armada in 1588, privateering on Spanish ships became big business until King James I came to the English throne in 1603 and put an end to it with his proclamation that any attacks on Spanish ships would be considered as piracy. He was as good as his word – seventeen English Barbary pirates were executed in London in 1609. But he held no sway over the raiders from Africa in the seventeenth century, and their presence shaped perceptions of the relationship between Islam and Christianity at that time. The European Christian west saw the corsairs of Barbary not as rebels from society, but as plain thieves and criminals, and their views were overtly racist and anti-Islamic. By the time James I became king in 1567, Islam was already being called 'the present terror of the world.'[2]

Ships' treasures and cargoes were only a part of the plunder. The pirates' most lucrative trade was the capture and enslavement of sea travellers – around one million Europeans and at least as many North African men, women and children lost their freedom in the seventeenth century. It was said that over 20,000 captives were held under lock and key in Algiers alone, and while the rich could sometimes be released by payment of a ransom, the poor had no such good fortune. They were kept in hot, overcrowded bagnios or prisons, which had chapels, hospitals and shops run by prisoners, whose only hope was to gain their freedom by converting to Islam.

Christianity and Islam collided and crossed over in the transitional maritime sphere of Mediterranean buccaneering, as identities were swapped and roles reversed. The lives of two unlikely corsairs reflect the ever-present backdrop of tensions between the two religions. The first started out as the governor of Tetouan in Morocco in the first half of the sixteenth century, a prominent political leader who was both privateer and overseer of pirate operations, who formed an alliance with the most notorious of sea-wolves, Hayreddin Barbarossa. This powerful politician and slave trader was a woman, a female figure of high status in the history of Islam's western empire, whose life story demonstrates how the conflict between Muslims and Christians in al-Andalus at times provoked vengeful and antithetical repercussions. Lalia Aicha bint Ali ibn Rashid al-Alami, otherwise known as Sayyida al-Hurra, was born in Granada around 1491, just before the surrender of the city to Christian forces. Her family came from the nobility of al-Andalus, and Sayyida was said to be the descendant of a Moroccan Sufi saint. Her parents fled to Morocco in the aftermath of the fall of Granada and settled in Chefchaouen, where Sayyida had a fine education and became fluent in several languages, including Spanish and Portuguese. She had been promised in marriage as a child to another Muslim refugee, Sidi al-Mandri, a friend of her father and then governor of Tetouan, who was also thirty years her senior.

When al-Mandri died in 1515, Sayyida, who was then about twenty-five, took over as governor of the city, a role she had experienced before when Sidi was away on business. Some years later, she married the sultan of Fez, Ahmed al-Wattasi, yet remained in her post as governor of Tetouan, and appointed her brother as al-Wattasi's vizier. In this way, she unified Morocco against the attacks of Christian Spain and Portugal, taking revenge on them for the exile of her people by operating her pirate fleet around Gibraltar. She supported and financed pirate ships, or provided them with supplies, enlisting Barbarossa's help to expand into the western Mediterranean, and grew rich from booty and captives' ransoms. Sayyida was feared by the Christians as a powerful queen of the Mediterranean Sea, and she ruled for thirty years, until her son-in-law overthrew her and she was forced to return to Chefchaouen bereft of property or influence, living in her father's home until she died, never having fulfilled her dream of returning to Andalusia.

The second improbable pirate and convert to Islam was an 'Englishman of the noblest blood', the knight Sir Francis Verney (1584–1615), born in Pendley Manor in Tring, Hertfordshire. He made an unusual Jacobean corsair, given his respected, noble ancestry and his complete lack of seafaring experience. His unlikely career was the consequence of a marriage, arranged when he was only fifteen, to Ursula St Barbe, the daughter of his stepmother, who was also now his mother-in-law. Soon after the marriage, records show he attended Trinity College, Oxford, where he amassed enormous debts and began to rebel against his enforced wedlock. When he was twenty, he became entangled in a dispute with his stepmother, Lady Mary Blakeney, over the ownership of a small field. The quarrel was debated in the House of Commons, which decided in her favour. Disillusioned and deep in debt, he sold his lands, abandoned his wife and, after travelling across Europe and visiting Jerusalem, ended up in Morocco, where he fell in with a band of English mercenaries led by a relation of his, Captain John Gifford. They were fighting for Mulay Sidan, a pretender to the Moroccan sultanate, whose father had friendly relations with Queen Elizabeth I of England and who aspired to reclaim al-Andalus from the Christian Spanish and return it to Islam.

Francis Cottington, the pro-Spanish, pro-Catholic English ambassador to Madrid, reported in 1609 that Verney was operating as a pirate, 'making havoc of his own countrymen, and carrying into Algiers prizes belonging to the merchants of Poole and Plymouth'.[3] There were rumours that he had captured a consignment of wine from Bordeaux, meant for King James I, who was so outraged that he sent a warship to the Barbary coast. At the time, Sir Francis was living in Tunis, in the company of the most infamous British pirate Captain John Ward and his band. A year later, the Venetian ambassador to Tunis spread the news that both men had 'turned Turk' by converting to Islam. Reports of Verney's new Muslim faith caused something of a sensation in England.

Verney's meteoric success as a corsair ended in an equally sudden fall from grace, after he lost several ships in just a few days and was once again reduced to poverty, this time because he was deeply in hock to the Turks. On his way home from Tunis in 1615, the Scottish traveller William Lithgow stopped over in Sicily, where he found Sir Francis on his deathbed in the hospital in Messina. He learnt that Francis had spent two years as a captive galley slave on a Sicilian ship, before being rescued by an English Jesuit, who made him promise to convert to Catholicism, a fate his family considered scarcely preferable to being a Muslim. Verney fell sick and died in hospital in September 1615; Lithgow arranged his burial and sent his turban, silk slippers, tunics and a pilgrim's staff back to his family home, where they remain to this day.

Swapped Identities and Rare Exchanges: The Strange Lives of Mediterranean Slaves

From Islam's earliest presence in Europe up to the transformation of Muslim al-Andalus into a Christian territory and the conquest of Istanbul by the Ottomans, a minority of Muslims had lived as slaves in areas of the western Mediterranean, mainly the Iberian peninsula, Italy and southern France. Outside al-Andalus, and Sicily in its Muslim era, Christian rulers had ceased to execute captive infidels, enslaving them instead, a process which involved forced conversion to Christianity and assimilation into Catholic society. Although in Christian territories conquered from al-Andalus after the eleventh century Muslims were allowed a degree of religious and cultural freedom, the only way for Muslims to free those enslaved elsewhere was by contracts of redemption, which had an equivalent in the redemption process for Christian captives imprisoned in Muslim territories. Exchanges of slaves were negotiated and implemented by 'redeemers' – who were known as *al-fakkāh* in Arabic, transliterated as *alfaqueques* in Christian Iberia – often merchants, often Jews, who took captives for exchange with them on their trading trips.

Captives living in conquered lands were not the only source of slaves, as many prisoners of maritime war became the prey of privateers in the Mediterranean. By the start of the sixteenth century, the seizure of foreign ships by the Barbary pirates, and their raids along the coasts of the Mediterranean, as well as England, the Netherlands and even Iceland, resulted in a highly lucrative trade in saleable prisoners. Many were condemned to live as galley slaves in the direst degrading conditions, or were relegated to prisons to await sale at the slave markets. Enslavement flourished across the religious divide. In the places of interchange, on the borders of European and North

African society, humans were bought and sold, swapped and bartered, redeemed and recaptured, and this tawdry trade led at times to the strangest of transformations and bizarre reversals of identity, to the embracing of reciprocities and the crossing of religious and cultural boundaries.

The Man with Two Names: al-Hasan Muhammad al-Wazzan, alias Leo Africanus

Al-Hasan al-Wazzan came from Granada, his father an Andalusian Muslim, his mother perhaps a Jewish convert to Islam. His birth coincided with the time of the Christian conquest of his city, when his family was exiled to Fez. Despite their brutal upheaval from al-Andalus, his family thrived as owners of vineyards in the Rif foothills and rented a castle in the mountains above Fez, with a base in the city too. Al-Hasan became a dedicated student at Kairouan University, after which he worked as a diplomat, employed as the emissary and ambassador to the sultan of Fez at the Mamluk court in Cairo, as well as in Constantinople. He ended up in Rosetta, where his return journey coincided with Sultan Selim's conquest of Egypt. His thirst for knowledge led him to carry books and writing materials in his pouch as he travelled, and he recounted how, late at night, on a Nile boat, he studied in his cabin by candlelight while everyone was asleep.

As he was returning by boat from Cairo to Fez in the summer of 1518, he was taken prisoner by Christian pirates. His abductor was a notorious Spanish raider, Pedro de Cabrera y Bobadilla, whose brother was the bishop of Salamanca. Cabrera was no fool, and realized how priceless his latest captive was as a North African diplomat, familiar with the Ottoman court. He sent al-Hasan al-Wazzan as a gift to Pope Leo X, along with his writing pouches, which proved a clever move, as al-Wazzan was kept under arrest in the Vatican fortress of Castel Sant'Angelo, but was soon allowed to borrow Arabic manuscripts from the Vatican library. He joined the small group of intellectual elite Muslim slaves who were useful in Christian circles because of their scholarship. Just over a year later, he was baptized in a grand ceremony at St Peter's Basilica in Rome, taking the name Giovanne Leone Africani, better known as Leo Africanus.

Leo Africanus devoted himself to scholarly writing. On 10 March 1526, his book *Cosmography and Geography of Africa* was published in Rome, in Italian. Later renamed *Description of Africa*, it was the first important source of geographic information on Muslim Africa in Europe, and in it he revised the existing idea of Africa on the basis of his European contacts and readings. Leo Africanus wrote relatively objectively about Islam and Christianity, moving freely across the two cultures. His work became part of the European canon of learned books, but was not translated into Arabic until 1982.

Leo also taught Arabic and worked as a translator, and by the mid-1520s was able to travel outside Rome, to Venice, Florence and Naples. Sometime around 1550, he found the opportunity to leave for Tunis and was thought to have reconverted to Islam, but he vanished from view, and it is not known when he died. Leo Africanus seems to have remained a Muslim at heart despite his conversion to Catholicism, and showed astonishing adaptability in moving between two worlds, cultures and religions. He was a shapeshifter and also a citizen of the world who embraced diverse languages and peoples. Yet, the colophon of his *Geography of Africa*, signed in Latin 'Joan Lione Granatino' ('John the Lion of Granada'), divulges his deep connection to his Andalusian origins.

*

In the reign of the Ottoman sultan Murat III (r. 1574–95), William Harborne from Great Yarmouth was appointed English ambassador to the Ottoman Empire by Queen Elizabeth I. He was awarded the position in 1582, after his coup of gaining the sultan's permission for trading rights for English ships in Ottoman ports in 1578. He also played an important role in dissuading the Ottomans from supporting Catholic Spain against the English Protestants. In June 1586, he wrote a letter on a sensitive matter to the eunuch and treasurer of Ottoman Algiers, Hassan Agha. He was requesting the release of some

Englishmen imprisoned by the Ottomans, a move that had previously put him in bad odour with the governor. What made this approach different was that Harborne was writing to another Englishman, one who in fact came from his own home town. Hassan Agha (d. after 1588) was born and baptized in Norfolk with the name Samson Rowlie, and he was taken prisoner on board a ship called the *Swallow* and later castrated and enslaved by the Ottomans. Samson converted to Islam from Christianity and adopted his Muslim name. All we know about him comes from this letter from William Harborne, and a chance watercolour portrait, dated 1588, painted by a German tourist in his notebook, which shows him pale-skinned and colourfully dressed, wearing a large turban.[4] It is presumed that he was murdered sometime after this date. This glimpse of a man from England who changed his religious and cultural identity under duress, yet rose to a powerful position in the Ottoman province of Algiers, under the rule of the beylerbey Uluç Ali Pasha (1519–87), himself an Italian galley slave who converted to Islam, is a striking counterpoint to the life of Leo Africanus, and reflects the numerous crossovers, or contrary transformations of religious identity, that took place on the margins of the Mediterranean.

Two Great Escapes: The Liberation of a Catholic and a Protestant

The redemption of slaves by the payment of a ransom was a lucrative business for the Barbary pirates, but a potential source of desperation for captives, since negotiations often failed, were delayed or never took place. The escape stories of two Christian prisoners in Muslim lands bring alive the vivid fears and hopes of myriad captive travellers like themselves who fell into the hands of sea brigands and privateers when piracy was at its peak. In 1571, Miguel de Cervantes Saavedra's great heroism at the Battle of Lepanto earned him promotion to the rank of elite trooper. Four years later, in Naples, he embarked on a galley, the *Sol*, with his brother Rodrigo, bound for Barcelona. The *Sol* was badly damaged in a storm and attacked by Barbary corsairs, who took its surviving passengers, including the brothers, as captives to Algiers.

On arrival, the letters of recommendation Miguel was carrying bore prestigious signatures, leading his captors to think he was an important personage for whom they could command a high ransom, which was promptly set at the unreasonable sum of 500 gold escudos. Cervantes was imprisoned in the bagnio and was given the standard treatment – threatened, chained and badly treated – before being thrown into a solitary cell in irons. After four or five months of confinement and maltreatment, he managed to escape in early 1576, setting out to reach the nearest Spanish fortress, in Oran on the Algerian coast, a walk of 400 kilometres during which he was assailed by hostile tribesmen, stalked by hyenas and wild cats, and found little food or drink. In the end, he was obliged to turn back to Algiers, where he was imprisoned again and held under much tighter guard.

Undeterred, a year later, he took fourteen other Christian captives and hid with them for five months in a cave on the edge of the city. There, they planned their rescue, aided and abetted by Cervantes's brother, whose freedom had been bought by the Mercedarian friars. It was arranged that the ship belonging to Viana, an experienced Mallorcan mariner, who knew every inch of the Barbary coast, would pass by and take them on board, but the vessel never materialized and the fugitives were betrayed to the new governor of Algiers, Hasan Pasha. Showing extreme courage, Cervantes refused to implicate any of his other companions in the plot when hauled up before Hasan, a man renowned for his cruel punishment of recaptured slaves. Once more, Cervantes escaped with his life and spent another five months in manacles in the slaves' prison.

Unthinkably, he made a third attempt to break free. In March 1578, from prison, he secretly sent a Muslim to the port of Oran with a letter for the governor, Don Martín de Cordoba, himself a former captive. But the letter never arrived, as the messenger was intercepted on entering Oran and sent back to Algiers. There, Hasan Pasha had the Moor impaled and Cervantes was sentenced to 2,000 lashes, effectively a death sentence. For unknown reasons, the sentence was never carried out, leaving Cervantes languishing in jail. After a fourth failed escape attempt in September 1579, on an armed frigate bought by a Spanish renegade, when Cervantes and his fellow rebels were betrayed once again, he was finally liberated in 1580 by the Trinitarian brotherhood, who paid his ransom. He returned to Madrid, later claiming he had written over twenty plays on his time as a captive in Algiers, some of which are enjoying critical attention today. His experiences living among Muslims also left a fundamental imprint on his great masterpiece, *Don Quixote*, the entirety of which the author tells us was based on an Arabic manuscript written by a historian, Cide Hamete Benengeli, that he discovered in a market in Toledo.

*

About sixty years later, in 1639, the ship on which an English Puritan named William Okeley was travelling, the *Mary* of London, was seized by pirates in the Atlantic Ocean. The vessel had been taking a consignment of cloth and a number of colonists to Providence Island, off the coast of what is now Nicaragua. Those seas were notorious for corsairs, anti-Catholic militants who preyed on Spanish fleets loaded with silver. The would-be settlers were kept in foul-smelling darkness for six weeks until they eventually arrived in Algeria. Okeley, who was fleeing religious persecution, had ranted and raved over Catholics, Turks and Jews, yet was beguiled by his first impressions of the beauty of Algiers, and praised its fine houses, magnificent temples and castles, and its baths. Slung into a deep cellar overnight, the next day he and the other captives were brought before the pasha, Yusuf II, who wore a red silk gown and enormous turban, and sat cross-legged on a blue tapestry cushion. The prisoners were strongly encouraged to convert to Islam and were taken back to the bagnio until market day, when Okeley was sold to a Morisco. His unwise criticism of Islam in his purchaser's house almost cost him his life, but he worked there for six months as a servant, until he was unexpectedly sent to sea in his master's pirate ship.

The crew tried their luck outside Gibraltar, much to Okeley's moral distress, given that they would be fighting his fellow Christians, but they returned empty-handed to Algiers, where his master threw him out and told him to get a job. After setting up a business selling lead, iron, tobacco and alcohol with a fellow slave, he was sold off by his Morisco owner to an old man in a country estate outside Algiers. Okeley recounted that, there, to his surprise, he was treated with respect, tenderness and compassion, and his master groomed him to take over the running of the estate. Yet, like Cervantes, William found the urge to escape too strong and spurned the promise of a comfortable life as an estate manager. He came up with the extraordinary plan to build a small boat, row or sail it 300 kilometres to the north-east coast of Spain, as far as Mallorca, and ask for the Spanish governor's help.

He and six other captives clandestinely fashioned the boat, which they waterproofed with tarred and pitched canvas. They planned to subsist on bread and water, and made water bottles out of two goatskins. The five men who were able to get into the boat without it sinking set off, but were soon in dire straits, as their bread got soaked and sea water seeped into the goatskins, making their contents undrinkable. Remarkably, they survived by catching a turtle and eating it, and six days later came ashore on Mallorca. Half dead, they were saved by the water and mouldy cake they were given by the locals, and limped the fifteen kilometres to Palma in two days. There, they contacted the viceroy of the island, who was so overcome by their story that he offered to look after them at his own expense until a sea passage to England could be organized. In what is one of the most astonishing captivity narratives of all, Okeley reported his return to England in September 1644, just over five years after he left for Nicaragua. Almost thirty years later, in 1675, he published a book about his Algerian experiences, which presented his captivity story as a Protestant parable about redemption.

★

Beyond traditional Islam and the strictures of Catholicism, in the wildernesses of land and sea, outsiders of all stripes – from pioneers to slaves to buccaneers – found places of interchange where religious and cultural rules were abandoned and new merged identities were forged. For 300 years, from the late fifteenth century onwards, antitheses, transpositions and reversals moulded new social and cultural relationships in the spaces between the Christian and Muslim worlds of Europe and North Africa. Some crossovers of identity became permanent, others were fluid and reversible, but all sought and found common ground instead of difference and otherness. Changing religions changed social status – Samson Rowlie rose to high rank, while Francis Verney went from lord to pirate. Pious reversals brought intellectual illumination too, and captivity in the lands of the infidel released a hybrid creativity that manifested itself in the great history of Africa of Leo Africanus, in the captivity narrative of William Okeley that formed his spiritual autobiography, and in one of the great masterpieces of western literature, the tale of the Knight of La Mancha, Don Quixote.

Chapter 21

A Debt Disowned: The Islamic Legacy of the European Renaissance

'If I have seen further than others, it is by standing on the shoulders of giants.'

Isaac Newton

'Finally we shall place the Sun himself at the centre of the universe.'

Nicholas Copernicus

Parallel Lines: An Early Oriental Renaissance

The Italian artist and architect from Urbino known in English as Raphael (1483–1520) painted a masterpiece entitled *The School of Athens* between 1509 and 1511. It portrays a gathered host of the greatest ancient philosophers and scientists, including Plato, Aristotle, Pythagoras, Ptolemy and Archimedes. The use of perspective and the celebration of the rebirth of Greek philosophy and scholarship in Europe represent stylistically and in subject matter the Renaissance spirit that burned brightly on the continent from the late fifteenth to the seventeenth centuries. Even so, *The School of Athens* includes an unexpected personage – the Andalusian philosopher and polymath Averroes, who leans over the shoulder of Pythagoras in the left middle ground. His portrayal creates an enigma that hints at a hidden history. Raphael honours Averroes as a medieval Muslim sage on a par with the most brilliant minds of ancient times; yet he is also the lone representative of the Islamic civilization and scholarship that determined much of Europe's cultural evolution.

The word *renaissance* means 'rebirth' and refers to the system of thought known as humanism that began in Italy in the fifteenth century and spread across Europe, the basis of which was the revival of classical Greek philosophy and learning. It brought great changes in art, architecture, politics, science and literature, and this period is often seen as the era of transition from the Middle Ages to modernity. The fifteenth-century renewal of interest in the literature and history of the ancient world, which seemed to bypass Arabic learning in favour of the rediscovery of original Greek scholarship, would lead to the start of the scientific revolution in Europe in the sixteenth century, that prepared the way for the birth of modern Europe.

Just thirty-nine years separated the Ottoman conquest of Constantinople in 1453 and the Catholic conquest of Granada in 1492, one the inverted image of the other and each leading to the establishment of major territories for Islam and Christianity. It seemed to polarize the continent into the Muslim East and the Christian West, and reinforced the perception of difference and opposition between the two religions and cultures. That awareness contributed to an increasing interest in Islamic culture and the Arabic language in western Europe, which evolved into an early version of orientalism. This was different from the later nineteenth-century expression of orientalism, which would represent Asia in a stereotyped way that at times reflected a colonialist attitude. Rather, it manifested itself in the creation of the first European professorship in Arabic in 1535, awarded to Guillaume Postel as royal lector in Greek, Hebrew and Arabic letters at the Collège de France in Paris. The following year, Postel went to Kostantiniyye as one of twelve French ambassadors to Suleiman I and returned with Arabic books, mainly on mathematics and medicine. A former ambassador, Savary de Brèves, also brought back to France a large collection of Arabic manuscripts.

Fifty years later, in 1584, the first Arabic printing press was established in Rome by Giovan Battista Raimondi, funded by the Medicis. Raimondi published Avicenna's *Canon of Medicine* in the original Arabic and provided Arabic grammars and texts for an Islamic audience. The Flemish scholar and printer Franciscus Raphelengius (d. 1598) wrote the first dictionary of classical Arabic, finally published in Leiden in 1613; in the same place, Thomas Erpenius (1584–1624) held the first Dutch Chair in Arabic and advocated the study of Arabic poetry; while, in Oxford, Edward Pococke, who had studied Arabic in Aleppo and owned many valuable manuscripts in the language, became the earliest Laudian Professor of Arabic, introducing Islamic historiography and Ibn Tufayl's philosophical novel to Europe.

Although the term 'orientalism' only appeared in English in 1779 and in French in 1799, these scholars built the foundations of the modern discipline of oriental studies, and their interest lay in the linguistic and religious underpinning of Islamic culture. Manuscripts were the key to a treasure house of knowledge, and they learnt Arabic to interpret Islamic scriptures and to combat Islam by translating Christian theology with the aim of using it to convert Muslims. By the sixteenth century, humanist education began to include a knowledge of Arabic, which the French writer Rabelais' character Gargantua recommends to his son Pantagruel, whom he urges to learn the 'Arabique' language.[1] There was also growing interest in the Koran itself. The first translation of a Koran into any European language was an Italian version, printed in Venice in 1547; a century later, in 1647, a French translation was published and was quickly followed by an English translation of the French version, attributed to the Scottish clergyman Alexander Ross (1592–1654). Ross was taken to court over his translation, whose publication the Council of State tried to prevent for fear that the Koran might become a pernicious influence in English society. Ross finally succeeded in having it printed in May 1649, making a swingeing attack in his afterword on the new English regime following the execution of King Charles I, in which he claimed that Muslims were far superior in terms of religious piety and in matters of social order.

Early orientalist thinking also flourished among the translators and diplomats who worked in the courts and ports of the Muslim world. The translators or dragomans had wide training in the three languages of the Islamic East: Arabic, Turkish and Persian. Antoine Galland (1646–1715) was a French diplomat whose translation of *One Thousand and One Nights* appeared in twelve volumes between 1704 and 1717, finding Europe-wide success, while an Austrian dragoman, Joseph von Hammer-Purgstall (1774–1856), wrote a monumental history of the Ottoman Empire and founded the first ever orientalist review at the start of the nineteenth century. In the Renaissance, intellectuals were acutely aware of the vastness and sophistication of the Ottoman Empire. Thomas Fuller, an English churchman and historian, wrote in his *Historie of the Holy Warre*, in 1639, that the Turkish empire 'lieth in the heart of the world, like a bold champion bidding defiance to all his borderers, commanding the most fruitfull countreys of Europe, Asia and Africa'.[2] Simon Ockley, an Oxford Arabist, published a history of the Saracens in 1708 that expressed his admiration for them. Many valuable historical works of the seventeenth century in French, English and Dutch often described Islam in positive terms, as rational, tolerant and civilizing, themes which would be picked up in the philosophy of the Enlightenment as ammunition against the Catholic Church.

In the world of western European political philosophy, there were ambivalent and often divergent views. Machiavelli's political treatise *The Prince* (1513) discussed and contrasted Ottoman and French regimes, and the term 'oriental despotism' came into use from 1630 as thinkers debated the view of Ottoman rulers as tyrants. The sixteenth-century political philosopher Jean Bodin (*c.* 1530–90) respected the Ottomans as worthy successors of the Romans, and even justified some of their controversial policies, such as fratricide in the royal family and the child levy, or *devshirme*, when children of Balkan Christians were forcibly recruited as Janissaries and bureaucrats and converted to Islam. In the following century, the French philosopher Voltaire changed his opinion on Islam, initially depicting the Prophet as a rogue in his tragedy *Muhammad and Fanaticism* (1742), before finally praising Islam's moderation and tolerance. The Swiss philosopher Jean-Jacques Rousseau admired Muhammad as a great lawmaker, but it was Islam's practice of religious tolerance that became a key philosophical element of the eighteenth-century intellectual movement known as the Enlightenment.

The Untold Story of the European Renaissance

The fascination with the roots of Islamic culture among western European thinkers and scholars belongs to a little-known story that turns our conventional understanding of the European Renaissance on its head. It revises the view that the great flowering of learning that led to the development of literature in Latin and in European vernaculars, and prompted political change and the ostensible scientific revolution, was ignited solely by Greek and Christian Latin knowledge. Sir Isaac Newton acknowledged the debt that scholars of his time, including himself, owed to those who went before, but on which giants' shoulders was he standing? He might have had the ancient Greek sages in mind, but was he also thinking of great Muslim scientists too? To answer these questions, we must turn to the intersection of Renaissance knowledge and the Muslim scientific legacy, and start with what is known as the scientific method.

Nowadays, the scientific method is described as 'the approach to investigating phenomena, acquiring new knowledge, or correcting or integrating previous knowledge, based on the gathering of data through observation and measurement, followed by the formulation and testing of hypotheses to explain the data.'[3] It is generally accepted that this process was first established in the Renaissance reign of the English king James I, by Francis Bacon (1561–1626), the Lord High Chancellor of England and an eminent scholar of Trinity College, Cambridge. Bacon set out his ideas on the modern scientific method in his book *New Method* (*Novum Organum*) (1620). His theory replaced Aristotle's ideas in *Organon*, and is based on what is known as inductive reasoning, where a principle can be generalized from a set of known facts; its rigorous purpose was to arrive at the truth of natural philosophy. In 1637, the French philosopher René Descartes (1596–1650) set out similar ideas in his *Discourse on the Method of Rightly Conducting One's Reason and of Seeking Truth in the Sciences* (*Discours *de la Méthode pour bien conduire sa raison, et chercher la vérité dans les sciences*), which also sought scientific truth through observed evidence. But the basic tenets of the scientific method were in fact created many centuries earlier.

Six hundred years ago, about AD 965, a boy was born in the southern Iraqi city of Basra who would become the greatest physicist since Archimedes. His name was Abu Ali al-Hassan ibn al-Haytham, known in the Latin world as Alhazen. Al-Haytham came from a prominent, well-to-do family and had a good education, excelling at mathematics and science at an early age. Around 1010, having worked in administration, he was summoned to Cairo by the Fatimid caliph al-Hakim to assist with the design of civil engineering works. He spent some years in an asylum feigning madness to escape the wrath of the caliph after his planned project to build a dam across the Nile came to nothing. Eventually, he settled in central Cairo, combining work as a tutor with his own scholarly research, conducting scientific experiments which he carried out meticulously, carefully recording the results. The scientific method he used was fundamental to his investigations, as he points out:

> We should distinguish the properties of particulars, and gather by induction what pertains to the eye and what is found in the manner of sensation to be uniform, unchanging, manifest and not subject to doubt. After which we should ascend in our enquiry and reasoning, gradually and orderly, criticizing premises and exercising caution in regard to conclusions – our aim in all that we make subject to inspection and review being to employ justice, not to follow prejudice, and to take care in all that we judge and criticize that we seek the truth and not be swayed by opinion.[4]

Like Bacon and Descartes, Ibn al-Haytham sought scientific truth through rigorous observation and analysis, and established the standard way of proving scientific theories, six centuries before his Renaissance counterparts. There is nothing to prove that Bacon or

Descartes had read the works of Muslim scientists, but it seems that Ibn al-Haytham was the true 'father of the scientific method'.

While he earned a living by teaching and as a scribe, Ibn al-Haytham worked obsessively on his research and wrote his greatest work, the *Book of Optics* (*Kitab al-Manathir*), published in seven volumes between 1010 and 1021. It was a science textbook with detailed descriptions of his experiments, through which he came to understand that human vision works through the refraction of light via the lens of the eye. Only in the seventeenth century did the German scientist Johannes Kepler (1571–1630) go a step further and explain how the eye worked like a camera. Ibn al-Haytham also worked on the refraction of light through the Earth's atmosphere, and, like his contemporary Avicenna, believed that the speed of light was finite, though Avicenna correctly inferred that it was made up of particles, a theory that Newton also supported and which Einstein proved in work for which he won the Nobel Prize in 1921, nearly a millennium after both Ibn al-Haytham and Avicenna.

The first Latin version of the *Book of Optics* was translated in the late twelfth century, had a great influence on the scientist Roger Bacon (*c.* 1214–*c.* 1292) and became widely known across Europe. A Latin printed edition was published in 1572 under the name *Opticae Thesaurus*, and Isaac Newton had a copy in his personal library, which laid the foundations for his own experiments with light. Newton is commonly thought of throughout the Christian and Islamic worlds as the father of modern optics, even among historians of science, but, while studies of the properties of light and lenses were significant in ancient Greek learning, Ibn al-Haytham's pioneering research was the bedrock of Newton's work on lenses and prisms and his study of the nature of light. Newton was also deeply interested in alchemy, and owned translations of works by another Arab Muslim scientist, the early alchemist Jabir ibn Hayyan (*c.* 721–*c.* 815), from Kufa in Iraq, whose book *Summa Perfectionis* (*Kitab al-Mulk*) had a great impact on Newton. Known as Geber the Alchemist in the west, he held very practical views on chemical research methods and processes, which led him to discover inorganic acids through an experiment that mixed nitric and hydrochloric acids which dissolved gold: a major development in the science of chemistry.

In the middle of the sixteenth century, the Renaissance world view was turned on its head by new discoveries in the field of astronomy. Once again, the research and experiments of earlier Muslim scientists formed the groundwork for new ways of thinking. In the eleventh century, the Andalusian Muslim mathematician Ibn Mu'adh wrote a book on twilight – the *Liber crepusculis*, in Latin translation. Using simple geometry and a value for the size of the Earth that had been calculated by Caliph al-Mamun's astronomers in the ninth century, he worked out the height of the Earth's atmosphere to be about fifty-two miles (eighty-three kilometres), which is not far from its actual height of sixty-two miles (one hundred kilometres). His work aroused great interest in the Latin Middle Ages and also in the Renaissance, along with what was the first ever treatise on spherical geometry, that explored the relationship between the sides and angles of spherical triangles.

Ibn Mu'adh's mathematical work on ratios appears to have made an impression on the German Renaissance mathematician known as Regiomontanus (1436–76), who, together with the Austrian scientist Georg Peurbach (1423–61), wrote several works that were central to the education of Nicholas Copernicus (1473–1543). Peurbach and Regiomontanus collaborated on the *Epitome of the Almagest*, a digest considered to be the finest textbook on Ptolemy's theories on astronomy ever written. Copernicus studied it very carefully, alongside a Latin translation of the *Almagest*, in an edition of Gerard of Cremona's famous translation into Latin from Arabic versions in Toledo, printed in Venice in 1515. In the *Epitome*, he learnt about the work of early Arab astronomers such as the ninth-century Iraqi Ibn Qurra and the Syrian al-Battani, whose life straddled the ninth and tenth centuries in the Islamic Golden Age, and he began to study the famous astronomical Toledan Tables.

Copernicus came from the kingdom of Poland, though his parents were German. A physician, economist, cathedral canon and cosmologist, he had studied at universities in Krakow, Bologna, Padua and Ferrara, and some time before 1514 he had been working on an idea that was to revolutionize the thinking of the Renaissance world. He called it his heliocentric hypothesis, and it harked back to the ideas of the Greek astronomer Aristarchus of Samos (*c.* 310 BC–*c.* 230 BC), who was the first to advance the theory that the Earth moved around the Sun, rather than being the centre of the solar system. The conflicting geocentric theory expounded in Ptolemy's *Almagest* rejected Aristarchus's ideas and placed the Earth at the centre of the solar system. It became the prevailing view of the Renaissance world, until Copernicus announced his findings in *On the Revolutions of the Celestial Spheres* (*De revolutionibus orbium coelestium*), published in 1543, the year of his death, though formulated long before. His revolutionary theory has its basis in the ancient Greek astronomy of Aristarchus and in a refutation of Ptolemy's ideas. Even so, it transpires that the Polish polymath mined other deep seams of astronomical knowledge that formed the foundations of what was known as the Maragha revolution, a system of ideas that sprang up in Persia in the thirteenth century with the aim of rising to Ibn al-Haytham's earlier challenge to scientists to overhaul Ptolemy's astronomy. Maragha, north-west of Tehran, became the world's greatest astronomy centre after an observatory was built there in 1259 by the khan Halagi for a Persian scholar born in the city of Tus, in east Persia, around 1200, known as al-Tusi.

In Maragha, al-Tusi assembled eminent astronomers from as far afield as China, and his famous book *Memoir on Astronomy* (*Al-Tadhkirah fi'ilm al-hay'ah*) became the most original and significant medieval text on astronomy. In the *Memoir*, al-Tusi developed ideas that revised Ptolemy's thinking, following the tenth-century tradition in Islamic astronomy that expressed doubts about the Greek's geocentric theory of the Earth. His diagram showing a small circle revolving round a larger circle allowed him to reformulate Ptolemy's planetary models and is known as the Tusi couple. What was quite unexpected was the similarity of the Tusi couple to Copernicus's geometric diagrams of planetary models, in which he even replaced al-Tusi's Arabic letters marking points on the circle with the corresponding Latin ones. In addition, Copernicus's lunar and solar models, and the model for the planet Mercury, are exactly the same as those created by al-Tusi and the Arab astronomer Ibn al-Shatir before him. This provides conclusive evidence that Copernicus borrowed from the work of these Islamic scientists, and, more significantly, could not have arrived at his final heliocentric theory without the mathematical models of the Maragha astronomers. They had worked out the correct mathematics, but Copernicus applied it with the correct interpretation, turning the philosophical concept of heliocentrism into a workable mathematical thesis.[5]

There is no clear path for the transmission of al-Tusi's work to Europe, and to Copernicus, but it is likely that the Persian's planetary models found their way via Constantinople to Italy. Several manuscripts of the Tusi couple exist in Italy, where Copernicus studied between 1496 and 1503, and he may have come across them then. But he is silent on the subject of Islamic astronomers. Renaissance science has been thought of as an exclusively European creation, unlike medieval science and philosophy, but across the continent there was a growing body of scholars who knew Arabic and could read sources in the original. It may even have been the case that Renaissance scientists were seeking out Islamic science for new ideas. Vesalius, the court physician to King Charles V from 1514 to 1564, certainly spoke of Arab science being as familiar as Greek knowledge, and even considered superior to it, once the failings of Greek science became apparent.

Reassessing Muhammad: Islam as Propaganda in Renaissance Europe

Amid the profusion of scientific, philosophical and Christian theological works in the personal library of Sir Isaac Newton, there are two striking titles. The first is the Latin translation of a biography of the Prophet Muhammad by Abulfeda, the thirteenth-century historian from Damascus, taken from Edward Pococke's manuscript in the Bodleian library in Oxford. The second is a history of the Saracens by the thirteenth-century Coptic Christian historian Ibn al-Amid, known as Georgius Elacinus, published in Latin. While

Newton was known to hold controversial religious views, and was even thought to be a heretic for his rejection of the doctrine of Trinitarianism, it is fascinating that he should have sought out two obscure Muslim works on the Prophet and the history of his peoples. Whatever Newton's views on Islam, the presence of such books in his library reflects a growing interest in the Muslim faith and the figure of Muhammad that was emerging across early modern Europe. The continent was wracked by religious wars in its German-, French- and English-speaking lands, as social, intellectual, political and military conflicts arising from the Reformation began to shape western Christendom's perception of the Prophet. At the same time, the Ottomans, whose capital city and over a third of whose territory lay in Europe, were both a military threat and a salutary model of political unity and tolerant religious diversity. The seductive allure of Islamic culture that had contrasted with its military menace in al-Andalus and Christian Spain was matched by the simultaneous fear of and fascination with things Turkish for early modern Christians.

In the bitter struggles between Catholics and Protestants, Islam suddenly became a yardstick against which to measure the failings of these conflicting versions of Christianity. The Muslim faith became less a direct source of antagonism and enmity, and more relative, just one religious sect among several, often viewed as heretical, but in some ways better than the rival Christian beliefs in question. There was a sea change that sparked debates about Muhammad and Islam among European Christians, alongside the continued depiction of him as a false prophet and impostor, although this negative portrayal was employed at times to contrast him with those who abjured the Catholic or Protestant cause and were consequently perceived as worse. On the Protestant side, Luther wrote that Muhammad seemed to be a saint compared with the pope. In his 'War Sermon against the Turks', he exclaimed: 'The Turk fills heaven with Christians by murdering their bodies, but the Pope does what he can to fill hell with Christians through his blasphemous teachings.'[6] John Calvin (1509–1564), the Protestant reformer, presented

Muhammad as a seducer and sorcerer, while, in retaliation, Catholics claimed Luther was no better, breaking his vow of celibacy and authorizing clerical marriage. Guillaume Postel, the first professor of Arabic in Europe, was a fervent Catholic, and in his polemical writings he denigrated and denounced Protestantism by identifying Luther with the Prophet Muhammad, and also with the Antichrist. He envisioned a world where the three peoples of the Book would be united, albeit under Christian rule, and claimed that Islam was only a branch of Christianity, a minor heresy that could be reintegrated.

The increasing interest in studying the Koran and other aspects of Islamic doctrine served to feed Christian polemics, fuelled by the use of the Prophet as a kind of rhetorical tool.[7] The Swiss humanist Bibliander's Latin edition of the Koran, published in 1452, was translated into Italian, German and Dutch, and provided a vital source of information to many European Christians. Islam began to be viewed as closer in some ways to perceived authentic Christianity than other deviant forms of that faith. Early in the Renaissance, Miguel Servet (1511–53), a humanist from Aragon, launched a punishing attack on the Christian doctrine of the Trinity in his essay 'On the Errors of the Trinity'. He declared that the concept of the Trinity – of God the Father, God the Son and God the Holy Ghost – was an innovation by fourth-century Church councils, and nothing that Jesus and his followers had ever spoken of. Servet advised paying attention to the words of Muhammad that deny the Trinity, a truth more reliable than a hundred Christian lies. He also believed Muhammad was a reformer who preached the unity of God, making him superior to Catholics and Protestants because his teachings were closer to those of Christ. Servet sadly had a bad end. He wrote to Calvin to explain his Unitarian views, and the Catholic inquisitor of Vienna had him arrested. He was condemned as a heretic by the Inquisition and burned at the stake on a pile of his books in 1553.

In parallel with revisionist thinkers, there was no shortage of European authors who discredited the Prophet and his religion in the sixteenth and seventeenth centuries. Although it circulated widely, in 1564 the Koran was placed on the index of prohibited books, first published by the Vatican's Sacred Congregation of the Roman Inquisition in 1559, and many copies were seized and burned. The conflicting opinions of Islam at this time bear witness to the extent to which the Muslim faith provoked controversy and uncertainty. One man who showed no vacillation in his opinions was the English royal physician, historian and dissident Henry Stubbe (1632–76), thought to be the most eminent Latin and Greek scholar of his era. In 1671, he wrote *An Account of the Rise and Progress of Mahometanism, and a Vindication of him and his Religion from the Calumnies of the Christians*, which was passed around in private circles as he was unable to publish it. It was the first full work in English to be sympathetic to Islam, and gives a shrewd, unbiased view of a non-Christian religion amid the turmoil of Restoration England.

Stubbe saw the history of religion from Christianity to Islam as a series of what he called 'great revolutions', cycles of transformation of society and culture, within which the Prophet's artful intelligence enabled him to evolve a religion perfectly suited to his place, time and traditions. He summarized Islam as: 'on the one hand, not clogging men's faith with the necessity of believing a number of abstruse notions which they cannot comprehend, and which are often contrary to the dictates of reason and common sense; nor on the other hand, loading them with the performance of many troublesome, expensive and superstitious ceremonies, yet enjoining a due observance of religion, as the surest method to keep men in the bounds of their duty both to God and man.'[8]

Stubbe compared the religious policy of Islam with that of the Christian Roman Empire and criticized the delegation of spiritual authority to priests by the emperors, separating it from civil authority, which in Stubbe's view caused the ultimate weakening of the empire. He pointed out that Muhammad brought together religion and civil authority in temporal rulers, with the opposite outcome.

He also praised Muhammad's forbearance in his refusal to force Islam on his peoples and his tolerance in allowing them to practise their own religions, which in Stubbe's opinion allowed Jews and

Christians to live side by side with Muslims, brought a great deal of money into the public treasury and encouraged non-Muslims to live in Islamic lands. He even went so far as to state that Christians in seventeenth-century Europe would prefer Muslim rule, if given the choice. Stubbe's radical yet persuasive theories, which sought to vindicate Islam and return to the unitarian origins of Christianity in the Middle East, were ahead of his time, and forged a kind of Muhammadan Christianity which finds echoes in the intentions of the Spanish Moriscos in fabricating the Arabic texts of the Lead Books of Granada. His *Account* was not published until 1911, by the Islamic Society.

While Henry Stubbe's controversial book was perhaps a step too far in his time, Muhammad appeared in Catholic debates in a positive light, as a witness to the Immaculate Conception of the Virgin. Whether or not the Virgin was conceived without sin had been an unresolved subject of fierce debate in the Catholic Church since the time of Bernard of Clairvaux and Thomas Aquinas in the twelfth and thirteenth centuries, both of whom opposed the idea. In the early seventeenth century, the archbishop of Granada, Pedro de Castro, had taken to promoting the idea that the Immaculate Conception of the Virgin had doctrinal proof in the texts of the Lead Books of Granada. The Morisco translators, and creators, of the Lead Books claimed that they explicitly stated that Mary was born without original sin, even though that is not in itself a Muslim belief, as Islam does not acknowledge the concept of original sin. The words 'Mary was untouched by original sin' were inscribed on the foundation stone of the Abbey of the Sacromonte in Granada, and the city commemorated Granada's devotion to the Immaculate Conception in a monument erected to the Virgin in the Plaza del Triunfo.

By the seventeenth century, Muhammad had been recruited as a Catholic ally who testified to the doctrine of the Virgin's Immaculate Conception. In a painting by Michele Luposignoli dated 1727, copied from an original by the artist Nicola Braccio, from Pisa, who worked in Dalmatia in the sixteenth century, the Virgin is surrounded by her learned Doctors of the Church. Muhammad sits in the bottom right corner, holding a scroll, opposite the ninth-century Arab astrologer Albumasar, who foresaw Mary's divine conception. The altarpiece resides in the Franciscan church in Poljud, in Split, in modern Croatia, and several other Italian paintings exist with a similar theme. The use of the image of the Prophet and of a learned Arab scholar as propaganda to promote the Virgin's Immaculate Conception, in both eastern and western Europe, underlines a change in the mindset of the Christians of Europe, who were no longer unified in their opposition to Islam and its founder.

*

The Bodleian library in Oxford held hundreds of Arabic manuscripts in the seventeenth century. They included Islamic law and Arabic grammar, Arabic poetry, medical works by Avicenna, al-Zahrawi and many others, scientific and philosophical texts and those on astronomy, alchemy, history and geography, as well as commentaries on the Koran. They are material evidence of the profound, widespread presence and influence of Muslim learning, at the deepest intellectual level, in an age which appeared to look the other way in asserting its revival and reformulation of classical knowledge. Beyond the realms of academic progress and major scientific experimentation, where it became fundamental to a new European world view, Islam was felt as a profound religious presence which seeped into the intellectual debates and conflicts that sought to redefine religious truth across Christian Europe. The new European world of the early modern era owes an unacknowledged debt to Islamic civilization, as witnessed in a Renaissance of both Greek and Arab Muslim learning deeply ingrained in the life of the continent of which it is an essential part.

Chapter 22

Coffee, Carpets and Tulips: Western Europe's Obsession with *Turquerie*

'Tis, methinks, faint defying
Old-Nick and his Works;
To be fond of a Berry,
Which comes from the Turks.'

"W.P.", 1631

'. . . here [Konya] they make the most beautiful silks and carpets in the world, and with the most beautiful colours.'

Marco Polo

In the 200 years from 1492 to the end of the seventeenth century, the eastern and western poles of European civilization came into an alignment more profound than any since the birth of Islam. It was not just in the more rarefied spheres of scholarly, scientific and theological interaction, but also in the private and public spheres of everyday life, across domestic as well as civic settings, that Christians and Muslims absorbed diverse aspects of each other's culture. The essence of Christian Europe's relationship with Muslims during this time was an ambivalence born of a psychological conflict similar to the one that had pervaded the society of Catholic Spain. In this case, the tension arose between a dread of the military might and perceived tyranny of the Ottoman state and a simultaneous enchantment with Islamic culture, both Turkish and North African. The effect of that allure was visible in the daily life of Christian Europe and in eloquent diplomacy demonstrated in two memorable Muslim embassies to the cold north-west of the continent.

The Coming of the Ambassadors

The earliest surviving portrait of a Muslim painted in England is held at the Shakespeare Institute at Stratford-upon-Avon and depicts Abd al-Wahid bin Mas'ud bin Muhammad Anun, the Moorish ambassador to England and secretary of the sultan of Morocco, al-Mansur. He wears a turban and robe of white linen, a black cloak, and a *nimcha*, or scimitar, and appears to be pointing at the weapon with his index finger. His stern, almost threatening expression, and a costume whose turban and sword would have seemed exotic to the English, reflect that perception of the Moor as fearsome yet fascinating. The forty-two-year-old Abd al-Wahid sailed on board the English ship *The Eagle* and arrived at the port of Dover on 8 August 1600, accompanied by his Andalusian interpreter, Abd el-Dodar, on an embassy from Sultan al-Mansur that purported to be a trade mission to Aleppo, with a perhaps unlikely stopover in London. But that was a cover story for what turned out to be a secret plan to negotiate an alliance against Spain with Queen Elizabeth I, whom the ambassador met twice. The queen declined his request for an English fleet to mount a joint invasion of Spain, but welcomed commercial agreements between England and Morocco. Abd al-Wahid stayed in England for six months, after which plans for combined military ventures continued to be discussed, but were thwarted by the deaths of both the queen and the sultan within two years, without any resolution.

*

There is another portrait, this time in Chiswick House in London, depicting a second Moroccan ambassador, Muhammad bin Haddu al-Attar, who came to England eighty years after Abd al-Wahid, in 1682, to discuss trade and peace. By then, Morocco was an independent state ruled by the Alawi dynasty from whom today's king of Morocco descends, and good diplomatic relations with England had lasted since the first visit by ambassador al-Wahid. As before, bin Haddu's trip lasted six months, and caused great intrigue and excitement among the English, who were very keen to see him in person. His ship, the *Golden Horse*, left Tangiers for Deal in Kent and arrived on 26 December 1681, after which he was taken amid gun salutes to a house specially prepared for him in the Strand. Bin Haddu met King Charles II for the first time on 11 January 1682, in the royal bedchamber, and caused a sensation by giving him two lions and thirty ostriches that he had brought with him from Morocco. The king fretted over the fact that he might only be able to offer a flock of geese in return.

The English writer and courtier John Evelyn (1620–1706) witnessed much of the ambassador's visit and made some interesting observations, including the fact that bin Haddu had an English mother. He reported that the ambassador was 'the fashion of the season', describing him as very handsome, with a wise expression and civil manners. His party was dressed in Moorish garments, including silk and calico shirts, white woollen cloaks, small turbans and short, highly embellished curved swords. Despite their air of grandeur, they ate and drank very modestly, never touching wine, but taking milk or water instead. During his visit, the ambassador travelled outside London, touring Newmarket, Windsor, Cambridge and Oxford, where he met the university's first professor of Arabic, Edward Pococke. He also enjoyed trips to the London theatre, where he saw *The Tempest* and *Coriolanus*, and behaved there, according to Evelyn, with great gravity and modesty. There were many official engagements, often in the presence of noisy, animated crowds who gathered just to catch a glimpse of the Muslims from Morocco, and whom the king's soldiers were unable to bring into line, much to the astonishment of the African visitors.[1] The English members of the Socinians, a group of non-Trinitarian Protestants who rejected the divinity of Christ, went so far as to write letters to Sultan al-Mansur for bin Haddu to take back with him, which praised the Islamic belief in one God and applauded the Prophet as the scourge of idol-worshipping Christians.

Despite the importance of the Moroccan embassy to England, the efforts to sign a peace treaty were to no avail. When Muhammad bin Haddu returned to Tangiers, he fell out of favour, and the Moroccans refused to agree to peace as long as the English remained a military presence there. Even so, the welcoming and honouring of two Muslim diplomats during the same century, by both the elite strata of English society and ordinary people, is strong evidence of the interest in and admiration for Muslim culture and diplomacy in the Christian realms of early modern Europe.

The Lure of the Mahometan Berry

From the outset, coffee was associated with Islam and the Turks in the Christian areas of Europe. The coffee bean was known as the Mahometan berry and came to the rest of the continent from the Ottoman Empire, where the drink was introduced to Istanbul from Yemen in the middle of the sixteenth century, along with its own institutions and instructions for use. At first, those new to coffee were appalled by its bitter flavour, but western Europeans began to acquire a taste for it because it represented the high society of Istanbul that they admired. There, it was a central part of polite ceremony, where the refinement of the way it was served, from the richly embroidered napkins down to the order of serving guests, held an irresistible appeal to the Western European aspirational upper echelons of society. Edward Pococke wrote a treatise on coffee, based on a medical handbook by a contemporary Ottoman Arab physician, praising the health benefits of the drink. Pococke himself became addicted to coffee and drank so much that he developed tremors. Jean de Thévenot, a French scholar who travelled widely in the east, was one of the first to take coffee to Paris, and he provided a Levantine recipe that specified the correct ratio of coffee to water and how to boil it.

Some travellers and writers were less enthusiastic. As early as 1600, the explorer William Parry had denounced coffee because it intoxicated the brain, while others felt its main danger lay in inducing men to convert to Islam. They warned that coffee had magical powers, 'an ugly Turkish enchantress' that conquered the Christian body and soul. The religious prejudice against coffee was most strongly expressed in England, where it was seen as Satan's drink, brewed with the connivance of the Turks to destroy Christendom. The broadsheet *A Cup of Coffee*, printed in 1663, suggested that merely imbibing the drink could give those who drank it a swarthy 'Moorish' complexion and the physical appearance of the Turks. It was seen as a secret Muslim weapon. Surprisingly, such extreme reactions to coffee were echoed by the Ottoman sultan Murad IV (r. 1623–40), who ordered all coffee shops in his empire to close because of their tendency to foster sedition. In his reign, coffee drinking was punishable by death.

Even so, Christian Europe's penchant for drinking coffee was undiminished. In the beginning, merchants who had travelled to the Ottoman Empire brought it back to drink privately at home, but European life was soon to be transformed by the institution of the public coffee house, based on the Ottoman model. The first of the original cafes probably opened in Venice in 1647, quickly followed by Oxford in 1650, London in 1652 and Paris in 1668, with those in Amsterdam and Hamburg appearing some years later. The London coffee house was started by Pasqua Rosée, the Italian former servant of an English merchant who traded in Smyrna (now Izmir). It was located in St Michael's Alley in the Cornhill, and boasted a signboard bearing the image of Rosée wearing a turban. He produced an accompanying pamphlet, a sales pitch, for drinkers to read about the medical benefits of coffee, which stated that: 'It is observed in Turkey where it is generally drunk that they are not trobled with the Stone, Gout, Dropsie or Scurvy and that their skins are exceeding clear and white'.[2]

Some coffee houses had waiters in Ottoman costume, who offered sherbet and another new introduction, tobacco, or they combined coffee with public baths, all according to Ottoman custom. The most important element of this Turkish Muslim legacy was the role of coffee houses in the exchange of news and ideas. Across north-west Europe they became thriving hubs of social communication and artistic activity, where all manner of people could meet and swap information, but also enjoy music, puppetry, poetry and story recitals. Some establishments in England, France and Germany circulated manuscripts, held lessons and read news aloud. They were bustling hives of conversation and places where business was transacted. Drinking coffee acquired a political dimension, as coffee houses took on the role of bourgeois public forums that assembled a highly diverse society. Political debate became so fundamental to the coffee house experience that, in a similar but less drastic way to Sultan Murad IV, England's King Charles II (r. 1630–85) feared social unrest and prohibited them in 1675, though the measure was repealed within ten days.

Women also took to coffee drinking, though they met in each other's houses for coffee mornings, a social institution familiar to us today. These regular meetings gave them the opportunity for companionship and the sharing of knowledge, which struck a new chord in the late seventeenth century, and met with the displeasure of more conservative husbands, who accused their wives of neglecting the domestic routine, though in fact it was the increasing empowerment of their wives that they feared. The devotion of women to drinking coffee is reflected in J. S. Bach's short comic opera the *Coffee Cantata*, composed around 1735 for the Zimmerman coffee house in Leipzig and dedicated to female coffee addicts. By this time in the eighteenth century, not just the bourgeoisie but also the impoverished social classes had adopted coffee drinking, marking a social change which saw poorer people choosing how they used their money, free of regulation by superiors. The translation of the cultural institution of coffee drinking from Turkish Muslim to Christian European society created a force for intellectual, social and political change that heralded the demise of old social structures and paved the way for a new bourgeois order.

Carpets, Tulips and the Craze for All Things Turkish

Between 1650 and 1750, the enchantment with Ottoman culture and style, known as *turquerie*, spread across the lands of Christian Europe, as new trade deals and closer diplomatic contacts with the Turkish empire brought a wider circulation of commodities and ideas. The vogue for coffee was just one of many aspects of a phenomenon that heightened western Europe's understanding of and engagement with the Muslim culture of the Ottomans. Though their military menace may have diminished after the failed siege of Vienna in 1683, the past showed that combat did not preclude cultural exchange, as war booty travelled to Europe with Ottoman troops, and commerce continued alongside conflict. By the sixteenth century, as the Ottomans sought to consolidate their empire rather than expand it further, their image began to change from fearsome warriors to patrons of opulence and luxury, to the epitome of cultural refinement.[3]

The vogue for Turkish fashion had begun much earlier. When Charles the Bold married Margaret of York in Bruges in 1468, the courtiers of Burgundy were attired in sumptuous Turkish costumes, while, a century later, in 1541, the French king Francis I appeared at a wedding among dancers dressed in Turkish-style gold brocade. As new trade deals were struck with France, England and the Dutch republic, the flow of goods increased in the sixteenth and seventeenth centuries, and included luxuries affordable to the middle classes, from printed engravings to other items of Ottoman-inspired home decor and clothing, widening the market for *turqueries* beyond the royal court and urban nobility. France was the first to embrace luxury items, such as sofas, a name taken from the Arabic *soffah*, meaning a raised seating platform with cushions and mats, and found in English usage from 1694. By the eighteenth century, seating terminology included Ottoman chairs and seats in Turkish style or in the style of the sultana, with rounded backs, scrolled armrests and canopies.

Turkish or oriental carpets became the symbols of style and luxury, rare commodities that were at times seen as markers of vanity and excess. Like the North African Berbers, many of whose carpets were produced in al-Andalus, the Turkish peoples of central Asia used carpets as part of their nomadic lifestyle, and the thirteenth-century blue and red floor coverings of the Anatolian Seljuks became famous. One hundred years later, the Muslim traveller Ibn Battuta praised Turkish carpets, remarking that they were traded across the world and enhanced the European palaces of aristocrats with their beauty. In Venice, Piazza San Marco was decked out with Ottoman carpets hanging from house windows on special occasions, and in 1506 the artist Albrecht Dürer wrote from Venice to a friend about his search for two broad Turkish carpets, plus some crane feathers, as props for his artistic compositions, though he never included them in his paintings.

Yet oriental carpets with their Islamic designs became not only a visual sign of all that was exotic, precious and opulent in the life of early modern Europe, but also featured in many works of art, where they were recreated in great detail, accuracy and with astonishing variety. Carpets formed a background for religious scenes, often emphasizing the holiness of a saint, the Virgin, or secular rulers, who were depicted standing on an oriental floor covering, separate from the world around, akin to celebrities on the modern red carpet. Andrea Mantegna's late-fifteenth-century painting of the Virgin, known as the *San Zeno Altarpiece*, shows an example of a Turkish carpet at her feet, and there are several fine paintings of the English king Henry VIII seated on an Anatolian carpet.

The artist Gentile Bellini's visit to the Ottoman court inspired him, and his brother Giovani, to paint prayer rugs decorated with typical keyhole motifs. It was an Islamic design of religious significance, and carpets of this kind became known in English as 'musket' carpets, which was a corruption of the word 'mosque'. The Ottomans made the carpets woven in their empire distinctive because of their flower motifs and medallion-shaped emblems that represented the sultanate. The Flemish artist Ambrosius Francken (1544–1618) used a Mamluk carpet as a wall hanging behind the figure of Christ in his painting of the Last Supper (*c.* 1573). Its central Ottoman-style medallion, whose shape reflects the halo around Christ's head, also asserts its Christian authority over Turkish secular culture. Many other artists used oriental carpets in their work out of context, to create visual exoticism and beauty, while their cultural origins were disregarded.

*

Istanbul is currently a city of thirty million tulips. In 2006, the city government planted three million red tulip bulbs in parks, avenues and on roundabouts, in a bid to revive the city's Tulip Age. Since then, the number has mushroomed, as giant swathes of the flowers were gradually laid out in front of the Blue Mosque and in other locations, and every April the city celebrates its annual Tulip Festival. The name 'tulip' comes from the Persian word for turban, and the flower has had unique significance in Turkish culture from the time when wild tulips that grew on the central plains where the Turkic tribes lived spread into Anatolia under the Ottoman Empire, which adopted the tulip motif as part of its visual symbolism. In tiles, pottery, carpets and tapestries, paintings and illuminated manuscripts, the flowers represent love, beauty and abundance, as well as offering protection against the evil eye in their use on talismans and in Islamic religious sites. Their name is also an emblem of the defining head-dress of Arab and Asian Muslims.

Ogier Ghiselin de Busbecq, the Flemish herbalist and diplomat who was Austrian ambassador to Constantinople, is credited with sending tulip bulbs back to the Netherlands sometime in the second half of the sixteenth century. Demand was high in the Dutch republic and quickly outstripped the supply, as tulip mania took hold across Christian Europe. The rarest, most highly prized bulbs could cost the annual wage of an artisan. Suddenly, tulips were everywhere, and the vogue for painting them in still lifes became a hallmark of the Dutch Golden Age. A man who owned tulip bulbs, or even a painting of the flowers, could expect great wealth – until the tulip market crashed in the 1630s. But the blooms still shone brightly in Dutch art for another century, as the Netherlanders adopted the Ottoman flower which came to represent their own culture, and still does.

In the 1700s, Kostantiniyye experienced a similar craze that began in the first decades of the century. For a short time between 1718 and 1730, known as the Tulip Age, the city enjoyed a peace that fostered the expansion of art and architecture, and the tulip flourished everywhere. Sultan Ahmed III (1673–1736) and his viziers began to reconstruct the image of the city, and the sultan's private passion for tulips was harnessed to Muslim piety in the promotion of the idea of the spiritual value of the garden, as well as suggesting nobility and prosperity. It was recorded that the grand vizier had half a million bulbs growing in his own garden, in a turnabout which saw tulips reimported from the Netherlands, and from Persia. His display was illuminated with coloured lamps and candles, but the sultan went one step further, allegedly strapping night lights to the backs of tortoises as they moved slowly among the blooms in his gardens, lighting up the flower heads.[4]

Impersonating the Enemy

To all intents and purposes, the Christians and Muslims of Europe seemed for a time to have swapped aspects of their identities and exchanged hostility for emulation. In England, high society, including the royal family, donned turbans and other Muslim clothes, and as contact with the Turks increased in the seventeenth century, oriental fashion also became familiar and public on the streets of London. That they should choose to adopt the turban, the most feared and imposing symbol of Islam, seems counter-intuitive. Along with the scimitar and the crescent moon, it was the essential symbol of Muslim power and dominance, appearing in Flemish and Italian paintings of Muslim rulers such as Suleiman the Magnificent and Mehmed the Conqueror. Turbans also took pride of place in wonderful print collections that displayed Turkish and other Muslim attire, the images drawn from the real-life experiences of visitors to Ottoman lands. The French geographer Nicolas de Nicolay (1517–1583), who travelled to Istanbul on a mission for the French government in 1551, wrote the first extensive guide to the customs and dress of the Ottomans in his *Travels in Turkey* (*Quatre premiers livres des navigations*), which became a bestseller and led to a profusion of costume books throughout Europe.

The fascination with adopting Turkish Muslim dress was nowhere more undisguised than in the costumes of monarchs. The portraits of Henry VIII wearing layered coats with silk braid in the style of

21. The funeral procession of Suleiman the Magnificent, 1579. From the *History of Sultan Suleiman*. Miniature depicting the architect Sinan middle left.

22. Example of the script of the Lead Books. Granada Plates, Scatola III/4v.

23. 'Portrait of a Humanist' (probably Leo Africanus) *c.* 15[illegible] Sebastiano del Piombo.

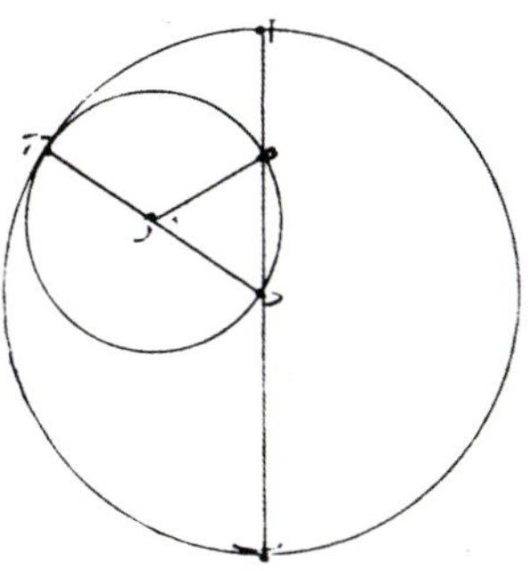

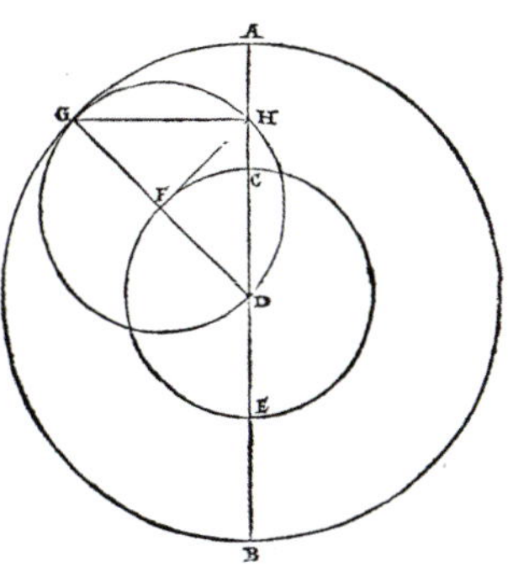

24. Comparison of The Tusi Couple, 13th century sketch by Nasir al-Din Tusi, and Copernicus' version.

25. Samson Rowlie as Hassan Agha, also Assan Agha, 16th century. Anon.

26. Abd el-Ouahed ben Messaoud ben Mohammed Anoun (1558 – ?), ambassador to the court of Queen Elizabeth I of England in 1600, to promote the establishment of an Anglo-Moroccan alliance. Anon.

27. 'Battle of Vienna', 1683. Anon.

28. Coat of arms of Isabella I of Castile and Ferdinand II of Aragon, after 1492.

29. 'Landing of Columbus', 1847. Jon Vanderlyn.

30. 'Bonaparte before the Sphinx', 1886. Jean-Léon Gérôme.

31. The first President of the Republic of Turkey, Mustafa Kemal Atatürk, in a top hat and white tie.

32. A British UN soldier in the UN buffer zone, Nicosia, Cyprus.

33. 'The Temple of All Religions', Tatarstan, by Ildar Xanov.

34. The Alhambra, Granada, Spain.

35. Berat, Albania.

Ottoman kaftans were matched by his garb at a banquet in Westminster in the first year of his reign, which he attended in Turkish dress of gold and silk brocade, with a crimson velvet turban. Henry's daughter Queen Elizabeth I was sent gifts of clothing from the sultan, and she too was painted, in an anonymous portrait of around 1575, wearing the braided bodice typical of Ottoman official dress. The queen's fascination with foreign clothing, especially in oriental style, was also a sign of respect for the Istanbul government with whom she was aligned against the Catholic Church.

English men and women began to imitate their queen, to a degree that some commentators believed provoked foreign derision. But European women saw Muslim women's dress as liberating in its looseness and lack of constraint, as well as luxurious, with its rich fabrics, use of fur and elaborate turbans. It gave them a new, informal style that spoke of opulence and ease. Yet wearing the turban continued to cause trouble. As Christian travellers between Christendom and Islamic lands knew very well, the turban was a demonstration of Islam that identified, in this case, the Turkish Muslim. The modest cloth headdress, which contrasts sharply with the grand, jewelled crowns of Christian monarchs, was laid above the tombs of Muslim rulers to denote their status and religion. In the conflicts between Catholicism and Protestantism, and Christianity and Islam, clothes stood for nationality, religion and social status, which is why, when Sir Robert Shirley, an English traveller, wore a turban to his audience with King James I, it nearly caused a diplomatic crisis, as Shirley's turban suggested his allegiance to another ruler.

*

As Christian Europeans both royal and bourgeois enacted Turkish Islamic identity at home and in public, Muslims became the protagonists of a different kind of performance. In novels and plays, the theme of the time was Moorish and Ottoman history, whose pageant of exotic characters trod the boards and enlivened fiction as writers male and female sought out those events that had greatest drama and pathos. The dramatist George Peele brought alive the defeat of the Portuguese by the Moroccans in 1578 in his play *The Battle of Alcazar*, and Shakespeare himself featured Moorish characters, most strikingly in *Othello* and *Titus Andronicus*. In France, the dramatist Corneille gave his loyal Spanish Moors a special role in the play *El Cid* (1636), while his rival Jean Racine's tragedy *Bajazet* (1672) dramatized the murder of Sultan Murad IV's younger brother Bayezid in Kostantiniyye at the sultan's orders in 1635. Set in the seraglio, the play encouraged the idea of the harem as a sensual, cruel place of crime and conflict between the personal and the political.

'A monstrous regiment': The Women who Sought Change

Ottoman history was central to the novel *Ibrahim* by the French writer Madame de Scudéry (1607–1701), which told the story of the execution of Ibrahim, Suleiman the Magnificent's grand vizier and great favourite, and many other women wrote Turkish-themed novels, and at times dramas, too. The setting of the harem awakened the notion of an alternative social order in which women had direct political influence. These ideas, and the liberty women found in adopting the outer appearance of Turkish Muslim identity, including coffee drinking, led to their engagement with polemical writings and the attempt to defend their rights. This change struck fear into the patriarchs of western Christendom, who decided in the sixteenth and seventeenth centuries that women needed to be monitored, and policed if necessary. They had a diametrically different view of Muslim women, not as a model of social and personal liberation for their Christian counterparts, but as the embodiment of female subservience. The segregation of Ottoman women in religious settings such as the mosque and their social relegation to domestic arenas met with approval among Christian writers such as the Scot Alexander Ross (1591–1654), who translated the Koran from French and claimed that, in the Turkish empire, 'Men and Women converse not together promiscuously, as among us'.[5]

European male writers found Muslim women virtuous and modest, as the German minister and humanist Joannes Boemus (*c.* 1485–1535) observed in his *Manners and Customs of all Nations*, in contrast with Christian women, who could be wily and untrustworthy. This and a litany of other criticisms of non-Muslim women – such as not suckling their own babies, using excessive make-up and causing their husbands great expense, unlike their Muslim peers – were used to present the indisputable superiority of Muslim womanhood by Christian men who needed to assert their power and authority over the female sex. There is an irony in the fact that those who were otherwise at war with the Ottomans and viewed Islam with hostility should have found common ground with the Muslims in a shared patriarchy.

*

The emulation of Ottoman fashions, tastes and ideas in western Christendom, especially in France, was reciprocated for a short time by the Ottoman court. Around the time of the Tulip Age, there was a craze in the capital for all things French – particularly Louis XV furniture, including clocks, mirrors and European-style chairs and settees, which seemed to have returned to their Turkish roots in a modified form. Sultan Ahmed III commissioned French craftsmen to decorate glamorous interiors, such as his Chamber of Fruits dining room in the seraglio of the Topkapı Palace. This desire to imitate the decor of the French court was encouraged by the lavish descriptions of the wonders of Versailles by the ambassador to France, Çelebi Mehmed Efendi, and these Frankish fashions became a transitory mirror image of *turquerie*.

In the fifteenth and sixteenth centuries, some scientific and technical knowledge came, for the first time, from west to east rather than vice versa, as the Ottomans acquired the latest western artillery and firearms, which fed the vast martial enterprise of the Ottomans up to the reign of Selim I. But, as a rule, the eastern European Muslims of the Turkish empire did not share the fascination of the west with a foreign culture and were reluctant to adopt their ideas. In Ambassador Busbecq's third Turkish letter, he laments the fact that the Ottomans 'have never been able to bring themselves to print books and set up public clocks. They hold that their scriptures, that is, their sacred books, would no longer be scriptures if they were printed; and if they established public clocks, they think the authority of their muezzins and their ancient rites would suffer diminution'.[6]

That said, a profound intermingling and integration of the Muslim culture of south-eastern Europe with western Christendom, on both public and private levels, took place from the end of the Middle Ages to the start of modernity, as western Christendom absorbed and performed oriental Muslim identity, and many Christians converted to Islam during that time. A bizarre yet radical imitation of the perceived religious and military enemy took place, as admiration and fascination overrode fear and prejudice. And, as Christian men and women at home, on the stage and in public disguised themselves in Muslim dress, they tested out a new identity that revealed both their disquieting outer differences and their common humanity. The textures, colours and styles of better-off Christian homes and palaces took on the appearance of Islamic culture, and for a time the Ottomans embraced the domestic and artistic innovations of the western Renaissance. Diplomacy, too, brought unexpected and mutually beneficial encounters on both sides, and for the first time a window of opportunity opened through which a different kind of European continent could be glimpsed, one of potential unity and collaboration between its Christian and Muslim peoples. Yet the ages of discovery, enlightenment and revolution in Europe were to bring changes that would shift the power balance of the western world and set Islam and Christianity on a less utopian footing.

Part Five

TURNING THE TABLES: CHRISTIAN EUROPE TAKES THE UPPER HAND

'Prayer', c. 1916–20. Étienne (Nasreddin) Dinet

Chapter 23

Thwarting the Ottomans: The Struggle for Western Europe

'An empire founded by war has to maintain itself by war.'

Montesquieu

'Oh, East is East, and West is West, and never the twain shall meet,
Till Earth and Sky stand presently at God's great Judgment Seat;
But there is neither East nor West, Border, nor Breed, nor Birth,
When two strong men stand face to face, though they come from
the ends of the earth!'

Rudyard Kipling

In September 2004, on the eve of the Turkish Muslim prime minister Recep Tayyip Erdoğan's visit to Brussels to make the case for Turkey's accession to the European Union, the *Guardian* correspondent Ian Traynor sat at a bar in the hills above Vienna, deep in conversation with a social worker named Helmut, whom he was interviewing.[1] Both Helmut and Gerhard, the owner of the bar, were against Turkey joining the European Union, not because of that country's human-rights record nor its economic status, but for religious and cultural reasons deeply rooted in Europe's early modern history. These two Viennese citizens feared losing their religious identity as Christians amid a wave of Muslim fundamentalism if Turkey became part of Europe. They pointed out that the hillside where they sat had been the theatre for the dramatic defeat of the Ottoman Turks by the Polish leader John III Sobieski in 1683, lifting the siege of Vienna and halting the Ottoman advance deep into central Europe. That ancient fear of the mighty Turk was also expressed in the headline 'The Turks at the Gates of Vienna', which appeared in the Viennese newspaper *Profil* the same week. The paper's editorial harked back to that ferocious battle for the city in the context of Turkey's application for membership of the EU. Just weeks before, the Dutch liberal European commissioner Frits Bolkestein had also forecasted the potential Islamization of Europe if Turkey became a member state. Since then, negotiations for Turkey's accession to the EU have proceeded slowly, until in 2019 the European parliament committee voted to suspend talks until further notice. This was not least because opposition to Turkey's admission increased after 9/11 and the upsurge of Islamic terrorism, and some member states remain uneasy about including a secularist country with a large majority Muslim population in what is perceived as a Christian polity. These dilemmas have their origins in the great struggle for western Europe that dominated the second half of the seventeenth century, when political and religious narratives in the continental history of Christians and Muslims overlaid the cultural and economic ones in the relentless contest of empires for supremacy.

Empires Built on Blood and Fire

The lands of Europe have been shaped by the politics and culture of empires since Roman times, through a counterpoint of intimidating violence and enduring associations formed of ethnic or religious communities, slaves, scholars, traders and migrants. Unlike the Chinese or early Romans, the Islamic caliphates founded their empires on a militant monotheism that was a branch of state power. The encounters between Christian and Muslim empires in both war and peace brought a competition, innovation and imitation that was most pronounced in terms of religion and its moral foundations. Those empires embraced many different peoples and their customs, as well as creating hierarchies between perceived insiders and outsiders; they were large political units that expanded, but also rose and fell. In European Christendom, popes challenged the power of kings, Islamic jurists became powerful, and schisms arose in both Christian and Muslim faiths. Their varied populations contrasted starkly with those of nation states such as the kingdom that emerged in Spain and Portugal after 1492, which purported to be a single people who spoke the same official language and followed the same religion, a unique political community in a sole territory under a monopoly of violence, until Spain created an empire of its own.

By the middle of the seventeenth century, the Ottoman Empire had taken centre stage, with its unique synthesis of the traditions of the Turks, Byzantines, Arabs, Mongols and Persians, evolving into an adaptable and long-lived superpower. Both violent and tolerant, its supremacy was won by a military prowess that struck fear into western Europe, and by the charm of its exotic lifestyle and opulence. But another imperial colossus was waiting in the wings in the shape of the Roman Catholic empire of the Habsburgs, who ruled from Vienna after the German king Rudolf I assumed Charlemagne's throne in 1273, although they did not take on the mantle of Holy Roman Emperors until Frederick III came to the throne in 1415. The final confrontation that loomed ominously between Europe's two potent religious and political actors was to prove definitive.

The Return of the Gazi

After the Islamic Millennium in 1592, year 1,000 of the Hijra, radical changes swept through the Ottoman state as a perplexing procession of unconventional sultans came and went. When Mehmed III (1566–1603) took the throne in 1595, he invoked the law of fratricide and ordered his deaf-mute servants to murder all nineteen of his half-brothers in a single night. His son and successor Ahmed I (r. 1603–16) became the first Ottoman sultan to break with that brutal custom and allow his own brother to live. Over the next thirty years, there was a dramatic shift in the balance of power at the head of government that manifested itself in a series of depositions and executions. The brother Ahmed saved from death, Sultan Mustafa I (r. 1617–18 and 1622–23), was mentally unstable and twice deposed, the first time by the chief eunuch of the harem, Mustafa Agha; the sultan became known as Mustafa the Mad and spent thirty-four of his thirty-eight years of life imprisoned as a lunatic. The resulting succession to the throne of Mustafa I's eighteen-year-old nephew Osman II in 1618 led to a revolt. The new sultan had ambitious dreams. He planned to make the foundering sultanate strong again by abolishing the highly esteemed Janissary corps and instating a cohort of musketeers instead. Osman also had plans to create a new Ottoman capital in Damascus instead of Istanbul, aligning the empire more with the Middle East than with Europe. Not surprisingly, the veteran Janissaries mounted a rebellion by storming the Imperial Palace and murdering Osman on the spot in 1622. By virtue of this insurgency, the power hierarchy was turned on its head. The sultan had become the servant of his subjects, of the army and of the legal authorities, and not vice versa; it was the beginning of the blueprint for a modern civil state.[2]

*

The reigns of two of Ahmed I's sons, the sultans Murad IV (r. 1623–40) and his younger brother Ibrahim I (r. 1640–8), did little to boost the diminishing prestige of the Ottoman dynasty. Murad was a mass of contradictions, banning the smoking of tobacco and opium and taking a hard line with coffee houses, while legalizing the sale and drinking of alcohol, even for his Muslim subjects. His mother ruled in his stead for nine years, until he was twenty, by which time Murad was overweight and a heavy drinker, and he died an early death from gout, aged twenty-nine. His only living male heir, his sibling Ibrahim, became the second sultan to be executed in a generation – strangled, with the approval of his mother, after devoting himself too much to the pleasures of the harem. Ibrahim was replaced by his oldest son Mehmed IV, who became sultan aged seven, in a reign initially overshadowed by royal women, including his grandmother, the regent Kösem Sultan, whose death warrant he signed after her plot to kill him was revealed.

Mehmed IV ruled from 1648 until 1687 and was cut from a different cloth to his immediate ancestors. He sought to revive that courage and superiority born of the desert nomads and to restore the model of the pious, manly, holy warrior sultan who led great military campaigns in Europe. Mehmed saw himself as a *gazi*, a virtuous fighter for Islam like the Prophet himself, pursuing conquest without compromise. He employed chronicle writers who wrote his life history as a great fighter for Islam, a redoubtable hero who destroyed the Christian enemy and rode into battle with his soldiers. He was known as Mehmed the Hunter, a falcon who swooped on 'the nest of the polytheist crows', though his epithet acquired a more derogatory meaning later.[3]

The sultan's militant approach had more than a whiff of religious intolerance about it. In 1660, a man smoking tobacco started an apocalyptic fire in Istanbul that devasted two thirds of the city and killed 40,000 inhabitants. In the aftermath, Mehmed and his viziers adopted a policy of Islamization throughout the city, in a mirror image of the attempted Christianization of Granada after 1492. An imperial decree was issued to banish Jews from the port and commercial district, where most of them lived, and many high-ranking Jews, including court physicians, were obliged to convert to Islam or lose their livelihoods. Further afield, Mehmed's first successful jihad, in Crete, in 1669, saw the bell towers of the conquered island converted to minarets, its churches to mosques or public baths. This policy was extended to all his conquered territories, as he swept through swathes of south-east Europe, conducting mass conversions to Islam of thousands of Christian and Jewish peasants, who acted as drovers for his lavish, Mongol-style hunting parties held en route.

Over the next decade, the Ottoman Empire under Mehmed's pioneering dominion expanded to its maximum range northward, with the conquest in 1672 of the storied White Castle at Kameniçe, seen as the gateway to Poland and Ukraine. This was buttressed by a successful campaign against the tsardom of Russia in 1678, after which a twenty-year peace treaty with Russia was signed in 1681. The Turks were riding high when Imre Thököly (1657–1705), a Hungarian Christian nobleman and military leader, became an Ottoman vassal and was awarded the title of King of Hungary by Mehmed in 1682. Their alliance was strengthened due to the Calvinist Thököly's opposition to the Catholic Habsburgs, and it encouraged the sultan to harbour a bold, possibly foolhardy, ambition to attempt something none of his ancestors had succeeded in achieving – the conquest of Vienna, some 1,500 kilometres to the north-west.

Crossing the Rubicon: The Contest for the Golden Apple

In the autumn of 1682, Mehmed IV reached the age of forty and had been Khan of Khans and Lord of the Two Continents since he was seven. His imperial name matched that of the greatest of Ottoman military leaders, Sultan Mehmed II, and his early obsession with chivalry and knightly deeds had moulded him as a ruler who exercised great power over a vast realm. But he still longed for an outstanding triumph that would rival or exceed those of his forebears. One hundred and fifty years before, the great Suleiman I had seized the city of Belgrade in August 1521, a significant victory followed by the devastating defeat of the Hungarians at the Battle of Mohács in 1526. Three years later, Suleiman was obliged to set off from Istanbul to Buda to meet the challenge of Ferdinand, archduke of Austria, who had retaken the Hungarian capital. Suleiman defeated the Austrians easily to reoccupy Buda, then stormed onwards to beleaguer Vienna, where, despite four assaults, he was compelled to lift the siege after almost a month and return home in October. This debacle was swept under the carpet – in the battle report in Greek that the sultan sent to the doge of Venice, Suleiman denied that he ever intended to take Vienna, and alleged he was merely chasing his enemy Ferdinand.[4]

Vienna's narrow escape and the shock of the Battle of Mohács had struck terror into western Europe, where the vastness of the Ottoman armies and their savagery were widely reported, casting a long shadow that gave Mehmed IV a psychological advantage. Yet it was crucial for Mehmed IV to take note of the reasons for Suleiman's failure; which were a combination of a lack of sappers and mining equipment to dig trenches and tunnels, and the misfortune of starting such a siege when winter was imminent, since the entire Ottoman army was forced to retreat through deep snow. In 1683, the challenges were no different – war in those mountainous regions or *balkans*, the Turkish word for 'mountain', was entirely governed by the weather, and the transportation of vast amounts of provisions, tents and the paraphernalia of war overland on carts and pack animals that had to ford streams and wide rivers was a logistical conundrum made more difficult by the early onset of the severe winters of south-east Europe.

So it was that, in August 1682, the sultan and his government council chaired by the grand vizier Kara Mustafa agreed to embark on a large-scale war against the Habsburgs, with the Ottoman army marching west on the Christian capital of Vienna and headed by the sultan himself. It was an Ottoman tradition that, once war was declared, the ancient banners of the warriors of the steppes, their ancestors, were put on public display. The historian Andrew Wheatcroft describes how seven long crimson poles were erected outside the Imperial Gate of the Topkapı Palace on the evening of 6 August 1682, each one gilded and adorned with horses' tails – black, chestnut and white – hanging from the golden orbs at the top of each pole.[5] It was a public symbol of the Commander of the Faithful's commitment to war, and a call to arms. The sultan's rust-red pavilions stood out in the new camp set up in fields outside the city walls, where troops, military tents and arms were marshalled with an order, complete silence and tranquillity that astonished the Habsburg ambassador to Istanbul, who was more accustomed to the filthy, unruly camps of the western Christian armies. These preparations, which included the fabrication of at least 15,000 war tents, must have alarmed the ambassador, who was only too aware of the inferior resources and lack of money and discipline of the Habsburg army.

In October 1682, at the start of the coldest winter in living memory in central and south-east Europe, Mehmed IV departed from Istanbul for Edirne mounted on a white horse decked out in jewelled trappings, in a parade that lasted over five hours. He was to spend the winter in the old capital, and would be joined in the early spring by the full army, whose cavalry had been boosted by the presence of the Crimean Tatars, crack horsemen impervious to weather, who could move ten times faster than ordinary troops and ford wide, fast-flowing rivers. They wore no armour and carried no firearms, relying solely on their astonishing speed and archery skills. Together, they would then head to the frontier of the Danube at the White Castle of Belgrade, up to which point Mehmed would be supreme commander. Surprisingly for a sultan who had led his troops in earlier conquests, he had elected to transfer that command to the grand vizier, who would lead the host north-west into Hungary. The ultimate objective, Vienna, had been kept secret from the troops. The stakes were high: if Kara Mustafa conquered the Habsburg capital, it would be a victory to match the conquest of Constantinople in 1453; but if he was defeated, the humiliation would be terrible.

Mehmed's departure from Edirne was delayed by the late arrival of the artillery, mired by the atrocious mud churned up in winter rains, so the army did not leave for Belgrade until late March. An evil omen unnerved the cavalcade when a sudden violent gust of wind blew off the sultan's turban as he ordered the march to begin. It was a sign of things to come. Nine days of torrential rain hampered their journey, rain that swept away bridges and poured down hillsides. Before the great procession reached Belgrade, Mehmed IV handed the Prophet's black wool banner to Kara Mustafa Pasha to symbolize the exchange of command, and the grand vizier steered his troops onwards to Vienna, 600 kilometres north-west.

At the Gates of the West: The Fifth Turning Point

The colossal retinue of the Ottoman war force, that included the Crimean khan and his Tartar horde, plus Imre Thököly's Hungarian hussars, struggled its way across marshy terrain to besiege Vienna, little knowing that the impending military conflict would mark the fifth, definitive turning point in the history of European Muslims and Christians. Posterity has seen the ensuing conflict in divergent ways – as a great religious struggle, as a bid for dominion and glory, and as a mission riddled with ambiguity – and in truth it was all these things. Despite the evident differences in religion, language and society between sultan and emperor as supreme commanders, they had several things in common. For Mehmed IV, Vienna was the irresistible Golden Apple, the object of desire which led him to scour the archives to learn from past lessons. The natural concomitant of his self-image as a *gazi* was to be the vanquisher of the city that would open a path to the west of Europe, an ambition which harmonized with his duty as leader of the Muslim world. To aspire to the conquest of the west was deeply entrenched in Ottoman political doctrine.

His direct antagonist was the emperor Leopold I (1640–1705), a man who, like Mehmed IV, had led a cloistered life in a youth devoted to learning. Born in Vienna, Leopold was fluent in four languages, had a passion for music and had received full ecclesiastical training for a senior role in the Catholic Church, but then his elder brother died unexpectedly. Erudite, pious and tolerant, he was next in line to the Habsburg throne and had been elected Holy Roman Emperor on 18 July 1658, at the age of eighteen, after which he ruled from Vienna. This illustrious title given to western Catholic kings was scorned by the Ottomans, who disavowed it on the basis that the true Holy Roman Emperor ruled from Istanbul, like Mehmed the Conqueror.

As leaders of the two oldest, most powerful states in Europe, aside from the pope, their lives were dictated by their courtiers and detached from everyday realities – so Mehmed IV was never informed of the advice of his local commanders in Hungary, especially the pasha of Buda, who had trenchantly opposed the Vienna siege plan. Likewise, Leopold did not understand the harmful repercussions of his repressive actions in Hungary in the 1670s until it was too late and the Hungarians had sided with his enemies.[6] The Habsburgs and the Ottomans had evolved the first empires with civic administration in Europe since the Roman Empire, yet, by the late seventeenth century, they were jaded as a result of a narrow continuity of dynastic rule that had lasted unrefreshed for almost 200 years.

*

In June 1683, the Ottomans set out on the road to Vienna wielding a devastating military power that was unmatched by the Habsburgs at that time. Yet that martial might was also to prove a big disadvantage. It was said that they formed a line ten kilometres wide across the horizon, and it was precisely the sheer scale of the army and its heavy baggage train that hampered its route to the Habsburg capital. On the other hand, the Habsburg army was lacking in manpower and had very poor military intelligence networks. They had no recent knowledge of the state of the marshy wildernesses south of the Hungarian town of Györ through which the Ottomans would need to pass, but the Crimean Tatars had sufficient information to report to the grand vizier that it was passable even for heavy artillery. The Ottomans also had good intelligence of the whereabouts of the Catholic army, while Leopold and his advisers could only guess what the enemy plans might be.

The commander of the Habsburg forces was Charles V, duke of Lorraine (1643–90), an experienced soldier in the imperial army. A native of Vienna, he had started out as a clergyman and became the abbot of Gorze Abbey near Metz, but, when his elder brother died, he became heir to Lorraine and took up a military career. By 1683, he had seen action in several major conflicts, including the Franco-Dutch War of 1672–8, and, as head of the armed forces, he had the hard task of coordinating the confusion of regiments, allies and mercenaries making up the Habsburg host. His counterpart at the head of the Ottoman army, the grand vizier Kara Mustafa Pasha (1634/5–83), was a controversial man of Albanian origin with a mercurial temperament, rumoured to own 700 black eunuchs and thousands of wild and exotic animals. He never wore silk, silver or gold, according to Islamic custom, and was entirely devoted to the Ottoman state. Yet, while his loyalty was never in question, his military inexperience would cost the Turks dearly.

On 13 July 1683, Kara Mustafa's army, who were suffering from the rigours of their arduous journey, arrived where Suleiman I had pitched his tent in 1529. A day later, they were outside the walls of Vienna. When Leopold saw the approaching dust cloud, he fled with his family, perhaps wisely, for Vienna was quickly surrounded by Ottoman tents and the citadel was soon being heavily bombarded.

Kara Mustafa's early success led to a degree of overconfidence, and his formal demand for surrender and conversion to Islam was ignored by the Viennese, who chose to fight on. The big problem for the Ottomans was that the city had very high walls and was encircled by a ditch twenty metres wide. Inside, there were also hundreds of pieces of heavy artillery. The grand vizier was nothing if not bold, and he was convinced his sappers would demolish the city walls and the Golden Apple would be his. Yet they tunnelled and exploded mines to bring down the thick ramparts of a weakened city, whose defenders were starving and desperate, without success. Three weeks after the initial attack, the Ottomans were still trying to break through the outer defences.

The two-month siege was shaping up to be a disaster for the Ottomans. They were again bedevilled by bad omens: reports arrived that the sultan's commander's palace in Istanbul had burned to the ground, and the sultan's mother had died. The usual immaculate discipline failed and, although it was Ramadan, contemporary Ottoman chroniclers wrote with disapproval of the widespread wine-drinking and fornicating of the increasingly disenchanted troops. Even so, by 8 September, it looked as if the Ottomans were at last poised to take the city, as they had managed to occupy part of the fortress and lower walls, and the defenders prepared for a battle inside the citadel. Vienna's fate hung on a knife-edge.

*

There were errors of judgment on both sides. Just as he was poised for victory, Kara Mustafa failed to gather intelligence about the Habsburg army's plans, nor did he protect his camp against attack on the west flank. Behind the scenes, Pope Innocent XI had financed what he hoped would be an army of liberation for Vienna, a coalition called the Holy League consisting of armed forces from various states and cities of the Holy Roman Empire and the cavalry led by the king of Poland. In Innocent's view, the relief of Vienna was the crucial chance to halt the advance of Islam, if both Catholic and Protestant states would work together. At the end of August, the key players had gathered at the castle of Stellendorf to plot the final battle to free Vienna. The vital element was the Polish army led by King John III Sobieski (1629–96), ruler of the multi-religious, multi-lingual Polish–Lithuanian commonwealth. His soldiers included the legendary 'winged horsemen', who rode into battle with a metre-high frame of angel-like wings made from the feathers of birds of prey, attached to their armour or saddles. These hussars were an elite force on a par with the Janissaries, heavy cavalry covered in chain mail and plate like medieval knights, equipped with lances five metres long, who could ravage infantry lines by striking at full gallop. Sobieski also brought a contingent of Sunni Muslim troops known as the Lipka Tatars, who were also to play an important part in the final encounter.

The Holy League gathered at 5 a.m. on 12 September, in the Vienna woods on the outskirts of the city, their troops flying the huge white flag with a red central cross that represented the avenging crusaders of Christ. Sixty thousand soldiers had taken a perilous route over rocks and down slopes, travelling in the extreme summer heat, and they outnumbered the Ottomans by two to one. Kara Mustafa's forces were swamped by 'an immense herd of furious boars that trampled and demolished them', according to the Ottoman master of ceremonies, who described the events in his diary.[7] Amid the fighting, the battle cry of the Christians was heard to be 'Jesus, Mary', and of the Ottomans 'Allah, Allah'. As soon as the winged hussars attacked the grand vizier's position, the sultan's army saw that the battle was lost and fled with Muhammad's banner. In a moment, thousands of Turks were running for the Hungarian border, and Kara Mustafa abandoned his post, leaving his luxury tent, jewelled daggers and swords to be seized by the Christians. The Ottomans had been thwarted once and for all, and the ultimate humiliation was the reforging of their captured cannons to make the bell of St Stephen's Cathedral in Vienna. Sultan Mehmed IV was furious and ordered Kara Mustafa's execution. He was strangled on Christmas Day 1683, using silken cords, in the Ottoman tradition, and his head was sent to Edirne to be displayed at the entrance to the sultan's palace. To western Christendom, Kara Mustafa's attack on Vienna was a manifestation of his deep hatred of the west, and his disastrous fall from grace was seen to represent the impending decline of the Ottomans.

Crusade and Reconquest Reprised

The Battle of Vienna could have gone either way. If Kara Mustafa had pressed home his advantage and taken the city, Europe might be a very different place today. As things turned out, the liberation of Vienna in September 1683 represented the historic end of Ottoman expansion further into the continent. When the emperor Leopold I returned to the capital from his bolthole in Passau, the sudden allied victory suggested to his pious nature that he was a man with a special, God-given mission to continue the recovery of Christian lands lost to the Ottomans, which his forebear the emperor Charles V of Spain had begun a century earlier, when he had besieged and conquered Tunis in 1535. Even before that, Charles's grandparents, Ferdinand and Isabella of Spain, had overcome the emirate of Granada to conclude the Christian reconquest of al-Andalus. Now, Leopold had an even greater possibility, which was to recover Kostantiniyye for Christianity and re-establish the Roman Empire.

His ambition was endorsed by Pope Innocent XI, who promised to bankroll another crusade. In March 1684, a new Catholic league was formed between Emperor Leopold, the king of Poland and the doge of Venice, as well as Orthodox Russia. It marked a commitment to fight the infidel in a defensive alliance against any future incursions by the Muslims. This was the bad news given to Sultan Mehmed IV at his palace in Edirne. Between 1683 and 1697, fifteen major battles were fought between the Turkish Muslims and the Christians, twelve of them won by the latter. Buda was finally reclaimed by the western allies on 2 September 1686, and Mohács, which had been the focus of a great Ottoman triumph a century earlier, fell to the Christians in 1687. The Treaty of Karlowitz was signed in 1699, ending hostilities between the Ottoman Empire and the Catholic league, and transferring Transylvania and the majority of Hungary back to Austrian rule.

*

In the wake of the military losses inflicted on the Ottoman Empire, Mehmed IV suffered a breakdown. He spent all his time hunting, refused to return to Istanbul and neglected his duties, both military and religious. The two titans of early modern Europe, the Ottomans and the Habsburgs, had locked horns in the struggle for western territory that came to be known as the Great Turkish War, but the fallout of their loss changed the Ottoman state irrevocably. As Mehmed persisted in ignoring his obligations, the Janissaries and religious leaders rebelled, asserting that it was entirely legal to dethrone a sultan who could not fulfil his duties. Mehmed was duly deposed and kept under house arrest in Edirne, to be succeeded by his younger brother Suleiman II. From that time on, obedience was due to the government, not to the sultan, and the state started to wield greater power than its ruler. Mehmed IV died of natural causes in 1693. Although he achieved great military successes, including the conquest of Crete, and expanded the Ottoman Empire into eastern Europe to reach its maximum range, he could not shake off the ignominy of the defeat at Vienna.

Staging a Multicultural Tragedy: Parallels, Parities and Reversals

In the last fifteen years of the seventeenth century, central and eastern Europe witnessed legion after legion of warriors clash and disengage, ranked in varied configurations of armies mustered under the banner of religious faith, as another of history's great slaughters played out in yet another drama of appalling loss of life, suffering and horror on a vast scale. Its motives appeared clear cut: a black and white struggle between Islam and Christianity for religious, political and territorial supremacy in Europe, in which the battle for Vienna was a defining moment in that long history of conflict. Men went to war believing they were fighting for Jesus Christ or Allah, and their foe was identified by their religious creed. Historians, chroniclers and holy men have since come to simplify and justify what proved to be a complex and contradictory struggle criss-crossed with ambiguities, parallels and mirror images.

At the heart of those ambiguities lay the perplexing and age-old conundrum regarding the extent to which religion was harnessed in the service of power-seeking. When the Catholic Monarchs believed they had defeated Islam in Spain and Portugal, their victorious crusade lent them moral virtue, but it also gave them access to great political power, and to a dominion that became international as the Spanish Empire was established. Their ambitions had parallels with those of Mehmed IV and Leopold I, in the sense that both men believed they were fighting a jihad or crusade respectively, and both aspired to great political glory. Had Mehmed achieved his dream of winning Vienna, it may well have led to greater expansion of his empire into the rest of western Europe and guaranteed his perennial renown in the annals of the Ottoman Empire. Likewise, the successful defence of Vienna opened a path for Leopold to pursue the crusade as far as Istanbul, which he envisioned restoring as the Christian city at the head of the Holy Roman Empire. Their ambitions were mirror images and suggest that, in their cases, religious and political pre-eminence were inseparable.

At no time was there a sense that western Christendom was united against the Ottomans, whose very own elite army, the Janissaries, had always been formed of converted Christians. Although the peace treaty of Westphalia, signed in 1648, had calmed the conflicts between different Christian European traditions by acknowledging Roman Catholicism, Lutheranism and Calvinism, Protestants were noticeably absent in the battle for Vienna. Neither was there political harmony in the west – Sultan Mehmed IV's association with the French Sun King Louis XIV continued the Franco-Ottoman alliance begun in the 1530s, which lasted until Napoleon's invasion of Egypt in 1798, making it the longest-lasting peace agreement in French history. In support of Mehmed IV, France sent troops to the Ottoman's western front during the siege of Vienna in 1683.

Political and personal loyalties often disregarded religion and ethnicity. After his famous victory at Vienna, the Polish king John III Sobieski wrote to his French wife Marie Casimire from his camp: 'Our Tatars are entertaining themselves with falcons they have brought with them; they are guarding the prisoners and are proving to be loyal and trustworthy.'[8] He was referring to the Lipka Tatars, whose light cavalry had been a vital force in his victory against the Ottomans. These men were Sunni Muslims, whom Sobieski had freed from all taxation in his country when he came to the throne in 1674. He had reinstated their former privileges lost during the Counter-Reformation, which included permission to rebuild their mosques. To ensure their loyalty in his army, he had also given them Crown estates in eastern Poland, near Bialystok, a multicultural city inhabited by people of diverse cultural and religious traditions, including Jews, Catholic Poles and Orthodox Belarusians.

During the final battle for Vienna, the Lipka Tatars wore straw sprigs in their helmets to avoid being mistaken for the Crimean Tatars fighting for the Ottomans, and they employed their key tactic of feigning retreat before suddenly turning to surround the enemy. Sobieski's battle lieutenant was a Lipka Tatar, Samuel Murza Krzeczowski, who saved his king's life three weeks later at a battle near the Danube as his army was chasing retreating Ottomans. Sobieski was on the point of being singled out and killed, but Krzeczowski saved him. As a reward, he was promoted to colonel and given an estate in eastern Poland, where the king later visited him personally to thank him. One of the many great ironies of this history is the fact that a Muslim soldier saved the life of the man credited with liberating Europe from the Ottomans. But Sobieski rose above religious and cultural hatred and remains the only European ruler to have established a lasting Muslim community in a non-Islamic European country.

The reversal of the balance of power between Habsburg Europe and the Ottoman Empire was a watershed in the history of continent. Although they remained strong, the Ottomans never advanced further into western Europe, and their polity was about to evolve in radical new ways and embrace educational and technological reforms as well as a different kind of government. Christian Europe's global imperial ambitions had emerged from its quest for the New World at the end of the fifteenth century, pioneered by Columbus and Portuguese explorers. To make sense of the growing feeling of European cultural superiority that would cast Islamic civilization into the shadows, we need to probe into the motives behind Columbus's first voyage of discovery in 1492.

Chapter 24

Changing the Guard: The Conquests of Colonialism

'Europe is the light of the world, and the ark of knowledge'

Edinburgh Review, 1802

'In religion, I see the mystery of the social order.'

Napoleon Bonaparte

'. . . the inversion of the innate and the elimination of the established; of horrors upon horrors and contradicting conditions; of the perversion of all precepts and the onset of annihilation'

Abdulrahman al-Jabarti, on the French invasion of Egypt

A Thirst for Conquest: The Great Crusade of Christopher Columbus

From January 1492, the Catholic Monarchs adopted a new coat of arms, bearing a pomegranate to symbolize their conquest of Granada. There was also a second addition to the design, in the form of the eagle of St John the Evangelist carrying the royal shield between its claws, purporting to represent Isabella's devotion to St John, but also echoing the Habsburg's imperial eagle and that of the Roman Empire before them. The insignia are important symbols of the first major defeat of Islam in Europe, which gave birth to imperial ambitions that rose from the ashes of the defeated Muslim civilization of al-Andalus. The surrender of the last emirate in western Europe prefigured the long-drawn-out erosion and repression of Muslim peoples on a global scale, stretching from the sixteenth to the nineteenth centuries and culminating in the era when imperialism was remodelled in the form of colonialism.

The Catholic Reconquest of Spain had created a country with a new sense of its power on the world stage, and fate presented Ferdinand and Isabella with just the man to expand their newly acquired taste for conquest beyond national boundaries. Christopher Columbus had witnessed the events of 2 January 1492 as he awaited Their Majesties' pleasure while they considered financing his proposed voyage of exploration across the Atlantic Ocean. He got on well with the queen, but had failed to convince her he was worth the investment. When she finally and suddenly changed her mind and agreed to sponsor Columbus's new venture, it became clear that they shared a common purpose: – a holy crusade to enlarge Christendom and eliminate Muslim power once and for all. He was, he assured her, 'devoted to the Holy Christian faith, and dedicated to its expansion and to combating the religion of Mahomet.'[1]

Columbus had grown up in Genoa, a hub for crusaders departing for Jerusalem, and as a youngster he had heard stories of the Crusades and the tales of Marco Polo's encounter with the Grand Khan, described in his travelogue *The Description of the World*. The Grand Khan was probably the Mongol emperor Kubla Khan, a man who fascinated Columbus because he aspired to become a Christian. Marco Polo also referred to the remarkable length of Eurasia, which led Columbus to suppose that the ocean route from the Canary Islands to Cipango, as Japan was known, would be relatively short. The Genoese seafarer had also heard the legend of the Seven Cities of Cíbola, said to have been built by Christian bishops fleeing the Muslim conquest of Spain in 711 and fashioned of pure gold – enough gold to fund a holy army to reclaim Jerusalem from the Saracens and bestow boundless wealth on its saviours. Columbus felt certain that these cities must exist somewhere across the Atlantic Ocean.

The nineteenth-century American writer Washington Irving was the first to draw attention to Columbus's crusading objectives, which were to sail west to the court of the khan, persuade him to make an alliance with Christian Europe, and reconquer Jerusalem, thereby defeating Islam permanently.[2] The Spanish priest Bartolomé de las Casas, who travelled to the New World in 1502 and wrote a devastating condemnation of the brutal treatment of the indigenous people by the Spanish conquistadors, cited Columbus's own words on his intended crusade in the prologue to his journals. The admiral hoped:

> there would be found a cask of gold, which those whom he left behind would have obtained by barter, and that they would have found the mine of gold and the spicery, and that in so great quantity that the Sovereigns (Ferdinand and Isabella) within three years would undertake and prepare to go and conquer the Holy Sepulchre . . . I declared to Your Highnesses that all the gain of this my enterprise should be spent in the conquest of Jerusalem; and Your Highnesses smiled and said that it pleased you, and that even without this you had that strong desire.[3]

Columbus believed he was the chosen Spanish messianic figure who would achieve the conquest of Jerusalem, in line with the prophecy of the twelfth-century mystic Joachim of Fiore, a conviction he set out for the Catholic Monarchs in a long letter, the *Lettera Rarissima*: 'Jerusalem and the Mount of Zion are now to be rebuilt through Christian hands . . . the Abbot Joachim said that this man was to come from Spain . . .'[4]

Bolstered by this dubious hypothesis, and over a million Spanish maravedis forwarded against funds to be raised by the sales of papal indulgences, Columbus set sail from Palos de la Frontera in August 1492, in ships fitted with lateen sails invented by Muslim maritime technology, and accompanied by interpreters who spoke Arabic and Hebrew, the languages of the peoples Ferdinand and Isabella were in the process of banishing. In a bizarre conjunction of imperial ambition and madcap maritime exploration, of chance, prophecy and opportunism, it turned out that a crusade to liberate Jerusalem from Islamic rule led to the revelation of the Americas to the peoples of Europe. Out of the triumph of Spain's Christian Reconquest came the rapid invasion and Europeanization of vast swathes of the American continent by a country ideally placed to vanquish, administer and Christianize the New World, since its Catholic society had been built precisely for the purpose of vanquishing, administering and 'Europeanizing' the inhabitants of al-Andalus for nearly eight centuries.[5]

The Ascent of Western Europe in the Age of Discovery

The boundaries of Europe's Christian and Islamic civilizations began to shift after 1492, and their transformation was reflected in the specific enterprise of Columbus and the Spanish Crown, in one decisive act in the changing world of global Christendom. Ferdinand and Isabella's patronage of Columbus's voyages chimed with the zeitgeist of their time, and the queen was well aware of the increasing rivalry between Spain and Portugal for supremacy in trade and colonial expansion, with Portugal in pole position. Portugal had been the first European nation to begin building a colonial trading empire, initially as its sailors and explorers discovered an eastern sea route to India. The Portuguese seized the Muslim port of Ceuta on the North African coast, a modest invasion which led them to the Atlantic islands that included Madeira, and on to the African coast; by 1487, they had rounded the Cape of Good Hope, laying open the path to India. In 1497, Vasco da Gama reached the Malabar coast bordering the western region of India, and, in 1500, the Portuguese crossed the Atlantic to Brazil, where they started sugar cultivation, the importation of brazilwood, and a trade in slaves.

Spain soon caught up with this colonial expansion, and by the middle of the sixteenth century had dominion over a vast empire that stretched from the Iberian peninsula as far as south-east Asia. The new Atlantic routes pioneered by Portugal enabled western traders to bypass land routes to Asia via the eastern Mediterranean, which were barred by the Ottomans as well as by Venice and Genoa, who were the agents of European trade in North Africa and the East. In this way, the newly emerging states of western Europe found much-needed finance through the increased wealth derived from eastern trade. This global configuration of power and resources took European navigators to Asia and also to the Americas, whose discovery was a lucky imperial accident with a transformational impact. In eastern Europe, the Ottomans remained resolute in their control of the Black Sea and Arabia, and grew rich on the trade from pepper, spices, silk and porcelain from China and cloth from India. But Europe's new involvement in long-distance maritime trade was essentially one of political and commercial rivalry, which depended on setting up trading enclaves and attempting to destroy those of others. One consequence was that maritime traders from the west ran up against rivals from an unknown cultural realm – as they sailed the southern seas, they found themselves in the preserves of Asian Islam. Yet new ways of thinking and new attitudes to exploration were poised to shift the emphasis from the possession of commercial power to the conquest and colonization of new lands.

The Cultural Revolution in the Age of Exploration and Enlightenment

As he travelled across the landscape of Mexico in the 1570s, the court physician to King Philip II of Spain, Francisco Hernández, recorded some 3,000 species of plants and animals unknown to the Old World. Hernández was a true Renaissance physician who had revived the principles of Galen and the rationalist philosopher and doctor Averroes. He had been sent to the Central American colonies by the king on what was the world's first scientific expedition overseas, conducting botanical and medical studies, as a result of which he introduced vanilla, chillies, cacao, tomatoes and tobacco to Europe. The Hernández expedition was the forerunner of the era of research-based exploration that flourished in the seventeenth and eighteenth centuries and emerged out of the Scientific Revolution of the Renaissance. Those centuries were infused with the spirit of the Enlightenment, which harnessed reason and evidence-based thinking as tools in the search for the knowledge deemed fundamental to the ideal of human progress. Scientific associations such as the British Royal Society were founded across Europe, and maritime expeditions of scientific exploration peaked in the eighteenth century, contributing to great advances in natural sciences based on the voyages of mariners like Captain Cook, who travelled to the Pacific, and French explorers like Bougainville, who discovered Tahiti. Experts of many different backgrounds usually collaborated on these maritime missions, creating a multicultural, multiracial team of researchers, and, by the middle of the nineteenth century, nearly all the land masses of the world had been explored and their coastlines charted.

As western Europe grew in confidence and knowledge, and its sense of cultural superiority increased as its hegemony extended worldwide, society benefited from improved education, mass printing, the emergence of museums and advances in health and sanitation in daily life. It also became increasingly secular, as thinkers such as Voltaire and Rousseau challenged a social order based on faith and Catholicism in favour of one based on reason, that replaced tradition with individualism. Although that clash between faith and reason had been examined and reconciled in much earlier Islamic philosophy, the Muslim world in Europe and beyond turned a blind eye to the cultural revolution taking place among its Christian counterparts. Muslim thinkers refused to question the established order of things, and the printing press was banned almost as soon as it appeared in the Ottoman capital, on the grounds that making the Koran available to all would lead to undesirable misinterpretations of the words of the Prophet. Later, printing became a capital crime. Diderot published his famous *Encyclopedia* between 1751 and 1772, which spread Enlightenment ideas far and wide, but Islam remained rigidly insistent on traditional religious doctrine, often infused with extreme mysticism.

Bonaparte in Egypt: The Sixth Turning Point

The French artist Jean-Léon Gérôme's painting of Napoleon standing before the Sphinx is a striking image of the confrontation between two worlds that arose when he invaded Egypt in 1798. His incursion amounted to a cultural collision between the modern western European Enlightenment and a Muslim country with a resonant ancient heritage that had little or no knowledge of the world outside Islam. It was also a political campaign in which appropriation and possession were disguised as exploration and discovery.

Egypt had been under Muslim rule since the defeat of the Byzantines only a couple of decades after the death of the Prophet, and had reached a zenith under the Fatimids in the eleventh century. It had been the breadbasket of the Ottoman Empire, which had ruled it since 1517, and was well placed strategically and geographically on the overland trade route to India. In the late eighteenth century, it was ruled by the Mamluks, the caste of former slaves who governed on behalf of the Ottomans using a regime of oppression and extortion. Egyptian society was stuck in a time warp, and its educational system was in disarray – it had a mere twenty schools, in contrast with the seventy-five it had boasted in the early 1400s.[6] Western Christendom had a sense, rightly or wrongly, that the Ottoman Empire was beginning to decline, especially after the triumph of Vienna, and the French invasion of Egypt began to dismantle the West's centuries-old deference to Muslim superiority.

Napoleon had cast himself in the mould of history's great conqueror, Alexander the Great, who had liberated Egypt from Persian rule in 332 BC and was regarded as a divinity in Africa, but the French emperor's motives and intentions arose more specifically from the political and cultural context in which he lived. In the afterglow of the French Revolution of 1789, an invasion of Egypt as a means of liberating a people oppressed by foreign tyrants appealed to radical idealists and merged with the more hard-headed aim to disrupt the British presence further afield in the Indian Ocean, an ambition endorsed fulsomely by Napoleon: 'To destroy England thoroughly, the time is coming when we must seize Egypt.'[7] He intended to create a permanent French colony there and set up a base for 60,000 soldiers who could attack British possessions, thereby opening up Asian markets to French goods. Napoleon also conceived of the expedition as one of scientific research, and, in the true spirit of the Enlightenment, it became a cultural and scientific event as well as a war of conquest.

The fleet that left France in May 1798 comprised 13 ships of the line and 400 transport vessels, the largest ever to sail the Mediterranean, loaded with all manner of paraphernalia, including astronomical telescopes, chemical apparatus, ballooning equipment and even a printing press set with Latin, Arabic and Syriac type, along with 4,800 bottles of red burgundy.[8] Like Alexander before him, Napoleon took over a hundred books in a specially constructed library, including Captain Cook's *Voyages* and Latin works by Livy, Tacitus and Julius Caesar, plus the Bible, the Koran and the Vedas to help him understand Muslims, Hindus and Christians. In addition to the armed forces, the passengers consisted of 167 scholars to organize and conduct the scientific research. In the emperor's mind, this was to be a kind of Greek odyssey, a colonization of land and culture that would finally lead to the banishment of the British from India.

The fleet reached Alexandria in July 1798, and easily quashed the Mamluks at what was known as the Battle of the Pyramids. The Muslim army was no match for the French in tactics, training or equipment, even after Napoleon had marched his soldiers across the sands in searing heat, in the first desert crossing by a modern western army. The exhausted host took over Cairo in October 1798, and, to win over its inhabitants, the French general pretended to support the Muslims against the pope. In a victory proclamation, whose rhythm and style imitated that of the Koran, he stated: 'I reverence God, his prophet Muhammad, and the Koran. Have we not destroyed the Pope, who made men wage war on the Muslims?' The French troops were ordered to behave respectfully and give no cause for jihad, and Napoleon continued to flatter the ulema and engage in discussions of the Koran. While he appeared to esteem Islam, what he really admired were the political and civil dimensions, and the potential of religion in general, which he saw as the key to social order, favouring Islam over Christianity because the former did not encourage conflict between the material and spiritual worlds.

Niqula al-Turk, a contemporary Egyptian historian, observed that many Muslims in Egypt believed Napoleon was the Mahdi or Guided One, sent to redeem Islam, and certainly the emperor went to remarkable lengths to confirm his allegiance to the Prophet. Despite the unexpected disaster of Admiral Lord Nelson's sinking of virtually the entire French fleet lying at anchor in Aboukir Bay in August 1798, Napoleon found the money to fund the celebrations for the Prophet's birthday in Cairo and other regions. In the capital, there were sideshows with live bears and monkeys, magicians, illuminated models of the Prophet's tomb in Medina and a feast for over a hundred Muslim clerics, at which their new overlord was declared to be an honorary son-in-law of the Prophet himself and was bequeathed the name Ali Bonaparte. It was said that the French soldiers laughed heartily at the farce when they returned to their quarters.[9]

All Napoleon's assiduous courting of the sultan and of Islam cut no ice with the Ottomans. Selim III sent his Tatar couriers to Cairo with a proclamation of war on the French, and the sultan circulated his own propaganda to the effect that he had at first hesitated to condemn France out of respect for their centuries-old alliance, but, he went on: 'those the (French) revolution brought to power have subverted under an illusive idea of liberty . . . every established government, . . . and caused the abolition of all religions, the destruction of every country'.[10] He claimed that Napoleon planned to divide Arabia into various republics, attack all Muslims and gradually extirpate them from the face of the Earth. Selim also warned the Egyptians that the French would incite the people to revolt, and then destroy all Muslims. His fears were realized when Napoleon fired on rebels in Cairo in October 1798, demolishing parts of the Al-Azhar Mosque and University and killing almost 3,000 Egyptians.

Alongside his impudent and insincere, if diplomatic, engagement with the Muslim faith, Napoleon's other cultural weapon was the power of reason as it manifested itself in scientific research. The Institut d'Égypte was opened in Cairo by the emperor in August 1798 to use the scientific equipment shipped over by the French. There, they set up laboratories and held scientific meetings every five days, in mathematics, physics, political economy and the arts. The contemporary Egyptian historian al-Jabarti, who looked on the

French invasion as a cataclysm of disaster and Allah's punishment for religious laxity, wrote in his *Marvels of Deeds in Annals and Lives*, an extensive history of Egypt from 1688 to 1821, that he deplored France as a country without religion and enslaved to the judgment of reason. Yet he visited the Institut d'Égypte and was captivated by their illustrated books, art, chemistry laboratories and military advances. Despite his fascination, he was downcast, for he had seen phenomena of which the Egyptians had no knowledge – electricity, anatomy and the printed word – and the backwardness of Egyptian life and the urgent need for modernity hit him forcefully.

⋆

By August 1799, Napoleon had lost interest in his Egyptian campaign and decided to return to France. The British joined forces with the Ottomans to defeat the remaining French troops at the Battle of Alexandria in March 1801, and the French commander General Menou ceded to the British in September, signing over to them all the priceless antiquities, including the Rosetta Stone, that the French had collected on their expeditions. By January 1802, Egypt was once again under Ottoman control. Despite the brevity and ultimate failure of Napoleon's campaign in Egypt, which never came close to achieving his ambitions, the scientific discoveries made there were recorded for posterity in a comprehensive, fully illustrated, multivolume work, the *Description of Egypt*, published between 1809 and 1821, which was at that time the largest known publication in the world. It roundly condemned the negligent government of Ottoman Egypt and its completely outdated science, and claimed that Islam did not allow the development of the mind. It also gave Europeans their first proper glimpse of a little-known country and aroused an intense fascination with ancient Egyptian culture, which created the field of Egyptology in Europe. A century and a half later, the Palestinian-American scholar Edward Said condemned the *Description of Egypt* as 'that great collective appropriation of one country by another', which formed the basis of the 'pernicious exercise in Western intellectual imperialism' that he criticized in his book *Orientalism*.[11]

So, Napoleon's great Egyptian campaign lasted just over three years, and ended not with the establishment of the large French colony and trading post and the ultimate ousting of the British from India envisaged by the emperor, but with the victory of the British–Ottoman alliance and the reinstatement of Ottoman control in Egypt, where Mamluk rule came to an end. But the impact of his occupation of Egypt on the Muslim world was powerful and led to fundamental social change, obliging the Muslim polity to acknowledge the urgent need to adopt western practices and technologies for their own survival. At this sixth turning point in the history of Christians and Muslims in Europe, the French cultural invasion of the Middle East reinforced a perceived Christian European supremacy over Islamic cultures in particular that would catalyse the relentless pursuit of colonialism by European powers.

Hybrid Communities: The Tidal Wave of Western Colonialism

Colonies are nothing new. The practice of gaining full or partial control over another country, occupying it with settlers and exploiting it economically started as far back as 1500 BC, when the Phoenicians, and later the Greeks, Romans and Arabs, all had trading colonies across the Mediterranean. The modern idea of colonialism began in the Age of Discovery with the Portuguese, who expanded their conquered territories, which were Christianized and plundered for their wealth. After 1492, the Portuguese and Spanish Empires became global and exploited their colonies in the Americas and the Far East, while England, France and the Netherlands gained territory worldwide in the sixteenth and seventeenth centuries, often in competition with each other. The Habsburg, Russian and Ottoman Empires continued to expand their dominions overland rather than overseas, by conquering neighbouring regions. What was unprecedented was the nineteenth-century invasion and colonization of most of Africa by western Europe, a process which divided up the continent among seven European countries, giving them a staggering 90 per cent control of Africa by the start of the First World War, which included the entirety of North Africa.

In 1827, the French consul Pierre Deval had an altercation regarding unpaid debts with the regent of Algiers, Hussein Dey, during which Hussein struck the consul with his flywhisk fan. This incident led to the French blockade of the port of Algiers for three years, after which, in 1830, the French army invaded and ousted the dey, who fled the capital, leaving the French in command, thereby ending over 300 years of Ottoman rule. Algeria remained a colony of France until 1848, when the largely Muslim country became a department of France itself. In 1881, the French also invaded Tunisia and established a protectorate there, and later the same happened in Morocco, which became a French protectorate in 1912, after a long military campaign, although Spain held certain strips of its territory at the same time. The term 'French North Africa' was adopted to describe three entirely different colonial regimes in separately governed Muslim territories. In the twentieth century, small Spanish colonies in North Africa also increased, while Libya became a colony of Fascist Italy in the Second World War. At the peak of the colonial era in the nineteenth century, Britain ended Mughal power and ruled Muslim-majority India, the Dutch commanded Muslim south-east Asia, including Java and Indonesia, and Spain ruled the Philippines, relegating Islam to the margins. Russia governed the Tatars of Crimea and was expanding eastwards into the Muslim lands of central Asia, where places that had been centres of Islamic civilization for twelve centuries became Russian colonies.

*

As western civilization spread globally, it came to scorn the great cultures and civilizations it confronted, and its progressive attitude seemed to disrespect the past, even if it was European. Faith in Christianity, which was part of western colonialism and spread by missionaries in a spiritual crusade, combined with or was superseded by a faith in western values and the material wealth of the West – piety and prosperity went hand in hand. The West was convinced of its superiority and aligned itself with the belief that history is the idea of Progress. At the same time, Christianity had been the original, defining model of western civilization, and while missionaries were often the fiercest critics of colonial powers, evangelizing zeal reinforced European imperialism, which could be defended because it upheld the conquests of the Cross. The *Edinburgh Review* of 1802 asserted that 'Europe is the light of the world, and the ark of knowledge.' It was a vision of Europe in which Muslims played no part.

An-Nahda: The Awakening

In 1801, the year the French evacuated Egypt, Rifaa al-Tahtawi was born in the Egyptian village of Tahta on the Nile; by the time he was sixteen, he had joined Al-Azhar, the foremost institution of Muslim learning in the Islamic world. Nine years later, in 1826, he was sent on an educational mission to Paris, in line with the contemporary tradition of sending Muslim students to study arts and sciences in western Europe. There, Rifaa wrote the first full description of modern France to be published in Arabic, and later translated into Turkish, which became famous across the Ottoman Empire. Its author also achieved great renown later in life and was known as the 'father of Egyptian identity'.

Once the Treaty of Amiens had been signed by Napoleon's brother Joseph Bonaparte and a British Army officer, Charles Cornwallis, in 1802, in an act that restored Egypt to the Ottoman Empire, Albanian-born Muhammad Ali Pasha became the Ottoman viceroy in Egypt from 1805 until 1849. He set about a programme of modernization to transform Egypt into a strong European-style state that would never again be subject to foreign rule. Ali Pasha successfully reformed the army using European military technology and ideas. He set up a printing press in Cairo that published European translations and Ottoman classics, and, for the first time in the Muslim world, he ordered the Koran to be typeset. Women were employed to spin yarn in the new factories, working veiled, as one of the earliest female workforces in Middle Eastern industry. His dramatic reforms and his purging of the final remnants of Mamluk power earned him a reputation as the founder of modern Egypt.

In 1766, an Egyptian of North African origin, Hassan al-Attar, was born in Cairo. He grew into a brilliant scholar, famed for his ability to memorize the Koran, and became a cleric at the renowned Al-Azhar institute. During Napoleon's occupation, he met the French scholars working at the Institut d'Égypte and was thrilled by his conversations with them though, as an imam, his enthusiasm for the philosophy of the infidel and admiration for their unexpected knowledge of Arabic culture and literature made him feel guilty. Hassan travelled to Istanbul to visit its libraries, and, enlightened by the discovery of his intellectual precursors al-Tusi, Avicenna and Ibn Khaldun, he studied astronomy, logic and mysticism, and went on to revive medieval Islamic learning. On his return to Cairo, he worked from his private house, instructing open-minded students, who became crucial to the modernization of Egypt's intellectual life, among whom was Rifaa al-Tahtawi. It was under these circumstances that the young scholar found himself in the land of the infidel, where, in his own words, every single thing was done differently.

Rifaa spent five years in France, reading the great writers of the day, including Voltaire, Montesquieu and Rousseau, who opened his eyes to a whole new world of ideas and experiences. He realized the need for the sciences and technologies of nineteenth-century Europe to be harnessed by the Islamic world and was a tireless advocate of the reconciliation of Islam with progressive ideas. On his return to Cairo, he ran several schools and set up a translation bureau at the Cairo School of Languages. A skilled translator himself, the movement he spearheaded enabled foreign thought to be read in Arabic, opening a window onto a world of knowledge that seemed to transcend the conflict between religions. Rifaa wrote books on political and moral philosophy that showed how European Enlightenment ideas such as secular authority, freedom and human rights had their roots in early Islam. He envisaged a world where there was cooperation rather than confrontation with foreign peoples and sought to bring together the tenets of Islam with European social principles, and to reconcile Christianity and Islam as a member of the *Nahda*, or Arab Enlightenment. Rifaa died in Cairo in 1873, a man of enlightened mind who left an important cultural legacy.

Other Muslim reformers strove to maintain the Islamic cultural identity and principles threatened by western colonial supremacy. The political activist Jamal al-Din al-Afghani (1839–97), born in Afghanistan, travelled through the Middle East, including Cairo, where he met one of his disciples, Muhammad Abduh (1849–1905), rector of Al-Azhar, who followed his lead in aspiring to reconcile Islam with modern European thought by encouraging Muslims to accept modern scientific advances as part of Allah's revelation. Al-Afghani continued to travel widely, preaching his radical views on reform, which advocated using the enemy and conqueror of Islam, the West, as a model to follow to enable the Muslim world to be liberated and reborn. He strongly criticized the prohibition of modern science by the conservative ulema, whom he saw as the true enemies of the faith.

*

Back in Europe, the Ottomans pursued a path laid by Sultan Selim III in the late eighteenth century, when he had updated his army with the latest French, Prussian and Russian advances, favoured European advisers and established the first permanent Ottoman embassies in Berlin, London, Paris and Vienna. In 1829, his cousin and second successor Sultan Mahmud II decreed that all civilians should wear a fez and western-style jackets; Mahmud was the first sultan who had a portrait of himself painted in this attire. After a series of military disasters, Mahmud decided the time had come to abolish the Janissaries, who rose up in understandable rebellion. The outcome was disastrous, as the 6,000-strong corps was slaughtered in less than thirty minutes. Mahmud also invested in telegraph technology and railways that centralized and improved government. But the Ottoman Empire was still unstable and under threat, this time from the eastern Balkan states, including Bulgaria and Macedonia, which revolted and fought for independence, inspired by the French and American revolutions. When Mahmud died of tuberculosis in 1839, his son Abdulmecid (r. 1839–61) made sweeping changes, the most significant being the granting of equality to all citizens of the empire, regardless of religion, in a move that did away with a social order that had lasted almost 600 years.[12]

From this time, the wide-ranging series of political and structural reforms known as the Tanzimat (1839–76) brought further changes, including the closure of the Istanbul slave market. This process of reorganization was symbolized by moving the sultan's official residence from the old Topkapı Palace built by Mehmed the Conqueror and overlooking the Golden Horn to a brand new European-style building, the Dolmabahçe Palace, along the Bosphorus. It was designed by an Armenian architect, Nikogos Balyan, with interior decoration by Charles Séchan, a painter and set designer who created the Paris Opéra. The Ottomans followed a similar pattern of secularization to that implemented by Muhammad Ali Pasha in Egypt, basing a new legal code on a French model that eliminated the need for recourse to sharia law for authority. Issues regarding the use of the veil, arranged marriages and women's visibility in public places were aligned with western values, amid pleas for an end to polygamy and for women's liberation and education.

European colonialism had created an unprecedented political and religious challenge to the Muslim world in so far as it upended a pattern of self-rule that had been in place since the time of the Prophet. Historically, despite wars, revolts and schisms, Islam had always remained triumphant, but its identity and social fabric now came under the threat of colonialism. A vast inversion of the power balance between the Muslim world and Europe had taken place, and despite the Muslim inclination to imitation and admiration of Enlightenment culture, the dominant note was of a conflict and competition that revived memories of the Crusades against Islam. This idea re-emerged in the rhetoric of war used by the French, who spoke of colonialism as the battle between the Cross and the Crescent, a clash symbolized by the French seizure of the Grand Mosque of Algiers and its conversion to the St Philippe Cathedral, flying the French cross on its minaret. Muslim responses to colonialism had ranged from outright rejection, to westernization, to Islamic modernism, the latter reflecting that ambivalence of attraction and repulsion that has distinguished relations between European Christians and Muslims down the centuries.

For all its reforms and endeavours of regeneration, the Ottoman Empire in Europe came under siege in the battle between the allied Turks, Britain and France against Russia in the Crimean War (1853–6), a mass slaughter which has been seen as a dress rehearsal for the First World War. New field reporting by journalists and the presence of photographers at the theatres of war graphically brought home the horror of the military engagement, provoked by Russian aggression mustered to protect the millions of Orthodox Christians in the Ottoman Empire. There were 750,000 fatalities, of which 450,000 were Russians, a total that left Russia burning for revenge on the Ottoman Empire, which Tsar Nicholas (r. 1825–55) described as 'the sick man of Europe'. Russia sought to replace the Ottoman Empire with a Christian kingdom, with Istanbul as centre of the Orthodox Church once more. But, far from being superseded, the Treaty of Paris, signed after the Crimean War in 1856, acknowledged the Ottoman Empire as an equal member among European states – the first time such an acknowledgement had been made in the 500 years that it had been part of the European continent. In revenge, the tsar expelled hundreds of thousands of Muslim Tatars from the Crimea, who fled to Ottoman lands.

This sixth turning point in the history of European Muslims and Christians was defined by invasion – military, political, cultural and religious – manifested in complex entanglements, disorder and inversion. The European pursuit of colonies had harnessed those basic tenets of the Enlightenment – faith and reason – to pursue its aims by means of conversion to Christianity, and via scientific discovery. The strong feelings expressed in the Egyptian al-Jabarti's description of the invasion of his country as 'the inversion of the innate and the elimination of the established; of horrors upon horrors and contradicting conditions; of the perversion of all precepts and the onset of annihilation' reflect an impact made by colonialism on the Muslim psyche that some historians see as dominating their subsequent history and affecting relations between Islam and western Europe to this day.[13] It redrew the map of the Middle East and imposed new leaders upon it, transforming the mutually beneficial trading relationships of the early modern era into bonds of economic exploitation that challenged the entire Muslim world view. Christian Europe's rationalization of its colonizing ambitions was bolstered by its incongruous impressions of Islam as both a threat and as a backward civilization. Even so, alongside the turmoil and upheaval in the Muslim world caused by the invasion of the Middle East, the close encounters with North Africa and with Ottoman civilization on the European continent ignited a lasting passion for oriental culture that found expression in the art, literature, music and material life of the Christian West.

Chapter 25

Travellers' Tales of the Orient: Colonial Contempt and the Allure of Islamic Culture

'The Orient is extraordinary . . . It escapes conventions, lies outside all disciplines, it transposes, it inverts everything.'

Eugène Fromentin, 1858

'If the grandeur of his ambition, the modesty of his means and the enormity of the result are the three criteria by which to measure man's genius, who could venture to compare as a human being any great man of modern history with Mahomet?'

Alphonse de Lamartine

The opulent frame strikes you at once. Its gilded calligraphy displays a garbled Arabic version of the motto of the Nasrid kingdom of Granada – *Wa la ghaliba illa-llah* (There is no conqueror but God) – on a crimson red ground that matches the colour of the Nasrid flag. Yet the painting inside the frame is not of Granada. Instead, it shows a Muslim man at prayer, set against the mountainous landscape of North Africa. He is standing, facing towards Mecca, in the *takhbir*, the first pose of the Muslim prayer ritual, in a state of calm, pious contemplation. The desert dweller appears detached from the viewer, the colours of his clothing merging with those of the natural landscape, his gaze fixed on things beyond our field of vision. Whether by chance or design, the reverent words of the Nasrid motto link the Islamic emirate of Granada to a Levantine Muslim worshipper making a gesture of submission to a higher power, aligning the medieval western Islamic emirate with its modern North African counterparts.

This compelling image was painted in the early twentieth century by a Parisian artist, Alphonse-Étienne Dinet (1861–1929), founder of the Society for French Orientalist Painters, whose purpose was to foster the depiction or imitation of the eastern world by western artists, and encourage French painters to travel to the Islamic lands of the East. After two trips to Algeria, in 1884 and 1885, when it was still under French colonial control, Dinet was sufficiently beguiled by the place to buy a house in Bou Saâda, in the foothills of the Saharan Atlas Mountains, where he lived for three quarters of each year. He became so enamoured of life in North Africa that he converted to Islam and changed his name to Nasreddine Dinet. Despite the colonial backdrop to his sojourns in Muslim lands, Dinet's portrait *Prayer* goes against the grain of conventional orientalism as it was seen through colonial eyes. The painting is an image of respect for and understanding of Islam on Dinet's part that contradicts nineteenth- and early twentieth-century western European views of Muslims as different and alien, and implies a more widespread, complex and sympathetic appreciation of Islamic culture at that time.

Complexity was the keynote of nineteenth-century encounters between western Christians and Muslims both inside and outside Europe. It arose from a series of connections that involved potent social and political forces, movements and perceptions that were remoulding human societies in Europe and in other parts of the Islamic world. Such upheavals were triggered by far-reaching transformations – the scientific approach of the Enlightenment, the Industrial Revolution, the rise of colonies, orientalism and its kindred Romanticism, and the evolving nature of world travel. A global continuum dominated by mobility and fluidity came into being in which established orders were upended as places real and imagined were recast and remodelled. As the order changed, and the relationship between the peoples of Islamic and Christian Europe and the Near East shifted, geographical sites of special fascination came into focus, outside and inside the European continent, which crystallized many crucial issues of the century that preceded the great World Wars.

Beyond Europe: Egypt and Colonial North Africa Under the Gaze of Orientalism

When the Egyptian scholar and reformer Rifaa al-Tahtawi recorded his experiences of living in Paris for five years in his book *An Imam in Paris*, he was deeply impressed with French cutting-edge science and technology, and was convinced the Islamic world needed to wake up and take note. When he returned to Cairo, a vital part of his work was to introduce the vocabulary of western progress and civilization into the Arabic language. He translated the word 'civilization' into the Arabic equivalent *tammadun*, from the word meaning a city, and was the first Arab to use the word *jumhuriyya*, meaning 'republic', as well as coining an equivalent term, *watan*, for 'nation'.[1] In this way, Rifaa began to incorporate key western ideas into everyday language in order to popularize new areas of knowledge he felt would befit Egypt and revitalize it.

His enlightened view of Islamic society was not shared by much of the nineteenth-century western world, who saw it as exotic and erotic, as well as frightening, inferior and unprogressive. Yet, in a world in thrall to but also alienated by the Industrial Revolution, the fantasy of escaping to the Orient began to appeal more and more to modern European bourgeois society. In the imagination, it seemed a place for adventurers, either seeking the thrill of military action, sexual freedom or the promise of scientific exploration. Such western European exploits often involved crossing racial and religious barriers by assuming a new Muslim identity that involved both physical disguise and a convincing knowledge of Islam and Muslim culture. One of the first westerners to study Arabia in the 1800s was the Finnish orientalist Georg Wallin (1811–1852), who travelled to Cairo in 1843 and then to Mecca in 1845, dressed as a Muslim and using the name Abd al-Wali. It was said that he later converted to Islam. Mecca was a city forbidden to non-Muslims, but neither Wallin nor the British Nile explorer and polymath Richard Burton (1821–1890) were deterred. Burton travelled to Mecca in 1853 disguised as a Muslim pilgrim, and, ten years later, the Hungarian traveller Arminius

Vámbéry (1832–1913) ventured from Istanbul across central Iran to Khorezm, in central Asia, in the guise of a dervish.

The deeper engagement of western Europeans with Muslim lands flourished in the wake of the changing nature of travel. The long-standing concept of travel as a quest for knowledge or scholarly study, its importance in trade and diplomacy, and its role in pilgrimage all continued in various forms, to which was added the enterprise of travel for leisure and entertainment. The western political environment fostered the commercial aspirations of France and Britain, the two principal colonists of North Africa and the Middle East, as the settlement of the Greek War of Independence in 1829 and extensive reforms inside the Ottoman Empire fuelled significant investment in international infrastructures for improved communication, including the opening of the Suez Canal in 1869 and the growth of railways. It was precisely the industrialization that had been instrumental in provoking the escapist dreams of western travellers that in fact allowed them to make their ambitions a reality.

New railway routes enabled young men, and sometimes women, from the European upper classes, along with artists and writers, to undertake a traditional rite of passage, the grand tour, an educational trip to the great cultural sites of continental Europe to seek the legacy of classical civilization and the Renaissance. They recounted their experiences in travelogues and sensational tales which inspired a western attraction for all things foreign. The grand tour, now seen as the start of modern tourism, had begun as early as the seventeenth century, and usually took in France, Germany, Switzerland and Italy. Now, it included not only Spain, but also the Middle East. The Orient became a vacation destination, and the English businessman Thomas Cook (1808–92) saw an opportunity in the growth of rail travel and opened his travel agency, which started organized, affordable tours in those regions. Gertrude Bell (1868–1926), the English archaeologist and writer, travelled to Arabia and recorded the presence of tourists even in remote towns, where she observed them bargaining for imitation Bedouin knives. Bell was a convinced colonialist who held a strong conviction of the necessity of British imperial rule in Muslim lands, based on their perceived inferiority to western culture, although she later supported their independence. She was not alone in her initial opinions, yet the revelation of eastern Islamic lands to the western mind was fraught with paradox. Despite their supposed backwardness, the fascination with both their material and intangible culture attracted people of the Romantic disposition and found expression in an imitation or presentation of the oriental world in art, literature and architecture that focused on the perceived differences between eastern and western civilizations.

*

The appropriation of Egyptian artefacts by Europeans had begun in the early nineteenth century, soon after Napoleon's brief jurisdiction. Many Egyptian sculptures and obelisks were removed from the Nile temples and sent to Europe, along with anything else transportable. The Italian explorer and archaeologist Gentile Belzoni was famed, or notorious, for succeeding in looting the colossal seven-ton bust of the Egyptian pharaoh Ramses II and shipping it to England, where it is still on display in the British Museum. Soon, Egyptian-style buildings, tombs and obelisks began appearing in various European countries, and the style of Egyptian and Islamic architecture was adapted for public buildings such as theatres and, later, cinemas. In 1851, Muslim culture came to the United Kingdom in the form of the Great Exhibition, the first of its kind in the world, a spectacular display where six million visitors to London could see examples of Islamic design. Goods from the Muslim world, mostly consisting of textiles and dyes from Persia, Algeria, Tunisia and Turkey, were on display. Three years later, Owen Jones, who was superintendent of works for the London exhibition, tuned in to contemporary trends and recreated the Alhambra of Granada's Court of the Lions in the London suburb of Sydenham. The Paris Exhibition of 1867 followed, where many Muslim countries were represented, among them the Ottoman Empire, Egypt and Tunisia.

The writers and artists of the Christian west constructed the Muslim east at this time as an entity that shrouded itself in a veil or disguised itself behind an impenetrable mask. As they travelled in antique lands, they stepped into a vast visual spectacle, a colourful and vibrant carnival of mysterious figures who inhabited a place both strange yet familiar, which they watched always as outsiders, excluded from the secrets and magic of the oriental spirit. Poets and novelists from the colonizing lands of Napoleon and Nelson eagerly boarded ships bound for Egypt and its environs, harbouring fears that the reality of the Orient might not match up to the foreign paradise of their imaginations. On arrival, in a mirror image of Rifaa al-Tahtawi's first impressions of France, they were confronted with a world where all that was familiar and stable was upturned, transposed and inverted, as Eugène Fromentin declared in the epigraph above.

The new generation of French writers who immersed themselves in oriental culture were also shaped by the artistic and intellectual movement of Romanticism, in part a reaction against modernity and the excessively scientific approach of the Enlightenment. The Romantics' disdain for extreme materialism and environmental destruction went hand in hand with an obsession with the heroic and sublime, with the mysterious and exotic, that generated imaginary evocations of the East in verse and prose and the often intensely charged narratives of travellers to the Orient. One inspiration had been François-René de Châteaubriand's travelogue *Journey from Paris to Jerusalem* (*Itinéraire de Paris à Jérusalem*), published in 1811. In it, the author writes as a pilgrim searching for traces of ancient civilizations in a present reality he largely ignores. The poet Gérard de Nerval and the novelist Gustave Flaubert, among many others, followed in his footsteps, but often as pilgrims of a different kind, come to worship at the shrine of sensual indulgence. Flaubert travelled to Egypt in 1849 in hope of discovering his true self, immersing himself in erotic delights and extreme experiences. He wrote to his mother that he loved the desert: 'We've spent the last six nights under a tent, living with Bedouins . . . eating turtledoves . . . and drinking buffalo milk'.[2] The highlight of his visit, the Al-Azhar Mosque in Cairo, was second only to his trip to the convent of dervishes, where he was captivated by the sight of an ecstatic monk rolling on the ground, dagger in hand.[3]

Flaubert's detailed descriptions of his sexual exploits as he travelled south of Cairo confirmed the unconstrained nature of sexual relations admired and desired by western male travellers. The harem and its pleasures also caught the eye of French and British artists who made the trip to Arabia, and it became a familiar subject for their art, alongside landscapes of ancient archaeological sites, the river Nile, the Holy Land and biblical scenes, the desert and its caravans, the bustle of cities and souks, and the religious manifestations of Islam. The sights and subjects of what became known as orientalism found perhaps their fullest expression in visual arts, where the new idea of the picturesque, combining beauty and sublimity, and the burgeoning scientific and historical interest in exploration that demanded accuracy of depiction, merged in a body of art that shaped public expectations of the Islamic world as a place of heightened drama and intense colour. The same sense of a world of theatrical illusion described by orientalist writers also bewitched western visual artists. The French painter Paul Marie Lenoir (b. 1841) described his arrival in Messina as raising a stage curtain on the great magical spectacle that is a journey to the Orient (*'lever du rideau de cette grande féerie qu'on appelle un voyage en Orient'*[4]). Alongside the drama and theatricality of life in the souks, harems and caravans of the Near East was a more peaceful, pastoral life in the Arab villages. There, artists such as Gustave Guillaumet, who spent a long time in remote southern Algeria, sensed an ancient biblical feel to those settlements which brought welcome relief from the pressures of western progress.

In the paintings of these artists, flamboyant fantasies of the seraglio vied with detailed architectural drawings of ancient ruins, each respective responses to the drive for scientific exploration and the desire to find personal freedom from the constraints of western European society. Converging with these subjects was a deeper seam of exploration into biblical and Islamic themes. This was in part a seeking after Christian truth in a concrete, observable reality, based on an assumption that life in the Near East had changed little since biblical times. Artists saw living images of Bible scenes in daily life – in Tissot's *The Annunciation*, the Virgin is barely visible beneath her Arab costume, outlined against an exotic setting. The urge to seek firm answers to religious questions was a burning issue in western Christendom, where the authority of the Bible had been seriously called into question by the publication of Darwin's *On the Origin of Species* in 1859, a work that confuted the account of Creation written in the first book of the Bible, Genesis, and which epitomized the gap between faith and the tenets of contemporary science.[5]

At the same time, there was a growing sympathy for Islam in the west, despite a prevalent view that the Muslim faith was bigoted, superstitious, immoral and corrupt. The paintings of orientalist artists refute those claims and confound the perception that their work showed an essentially colonialist relationship between Christians and Muslims. Their subjects were Muslims at prayer, in the mosque, at a tomb, on the pilgrims' caravan to Mecca. Jean-Léon Gérôme's beautiful *Prayer in the Mosque of 'Amr* (c. 1872) is a masterpiece of architectural draughtsmanship, but it is also a solemn and respectful religious declaration of the power of Islam. Gustav Deutsch's work *The Prayer at the Tomb* (1898), showing a Muslim paying his respects at a sepulchre, conveys profound solemnity, dignity and deference. These and many others like them are not depictions of colonial superiority or disdain, but show a powerful desire to understand the Islamic faith and its rituals that moves beyond prejudice.

Orientalism has suffered from very negative implications since Edward Said published his critique *Orientalism* in 1978. The meaning of the word originally referred to scholarly interest in the language, history and culture of the Islamic world, but by the nineteenth century it had come to signify the study of the oriental world in the service of imperialism, where perceived eastern backwardness was contrasted with progress, autocracy with liberal politics, servitude with liberty. Under the lens of colonialism, the depiction of ancient ruins decried the inherent deterioration of eastern culture, and orientalist art and writing was seen ultimately as a patronizing statement made by a superior power. Quite contrary to this view, the Orient often served as a great inspiration to those western travellers to Muslim territories abroad, whose art and writing suggest a far more complex, ambiguous dialogue and exchange of ideas and beliefs. Their engagement with the Muslim culture of the east lends a much more positive meaning to orientalism, as it emerged through not solely scientific but also creative exploration, which challenged the colonial gaze and probed issues of religious and cultural ambiguity and identity.

Inside Europe: The Eastern Islamic Lands of Kostantiniyye and the Balkans

The Islamic world inside Europe exerted an equal fascination upon western travellers. There were important differences in comparison with the Levantine Orient – Turkey and the Balkans were not colonized by Christian Europeans but ruled by the Ottomans, although there was an increasing awareness of a dying cadence in the eastern realms as western Europe gained the whip-hand. Kostantiniyye, or Istanbul, remained entrancing for the west, and the Balkan states, still unknown and mysterious to most western Europeans, were increasingly explored by intrepid travellers in the nineteenth century. There had been travellers' tales from the Ottoman Empire from the time of the Crusades, and by the seventeenth and eighteenth centuries, British commercial interests in the area involved frequent visits to Kostantiniyye. In Lady Mary Wortley Montagu's famed *Turkish Letters* of 1763, she described her travels through Serbia and Bulgaria en route to the Ottoman capital, where her husband was ambassador. By the end of the eighteenth century, both Kostantiniyye and the Balkans had become destinations in their own right for western continentals.

'A languid eye, a thrilling hand': Kostantiniyye the Enchantress

The exchanges between western and eastern Europe proved rich and promising and were strengthened by civil engineering breakthroughs. Buoyed by his recent victory over Russia and the modernizing reforms of the Tanzimat, in 1867 Abdulaziz I undertook what was the first visit of an Ottoman sultan to western Europe, taking in well over a dozen cities, including Vienna, Paris, where he saw the Universal Exhibition, and London. He travelled in a railway carriage lavishly appointed in blue and gold, which had been built by the Metropolitan Carriage and Wagon Company in Birmingham. In London, he met the Prince of Wales and the Queen and was invested as a Knight of the Garter. Two years later, the sultan was visited by several western European monarchs who were travelling to the opening of the Suez Canal, and Britain's Prince of Wales twice toured Kostantiniyye. Trade as well as diplomacy flourished between the Christian west and Muslim east, and prevailed over internal trade, as modern roads replaced caravan trails, and railways linked ports like Jaffa and Beirut to the European continent. Sea ports old and new connected key cities and became hubs for commerce in merchandise and raw materials. Geographical sites were being reconfigured by the technological developments of the Industrial Revolution, opening up new vistas and realizations north, south, east and west of the European continent.

At the very end of the eighteenth century, the Dutch philosopher and interior designer Thomas Hope went on a grand tour that lasted eight years, during which he travelled through Europe, Asia and Africa, including Kostantiniyye. His favourite portrait of himself was painted some years later, wearing Turkish costume, with a waistcoat embroidered in Arabic, and with a mosque in the background. Hope was captivated by the Ottoman capital and created over 350 exquisite drawings, not just of buildings and the daily life in its markets and coffee shops, but also of local costumes. His visual recordings of Ottoman dress provided invaluable insights into life in Kostantiniyye and formed part of the tradition of the pictorial category of costume books, colourful albums produced by European and Ottoman artists for both western and eastern audiences, which inspired the orientalist craze for wearing Turkish dress, but which also presented vivid images of a fundamentally multicultural society. A varied pageant of peoples posed in costumes that reflected their culture, ethnicity or religion – Muslim dervishes, Jews, Turks, Greek monks, Venetian women, Arab merchants, Persian men about town, European ambassadors. They debunked western myths of an unvarying Muslim east, instead revealing its profuse multitude of cultural identities.

The English Romantic poet Lord Byron (1788–1824) also travelled extensively in eastern Europe, from 1816 to 1824, bringing his dramatic and vividly recollected scenes of Istanbul into the English drawing room. Poetic tales of Ottoman pirates, the slave market and the 'languid eye' and 'thrilling hand' of the harem were potently evoked in his classic narrative poem *Childe Harold's Pilgrimage*. Byron, heroic and swashbuckling, was widely read and his descriptions of the Ottoman capital were incredibly popular. His poetry books, printed with illustrations and engravings of Istanbul, were available on the mass market, and began to shape lasting western ideas of the exoticism of the city. Nearly thirty years later, in 1852, the French writer Théophile Gautier also visited Istanbul, writing an account of his impressions of the city in his travelogue *Constantinople*. In the same way that Flaubert, Nerval and Fromentin had dramatized Cairo in their writing, Gautier presented Istanbul as a mirage or dream, a fantastical opera performance. The city was intriguing and inscrutable, an alien and at times shocking place, whose real nature escaped his comprehension. The orientalist aura of both Gautier's and Byron's interpretations of Ottoman life, along with those of other Romantic writers, reinforced and promoted the sense of an unbridgeable gap between western Christendom and eastern Islamic Europe.

*

In Victor Hugo's house in the Place des Vosges in Paris, there is a small desk displaying four inkwells, a donation from the author to a children's charity. The inkwells belonged to, and united, the great French writers of the day, Alphonse de Lamartine, Alexandre Dumas, George Sand and Hugo himself. At a time when the well-known British Arabist and historian of Islam, Sir William Muir, had recently written an article, 'The Mohammedan Controversy', describing the Christian west's hostility to Islam as 'the only undisguised and formidable antagonist of Christianity', Hugo had praised the Prophet Muhammad in his poetry collection *The Legend of the Centuries* (*La légende des siècles*) (1859–83) and Dumas had written of the 'genius of Mahomet' in his travelogue *Diary of a Journey to Arabia* (*Journal d'un voyage en Arabie*) of 1891.[6] Their admiration for Islam was echoed by other French writers, including Auguste Comte, Stéphane Mallarmé and Jules Verne, who wrote a poem entitled 'The Koran'. They took their lead from the oldest of their generation, Alphonse de Lamartine (1790–1869), a friend of Hugo, who was one of the most ardent and unexpected advocates of Islam in western Europe. Poet and politician, Lamartine was a royalist nobleman who became a left-winger, a European imperialist who later espoused anti-colonialism, and a staunch Catholic who extolled the founder of Islam.

Lamartine first travelled to the East in 1832, on a trip through Greece, Palestine, Syria, Lebanon and Constantinople, where he was dazzled by the Ottoman capital and stayed for several weeks. Appalled by the violence associated with the colonization of Algeria, Lamartine abandoned his advocacy for colonialism and began to defend the Ottomans, and all Muslims, whose religious tolerance he praised in his travel account *Voyage en Orient*: 'Mahometanism is capable of entering, effortlessly and painlessly into a system of religious and civil liberties; . . . it is accustomed to living in peace and harmony alongside Christian faiths'.[7] In 1854, he published an eight-volume history of Turkey, *Histoire de la Turquie*, one volume of which was devoted entirely to the life of Muhammad. It was translated into Arabic and is a work little known today outside the Muslim world, yet it contains what must be one of the most compelling eulogies of the Prophet ever made by a non-Muslim. It concludes: 'Philosopher, orator, apostle, legislator, warrior, conqueror of ideas, restorer of rational dogmas, of a cult without images; the founder of twenty terrestrial empires and of one spiritual empire, that is Mahomet. As regards all standards by which human greatness may be measured, we may well ask, is there any man greater than he?'[8]

At the end of his political life as minister for foreign affairs, Lamartine was deep in debt and envisaged emigrating to Turkey to end his days there. He wrote a letter to Sultan Abdulmecid asking if he might purchase a plot of land near Smyrna. Sadly, despite being granted his wish, he failed to raise the capital to make the sale and died in Paris some years later. Lamartine and those other French writers inspired by Islam lived at a time when they could still freely express their esteem for the Muslim way of life. Lamartine in particular saw beyond the surface glamour and distancing strangeness beloved of orientalism to find equivalences between the multicultural world of the Ottoman Empire and his own country, which he declared was also a mix of 'races, blood types, languages, mores, legislations and religions', a diversity he believed was shared with the Muslim lands of eastern Europe.

*

The nineteenth century saw increasing numbers of western travellers to the Ottoman Balkans, regions that had a reputation for wildness and barbarity, as the British explorer Harry de Windt confirmed in his narrative of a journey through the Balkans and eastern Russia, *Through Savage Europe*, published in 1907. In 1809, Byron and his friend John Hobhouse had ventured into Albania, where the first thing they saw was a severed arm hanging from a tree. The scholarly and scientific travel accounts were a sharp contrast with Byron's narratives of these adventures, in which he wrote of the rugged beauty of the landscape, his fascination with its culture and its complexity under Ottoman rule. As with Istanbul, Byron's tales from Albania created its romantic image in western Europe, one which dwelt on its folklore and superstitions. Romantic writers admired the ferocity of the Balkan mountain dwellers and started a movement of support for specific Balkan nations against the Ottomans, often fighting on their behalf and dressing up in the relevant Balkan costume. Such partisans were not only men – in 1900, when she was thirty-seven, a British artist and anthropologist, Edith Durham, sailed down the Adriatic coast and into the Albanian highlands, where she found an opportunity to engage politically by championing the Albanian cause in the twentieth century.

In his account *Studies of Albania* (*Albanesische Studien*) of 1854, the Austrian diplomat and specialist in Albanian history, language and culture Johann Georg von Hahn favoured observations on Islam and Christianity over exoticism and politics. As he travelled in the region of Gjirokastra, he noticed the strict isolation between groups of Greek Christians and Albanian Muslims, both of whom only married within their own communities. In the area of Elbasan, then inaccessible by rail, he remarked on the progress made there by Islam, to the detriment of the Catholic and Orthodox Churches. The town of Elbasan itself had 2,000 Muslim and 200 Christian houses, along with resident gypsies who professed Islam and worked as blacksmiths. He recalled a local anecdote about Thomas, a poor Christian tobacco cutter, who set up shop in the bazaar. Thomas was unaware of the warning sent out that the shops of Christian merchants were to be plundered by Muslims, and he carried on selling his wares. The Muslims duly turned up and hanged him on the spot. Hahn's travel narrative recorded overall a Muslim majority who in odd instances lived harmoniously with Christians, while both groups mostly existed in a state of segregated hostility which manifested itself in petty crimes, revenge, feuds and murder. Hahn's work, and other reports of travellers from the west, contributed to a growing knowledge and awareness of the political and religious climate of the mountainous Balkans in those European countries outside the Ottoman Empire, and enlisted their sympathies as those regions in thrall to Turkish rule began to fight for independence and the creation of a new Balkan identity.

Inside Europe: The Outsider's Gaze on Western Europe's Islamic Past

Spain had not initially been part of the grand tour, but in the nineteenth century that all changed – suddenly it was the place to visit, and Granada became the high point of the experience. A view arose of a romantic city elevated in the imagination of outsiders to the paragon of a place whose past was plainly visible in its ruined monuments, a past which had more value and interest than its present or future. Unlike either North Africa, the Middle East or Istanbul, Granada held the charm of an ancient paradise now lost, and it led the first early tourists to Andalusia. Among them was Wilhelm von Humboldt, founder of the University of Berlin, who travelled to Spain with his wife Caroline, and arrived in Granada in the middle of February 1800. Humboldt was keenly aware of the otherness of the place, and his precise, factual account at times expressed a dislike of what he saw. The Court of the Lions in the Alhambra was not to his taste, typically Arabic, but 'decidedly not beautiful'. Humboldt's words would find an echo in the observation of Walter Gropius, founder of the Bauhaus school of architecture, who likened the structure of the Alhambra patios to a campaign tent whose hanging carpets were the intermediate arches and the pillars the tent poles. It was the style, he declared, of a nomad people in a country of burning heat. The British baronet Sir Arthur de Capell Brooke expressed a rather different view in his *Sketches in Spain and Morocco* of 1831, which affirmed the city's international fame at that time: 'Who has not heard of Granada, and does not long to climb its mountain barriers and visit this romantic city, once the last refuge of an enlightened and high-minded people, who . . . reached that height of civilization so remarkable when contrasted with the barbarism of the rest of Europe . . .'[9] What interested him most was the nature of the Granadan Muslims, whom he considered to be culturally superior to other Europeans, and also the difference between the Catholic Spain of his time and its Muslim past, a contrast about which he was scathing: 'It is true that Christianity has taken the place of the religion of Mahomet; but how much lower on the animal scale does the bigoted Spaniard of the present day appear when compared with the enlightened and liberal Mussulman of former ages!'[10] He was not the only traveller to Granada at this time who criticized contemporary Spanish Catholicism, to the extent that, rightly or wrongly, the Alhambra came to symbolize racial and religious tolerance, and to express medieval culture's highest degree of civilization.

The Alhambra also became the focus of an extraordinary polemic on the Islamic roots of Gothic architecture. Sir Christopher Wren had set out his theory of the Saracen origins of Gothic style, the crucial feature being the pointed arch, which he believed the crusaders had brought to Europe from Jerusalem. Around 1800, as more European travellers explored Spain, a debate arose surrounding the idea that the origin of Gothic lay in the Spanish Muslim kingdoms, and not the Near East. British visitors went to Spain with that preconception and searched for evidence of the theory in the Muslim architecture of Andalusia, and of Granada specifically. When the Scottish painter David Roberts returned to London with a portfolio filled with sketches, among them were several views of a 'Gothicized' Alhambra. The perception of the Moorish palace as a source of Gothic inspiration was far-reaching. At the Great Exhibition of 1851, a design for stained-glass windows featured an inner area decorated with Christian symbols as well as acanthus motifs that echoed not only Roman, but also Nasrid style, with borders embellished with ornamental patterns inspired by the Alhambra. It was a triumphant cultural exchange between east and west in glass and stone.

Another British traveller, Richard Ford (1796–1858), stayed in the city during the summers of 1831 and 1833. Ford's account of his time there is a masterpiece of travel writing from a privileged position as a resident of the Alhambra, where the governor lent him a suite of rooms in the palace. Ford rekindled the image of the province of Granada as a paradise, divided by its wealth-bringing river water, like a Rubicon, from the desert beyond the *vega*, green and fruitful while all beyond is barren and tawny. His descriptions of its geography abound in intense contrasts; it is a place where, he says, eternal snow and the blood-heat of Africa mingle. He also voiced strong opinions about the history and society of Granada: 'Under the Moors, Granada was rich, brilliant, learned, industrious and gallant and now it is poor, dull, ignorant, indolent and dastardly. The Spaniards have indeed laboured hard to neutralize the gifts of a lavish nature, and to dwarf this once proud capital down to a paralysed provincial town.'[11] Although his overall perspective was a Christian one, he condemned Philip III's expulsion of the Moriscos as a great crime, rather than a great glory. But on entering the Alhambra site, the traveller, Ford affirmed, came under 'the magical jurisdiction of this fairy palace', despite its neglected and ruinous condition, a prolonged degradation dating, in his view, from 2 January 1492, when the Catholic Monarchs ordained the whitewashing of walls to remove Moorish symbols.[12]

Théophile Gautier, the French writer, also visited Granada and certainly had a more optimistic perspective on the city. Like Ford, Gautier saw a paradise in Granada: 'This mixture of water, snow and fire renders the Granadan climate unparalleled throughout the world, and makes Granada a real terrestrial paradise.'[13] The Generalife gardens delighted him most of all, with their overwhelming perfume of aromatic plants, all irrigated by the ever-present running water. The Arab skill in hydraulics was a sign to Gautier of the most advanced state of civilization, and he claimed that the sophisticated irrigation system in the city had created its reputation as the Paradise of Spain.[14]

The Alhambra became picturesque, poetic in its dereliction. The New Yorker Washington Irving (1783–1859), considered the first American Hispanist, is famous for intensifying the romantic image of Granada and the Alhambra adopted by nineteenth-century travellers. To him, as to other travellers, it was a sacred place: 'To the traveller imbued with a feeling for the historical and poetical, the Alhambra of Granada is an object of veneration as is the Kaaba or sacred house of Mecca to all true Moslem pilgrims'.[15] Granada and its famous palace had become a paradise of the mind and a unique destination for those who hoped to find or rediscover a lost Eden there. Nineteenth-century western perceptions of the last Islamic emirate in Spain bore little resemblance to those of its Muslim colonial territories, where a sense of triumph and cultural superiority tended to prevail, nor to those of the Ottoman Empire, admired but still feared. Instead, there was a surprising sense of nostalgia, mingled with deep admiration for the peerless Islamic culture seemingly lost to western Europe.

Part Six

THE ECLIPSE AND REASCENDANCY OF THE STAR AND CRESCENT

'Abdul Hamid II, le sultan rouge', c. 1900. Auguste Roubille

Chapter 26

A Fading Glory: The Vanquishing of the Ottoman Empire

'One of the most important, most visionary and most strategic-minded individuals to make his mark in the last one hundred and fifty years'

Recep Erdoğan on Sultan Abdul Hamid II

'One day the great European war will come out of some damned foolish thing in the Balkans.'

Otto von Bismarck, 1888

The World's Desire, the Abode of Felicity – that diamond set between two sapphires and two emeralds that Osman saw in a dream – was heading for decline and disaster. The 600-year-old Muslim empire of the Ottomans with its European capital in Kostantiniyye and a global reach found itself in thrall to potent forces outside its control. Across the European continent of the nineteenth and early twentieth centuries, the rage for progress and modernization, the rise of nationalism, fascism and ultimately world war determined the demise of a famous empire and the decline of Islamic power in Europe. It was a matter of destiny, a colossal shift in the power structures of society and politics that manifested itself in fissures, fault lines and crumbling traditions, reconfiguring the religious landscape and turning Europe's Muslim population into a minority group of exiles and migrants.

The Red Sultan: Reform and Regression in the Reign of Abdul Hamid II

On 31 August 1876, the thirty-fourth sultan of the Ottoman Empire, Abdul Hamid II, rode virtually unattended to the Eyüp Sultan

Mosque, where he was presented with the Sword of Osman, the ceremonial weapon marking the enthronement of a new sovereign. His accession followed the overthrow of his brother Murad V and led to an absolute monarchy that lasted three decades, until his own deposition in 1909. His ambivalent legacy is reflected in the twenty-first century Turkish president Erdoğan's view of him as visionary and strategic-minded, and his contrasting image in twentieth-century western Europe as the Red Sultan, the man responsible for the horrific slaughter of 300,000 Armenian people in the Hamidian massacres of 1893. Abdul Hamid was urbane and well educated, a lover of fine champagne who spoke French fluently and admired western European classical music and comic opera.[1] He was also a devout Muslim who sought ways to save the Ottoman Empire and reconcile modernity with Islam. At once progressive and brutal, he presided over an era of unparalleled decline in Ottoman power, as the empire was ravaged by conflicts in the Balkans and a serious war with the Russian Empire, leaving it diminished by the loss of large swathes of territory.

In a drive to modernize the Ottoman polity, the new sultan built on the reforms begun with the Tanzimat earlier in the nineteenth century, resulting in a more up-to-date conscripted army, improved banking systems, the legitimizing of homosexuality and the replacement of religious law with secular law. Abdul Hamid's most extensive improvements were in education, with the creation of professional schools for law, arts, trades, science and farming, as well as primary, secondary and military schools across the empire. Yet this expansion created a simmering antagonism, as the Christian population began to acquire a higher general educational level than the Muslim majority, who devoted much of their education to learning Arabic and Islamic theology. Despite such widespread and enlightened reorientation, Abdul Hamid had inherited severe financial difficulties when he came to the throne. The Ottoman government was still reeling from the mass immigration into their realms of some 200,000 Crimean Tatars displaced after the Crimean War (1853–56), along with over half a million Circassians ethnically cleansed and exiled from the Caucasus. In 1875, the Ottoman state had declared bankruptcy due to the rising debts incurred to cope with the huge increase in population.

On the political front, Abdul Hamid supported the Young Ottomans, the intellectuals who wanted to take the Tanzimat reforms further and establish a modern western-European-style constitutional government that incorporated Islamic elements. The sultan had to deal with the negative backlash from the rest of Europe over the Ottoman government's brutal response to the nationalist uprisings in some of the Balkan states in 1875. Many Muslims were massacred in Bosnia, Herzegovina, Montenegro and Bulgaria, and the Ottomans had retaliated by slaughtering tens of thousands of Bulgarians in April 1876, just months before Abdul Hamid became sultan. As a result, and by way of showing his liberal thinking, he enforced a constitution and a parliament in December of that year, leading to the first ever Ottoman election in 1877. But events conspired to turn Abdul Hamid from liberal reformer to dictator. In February 1878, the Ottoman armies were defeated by Russia in a major military encounter. Soon after, in the small village of San Stefano near Kostantiniyye, a treaty was signed in which the Ottoman Empire was obliged by Russia to give autonomy to Bulgaria and independence to Serbia and Montenegro.

At the conclusion of the war, Abdul Hamid dissolved parliament after just one session and instigated a dictatorship that lasted for the next thirty years. Believing Islam was the only way to unite the diverse peoples of his empire, he promoted a new ideology, pan-Islamism, which encouraged Muslims in Europe to unite under one political system. The reform endeavour continued with its focus on education, and, in 1900, what would become Istanbul University was founded. In the twelve years between 1882 and 1894, over fifty secondary schools were built in a move to conquer any foreign influence, although western European teaching techniques were still used to promote Islamic morality and a sense of Ottoman identity in their pupils. Yet the drive for progress was countered by an equal force of political regression which gained Abdul Hamid a reputation as the bogeyman of Europe. He quelled the rebellion of Armenian revolutionary groups against the Ottoman Empire in the last decade of the nineteenth century in the most savage terms. From 1894 until 1896, between 100,000 and 300,000 Armenians living in Ottoman territories were exterminated by the state, provoking horrified reactions in western Europe, where Abdul Hamid appeared in political cartoons with blood dripping from his hands. In 1905, the sultan narrowly avoided assassination by a car bomb set by the Armenian Revolutionary Federation in an act of revenge that misfired when the bomb exploded early, killing twenty-six civilians. Just three years later, in 1908, he was deposed in a coup masterminded by the group of intellectuals known as the Young Turks, who had been educated at the very institutions the sultan had sponsored. He was succeeded by his half-brother, who was enthroned as Sultan Mehmed V.

Fragmentation and Despair: The Fervour for Nationalism and the First Balkan Wars

The Balkans are only a couple of hundred years old. Before that, their territories were called 'Rumeli', Roman lands ruled by the Ottomans since the conquest of Constantinople in 1453. Many of the European subjects of the Turkish empire were Orthodox Christians, peoples who hailed from a civilization quite different from western Europe and spoke languages other than Latin and Germanic tongues – Ottoman Turkish, Albanian, Tatar, Arabic, Ladino, Romani. Their geography, too, looked more eastwards than westwards, in a region focused on the river Danube and sheltered by mountains and forests. The Balkans had embodied the inherent uniqueness of Europe in the east, even before its centuries of Ottoman rule. Its inhabitants were frontier settlers in a land of frequent warfare, and as Christians under Muslim domination they led lives in a zone of cultural transition between Europe and Asia quite unlike those of western Europeans. These were multilingual, complex Muslim societies who lived among equally heterogeneous groups of Christians and Jews.

The big change had come in the hundred years between 1815

and 1919, when the map of Europe was redrawn as the concept of nationalism took fire, and countries were reconfigured as a collection of nation states. Already presaged by the unity of state and nation in late fifteenth-century Catholic Spain, nationalism became the political master-idea of the nineteenth and twentieth centuries. Greece was the first new nation to emerge from the Ottoman Empire when it won independence in 1821 after the Christian Orthodox peasants living in the southern region of the Peloponnese slaughtered almost 20,000 Muslims in just a few months. It set a pattern of atrocity that scarred the future wars of liberation in the Balkans in an unparalleled way. Greece was followed by the new independent nations of Belgium, Italy and Germany by 1871. The Ottoman Balkans then fragmented into a patchwork of many smaller states, from which the term 'balkanize' was coined; by 1914, the modern Balkans had come into being, with nationalism replacing dynasticism as the organizing principle of European politics, and challenging imperial power. That great reconstitution of peoples and lands touched on perceptions buried deep in western thought that emanated from religious tensions between Orthodox and Catholic Christians, and from the persistent rift between Muslim and Christian worlds. It was to have profound repercussions for European Muslims.

In October 1912, the former Ottoman provinces and the by then independent states of Bulgaria, Greece, Montenegro and Serbia declared war on the Ottoman Empire. Their aim was to drive the Ottomans out of Europe and liberate their few remaining provinces, but the populations of those independent states remained a Christian minority in Ottoman Europe, where 51 per cent were Muslims, mostly Albanians in the west and Turks in the east. Seeing that Muslim majorities would threaten their minority rule, the new nations resolved to expel and eliminate them. The Ottomans were trenchantly defeated, resulting in the mass exodus of south-east European Muslims to what remained of the failing empire. Nine months later, in June 1913, the Balkan states turned on each other, and all those involved then attacked Bulgaria. One outcome of these conflicts was the loss of almost all remaining Ottoman lands in

Europe, including Albania, Macedonia and western Thrace, which had been under Muslim rule as early as the fourteenth century. The Ottomans managed to hang on to Kostantiniyye and recaptured Edirne and eastern Thrace in June 1913, which is today's modern Turkey, but all else in Ottoman Europe was lost.

In the aftermath, the fate of the Muslims of Ottoman Europe, soldiers and civilians, was grim. As many as 125,000 Ottoman soldiers died from disease, starvation or murder. Sir Harry Lamb, British consul, reported on the former Ottoman territories: 'Throughout the districts of Kilkish, Doiran and Ghevgheli nearly all the leading Mussulmans have been put to death in one form or another, their property pillaged or destroyed and their farms and dwelling-houses burned.'[2] Muslim civilians could not escape, as armies blocked their routes, and it was a similar situation in every region. The Bulgarians destroyed nearly all the Muslim villages in Thrace, and the Montenegrins sacked northern Albania, leaving devastation in their wake. Villagers had no food and starved, and those who could flee to Anatolia lost their land, houses, businesses and their animals, and no compensation was ever forthcoming. Over 800,000 Muslims finally settled in what was left of Ottoman territory, mostly in Anatolia. 632,000 Muslims from the Ottoman Empire, 27 per cent of its population, had died, making it the worst civilian mortality in any modern European war.[3]

From Muslim Ideal to Dark Alliances

Like the Ottoman sultans before him, Mehmed V was girded with the Sword of Osman at his accession ceremony, after which he rode in his royal carriage to visit the tomb of Mehmed the Conqueror in the Fatih Mosque in Kostantiniyye. After pledging his oath of allegiance, Mehmed proclaimed: 'I am the first sultan of liberty and proud of it', and he became known as the Constitutional Sultan. Yet Mehmed V came to the throne when he was sixty-five and had no experience of matters of state. What seemed a point of rejuvenation and freedom for the Ottomans became a catastrophic falling from grace. The ethnically and ideologically diverse intellectuals that formed the Young Turks movement in opposition to Abdul Hamid's dictatorial reign believed in the power of a constitution to strengthen and modernize the Ottoman state and make it a worthy match for foreign threats. In what was known as the Second Constitutional Era, not only was the constitution restored but a system of multiparty politics and electoral voting was implemented. There was hope for the future, and for the peaceful reconciling of the empire's many peoples. Yet the formation of the Committee of Union and Progress (CUP) party in 1908 was to transform Ottoman life in a very different way.

In 1913, two members of the CUP staged a coup in a surprise raid on the Sublime Porte, seizing control of the government. The empire fell into the hands of Enver Pasha, the minister of war, Cemal Pasha, commander of the Fourth Army and governor of Syria, and Mehmed Talat Pasha, the interior minister. Together they formed a one-party dictatorship, a military regime that confounded the ideals of the Young Turks and plotted to reforge the Muslim empire by means of demographic engineering. Ethnic cleansing had already reared its head in the Balkan Wars in the form of population exchange, when the Ottomans had retaliated for the Balkan expulsion of hundreds of thousands of Muslims by driving equally vast numbers of Christians out of western Anatolia. The rule of the pashas allowed them to execute their theory of social Darwinism predicated on the survival of the fittest, which in their scheme of things would guarantee the future of the Ottoman Empire. It was a social engineering project that transformed the ethos of the imperial state from one of tolerance and respect for difference into a hardline intolerant Islamic regime that fostered perpetual war, killed all enemies, real and perceived, stifled dissent and murdered civilian men, women and children alike.

World War and the Armenian Genocide

Meanwhile, the threat of violent international conflict presaged by the warring Balkans became a reality when Serbian militants assassinated Archduke Ferdinand in June 1914. Sultan Mehmed V had no desire to be part of the great global conflagration that followed, although he made overtures to Britain and France to form an alliance against Serbia, which they rejected. But Enver and Talat Pasha, who had previously encouraged strong military ties with Germany, made a secret agreement in that same month of August 1914 to join the war on the side of the Central Powers, comprising the German Empire, Austria-Hungary, Bulgaria and the Ottomans against the British and Russian Empires and their ally France. Despite his abhorrence of the pashas' pro-German leanings, Mehmed V found himself obliged to formally declare a jihad against the Allied Powers in November of that year, describing the Allied forces as an oppressive entity 'whose national pride takes extreme pleasure in the subjection of thousands of Muslims.'[4] Germany had worked hard to secure the alliance of the Ottomans, tempting them with gold and state-of-the-art ships and purporting to support the Ottoman ideology of pan-Islamism, for they knew that such a connection would ease their access to Russia and Egypt. For the Ottomans, the strongest motive for joining the war on the side of Germany was that it gave them the opportunity to seek revenge against an old foe, Russia. The combined Ottoman and German forces launched a minor surprise attack on the Black Sea coast of the Russian Empire in late October 1914, which provoked Russia to declare war.

At one of the darkest times in human history, under cover of a world war, the ruling CUP party, with the help of Kurdish tribes remaining in the empire, began to implement their policy of ethnic cleansing and deportation, demonstrated in the systematic extermination in 1915 of between one million and one and a half million Armenians living in Ottoman lands. The Ottoman cabinet minister Mehmed Cavid described it as 'monstrous murder', as brutality on the vastest scale ever known in the history of his people, which left 'an inextinguishable stain' on the Ottoman government.[5] During and after the world war, the mass murder of the male population and the inhuman conditions of forced labour were succeeded by the deportation of women, children and the old and infirm on death marches into the Syrian desert. En route, they were deprived of food and water, and were subjected to robbery, rape and execution. Similar widespread massacres of the Ottoman Empire's Greek and Assyrian minorities also took place as part of the ethnic-cleansing drive.

There were few who lived to tell the tale, but one, Arshaluys Martikian, survived to recount her bid for freedom and died at the age of ninety-two. She had been born in 1901 in Çemişgezek, in the modern Tunceli province of Turkey, the third of eight children of a prosperous Armenian silk manufacturer. When the horrors of 1915 began to unfold, she was a promising student and talented violinist. She witnessed the murder of her father and one of her brothers, and was taken with her mother and sisters to the Syrian desert during the mass deportation of Armenian women. Arshaluys was sold for a pittance to a tribal leader for his harem, but she somehow escaped and found her way over the Dersim mountain range, hiding in caves and woods and eating plants and roots. Eighteen months later, she turned up in rags, barefoot and starving, in Erzerum, then under Russian control. There, she was looked after by American missionaries and was eventually adopted by an Armenian family in New York. Arshaluys' account of the genocide appeared in newspapers in New York and Los Angeles in 1918, and was published in a book, *Ravished Armenia*, which sold not far off a million copies and was made into a silent film. At that time, she changed her name to Aurora Mardiganian to protect her identity and played the leading role in the film herself. Ten years later, she married an Armenian immigrant, and they had a son in 1931. No known complete copy of the film still exists.

In its twilight, Ottoman imperial rule had degenerated into an unprecedented brutality towards some of its peoples that was the antithesis of its centuries-old policy of forbearance and open-mindedness. The mass murder of Armenians, Greeks and Assyrians appeared not to be a religious issue, as the CUP ignored the Islamic prohibition of genocide, but rather an element in their transformation of Ottoman society that would save the empire from destruction and eliminate the part of that society perceived to be traitors who conspired with Russia. It proved to be one of several ruinous choices that had quite the opposite effect, bringing about the downfall of the Ottoman superpower.

Spain, North Africa and the Arab Revolt

As Europe's eastern Islamic world fractured and disintegrated, the Islamic past of western Europe came back into focus amid an era of unrest in North Africa, which in turn would have grave consequences for the Turkish empire. In November 1912, Morocco became a protectorate of Spain, retaining its autonomy in general affairs yet under the sovereignty of the Spanish government. While western Europe was expanding its empires, Spain had lost the last remnants of its once great imperial power in 1898, when it relinquished Cuba and the Philippines in the Spanish–American War. The psychological shock of this defeat played its part in prompting Spain to embark on an invasion of Morocco in 1908, starting from the Spanish enclaves of Ceuta and Melilla on the Moroccan coast, which led to their occupation of the whole northern region of Morocco until 1956. The plausible political motives for such a late colonial enterprise were linked to investment potential, laced with a strong dose of competitiveness with France and Britain, who each controlled areas of North Africa. A deeper motive lay beneath the surface too: it was an act of revenge for the Muslim conquest of 711, a revenge which had begun with the Christian reconquest of al-Andalus and had spread across the Strait of Gibraltar to North Africa by the late fifteenth century, with the pope's blessing.

At the start of the twentieth century, Morocco had a sultanate, ruled by the reformer Abd al-Aziz bin Hassan of the Alawi dynasty, who abdicated in favour of his brother Abd al-Hafid in 1908. The Moroccans regarded the Spanish as entrenched opponents of Islam who had waged war on them over the centuries, and Spaniards saw the Moroccans as their long-standing adversaries, closely associated with war. In traditional festivals held in Spanish towns and villages, mock battles between Christians and Moors were staged, and Moors were often depicted as targets on fairground firing ranges. Even matchboxes used by Spanish soldiers bore images of Moors on one side.[6] In the early years of the protectorate, the Spanish adopted the attitude of the European colonizer, dismissing the strong connections between the cultures of Spain and Morocco, believing they were bringing the benefits of progress to an unsophisticated people. Yet their occupation of Moroccan territory was to take a dramatic turn two decades later, as Spain turned to civil war.

In the late 1930s, General Franco harnessed medieval history as political propaganda in his campaign to create a national Catholic state in Spain, lauding the Catholic Monarchs for their victory over the Muslim infidel in 1492, but the logic of his political mythology was outweighed by practical necessity. The recruitment of Moroccan troops became vital to his Nationalist cause, since his Army of Africa was the only crack unit in the Spanish military, rising against the Second Republic of Spain in the 1936 coup that brought Franco to power. Suddenly, the traditional Muslim foe was in fact fighting on Spain's side to liberate it from an internal Other that Franco presented as atheist and communist. The caudillo or military leader, as he was called, saw Muslims and Catholics as united in a holy war, a crusade against the enemy within, and he went to extraordinary lengths to organize and fund a pilgrimage by boat to Mecca.[7] At the same time, Franco's regime played on historical memory of the reputed fearsome barbarity of the Moors, to the degree that the very sight of the coloured turbans and white uniform of the Moroccan troops struck terror into the hearts of those who saw them. In this way, the profoundly interwoven histories of Christians and Muslims in far western Europe played out in bolstering a twentieth-century political policy of disinformation that promoted a catastrophic civil war.

*

As Spain flexed its colonial muscles in Morocco, the Ottoman lands of the Near East rose up in a nationalist rebellion that struck a fatal blow for the Muslim empire. It began in Mecca, the heart of Islam, in June 1916, following a pact between the sharif of Mecca, Hussein bin Ali, and the British government to rebel against Ottoman rule and forge a unified, independent Arab state stretching from Syria to Yemen. The sharif's army, aided and abetted by British troops in Egypt, fought and defeated Ottoman troops in the Hejaz and most of what is present-day Jordan. By 1917, the Ottomans had lost not only Mecca, but also Baghdad, Damascus, Medina and Jerusalem, captured by the British in 1917 after 400 years of Muslim rule. The seizing of the prized holy cities of Islam and their surrounding territories weakened the Ottoman regime even further, materially and psychologically. Even so, the Arab nationalist dream was not fulfilled – after the revolt, the British and French partitioned the Middle East into what were known as mandate territories, arising from an authorization granted by the League of Nations to member nations to govern a former German or Turkish colony after the First World War. Palestine, Iraq and Lebanon passed from Ottoman sovereignty to British and French rule, bypassing the Arab nationalists and provoking their outrage.

A War of Empires: The Demise of the House of Osman

The First World War was a battle of empires, and the Ottomans picked the losing side, along with the Habsburg and German Empires and Bulgaria. The Ottoman Empire did not die because of its imperial structures, nor because it had lost relevance. On the contrary, the presence of its empire as a European power in the Great War reshapes the more familiar perception of that conflict, shifting the focus towards eastern Europe rather than solely upon its western actors. The theatre of war was larger than the Western Front; the struggle was enacted from Britain to Istanbul, and from Moscow to North Africa, west to east, north to south, and it involved soldiers, both Christian and Muslim, from as far afield as India, Siam (now Thailand) and Australia. The last sultan of the Ottoman Empire, Mehmed VI, came to the throne in July 1918, four months before the end of the world war and the defeat of his dynasty. On 30 October, on the Greek island of Lemnos, the Armistice of Mudros was signed, ending hostilities between the Ottomans and the Allied powers, and Kostantiniyye, a Muslim capital for 465 years, was occupied by combined Allied forces. The World's Desire had finally been vanquished.

The dissolution of the Ottoman Empire happened quickly. At the Treaty of Sèvres, signed in the town's famous porcelain factory in 1920, the partition of the territory between France, Great Britain, Italy and Greece was finalized and the sultan was allowed to keep his position and title. Soon, a provisional government was established in Ankara by Mustafa Kemal Pasha, the sultan's top military man, and, just two years later, in November 1922, the Grand National Assembly of Turkey, presided over by Mustafa Kemal, declared that the sultanate was to be abolished. Mehmed VI could only acquiesce, and he left in secret on a British battleship for Malta, then Italy, where he lived in exile until his death in 1926. Two weeks later, the Grand Assembly elevated Abdulmecid II as caliph, the supreme religious and political leader of Muslims across the globe. But, in 1924, the Grand Assembly voted to abolish the caliphate on the grounds that it was no longer necessary, and to expel all members of the Ottoman dynasty. The last caliph, his wife and two children were exiled to Paris with heavy hearts, since Abdulmecid believed the end of the caliphate would bring chaos, extremism and disaster. Yet his voice was silenced, and he sought refuge in a life as an artist and musician until his death in the French capital in 1944.

*

The long decline and fall of Europe's Islamic empire in the east was life-changing for its Muslim inhabitants. Not only had they endured terrible loss of life due to war, disease and starvation, but they had become exiles, migrants in lands both familiar and now strange. The biggest challenge for Muslim survivors of the Balkan Wars and the First World War was how they, a former majority group in south-eastern Europe, could integrate into the new European way of life as a minority. The demographic configuration of eastern Europe in particular had changed dramatically, and those Muslims living in former Ottoman lands dwelt in a state of ambiguity. Although they now formed part of new polities and societies, where they paid taxes and sent their children to school, many migrant Muslims saw themselves in terms of their religious identities rather than as citizens of a particular nation to whom they owed loyalty in exchange for its legal protection. They were obliged to reconsider their place in the new European world where they found themselves, and to ponder what they could do to acquire power and agency.

After the First World War, many Muslim communities lived in fear, afraid of losing their property, their identity, of the elimination of the elements of Islamic life they espoused, and afraid of expulsion. In the post-war world of the early twentieth century, the Muslim population was perceived as a problem for which solutions had to be found. These included resettlement, population transfers, voluntary migration and forced assimilation. One such solution, decreed by the Treaty of Lausanne in 1923, dictated transfers of Muslims from Greece, and Greek Orthodox Christians from Turkey, on the bizarre basis that these two populations were incompatible.

For a while, the new Yugoslav state seemed to hold out hope for Europe's besieged religious minority, as it did not deport its Muslims, and became a multilingual, multi-religious state. A small victory was won in the Shari'a Mandate that formed part of the Constitution of the Kingdom of Serbs, Croats and Slovenes, through which Muslims came to define a legal framework for a Muslim minority in Europe.[8] The brave new Europe of the 1920s did not embrace its Muslim communities, who were viewed with suspicion as people who lived according to an entirely different world view, with different social and religious structures and legal systems, all at odds with Christian European societies, laws and ethics. For the Muslims, this encounter gave them not only a wish to be free from European domination, but also a heightened awareness of belonging to Muslim civilization, however diverse it may have been globally, that could be compatible with ethnic and national identities. Yet it was nevertheless a Muslim civilization that had been and remained an ineradicable part of European history too.

Chapter 27

Abandoning the Islamic Past: Mustafa Kemal Atatürk and the New Turkey

'A star in the darkness.'

Adolf Hitler on Mustafa Kemal Atatürk

'Peace at home is peace in the country. Peace in the country is peace in the world.'

Mustafa Kemal Atatürk

'. . . the story of massive mortality and one of history's great migrations.'

Justin McCarthy

At the entrance to a smart bakery in the seaside resort of Ayvalık, a Muslim town on the north-west Aegean coast of Turkey, a large black and white photo of Mustafa Kemal Atatürk commands attention. It is one of many representations of the Turkish statesman across the nation in the form of posters, portraits, snapshots and monuments that appear today in shops, cinemas, petrol stations and other public places. Both loved and hated, Atatürk was and remains a controversial figure, who snatched victory from the jaws of defeat by creating a modern, independent Turkish republic out of the ashes of the old Ottoman Empire. It was a majestic yet brutal experiment, tempered by great enlightenment, that created continuity amid violent change and left an ambiguous legacy. The price paid for Turkish independence and self-definition was a suppression of history and religion that aimed to erase the Ottoman past while anchoring Turkey's rightful place in Europe.

The Era of Transition: From Soldier of the Muslim Empire to Secular Statesman

In the ten years or so between 1881 and 1892, four men were born who had a permanent impact on Europe. All served in the army in varying degrees, and three of them, Benito Mussolini, Adolf Hitler and Francisco Franco, became fascist dictators. The fourth, Mustafa Kemal (1881–1938), later known as Atatürk, believed in peace and admired the concept of a world civilization; he became the liberator of the Turkish nation. Kemal was born around 1881 in Salonica (now Thessaloniki), into a Muslim, Turkish-speaking, lower-middle-class family with some Albanian roots. His father was a junior civil servant who died of drink, and his mother was a farmer's daughter and devout Muslim. When he entered the world, the Ottoman Empire, one of the largest states incorporating adjoining territories that had ever existed, had returned to the reign of despotism after unsuccessful attempts at reform, and its government had silenced all political discussion. As it was forbidden to debate issues of westernization and modernization, opponents of the Ottoman regime turned to subversion, and the CUP party, known abroad as the Young Turks, many of whom were army officers, came to power under the aegis of the disempowered sultan.

Against such a backdrop came the startling, dramatic advent of Mustafa Kemal, the soldier from Salonica who led a national resistance from 1919 to 1922 that defeated the attempts of England, France and Russia to divide up Ottoman lands. The seeds of his remarkable rise were sown early in his life, when certain important elements combined to form the character and beliefs that would define him. His home town had a rich, diverse culture and religious population, which from the start encouraged the development of his cosmopolitan world view; Mustafa Kemal was alert to the clash between traditional Islam and European free thought from early on. Against his mother's wishes, he signed up as a soldier and entered the Istanbul War College in 1899, when he was eighteen. He wrote later: 'It was when I entered the military preparatory school and put on its uniform that a feeling of strength came to me, as if I had become master of my own identity.'[1] The close connection between dress and identity was to become important to Kemal, both personally and in his political policies, but at first he saw himself fundamentally as a soldier, a career path that bolstered his innately masterful nature.

His thirteen years of military service involved armed combat on three continents, and he earned a celebrated reputation as an exceptional commander, in particular for his courageous exploits at Gallipoli in 1915, where he and his troops contained the combined Australian and New Zealand forces at his own initiative, earning an outstanding victory for which he was awarded the Ottoman Silver Medal of Battle Service and the German Iron Cross. His study of battle strategy and his belief in the importance of military instruction led him to write various treatises on war tactics. This specialized logistical knowledge and the study of human psychology that accompanied it were skills that he transferred to other spheres of life. Kemal had joined the Young Turks and moved in the underworld of secret political societies. His tall, imposing presence, with piercing blue eyes and fair hair, made him a powerful figure. He was a natural leader of boundless energy and remarkable force of will, waiting in the wings for the right opportunity.

*

The breakthrough came when he was posted to Anatolia to inspect troops on the Black Sea coast and saw at once the opportunity to gain control of the region. Harnessing the support of local resistance groups, he formed a national movement whose new seat of government was not in Istanbul but in Ankara (formerly Angora), in central Anatolia, where its first assembly met in 1920. The ambition of the rebels was to overthrow the sultan and liberate Turkish lands from foreign threats. In 1922, Kemal's men defeated Greek invaders who had been promised territories by the Allies after the First World War, and who felt their claim was justified since Anatolia had been part of ancient Greece. Kemal's victory made him a popular hero, known as Ghazi, Champion of the Faith. The same year, his forces entered Istanbul, upon which the sultan fled his country on a British battleship and a new peace treaty was negotiated with the Allies. It was the only peace treaty after the First World War not to have been agreed with a defeated power, and in general terms it remains unbroken today. The following year, 1923, a Turkish republic was proclaimed, and Kemal became its first president. His impressive transition from soldier to statesman coincided with the moment the Ottoman Empire became a Turkish republic.

The Metamorphosis of a Nation

To reach the new seat of power in Ankara, Mustafa Kemal rowed himself across the Bosphorus from European Turkey to Anatolia in a small wooden dinghy.[2] It was a political statement that disassociated him from the Ottoman sultans who crossed the Bosphorus in golden barges, aligning him instead with the community that formed the new nation. In Kemal's view, the now superseded Ottoman Empire had originally been established by the Turkish nation, but it had lost its identity, and his aspiration was to create a modern, independent Turkish nation state. Nationalism was a key tenet of his political ideology, which came to be known as Kemalism; he believed Turkishness would unite the country, bestow pride and a sense of purpose after the devastation of the world war, and fend off western imperialism. Not only did nationalism drive a nail into the coffin of the Ottomans, but it also covered the traces of their European heritage. History lay at the core of this critical remoulding of a people. The new president of the Turkish Republic had claimed that 'nations which are unaware of their history are obliged to die out' – so, under Kemal's aegis, Turkish history was recast and reinterpreted. In June 1930, the Committee for the Investigation of Turkish History met to draw up plans for a new, comprehensive Turkish history, from its origins to the twentieth century, and Kemal was involved in its work. The shorter version of the two works written, *Introduction to the Main Outline of Turkish History*, appeared in January 1931, and a total of 70,000 copies were printed. It described central Asia as the homeland of the Turks and the cradle of human civilization, a theory that coincides with current thinking, which locates the earliest human civilization in the Neolithic site of Göbekli Tepe, in south-east Anatolia. The *Introduction* also emphasizes that the Turks accepted Islam in due time and rejuvenated Muslim civilization.

Hand in hand with the clarification and modernization of Turkish history was the reform of language, which underlined the unfolding official national history. The reforms proved to be highly controversial, not to mention dramatic. The name 'Turkey' was unknown to its people. It originates in medieval Latin, and was used by Chaucer in the fourteenth century, deriving from the native name for the Turkish people, 'Türk', first found in a Mongolian inscription of the sixth century BC. Its use in the western continent was adopted by the new Republic in 1923, aligning the nation with Europe by its very designation. Mustafa Kemal was a consummate linguist himself and a fine writer in high imperial Ottoman prose, and also Arabic. He believed language was vital in the formation of a national identity, citing the Persian epic *Shahname*, 'The Book of Kings', as key to the preservation of Persian identity in the twentieth century. The 1924 Turkish constitution had proclaimed Turkish as the only official language, and its reform was focused on changing the alphabet and including the Turkish vernacular to create the new idiom. These were ideas that had been mooted towards the end of the Ottoman era, and both Muslim Albania and Azerbaijan had already adopted the Latin alphabet in their foreign-language publications. So, in May 1928, Kemal put forward a proposal for a Latin alphabet, which was accepted by the government in August. The new language would have a revised Turkish alphabet of twenty-nine letters, and the president wanted everyone to learn the script within two years. As of June 1929, Turkish letters taken from Latin script were used in all public transactions. At the same time, all other languages were prohibited, and foreign words, especially in Arabic or Persian, were replaced with Turkish ones. The results were radical and far-reaching. On a practical level, new printing presses had to be constructed, all school textbooks had to be printed in Latin script and, from September 1929, Arabic and Persian were taken off the school curriculum. This had the effect of denying access to Ottoman literature for those who grew up with the new language, and left them unable even to read the inscriptions on the gravestones of their ancestors. In general terms, the remaking of Turkish was intended to encourage a contemporary mindset; it also reinforced a western orientation and eroded cultural links with Arab and Persian culture.

The new Law of Family Names, enacted in June 1934, was in a similar vein, though with even more drastic repercussions. The law enforced compulsory surnames, which obliged everyone including Muslims, who rarely had family names, to adopt one. It prohibited any name that suggested a rank, a tribe, foreign race or nation, and it had to come from the Turkish language. The minority group of Kurds, who had been recognized as a nation before the Turkish Republic, found their autonomy and language were repressed by the government in retaliation for several forceful Kurdish rebellions. All Kurdish dialects were forbidden, the letters *J* and *X* were not included in the Turkish alphabet, so that Kurdish names could not be written, and it became a crime to mention Kurds or Kurdistan. At the same time, Kemal continued the CUP policy of changing all Armenian, Kurdish, Arabic or Laz place names into Turkish, including towns, villages, mountains and rivers. Even the name of the great city of Constantinople, known for so long to the Turks as Kostantiniyye, was finally changed to Istanbul in May 1930. Because of this, one negative consequence of Kemal's drive for Turkish nationalism was the aggravation of ancient tribal and ethnic differences. Kurds and Armenians were felt to threaten the unity of the nation, and he uncompromisingly resorted to a military solution in the form of cycles of violent repression, which lent a dark, tragic side to his reforms.

Like Spain at the end of the fifteenth century, the Turkish Republic became a country with a single language and identity, shunning the multicultural and pluralistic society of the Ottoman

Empire. The imposition of a new language had the undesirable effect of deterring communication with the world outside. In that regard, it was light years away from the diverse, multilingual society of medieval Spain, where skilled linguists from many countries translated between languages to encourage scholarship and community. On the contrary, the new mother tongue may have united the Turkish people, but it also isolated them.

The third element of the metamorphosis of Turkey was the great push for education. Mustafa Kemal was a man of great intellectual curiosity, who embraced a vast range of knowledge that included literature, history, poetry, religion, philosophy and sociology. He knew the value of education, setting out in August 1928 to introduce the new alphabet to the people, travelling from town to town and explaining the new system using a blackboard and chalk. When British journalist Grace Ellison visited Ankara in 1927, she was astonished to hear Kemal quote verbatim passages from the English writer H. G. Wells's *Outline of History*, a book he had read and ordered for use in schools.[3] A progressive education system began in Anatolian villages. Peasant children were taught to play western instruments, including the violin, and they learnt to recite Shakespeare. In this educational experiment that lasted a decade, village children acted out Greek tragedies in the lands where those plays were originally set.[4]

Universities did not fare so well due to a series of repressions and purges that fed Kemal's desire to establish absolute control over Turkish society, creating a kind of political and intellectual censorship. Despite this, Kemal's inspirational manner and his vision of a secular, independent Turkey empowered a great many writers, teachers, doctors and others, who saw themselves as an elite, to guide their uneducated fellow countrymen, and they often worked hard, with considerable personal sacrifice, for those ideals. But, while the president had forged ahead in reconfiguring Turkish history, language and education with significant success, the recasting of politics and religion would turn out to be a greater challenge.

Becoming Western European: Veiling Religion, Changing Costumes and Freeing Women

Mustafa Kemal's lodestar was the civilization of western Europe, and specifically the French Revolution of 1799 and its Declaration of the Rights of Man and the Citizen which was his lifelong guiding principle. He spoke of European civilization in the west as all consuming, a force that 'pierces the mountains, flies across the heavens, sees everything, even stars invisible to the naked eye . . . to whose seething torrent it is vain to offer resistance.'[5] When he was a student at the military academy, two of his fellow students had introduced him to literature and philosophy. Ömer Naci, a young poet, shared his love of verse and literature with him, and, despite government censorship, his friend Ali Fethi introduced him to the works of the French philosophers, including Voltaire, Rousseau, Auguste Comte and Montesquieu. His reading led him to believe in the importance of secularism, inspired by the French concept of laicism that separated Church from State in France after the revolution. Kemal believed that religion should be a private matter, without the mentorship of religious leaders: 'The lessons provided by our mothers and fathers are sufficient for explaining the foundations of our religion.'[6] It was to be a matter of personal choice and conscience, practised in public in the mosque. In this way, Kemal sought to take Islam out of the political sphere and elevate its status as a private form of spiritual worship. This way of thinking was inevitably at odds with the essential tenets of Islam, which hold that the Koran is both a moral guide and a state constitution created by the Prophet that contains its civil and criminal law. To deny this was a radical, revolutionary act for a Muslim, but Mustafa Kemal had decided that religion should have no part in government.

Bolder than those before him, his first step was to abolish the caliphate in 1924, ordering the caliph to be woken in the night and compelling him to leave the country by 5 a.m. The religious courts were closed and religious teaching in state schools was abandoned. A new civil law code based on the Swiss model was implemented and any reference to Islam was removed from the constitution. In 1925, religious shrines, or *türbes*, and dervish convents, *tekkes*, were closed, Sufism was made illegal and, in 1934, the Hagia Sophia was turned into a museum. All of this provoked public resistance, since these places and beliefs played a significant role in daily life. The Gregorian calendar used by the Catholic Church was adopted, further aligning Turkey with the west. In a tactical move, Kemal retained the official see of the Christian Orthodox Ecumenical Church in Istanbul, since to banish the Christian Orthodox Church would have provoked an undesirable diplomatic crisis with western Europe. The dissolution of the caliphate was a bombshell for the Muslim world; it ended thirteen centuries of Islamic history, and no obvious candidate has since arisen to reclaim it.

The secularization of Turkey prompted a crisis of faith and identity among its many Muslims. Islam had deep roots in Ottoman life and had fashioned its political and legal fabric. In the 1927 census, Muslims made up 97 per cent of the population, composed of diverse groups. Kemal needed to reconcile those devout and conservative Muslims who were deeply troubled by the new conformation of their world, as he shaped a new kind of Islam that had no part in politics and existed mainly in mosques, in private homes, and was nationalized in public places. Islam developed in parallel with secular society, and, however unviable it appeared in theory, the new configuration gradually came to work in practice. Although Kemal himself was brought up as a Muslim, his adult life suggests he had few religious convictions. Even so, he had a noble ideal in his dream of a universal religion, an aspiration he explained in a speech given in October 1927, which stated that 'mankind would abandon Christianity, Islam, Buddhism; and . . . a pure, spotless, simplified religion, understood by all and of a universal character, will be established.'[7]

*

Rules were gradually introduced to eliminate the wearing of religious dress and other markers of a religious nature, such as the special headgear of Muslim scholars or ulema. Laws did not ultimately ban the wearing of veils or headscarves for women, but focused on the prohibition of turbans outside places of worship. Mustafa Kemal had seen the power of dress in defining personal identity as a young soldier, and now he set about imposing western clothing on the Turkish nation. He began by making the wearing of hats compulsory for civil servants, a move followed up by the drastic Hat Law of November 1925, which decreed that all men should wear western-style hats or caps and abandon the traditional Turkish fez. Images in school textbooks that showed men wearing fezzes were substituted by pictures of men wearing hats. Not surprisingly, this new ruling sparked a rebellious attitude among those Muslims who saw the western hat as a symbol of Christian Europe, and many refused to don a brimmed hat, as it interfered with praying. In reaction to this, under the Law of the Maintenance of Order, Kemal commanded the arrest of almost 7,500 men, and 660 of them were executed. It was a telling, if excessive, reminder that the authority of Kemal and the republican government could not be undermined, and that progress and westernization were inexorable.

⋆

In 1932, the Turkish model, pianist and beauty queen Keriman Halis Ece was crowned Miss Universe. Her triumph was considered a great Turkish victory, and Keriman became a symbol of the new freedom of women in the Middle East, where she was celebrated in the Egyptian Arab press. Mustafa Kemal was thrilled that an international jury had chosen a Turkish woman, and congratulated her for demonstrating the beauty of the Turkish race. The fact that it was even possible for Keriman Halis to be a candidate in a world beauty contest was the result of reforming ideas expressed by many Muslim thinkers at the start of the twentieth century. Their view was that, as women made up half a country's population, if their talents were not used, then the evolution of society would be thwarted. Kemal shared this point of view, and the emancipation of women became a keystone in his transformation of Turkish society.

Towards the end of the Ottoman era, women had begun to wear

European clothing in public in the cities and many rejected the veil. In 1910, a book was published on the subject of feminism in relation to Islam.[8] Female activism had taken hold during the Balkan Wars and the First World War, when so many women had taken over the jobs of men who were away fighting, and Mustafa Kemal had encouraged the mobilization of women. On the eve of the First World War, university education was made available to Turkish women; three years later, eighteen women graduated, some of whom became teachers. Over the decade from 1924 until 1935, schools became co-educational, and, in December 1934, women received the right to vote in national elections, ten years before women in France. Turkey was also decades ahead of other Muslim countries in appointing women as judges – in 1934, there were around fifty female lawyers and twenty-five women judges in Turkey, one of whom, Muazzez Halet, became the first woman criminal judge in the country.

Mustafa Kemal thought that the use of the veil was isolating, leaving a bad impression on foreigners, and that men should not be able to oblige their wives to cover their faces. He wanted women to wear hats so that they looked more European, modern and civilized, but he avoided banning the veil completely. Despite these reforms, Turkey was still a patriarchal country, but there had undoubtedly been a transformation in women's status and there had been great progress in the liberation of women in society, a change Kemal had achieved by breaking ties with religious law and decreeing sexual equality.

Saving Turkey: The Legacy of War and Peace

To conform to the new Law of Family Names that came into force in 1934, Mustafa Kemal adopted the surname Atatürk, meaning 'Father of the Turks', a name he is remembered by, which represents what post-war Germany saw as his miraculous achievement in building a secular Turkish nation state, a coalition of its majority population of Muslims that kept religion separate from government and remained fully part of Europe. Religion might have seemed on the margins in the years before, during and after the First World

War, but Muslims and Christians alike found themselves reeling in the aftermath of the rebuilding and political restructuring of the continent. The material horrors of the mass migrations enforced by population exchanges on both sides were compounded by the psychological distress arising from adjustment to new ways of life and thinking, which challenged the role and validity of Christianity and overturned the Islamic world view. No exclusively religious cause motivated the warring nations. When the Ottomans made a reluctant alliance with the Germans in 1914 and proclaimed a jihad, their engagement in the conflict bore no resemblance to the holy Islamic wars of the Middle Ages, but was focused on the preservation of the Ottoman Empire at all costs. In contrast, the German war discourse was full of spiritual exaltation and presented German involvement as divine will. German preachers and theologians revelled in the combat, and Christian leaders saw their country as playing a messianic role in Europe and the world.[9] Britain and the USA also entered the war using crusading vocabulary – the British prime minister David Lloyd George declared it 'a great crusade', words echoed by an American rector when the USA entered the war in 1917: 'It is in the profoundest and truest sense a holy war.'[10] Yet the old order collapsed after 1918. Countries were physically rebuilt and their populations reconfigured, while the new political order in the Middle East that arose out of Arab nationalism and the Islamic revival made minority Christians fearful of persecution by the Muslim majority.

Back in Turkey, what emerged from the at times questionable means to achieve ends that included conspiracy and the use of violence to achieve power, the dominance of the military, the sacrifice of religious principles to nationalism and the ensuing disenchantment of liberals and minorities was a country at peace, free from the occupation and attempted partition of its lands, and with an unprecedented degree of internal order. For this, Atatürk earned his place in history as one of the great leaders of men, who worked consistently for peaceful relations with neighbouring countries and cooperated internationally to preserve peace. Turkey earned a new self-respect, independence and a new national purpose, but it paid a great price for it. There was a traumatic rift between the continuity of Islamic culture and the needs of modernity and progress. Kemalism broke completely with Turkey's Muslim heritage, which it identified with Arab culture, and part of that fracturing of the Islamic past involved the rejection of the pluralism which had made the Ottoman Empire a multi-ethnic, multi-religious place of many tongues. There was a clash between the identity imposed by the new Republic and the identity its majority Muslims continued to cling to – Turkey's modern national destiny excluded Islam, but Turkish Muslims persisted in their old ways, laying the ground for future backlashes.

When Atatürk died at fifty-seven, in 1938, of cirrhosis of the liver, Turkey was still poor and relatively underdeveloped, but he had left behind him the structure of a democracy which paved the way for a swift rise in standards of living after the Second World War. All the same, there were inevitably downsides to such a radical social experiment. Minority groups got short shrift as ethnic origins became a private matter in a polity that now held all citizens of the Republic to be Turks, although millions of Christians and the Kurdish members of society clung to their ethnic identity. Atatürk's presidency was at times blackened by the imposition of internal exile, censorship and political murder, as well as the periodic infliction of violence and death upon those who disobeyed the laws of the new regime. Yet such an all-encompassing social transformation had to be absolute – there was no room or time for a gradual acclimatization which might have created rebellion.

It was also unfortunate that Mustafa Kemal Atatürk's success story fuelled Nazi strategies in Germany, a country obsessed with events in Turkey after the First World War. Adolf Hitler described Atatürk as a 'star in the darkness' and Turkey a light from the East – in 1921, the Nazi newspaper *Völkische Beobachter* featured an article on events there with the headline 'Turkey – Role Model'. Although the Turkish state system was in essence an autocratic, single-party democracy, there was a perceived affinity between Kemalism and

German National Socialism in the early 1930s. The Nazis considered Turkey as vibrant and hypermodern, since, in their view, it obeyed its leader without question and had resolved the issue of ethnic minorities and separated religion from politics. Lamentably, Atatürk's policy on small ethnic groups was manipulated as Nazi propaganda for an absolute German state, with all its future ramifications. In reality, Hitler's regime was very far from the philosophy of the first Turkish president, whose idealistic vision was for East to meet West on the common ground of universal, secular values and mutual respect, and whose belief was that nationalism was compatible with peace.[11] Atatürk was posthumously honoured by UNESCO in 1979 as 'an outstanding example in promoting the spirit of mutual understanding between peoples and lasting peace between the nations of the world, having advocated all his life the advent of an age of harmony and co-operation in which no distinction would be made between men on account of colour, religion or race.'[12]

The evolution of the Islamic world in the twentieth and twenty-first centuries originated in world events that took place between the end of the nineteenth century and the Second World War, among which the demise of the caliphate under the aegis of Atatürk was paramount. It has been said that the way rulers of Islamic peoples, among whom were Atatürk and Reza Shah of Iran, responded to western power and the urge for secular progress is the source of much of the anger and violence in the Islamic world nowadays. After the First World War, the Muslim call to identify new kinds of authority generated the creation or resurrection of the Muslim movements of the contemporary world. The Republic of Turkey was unique within that evolution in preserving the independence of its traditional Muslim society, although not its religion or values. Atatürk remains an ambiguous figure in Turkey, which owes him its freedom and sovereignty, yet which finds it hard to pinpoint the identity of the country he created, poised between two continents. One thing is certain – Mustafa Kemal's Turkey is an indisputable part of Europe, as it has been for centuries.

Chapter 28

Imprints of Islam: Three Portraits of Hostility, Hybridity and Harmony

'The island of Cyprus is shared between Greeks and Saracens' ('*insulam Cyprum quae est inter Graecos et Saracenos*')

Willibald the pilgrim, AD 723

'In Malta the Wars of Religion reached their climax. If both sides believed they saw Paradise in the bright sky above them, they had a close and very intimate knowledge of Hell.'

Ernle Bradford

'All people are our people. Nobody came here from a different planet.'

President Shaimiev of Tatarstan

Cyprus: The Shattered Mirror

Cyprus is a place whose history and geography align, its urban and rural landscapes creating a visual story of the island's past and present. The most striking and dramatic manifestation of that narrative is a no man's land, a region that spans the landscape, stretching 180 kilometres east to west, its width varying from less than twenty metres to over seven kilometres. It runs through the heart of the capital city, Nicosia, dividing the island into the Muslim Turkish Republic of Northern Cyprus and the Greek Orthodox Republic of Cyprus in the south. This buffer zone, controlled by UN peacekeeping forces, came into being just after Christmas 1963, after episodes of brutal violence between Greek and Turkish communities, and is known as the Green Line in recollection of the ceasefire line drawn on a map with a green chinagraph pencil by General Young of the British Joint Force sent to restore order.

Entry to the buffer zone through the centre of Nicosia is prohibited, although citizens can cross to the other side via a series of checkpoints. Inside the Green Line there is a post-apocalyptic feel to the abandoned streets and half-derelict buildings; it is a ghost town of deserted shops, where cobwebbed goods still lie waiting for customers. Over fifty forsaken cars, once brand new, sit rusting in a strange, silent street of personal memories. Nicosia Airport, opened in 1968, was located inside the buffer zone, where now planes sit empty on the weed-strewn tarmac in a liminal land reclaimed by wild creatures, plants and trees. An air of sudden abandonment combines with a sense of imminent conflict – the Turkish army has built a barrier to the north using barbed wire, watchtowers, anti-tank ditches and minefields, and, in March 2021, a barbed-wire fence was erected around the entire Green Line to curb immigration. Outside the capital, some 10,000 people live in villages inside the buffer zone, and one of them, Pyla, is unique in being one of the few remaining in Cyprus where Greek and Turkish Cypriots coexist. The island, with its landscape of mosques and churches, has been divided for just half a century of its long history, which is at once the origin of its present dilemmas and also its hope for the future.

*

The geographical location of Cyprus is in west Asia, but politically it is part of Europe, while its culture and religions belong to both continents. Its situation in the far east of the Mediterranean, just over a hundred kilometres from Syria by sea and seventy-five from Turkey, has encouraged a past of trade and invasion. The island cult of the goddess Aphrodite reflects its early Greek heritage fashioned by immigrants to Cyprus in the late Bronze Age of the mid-fifteenth to the fourteenth century BC, who made it an important centre of

Greek culture. Briefly ruled by Persia and then Egypt, it became a Roman province in 35 BC, which it remained for 600 years. At the division of the Roman Empire into its western and eastern halves, the inhabitants of Cyprus became part of the Byzantine Empire and adopted Orthodox Christianity. There is a legend that the emperor Constantine's mother, Helen, founded churches and monasteries on the island on her way back from Jerusalem in AD 326, which she endowed with pieces of the Holy Cross.

Cyprus had first become Christian in AD 45–6, when its peoples were converted by St Paul and the Cypriot apostle St Barnabas, who died a martyr's death on the island at the hands of the Jews of Salamis. Barnabas was the alleged author of an apocryphal gospel, possibly medieval in origin, in which Jesus prophesies the coming of Muhammad, and which has links with the Spanish Moriscos and the Lead Books of Granada. In AD 488, Anthemius, the archbishop of Cyprus, allegedly uncovered the tomb of St Barnabas, whose corpse lay inside with a copy of the Gospel of Matthew on its chest, and the archbishop took advantage of his discovery to assert the independence of the Church of Cyprus. Even so, over the centuries, the Cypriot Church often struggled for autonomy and as a result developed both the strong local spirit and important political role that it retains today.

Commerce and religion wrought lasting changes to life on the island. The name 'Cyprus' derives from the Latin word for copper, *cuprum*, of which there were rich seams on the island. From earliest times, it was the hub of a busy commercial network and created great prosperity selling copper across the Mediterranean, from Italy to Mesopotamia, Anatolia to Egypt, along with other goods such as olives and ceramics. Arab traders were frequent visitors, until the advent of Islam and its aftermath triggered dramatic new events. The first Muslim raid came in 649, when the capital Constantia was sacked, the basilica destroyed and many citizens killed or imprisoned. A second attack came around 649–50, by Arabs from the Syrian coast, its purpose to quell the perceived threat of Byzantine Cyprus in the framework of a wider plan to conquer Constantinople. There are reports in Arab accounts by Abn l-Mahasim and Ibn al-Athir of the death in Cyprus of the Prophet's aunt, Umm Haram, who had accompanied the raiders, but fell from her mule and died near the salt lake at Larnaca, where she was buried.[1] In Ottoman times, the Hala Sultan *tekke* was built round her tomb and stands today.

As a result of these incursions, in 688, the Byzantine emperor and the Arab caliph came to an unprecedented kind of agreement to run the island as a shared space between Arabs and Byzantines, and to share its tax revenues too. There may also have been the first division of the island into two parts. The result was that Muslim Arabs began to live amicably on Cyprus alongside Orthodox Christians, creating an environment of religious and ethnic coexistence. The English pilgrim Willibald, who travelled there soon after 724, wrote of the good relationships among its peoples: 'They were seated among Greeks and Saracens, who were unarmed, since there was great peace and good will between them.'[2] Ibn Hawqal, a tenth-century Muslim traveller and chronicler, also referred to the friendliness between Muslims and Christians in Cyprus two or three centuries later, describing how the Muslim authorities were pleased with the Christians they protected, who behaved towards them as if they were fellow inhabitants.[3]

Cyprus retained a dual identity, one part Byzantine, one part Arab, with a military leader and governor, until the time of the Third Crusade (1189–92), when Richard I of England sold the island briefly to the Knights Templar, who had a brutal crusading mentality and kept Muslims as slaves. They returned the island to Richard, who then passed it on to the French Lusignans until 1389, when a Genoese nobleman, Janus, took the throne on the death of his father James I of Cyprus. Janus lost a battle with the Sunni Muslim Mamluks in Egypt in 1426 and the island became a tributary state. For a long time, Venice had desired control of Cyprus, and its government finally bought it in 1489 from Janus's widow, and ruled it for eighty-two years.

*

Three hundred years of foreign Christian rule ended in 1570, when the Ottoman sultan Selim II conquered Cyprus as a former land of Islam. Selim captured Nicosia in defiance of the threat posed by the Venetian alliance with the Christian Holy League, and Cyprus became an Ottoman province. Venice was the Turks' great commercial rival at that time, so, on the island, it was the Latin Catholic Church that was now oppressed, while the Greek Orthodox religion flourished and enjoyed its autonomy and its own legal systems. The archbishop of Cyprus was reinstated and became the religious and ethnic leader of the Greek Cypriots, a status bestowed by the Ottoman sultan that was to have far-reaching repercussions in the twentieth century.[4] The Venetians had ruled Cyprus by means of a feudal system of serfs working on the estates of noblemen, which caused such discontent that Greek Cypriot workers' delegations went, on two occasions, to Constantinople to discuss the likelihood of the Turks conquering their homeland, under whose jurisdiction they rightly anticipated a far more liberal, tolerant regime. As expected, the Ottomans banned serfdom and the Cypriots were given their freedom, the right to own property and transfer its ownership, and to live a life without oppression. As they had under the Arab government of the eighth century, Christians and Muslims fostered good relations – they lived in the same villages and shared daily life, and both communities even cooperated at times in uprisings, mainly against Greek clergy and Ottoman taxes. There followed 300 years of flexibility and tolerance in ethnic, religious and political matters, of collaboration and peaceful connection.

All that changed when the Ottomans were defeated by Russia in 1870. After the British occupied Cyprus in July 1878, there followed a secret agreement known as the Cyprus Convention, in which the Ottoman government agreed to cede administration to them in exchange for Britain using bases on the island to protect the Turks from Russian threats. This new arrangement brought Cyprus into the orbit of western European civilization, yet neither the Sunni Muslim Turkish population of Cyprus nor its Greek Orthodox Christians liked their new overlords, who exploited them for financial and political gain, and finally annexed the island to the British Empire at the end of the First World War.

By the 1950s, Cyprus had fallen prey to a virulent form of nationalism that destroyed any harmony that had existed between Greek and Turkish Cypriots. In thrall to Greek pressure, and the wiles of the Greek archbishop Makarios (1913–77) and his fascistic, brutal sidekick, the retired army officer Georgios Grivas, the Greek Cypriot population found favour in their plan to unite Cyprus with Greece, and they set about purging the island of any Turkish Muslim elements. Turkish Cypriot villagers were chased from their homes by Greek Cypriots, while local councils changed street names to Greek versions and removed the tombs of notable Muslims in what they called a street-widening project.[5]

The first Republic of Cyprus was formed in 1960, with Archbishop Makarios as its president, making the island independent from Britain. The new Greek Cypriot state was the prelude to the future physical separation of its two groups of inhabitants, with Britain, Greece and Turkey acting as guarantor powers if intervention became necessary, which it did. The terrible violence that surfaced at the end of 1963 became known as Bloody Christmas. There were attempts at genocide against the Turkish population; over 25,000 Turkish Cypriots were displaced, their houses destroyed, and it was reported that 364 Turkish and 174 Greek Cypriots were killed. This was the tipping point, when the urgent need for a solution to the violence created the buffer zone that cut Nicosia in half. When Greece's short-lived right-wing dictatorship seized Cyprus in July 1974, Turkey intervened five days later, landing 25,000 soldiers and taking 7 per cent of the island back under its control, which later increased to 36 per cent after further Turkish military action to quell the appalling atrocities committed by Greek Cypriots.

The independent Turkish Republic of North Cyprus, formed on 15 November 1983, was semi-presidential and democratic, but the United Nations declared it to be illegal. To this day, it suffers from severe restrictions that leave it isolated internationally and obliged to pass all imports, exports and even flights through Turkey, the only country that acknowledges it as a sovereign state. All attempts to solve the dilemma of the division of Cyprus have so far failed, on an island where Turkish Muslims and Greek Christians coexisted in harmony for many centuries, as mirror images of each other. Yet there is a clear distinction between the official political line and the reality for many Cypriots in their daily lives. The checkpoints in Nicosia are always busy with locals crossing over, often to socialize with their friends across the divide and visit their old villages. In this landscape where mosques and churches often stood side by side, many harbour hopes for reconciliation. The mufti of the Islamic community in southern Cyprus, Imam Shakir Alemdar, claims that Cypriot Muslims and Christians respect each other's faiths, and he regularly attends both Christian and Muslim ceremonies with the Orthodox archbishop. Even so, both local and international antagonisms hinder any reconcilement of the religious conflict that has dominated the vexed issue of Cypriot identity. Yet today's fractured reflection of Cyprus's past has not emerged out of religious and ethnic hostility alone, but also out of international wars and conflicting political interests, nationalism and the pressures of immigration, whose legacy is an enduring and intractable segregation.

Malta: An Island with a Hybrid History

In 1984, the Libyan president Muammar Gaddafi opened a brand-new mosque in the town of Paola, on Malta. It was the first mosque to be built on the island since the knights of the Order of St John had built one inside a prison for Turkish slaves in 1702. The very name of the modern temple – Mariam Al-Batool, or Virgin Mary Mosque – proclaims the close association of the religions of Islam and Christianity through their reverence for the mother of Christ. The mosque stands on the crest of Corradino Hill, close to the remains of a Phoenician temple and a line of fortifications built by Malta's British overlords in the nineteenth century, and has the Islamic Cultural Centre and Malta Islamic cemetery within its precincts. Its conception and construction were part of the Treaty of Friendship and Cooperation signed with Libya at that time, and it has come to represent the revival of Islam in Malta, welcomed by many, though seen by some as the start of a modern Muslim invasion, or as sinister evidence that Malta became Libya's bridge to Europe after the Lockerbie plane bombing by Libyan terrorists in 1988. On an island whose official religion is Catholicism, the new mosque also symbolizes the historical presence of Islam, whose profound cultural influence began long ago on Malta, in the eighth century.

*

Malta is an island of mixed identity, an archipelago located almost at the midpoint of the Mediterranean, within striking distance of Tunisia and Libya, and only eighty kilometres south of Sicily. For centuries, it was seen as North African, and Maltese is the only Semitic language with official status in the European Union, or in any European country. Like Sicily and Cyprus, it has been ruled by many foreign powers on account of its special strategic importance at the centre of the Great Sea. All three islands experienced Muslim Arab raids in the ninth century, though Malta did not come under Arab rule until 870–1, or at least no surviving historical accounts refer to earlier raids. The island was a key element in the Byzantine Empire's defence system and was ruled from Constantinople as an Orthodox Christian society, as its abundance of Christian catacombs suggest.

In 870, the North African Aghlabids, who were Sunni Muslims and vassals of the Abbasid caliphate, took control of all three adjacent islands – Malta, Gozo and Comino – and set up their capital in Mdina, introducing Islam and laying the foundations of today's Maltese language. Records of life on Malta from this time until the late eleventh century are vague and fragmented, yet there are signs that, while the population was very small, Arab Malta was fully involved in the cultural and economic interactions between Sicily and the Maghreb, since plentiful remnants of high-quality imported ceramics dating from the tenth and eleventh centuries have been found in town and country. There is a good chance that a fugitive Muslim community from Sicily fled to Malta to escape the threat of conquest by the Byzantine general George Maniakes in 1038, forming a colony. As they had in al-Andalus and Sicily, the Muslims brought new crops of spices, citrus fruits, almonds and figs, as well as cotton, which became crucial to Malta's economy for centuries. The crops were terraced according to ancient Arab husbandry and watered by their innovative irrigation techniques, including the waterwheel – vital resources for an island that lacks permanent rivers or lakes.

*

Majmuna, daughter of Hassan, son of Ali al-Hudali, an Arab girl from Gozo or Tunisia, is believed to have died on the island on Thursday, 21 March 1174. Nothing else is known of her beyond these details written on a marble tombstone displayed in Gozo Museum of Archaeology. It was once a Roman tombstone, sculpted with a rose in relief in Roman style, but it was reused by a Muslim family and is engraved all over with a sombre funerary inscription in Kufic Arabic. It is unique in Malta as the only Islamic tombstone surviving intact and with a date. Poignant as an emblem of personal grief, it is also important in reinforcing the idea that Islam remained the majority religion for several generations after the Norman invasion of Malta in 1091, when it became part of the kingdom of Sicily. It was the last Arab stronghold in the area to be reclaimed by a Christian ruler, in this case Count Roger I of Sicily, who liberated many Greeks and other Christians, but retained the Arab system of administration headed by a local qadi, allowing Muslims to continue to practise their faith unrestricted. The emir remained as ruler, subject to paying a yearly tribute, an arrangement which enabled Malta's majority of Muslims to dominate the island in terms of commerce for over 150 years after the Christian conquest. The bishop of Strasbourg, Burchard, visited the archipelago in 1175 and declared that its people were mainly Saracens, though there was an Arabic-speaking Christian community too. The 300-year presence of Arabs on the islands of Malta left a deep imprint. As time went on and Catholicism became more embedded, many Maltese Muslims converted, but their colloquial Arab-Berber language remained in proverbs, riddles, surnames and place names.

In 1266, Malta confronted its third change of rulers since the first Arab incursion of 870, when that Renaissance man, the emperor Frederick II, passed the island to the French house of Anjou under Charles I, whose loathing for all religions except Catholicism jeopardized its peaceful coexistence with Islam on the island. Even so, Malta kept strong ties with North Africa until it came under the control of the Spanish Crown of Aragon in 1283. By the late fifteenth century, hot on the heels of the conquest of Granada, Spain ordered the conversion of all Maltese Muslims to Catholicism, and, like the Spanish Moriscos, they found themselves obliged to live a hidden life and disguise their identities. Islam went underground.

In a fourth change of regime in 1530, the military order of the Knights Hospitaller of St John took charge of Malta, Gozo and Tripoli in Libya as a fiefdom, in exchange for which they agreed to an annual payment of one Maltese falcon to Charles V, Holy Roman Emperor and king of Spain. They faced a powerful enemy when the Ottoman sultan Suleiman I attacked the island in 1565 as part of his policy to expand his territory across the Mediterranean. Only Malta stood between Suleiman and total domination of the Great Sea. In what was known as the Great Siege of Malta, 6,000 islanders and Knights of St John took on 50,000 highly trained Janissaries throughout the summer, resisting doggedly against the odds until Suleiman finally withdrew the army. It was a famous, if harrowing, victory, and the sultan's last defeat before he died in 1566, just six years before the disastrous sea Battle of Lepanto in 1571, when the Ottomans were roundly beaten by Christian navies.

Over the two and a half centuries of their stewardship, the Knights captured thousands of Muslim slaves in maritime raids, taking them to Malta, where they lived in relative freedom, gathered for prayers and worked at various trades. The new mosque was built inside the slaves' prison during this time, in 1702, though no trace of it remains. But when a plot by Muslim slaves to assassinate the grand master was foiled, the Hospitallers imposed tough laws and restrictions on their movements. These measures coincided with a concerted and deliberate disinformation campaign led by the Catholic clergy, through which they sought to construct a history of the island that shrugged off its past links with Islam and North Africa. It was a ploy that influenced the nature of Maltese history writing for 300 years.

*

In 1814, Malta became part of the British Empire, as agreed in the Treaty of Paris, and the British took full advantage of the island's important position between Gibraltar and Egypt, as a way station on their main trade route to India. At the end of the nineteenth century, Ottoman sultan Abdulaziz commissioned a new Muslim cemetery on Malta, designed by the Maltese architect Emanuele Galizia in a Moorish Revival style unique to the island, that created a picturesque landmark. It became the only public prayer site for Muslims until the 1970s.

After 150 years under British jurisdiction, Malta finally became an independent state in 1964, breaking off relations with NATO and turning to face Africa in the south after nearly a millennium of close contact with Europe. It was at this time that the Maltese government courted the dubious friendship of Libya under the leadership of the left-wing prime minister Dom Mintoff. The narrative of history-writing began to change as it explored the close cultural and ethnic connections of Malta with North Africa, and for a time Arabic was a compulsory subject in Maltese schools. Many of Malta's Sunni and Ahmadiyya Muslim men married Maltese women, creating a new Islamic community.* In political life, the civil servant Mario Farrugia Borg became the first Maltese person in public office to take an oath on the Koran, when he joined the local council in 1998.

The main imam of the Mariam Al-Batool Mosque, Sheikh

---

* The Ahmadiyya Muslim community began in British India in the nineteenth century and seeks to revitalize Islam and restore it to its original form, creating a moral and ethical path to peace.

Muhammad El-Sadi, estimates that there are around 6,000 Muslims living on Malta currently, most of whom are Libyan Sunnis, while the rest are from North Africa, the Middle East and Europe.[6] While there is some prejudice and racism relating to concerns about the arrival of illegal Muslim immigrants, the Maltese public and the Muslim community are well integrated. Although Malta's official religion is Catholic, religious freedom is guaranteed, and there are plans to build a second mosque on the island. Today, Malta has cemented its status as a bridge between Europe and North Africa, a hybrid land bearing the living legacy of its Islamic culture.

Land of Tolerance: Tatarstan and the Tatars

The republic of Tatarstan lies at the time-honoured meeting point of Europe and Asia, where the great river Volga joins its tributary, the river Kama, amid a landscape wooded with aspen, birch and Scots pine that extends as far east as the Ural Mountains. At the easternmost border of Europe, Tatarstan is little known in the west, although its territory has been inhabited since prehistoric times. By the start of the eighth century, its people had developed an advanced mercantile state that traded as far afield as the Middle East and the Baltic, a multi-ethnic community composed of Scandinavians, Slavs and the semi-nomadic Turkic tribes known as the Bulgars, hence its first designation as Volga Bulgaria. That state retained its independence until 1238, when it fell to the armies of the Mongol leader Batu Khan.

Earlier, in the year 921, at the time when Abd al-Rahman III ruled the sophisticated and advanced caliphate of Cordoba in the west of the Islamic empire, Ahmad ibn Fadlan, who was born in Baghdad and worked as secretary to the ambassador of the Abbasid caliph al-Muqtadir, left his native city with a party of diplomats to travel to Volga Bulgaria to meet its king. His journey of almost 5,000 kilometres, over deserts, mountains, rivers, snows and freezing weather, is recounted in the unique travelogue he wrote, his *risala*, the manuscript of which has survived. Ibn Fadlan undertook to swap the luxury and comfort of tenth-century Baghdad for a rough-and-ready yurt in the lands of the Bulgars. The perilous journey was prompted by the recent conversion of the Volga peoples to Islam by Muslim missionaries from Baghdad, upon which the Volga king Yiltawar had written to al-Muqtadir requesting instruction in the correct laws and rituals of Islam, as well as soliciting a mosque, minbar and fortress. The requests were granted and the diplomatic mission was sent out to accept the king and his peoples formally as part of the Islamic community. Ibn Fadlan and his party reached their destination on 12 May 922, after almost a year of travel; they were lodged in Bulgar tents and gave Islamic instruction to the local community, via two interpreters, one from each side, who were familiar with Arabic. Ibn Fadlan found Volga customs and culture crude and shocking at times, despite the genuine desire of the people to learn Muslim ways. He was fearful of the demeanour of the Volga king, but overcame his trepidation and succeeded in advising him on how to conduct the muezzin's call to prayer and on the correct proclamation to be made from the new minbar.

Over several centuries, Volga Bulgaria came to develop a culture greatly influenced by the Muslim Middle East, and it was the first Muslim state in future Russian lands. After the conquest of their state by the Golden Horde in 1238, the Volga peoples, by then known as Tatars, regained independence around 1430 under the Tatar Turkic khanate, based in the capital Kazan, not far from the ruined Bulgar capital on the Volga river. In 1550, around the time the Süleymaniye Mosque of Istanbul was founded, the khanate of Kazan was facing constant conflict with Russia, until it was eventually conquered by the troops of the Russian Prince Ivan the Terrible (1530–1584), who overran Kazan in 1552, using siege towers and battering rams to enter the city and massacre most of the population. After his victory, Ivan was reported to have ordered the crescent of Islam to be placed underneath the Christian cross on the domes of all Orthodox Christian churches. In Kazan itself, a bishop arrived to baptize the local people by forcible conversion to Christianity; churches and monasteries were built, and many of the Tatar nobility endured baptism in order to keep their aristocratic privileges. By 1593, all mosques were destroyed and the Russian government forbade the construction of new ones. The Volga Tatar Muslims were compelled to become Christians.

When Catherine the Great became empress of Russia in 1762, Muslims had been living in Moscow under duress since the late fifteenth century. The empress reversed the policy, in force since Ivan's time, of excluding Muslims and repressing Islam, and in line with her Enlightenment views became the first Russian ruler to be tolerant of Muslim religious and cultural identity in her territories, issuing a Toleration of All Faiths edict in 1773. The Moscow Cathedral Mosque was built in her time as a symbol of friendship between the Russian and Tatar people, and Catherine lifted the prohibition on mosque building in 1785, enabling the Tatar people of the Volga to rebuild their Muslim identity. The lands that would become Tatarstan formed one of the centres of an Islamic movement known as Jadidism, promoted by a Crimean Tatar, Ismail Gasprinski (1851–1914), whose aim was to spread the reform of religious education using his 'new method' or *jadid*. He and his followers, such as Musa Bigeev (*c.* 1870–1949), who was educated in Kazan, believed in religious reform and modernization, and they linked elements common to both Islam and Communism. Eventually, the Soviet government was to clamp down on Muslim institutions, and the Jadids became the main target of its bloody anti-Islam campaign before Islam went underground in the Soviet Union.

During the upheavals of the Russian Revolution, Tatar nationalists for a short time established an independent republic, but, in May 1920, the Tatar Autonomous Soviet Socialist Republic was declared. Under Stalin, the national culture and language of the Tatars were repressed, as was Islam. It was not until 1990 that the status of Tatarstan was changed, and a declaration of sovereignty of the Tatarstan Soviet Socialist Republic was made. The idea of Tatarstan as a sovereign state was not to Soviet liking, and the constitution was changed to define it as part of the Russian Federation, removing its autonomy, until a special agreement was signed in 1994, when the country officially assumed the name of

Tatarstan. In 2008, the Tatar people claimed independence for Tatarstan, but their aspiration was ignored by the United Nations and the Russian government; it remains part of the Russian Federation.

*

The enlightened ideas of the empress of Russia and Tatarstan's forward-thinking, reformist past seem to have played a vital part in making the country what it is today. Not only does its population of four million citizens belong to a democratic state which is one of the most economically advanced regions of Russia, but it is also an important cultural and religious centre, with two UNESCO World Heritage Sites: the Kazan Kremlin and the Assumption Cathedral and Monastery. Tatarstan's crowning glory is an awe-inspiring building, the Temple of All Religions, or Universal Temple, in the heart of the capital city. Its creator, Ildar Khanov, was born in 1939, on the eve of the Second World War, and spent much of his life in Kazan, where he worked as an artist, architect and healer. Living on small donations and very little sleep, he treated alcoholics and drug addicts, many of whom he conscripted to work on his architectural projects as part of their rehabilitation. Khanov was a highly spiritual man with an intense desire to foster unity among religions, and his temple is a testament to those beliefs. It combines architectural styles from various faiths, including Islam, Christianity, Judaism and Buddhism, and houses an Orthodox church, a mosque and a synagogue in the same building. Its mission as he saw it was to exist as a 'temple of culture and truth', and he aspired in the future to incorporate sixteen cupolas into the structure, corresponding to the sixteen major world religions, including those of the past, now defunct. He was still working on the temple when he died, aged seventy-four, in 2013.

The temple is the eloquent symbol of Tatarstan's cultural and religious ethos, which takes pride in the peaceful combination of different cultures and religions – Islamic Tatar, Orthodox Russian, Jewish and others – throughout its lands. Although today religion and state are separate, Tatarstan citizens comprise just over half Sunni Muslims, who worship at over a thousand different mosques, and the rest are Russian Orthodox or secular. Out of a history of conflict between Islam and Orthodox Christianity, it has forged a society akin to the religiously tolerant and stable polity of the caliphate of Cordoba, yet unique in today's world. At all public events, an Orthodox priest and a Muslim mufti are always present. Since 1992, the Kazan Kremlin has been the centre of the presidency of Tatarstan, which incorporates among its buildings the Kul-Sharif Mosque and a revitalized and ancient Annunciation Cathedral. Both buildings were reconstructed simultaneously, and mark a new era of understanding and cooperation between Islam and Christianity in the name of peace between ethnic groups and in Russia. They are testament to the widespread tolerance and cooperation that prevails in Tatarstan under the aegis of its enlightened President Shaimiev. He is the only Russian statesman to hold the highest orders of both the Russian Orthodox Church and the Spiritual Board of Russian Islam, awarded for his work for inter-religious peace and understanding.

Tatarstan has achieved harmony and stability in society, among religions and ethnic groups, to a degree unthinkable in many other countries, and its multiculturalism constitutes a workable social model, which greatly impressed the American ambassador William Burns, who visited Kazan in 2006. He concluded: 'It seems to me that the entire world must follow your example and traditions of inter-religious tolerance,' an objective which, Burns believed, all countries should aspire to.[7] Tatarstan's utopian example sends a message of hope precisely because it shows the world that religious tolerance and coexistence is not only conceivable, but actually works in a democratic and economically stable human society.

Reverberations

Three brief histories, three snapshots of lands that are microcosms of a greater picture of the divergences and convergences of European Muslims and Christians down the centuries, tell eloquent stories that resonate in the present. In Cyprus, the peaceful coexistence of both peoples has descended into divisions and hatreds that remain unresolved. In contrast, Malta's Muslim past extends into life today in a fusion of native and Islamic cultures manifested in the Maltese language, popular culture and architecture, as the islanders seek to build a relationship of tolerance and cooperation between its Christian and Muslim communities. The republic of Tatarstan stands alone in building a model community of interfaith harmony and diversity out of its turbulent religious past. These are three small countries within the great expanse of the continent of Europe, yet their portraits are food for thought for the interfaith conversations of the future.

Part Seven

THE CRUCIBLE OF LIGHT

'General View of the Alhambra', c. 1862

Chapter 29

Forging the Future of Europe

'Your identity is like your shadow: not always visible and yet always present.'

Fausto Cercignani

'Since my origin is of the earth, all the Earth is my country and all the people of the world are my kin.'

Abu-d-Salt, eleventh-century poet from Denia

At the heart of this book is an image, a metaphor whose source lies in ancient science. Long ago, near the time this history began, a Byzantine monk from Alexandria named Morienus travelled to Homs in Syria in the hope of converting the Umayyad prince Khalid ibn Yazid (*c.* AD 668–704) to Christianity. Khalid had no wish to forsake Islam, but he did have a burning desire to learn the secrets of alchemy and witness the alchemical production of gold. Morienus had been the disciple of a renowned alchemist, Stephanos of Alexandria, and was skilled in the art of the crucible, so he agreed to perform a successful transmutation of base metals into gold. The two men from different worlds met on the common ground of scientific discovery, as teacher and student, their religious differences set aside in their mutual search for knowledge and illumination. Khalid's new learning led him to write a number of alchemical poems and develop a lifelong fascination with the subject. The early Arabic *Book on the Composition of Alchemy*, possibly written by Morienus himself, told the story of the encounter between the monk and the caliph's son, and was the first work on this subject to appear in Latin Europe, in a translation by Robert of Chester, dated 1144.

As a result, Khalid became the earliest figure in both Muslim and Christian European alchemy.

For both Arab alchemists and their Latin European counterparts, alchemy was not just a scientific process. The physical transmutation of base metals into gold through the fire of the crucible was interpreted metaphorically, as a symbol of man's regeneration and transformation into a higher, more spiritual state. The crucible itself became a figure of speech, used often in relation to wars and conflicts, to express the idea of a place or situation in which people or their beliefs were tested severely, often creating something new and transformational in the process. In this book, the crucible corresponds to the continent of Europe, whose evolving, hybrid identity has been forged over centuries in myriad encounters between its Muslims and Christians in both war and peace. And, in that crucible, the darkness and light of European history are fashioned into a radical alternative.

Seven Crossroads on the Highway to the Twenty-First Century

Over 1,300 years, the history of those encounters between Muslims and Christians has been driven by seven decisive moments of reversal and evolution. These revolutionary moments involve the birth and death of great empires – Persian, Roman, Ottoman and Islamic; the creation of a new global religion; the fall of caliphs and emirs in al-Andalus and the rise of Catholic domination; the conquest and defence of great cities – Constantinople and Vienna; the invasions of colonialism and the devastation of mighty conflicts, most crucially the Crusades and the First World War. The titanic global shifts that reconfigured European political and religious history run parallel with a story of cultural and economic expansion that centres not on conflict, but on the prospect of multicultural harmony and tolerance. The seventh crossroad was reached when the Ottoman Empire was dissolved in 1923. A new Turkish state emerged alongside the regions of Europe redesignated as nation states, all of which wrought profound upheaval for Europe's Muslim population, which became at once dispersed yet gathered and concentrated in restricted locations. The dust was only beginning to settle when the western continent found itself, incomprehensibly, in the throes of a Second World War, whose aftermath raised crucial questions about the nature and status of Europe, with weighty repercussions for twenty-first-century relations between its Christian and Islamic peoples.

The Quest for European Identity and the Foundation of the European Union

In reaction to the horrors of the Second World War, Europe, for a time, sought peace and unity. The European Coal and Steel Community (ECSC), founded in 1951 to prevent the manufacture of weapons of war by a single country, was the precursor of a European Union conceived as a peace project aiming to reorientate 'Europe's bellicose history towards the goal of reconciliation and pacification.'[1] It fulfilled that aim to a degree, and was rewarded with the Nobel Peace Prize in 2012. Despite those strongly expressed, idealistic ambitions and their practical manifestations, the language of religious and cultural difference returned to exert a divisive influence as early as 1950, when the German city of Aachen founded the Charlemagne Prize for service to European unification. Its first winner, the politician and philosopher Richard Coudenhove Kalergi, described the ECSC as the start of the revival of Charlemagne's Carolingian Empire, of which it was the perceived continuation.[2] His words clearly aligned the new post-war Europe with a Catholic imperial power.

By the Cold War of the 1960s, Churchill and others spoke of the communist threat to Christian, or at times to Judaeo-Christian, civilization, while the German chancellor Konrad Adenauer and the Italian politician Alcide de Gasperi, both on the Catholic centre right, made it clear that Christianity was at the core of European identity. Even so, since the Treaty of Rome of 1957 which founded the European Economic Community, western Europe has presented itself as increasingly secular. Church attendance has dropped dramatically, although private religious belief has not. In line with the political zeitgeist, the fact that many Europeans still consider themselves Christians exposes the continuing awareness of an implicit Christian cultural distinctiveness.[3]

At the same time, the EU's expansion into central and eastern Europe has complicated the question of European identity. The Czech Republic, Slovakia and Poland joined the community in 2004 and attempted to introduce a reference to 'Christian tradition' into the acceptance documents, which were eventually modified in more general terms to include the cultural, religious and humanist inheritance of Europe.[4] A more extreme view of the continent as exclusively Christian has been voiced by the Hungarian prime minister, Viktor Orbán, who envisages a Europe 'free from the ravages of Islamization.'[5] For all that, the narrative of a uniquely Christian Europe is undermined by those EU countries with a Muslim population, either past or present. Greece joined the Common Market in 1981 when it was a formerly Balkan Ottoman country, then espousing Orthodox Christianity, and which only became an independent nation in the nineteenth century.[6] Almost all the former Ottoman Balkan countries are or will be EU members, except for Albania, Serbia and North Macedonia. But the issue of the acceptance of Turkey as an EU country remains a stumbling block and continues to generate great controversy. While its size and human-rights record are the official reasons for its non-acceptance, its cultural and religious identity as both secular and Muslim is an obstacle for France and Germany, who opposed its admission since it failed to square with the idea of Europe as a Christian polity.

After the 9/11 terrorist attacks, European hostility towards Turkey increased due to its mainly Muslim population. That hostility is exemplified by the European commissioner Frits Bolkestein, the liberal Dutch politician who controversially warned of the imminent Islamization of Europe, adding that, if Turkey were admitted to the EU, then 'the liberation of Vienna in 1683 would have been in vain.'[7] The attitudes and comments of certain senior European politicians raise a fundamental question: does Europe define itself primarily by its Latin Christian heritage, or by democracy, global human rights, and liberal values that must include the full recognition of its multicultural, multi-religious past?

The Fallacy of the Muslim Threat: Immigration and Islamophobia

Since the 1970s, the curtain has risen on a scene both new and very ancient, in which European Christians and Muslims are silhouetted against a backdrop of simmering hostilities, a sense of imminent threat, and deep confusion over the true nature of European civilization. That hostility, apprehension and confusion are provoked by the key players: Muslim immigrants on the one hand, and, on the other, radicalized Muslim terrorists, creating the notion that immigration in Europe relates almost exclusively to Muslims. The suspicion is mutual, as European Muslims are acutely aware that their presence in the western continent is rejected by many non-Muslim Europeans, that their religion is caricatured, and that they are often regarded as aliens even when immigrant families have been resident for two or three generations. Such antagonism takes no account of the fact that Muslims have lived on the continent for many centuries, nor that, along with immigrants, there exists a thriving indigenous Muslim population in central and eastern European lands.[8]

Most Muslims living in the European Union today immigrated after the Second World War. In the aftermath, the resulting severe labour shortages were eased by inviting immigrants from former colonies – North Africa, the Far East, India and Pakistan – to join the workforce in France, the UK, Holland and also Germany, where Turkish and Kurdish workers were employed. In the 1950s and 1960s, these mainstays of the European work effort, who built roads, worked in mines and cleaned streets and offices, came on a temporary basis and contributed to an economic boom. It is a deep irony that after the Second World War with its appalling loss of life, in which many thousands of Muslims fought and died for the Allies against the Nazis, up until 1970, immigrants, Muslim or not, were seen as a blessing rather than a threat. Then things changed. In 1973, European states brought in laws to restrict regular migration, but relaxed restrictions on family reunification. Families of migrants joined them in Europe, the population increased, and those who were Muslim became more visible in society as mosques were built, women wore veils and Muslim children went to local schools. The backlash came from new right-wing parties who now deemed immigration to be a threat, particularly as illegal migrants began to arrive in thousands, initially in Spain and Italy, a figure more recently added to by asylum seekers fleeing from devastated countries such as Syria and Iraq.

In 2024, roughly forty-four million Muslims were living in Europe, twenty-five million of whom reside in EU countries, plus seventy-seven million in Turkey. In a European population of some 744 million, excluding Turkey, that accounts for a non-threatening 6 per cent. Yet there is a prevalent opinion among politicians, the media and right-wing populists that Europe is being invaded by Muslims who will not adapt to European life and culture and who espouse a religion incompatible with western values. No heed is paid to the great diversity of Muslim communities in Europe, who speak different languages, have different ethnicities and have diverse views on Islam itself. But the irrational fear of and prejudice against Muslims in Europe that we now call Islamophobia has existed since the earliest writings of John of Damascus and the Venerable Bede in the eighth century. It is a key factor in the rise of right-wing politicians and polemicists, such as the British Reform UK leader, Nigel Farage, who has spoken of the need to preserve Britain's 'Judaeo-Christian tradition', and it has spawned the publication of a whole raft of bestsellers critical of Islam.[9]

Today's Islamophobia is no less virulent than the hostility and antagonism towards Islam expressed by those medieval Christian writers, and is stoked by rhetoric in much the same way, though with the added animosity and global reach of contemporary European media. British press and broadcasting have been criticized for promoting negative Muslim stereotypes and fuelling Islamic prejudice that has turned its resident Muslims into scapegoats to rationalize the UK's current economic and political problems. Many west European politicians now speak the language of Samuel P. Huntington's 'clash of civilizations' and assert the idea that the civilized world is fighting radical Islam, and history can appear to bear out that viewpoint. From the first Muslim conquests to the Crusades, the siege of Vienna, the wars between the Arabs and Israelis, and from images of modern-day Muslim tyrants like Muammar Gaddafi and Saddam Hussein wielding Islamic swords to death threats and terrorist atrocities – all conspire to justify a fear of violent and militant Islam.[10] Yet the British journalist Peter Oborne is outspoken in his belief that these views have encouraged western Europe and its US allies to undertake illegal wars, use torture and display a contempt for democracy, human life and the rule of law on a par with that of al-Qaeda.[11] As he points out, the prophecy of such a clash of civilizations has so far come to nothing – not one of the world's fifty Muslim-majority countries has declared war on the US, or on Europe for that matter.[12] In fact, the reverse has happened. At the same time, the rhetoric of militant Islamic groups is one of hatred of and opposition to western culture, and Islamic revivalists seek the complete merger of religious and political power which is fundamental to Islam, but at odds with the contemporary European state system. Even so, most of their energy is expended on battling with their own state rulers, the Gulf emirs and the international business classes of Cairo and Istanbul, rather than with western Europe. In an era of great social and political instability, with antipathy predominating over mutual friendship, European Christians and Muslims have reached a new crossroads in their long history, and the right path to take is not clearly signposted.

The Islamic Past that Lives On in the Present and Leads to the Future

It is impossible to comprehend Europe's past or imagine its future without grasping the full extent of the intense relationship between its Muslim and Christian citizens that has been forged by war and by peace for almost one and half millennia. Each owes a moral and cultural debt to the other in different ways, a debt that has accrued on their long, shared journey into the present. Europe's Muslims owe to the Christian West the gift of a technological and scientific development that enabled them to stand on a firm footing in the modern world, a bestowal offset by the disenchantments of colonization and what has been judged to be progress. Christian Europe has a greater debt, since it owes to Islamic civilization the knowledge that kick-started the entire cultural revolution of western Europe in the first place. The acknowledgement of that debt is not part of the dominant narrative of the development of European civilization. With some exceptions, such as the majestic history of Spain's Islamic empire by the early twentieth-century American scholar S. P. Scott, historians of western Europe, such as Arnold Toynbee and even the French historian Fernand Braudel, espouse a strongly Eurocentric view of the cultural evolution of the continent as a movement from classical antiquity to capitalism, owing little to outside influences. There is scant sense of the importance of the contribution of the Arab-Islamic empire. The leading contemporary philosopher Nayef Al-Rodhan underlines how that insistence on the superiority of western European civilization in fact uncovers a profound anxiety over its true character.[13]

That character has unquestionably been formed by the manifold exchanges between Muslims and Christians, at war and in peace, that have conferred a shared identity on the continent. This is a reality that shakes the perceived foundations of European selfhood, yet it is recognizable all around us, across twenty-first-century Europe, from east to west. It turns up in our daily lives, in our use of knives and forks, in many of the words we speak, such as 'algebra' or 'sugar', in the numerals we use for counting, in our reliance on antiseptics, pioneered by medieval Muslim physicians who used alcohol or vinegar to sanitize wounds. Our banking and insurance systems, the use of cheques, bills of exchange and written trading contracts, all often attributed to the Italians, originated in the Islamic and pre-Islamic Middle East. The Commercial Revolution from the late Middle Ages until the Industrial Revolution was founded on elements crucial to Muslim commerce – the lateen sail and the astrolabe that were vital to maritime trade, the use of the number zero in accounting and business dealings, paper and textile manufacture – all of which can be credited to the Middle and Far East, and China.[14]

The depth and resonance of those confluences is vivid in the legacy of past encounters between Muslims and Christians across the continent, east and west. It appears in tangible form in the preserved materiality of war, in the landscape, in structures and spaces, and in the performance of ceremonies that re-enact or celebrate historic events. In Bratislava, the capital of modern Slovakia, with a majority Christian population, a Slovak military plaque on the Church of Our Lady of the Snows preserves the memory of the Battle of Kahlenberg that ended the second siege of Vienna in 1683 and celebrates the Christian victory over the Ottomans.[15] In neighbouring Poland, with its almost exclusively Catholic society, there appears on the surface few vestiges of its Muslim heritage, yet rare traces emerge in the form of historic wooden mosques and Muslim gravestones, remnants of those Muslim Tatars from Lithuania who settled in Polish territory in the seventeenth century. Only two historical Tatar mosques remain in Poland today, but once there were many more. Newly explored Tatar cemeteries have revealed Muslim inscriptions on tombstones in Arabic, often with quotations from the Koran, along with gold arabesque ornamentation and metal crescents that lay bare a history previously overlaid by Russian inscriptions. Professor Agata S. Nalborczyk has written eloquently about Poland's concealed Muslim past, which she describes as 'the cultivation of local space by elements of material and symbolic Islamic legacy embedded in the landscape and local society for centuries – not alien, but familiar and settled.'[16]

Other Balkan countries today are powerful reminders of a living indigenous Muslim Europe, whose modern citizens declare that they have been happily Muslim and European for almost six centuries.[17] Bosnia Herzegovina, Kosovo and Albania have majority Muslim populations, while Serbia, North Macedonia and Montenegro have centuries-old Muslim communities. After the horrifying Bosnian war of 1992, which was a confrontation between Orthodox and Catholic Serb, Bosnian and Croat forces against citizens in a once Ottoman land which prided itself on being a multi-ethnic state, two borderless nations, both part of one country, came into being, each with its own parliament and capital. Bosnia and Herzegovina is Bosniak and Muslim, and the Republic of Sprska is mainly ethnic Serbian and Orthodox Christian. In the Bosnian capital of Sarajevo, an Ottoman city, the call to prayer is a normal part of daily life; its magnificent mosque was built in 1531, in the era of the architect Sinan. The town hall, built by the Austro-Hungarians, is designed using red and white horseshoe arches inspired by the famous Umayyad mosques of Damascus and Cordoba.

Further down the Adriatic coast in Albania, the old town of Gjirokaster, once the heart of Sufism and Islamic scholarship in that region, is now a UNESCO World Heritage Site, presided over by the Memi Bey Mosque, built in 1757, and an old Ottoman bazaar. The lovely village of Berat, also a UNESCO World Heritage Site, boasts a unique architectural legacy of Ottoman mosques and Byzantine churches. The Muslim traveller Evliya Çelebi visited the town in 1670 and praised its famous mosques, madrasas and Sufi lodges, and its mixed population of Muslims, Christians and Jews. Today, it is one of Albania's main cultural centres.

The case of Turkey is in some ways exceptional. Geographically in both west Asia and south-eastern Europe, and technically a secular state with no official religion, its population of some eighty-five million is almost entirely Muslim. In the twenty-first century, it has experienced almost a complete reversal of Atatürk's cultural revolution, as the Ottoman traditions previously censored have returned to the forefront of state policy. President Recep Erdoğan's Justice and Development Party, the AKP, founded in 2002, has turned Islam and Turkey's Muslim past into a central pillar of his domestic and foreign strategy. Parallel with, but opposite to Atatürk's reforms, Ottoman buildings have been renovated, including the Hagia Sophia and the Egyptian bazaar, and new mosques have been erected, while street names have been changed back to reflect Turkey's Ottoman heritage. Atatürk's rewriting of history has been reverse-engineered to revive the memory of the great sultans: Mehmed the Conqueror, who represents a return to Islamic traditions; Selim I and Suleiman the Magnificent, both greatly admired by Erdoğan and promoted in mass media; and Abdul Hamid II, the controversial Red Sultan, whose social and political outlook the president shares. In his reconversion of the Hagia Sophia from museum to mosque, the use of crusading rhetoric to extol the heroes of Gallipoli and his adept designation of Atatürk as a man who respected Islam, Erdoğan espouses the image of a defender of Muslims, despite the social tensions and international outrage sparked by his political agenda.[18]

Attestations to the inheritance of Ottoman life and culture are being celebrated and restored across the Muslim lands of the Balkans and Turkey, and university degrees in Islam are now available there. Their peoples are as European as they are Muslim, though western Europe has persistently ignored or resisted this fact, either intentionally or through lack of knowledge, and looks on them as outsiders.

*

The broad sweep of Europe's Islamic history is plainly visible, from the small utopian state of Tatarstan on the easternmost reaches of the continent, to Turkey and the Balkans, then as far north as France and Great Britain and as far south and west as Sicily and Spain. It lives on in modern Spanish, Balkan and Turkish politics, where Islam's medieval past is mobilized to reconfigure contemporary government agendas. Nowhere is it more arresting, tangible and powerful than in the structures, stones and spaces of the three greatest monuments to Islamic civilization in Europe: Istanbul's Hagia Sophia, a mosque for around 500 years; Cordoba's Great Mosque, where Muslims prayed for 600 years; and the Alhambra of Granada, a Muslim fortress and palace from the thirteenth century to the present. Each building is material proof of the sustained presence of Muslim life in Europe, and each symbolizes the persisting conflict and ambiguity of the relationships between Muslims and Christians. The Hagia Sophia began as a Byzantine basilica, became an Ottoman mosque in 1453, then a museum in the 1930s and is now a mosque once more. The Great Mosque of Cordoba, built in the eighth-century reign of Abd al-Rahman I, was nominally converted to a Christian building in 1236, until the sixteenth century, when it suffered the construction of a Renaissance cathedral in its very centre; today, it is still officially designated as a place of Christian worship which prohibits Islamic prayer inside the temple. The Alhambra has been an Islamic palace since its earliest incarnation in the thirteenth century, and remains a powerful witness to the fall of Granada's emirate to Catholic power in 1492.

Europe Reimagined

The epic story of the European encounters between Islam and Christianity from the fall of the Persian and Roman Empires and the birth of Islam up to the twenty-first century illuminates the compelling need for new ways of thinking and better kinds of social, cultural and political interaction between Europe's Christians, non-Muslims and Muslims. Their history makes it crystal clear that inter-religious, inter-racial violence never ends well, and that negotiation, discussion and compromise can save many lives. It also lays bare the essential importance of a new paradigm, a new way of seeing the continent of Europe. At the start of the twenty-first century, the historian Richard Bulliet put forward the idea of an 'Islamo-Christian civilization', a concept which he believed eliminates the idea of difference and annuls feelings of civilizational superiority and inferiority.[19] The problem is that 'Islamo-Christian' still marks opposition and separation. In contrast, the irrefutable proposition that the identity of Europe is and has been both Christian and Muslim since the eighth century, as its history suggests, unites the two in a single polity, culture and civilization that is still evolving as part of an ongoing intercultural, interfaith dialogue that celebrates the richness of hybridity. There is still a place for difference, for Sufi *tekkes*, Renaissance poetry, for Isaac Newton and Avicenna, and each element becomes vital to the development of the whole. Embracing an identity can bring limitation and restriction, as the negative forms of nationalism show, but to espouse a European identity that is both

Christian and Muslim might conversely be a path to liberation from prejudices and misconceptions.

The overlooking, passing over or forgetting, wilful or not, of a cultural heritage established over the course of a millennium that is shared with Muslim civilization is countermanded by the narrative of entwined philosophical, technological, scientific, artistic and commercial histories. The European past has seen appalling religious conflicts between Islam and Christianity, but also remarkable convergences in a long-standing and ongoing interdependence. Knowing the story of our common cultural past brings us together and forms a basis for greater understanding and reconciliation.

The Crucible of Light

The Alhambra of Granada is the most poignant, tangible reminder of a place where Arab Islamic civilization once flourished in a European land, and it holds the key to the re-envisioning of the great encounter between Christians and Muslims of all stripes. That civilization illuminated the medieval world, not just of Spain, but also of Europe, by virtue of its advanced knowledge of science, agriculture, architecture and philosophy, and its living Andalusian monuments are an undeniable and impressive testimony to that brilliance. The Iberian peninsula is at the heart of Europe's Muslim past – it is the place in Europe where Islamic rule and civilization in its various forms persisted the longest, and it has the greatest importance because it was the cradle of a culture and learning that was to transform the continent permanently.

Granada may be the gateway to the future. The importance of the city and the province, its history and culture, are pre-eminent, since no other single settlement in the peninsula, or indeed in Europe, can claim such a varied multicultural heritage. Granada was the place where Islamic rule finally ended in western Europe after almost 800 years, and where Spanish Catholicism became all-powerful. The longest-lasting and predominant culture in its multicultural history has been the Islamic one, which galvanized Granada's distinctive fusion of Muslim and Hispanic heritages. In this respect, Granada reflects the ambivalent identity not only of Spain, but also of Europe, and unlocks its significance in the vexed contemporary debates on just how that identity should be perceived.

In June 2018, a year before the announcement in August 2019 that Granada would bid for the award of European Capital of Culture 2031, a delegation from five EU countries, Cyprus, France, Greece, Portugal and Spain, met at the Alhambra to discuss the challenges facing the EU in the spheres of foreign affairs and defence, in which the ever more important need for dialogue with the Islamic world was on the agenda. Granada was chosen because of its historic multiculturalism, special relations with the Arab world and the universality of its links with Islamic civilization. At a meeting which led to the signing of the Declaration of Granada, whose aim is to bolster the fight against people trafficking and guarantee the rescue of migrants, the delegates reflected that few places in the world could be more inspiring in fostering cultural understanding and enabling a future of cooperation, peace and development. It was held up to other European parliaments as an example of peaceful coexistence deriving from its history as a place of confluence of many cultures, among which Muslim culture predominates. Granada is a place of overwhelming possibility as an influence for good, with the Alhambra, majestic in its global power as a touristic and cultural reference point, and above all as the hallmark of Europe's true heritage, and a guiding light for the multicultural values of the present and future.

In 1999, the Palestinian-American intellectual Edward Said and the Argentinian-Israeli conductor Daniel Barenboim founded the West–Eastern Divan Orchestra, originally based in Seville, which brought together musicians from the Muslim, Christian and Jewish countries of the Middle East and Spain with the aim of promoting understanding between nations. At the opening concert, Barenboim stressed the value of mutual comprehension: 'You can't create peace with an orchestra, but one can create the conditions for understanding and awaken the curiosity of each individual to listen to the narrative of the other.'[20] In a parallel way, the long story of conflict and cooperation between Muslims and Christians that has shaped European civilization through places, monuments and individual histories may sow the seeds of understanding, reconciliation and respect, and inspire a recognition of the power and value of the multicultural society that makes Europe what it is today. The symbolic vehicle of the evolution and transmutation of European civilization is not just a crucible of war. It is a crucible of light, a vessel in which an identity has been cast that confers an extraordinary richness and singularity on the continent, which demands that its citizens reconsider its true nature and acknowledge a history that has always been both Christian and Muslim. Then, the path ahead may lead to acceptance and mutual enlightenment.

Acknowledgements

The creation of a book from its conception to publication is an enormous team effort. I would like to record my sincere thanks to all the people who have been involved in this book, and who have worked so very hard to bring it into the world. As always, it has been a pleasure and privilege to work with my inimitable agent at AM Heath, Bill Hamilton, who encouraged me to write this book and whose faultless guidance, advice and perceptive understanding of the project I deeply appreciate. Warmest thanks are due also to my editor Georgina Morley, who believed in the book from the start and has been unfailingly encouraging, kind and supportive, as well as making numerous, wise improvements to the manuscript. Thanks to Gillian Stern for her editorial input, to Rosie Shackles and James Taylor for their excellent work on the images, and to Penelope Price, whose consummate copyediting is greatly valued. Thanks also to all the marvellous production team at Picador who have made this book a reality, including Nicholas Blake, with his prompt assistance, clarity and reassurance; Lindsay Nash for her text design; Martin Lubikowski for the clear, coherent maps; Moesha Parirenyatwa for the beautiful cover; and senior communications executive Kieran Sangha for his energy and enthusiasm. Above all, heartfelt gratitude as always to my husband Kiernan Ryan, who is my inspiration and kept me going whenever I flagged, and to my daughter Fiona for her unfailing support, encouragement and enthusiasm, as well as for her computing expertise.

Bibliography

Abulafia, David, *The Great Sea: A Human History of the Mediterranean* (London: Penguin, 2002)

Ackroyd, Peter, *Venice: Pure City* (London: Vintage, 2009)

Ágoston, Gábor, *The Last Muslim Conquest: The Ottoman Empire and its Wars in Europe* (Princeton: Princeton University Press, 2021)

Akhbar Machmua fi Fath al-Andalus wa Dhikri Umara'iha, ed. Emilio Lafuente y Alcántara (Madrid: n.p., 1867)

Aksan, Victoria, *The Ottomans 1700–1923: An Empire Besieged* (Abingdon and New York: Routledge, 2022)

Albrecht, Peter, 'Coffee-drinking as a symbol of social change in continental Europe in the seventeenth and eighteenth centuries', *Studies in Eighteenth-century Culture*, vol. 18, no. 1, 1989, pp. 91–103

Al-Hassani, Salim T. S., *1001 Inventions: Muslim Heritage in Our World* (Manchester: Foundation for Science, Technology and Civilization, 2006)

Al-Khalili, Jim, *Pathfinders: The Golden Age of Arabic Science* (London: Penguin, 2012)

Alkhateeb, Firas, *Lost Islamic History: Reclaiming Muslim Civilization from the Past* (London: C. Hurst and Co., 2014)

Al-Maqqari et al., *The History of the Mohammedan Dynasties in Spain* (London: Routledge Curzon, 2002)

—, *Analectes sur l'histoire et la littérature des arabes d'Espagne (Nafh al-tib)*, ed. R. Dozy, G. Dugat, L. Krehl, W. Wright, 2 vols in 3 (Leiden: Brill, 1855–61; repr. London: Oriental Press, 1967)

Al-Rodhan, Nayef R. F., ed., *The Role of the Arab-Islamic World in the Rise of the West: Implications for Contemporary Trans-Cultural Relations* (Basingstoke: Palgrave Macmillan, 2012)

Ansari, Sarah, 'The Islamic World in the Era of Western Domination', in *Cambridge Illustrated History of the Islamic World*, ed. Francis Robinson (Cambridge: Cambridge University Press, 1996; repr. 2009)

Ansary, Tamim, *Destiny Disrupted: A History of the World through Islamic Eyes* (New York: Public Affairs, 2009)

Appiah, Kwame Anthony, 'There is no such thing as western civilization', *The Guardian*, 9 November 2016 (https://www.theguardian.com/world/2016/nov/09/western-civilisation-appiah-reith-lecture)

—, 'Misunderstanding cultures: Islam and the West', *Philosophy and Social Criticism*, 38(4–5), 2012, pp. 425–33

Arjana, Sophie Rose, *Muslims in the Western Imagination* (Oxford: Oxford University Press, 2015)

Asbridge, Thomas, *The Crusades: The War for the Holy Land* (London: Simon and Schuster, 2010)

Ayala Martínez, Carlos de, 'La Escuela de Traductores de Toledo: ¿mito o realidad?', Al-Andalus y la Historia (website), 11 February 2022, (https://www.alandalusylahistoria.com/?p=3348)

Aziz, Sahar F., *Global Islamophobia and the Rise of Populism* (Oxford: Oxford University Press, 2024)

Baer, Marc David, *The Ottomans: Khans, Caesars and Caliphs* (London: Basic Books, 2021)

Bale, Anthony, ed., *The Cambridge Companion to the Literature of the Crusades* (Cambridge: Cambridge University Press, 2019)

Balfour, Sebastian, *Deadly Embrace: Morocco and the Road to the Spanish Civil War* (Oxford: Oxford University Press, 2002)

Barrucand, Marianne and Achim Bednorz, *Moorish Architecture in Andalusia* (Cologne: Taschen, 2007)

Barry, Michael, 'Renaissance Venice and her "Moors"', in *Venice and the Islamic World 828–1797*, ed. Stefano Carboni (New Haven and London: Yale University Press, 2006; English translation 2007), pp. 146–73

Bartlett, Robert, *The Normans*, BBC TV series, dir. Charles Colville, April 2015

Barton, Sholod, *Charlemagne in Spain: The Cultural Legacy of Roncesvalles* (Geneva: Droz, 1966)

Beck, Ulrich and Edgar Grande, *Cosmopolitan Europe* (Cambridge: Polity Press, 2006)

Bede, *Commentarius in Genesim* [Clavis Patrum Latinorum 1344] Corpus Christianorum Series Latina 118A (Turnhout: Brepols, 1995)

Behrends, Frederick, ed., *The Letters and Poems of Fulbert of Chartres*, Oxford Medieval Texts (Oxford: Oxford University Press, 2022)

Bellaigue, Christopher de, *The Lion House: The Rise of Suleyman the Magnificent* (London: Bodley Head, 2022; Vintage, 2023)

Benaboud, Muhammad, 'La imagen del Cid en las fuentes históricas andalusís', in *El Cid, Poema y Historia, Actas del Congreso Internacional (12–16 de julio, 1999)*, coordinator: César Hernández Alonso (Burgos: Ayuntamiento de Burgos, 2000), pp. 115–27

Bennett, Christopher, *Yugoslavia's Bloody Collapse: Causes, Course and Consequences* (London: C. Hurst and Co., 1995)

Bennison, Amira, *The Almoravid and Almohad Empires* (Edinburgh: Edinburgh University Press, 2016)

Berger, Maurits S., *A Brief History of Islam in Europe: Thirteen Centuries of Creed, Conflict and Coexistence* (Leiden: Leiden University Press, 2014)

Bernabé Pons, Luis, 'Introduction: Empires, wars and languages. Islam and Christianity in 17th-century western and southern Europe', in *Christian–Muslim Relations: A Bibliographical History, Volume 9. Western and Southern Europe (1600–1700)*, eds David Thomas and John Chesworth (Leiden and Boston: Brill, 2017), pp. 1–15

—, *Los moriscos: conflicto, expulsion, diaspora* (Madrid: Los Libros de la Catarata, 2009)

Bernstein, William, *A Splendid Exchange: How Trade Shaped the World* (London: Atlantic Books, 2009)

Bevilacqua, Alexander and Helen Pfeifer, 'Turquerie: culture in motion, 1650–1750', *Past and Present*, no. 221 (November 2013), pp. 75–118, doi: 10.1093/pastj/gtt019

Bisaha, Nancy, *Creating East and West: Renaissance Humanists and the Ottoman Turks* (Pennsylvania: University of Pennsylvania Press, 2004)

Blair, Sheila M. and Jonathan M. Bloom, 'The Mirage of Islamic Art: Reflections on the Study of an Unwieldy Field', *The Art Bulletin*, vol. 85, no. 1 (March 2003), pp. 152–84

Blanks, David R. and Michael Frassetto, *Western Views of Islam in Medieval and Early Modern Europe: Perception of Other* (Basingstoke: Macmillan, 1999)

Bleda, Jaime, *Chronicle of the Moors of Spain (Crónica de los moros de España)* (Valencia: Felipe Mey, 1618)

Blin, Louis, 'Lamartine, in the forgotten years of French Islamophilia', Middle East Directions Programme Blog, 17 October 2023 (https://blogs.eui.eu/medirections/lamartine-in-the-forgotten-years-of-french-islamophilia/)

Bloom, Jonathan M., *Architecture of the Islamic West: North Africa and the Iberian Peninsula 700–1800* (New Haven and London: Yale University Press, 2020)

Boloix Gallardo, Bárbara, *Ibn Al-Ahmar: vida y reinado del primer sultán de Granada* (Granada: Editorial Universidad de Granada, 2017)

Booms, Dirk and Peter Higgs, *Sicily: Culture and Conquest* (London: British Museum Press, 2016)

Boyar, Ebru and Kate Fleet, *A Social History of Ottoman Istanbul* (Cambridge: Cambridge University Press, 2010)

Bragg, Melvyn, 'Constantinople: siege and fall', *In Our Time*, BBC Radio 4, 28 December 2006 (https://www.bbc.co.uk/programmes/p0038xbd)

Brooke, Arthur de Capell, *Sketches in Spain and Morocco*, vol. II (London: H. Colburn and R. Bentley, 1831)

Brown, Frederick, 'Flaubert in Egypt', *New England Review*, vol. 25, no. 4 (Fall 2004), pp. 40–63

Brummett, Palmira Johnson, *Mapping the Ottomans: Sovereignty, Territory, and Identity in the Early Modern Mediterranean* (Cambridge: Cambridge University Press, 2020)

Bukharaev, Ravil, *Tatarstan: President Mintimer Shaimiev and the Power of Common Sense* (Boston: Brill, 2006)

Bulliet, Richard W., 'The Other Siege of Vienna and the Ottoman Threat: An Essay in Counter-Factual History', *ReOrient*, vol. 1, no.1 (Autumn 2015), pp. 11–22

—, *The Case for Islamo-Christian Civilization* (New York: Columbia University Press, 2004)

Burbank, Jane and Frederick Cooper, *Empires in World History: Power and the Politics of Difference* (Princeton: Princeton University Press, 2010)

Burnett, Charles, 'The Second Revelation of Arabic Philosophy and Science: 1492–1562', in *Islam and the Italian Renaissance*, eds Charles Burnett and Anna Contadini (London: The Warburg Institute, 1999), pp. 185–98

Burns, E. Jane, 'Saracen Silk and the Virgen's Chemise: Cultural Crossings in Cloth', *Speculum*, vol. 81, no. 2 (April 2006), pp. 365–97

Burns, Robert I., 'Paper-making comes to the west, 800–1400)', in *Europäische Technik im Mittelalter: 800 bis 1400. Tradition und Innovation: ein Handbuch*, ed. Uta Lindgren (Berlin: Gebr. Mann, 2001), pp. 415–17

Calic, Marie-Janine, *The Great Cauldron: A History of Southeastern Europe* (London and Cambridge, MA: Harvard University Press, 2019)

Calvo Capilla, Susana, 'The Visual Construction of the Umayyad Caliphate in Al-Andalus through the Great Mosque of Cordoba', *Arts*, 7, 2018 (Basel), p. 36

—, 'Los espacios del conocimiento en el Islam: Mezquitas, Casas de la

Sabiduría y Madrasas', in *Domus Hispánica. El real colegio de España y el cardenal Gil de Albornoz en la Historia del Arte*, ed. M. Parada López de Corselas (Bologna: Bononia University Press, 2018), pp. 179–94

Čapeta Rakič, Ivana and Giuseppe Capriotti, 'Two Marian Iconographic Themes in the Face of Islam on the Adriatic Coast in the Early Modern Period', *Ikon*, 10, 2017, pp. 169–86

—, eds, *Images in the Borderlands: The Mediterranean between Christian and Muslim Worlds in the Early Modern Period* (Turnhout: Brepols, 2022)

Carboni, Stefano, ed., *Venice and the Islamic World 828–1797* (New Haven and London: Yale University Press, 2006; English translation 2007)

Carboni, Stefano, Elizabeth Marwell and Trinita Kennedy, 'Venice and the Islamic World: Commercial Exchange, Diplomacy and Religious Difference', Metropolitan Museum of Art (website), 1 March 2007 (https://www.metmuseum.org/essays/commercial-exchange-diplomacy-and-religious-difference-between-venice-and-the-islamic-world)

—, 'Islamic Art and Culture: The Venetian Perspective', Metropolitan Museum of Art (website), March 2007 (https://www.metmuseum.org/essays/islamic-art-and-culture-the-venetian-perspective)

—'Venice's Principal Muslim Trading Partners: The Mamluks, the Ottomans and the Safavids', Metropolitan Museum of Art (website), March 2007 (https://www.metmuseum.org/essays/venices-principal-muslim-trading-partners-the-mamluks-the-ottomans-and-the-safavids)

Carr, Helen and Suzannah Lipscomb, *What is History, Now?* (London: Weidenfeld and Nicolson, 2021)

Carr, Matthew, *Blood and Faith: The Purging of Muslim Spain 1492–1614* (London: C. Hurst and Co., 2009)

Casanova, José, 'Religion, European secular identities and European integration', in *Religion in the New Europe*, ed. Krzysztof Michalski (Budapest and New York: Central University Press, 2022), pp. 23–43

Cassar, Carmel, 'Malta', in *Encyclopaedia of Islam Three Online*, eds Kate Fleet, Gudrun Krämer, Denis Matringe, John Abdallah Nawas, Everett K. Rowson (Leiden: Brill, 2007)

—, *A Concise History of Malta* (Msida, Malta: Mireva Publications, 2000)

Catlos, Brian, *Muslims of Medieval Latin Christendom c. 1050–1614* (Cambridge: Cambridge University Press, 2014)

Chaudhuri, K. N., 'The Economy in Muslim Societies', in *Cambridge Illustrated History of the Islamic World*, ed. Francis Robinson (Cambridge: Cambridge University Press, 1996; repr. 2009), pp. 124–63

Christ, Georg, 'Unread News, Crusade and Byzantine Continuity: Venetian Perceptions of the Ottomans Around the Turkish-Venetian Wars (1498–1503)', paper given at a panel discussion under the aegis of the European Quran Project, 15 November 2021 (https://teol.ku.dk/afd/the-european-quran/conference-2021/TurkishWars_conferenceprogramme_final.pdf)

Chroniques Ottomanes (website) 'Alphonse de Lamartine et l'empire Ottoman sous Abdulmecid', 9 March 2021 (https://chroniquesottomanes.fr/co-lamartine-empire-ottoman/)

Clark, Tommy, *A Brief History of Cyprus: The Story of a Divided Island* (Manchester: Upper Street Press, 2020)

Clarke, Nicola, *The Muslim Conquest of Iberia: Medieval Arabic Narratives* (Abingdon: Routledge, 2012)

Classen, Albrecht, ed., *East Meets West in the Middle Ages and Early Modern Times: Transcultural Experiences in the Premodern World* (Berlin/Boston: Walter de Gruyter, 2013)

Coleman, David, *Creating Christian Granada: Society and Religious Culture in an Old World Frontier City 1492–1600* (Ithaca and London: Cornell University Press, 2003)

Coles, Paul, *The Ottoman Impact on Europe* (London: Thames and Hudson, 1968)

Collins, Roger, *Early Medieval Spain: Unity in Diversity, 400–1000* (London: Macmillan, 1983)

—, *The Arab Conquest of Spain 710–797* (Oxford: Blackwell, 1989)

Conde Solares, Carlos, 'The Moral Dimensions of Sufism and the Iberian Mystical Canon', *Religions*, 11(15), 2020, pp. 1–14, doi: 10.3390/rel11010015

Cook, Michael A., *A History of the Muslim World: From its Origins to the Dawn of Modernity* (Princeton: Princeton University Press, 2024)

Cook, Robert F., *The Sense of the Song of Roland* (Ithaca: Cornell University Press, 1987)

Cordingly, David, *Under the Black Flag: The Romance and the Reality of Life Among the Pirates* (New York: Harvest Books, 1997)

Correa, Pedro, ed., *Los romances fronterizos I* (Granada: University of Granada, 1999)

Crane, Howard and Esra Akin, eds, preface by Gülru Necipoğlu, *Sinan's Autobiographies: Five Sixteenth-Century Texts* (Leiden: Brill, 2006)

Crawford, Peter, *The War of the Three Gods: Romans, Persians and the Rise of Islam* (Barnsley: Pen and Sword Books Ltd, 2013)

Creasy, E. S., *History of the Ottoman Turks: From the Beginning of their Empire to the Present Time* (London: R. Bentley, 1854)

Creswell, K. A. C., *Early Muslim Architecture: Umayyads A.D. 622–750*, 2 vols (Oxford: Clarendon Press, 1969)

Crichfield, Grant, 'Gautier's Orient: Mask, Mirage, and "Décor d'opéra" in Constantinople', *Romance Notes*, vol. 32, no. 3, 1992, pp. 263–70 (http://www.jstor.org/stable/43802163)

Crone, Patricia, 'The Rise of Islam in the World', in *Cambridge Illustrated History: Islamic World*, ed. Francis Robinson (Cambridge: Cambridge University Press, first edition 1996; repr. 1998, 2002, 2005, 2009), pp. 2–31

Cufurovic, Mirela, 'Fully known yet wholly unknowable: Orientalising the Balkans', *Australian Journal of Islamic Studies*, vol. 2(1), 2017, pp. 39–54

Czernin, Monika, dir., *Atatürk: The Father of Modern Turkey*, documentary film, 2018 (https://www.youtube.com/watch?v=OJad3EtoWuM)

Dalrymple, William, 'The Ottoman Empire: A Forgotten Giant of Western History. A remarkable new history of the Ottomans restores the empire's central role in shaping European culture', *Financial Times*, 24 November 2021

Darke, Diana, *Stealing from the Saracens: How Islamic Architecture Shaped Europe* (London: C. Hurst and Co., 2020)

Daskas, Beatrice, 'Competing iconographies: Hagia Sophia, ideology, and the construction of a cultural icon then and now', *Word and Image – A Journal of Verbal/Visual Enquiry*, 39:1, pp. 63–73 (https://doi.org/10.1080/02666286.2023.2168467)

Davies, C. S. L., 'The Youth and Education of Christopher Wren', *The English Historical Review*, vol. 123, no. 501, April 2008, pp. 300–27

Davis, Natalie Zemon, *Trickster Travels: The Search for Leo Africanus* (London: Faber and Faber Ltd, 2007, pbk 2008)

Davis-Secord, Sarah, *Where Three Worlds Met: Sicily in the Early Medieval Mediterranean* (Ithaca: Cornell University Press, 2017)

Day, David, *Conquest: How Societies Overwhelm Others* (Oxford: Oxford University Press, 2008)

Deliömeroĝlu, Yakup, *Tatars and Tataristan* (Ankara: Eurasia Development Association Publications, 1997)

Dodds, Jerrilyn, ed., *Al-Andalus: The Art of Islamic Spain* (New York: Metropolitan Museum of Art, 1992)

—, 'The Arts of Al-Andalus', in *The Legacy of Muslim Spain*, vol. 2, ed. Salma Jayyusi (Leiden: Brill, 1994), pp. 599–620

Doubleday, Simon, *The Wise King: A Christian Prince, Muslim Spain and the Birth of the Renaissance* (New York: Basic Books, 2015)

Draper, Peter, 'Islam and the West: The Early Use of the Pointed Arch Revisited', *Architectural History*, vol. 48, 2005, pp. 1–20

Drayson, Elizabeth, ed., *Europe's Islamic Legacy: 1900 to the Present, Proceedings of the Online Conference Hosted by the University of Cambridge on 20 October 2020* (Leiden: Brill, 2023)

—, *Lost Paradise: The Story of Granada* (London: Head of Zeus, 2021)

—, *The Moor's Last Stand: How Seven Centuries of Islamic Rule in Spain Came to an End* (London: Profile Books, 2017, pbk 2018)

—, *The Lead Books of Granada* (New York and Basingstoke: Palgrave Macmillan, 2013; pbk 2016)

—, *The King and the Whore: King Roderick and La Cava* (New York and Basingstoke: Palgrave Macmillan, 2007)

Dronke, Peter, ed., *The History of Twelfth Century Western Philosophy* (Cambridge: Cambridge University Press, 2011)

Ecker, Heather, 'The Great Mosque of Córdoba in the Twelfth and Thirteenth Centuries', in *Muqarnas*, vol. 20, 2003, Brill, pp. 113–41 (https://www.jstor.org/stable/1523329)

Esber, Rose M., 'The Poet-King of Seville', *Saudi Aramco World*, vol. 44(1), January/February 1993 (https://archive.aramcoworld.com/issue/199301/the.poet-king.of.seville.htm)

Escudero Aranda, José and María Dolores Baena Alcántara, 'Notas sobre al-Ándalus y su cultura material: de los Omeyas a los almohades', *AWRAQ*, no. 7, 2013, pp. 105–120 (http://www.awraq.es/blob.aspx?idx=6&nId=91&hash=d3a891ff0fd317c48f61054c41540fbd)

Esposito, John, *The Islamic Threat: Myth or Reality?* (New York and Oxford: Oxford University Press, 1992)

Ettinghausen, Richard, Oleg Grabar and Marilyn Jenkins-Madina, *Islamic Art and Architecture 650–1250* (New Haven and London: Yale University Press, 2001)

Euben, Roxanne L., *Journeys to the Other Shore: Muslim and Western Travellers in Search of Knowledge* (Princeton: Princeton University Press, 2006)

Fairchild Ruggles, D., 'The Stratigraphy of Forgetting: The Great Mosque of Cordoba and Its Contested Legacy', in *Contested Cultural Heritage: Religion, Nationalism, Erasure, and Exclusion in a Global World*, ed. Helaine Silverman (London and New York: Springer, 2011), pp. 51–60

—, *Gardens, Landscapes and Vision in the Palaces of Islamic Spain* (Pennsylvania: Pennsylvania State University Press, 2000, pbk 2003)

Falk, Avner, *Franks and Saracens: Reality and Fantasy in the Crusades* (London: Routledge, 2018)

Falk, Seb, *The Light Ages: A Journey of Medieval Discovery* (London: Penguin Books, 2020)

Fernández Guerra, Aureliano, *Caída y ruina del Imperio Visigótico español: primer drama que las representó en nuestro teatro* (Madrid: Manuel G. Hernández, 1883)

Fernández Valverde, Juan, introduction, translation, notes and indices, *Historia de los hechos de España* (Madrid: Alianza Editorial, 1989)

Ferraro, Joanne, *Venice: History of the Floating City* (Cambridge: Cambridge University Press, 2012), published online (https://doi.org/10.1017/CBO9781139029933.004)

Finkel, Caroline, *Osman's Dream: The History of the Ottoman Empire* (London: John Murray, 2006)

Fletcher, Richard, *The Quest for El Cid* (London: Century Hutchinson Ltd, 1989)

Florescu, Radu R., and Raymond T. McNally, *Dracula, Prince of Many Faces: His Life and His Times* (Boston: Little, Brown & Co., 1989)

Ford, Richard, *Granada: An account illustrated with unpublished original drawings*, text in Spanish and English, Spanish version and notes by Alfonso Gámir (Granada: Patronato de la Alhambra y Generalife, 1955)

Fossier, Robert, ed., *Cambridge Illustrated History of the Middle Ages: 950–1250* (Cambridge: Cambridge University Press, 1982, trans. 1997)

Fowden, Garth, *Empire to Commonwealth: Consequences of Monotheism in Late Antiquity* (Princeton: Princeton University Press, 1993)

—, *Qusayr Amra: Art and Umayyad Élite in Late Antique Syria* (Berkeley and London: University of California Press, 2004)

—, 'Late Antiquity, Islam, and the First Millennium: A Eurasian perspective', *Millennium*, vol. 13, no. 1, 2016, pp. 5–28 (https://doi.org/10.1515/mill-2016-0002)

Frankopan, Peter, *The Silk Roads: A New History of the World* (London: Bloomsbury, 2015; pbk 2016)

Freely, John, *The Grand Turk: Sultan Mehmet II – Conqueror of Constantinople, Master of an Empire and Lord of Two Seas* (London: I. B. Tauris and Co. Ltd, 2009)

Freely, John and Augusto Romano Burelli; photographer Ara Güler, *Sinan: Architect of Süleyman the Magnificent and the Ottoman Golden Age* (London: Thames and Hudson, 2015)

Futter, Catherine L., '"Beautiful as a poet's dream . . .": Islamic influence on European Design', in *Inspired by the East: How the Islamic World Influenced Western Art*, ed. William Greenwood and Lucien de Guise (London: The British Museum Press, 2019), pp. 66–81

Gambra, Andrés, 'Alfonso VI y El Cid. Reconsideración de un enigma histórico', in *El Cid, Poema y Historia, Actas del Congreso Internacional (12 – 16 de julio, 1999)*, coordinator: César Hernández Alonso (Burgos: Ayuntamiento de Burgos, 2000), pp. 189–204

Garcés, María Antonia, *Cervantes in Algiers: A Captive's Tale* (Nashville: Vanderbilt University Press, 2002)

García Fitz, Francisco, 'El Cid y la guerra', in *El Cid, Poema y Historia, Actas del Congreso Internacional (12–16 de julio, 1999)*, coordinator: César Hernández Alonso (Burgos: Ayuntamiento de Burgos, 2000), p. 383–418

García Mercadal, J., trans. and notes, *Viajes de extranjeros por España y Portugal desde los tiempos más remotos hasta los fines del siglo XVI* (Madrid: Aguilar, 1952)

Gawrych, George W., *Atatürk: Father of the Republic of Turkey* (London: I. B. Tauris, 2023)

Gaynor, Ian, 'In 1683 Turkey was the invader. In 2004 much of Europe still sees it that way', *The Guardian*, 22 September 2004 (https://www.theguardian.com/world/2004/sep/22/eu.turkey?CMP=share_btn_url)

Geoffrey of Malaterra, *The Deeds of Count Roger of Calabria and Sicily and of his brother Duke Robert Guiscard*, trans. Kenneth Baxter Wolf (Ann Arbor: University of Michigan, 2005)

Gibb, Elias John Wilkinson, *Ottoman Poems*, translated into English verse in the original forms, with introduction, biographical notices, and notes (London: Trubner and Co., 1882)

Gibbon, Edward, *The History of the Decline and Fall of the Roman Empire* (1782, revised 1845) (http://www.gutenberg.org/files/25717/25717-h/25717-h.htm#Elink52noteref-50)

Gil, José S., *La escuela de traductores de Toledo y sus colaboradores judíos* (Toledo: Instituto Provincial de Investigaciones y Estudios Toledanos, Diputación Provincial, 1985)

Gill, John, *Andalucía: A Cultural History* (Oxford: Signal Books Limited, 2008)

Glenny, Mischa, *The Balkans 1804–1999: Nationalism, War and the Great Powers* (London: Granta Books, 1999)

Goldsworthy, Vesna, 'The Balkans in nineteenth-century British travel writing', in *Travel Writing in the Nineteenth Century: Filling the Blank Spaces,* ed. Tim Youngs (London: Anthem Press, 2006), pp. 19–35

González-Ferrín, Emilio, 'Al-Andalus. The First Enlightenment', *Critical Muslim*, 6, April 2013, pp. 1–10

Goodwin, Jason, *Lords of the Horizons: A History of the Ottoman Empire* (London: Vintage Books, 1998)

Goody, Jack, *Islam in Europe* (Cambridge: Polity Press, 2004)

Gow, David and Ewan MacAskill, 'Turkish accession could spell end of EU, says commissioner', *The Guardian,* 8 September 2004 (https://www.theguardian.com/world/2004/sep/08/turkey.eu)

Grabar, Oleg, *The Alhambra* (London: Allen Lane, 1978)

—, 'Two paradoxes in the Islamic Art of the Spanish Peninsula', in *The Legacy of Muslim Spain*, vol. 2, ed. Salma Jayyusi (Leiden: Brill, 1994), pp. 583–91

Graham-Dixon, Andrew, *The Art of Spain*, TV series for BBC Worldwide Limited, 2010

Granara, William, *Narrating Muslim Sicily: War and Peace in the Medieval Mediterranean World* (London: Bloomsbury, 2019)

Greble, Emily, *Muslims and the Making of Modern Europe* (Oxford: Oxford University Press, 2021)

Greenwood, William and Lucien de Guise, eds, *Inspired by the East: How the Islamic World Influenced Western Art* (London: The British Museum Press, 2019)

Griffith, Sidney H., 'Faith and reason in Christian *kalam*: Theodore Abu Qurrah on discerning the true religion', in *Christian Arabic Apologetics during the Abbasid Period (750–1258)*, eds S. K. Samir and J. S. Nielson (Leiden: Brill, 1994), pp. 1–43

Grimau, Rodolfo Gil, 'Sayyida al-Hurra, mujer marroquí de origen andalusí', *Anaquel de Estudios Árabes*, 11, 2000, pp. 311–20

Guedalla, Philip, *If It Had Happened Otherwise* (London: Longmans Green Ltd, 1931)

Günay, Reha, *Sinan the Architect and His Works*, trans. Ali Ottoman (Istanbul: Yapı-Endüstri Merkezi Yamları, 1998)

Hahn, Johann Georg von, *The Discovery of Albania: Travel Writing and Anthropology in the Nineteenth-Century Balkans*, selected texts, introduction and translation Robert Elsie (London: I. B. Tauris, 2015)

Hamdani, Abbas, 'Columbus and the Recovery of Jerusalem', *Journal of the American Oriental Society*, vol. 99, no. 1, January–March 1979, pp. 39–48

Hamilton Abrams, Ray, *Preachers Present Arms* (New York: Round Table Press, 1933)

Harvey, L. P., 'The Mudéjars', in *The Legacy of Muslim Spain Volume I*, ed. Salma Khadra Jayyusi (Leiden: Brill, 1994), pp. 176–87

—, 'The Alfonsine School of Translators: Translations from Arabic into Castilian produced under the patronage of Alfonso the Wise of Castile (1221–1252–1284)', *Journal of the Royal Asiatic Society of Great Britain & Ireland*, 109(1), 1977, pp. 109–17

Hay, Denys, *Europe: The Emergence of an Idea*, revised edition (Edinburgh: Edinburgh University Press, 1968)

Hazleton, Lesley, *After the Prophet: The Epic Story of the Shia–Sunni Split* (New York: Anchor Books, 2009)

Henderson, George, *Gothic* (London: Penguin, 1967)

Herbjørnsrud, Dag, 'The Real Battle of Vienna', Aeon (website), 24 July 2018 (https://aeon.co/essays/the-battle-of-vienna-was-not-a-fight-between-cross-and-crescent)

Hernández Alonso, César, *El Cid, Poema y Historia, Actas del Congreso Internacional (12–16 de julio, 1999)* (Burgos: Ayuntamiento de Burgos, 2000)

Hernández Pérez, Azucena, 'Tocar el cielo y medir lo invisible. Astrolabios medievales, paradigma de arte y ciencia, símbolo de estatus e imagen del Universo', *Goya. Revista de Arte,* 363, 2018, pp. 91–109

Herold, J. Christopher, *Bonaparte in Egypt* (London: Hamish Hamilton, 1963)

Hillberg, I., ed., *Corpus Scriptorum Ecclesiasticorum Latinorum 54* (Vienna-Leipzig: Tempsky, 1910)

Hinrichsen, Laura, '"Alcoranus ex direptione Tunnetana": Arabic Manuscripts in Europe after the Sack of Tunis (1535)', paper given at a panel discussion under the aegis of the European Quran Project, 15 November 2021 (https://teol.ku.dk/afd/the-european-quran/conference-2021/TurkishWars_conferenceprogramme_final.pdf)

Hitti, Philip Khuri, *The Origins of the Islamic State: Being a Translation from the Arabic Accompanied with Annotations, Geographic and Historic Notes of the Kitâb FutûḤ al-Buldân of al-Imâm Abu-l 'Abbâs Aḥ Mad Ibn-JâBir al-BalâDhuri* (Beirut: Khayats, 1966; Khayats Oriental Reprint, no. 11) p. 237

Howard, Deborah, 'Venice as an "Eastern" city', in *Venice and the Islamic World 828–1797*, ed. Stefano Carboni (New Haven and London: Yale University Press, 2006; English translation 2007), pp. 59–71

Howard-Johnston, James, *The Last Great War of Antiquity* (Oxford: Oxford University Press, 2021)

Hughes, Bettany, *Istanbul: A Tale of Three Cities* (London: Weidenfeld and Nicolson, 2017)

Huntington, Samuel P., *The Clash of Civilizations and the Remaking of World Order* (London: The Free Press, 1996, 2nd edition 2002)

Hussain, Tharik, *Minarets in the Mountains* (Chesham: Bradt Guides Ltd, 2021)

Ibn al-Faqīh, *Kitāb al-buldān*, ed. M. J. de Goeje (Leiden: Brill, 1885)

Ibn al-Hayyan, *Al-Muktabis: Chronique du régne du calife umaiyade Abd Allah a Courdoue*, ed. P. Melchor M. Antuña (Paris: P. Geunthener, 1937)

Ibn Faldun, Ahmad, *Mission to the Volga*, trans. James E. Montgomery, foreword by Tim Severin (New York: New York University Press, 2017)

Ibn l'Athir, 'The story of Umm Haram', *Journal of the Royal Asiatic Society*, XXVIII, 1897, p. 84

Ibrahim, Raymond, *Sword and Scimitar: Fourteen Centuries of War between Islam and the West* (New York: Da Capo Press, 2018)

Ihrig, Stefan, *Atatürk and the Nazi Imagination* (Cambridge, MA and London: Harvard University Press, 2014)

Irujo, Xabier, *Charlemagne's Defeat in the Pyrenees: The Battle of Rencesvals* (Amsterdam: Amsterdam University Press, 2021)

Jackson, Peter, 'The Crusade against the Mongols', *Journal of Ecclesiastical History*, vol. 42, no. 1, January 1991, pp. 1–8

Jacob, James R., *Henry Stubbe, Radical Protestantism and the Early Enlightenment* (Cambridge University Press online, 14 October 2009)

James, David, ed., *Early Islamic Spain: The History of Ibn al-Qutiyya* (London: Routledge, 2009)

Jeauneau, Édouard, *Rethinking the School of Chartres*, trans. Claude Paul Desmarais (Toronto: Toronto University Press, 2009)

Jelavich, Charles and Barbara, eds, *The Balkans in Transition: Essays on the Development of Balkan Life and Politics Since the Eighteenth Century* (Berkeley and Los Angeles: University of California Press, 1963)

Jenkins, Philip, *The Great and Holy War: How World War I Changed Religion Forever* (Oxford: Lion Hudson, 2014)

Jirousek, Charlotte A., with Sara Catterall, *Ottoman Dress and Design in the*

West: A Visual History of Cultural Exchange (Bloomington, Indiana: Indiana University Press, 2019)

John of Damascus, *Saint John of Damascus: Writings*, translated by Frederic H. Chase Jr. (Washington D.C.: Catholic University of America Press, 1958, 1999 printing)

Johnson Brummett, Palmira, *Mapping the Ottomans: Sovereignty, Territory and Identity in the Early Modern Mediterranean* (Cambridge: Cambridge University Press, 2015)

Jones, Dan, *Crusaders: An Epic History of the Wars for the Holy Lands* (London: Head of Zeus, 2019)

Kalmar, Ivan, *Early Orientalism: Imagined Islam and the Notion of Sublime Power* (Abingdon: Routledge, 2012)

Kamen, Henry, *Spain's Road to Empire: The Making of a World Power 1492–1763* (London: Penguin, 2002)

Kendall, Bridget, 'Süleyman the Magnificent: longest-reigning Ottoman sultan', *The Forum*, BBC Sounds, World Service, 20 October 2022 (https://www.bbc.co.uk/sounds/play/w3ct38t1)

Khader, Bichara, 'Muslims in Europe: the Construction of a "Problem"', in *The Search for Europe: Contrasting Approaches* (Bilbao: BBVA, 2015), pp. 3–24

Khadra Jayyusi, Salma, ed., *The Legacy of Muslim Spain Volume I* (Leiden: Brill, 1994)

—, ed., *The Legacy of Muslim Spain Volume II* (Leiden: Brill, 1994)

Khemir, Sabiha, 'The Arts of the Book', in *Al-Andalus: The Art of Islamic Spain*, ed. Jerrilyn Dodds (New York: Metropolitan Museum of Art, 1992)

Khoury, Nuha N. N., 'The Meaning of the Great Mosque of Cordoba in the Tenth Century', *Muqarnas*, vol. 13, 1996, pp. 80–98

King, Rachel, 'Divine Constructions: A Comparison of the Great Mosque of Cordoba and Notre-Dame de Chartres', Boston College: electronic dissertation, 2007 (https://dlib.bc.edu/islandora/object/bc-ir:102369)

Klára, Hegyi, *The Ottoman Empire in Europe*, illustrations selected by Vera Zimányi, trans. Ildikó and Christopher Hann (Budapest: Corvina, 1989)

Krisciunas, Kevin and Belén Bistúe Conicet, 'Where did Copernicus Obtain the Tools to Build his Heliocentric Model? Historical considerations and a guiding Translation of Valentin Rose's "Ptolomaeus und die Schule von Toledo" (1874)', at arXiv:1712.05437 [physics.hist-ph], 2017

Kritzeck, James Aloysius, *The School of Toledo* (Princeton: Princeton University Press, 1964; 2016)

Kujawa, Karol, 'Turkey and the Politics of Memory: Consequences for Domestic and Foreign Affairs and Security in the Region', in *Europe's Islamic Legacy: 1900 to the Present, Proceedings of the Online Conference Hosted by the University of Cambridge on 20 October 2020*, ed. Elizabeth Drayson (Leiden: Brill, 2023), pp. 9–28

Kundnami, Hans, *Eurowhiteness: Culture, Empire and Race in the European Project* (London: C. Hurst and Co., 2023)

Kyrris, Costas P., *History of Cyprus with an Introduction to the Geography of Cyprus* (Nicosia: Nicocles Publishing House, 1985)

Lamartine, Alfonse de, *Histoire de la Turquie*, vol. I (Paris: Constitutionnel, 1854)

—, *Voyage en Orient*, ed. Sophie Basch (Paris: Gallimard, 2011)

Laurens, Henry, 'Civilization or Conquest?', in *Europe and the Islamic World: A History*, eds John Tolan, Gilles Veinstein and Henry Laurens (Princeton: Princeton University Press, 2013), pp. 277–94

—, 'The Great War and the Beginning of Emancipation', in *Europe and the Islamic World: A History*, eds John Tolan, Gilles Veinstein and Henry Laurens (Princeton: Princeton University Press, 2013), pp. 338–59

—, 'Contemporary Issues', in *Europe and the Islamic World: A History*, eds John Tolan, Gilles Veinstein and Henry Laurens (Princeton: Princeton University Press, 2013), pp. 387–404

Lehning, James R., *European Colonialism Since 1700* (Cambridge: Cambridge University Press, 2013)

Levering Lewis, David, *God's Crucible: Islam and the Making of Europe, 570–1215* (New York: Liveright Publishing Corporation, 2008)

Lévi-Provençal, E. and E. García Gómez, eds, *Crónica anónima de 'Abd al-Raḥmān III al-Naṣīr* (Madrid-Granada: CSIC, 1950)

Lévi-Provençal, E. and Emilio García Gómez, trans. and introducción, *El siglo XI en primera persona: las 'Memorias' de Abd Allah, último rey Zirí de Granada, destronado por los Almorávides (1090)* (Madrid: Alianza Tres, 1981)

Lewis, Bernard, *Islam and the West* (Oxford: Oxford University Press, 1993)

Lomax, Derek W., *The Reconquest of Spain* (London: Longman, 1978)

Loop, Jan, 'The Turkish Wars and the study of Islam in early modern Europe', paper given at a panel discussion under the aegis of the European Quran Project on 15 November 2021 (https://teol.ku.dk/afd/the-european-quran/conference-2021/TurkishWars_conferenceprogramme_final.pdf)

López Pereira, José Eduardo, ed. and trans., *Crónica mozárabe de 754*, (Zaragoza: Anubar, 1980)

Loucaides, Darren, 'Searching for Cyprus: Two halves of a divided island have more in common than you might think', *Slate* (website), 10 April 2017 (https://slate.com/news-and-politics/2017/04/cyprus-has-been-divided-in-two-for-40-years-do-its-people-still-have-anything-in-common.html)

Lunde, Paul, 'Ishbiliya: Islamic Seville', *Aramco World*, vol. 44, no. 1, January/February 1993, pp. 20–31

Lyndon, Donlyn and Charles W. Moore, *Chambers for a Memory Palace* (Cambridge, MA and London: The MIT Press, 1994)

Lyons, Jonathan, *The House of Wisdom: How the Arabs Transformed Western Civilization* (London: Bloomsbury, 2009)

Maalouf, Amin, *The Crusades Through Arab Eyes*, trans. Jon Rothschild (London: Al Saqi Books, 1994)

Mack Smith, Denis, *A History of Sicily: Medieval Sicily 800–1713* (London: Chatto and Windus, 1968)

Mackintosh-Smith, Tim, *Arabs: A 3000-Year History of Peoples, Tribes and Empires* (New Haven and London: Yale University Press, 2019)

Madden, Thomas F., *Venice: A New History* (New York: Viking, 2012)

Maíllo Salgado, Felipe, ''Abd al-Rahman I: biografía', *Real Academia de la Historia*, 2018 (https://historia-hispanica.rah.es/biografias/128-abd-al-rahman-i)

Malcolm, Noel, *Useful Enemies: Islam and The Ottoman Empire in Western Political Thought 1450–1750* (Oxford: Oxford University Press, 2019)

Mallinson, William, *Cyprus: A Modern History* (London: I. B. Tauris, 2010)

Mango, Andrew, *Atatürk* (London: John Murray, 1999)

Manji, Fatima, *Hidden Heritage: Rediscovering Britain's Lost Love of the Orient* (London: Chatto and Windus, 2021)

Marcos Cobaleda, María, *Los almorávides: arquitectura de un imperio* (Granada: University of Granada, 2015)

Mármol Carvajal, Luis del, *Historia del [sic] rebelión y castigo de los moriscos del Reino de Granada*, (Edición digital: Alicante: Biblioteca Virtual Miguel de Cervantes, 2001)

Martínez Díez, Gonzalo, *El Condado de Castilla, 711–1038: la historia frente a la leyenda, vol. 2* (Madrid: Marcial Pons Historia, 2005)

—, 'Semblanza de Rodrigo Díaz de Vivar', in *El Cid, Poema y Historia, Actas del Congreso Internacional (12–16 de julio, 1999)*, coordinator: César

Hernández Alonso (Burgos: Ayuntamiento de Burgos, 2000), pp. 93–103

Matar, Nabil, 'Renaissance England and the Turban', *Images of the Other: Europe and the Muslim World before 1700*, ed. David Blanks, Cairo Papers in Social Science, vol. 19, no. 2, 1996, pp. 39–54

—, 'The Representation of Muslim Women in Renaissance England', *The Muslim World*, vol. LXXXVI, no. 1, January 1996, pp. 50–61

—, *Islam in Britain 1558–1685* (Cambridge: Cambridge University Press, 1998)

Mazower, Mark, *The Balkans: A Short History* (London: Weidenfeld and Nicolson, 2000)

McCarthy, Justin, *Death and Exile: The Ethnic Cleansing of Ottoman Muslims 1821–1922* (Princeton, New Jersey: The Darwin Press, Inc., 1995)

—, *1912–13 Balkan Wars: Death and Forced Exile of Ottoman Muslims. An Annotated Map*, Turkish Coalition of America (website) (https://www.tc-america.org/files/news/pdf/balkan-wars-map.pdf)

McCormick, Michael, 'New Light on the 'Dark Ages: How the slave trade fuelled the Carolingian economy', *Past and Present*, vol. 177(1), November 2002, pp. 17–54

Melitzki, Dorothee, *The Matter of Araby in Medieval England* (New Haven and London: Yale University Press, 1977)

Melville, Charles and Ahmad Ubaydli, eds, *Christians and Moors in Spain, Volume III: Arabic Sources* (Warminster: Aris and Phillips, 1992)

Mendola, Louis and Jacqueline Alio, *The Peoples of Sicily: A Multicultural Legacy* (New York: Trinacria Editions, 2013)

Menéndez Pidal, Ramón, ed., *Primera crónica general de España*, 2 vols (Madrid: Gredos, 1955)

Menocal, María Rosa, *The Ornament of the World: How Muslims, Jews, and Christians Created a Culture of Tolerance in Medieval Spain* (New York and Boston: Little, Brown and Company, 2002)

Merlet, René, *The Cathedral of Chartres* (Paris: Henri Laurens, 1926)

Metcalfe, Alex, *Muslims and Christians in Norman Sicily: Arabic speakers and the end of Islam* (London: RoutledgeCurzon, 2003)

Mikhail, Alan, *God's Shadow: The Ottoman Sultan who shaped the Modern World* (London: Faber and Faber, 2020)

Mitchell, Colin Paul and Karl A. Roider, eds, *The Turkish Letters of Ogier Ghiselin de Busbecq: Imperial Ambassador at Constantinople, 1554–1562*, translated by Edward Seymour Forster (Baton Rouge, LA: Louisiana State University Press, 2005)

Moller, Violet, *The Map of Knowledge: How Classical Ideas were Lost and Found* (London: Picador, 2019)

Morey, Peter, Amina Yaqin and Alaya Forte, eds, *Contesting Islamophobia: Anti-Muslim Prejudice in Media, Culture and Politics* (London and New York: I. B. Tauris, 2019)

Muir, Sir William, 'The Mohammedan Controversy', in *Biographies of Muhammad, Sprenger on Tradition, the Indian liturgy and the Psalter* (Edinburgh: T & T Clark, 1897; repr.)

Naff, Thomas and Roger Owen, eds, *Studies in Eighteenth-century Islamic History* (Carbondale and Edwardsville: Southern Illinois University Press, 1977)

Nalborczyk, Agata S., 'Mosques and Cemeteries of the Polish Muslim Tatars as an example of the Islamic Legacy in the Central Eastern European landscape of the twenty-first century', in *Europe's Islamic Legacy: 1900 to the Present, Proceedings of the Online Conference Hosted by the University of Cambridge on 20 October 2020*, ed. Elizabeth Drayson (Leiden: Brill, 2023), pp. 98–129

Necipoğlu, et al., *Treasures of Knowledge: An Inventory of the Ottoman Palace Library (1502/3–1503/4)*, Studies and Sources in Islamic Art and Architecture, 2 vols (Leiden: Brill, 2019)

Nerval, Gérard de, *The Women of Cairo: Scenes of Life in the Orient*, vol. I, translation of *Voyages en Orient*, intro. Conrad Elphinstone (Guildford: Billing and Sons Ltd, 1930)

Nielsen, Jørgen et al., *Yearbook of Muslims in Europe, Volume 4* (Leiden: Brill, 2012)

Norwich, John Julius, *A History of Venice* (Harmondsworth: Penguin, 1983)

Oborne, Peter, *The Fate of Abraham: Why the West is Wrong about Islam* (London: Simon and Schuster, 2022)

O'Callaghan, Joseph, *A History of Medieval Spain* (Ithaca: Cornell University, 1975; 5th repr. 1994)

Öztunali, Olcay, 'The Intercultural Place and Importance of Studies Taking Place in the "Toledo School of Translators"', *Ankara Üniversitesi Dil ve Tarih-Coğrafya Fakültesi Dergisi*, vol. 57(2), 2017 (https://searchworks.stanford.edu/articles/edsdoj__edsdoj.47f5284146ac4d2382f1dba6a28b2ca0)

Palmer, Alan, *The Decline and Fall of the Ottoman Empire* (London: Faber, 2011)

Pandit Laisram, Pallavi, *Viewing the Islamic Orient: British Travel Writers of the Nineteenth Century* (London: Routledge, 2006)

Panofsky, Erwin, *Gothic Architecture and Scholasticism* (London: Thames and Hudson, 1957)

Parker, Geoffrey, *Imprudent King: A New life of Philip II* (New Haven and London: Yale University Press, 2014)

Partearroyo, Cristina, 'Almoravid and Almohad textiles', in *Al-Andalus: The Art of Islamic Spain*, ed. Jerrilyn Dodds (New York: Metropolitan Museum of Art, 1992)

Parvev, Ivan, *Habsburgs and Ottomans between Vienna and Belgrade (1683–1739)* (New York: Columbia University Press, 1995)

Petrovich, Michael Boro, *A History of Modern Serbia 1804–1918*, 2 vols (New York and London: Harcourt Brace Jovanovich, 1976)

Pirický, Gabriel, 'The Legacy of the Ottoman (Turkish) Age in Slovakia', in *Europe's Islamic Legacy: 1900 to the Present: Proceedings of the Online Conference Hosted by the University of Cambridge on 20 October 2020*, ed. Elizabeth Drayson (Leiden: Brill, 2023), pp. 29–47

Poppick, Laura, 'The Story of the Astrolabe, the Original Smartphone', *Smithsonian Magazine*, special report, 31 January 2017 (https://www.smithsonianmag.com/innovation/astrolabe-original-smart-phone-180961981/, accessed 10 October 2022)

Powell, James M., *The Crusades, the Kingdom of Sicily, and the Mediterranean* (Burlington, VT: Ashgate Publishing Company, 2007)

Puzon, Katarzyna, Mirjam Shatanawi and Sharon MacDonald, eds, *Islam and Heritage in Europe: Pasts, Presents and Future Possibilities* (London and New York: Routledge, 2021)

Raby, Julian, 'The Serenissima and the Sublime Porte: Art in the Art of Diplomacy 1453–1600)', in *Venice and the Islamic World 828–1797*, ed. Stefano Carboni (New Haven and London: Yale University Press, 2006; English translation 2007), pp. 90–119

Real Academia de la Historia, *Memorial histórico español: colección de documentos, opúsculos y antigüedades que publica la Real Academia de la Historia* (Madrid: La Academia, 1851)

Reeves, Minou and P. J. Stewart, *Muhammad in Europe: A Thousand Years of Western Myth-Making* (New York: New York University Press, 2003)

Reich, Robin, 'Multiculturalism and *convivencia* in medieval Sicily', The Study of Antiquity and the Middle Ages, interview, 7 April 2020 (https://www.youtube.com/watch?v=lhXbvo4PL7I)

Ríquer, Martín de, *Chanson de Roland, Cantar de Roldán y el Roncesvalles Navarro* (Barcelona: El Festín de Esopo, 1983)

Rius Piniés, Mònica, 'Qurtuba y la ciencia medieval. Reminiscencias del pasado en el presente', *Awraq*, 7, 2013, pp. 143–61

Roberts, Andrew, *Napoleon the Great* (London: Penguin Books, 2015)

Roberts, J. M., *The Triumph of the West* (London: BBC, 1985)

Robinson, Douglas, *Translation and Empire: Postcolonial Theories Explained* (Manchester: St Jerome Publishing, 1997)

Robinson, Francis, ed., *Cambridge Illustrated History: Islamic World* (Cambridge: Cambridge University Press, first edition 1996; repr. 1998, 2002, 2005, 2009)

Rodinson, Maxime, *Islam and Capitalism* (Harmondsworth: Penguin Books, 1977)

Rogan, Eugene, *The Fall of the Ottomans: The Great War in the Middle East 1914–1920* (London: Allen Lane, 2015)

Rogers, J. M., *Sinan* (London: I. B. Tauris and Co. Ltd and Oxford University Press, 2006)

—, and R. M. Ward, *Süleyman the Magnificent* (London: British Museum Publications, 1988)

Rorlich, Azade-Ayse, *The Volga Tatars: A Profile in National Resilience* (Stanford, CA: Hoover Institution Press, Stanford University, 1986)

Said, Edward W., *Orientalism* (London: Penguin Books, 2019)

Saliba, George, *Islamic Science and the Making of the European Renaissance* (Cambridge, MA: MIT Press, 2007)

Samir, S. K. and J. S. Nielson, *Christian Arabic Apologetics during the Abbasid Period (750–1258)* (Leiden: Brill, 1994)

Samso, Julio, 'The early development of astrology in al-Andalus', *Journal of the History of Arabic Science*, vol. 3, 1979, pp. 228–43

Saoud, Rabah, *Sinan: A Great Ottoman Architect and Urban Designer* (Manchester: Foundation for Science, Technology and Civilisation, June 2007), pp. 1–15

Schmidt-Arcangeli, Catarina, '"Orientalist" painting in Venice, 15th–17th centuries', in *Venice and the Islamic World 828–1797*, ed. Stefano Carboni (New Haven and London: Yale University Press, 2006; English translation 2007), pp. 120–39

Scott, Samuel Parsons, *History of the Moorish Empire in Europe*, 3 vols, intro. Elizabeth Drayson (London: Bloomsbury Academic, 2021)

Singer, Isidore and Cyrus Adler, *The Jewish Encyclopedia: a descriptive record of the history, religion, literature, and customs of the Jewish people from the earliest times to the present day* (New York and London: Funk and Wagnalls, 1901)

Sirry, Mun'im A., 'Early Muslim–Christian dialogue: a closer look at major themes of the theological encounter', in *Islam and Christian Muslim relations*, vol. 16(4), 2005 (Colchester: Routledge), pp. 361–76

Smith, Colin, ed., *Christians and Moors in Spain, Volume I:* AD *711–1150* (Warminster: Aris and Phillips, 1988)

—, *Christians and Moors in Spain, Volume II: 1195–1614* (Warminster: Aris and Phillips, 1989)

Spackman, Barbara, *Accidental Orientalists: Modern Italian Travellers in Ottoman Lands* (Liverpool: Liverpool University Press, 2017)

Steffens, Bradley, *Ibn al-Haytham: First Scientist* (Greensboro, NC: Morgan Reynolds Publishing, 2005)

Stevens, Mary Anne, *The Orientalists: Delacroix to Matisse, European Painters in North Africa and the Near East* (London: Royal Academy of Arts, 1984)

Stoye, John, *The Siege of Vienna: The Last Great Trial between Cross and Crescent* (Edinburgh: Birlinn, 2012)

Streit, J. R., 'Penitence and Crusade in the Assumption Chapel of the Real Monasterio de Las Huelgas, Burgos', *Medieval Encounters*, 26(6), 2021, pp. 578–606. doi: https://doi.org/10.1163/15700674-12340089

Stubbe, Henry, *An Account of the Rise and Progress of Mahometanism: With the Life of Mahomet and a Vindication of Him and His Religion from the Calumnies of the Christians*, from a manuscript copied by Charles Hornby of Pipe Office, in 1705, with some variations and editions, edited with an introduction and appendix by Hafiz Mahmud Khan Shairani (Lahore: Orientalia, 1954)

Sutter Fichtner, Paula, *Terror and Toleration: The Habsburg Empire confronts Islam, 1526–1850* (London: Reaktion Books, 2008)

Talbot, C. H., trans. and ed., *The Anglo-Saxon Missionaries in Germany: Being the Lives of SS. Willibrord, Boniface, Sturm, Leoba, and Lebuin, together with the Hodoeporicum of St Willibald and a selection from the correspondence of Saint Boniface* (London: Sheed & Ward, 1981)

Tinniswood, Adrian, *Pirates of Barbary: Corsairs, Conquests and Captivity in the Seventeenth-Century Mediterranean* (London: Jonathan Cape, 2010)

Tolan, John V., *Saint Francis and the Sultan: The Curious History of a Christian–Muslim Encounter* (Oxford: Oxford University Press, 2009)

—, *Saracens: Islam in the Medieval European Imagination* (New York: Columbia University Press, 2002)

—, 'In Search of Egyptian Gold: Traders in the Mediterranean', in *Europe and the Islamic World: A History*, eds John Tolan, Gilles Veinstein and Henry Laurens (Princeton: Princeton University Press, 2013), pp. 70–86

—, 'On the Shoulders of Giants – Transmission and Exchange of Knowledge', in John Tolan, Gilles Veinstein and Henry Laurens, *Europe and the Islamic World: A History* (Princeton: Princeton University Press, 2013), pp. 87–107

—, Gilles Veinstein, Henry Laurens, *Europe and the Islamic World: A History* (Princeton: Princeton University Press, 2013)

—, *Faces of Muhammad: Western Perceptions of the Prophet of Islam from the Middle Ages to Today* (Princeton: Princeton University Press, 2019)

Treptow, Kurt, ed., *Dracula: Essays on the Life and Times of Vlad Ţepeş* (New York: Columbia University Press, 1991)

Trow, M. J., *Vlad the Impaler: In Search of the Real Dracula* (Stroud: Sutton Publishing, 2003)

Turner Johnson, James, *The Holy War Idea in Western and Islamic Traditions* (Pennsylvania: Pennsylvania University Press, 1997)

Van Koningsveld, Peter, 'Muslim Slaves and Captives in Western Europe during the Late Middle Ages', *Islam and Christian–Muslim Relations*, vol. 6, no. 1, 1995, pp. 5–21

Veinstein, Gilles, 'Part II: The Great Turk and Europe', in *Europe and the Islamic World: A History*, eds John Tolan, Gilles Veinstein, Henry Laurens (Princeton: Princeton University Press, 2013, pp. 111–256

Velázquez Basanta, Fernando Nicolás, 'La relación histórica sobre las postrimerías del Reino de Granada según Ahmad al-Maqqari (s. XVII)', in *En el epílogo del Islam andalusí: La Granada del siglo XV*, ed. Celia del Moral (Granada: Grupo de Investigación "Ciudades Andaluzas bajo el Islam", col. Al-Mudun, no. 5, 2002), pp. 481–555

Vélez León, Paulo, 'Sobre la noción, significado e importancia de la Escuela de Toledo', *Disputatio*, Madrid, vol. 6(7), 2017, p. 537

Vernet, Juan, Leonor Martínez Martín and Ramón Masats, *Al-Andalus: el Islam en España* (Barcelona and Madrid: Lunwerg Editores S.A., 1987, 2nd edition 1999)

Viguera Molins, María Jesús, 'Cuando Córdoba pasó a ser capital de al-Ándalus', *Revista al-Mulk*, no. 15, 2017, pp. 13–43 (https://www.academia.edu/35658453/CUANDO_CÓRDOBA_PASÓ_A_SER_CAPITAL_DE_AL_ANDALUS)

Villalba Sola, Dolores, *La senda de los Almohades: arquitectura y patrimonio* (Granada: Universidad de Granada, 2015)

Wallin, Georg August, *Notes taken during a Journey through Part of Northern Arabia in 1848* (Royal Geographical Society, 1851) (https://archive.org/details/jstor-1798039)

Warren, Andrew, *The Orient and the Young Romantics* (Cambridge: Cambridge University Press, 2014)

Watt, W. Montgomery and Pierre Cachia, *A History of Islamic Spain* (Edinburgh: Edinburgh University Press, 1965, 1996, digital 2007)

Wheatcroft, Andrew, *The Enemy at the Gate: Habsburgs, Ottomans and the Battle for Europe* (London: Pimlico, 2008)

—, *Infidels: The Conflict between Christendom and Islam 638–2002* (London: Viking, 2003)

Wickham, Chris, *Medieval Europe: From the Breakup of the Western Roman Empire to the Reformation* (New Haven and London: Yale University Press, 2016)

Williams, John, *Early Spanish Manuscript Illumination* (London: Chatto and Windus, 1977)

Wolf, Eric R., *Europe and the People Without History* (Berkely and Los Angeles: University of California Press, 1982, 1997)

Wright, Owen, 'Music in Muslim Spain', in *The Legacy of Muslim Spain*, vol. 2, ed. Salma Jayyusi (Leiden: Brill, 1994), pp. 558–9

Yeager, Suzanne M., 'The Earthly and Heavenly Jerusalem', in *The Cambridge Companion to the Literature of the Crusades*, ed. Anthony Bale (Cambridge: Cambridge University Press, 2019), pp. 121–35

Zaghloul, Ahmed Kamal and Adel Mohamed Nasr, 'El movimiento de traducción en la Casa de Sabiduría de Bagdad y la escuela de traductores de Toledo', *Entreculturas. Revista de tradicción y comunicación intercultural*, vol. 1(10), 2020, pp. 57–68

Zuccato, Marco, 'Rethinking the Ninth-Century Islamic Presence in Peninsular Italy: A Perspective Through Islamic History and Politics', *Al-Masāq*, 2023 (https://www.tandfonline.com/doi/full/10.1080/09503110.2023.2287955)

Zürcher, Erik J., *Turkey: A Modern History* (London: I. B.Tauris, 1993, 4th edition 2017)

Notes

Introduction: Perspectives Past and Present

1 Samuel P. Huntington, *The Clash of Civilizations and the Remaking of World Order* (London: The Free Press, 1996, 2nd edition 2002)

Chapter 1: Fire, Wood and Stone: A Phoenix Ascends

1 Peter Crawford, *The War of the Three Gods: Romans, Persians and the Rise of Islam* (Barnsley: Pen and Sword Books Ltd, 2013), p. 15

2 From Strategius, c. 24.9; Nic., c. 18.8–16, quoted in James Howard-Johnston, *The Last Great War of Antiquity* (Oxford: Oxford University Press, 2021), online text, note 99

3 Since the time of Muhammad, the stone has broken into fragments and is now set in a silver frame inside the Ka'aba. The silver frame and the black cloth, or *kiswah*, that covers the Ka'aba were maintained for centuries by the Ottoman sultans, who were Custodians of the Two Holy Mosques. Frames that wore out over time because of the constant handling by pilgrims were replaced, the worn-out ones taken to Istanbul to reside among the sacred relics of the Topkapı Palace.

4 David Levering Lewis, *God's Crucible: Islam and the Making of Europe, 570–1215* (New York: Liveright Publishing Corporation, 2008), p. 73

5 Patricia Crone, 'The Rise of Islam in the World', in *Cambridge Illustrated History: Islamic World* (Cambridge: Cambridge University Press, first edition 1996; repr. 1998, 2002, 2005, 2009), p. 10

6 Maurits S. Berger, *A Brief History of Islam in Europe: Thirteen Centuries of Creed, Conflict and Coexistence* (Leiden: Leiden University Press, 2014), p. 36

7 Violet Moller, *The Map of Knowledge: How Classical Ideas Were Lost and Found* (London: Picador, 2019), pp. 20–1

CHAPTER 2: THE KING AND THE SLAVE: RODERICK, TARIQ AND THE GREAT BATTLE OF 711

1 For further details, see Richard Ettinghausen, Oleg Grabar, Marilyn Jenkins, *Islamic Art and Architecture 650–1250* (New Haven and London: Yale University Press, 2001); K. A. C. Creswell, *Early Muslim Architecture: Umayyads A.D. 622–750*, 2 vols (Oxford: Clarendon Press, 1969); Garth Fowden, *Qusayr 'Amra: Art and Umayyad Élite in Late Antique Syria* (Berkeley and London: University of California Press, 2004). For a detailed overview, see Elizabeth Drayson, 'Ways of Seeing: the first medieval Islamic and Christian depictions of Roderick, last Visigothic king of Spain', *Al-Masaq* 18:2, 2006, pp. 115–28 (https://doi.org/10.1080/09503110600863443)

2 Aureliano Fernández-Guerra discusses the Visigothic monarchical system in Spain in some detail, underlining the fact that the crown was elective, not hereditary, although Spanish nobles maintained that it ought to be and fought to change it. When Witiza died, Roderick had been Duke of Bética (contemporary Andalusia) for a number of years. The senate did not want the sons of an unworthy king to reign, and Roderick was thus anointed king in the basilica of San Pedro y San Pablo. See Fernández-Guerra, *Caída y Ruina del Imperio Visigótico Español: primer drama que las representó en nuestro teatro* (Madrid: Manuel G. Hernández, 1883), pp. 38–45

3 'Rudericus tumultuose regnum ortante senatu inuadit'. José Eduardo López Pereira (ed. and trans.), *Crónica mozárabe de 754* (Zaragoza: Anubar, 1980)

4 Ibn al-Qutiyya's version of what happened is one of the first in Arabic: 'The merchant's wife died, and he was left with his beautiful daughter. Roderick ordered him to proceed to north Africa, but Julian excused himself on the grounds that his wife had died and he had no-one with whom he could leave his daughter. He ordered her to be brought to the palace. When Roderick saw her, she pleased him greatly, and he took her.' Quoted in Charles Melville and Ahmad Ubaydli (eds and trans.), *Christians and Moors in Spain Volume III: Arabic sources* (Warminster: Aris and Phillips, 1992), pp. 3–5

5 David Levering Lewis, *God's Crucible: Islam and the Making of Europe 570–1215* (New York: Liveright Publishing Corporation, 2008), p. 103

6 Tariq's speech is spurious but reflects the Arabization of Tariq and his Berber troops by al-Maqqari. See Avner Falk, *Franks and Saracens: Reality and Fantasy in the Crusades* (London: Routledge, 2018), p. 47; Tim

Mackintosh-Smith, *Arabs: A 3,000-Year History of Peoples, Tribes and Empires* (New Haven: Yale University Press, 2019), p. 255

7 For a full study of the legend of King Roderick through the ages, see Elizabeth Drayson, *The King and the Whore: Roderick and La Cava* (New York and Basingstoke: Palgrave Macmillan, 2007)

8 Charles Melville and Ahmad Ubaydli, *op. cit.*, p. 7

9 M. J. de Goeje (ed.), Ibn al-Faqīh, *Kitāb al-buldān* (Leiden: Brill, 1885), pp. 82–3

CHAPTER 3: WORDS OF HOSTILITY: THE FABRICATION OF OTHERNESS

1 Mun'im A. Sirry, 'Early Muslim–Christian dialogue: a closer look at major themes of the theological encounter', *Islam and Christian–Muslim Relations*, vol. 16 (4), 2005, p. 10. Timothy's words are quoted in S. H. Griffith, 'Faith and reason in Christian *kalam*: Theodore Abu Qurrah on discerning the true religion', in S. K. Samir and J. S. Nielson (eds), *Christian Arabic Apologetics during the Abbasid Period (750–1258)* (Leiden: Brill, 1994), pp. 15–16

2 John V. Tolan, *Saracens: Islam in the Medieval European Imagination* (New York: Columbia University Press, 2002), p. 40

3 Bede, *Ecclesiastical History of the English People (Historia ecclesiastica gentis Anglorum)*, trans. L. Sherley-Price (London: Penguin, 1955, 1990), 5:23, p. 323, quoted in John V. Tolan, *Saracens: Islam in the Medieval European Imagination* (New York: Columbia University Press, 2002), p. 74

4 P. Melchor Martínez Antuña (ed.), Ibn Hayyan, *Al-Muktabis: Chronique du régne du calife umaiyade Abd Allah a Courdoue* (Paris: P. Geuthner, 1937)

5 The historian Roger Collins challenges this date, which is the generally accepted one, placing it about a year later, in 733. See Roger Collins, *The Arab Conquest of Spain 710–797* (Oxford: Basil Blackwell Ltd, 1989), pp. 90–1

6 Roger Collins, *Early Medieval Spain: Unity in Diversity, 400–1000* (London: Macmillan, 1983), pp. 167, 254

7 Philip Guedalla, 'If the Moors in Spain had won', in J. C. Squire (ed.), *If It Had Happened Otherwise* (London: Longmans, Green, Ltd, 1931), pp. 1–22

8 David Levering Lewis, *God's Crucible: Islam and the Making of Europe, 570–1215* (New York: Liveright Publishing Corporation, 2008), p. 174

9 It is possible that a few Muslims were involved in the attack in order to liberate the governor of Zaragoza, Sulayman, captured by Charlemagne,

but the majority of the rebel fighters were Basques. See Joseph O'Callaghan, *A History of Medieval Spain* (Ithaca: Cornell University Press, 1975), p. 102

10 David Levering Lewis, *op. cit.*, p. 252

11 'Prospiciunt Europeenses Arabum tentoria ordinata . . .' ('The Europeans could make out the well-ordered tents of the Arabs . . .'). The full text of the *Crónica mozárabe de 754* may be consulted in the Spanish edition and translation by José Eduardo López Pereira (Zaragoza: Anubar, 1980).

CHAPTER 4: CITY OF ILLUMINATION: CORDOBA

1 Ahmed ibn Muhammad al-Maqqari, *The History of the Mohammedan Dynasties in Spain*, vol. 2 (London and New York: Johnson Reprint Co., 1964; first published 1840), p. 60

2 David Levering Lewis, *God's Crucible: Islam and the Making of Europe, 570–1215* (New York: Liveright Publishing Corporation, 2008), p. 198

3 Violet Moller, *The Map of Knowledge: How Classical Ideas Were Lost and Found* (London: Picador, 2019), p. 109

4 Ibn Idhari, *al-Bayan*, vol. II, p. 60, translated from the Arabic by D. Fairchild Ruggles, *Gardens, Landscape and Vision in the Palaces of Islamic Spain* (University Park: Pennsylvania State University Press, 2000, 2003), p. 42

5 David Levering Lewis, *op. cit.*, p. 202

6 This anecdote appears in the long historical work *The Unique Necklace* by the Muslim Andalusian Ibn abd-Rabbih (860–940).

7 The Latin text appears in Andreas Schott (ed.), *Hispana illustrata IV* (Frankfurt, 1608), pp. 237–8, quoted in Colin Smith, *Christians and Moors in Spain, Volume I: AD 711–1150* (Warminster: Aris and Phillips Ltd, 1988), pp. 43–7.

8 Owen Wright, 'Music in Muslim Spain', in Salma Khadra Jayyusi (ed.), *The Legacy of Muslim Spain*, vol. 2 (Leiden: Brill, 1994), pp. 558–9

9 R. Dozy, G. Dugat, L. Krehl, W. Wright (eds), Al-Maqqari, *Analectes sur l'histoire et la littérature des arabes d'Espagne (Nafh al-tib)*, 2 vols in 3 (Leiden: Brill, 1855–61; repr. London: Oriental Press, 1967), vol. I, p. 346

10 Quoted by Edward Gibbon in *The History of the Decline and Fall of the Roman Empire*, 1782, revised 1845, Chapter LII (http://www.gutenberg.org/files/25717/25717-h/25717-h.htm#Elink52noteref-50)

CHAPTER 5: A SPACE OF AMBIGUITY: THE GREAT MOSQUE

1 See, for example, Emilio Lafuente y Alcántara (ed.), *Akhbar Machmua fi Fath al-Andalus wa Dhikri Umara'iha*, (Madrid: 1867), p. 61

2 Al-Maqqari, *Shihân al-Dîn Abû l- 'Abbas Ahmad b. Muhammad Ahmad b. Yahyâ al-Qurashî al-Tilimsanî al-Fasî al-Mâlikî (1577–1632) Nafh al-tîb* (Cairo: 1949, 10 vols), partially translated by P. de Gayangos, *The History of the Mohammedan Dynasties in Spain* (London: Routledge Curzon, 2002), vol. 1, p. 232 and ff. Available online at The history of the Mohammedan dynasties in Spain; extracted from the Nafhu-t-tíb min ghosni-l-Andalusi-r-rattíb wa táríkh Lisánu-d-Dín Ibni-l-Khattíb : Maqqarī, Aḥmad ibn Muḥammad, d. 1631 or 2 : Free Download, Borrow, and Streaming : Internet Archive
The pomegranate is considered one of the golden fruits of the trees of the Islamic paradise.

3 Ibn Idhari, *Al-Bayan al-mughrib fi akhbar al-Andalus wa l-Maghrib* (trans. Fagnan), II, 392, quoted in Jerrilyn Dodds, 'The Arts of al-Andalus', in Salma Jayyusi (ed.), *The Legacy of Muslim Spain Volume II* (Leiden: Brill, 2012), p. 602

4 Susana Calvo Capilla, 'The visual construction of the Umayyad Caliphate in al-Andalus through the Great Mosque of Cordoba', *Arts*, 2018, 7(3), 36, doi: 10.3390/arts7030036

5 Quoted in Joseph F. O'Callaghan, *A History of Medieval Spain* (Ithaca: Cornell University Press, 1975), p. 130, from A. R. Nykl, *Hispano-Arabic Poetry and its Relations with the old Provencal Troubadours* (Baltimore: np, 1946; repr. New York: Hispanic Society, 1970), p. 55

6 *Historia silense*, quoted in Gonzalo Martínez Díez, *El Condado de Castilla, 711–1038: la historia frente a la leyenda, vol. 2* (Madrid: Marcial Pons Historia, 2005)

7 Quoted in Heather Ecker, 'The Great Mosque of Córdoba in the Twelfth and Thirteenth Centuries', *Muqarnas*, vol. 20, 2003, Brill, pp. 113–41, p. 116

8 See *De rebus Hispaniae*, in *Historia de los hechos de España*, introduction, translation, notes and indices by Juan Fernández Valverde (Madrid: Alianza Editorial, 1989), p. 17

9 Heather Ecker, *op. cit.*, p. 126

10 Jerrilynn D. Dodds, 'The Great Mosque of Córdoba' in Jerrilynn D. Dodds (ed.), *Al-Andalus: the Arts of Islamic Spain* (New York: The Metropolitan Museum of Art, 1992), pp. 11–27, p. 25

CHAPTER 6: THE PATHS TO ENLIGHTENMENT: BOOKS, SCHOLARS AND THE SEARCH FOR KNOWLEDGE

1 Although paper was imported into Christian Spain and used in works like the *Breviary of Silos*, composed in 950, its manufacture came late to western Europe, starting with France in the mid-fourteenth century. See Robert I. Burns, S.J., 'Paper-making comes to the west, 800–1400' in Uta Lindgren (ed.), *Europäische Technik im Mittelalter: 800 bis 1400. Tradition und Innovation: ein Handbuch* (Berlin: Gebr. Mann, 2001), pp. 415–17

2 Susana Calvo Capillo, 'Los espacios del conocimiento en el Islam: Mezquitas, Casas de la Sabiduría y Madrasas', in M. Parada López de Corselas (ed.), *Domus Hispanica: El Real Colegio de España y el cardenal Gil de Albornoz en la Historia de Arte* (Bologna: Bononia University Press, 2018), p. 184

3 For details of the fascinating conversation between Hisham I and al-Dabbi, see Julio Samso, 'The early development of astrology in al-Andalus', *Journal of the History of Arabic Science*, vol. 3, 1979, pp. 228–43, pp. 228–9

4 Salim T. S. Al-Hassani (chief ed.) and Elizabeth Woodcock and Rabah Saoud (eds), *1001 Inventions: Muslim Heritage in Our World* (Manchester: Foundation for Science Technology and Civilisation, 2006), p. 294

5 Laura Poppick, 'The Story of the Astrolabe, the Original Smartphone', *Smithsonian Magazine*, special report, 31 January 2017 (https://www.smithsonianmag.com/innovation/astrolabe-original-smartphone-180961981/)

CHAPTER 7: SICILY: CROSSROADS OF CIVILIZATIONS

1 Ibn Hawqal, *Portrait of the World*, trans. Alex Metcalfe, quoted in Dirk Booms and Peter Higgs, *Sicily: Culture and Conquest* (London: British Museum Press, 2016), p. 160

2 Geoffrey of Malaterra, *The Deeds of Count Roger of Calabria and Sicily and of his brother Duke Robert Guiscard* 2.36, trans. Kenneth Baxter Wolf (Ann Arbor: University of Michigan, 2005), p. 114

3 *Ibid.*, p. 15

4 Quoted in Booms and Higgs, *op. cit.*, p. 198

5 *Ibid.*, p. 222

CHAPTER 8: NOMADS OF WAR: CHRISTIAN HEROES, MUSLIM PURITANS

1 Joseph O'Callaghan, *A History of Medieval Spain* (Ithaca and London: Cornell University Press, 1975), p. 197

2 For a full description, see S. P. Scott, *History of the Moorish Empire in Europe*, vol. II (London: Bloomsbury Academic, 2021), p. 164

3 Joseph O'Callaghan, *op. cit.*, p. 209

4 E. Lévi-Provençal and Emilio García Gómez (trans. and intro.), *El siglo XI en primera persona: las 'Memorias' de Abd Allah, último rey Zirí de Granada, destronado por los Almorávides (1090)* (Madrid: Alianza Tres, 1981), p. 272

CHAPTER 9: SEVILLE: CITY OF TRIUMPH AND TRANSITION

1 Al-Himyari's account of al-Mansur Ya'qub and the Battle of Alarcos is quoted in Charles Melville and Ahmad Ubaydli, *Christians and Moors in Spain, Volume III: Arabic Sources* (Warminster: Aris and Phillips Ltd, 1992), pp. 135–6

2 J. R. Streit, 'Penitence and Crusade in the Assumption Chapel of the Real Monasterio de Las Huelgas, Burgos', *Medieval Encounters*, 26(6), 2021, pp. 578–606 (https://doi.org/10.1163/15700674-12340089)

3 David Levering Lewis, *God's Crucible: Islam and the Making of Europe, 570–1215* (New York: Liveright Publishing Corporation, 2008), p. 373

4 Adapted from Ramón Menéndez Pidal (ed.), *Primera crónica general de España*, 2 vols (Madrid: Gredos, 1955), vol. 2, pp. 768–9, ch. 1128

5 W. Montgomery Watt and Pierre Cachia, *A History of Islamic Spain* (Edinburgh: Edinburgh University Press, 1965, 1996, digital 2007), p. 171

6 Quoted by Joseph O'Callaghan, *A History of Medieval Spain* (Ithaca and London: Cornell University Press, 1975), p. 356

CHAPTER 10: THE PAGEANT OF DEATH: CRUSADES, CONQUESTS AND COLONIZATION

1 Quoted in Bettany Hughes, *Istanbul: A Tale of Three Cities* (London: Weidenfeld and Nicolson, 2017), p. 347

2 *Ibid.*, pp. 361–4

3 Peter Frankopan, *The Silk Roads* (London: Bloomsbury, 2014), p. 148

CHAPTER 11: A SPACE OF ENIGMAS: CHARTRES CATHEDRAL

1 Quoted in Erwin Panofsky, *Gothic Architecture and Scholasticism* (London: Thames and Hudson, 1957), p. 4

2 Quoted in C. S. L. Davies, 'The Youth and Education of Christopher Wren', *The English Historical Review*, vol. 123, no. 501, April 2008, p. 303

3 I am grateful for the insights in E. Jane Burns's article, 'Saracen Silk and the Virgin's Chemise: Cultural Crossings in Cloth', *Speculum*, vol. 81, no. 2, April 2006, pp. 365–97. The article contains a detailed account of the riddle of the Virgin's chemise.

4 Frederick Behrends (ed.), *The Letters and Poems of Fulbert of Chartres*, Oxford Medieval Texts (Oxford: Clarendon Press, 1976), poem 148, in English translation from Latin.

5 *Ibid.*, p. 50

CHAPTER 12: THE LIGHT FROM THE EAST: TRANSLATION, TRANSMISSION, TRANSITION

1 Toledo was also viewed with suspicion outside the Iberian peninsula, in part because many considered the scientific and philosophical knowledge of the Muslims as diabolical, and because the city had a reputation as a centre of black magic, which brought condemnation from some intellectuals. See Carlos de Ayala Martínez, 'La Escuela de Traductores de Toledo: ¿mito o realidad?', Al-Andalus y la Historia (website), 11 February 2022, (https://www.alandalusylahistoria.com/?p=3348)

2 Quoted in José S. Gil, *La Escuela de Traductores de Toledo y sus colaboradores judíos* (Toledo: Instituto Provincial de Investigaciones y Estudios Toledanos, Diputación Provincial, 1985), p. 29

3 Quoted in Violet Moller, *The Map of Knowledge: How Classical Ideas Were Lost and Found* (London: Picador, 2019), p. 146

4 Peter Dronke (ed.), *The History of Twelfth Century Western Philosophy* (Cambridge: Cambridge University Press, 2011), p. 113

5 *Memorial histórico español*, I (Madrid: Real Academia de la Historia, 1851), p. 54

6 'quasi captiuous sensus in suam linguam uictoris iure transposit', Jerome, *Epistola 57*, in *Sancti Eusebii Hieronymi epistulae*, I. Hillberg (ed.), *Corpus Scriptorum Ecclesiasticorum Latinorum 54* (Vienna-Leipzig: Tempsky, 1910), p. 512

7 Quoted by Douglas Robinson, *Translation and Empire – Postcolonial Theories Explained* (Manchester: St Jerome Publishing, 1997), p. 57

CHAPTER 13: GRANADA: A PLACE OF DESTINY

1 Quoted in Bárbara Boloix Gallardo, *Ibn Al-Ahmar: vida y reinado del primer sultán de Granada* (Granada: Editorial Universidad de Granada, 2017), p. 94
2 *Ibid.*, p. 87
3 Pedro Correa (ed.), *Los romances fronterizos I* (Granada: University of Granada, 1999), p. 297. To hear a performance of the ballad, go to: https://www.youtube.com/watch?v=EqvpTWS_ths
4 *Ibid.*, p. 63
5 *Viajes de extranjeros por España y Portugal desde los tiempos más remotos hasta los fines del siglo XVI*, translation and notes by J. García Mercadal (Madrid: Aguilar, 1952), p. 248

CHAPTER 14: 1492: A YEAR THAT CHANGED THE WORLD

1 Fernando Nicolás Velázquez Basanta, 'La relación histórica sobre las postrimerías del Reino de Granada según Ahmad al-Maqqari (s. XVII)', in Celia del Moral (ed.), *En el epílogo del Islam andalusí: La Granada del siglo XV* (Granada: Grupo de Investigación 'Ciudades Andaluzas bajo el Islam', col. Al-Mudun, no. 5, 2002), p. 486
2 Quoted in Elizabeth Drayson, *The Moor's Last Stand: how seven centuries of Islamic rule in Spain came to an end* (London: Profile Books, 2017), p. 55
3 For a full account of the life and times of Sultan Muhammad XI, Boabdil, see Elizabeth Drayson, *The Moor's Last Stand: how seven centuries of Islamic rule in Spain came to an end* (London: Profile Books, 2017, pbk 2018).

CHAPTER 15: GUARDIANS OF THE PAST, ARCHITECTS OF THE FUTURE: THE RISE OF THE OTTOMANS

1 Quoted in E. S. Creasy, *History of the Ottoman Turks: From the Beginning of their Empire to the Present Time* (London: R. Bentley, 1854), pp. 10–11
2 Marc David Baer, *The Ottomans: Khans, Caesars and Caliphs* (London: Basic Books, 2021), p. 27
3 Caroline Finkel, *Osman's Dream: The History of the Ottoman Empire* (London: John Murray, 2006), p. 13

4 Ebru Boyar and Kate Fleet, *A Social History of Ottoman Istanbul* (Cambridge: Cambridge University Press, 2010), p. 21
5 Quoted in Marc David Baer, *The Ottomans: Khans, Caesars and Caliphs*, p. 69
6 Radu R. Florescu and Raymond T. McNally, *Dracula, Prince of Many Faces: His Life and His Times* (Boston: Little, Brown & Co., 1989), p. 132
7 M. J. Trow, *Vlad the Impaler: in search of the real Dracula* (Stroud: Sutton Publishing, 2003), p. 185
8 *Ibid.*, p. 206

Chapter 16: Istanbul: City of Manifold Meanings

1 Charles F. Horne, ed., *The Sacred Books and Early Literature of the East*, (New York: Parke, Austin, & Lipscomb, 1917), vol. VI: *Medieval Arabia*, p. 277
2 Quoted in Nancy Bisaha, *Creating East and West: Renaissance Humanists and the Ottoman Turks* (Philadelphia: University of Pennsylvania Press, 2006), p. 110
3 For full details of this astonishing library, see Necipoğlu, Kafadar and Fleischer (eds), *Treasures of Knowledge: An Inventory of the Ottoman Palace Library (1502/3–1503/4)* (Leiden: Brill, 2019) (https: //doi.org/10.1163/9789004402508)
4 Isidore Singer and Cyrus Adler, *The Jewish Encyclopedia: a descriptive record of the history, religion, literature, and customs of the Jewish people from the earliest times to the present day*, vol. 2 (New York and London: Funk and Wagnalls, 1912), p. 460
5 For an ambitious and surprising biography of Selim I, see Alan Mikhail, *God's Shadow: the Ottoman sultan who shaped the modern world* (London: Faber and Faber, 2020)

Chapter 17: Trading Titans: Venice and Constantinople in Commerce and Conflict

1 William J. Bernstein, *A Splendid Exchange: How Trade Shaped the World* (London: Atlantic Books, 2001), p. 71
2 John Tolan, 'In Search of Egyptian Gold: Traders in the Mediterranean', in John Tolan, Henry Laurens and Gilles Veinstein, *Europe and the Islamic World: a History* (Princeton: Princeton University Press, 2013), p. 81

3 Stefano Carboni (ed.), *Venice and the Islamic World 828–1797* (New Haven and London: Yale University Press, 2006; English translation 2007), p. 16
4 Peter Ackroyd, *Venice: Pure City* (London: Vintage, 2009), p. 84
5 There is an anonymous woodcut of Suleiman wearing the jewel-studded headdress in the Metropolitan Museum of Art in New York. See Stefano Carboni, *op. cit.*, pp. 26–7
6 Deborah Howard, 'Venice as an "Eastern" city', in *ibid.*, p. 64
7 For more detail on painting Muslim subjects in Venice, see Catarina Schmidt-Arcangeli, '"Orientalist" painting in Venice, 15th–17th centuries', in *ibid.*, pp. 120–39
8 Michael Barry, 'Renaissance Venice and Her "Moors"', in *ibid.*, p. 167

Chapter 18: An Architecture of Power and Faith: Islam's Michelangelo in the Reign of Suleiman the Magnificent

1 Howard Crane and Esra Akin, *Sinan's Autobiographies: Five Sixteenth-Century Texts* (Leiden: Brill, 2006), Preface
2 J. M. Rogers and R. M. Ward, *Süleyman the Magnificent* (London: British Museum Publications, 1988), p. 27
3 *Ibid.*, p. 29
4 For more detail see Marc David Baer, *The Ottomans: Khans, Caesars and Caliphs* (London: Basic Books, 2021), p. 148
5 *Ibid.*, p. 153
6 *Ibid.*, p. 215
7 J. M. Rogers, *Sinan* (London: I. B. Tauris and Oxford University Press, 2006), p. 137
8 Quoted in Andrew Wheatcroft, *Infidels: A History of the Conflict between Christendom and Islam* (London: Penguin Books, 2004), p. 34

Chapter 19: A People Betrayed: The Spanish Moriscos and the Repression of Western European Islam

1 *Viajes de extranjeros por España y Portugal desde los tiempos más remotos hasta los fines del siglo XVI*, translation and notes by J. García Mercadal (Madrid: Aguilar, 1952), p. 364
2 Quoted in Luis Bernabé Pons, *Los Moriscos: Conflicto, expulsion y diaspora* (Madrid: Los Libros de la Catarata, 2009), p. 27

3 L. P. Harvey, *Muslims in Spain 1500–1614* (Chicago and London: University of Chicago Press, 2005), p. 13

4 Luis del Mármol Carvajal, *Historia del [sic] rebelión y castigo de los moriscos del Reino de Granada* (Alicante: Biblioteca Virtual Miguel de Cervantes, 2001; originally published Madrid: M. Rivadeneyra, 1852), Capitulo XXVII, p. 278

5 David Coleman estimates that, by 1571, the capital city had lost about a third of the overall population, i.e. between 15,000 and 20,000 Moriscos, leaving around 3,000 or 4,000 behind. See David Coleman, *Creating Christian Granada: Society and Religious Culture in an Old-World Frontier City 1492–1600* (Ithaca and London: Cornell University Press, 2003), p. 185

6 For a full, detailed account of the story of the Lead Books, see Elizabeth Drayson, *The Lead Books of Granada* (Basingstoke and New York: Palgrave Macmillan, 2013, 2016)

7 Darío Cabanelas, 'Cartas del Morisco granadino Miguel de Luna' in *Miscelánea de Estudios Árabes y Hebraicos* XIV–XV (1965–1966), pp. 31–47; letter 19

8 Jaime Bleda, *Coronica de Los Moros de España : Diuida En Ocho Libros* (Valencia: Felipe Mey, 1618), available online at: Coronica de los Moros de España [Chronicle of the Spanish Moors] : Jaime Bleda : Free Download, Borrow, and Streaming : Internet Archive

9 Matthew Carr, *Blood and Faith: The Purging of Muslim Spain 1492–1614* (London: C. Hurst and Co., 2009), p. 309

Chapter 20: Beyond the Pale: Sufis, Slaves and Pirates

1 Marc David Baer, *The Ottomans: Khans, Caesars and Caliphs* (London: Basic Books, 2021), p. 63

2 Adrian Tinniswood, *Pirates of Barbary: Corsairs, Conquests and Captivity in the 17th-Century Mediterranean* (London: Jonathan Cape, 2010), p. 6

3 David Cordingly, *Under the Black Flag: The Romance and the Reality of Life Among the Pirates* (New York: Harvest Books, 1997), pp. 17–18

4 New research, so far unpublished, by Daniel J. Bamford, hints at Hassan Agha's continued contact with fellow Englishmen and his premature death in sinister circumstances.

CHAPTER 21: A DEBT DISOWNED: THE ISLAMIC LEGACY OF THE EUROPEAN RENAISSANCE

1 This comes in a letter to his son in his great work *Gargantua et Pantagruel*, 5 vols (1532–64), quoted in Gilles Veinstein, 'The Great Turk and Europe', in John Tolan, Gilles Veinstein and Henry Laurens (eds), *Europe and the Islamic World: A History* (Princeton: Princeton University Press, 2013), p. 245
2 Quoted in Nabil Matar, *Islam in Britain 1558–1685* (Cambridge: Cambridge University Press, 1998), p. 14
3 Jim al-Khalili, *Pathfinders: The Golden Age of Arabic Science* (London: Penguin, 2012), p. 170
4 Bradley Steffens, *Ibn al-Haytham: First Scientist* (Greensboro, NC: Morgan Reynolds Publishing, 2005), p. 62, quoted in Jim Al-Khalili, *Pathfinders*, p. 170
5 I am indebted to the clarity and thoroughness of Jim al-Khalili's exposition of these issues in his book *Pathfinders*, where more detailed information can be found on pp. 215–20.
6 Quoted in John Tolan, *Faces of Muhammad* (Princeton and Oxford: Princeton University Press, 2019), p. 109
7 *Ibid.*, p. 103
8 Quoted in James R. Jacob, *Henry Stubbe, radical Protestantism and the early Enlightenment* (Cambridge: Cambridge University Press, 1983; online version 14 October 2009), p. 71. I am indebted to James Jacob's illuminating study of Henry Stubbe.

CHAPTER 22: COFFEE, CARPETS AND TULIPS: WESTERN EUROPE'S OBSESSION WITH *TURQUERIE*

1 For a full account of Ambassador bin Haddu's visit to England, see Fatima Manji, *Hidden Histories: Rediscovering Britain's Lost Love of the Orient* (London: Chatto and Windus, 2021), pp. 11–27
2 *Ibid.*, p. 111
3 Alexander Bevilacqua and Helen Pfeifer, 'Turquerie: culture in motion, 1650–1750', *Past and Present*, no. 221 (November 2013), p. 88
4 Bettany Hughes, *Istanbul: A Tale of Three Cities* (London: Weidenfeld and Nicolson, 2017), p. 476

5 Quoted in Nabil Matar, 'Muslim Women in Renaissance England', *The Muslim World*, vol. LXXXVI, no. 1, January 1996, p. 51

6 Edward Seymour Forster (trans.), *The Turkish Letters of Ogier Ghiselin de Busbecq* (Baton Rouge: LSU Press, 2005), pp. 135–6

Chapter 23: Thwarting the Ottomans: The Struggle for Western Europe

1 Ian Traynor, 'In 1683 Turkey was the invader. In 2004 much of Europe still sees it that way', *The Guardian*, 22 September 2004, https://www.theguardian.com/world/2004/sep/22/eu.turkey?CMP=share_btn_url

2 Marc David Baer, *The Ottomans: Khans, Caesars and Caliphs* (London: Basic Books, 2021), p. 264. Baer also notes that the regicide of Osman II had parallels with that of England's King Charles I in the seventeenth century, both of which led to a limitation on the power of the monarch and more devolved government.

3 Yusuf Nabi, *Fethname – I Kamaniça*, MS Hazine 1629, fol. 28, Topkapı Palace Museum Library, quoted in Marc David Baer, *op. cit.*, p. 280

4 Richard W. Bulliet, 'The Other Siege of Vienna and the Ottoman Threat: An essay in Counter-Factual History', *ReOrient*, vol. 1, no. 1 (Autumn 2015), pp. 11–22; Bulliet makes an interesting case for the first Ottoman siege of Vienna in 1529 to be considered as an equivalently crucial event which might almost have succeeded in overthrowing Vienna, a close call that could have resulted in a prolonged Ottoman presence deep in German territory, obliging western Europe to see the Muslim state as part of the European state system.

5 Andrew Wheatcroft, *The Enemy at the Gate: Habsburgs, Ottomans and the Battle for Europe* (London: Pimlico, 2008), p. 13

6 *Ibid.*, p. 101

7 Richard Kreutel (ed.), *Kara Mustafa vor Wien: Das türkische Tagebuch der Belagerung Wiens, 1683, verfasst vom Zeremonienmeister der Hohen Pforte* (Munich: Deutscher Taschenbuch, 1967), p. 76, quoted in Marc David Baer, *op. cit.*, p. 304

8 Dag Herbjørnsrud, 'The Real Battle of Vienna', Aeon (website), 24 July 2018, at https://aeon.co/essays/the-battle-of-vienna-was-not-a-fight-between-cross-and-crescent

CHAPTER 24: CHANGING THE GUARD: THE CONQUESTS OF COLONIALISM

1 Alan Mikhail, *God's Shadow: The Ottoman Sultan Who Shaped the Modern World* (London: Faber and Faber, 2021), p. 117
2 Abbas Hamdani, 'Columbus and the recovery of Jerusalem', *Journal of the American Oriental Society*, January–March 1979, vol. 99, no. 1, p. 40
3 *Ibid.*, pp. 43–4
4 *Ibid.*, pp. 43–4
5 D. W. Lomax, *The Reconquest of Spain* (London: Longman, 1978), p. 178
6 Christopher de Bellaigue, *The Cultural Enlightenment: The Modern Struggle between Faith and Reason* (London: Vintage, 2017), p. 5
7 Quoted in Andrew Roberts, *Napoleon the Great* (London: Penguin Books, 2015), p. 162
8 *Ibid.*, p. 166
9 *Ibid.*, p. 176
10 Virginia H. Aksan, *The Ottomans 1700–1923: An Empire Besieged* (Oxford and New York: Routledge, 2022), p. 104
11 Edward W. Said, *Orientalism* (London: Penguin Books, 2019), p. 84
12 Marc David Baer, *The Ottomans: Khans, Caesars and Caliphs* (London: Basic Books, 2021), p. 344
13 For example, see John L. Esposito, *The Islamic Threat: Myth or Reality?* (New York and Oxford: Oxford University Press, 1992), pp. 46–7

CHAPTER 25: TRAVELLERS' TALES OF THE ORIENT: COLONIAL CONTEMPT AND THE ALLURE OF ISLAMIC CULTURE

1 Christopher de Bellaigue, *The Islamic Enlightenment: The Modern Struggle Between Faith and Reason* (London: Bodley Head, 2017), p. 43
2 Quoted in Frederick Brown, 'Flaubert in Egypt', *New England Review*, Fall 2004, vol. 25, p. 50
3 *Ibid.*, p. 53
4 Quoted in Mary Anne Stevens (ed.), *The Orientalists: Delacroix to Matisse – European Painters in North Africa and the Near East* (London: Royal Academy of Arts, 1984), p. 18
5 For a full account of the controversy, see *ibid.*, pp. 34–5.
6 Sir William Muir, 'The Mohammedan Controversy', in *Biographies of Muhammad, Sprenger on Tradition, the Indian liturgy and the Psalter* (Edinburgh: T. & T. Clark, 1897, repr.), p. 2

7 Sophie Basch (ed.), Alphonse de Lamartine, *Voyage en Orient* (Paris: Gallimard, 2011), p. 552

8 Alphonse de Lamartine, *Histoire de la Turquie*, vol. I (Paris: Constitutionnel, 1854), pp. 276–7. The entire statement is as follows:

Never has a man set for himself, voluntarily or involuntarily, a more sublime aim, since this aim was super human; to subvert superstitions which had been imposed between man and his Creator, to render God unto man and man unto God; to restore the rational and sacred idea of divinity amidst the chaos of the material and disfigured gods of idolatry, then existing. Never has a man undertaken a work so far beyond human power with so feeble means, for he Muhammad had in the conception as well as in the execution of such a great design, no other instrument than himself and no other aid except a handful of men living in a corner of the desert. Finally, never has a man accomplished such a huge and lasting revolution in the world, because in less than two centuries after its appearance, Islam reigned over the whole of Arabia, and conquered, in God's name, Persia, Khorasan, Transoxania, Western India, Syria, Egypt, Abyssinia, all the known continent of Northern Africa, numerous islands of the Mediterranean Sea, Spain and part of Gaul.

If greatness of purpose, smallness of means, and astounding results are the three criteria of human genius, who could dare to compare any great man in modern history with Muhammad? The most famous men created arms, laws and empires only. They founded, if anything at all, no more than material powers which often crumbled away before their eyes. This man moved not only armies, legislations, empires, peoples and dynasties, but millions of men in one-third of the then inhabited world; and more than that, he moved the altars, the gods, the religions, the ideas, the beliefs and souls . . . his forbearance in victory, his ambition, which was entirely devoted to one idea and in no manner striving for an empire; his endless prayers, his mystic conversations with God, his death and his triumph after death; all these attest not to an imposture but to a firm conviction which gave him the power to restore a dogma. This dogma was twofold, the unity of God and the immateriality of God; the former telling what God is, the latter telling what God is not; the one overthrowing false gods with the sword, the other starting an idea with words. Philosopher, orator, apostle, legislator, warrior, conqueror of ideas, restorer of rational dogmas, of a cult without images; the founder of twenty terrestrial empires and of one spiritual empire, that is Mahomet. As regards all standards by which human greatness may be measured, we may well ask, is there any man greater than he?

9 Arthur de Capell Brooke, *Sketches in Spain and Morocco*, vol. II (London: H. Colburn and R. Bentley, 1831), p. 220

10 *Ibid.*, p. 255

11 Richard Ford, *Granada: An account illustrated with unpublished original drawings*, text in Spanish and English, Spanish version and notes by Alfonso Gámir (Granada: Patronato de la Alhambra y Generalife, 1955), p. 182. Ford's handbook for travellers in Spain was first published in 1845.

12 *Ibid.*, p. 196

13 Théophile Gautier, *Wanderings in Spain*, trans. Thomas Robert McQuoid (London: Ingram Cooke, 1853), p. 166

14 *Ibid.*, p. 172

15 Washington Irving, *Tales of the Alhambra* (Granada: Ediciones Miguel Sánchez, 1994), p. 31

Chapter 26: A Fading Glory: The Vanquishing of the Ottoman Empire

1 Marc David Baer, *The Ottomans: Khans, Caesars and Caliphs* (London: Basic Books, 2021), p. 363

2 Justin McCarthy, '1912–13 Balkan Wars: Death and Forced Exile of Ottoman Muslims. An Annotated Map', Turkish Coalition of America (website), https://www.tc-america.org/files/news/pdf/balkan-wars-map.pdf

3 *Ibid.*

4 Quoted in Henry Laurens, 'The Great War and the Beginning of Emancipation', in John Tolan, Gilles Veinstein and Henry Laurens (eds), *Europe and the Islamic World* (Princeton and Oxford: Princeton University Press, 2013), p. 361

5 Marc David Baer, *The Ottomans*, p. 444

6 Sebastian Balfour, *Deadly Embrace: Morocco and the Road to the Spanish Civil War* (Oxford: Oxford University Press, 2002), p. 195

7 *Ibid.*, p. 281. I am grateful to Sebastian Balfour for his insights into Franco's deployment of Moroccan troops in the Spanish Civil War.

8 For an excellent detailed account of the issue of Muslims in post-war Europe, see Emily Greble, *Muslims and the Making of Modern Europe* (Oxford: Oxford University Press, 2021), p. 131 ff.

CHAPTER 27: ABANDONING THE ISLAMIC PAST: MUSTAFA KEMAL ATATÜRK AND THE NEW TURKEY

1 Quoted by Andrew Mango, *Atatürk* (London: John Murray, 1999), p. 33
2 Bettany Hughes, *Istanbul: A Tale of Three Cities* (London: Weidenfeld and Nicolson, 2017), p. 593
3 George W. Gawrych, *Atatürk: Father of the Republic of Turkey* (London: I. B Tauris, 2023), p. 3
4 Bettany Hughes, *op. cit.*, p. 594
5 Maxime Rodinson, *Islam and Capitalism* (Harmondsworth: Penguin Books, 1977), p. 12
6 George W. Gawrych, *Atatürk: Father of the Republic of Turkey*, pp. 115–16
7 *Ibid.*, p. 112
8 *Ibid.*, p. 156. I am grateful to George W. Gawrych for his numerous insights into and illumination of the Kemalist regime.
9 Philip Jenkins, *The Great and Holy War: How World War I Changed Religion Forever* (Oxford: Lion Hudson, 2014), pp. 11–12
10 Quoted in Ray Hamilton Abrams, *Preachers Present Arms* (New York: Round Table Press, 1933), p. 55, cited in Jenkins, *op. cit.*, p. 10
11 For this insight, I am grateful to Andrew Mango, *Atatürk* (London: John Murray, 1999), p. 539
12 United Nations Resolution 3/1.5 and 2.3/4

CHAPTER 28: IMPRINTS OF ISLAM: THREE PORTRAITS OF HOSTILITY, HYBRIDITY AND HARMONY

1 See *Journal of the Royal Asiatic Society* XXVIII, 1897, p. 84 and Philip Khuri Hitti, *The Origins of the Islamic State: Being a Translation from the Arabic Accompanied with Annotations, Geographic and Historic Notes of the Kitab̂ FutuḤ̂ al-Buldan̂ of al-Imam̂ Abu-l 'Abbaŝ AḫMad Ibn-JaB̂ir al-BalaD̂huri* (Beirut: Khayats, 1966; Khayats Oriental Reprint, no. 11), p. 237
2 'Sedebant inter Graecos et Saracenos et inermes fuerunt, quia pax maxima fuit et conciliatio inter Saracenos et Graecos', *The Hodoeporicam of Willibald*, written by the nun Huneberc and dictated by Willibald, p. 116
3 Costas P. Kyrris, *History of Cyprus with an Introduction to the Geography of Cyprus* (Nicosia: Nicocles Publishing House, 1985), p. 190
4 Tommy Clark, *A Brief History of Cyprus: The Story of a Divided Island* (Manchester: Upper Street Press, 2020), p. 21

5 *Ibid.*, p. 51
6 Jørgen Nielsen et al., *Yearbook of Muslims in Europe, Volume 4* (Leiden: Brill, 2012)
7 Quoted in Ravil Bukharaev, *Tatarstan: President Mintimer Shaimiev and the Power of Common Sense* (Boston: Brill, 2006), pp. 184–5

CHAPTER 29: FORGING THE FUTURE OF EUROPE

1 Beck, Ulrich and Edgar Grande, *Cosmopolitan Europe* (Cambridge: Polity, 2006), p. 79
2 Hans Kundnani, *Eurowhiteness: Culture, Empire and Race in the European Project* (London: C. Hurst and Co., 2023), p. 80. I am indebted to the research of Hans Kundnani, on which I draw here.
3 José Casanova, 'Religion, European Secular Identities and European integration', in Krzysztof Michalski (ed.), *Religion in the New Europe* (Budapest: Central European University Press, 2022), p. 26
4 Kundnani, *op. cit.*, p. 116
5 *Ibid.*, p. 141
6 Henry Laurens, 'Contemporary Issues', in John Tolan, Gilles Veinstein and Henry Laurens (eds), *Europe and the Islamic World: A History* (Princeton: Princeton University Press, 2013), p. 402
7 Quoted in David Gow and Ewen MacAskill, 'Turkish accession could spell end of EU, says commissioner', *The Guardian*, 8 September 2004 (https://www.theguardian.com/world/2004/sep/08/turkey.eu)
8 For a fuller account, see Bichara Khader, 'Muslims in Europe: the construction of a problem', in Daron Acemoglu et al., *The Search for Europe: Contrasting Approaches* (Bilbao: BBVA, 2015), p. 5.
9 Bichara Khader, as above, cites the examples of the Italian intellectual Oriana Fallaci, *La rabbia e l'orgoglio*, 2001, the German Thilo Sarrazin, *Deutschland schafft sich ab*, 2010, the French writer Michel Houellebeq's 2015 novel *Soumission* and the Norwegian-American Bruce Bawer's *While Europe Slept: How Radical Islam is Destroying the West from Within*, 2006.
10 John Esposito, *The Islamic Threat: Myth or Reality?* (New York and Oxford: Oxford University Press, 1992), p. 171
11 Peter Oborne, *The Fate of Abraham: Why the West is Wrong About Islam* (London: Simon and Schuster, 2022), p. 376
12 *Ibid.*, p. 375
13 Nayef R. F. Al-Rodhan (ed.), *The Role of the Arab-Islamic World in the Rise*

of the West: Implications for Contemporary Transcultural Relations (Basingstoke: Palgrave Macmillan, 2012), p. 111

14 *Ibid.*, p. 11

15 Gabriel Pirický, 'The Legacy of the Ottoman (Turkish) Age in Slovakia', in Elizabeth Drayson (ed.), *Europe's Islamic Legacy: 1900 to the Present: Proceedings of the Online Conference Hosted by the University of Cambridge on 20 October 2020* (Leiden: Brill, 2023), p. 35

16 Agata S. Nalborczyk, 'Mosques and Cemeteries of the Polish Muslim Tatars as an example of Islamic legacy in the central Eastern European landscape in the twenty-first century', in Elizabeth Drayson (ed.), *op. cit.*, p. 112

17 See Tharik Hussein's important book *Minarets in the Mountains* (Chesham: Bradt Guides, 2021), p. 322

18 For a detailed analysis of these issues, see Karol Kujawa, 'Turkey and the Politics of Memory: consequences for Domestic and Foreign Affairs and Security in the Region', in Elizabeth Drayson (ed.), *op. cit.*, pp. 9–28.

19 Richard W. Bulliet, *The Case for Islamo-Christian Civilization* (New York: Columbia University Press, 2004)

20 Ed Vulliamy, 'Bridging the gap, part two', *The Guardian*, 13 July 2008, (https://www.theguardian.com/music/2008/jul/13/classicalmusicand-opera.culture)

Index